Asian Christian Theologies
A Research Guide to Authors, Movements, Sources

The Catholic Theological Union
LIBRARY
Chicago, Ill.

Asian Christian Theologies
A Research Guide to Authors, Movements, Sources

Edited by
John C. England, Jose Kuttianimattathil sdb,
John Mansford Prior svd, Lily A. Quintos rc,
David Suh Kwang-sun, Janice Wickeri

VOLUME 2
Southeast Asia

ISPCK/Claretian Publishers/Orbis Books
2003

Asian Christian Theologies–Vol. 2—Published by the Rev. Ashish Amos of the Indian Society for Promoting Christian Knowledge (ISPCK), Post Box 1585, Kashmere Gate, Delhi-110006 in association with Claretian Publishers, Quezon City; Orbis Books, Maryknoll, NY.

First Published 2003

© The Editors 2003

Library of Congress Control Number: 2003040526

ISBN: 1-57075-482-9

Cover design: TONY SMITH

Laser typeset and cover design by **ISPCK,** Post Box 1585, 1654 Madarsa Road, Kashmere Gate, Delhi-110006, Tel: 23866323, Fax: 91-11-23865490.
E-Mail–ispck@nde.vsnl.net.in, Publishing@ispck.org.in
Internet-www.ispck.org.in
Printed at Cambridge Press, Kashmere Gate, Delhi–110006

*Dedicated by the editors to
their forebears throughout the region
who have handed on the
rich heritage of Asian theologies,
and to colleagues in all Asian countries who,
despite few resources and every obstacle,
persevere in writing, teaching and living
Asian theology with people in context.*

Contents

The Genesis of this Work	ix
Table of Contents vols. 1 & 3	xi
Acknowledgements	xiii
Foreword 1: Anna May Say Pa	xvii
Foreword 2: Jose de Mesa	xxi
A Note on Languages, Terms, Style	xxv
Abbreviations	xxx
Note on Illustrations & Artists	xl
Illustrations	xlii-a
Introduction	xliii
1 Contextual Christian Theology in Asia (Summary)	1
2. Groundwork for Asian Christian Theologies: Southeast Asia	9
3. Contextual Theology in Burma / Myanmar 1800-2000	25
4. A note on Contextual Theology in Cambodia and Laos	108
5. Contextual Theological Reflection in Indonesia 1800-2000	122
6. Contextual Theology in Malaysia and Singapore 1800-2000	244
7. Contextual Theology in the Philippines 1800-2000	331
8. Contextual Theology in Thailand 1800-2000	498
9. Contextual Theology in Vietnam 1800-2000	556
Key Bibliographic Sources	656
Contributors to Volume 2	658
Editors	660
Index of Persons	663

The Genesis of this Work

During the last twenty years the extent of our knowledge of Asian Christian theologies and of their extensive written sources, has greatly increased, as has the number of those studying these and of the courses offered for them in seminary or university. There has been, however, no attempt as yet to provide an Asia-wide and comprehensive guide to study or research in these theologies, despite a growing tide of deep interest, study and teaching. Some of this concern has been fostered through the work of the Commission for Theological Concerns (CCA-CTC), the publications of the Federation of Asian Bishops' Conferences (FABC), the Theological Seminar-Workshops held regularly over the past 17 years by the Programme for Theology and Cultures in Asia (PTCA), and activities of regional bodies such as the Asia-Pacific Association for Missiological Research (ASPAMIR).

Impetus came from all these, along with the more recent Congress of Asian Theologians (CATS), for the undertaking at last of a more comprehensive and fully ecumenical guide to study and research, despite the scale and the complexity of work necessary for such a project. A small group shared by mail their enthusiasm and commitment for this in mid 1997, and in early 1998, a team of co-editors was forming in order to initiate the writing. A fully ecumenical team of contributors was sought with participation from each country in the region and the co-editors first met for planning and co-ordination in December, 1998.

Approaches were made to CCA, ASPAMIR and PTCA for their approval, and to MWI-Missio (Aachen) and the Council for World Mission (CWM, London) for seed funds to assist in co-ordination and publication.

Principal concerns have throughout been to make available as wide a range as possible of Asian Christian theologies in all their varied forms, and to provide adequate guidance for their discovery, study and research .

The demanding work of obtaining adequate contributions from across the region, and of themselves preparing major sections of the text, demanded considerable dedication of the editors and co-ordinator over the next three years along with the work of many other colleagues across the region who have assisted with information, bibliographies, translations and advice.

Table of Contents: Volumes 1 & 3

Volume 1 - Regional, South and Austral Asia.
Forewords
Introduction
I **Asia as Region.**
  1 Groundwork for Asian Theology 1 (7-15th Cents)
  2 Groundwork for Asian Theology 2 (16-18th Cents)
  3 Asia-wide and Ecumenical Theologies .
II **South Asia**
  4 Contextual Theology in Bangla Desh
  5 Contextual Theology in India
  6 A Note on Nepal
  7 Contextual Theology in Pakistan
  8 Contextual Theology in Sri Lanka
III **Austral Asia**
  9 Contextual Theology in Aotearoa New Zealand
  10 Contextual Theology in Australia
Key Bibliographic Sources
Indexes; Contributors

Volume 3 - Northeast Asia
Forewords
Introduction
1. Asia Regional Survey (summary)
2. Northeast Asia 16th-18th centuries
3. Contextual Theology in China
4. Contextual Theology in Hong Kong
5. A Note on Inner Asia
6. Contextual Theology in Japan
7. Contextual Theology in Korea
8. A Note on North Korea
9. A Note on Macau
10. Contextual Theology in Taiwan
Indexes; Contributors

Acknowledgements

The following chapters represent the work of an almost countless number of colleagues throughout the region, and also in other countries, who have in their writings, teaching and co-operative study made possible the compilation of this pioneer Guide to the study of Asian theologies. Some have provided personal knowledge and counsel, while others have given indispensable assistance in the research, drafting and compilation of particular sections. Many eminent theologians, writers and activists throughout the Asian region and beyond have given valued encouragement and advice, and librarians both of theological colleges and of universities in many countries have also provided wide-ranging support. It is of course impossible to acknowledge by name here all who have assisted with their expertise and sustaining help.

Amongst the many colleagues who have given particular assistance, the following at least, must be mentioned for this volume:

Dr Hope Antone, Asian Women's Resource Centre for Culture and Theology, Hong Kong; Dr Melanio LaG. Aoanan, Union Theological Seminary, Das Marinas, Cavite, Philippines; Fr Bruno Arens, Nakhonsawan Diocese, Thailand; Fr Catalino G. Arevalo sj, Loyola House of Studies, Quezon City, Philippines; Sr Mary Rosario Battung rgs, Co-ordinator of FIDES (Forum for Interdisciplinary Endeavors and Studies), Philippines; Mrs Louise Buhler of Bread for the World, Hanoi, Vietnam; Dr Noriel Capulong, the Divinity School, Silliman University, Philippines; Fr Siripong Charatsri, the Major Seminary, Samphran, Bangkok; Ms Porntip Chaweephath, Payap University, Chiangmai, Thailand; Dr Roland Chia, Trinity Theological College, Singapore; U Chit Pe, Assumption University, Bangkok; Ms Patricia Sandar Chit, Yangon, Myanmar; Fr Jean Dantonel, the Major Seminary, Samphran, Bangkok; Dr Jose de Mesa, De La Salle University,

Manila, Philippines; Rev'd Mark Maung Doe, Principal of Holy Cross College, Yangon, Myanmar; Dr Mary Dun, Principal of the Burman Theological Seminary, Insein, Myanmar; Fr Fung Jojo sj, the Arrupe Jesuit Community in Taman Rinting, Johor, Malaysia; Hoang Gia Khanh, Historian of Vietnamese Theology, HCMV, Vietnam; Dr Alle Hoekema, University of Amsterdam, Netherlands; Dr Hwa Yung, Principal, Seminari Teologi Malaysia; Dr Cecilia Ing of *Women's Voice,* Petaling Jaya, Malaysia; Rev'd Peter Joseph, Association for Theological Education, Myanmar; Ms Delia Kwong, Seminari Teologi Malaysia; Dr Lahpai Zau Lat, Myanmar Institute of Theology, Insein, Myanmar; Fr O.C. Lim sj, Director of the Catholic Research Centre, Kuala Lumpur, Malaysia; Rev'd Reuel Marigza, the Divinity School, Silliman University, Philippines; Dr Salvador Martinez, Payap University, Chiangmai, Thailand; Ng Chinh Ket, Theological scholar and writer, HCMV, Vietnam; Nguyen van Nghi of the Institut des Sciences Sociales, HCMV, Vietnam; Sr Amelie Nguyen, of the Congregation de Notre Dame HCMV, Vietnam; Rufus Bruno Perera, Catholic Research Centre, Kuala Lumpur, Malaysia; Gerard Pham Dinh Thai of *United Catholic Asia News*, Vietnam; Fr Phan Khac Tu, of Vuon Xoai Church, HCMV and the United Catholic Committee, Vietnam; Dr Peter Phan of the Catholic University of America, Washington, USA; Alan Po, Librarian, Myanmar Institute of Theology, Insein, Myanmar; Prasit Pongudom, Office of Church History, CCT, Chiangmai, Thailand; Willi Riedel svd, SOVERDI, Jakarta, Indonesia; Anthony Rogers fsc, National Director of the Office for Human Development, Kuala Lumpur, Malaysia; Bp Louis Chamniern Santisukniran, Nakhonsawan Diocese, Thailand; Alan Saw U of the Myanmar Christian Literature Society, Yangon, Myanmar; Michael Saw U, of the Catholic Literature Service, Myanmar; Dr Hermen Shastri, General Secretary of the Council of Churches, Malaysia; Dr Gerrit Singgih, Dean of Post-graduate Studies, Duta Wacana Christian University, Yogyakarta, Indonesia; Dr Richard Siwu, General Secretary MIBM Church, Sulawesi Utara, Indonesia; Achara Somsaengsruang, of the Ubon-Ratchathani Diocesan Office, Thailand; Mrs Gwyneth Squires, University of Pnom Penh, Cambodia; Dr Karel Steenbrink, Inter-University Institute for Missiological and Ecumenical Research ,

Acknowledgements

Utrecht, Netherlands; Dr Herbert R. Swanson, Office of Church History, CCT, Chiangmai, Thailand; Ms Corazon Tabing-Reyes, Executive Secretary for Women's Concerns, CCA; Dr Pradit Takerngrangsarit, Payap University, Chiangmai, Thailand; Dr Tam Kim Huat, Trinity Theological College, Singapore; Dr Stephen Tan, formerly Principal of Trinity Theological College, Singapore; Fr Thomas Than Thien Cam op, Director of Studies for the Dominican Order, Vietnam; Sr. Mai Thanh of the Congregation de Notre Dame HCMV, Vietnam; Tran Duy Nghien, professor in the University of Law, HCMV, Vietnam; Fr Truong Ba Can, Editor, *Cong giao vao Dan toc*, HCMV, Vietnam; Dr Voon Choon Khing, Seminari Teologi, Seremban, Malaysia; Vuong Dinh Chu of the *Cong giao vao Dan toc*, HCMV, Vietnam; Dr Albert Walters, Seminari Teologi Malaysia; Fr. Joseph Maung Win of the Conference of Catholic Bishops, Myanmar; Dr A.A.Yewangoe, President of the Artha Wacana University, Kupang, Timor; Ms Yong Ting Jin, Co-ordinator of the Asian Women's Resource Centre for Culture and Theology, Kuala Lumpur, Malaysia.

Thanks must go especially to those colleagues who have greatly assisted in the final editing of country chapters: Dr Anna May Say Pa and Dr Jose de Mesa, both of whom also generously contributed Forewords, along with Delia Kwong, Alan Po, Nguyen Chin Ket, Tran Duy Nhien and Dr Herbert Swanson. Dr Judo Poerwowidagdo and the staff of the Asian Christian Art Association have again assisted with the illustrations here included. Special mention must also be made of the additional editorial work done by Dr John M. Prior svd, of the professional services as copy and detail editor in addition to her other editorial responsibilities given by Janice Wickeri and to Rita M. England who has undertaken supplementary research, editorial and proof-reading responsibilities at every stage. General Editors for this volume, as for the other volumes, have also included Dr Lily A. Quintos, Dr David Suh Kwang-sun and Dr Jose Kuttianimattathil. Co-ordination of writing and editing has been done by John C. England. The Editors wish to also acknowledge the careful work of the Rev'd Ashish Amos, Rachna Singh and their staff at the ISPCK, throughout the production of these volumes.

Foreword 1

Christianity in Southeast Asia has been alive and vibrant since its early beginnings. However it is difficult to capture in print alone the life, spirit and thought of the peoples of Southeast Asia who call themselves Christians. Faith in many Asian cultures is expressed in graphic art, music, dance, drama, ritual and symbolic actions. We are inheritors of an oral culture, receiving stories, songs, legends, myths, proverbs and genealogies from generation to generation. It was only in the 19th century that some ethnic groups in Myanmar for example, like the Chins, Karens and Kachins received the written script from missionaries and national scholars, and for the first time could write down and read what for centuries had been passed down by word of mouth. The Bible could then be translated into the different languages and be read and interpreted. Even today some ethnic minorities in Myanmar such as the Kayahs, Kayans and Mros do not have a written script. They look forward to the day when they, too, can share their traditions and history in print. This is the situation of many ethnic groupings in Southeast Asia and the theological writings we select for study therefore must be seen as select and representative examples of this much larger body of thought and life. Yet it is of course of vital importance that we have such examples, and the guidance for research, which this volume provides.

As can be seen in the chapters which follow, Christian presence is recorded in many parts of Southeast Asia long before the 16th century, and in following centuries Christian literatures developed in growing streams for each country. Asian Christians from the earliest period have felt the need not only to proclaim the Gospel by life and word of mouth but also in manuscript and print. Roman Catholic writers and printing presses date from the 16th and 17th centuries in Indochina, Siam, Burma and the Philippines, and along with Protestant undertakings, in the Malay Peninsula and

Archipelago. The 19th century would see large increases in Christian writing and publishing, especially by Protestants, in most countries of the region. In Myanmar, not many years after Dr. Adoniram and Mrs. Ann Judson arrived in 1813 as the first missionaries of the Baptist churches of America, William Carey and the English Baptist mission in Serampore, India, sent a printing press as a gift. Soon after, George Hough was sent from America to take charge of the press and the work of printing of tracts, pamphlets and passages and books of the Bible was begun in 1817. Writings also came from Burmese Christians, the first then being the letter of Maung Naw who in 1819 asked for baptism.

Although each people of Southeast Asia possesses unique cultural and Christian traditions they also share many historical and cultural experiences. These include the long years of feudal kingship with its wars and subjugation of ethnic minorities and their cultures, the colonization by the western nations and the struggles for selfhood and independence. Over many centuries they have been introduced to new religions such as Buddhism, Hinduism, Islam and Christianity, all of which learnt in varying degrees to co-exist with the traditional faiths of the peoples. Christian communities in each of these histories have shared in the vicissitudes and experiences of their peoples and out of these have emerged living theologies and expressions of faith. These rich cultural, historical and religious resources have now been brought together in the Research Guides providing an invaluable service for students, teachers and all earnest seekers of information. It is to be noted that resources in national languages are included, as well as materials in a wide variety of form and content from many diverse peoples and contexts. The Research Guide is thus a fully inclusive and representative endeavour.

Here at Myanmar Institute of Theology, students are encouraged to do research on histories of their ethnic peoples and their churches, to describe Christian thought and life amidst varied cultural and religious traditions and to do theology in their own Asian context using Asian resources. In the courses on Feminist Theology students have begun collecting the experiences and writings of women which

Foreword 1

for so long had been hidden or lost. They attempt to recover the forgotten histories of their foremothers. All these diverse resources are given full recognition in the chapters which follow. There is no doubt that the Research Guides will be valuable tools for such study and research, breaking new ground in the presentation and study of contextual theology in our region.

Anna May Say Pa
Myanmar Institute of Theology, Yangon

Foreword 2

The publication of this Research Guide is inspiration, confirmation and challenge. The collection is an inspiration as it is a telling statement that Christianity is Asian, not a religion that requires Asians to turn their backs on their peoples by denying who they are. Although this is a perception which has had historical causes whose effects linger up to now, the material from Southeast Asia in this volume shows that Christianity is rather a faith that in the long run promotes both truthfulness to the Gospel and rootedness of Christians in their cultural and historical situations. The theological voices represented here, when one surveys the whole development, are ultimately those of Asians grounded in their culture and history, not of locals speaking to represent and defend a religion from the West. Understandably, for various cultural and historical reasons, it had taken a long time, to shift focus from the culture and history of the church that made Christianity known locally, to the local culture and history themselves.

This Research Guide is thus a significant contribution to dispel the distortion that faith in Jesus Christ is anti-Asian. The views on Christianity represented here speak of a genuine re-appropriation, within concrete Asian settings, of faith in Jesus the Christ in its many dimensions. Rather than just imaginative local translation of what has been formulated elsewhere and from another time, they recall the contemporaneity of the early Christians' witness regarding the life-giving Word: "what we have seen, heard, looked upon and touched with our hands, this is what we proclaim to you" (cf. 1 Jn. 1: 1-4). And as can be gleaned from the histories of the churches, for example, in Cambodia, Laos, Thailand and Vietnam, Christian witness was not only through words but with deeds of courage and perseverance under severe conditions such as persecution and possible martyrdom.

In addition to the theological insights, the various interpretations of the complex Asian setting, from the theological perspective, yield not only knowledge about Christianity in Asia, but also insights into the Asian situation itself complementing analyses made within other human disciplines. Any understanding of the Asian condition cannot afford to ignore the present-day situation which characterizes the region: widespread poverty and social injustice, which particularly affect women and children negatively; the pluriformity of cultures, which require better comprehension of cultural dynamics; and the presence and deep significance of religions which constantly remind people of what life is all about. It is not a surprise therefore, that we find themes related to these in this collection. Concern for just relationships in society - including those of women and men - and care of our ecologically endangered earth, the continuing search for cultural identity and integrity, and dialogue among religions to achieve mutual respect and harmony are indispensable elements of the agenda in the work and thinking of the Asian churches and of individual Asian Christians today. There is no doubt that information and insight on these are relevant even to a secular reading of what Asia is today.

The Guide is a confirmation of Asian theology. The present volume(s) show clearly that Asian theology is no longer just a promise of things to come and of projects still to be realized. Not that there are no more dreams awaiting fulfillment. But much is already here, particularly when one considers that the major elements of contextual theologizing are reflected in these volumes. Material about particular issues taken up or questions raised and answered; presuppositions of local thought and method which have been incorporated in the reflection about Christian faith; thought patterns which are operational in a specific culture, religion or society that have been utilized in doing theology; and explorations of vocabulary locally available for theological purposes.

The Research Guide is a challenge because the wealth of information contained in it offers an invitation to dialogue. First of all, among Asian Christians themselves. For a long time they had been held in some form of "Western theological captivity" and could only exchange insights mainly about Western theologies they had adopted. The past is replete with examples of Asians communicating with the West - learning mostly from and speaking sometimes to Western mentors. Without cultural voices of their own, they could hardly share their understanding of being and becoming Christians in Asian terms and Asian ways. A genuine intra-Asian dialogue among Christians is not yet given. The present publication is an invitation to mutually explore, discover and be enriched by each other's theological treasures. Hopefully, a process of sustained exchange and collaboration will be triggered by this work. If so, then one may expect at times that themes locally worked on will be corroborated by others in another country or, perhaps, enriched by another perspective or even confronted with a counterpoint. Through comparison, the sophistication of various theological methodologies employed may be honed. Knowledge of what is being done in another setting may provide the stimulus to undertake the same or a similar task in one's own setting. In any case, mutual learning will surely happen as Christian churches of Asia learn of each other's experiences and reflection, and discover each other's genius and wisdom.

The dialogue may even entice a number of theological practitioners to learn each other's language, enough to comprehend local articulation - written or oral - expressed in the vernacular. After all, there is truly a value in the study of texts or other material in the original language, especially when we consider its hermeneutical implications. Resources in national languages have been included in these volumes for that reason. The Research Guide also provides an Asian life-setting to the material in the collection by including personal and background information to introduce Asian churches and Christians to each other.

With the material provided in the volumes, a more accurate picture of what is truly shared commonly by Asians in their respective worldviews (or *worldfeel* for cultures in which the affective is more valued than the cognitive) will be made clear. This will surely be a step forward from the contemporary recognition that situationally Asia is poor, culturally diversified and home to different religions. This is commonality, to be sure. But with the Research Guide, what is spoken of in general terms will have the chance of being discussed in particulars - specific beliefs, particular values, definite patterns of behavior or concrete structures. There will be more substance to the adjective "Asian" because a conscious common agreement - in theology and practice - among Asian Christians will undergird its use. As further investigation of the Judaeo-Christian Tradition is made in the light of Asian realities, there will be more depth when *Asian* Christianity is spoken of and, perhaps, even when *Christianity* is spoken of elsewhere in the world. The very particularity of Asia is apt to bring to the surface aspects and meanings of the Gospel which may have receded into the background in other cultural and historical contexts.

The Research Guide is also an invitation to Christians in the West, particularly those engaged in the theological enterprise, to learn a lesson or two about what it means to do theology today in one's context, especially in very difficult circumstances. Asian Christians, as this collection shows, are no longer their theological tutees, but equal theological partners. Asian contextual theologizing is a reminder to fellow Christians in the West that their theologies have never been and still are not other than contextual or inculturated theologies.

Finally, heartfelt appreciation for this publication and deep gratitude to all who have collaborated in this most important project on Asian theology, particularly its editors, are most appropriate. Putting together a Research Guide of this magnitude may have appeared impossible in the beginning were it not for the conviction and dedication of everyone engaged in the project to see to its completion. May our fruitful use of this work, then, be a way of constantly thanking the God and Father of our Lord Jesus Christ who has blessed us with such rich resource to understand our faith.

José M. de Mesa
De La Salle University, Manila

A Note on Languages, Terms, Style

Languages

Much of the theological writing and scholarship in the Southeast Asian region, is written or published in English, although the major amount of Christian writing in countries such as Burma/Myanmar, Indonesia, Thailand and Vietnam has always been in the vernacular. However, as Michael Amaladoss points out in his Foreword to volume 1, English is the link language of Asia, "less an embodiment of culture than a medium of communication." The grounding of this Guide in what has become the default language of international communication will, we hope, make these resources more broadly available within the region itself. Translation into local languages could well follow.

The English language, however, and by extension the varieties in use in Asia, is far from uniform. Its varieties give only a hint of the greater linguistic and cultural diversity in which they exist. The history of a community, often its experience of colonisation, and the unique character of its encounter with Christianity all bear on the choice of 'Englishes'. We have avoided standardization beyond the chapter level, for the multiplicity of usage, punctuation and spelling that a work of this scope embraces reflects, in its sometimes jarring, hybrid nature, the realities and diversities of the Asian region. A brief note only on these diversities is possible here.

Extensive research has been undertaken to ensure that, in particular, a wide range of vernacular materials are included and outlined. Care has been taken to provide translation where necessary, along with accepted forms for romanization. It is to be noted in Southeast Asia that while mainland peoples such as Burmese and Siamese early borrowed alphabets of Indian origin, Malay peoples adopted Arabic characters to represent their languages. These were later romanized in varying ways although those in general use for Burmese, Malay and Siamese, such as the Hunterian, give roughly Italian values for vowels and English values for consonants. Where diacritics are highly complex in a particular language, such as Vietnamese, these have been simplified in accord with more general usage. Where more than one form of romanization appears in the references for writings in Chinese, for example (see also volume 3), the alternative form will be given in parentheses where necessary. In very many cases, alternative forms are widely used in the region, both for key terms in discourse and for personal names, and these proliferate further in secondary language sources.

In Burma/Myanmar, The Burmese (Tibeto-Burman) language is widely spoken not just by Burmans, and is used for the majority of references given here. Honorifics include U (" elder" or "uncle"), Daw ("lady" or "auntie"), Ma (younger woman) and Saya (teacher), along with such ethnic parallels as Saw, Naw, and Thra.

Multiple personal names and titles are commonly used in Indonesia: most Indonesians have a single personal name; in some areas outside Java also a clan name. Most people also have a nickname, often more commonly used, even in print. Christians rarely make use of their baptismal name. The official personal name - with baptismal name - is used in the headings, while the most commonly used "nickname" is used in the text. Many personal names use pre-1972 spelling, others post-1972 spelling; whichever is more commonly used is given in the text. Many names are preceded by a honorific - for instance *Ibu* or *Bu* for women ("mother") and *Bapak* or *Pak* for men, or *Romo* for Catholic priests.

Malay is the national language of Malaysia and is closely similar to that spoken in Sabah and to Bahasa Indonesia. In 1972 a joint Malaysian-Indonesian spelling reform was adopted. English is also widely used, with Tamil and a number of Chinese dialects being spoken by large minorities.

There are three official languages in the Philippines: Tagalog, Spanish and English. Tagalog has been chosen as the basis of the national language (Pilipino), though its speakers form only the second largest cultural-linguistic group. The largest group is

Cebuano-speaking, but Cebuano has been less used as a literary language.

For countries such as Thailand, Cambodia and Laos, personal names are normally cited complete (i.e.) under the "first" name, without division into what are elsewhere termed "given" and "family" names.

For Vietnamese, earlier writing systems which derived from Indian scripts, have been replaced by the forms of *quôc-ngu* (national language) which were simplified early in the 19th century. But Chinese characters, sometimes in the earlier *Chu nôm* (southern characters) form have also been often used by scholars. Transliteration has been influenced both by French and American English. Family names normally appear first although Christian names sometimes precede these.

Geographical and Historical Terms

The complex cultural and colonial history, along with ethnic diversity, of Southeast Asia are reflected in the variety of geographical names and ethnic groups encountered throughout the text. A simple "mini-glossary" of these may serve as a guide:

Indochina (Indochine), comprising Vietnam, Laos and Cambodia, was conceived of as a region by the French, who ruled there between 1858 and 1893 and created the first Indochinese Union to govern it (Vietnam remaining an integral part of France until 1954). **Tonkin (Tonquin)** was the French colonial term for northern Vietnam. **Annam** (meaning "pacified south") was the Chinese name for central Vietnam and was adopted by the French to refer to both central Vietnam and Vietnam as a whole. The Vietnamese people were also referred to as the Annamese. **Cochinchina (Cochine)** was the name the French gave to the southern part of Vietnam.

Burma was declared the Union of **Myanmar** in 1989 to recover earlier historic symbolism, although for many in the country this remains only a fiat of the military government. **Yangon** ("end of strife") is the historical name of the capital city of Myanmar, which the British, in 1851, called **Rangoon.** Such peoples as the **Karen, Lao, Shans, Lisu, Akha, and Lahu** - to mention only a few - are minority peoples living in a number of states on the Southeast Asian mainland, many of whom suffer discrimination or persecution.

Siam became Thailand in 1939 (the constitutional monarchy was established following a coup in 1932), although Siam remains the preferred name for many nationalists and scholars. Thai is, like some other languages in "Indochina", mono-syllabic and tonal with diverse dialect forms in, for example, northern Thailand.

The **East Indies** was used by the West as a collective term for the area which included Indonesia and the Philippines as well as parts of Malaysia (Sarawak and Sabah), Brunei, Papua New Guinea and Portuguese Timor. **Dutch East Indies** referred, until 1945, to the over 7,000 islands of Indonesia. **Indonesia** comprises all areas of the former Dutch colonies, except East Timor, although struggles for autonomy or independence continue in areas such as Acheh, Kalimantan and West Papua.

The **Malay Peninsula,** comprises southwestern Thailand, western Malaysia and Singapore. Its inhabitants include Malays, Indians and Chinese, as well as ethnic minorities such as the Orang Asli. The **Malay States** came under Dutch influence via Acheh in Sumatra in 1620. British influence grew subsequently, with Britain gaining control of Penang in 1786; Malacca in 1795; and Singapore in 1824 (the **Straits Settlements**). **Malaya** gained independence in 1957. **Malaysia** was formed in 1963 by Singapore, Malaya (now West Malaysia), Sarawak and Sabah (now East Malaysia). **Singapore** had achieved self-rule in 1959, and became an independent republic in 1965.

The **Malay Archipelago** is the largest group of islands in the world, comprising **Indonesia** and the **Philippines.** The Philippines includes over 13,000 islands and gained political independence from the United States of America in 1946. Principal regions include Luzon (northern Philippines), the Visayas (central Philippines), and Mindanao and the Sulu Achipelago in the south. The Filipino people have been enriched by tribal, Malay, Chinese and Spanish ethnic strands, along with Islamic culture in the south where struggles for autonomy are endemic.

A Note on Languages, Terms, Style

English spelling and punctuation follow that which is customary within the country under consideration. Apart from some minor variations made necessary by particular cultural traditions, the style followed is that of *The Chicago Manual of Style*. Particular terms and usages - and in some cases formats - native to the area concerned have been retained where possible, both to remain true to the wide diversity of texts and authors, and also to signify important aspects of localised context and reflection. A Glossary, which can be only partial for such vast geographical areas and such immense bodies of writing, is provided for abbreviations, special terms and acronyms, along with full indexes to subjects and to personal names.

Note: In bibliographies full publishing details are given for only the first occurrence of a work.

Abbreviations

ABF	-	Association des bibliothécaires français.
ABM	-	American Baptist Mission
ACAA	-	Asian Christian Art Association
ACFOD	-	Asian Cultural Forum for Development
ACISCA	-	Association of Christian Institutes for Social Concern in Asia
ACS	-	Asian Christian Service (EACC-CCA)
AKKAPKA	-	Action for Peace and Justice, Philippines
AMRSP	-	Association of Major Religious Superiors in the Philippines
APNIEVE	-	Asia Pacific Network for International Education and Values Education
ASPAMIR	-	SVD Asian Pacific Association of Mission Researchers
ATEM	-	Association for Theological Education Myanmar
ATESEA	-	Association for Theological Education in Southeast Asia
AWIT	-	Association of Women in Theology, Philippines
AWRC / AWRCCT	-	Asian Women's Resource Centre for Culture and Theology
Balitbang-PGI	-	Research and Study Unit of the Communion of Churches Indonesia.
BBC	-	Burma Baptist Convention
BCC	-	Basic Christian Communities
BCCM	-	Basel Christian Church of Malaysia

Abbreviations

BDS	-	Burma Divinity School
BEC	-	Basic Ecclesial Communities
BEFEO	-	Bulletin de l'Ecole Francaise d' Extrême-Orient
BFM	-	Board of Foreign Missions (USA)
BISA	-	Bishops' Institute for Social Action (FABC)
BIT	-	Burma Institute of Theology (now MIT)
BPK	-	Gunung Mulia - Badan Penerbit Kristen (the name of "Gunung Mulia" was added to BPK in 1967) Indonesian Christian Publisher
BRE	-	Bachelor of Religious Education (Myanmar)
BSEI	-	Bulletin de la Société des Etudes Indochinoises
C & MA	-	Christian and Missionary Alliance
CAN	-	*Catholic Asian News*
CARE	-	Christian Association for Relief, Malaysia
CBCM	-	Catholic Bishops' Conference of Myanmar
CBCP	-	Catholic Bishops' Conference of the Philippines
CBCT	-	Catholic Bishops' Conference of Thailand
CBMS	-	Conference British Mission Societies
CCA	-	Christian Conference of Asia
CCA-CTC	-	CCA Commission of Theological Concerns
CCA-URM	-	CCA Urban Rural Mission
CCHD	-	Catholic Commission for Human Development, Thailand

CCM	- Council of Churches Malaysia
CCT	- Church of Christ in Thailand
CCWA	- Cambodian Christian Women's Association
CEER	- Commission on Evangelism and Ecumenical Relations, Philippines
CFA	- Media Group, Philippines
CFM	- Christian Federation of Malaysia
CGDT / CG	- *Cong Giao va Dan Toc* (Catholicism and Nation) National Catholic Weekly, Vietnam
CIAM	- International Center of Missionary Animation
cicm	- Scheut Missionaries, Louvain
CIIR	- Catholic Institute for International Relations
CJPC	- Catholic Justice and Peace Commission, Thailand
CLS	- Christian Literature Society
CMKI / GMKI	- Student Christian Movement Indonesia
cnd	- Congregation de Notre Dame
CNL	- Christians for National Liberation, Philippines
CPDSK	- Churches' Participation in Development in Shan, Kayah and Karen States
CSM	- College Student Ministries, Philippines
CSO	- Civil Society Organizations, Philippines
cssr	- Redemptorists (Congregation of the Most Holy Redeemer)
DAGA	- Documentation for action Groups in Asia
DCL	- Doctor of Canon Law

Abbreviations

DDK	-	*Dai Doan Ket (*Movement for Greater Solidarity), Vietnam
DGI/PGI	-	The Communion of Churches in Indonesia
DIWA	-	SVD Theological Journal from Tagaytay, Philippines
EACC	-	East Asia Christian Conference
EAPR	-	East Asia Pastoral Review
EATWOT	-	Ecumenical Association of Third World Theologians
EBF	-	Ecumenical Bishops' Forum, Philippines
ECPAT	-	End Child Prostitution in Asian Tourism.
ECTWT	-	Ecumenical Coalition on Third World Tourism
EFT	-	Evangelical Fellowship of Thailand
EMW	-	Evangelische Missionswerk
FABC	-	Federation of Asian Bishops' Conferences
FABC-OHD	-	Federation of Asian Bishops' Conferences Office for Human Development
FFW	-	Federation of Free Workers, Philippines.
FIDES	-	Forum for Interdisciplinary Endeavours and Studies, Philippines
FME/IDOC	-	Future of the Missionary Enterprise - IDOC
fsc	-	De La Salle Brothers
GCF	-	Graduates' Christian Fellowship
GFVN	-	Government of Free Vietnam
GKE	-	Evangelical Church in Kalimantan Indonesia.
GKI	-	Protestant Church in Irian Jaya (West Papua)
GKP	-	Pasundan Protestant Church Indonesia.

GKPB	- Protestant Church in Bali
GMIM	- Protestant Church in Minahasa Indonesia
GMIT	- Protestant Church in Timor Indonesia
GPIB	- Protestant Church in Macassar Indonesia
GCF	- Graduates' Christian Fellowship
HCMV	- Ho Chi Minh Ville, Vietnam
HKBP	- Batak Protestant Church Indonesia.
HMI	- Modernist Muslim Student Association Indonesia.
IEMELIF	- Iglesia Evangelica Metodista en las Islas Filipinas, Philippines
IF	- IGOROTA Foundation, Philippines
IFI	- Iglesia Filipina Independiente
IIRFWP	- International and Inter-Religious Federation for World Peace
ij	- Sisters of the Infant Jesus
IMC	- International Missionary Council
IMCS	- International Movement of Catholic Students
IRC	- Institute for Religion and Culture, Philippines
IRM	- International Review of Mission
ISA	- Internal Security Act (Malaysia)
ISACC	- Institute for Studies in Asian Church and Culture, Quezon City Philippines
ISO	- Institute for Social Order, Manila, Philippines.
IVP	- Intervarsity Press
IWA	- International Writers' Association
IWS	- Institute of Women's Studies, Philippines
JEC	- Jeunesse éstudiante Catholique

JMBRAS	- Journal of the Malay Branch Royal Asiatic Society
JMP	- *Jaringan Mitra Perempuan* (Women's Partnership Network)
JPC	- Justice and Peace Commission of the Catholic Church
JSBRAS	- Journal of Singapore Branch Royal Asiatic Society
KBC	- Karen Baptist Convention
KITLV	- Royal Institute of Linguistics and Anthropology, Leiden.
KOPTARI	- The Indonesian Religious Leadership Conference (formerly MASRI).
KPS	- *Kelompok Perempuan Sadar* (Association for Women's Awareness Indonesia).
LAI	- National Bible Society Indonesia.
LBI	- Catholic Biblical Institute Indonesia.
LMS	- London Missionary Society (now CWM)
LPPS-KWI	- Social Research Unit of the Indonesian Catholic Bishops' Conference
LST	- Loyola School of Theology, Quezon City, Philippines.
LWF	- Lutheran World Federation.
MAKIBAKA	- *Malayang Kilusan nh Bagong Kababaihan* (Free Movement of New Women), Philippines
MAWI, KWI	- Indonesian Conference of Bishops
MBC	- Myanmar Baptist Convention
MCC	- Malayan Christian Council
MCC	- Myanmar Council of Churches

MCCBCHS	- Malaysian Consultative Council for Buddhism, Christianity, Hinduism and Sikhism.
mep	- Missions Etrangère de Paris
MICT	- Myanmar Institute of Christian Theology
MIN, UMNO, MCA	- (Political Parties, Malaysia)
MIRO	- Malaysian Inter-religious Association
MIT	- Myanmar Institute of Theology
MST Review	- Maryhill School of Theology Review, Manila Philippines
NASSA	- National Secretariat of Social Action, Justice and Peace, Philippines
NCCP	- National Christian Council of the Philippines
NECF	- National Evangelical Christian Fellowship, Malaysia
NGO	- Non-Government Organisation
NthT	- Nederlands Theologisch Tijdschrift
ocd	- Discalced Carmelites
ofm	- Order of Friars Minor
OMF	- Overseas Missionary Fellowship
op	- Order of Preachers (Dominicans)
osb	- Order of St Benedict
osu	- Order of St Ursula
PACT	- People's Action for Cultural Ties
PAN	- *Partai Amanat Nasional* (Indonesian National Mandate Party)
PCP II	- Plenary Council of the Philippines
PDIP	- Democratic Party of Struggle Indonesia.
PEN	- World Association of Writers

Abbreviations

PERSETIA	- *Perhimpunan Sekolah Teologi Indonesia* (The (Protestant) Association of Theological Schools in Indonesia)
PERWATI	- Association of Women with Theological Education in Indonesia
PGI	- The Communion of Churches in Indonesia
PMPC	- Peninsula Malaysia Pastoral Council
PMRI	- Catholic Student Movement, Indonesia.
PMV	- Pro Mundi Vita
PPIP	- Research Institute of Duta Wacana Protestant University, Yogyakarta Indonesia.
PTE	- Programme on Theological Education WCC
rc	- Religious Sisters of the Cenacle
rgs	- Sisters of the Good Shepherd
rscj	- Religious Sisters of the Sacred Heart
SCM	- Student Christian Movement
SCS	- Society for Christian Service (Sarawak)
SEAATS	- Southeast Asia Association of Theological Schools (now ATESEA)
SEAGST	- Southeast Asian Graduate School of Theology
SEAJT	- *Southeast Asian Journal of Theology* (now *Asia Journal of Theology)*
sj	- Society of Jesus
SPCPD	- Southern Philippines Council for Peace and Development.
SPI	- Socio-Pastoral Institute, Manila
ssps	- Sisters of the Holy Spirit
STM	- Seminari Theoloji Malaysia (Seremban)
STT	- Sekolah Tinggi Theologia, Graduate School of Theology, Jakarta.

svd	- Society of the Divine Word
TBAVHM / BAVH	- *Trong Bulletin des Amis du Vieux Hué*, Vietnam
TEE	- Theological Education by Extension
TESDA	- Technical Education and Skills of the government's Development Authority, Philippines
THRUST	- Theologians for Renewal, Unity and Social Transformation, Philippines
TICD	- Thai Inter-Religious Commission for Development
TTTH	- *Tuyen Tap Than Hoc* (Theological Selection), Vietnam.
UCAN	- *Union of Catholic Asian News*
UCCP	- United Church of Christ in the Philippines
UIF	- Union de Impresores de Filipinas / Union Obrera Democratica (UOD in 1902, later the Union Democratica de Filipinas)
UILD	- Urban Industrial League for Development
UIM	- Urban Industrial Mission
UKIT	- Christian University at Tomohon Indonesia
UMI	- University Microfilms International
VOC	- Dutch East India Company
WACC	- World Association of Christian Communication
WCC -CCPD	- World Council of Churches Commission on the Churches' Participation in Development
WPF	- World Peace Federation
WSCF A-P	- World Student Christian Federation Asia-Pacific.

Abbreviations

YCW /JOC	- Young Catholic Workers
YMCA	- Young Men's Christian Association
YWCA	- Young Women's Christian Association
ZBC	- Zomi Baptist Convention

ILLUSTRATIONS
Volume Two: Southeast Asia

1 Saw Edward - Myanmar
Print: THE LOST COIN
Source: *The Bible Through Asian Eyes,* p.115.

Saw Edward was born in Myanmar in 1945 and studied art at the Myanmar State School of Fine Art. He has been working for the Episcopal Church in the Province of Myanmar as Communications Director, and has done illustrations for church publications and some oil paintings of Biblical themes. He uses the traditional Burmese style of art in order to communicate more directly with the local people. This work is based on rhythm of lines, the same tone in colours, no light or shade, and very little perspective. "The Lost Coin" is painted in oil on canvas.

2 Bagong Kussudiardja - Indonesia
Print: THE ASCENSION
Source: *The Bible Through Asian Eyes,* p.165.

Bagong Kussudiardja was born in Indonesia in 1928 and brought up among artists. He began to study the classical dances of Java at the age of 18 and his love of dance has always been foremost in his life. After the proclamation of independence in 1945, Bagong began to experiment with dances which would reflect the new spirit in Indonesia. Always creative and innovative, he had many critics but just as many supporters. He wrote: "Art is a part of my life. I feel that one needs art just as one needs food, clothing and shelter. I live every day receptive to everything surrounding me, open to the past and the things inherited from my ancestors, the present and the future. Even though something may be very small, I try to understand it completely, since human life must be able to appreciate the vitality of all things."

Bagong takes a close interest in all aspects of the arts. He is a skilled batik painter and, as "The Ascension" indicates, his oil

Saw Edward – The Lost Coin

Bagong Kussudiardja – The Ascension

Pracoyo – Confrontation. Wood cut print

Hanna C. Varghese–Who Will Roll Away the Stone. Batik painting.

Jonathan T. Carpio – Christ Our Peace

Sawai Chinnawong – Pentecost

paintings also rank with the finest. His painting of the dancing Christ ascending to heaven was prepared for the Second Conference of the ACAA held in the Philippines. Bagong currently heads a dance training centre and an education institute in Jogjakarta.

3 Pracoyo - Indonesia

Print: CONFRONTATION. Wood cut print.
Source: *CATS III Art Exhibition,* Jogja 2001.

Pracoyo was born in Jogjakarta, central Java, in 1959. He still lives in Jogja five kilometres up the 30-kilometre long Kaliurang Road that links the Sutan's Place (Kraton) and the foot of Merapi Volcano. "Confrontation" expresses the verve of the student insurrection that toppled Soeharto in May 1998 and the courage of the faith-inspired grass-roots movements in their ongoing confrontation with entrenched militarism.

4 Hanna C. Varghese - Malaysia

Print: WHO WILL ROLL AWAY THE STONE. Batik painting.
Source: *Image 82,* p.3.

Hanna Varghese was born and brought up in Malaysia. Hanna comes from the Orthodox Church and discovered her vocation as an artist early in life. She has been an active supporter of the ACAA for many years and has now become a committee member.

Painting and drawing has been Hanna's great passion for as long as she can remember. Hanna presently dyes batik cloth pictures and paints mainly in acrylics. Hanna says: "Visual images reveal more of one's mind than words. Art (images/icons) has been used in education, contemplation, meditation and veneration in Christian tradition. I hope to continue expressing my Christian faith in art."

5 Jonathan T. Carpio - Philippines

Print: CHRIST OUR PEACE
Source: *The Bible Through Asian Eyes,* p.179.

Jonathan T. Carpio studied art in Manila. The theme of the Ninth Assembly of the Christian Conference in Asia (CCA) in June 1990 was "Christ our Peace". Carpio won first prize in a competition for an art work to illustrate this theme. In his acrylic painting he expresses how Christ has made all one, by showing tribal people from different parts of the Philippines coming together through the power of God's Spirit.

6 Sawai Chinnawong - Thailand
Print: PENTECOST
Source: *The Bible Through Asian Eyes,* p.167.

Sawai Chinnawong was born in Thailand in 1959. He grew up in the Buddhist tradition and it was the enjoyment of Buddhist paintings which made him determined to become an artist. During high school he converted to Christianity, and after studying art at the Taiwichitsin Institute in Bangkok he entered the McGilrary Faculty of Theology at Payap University, Chiang Mai. He graduated with arts and theology degrees in 1989. Since then he has been part of the Church Arts Programme of the Church of Christ in Thailand, an innovative programme supporting indigenous Christian art. Sawai is the first Resident Artist in the programme. His paintings use traditional Thai art forms and images to convey the Christian message in a way local people will understand.

Introduction

The central aim in preparing this Research Guide has been to introduce and chart the range and significance of Asian Christian theologies in historical context, and to provide the resources and tools for their study.

It is of course impossible within even three volumes to provide an exhaustive coverage of Christian reflection and writing from half the Christian world over more than fifteen centuries. Within scores of diverse cultures and religious traditions - Shinto or Taoist, Primal Hindu, Confucian, Buddhist or Islamic - Christian faith has lived and interacted since the earliest centuries. From this presence has come

- bodies of Christian writing from at least the 4th century with particular creativity in the periods of the 4th-5th centuries (west Asia in particular), 7th-8th-centuries (west and central Asia), 16th-17th centuries (east and south Asia), late 19th century and second half of the 20th century (throughout the region).

- writings in a wide variety of literary and oral-record forms - frequently shaped by local tradition - along with richly diverse expressions in art, architecture and community life.

- reflection, scholarship, and devotion amidst the widest range of movements and endeavours for not only spiritual nurture and 'church-planting', 'leadership training', and many-sided educational and medical programmes, but also in community and inter-religious movements for social reform or political reconstruction, for rural development and environmental protection, for women's concerns and human rights, for peace, social justice, community reconciliation, and the empowering of the destitute and powerless.

A Different Focus

A large part of this theological work and writing can indeed be studied with the help of resources here provided, but the primary focus in the following sections is more limited. It is rather to outline the key sources for a study of 'Asian theologies' which have arisen from, and fed, Christian life in a particular country and region; 'reflective' responses to God's historic and present work in Tamilnadu or Tomohon, Guangdung or Luzon, Cholla, or Kyushu. The focus is therefore upon contextualizing, incarnational or 'local' theologies which discover within a people's present struggle and aspiration, and in their creative cultural and religious traditions, the presence of the same liberating and transforming Spirit known in Jesus the Christ.

From early centuries on, and now in the midst of sharp socio-economic and cultural discord, we can recognise theological reflection and construction which is both critical and doxological, non-dualistic and communitarian, dialogical and confessional, dissident and devotional, historical, incarnational, pilgriming, heuristic and pragmatic. Beyond the motives of communicating the faith or nurturing believers, creative theological reflection is here often a wrestling with such issues as:

- "what understanding of Christian faith in our culture will make possible social reconstruction and spiritual reform for our nation and people?" (in the seventeenth or eighteenth centuries: such authors as Yang Ting Yun, Fucansai Fabian, and Chong Yak Jong; in the nineteenth and early twentieth centuries: such authors as Krishna Mohab Banrjea, Jose Burgos, Nguyen Truong To and Kozaki Hiromichi, amongst many others);

- or "what faith and spirituality will nourish our people in prophetic and holistic mission?" (in the twentieth century: such theologians - out of very many - as C.L. Wickremasinghe, Khin Maung Din, Park Sun-ai, T.B. Simutupang, Shoki Coe, Horatio de la Costa).

Such bodies of reflection and insight are not easily classified according to non-Asian theological movements or western theological disciplines. The long and autonomous traditions of Asian theologies have not only other sources and intentions, but frequently question, even reject, the elements or frameworks of western or westernising theologies. In this, many Asian theologies are "post- (or pre-) colonial", and reject either explicitly or implicitly the categories of imperial or neo-imperial theories and theologies, especially where these would claim an "objective" or normative role in assessing or interpreting theological reflection.

Whatever similarities can be found to the theologies of other regions, those of Asia have long held quite distinct qualities. There is in Asia a special seriousness of concern for indigenous culture and religion, and a particular apprehension of life in community as it is shaped by these. The vast scale of human suffering in Asian countries and the sharpness of the struggle for human survival has yielded also a vitality of prophetic insight and an immediacy in gospel interpretation, while the unrivalled diversity of peoples, of Christian tradition and of historical experience in the region give a unique character to each of Asia's theologies.

In this sense, these theologies, like all others, are local theologies. They arise at a particular point of history, in the dynamic interaction of gospel, church, and culture. They grow out of and serve national or regional Christian traditions and retain the marks of a unique cultural experience. This can be thought to undermine the universality of the Christian gospel only by ignoring the particularity and historicity of God's dealings with Israel and of the life of Jesus himself. Those who would reject the localised character of theological construction are often in fact imposing their own formulations as in some sense normative for all others. This often veils only thinly a westernising or ethnocentric oppression brought about by cultural (and economic) domination.

Theological reflection is Asian therefore, not because of the characteristics shared with other parts of the region: far less because of the nationality or geographical location of the theologian. Rather it will be Asian, and a witness to the one God, in so far as it discerns and responds to the unique incarnation of the Gospel in a local Asian context. 'The Lord' has a personal and particular controversy with the people of Thailand or Sri Lanka, the Philippines or Korea as much as with Israel; with the people of Indonesia or Vietnam, India or Japan as with Judah. And in each of Asia's peoples, this controversy comes as a different summons.

In their vast extent, their wisdom and witness, such writings and reflections are also a continuing challenge to any assumptions that Asian 'theologies' are of secondary importance or that western theologies are somehow normative for all others. Extensive libraries of Christian writing, from many countries over many centuries, and the vitality of reflection and insight they contain, demonstrate that Asian 'theology' is a major study in its own right, with independent sources and experience and with its own autonomy of intention and interpretation.

It must be recognised, however, that the thought patterns, the terminology, and the interpretive principles used in incarnational Asian theologies are frequently markedly different from those which are often assumed to be normative in some other regions. The systematic metaphysical construction that emerged in the post-medieval West for example, has seldom been an indispensable - or even recognised - element in incarnational Asian theologies. And it will be clear throughout this Guide that Asian Christians have long possessed different models - of insight and wisdom, discernment and truth-seeing, of heart-knowledge and life-shaping - by which they "do theology", reflecting upon and living the faith.

The forms of thought and writing included for study here, include therefore not only treatises and volumes, articles and theses, but also many other forms, including letters and poetry, liturgies, homilies and confessions, declarations, meditations, and life-stories. And because 'spirituality' and devotion has from the earliest centuries been integral to the doing of theology in Asian cultures, the 'theology' presented often demonstrates a unity of life-experience and mysticism, of cultural identity and critical reflection, which goes beyond particular 'disciplines' while also drawing on a wide range of Christian resources. The reflection and writing may in fact be incidental to ministry, to vocation or to activism, arising from present needs to "take the next step in pilgrimage", rather than from any desire to contribute to systematic thought, although this too will appear in many entries. Certainly it will be seen that 'theology' in Asian countries includes all deeply human issues and concerns within its content, and that it arises as much

Introduction

in a dynamic unity of words and life - an alternative hermeneutic of prophetic witness - as in the formulation of creative expositions.

Charting Resources

Scores of national bibliographies, surveys, histories, and anthologies have attempted to introduce sections of these large bodies of material, and many regional studies, collections, and surveys have been published in recent decades. In addition there are now over two hundred theological journals published regularly in the region along with publications by networks of Christian publishers, Study and Social Concern Centres, People's Movements, Pastoral Institutes, and Theological Schools. A guide-to-study which attempts to be more comprehensive, and practical, in aim has become increasingly necessary in order to introduce and chart a fuller range of the resources available. And such a charting must be based on careful work, to assemble as well as reclaim a wide spectrum of theological sources which are genuinely contextualizing or incarnational. These include both unique national and local bodies of thought and witness, and also the writings which have arisen from regional movements and complex theological interactions. We recognise the significance not only of creative individuals, and scholarly teachers, but also of groups and collectives, of 'non-professional'/lay women and men, and of thinkers, witnesses or activists, some having only tenuous relationship to an institutional church. The attempt has also here been made to include such thought and writings from those of 'Orthodox', 'Catholic' or 'Protestant' communions, in all parts of Asia/Austral-Asia, from all cultural traditions and from the period of the seventh to twentieth centuries.

In order to do this, the approach chosen for this 'guide-to-study' presents study-outlines by country and region. These may include brief historical introductions, mini-studies of selected texts and writers, and bibliographies for these as well as for additional sources. Although most sections appear in the form of individual, group or theme entries, followed by selected references, some are largely annotated and categorised bibliographies. In view of the wide diversity of theological context and tradition being included, such minimum diversity in format is appropriate. Supplementary bibliographies are also provided where necessary; further works by authors cited can be found in such serials as *Theology in Context* (Bi-annual, Aachen); *International Review of Mission* (Quarterly, Geneva); *Bibliographia Missionaria* (Annual, Rome); and *PTCA Bulletin* (Bi-annual, Kyoto and Chiangmai). Special attention has been given to, but is not limited to, the work and writings of nationals, both 'lay' and professional, with particular recognition of women's thought and work. But the primary reason for inclusion in all cases has been the intention by the author(s) to 'incarnate' the gospel in a particular Asian context in response to the realities of a people's life and God's presence within them.

It is hoped that the combination of historical contexts, textual and biographical notes, bibliographies and other tools will form a practical guide to the people, movements, and literatures which offer, for the life of our people now, the wealth of Asian theological reflection and insight.

Use of the Guide

A chapter for each country of Southeast Asia is here provided, comprising entries for individuals, groups and movements, as well as for historical contexts and diverse categories of writing. These all include selected bibliographies which are enlarged in extensive supplementary bibliographies for each country. Quick reference to particular authors, movements, sources or contexts can be found by use of the listing that commences each chapter and/or by use of the indexes.

In using this guide for individual or group study, the following approaches are suggested:
   i) Country studies - centred in theological movements and leaders within a particular period.
   ii) Thematic studies - selecting writings on Christian ethics; theologies of struggle, spirituality or mission; cross-cultural or inter-faith interpretation ... within a group of countries.
   iii) Study of regional movements in women's theology, story theology, contextualizing/incarnational theologies, ecumenical action and reflection, biblical hermeneutics.

Introduction

iv) Study of selected texts, by country, period or movement - or surveys of theological literature within a particular historical context.

v) Research that uses this Guide as basis for the investigation of further primary sources from a country, movement or period.

A note must be added concerning the accessibility of many materials here referred to. Few theological libraries in Asia have as yet any comprehensive collection of the sources, and although some libraries in other regions have selected items, these collections also are individually fragmentary. For most countries there are extensive sources held outside the region which should be copied and returned. It has been thought best, however, to include reference to any source which is important for the further study of Asian 'theologies', regardless of its location, so that at least the necessary signposts for subsequent research are given.

The Tasks Ahead

The editors have no illusions that these volumes offer an exhaustive guide to Asian theologies but believe them to be thoroughly representative of their range and content. No similar guide has yet been attempted, and it has become increasingly clear during preparation of this study-guide that large tasks remain if the full extent and significance of the region's reflection and writing is to be recognised (and included in such a Research Guide). This work is therefore also a signpost, and hopefully a stimulus, to some of the major investigation which still needs to be undertaken.

For some countries, peoples and historical periods, we are still in the 'excavatory' stage of discovering and identifying texts and authors: much research and reclaiming is still needed, not least because the writings of nationals, of lay-people, clergy, or of women have often been disguised, or even suppressed. Many studies of writings, as yet unrecognised or interpreted in their context, wait to be done. We warmly invite you to collaborate in this venture to unearth, collect, and share theological sources in our region, assuring you that the Editors will gratefully acknowledge all contributions sent to:

Research Guide to Asian Theologies,

[Either at]   Puslit Candraditya, Jalan Lero Wulan No. 1,
              Wairklau - Maumere 86112, Flores NTT, Indonesia;

[Or at]   13 Hilldale Place, Christchurch 8002, New Zealand.

It is now the time to give priority to the study of Asia's many living theologies, within the life of our societies - through carefully planned courses both in 'academic' and non-formal settings, in local or national seminars and workshops, and in programmes of study by individuals or groups. Increasing numbers of our colleagues beckon us to do this, and partners beyond the region ask us to share our resources with them.

The related tasks of collection, translation, publication or reprinting call for much fuller commitment and active promotion if our libraries are to possess any significant body of even fundamental texts. And for this we must seek active co-operation with the librarians of our seminaries, institutes, study and social concern centres, and with translators, publishers, and distributors. For despite the collaboration of scores of scholars from the region and the very extensive research which has made this Guide possible, it remains only the first wide-ranging attempt to chart the vast materials of Asian theologies.

There then remains for us the enriching exchanges, across cultures, the reinterpretation shaped by our people's struggles, and the collaboration in putting-theology-to-work, by which we together seek the transformation of society, culture, and faith which God's coming Commonwealth brings.

The Editors

1 Contextual Christian Theology in Asia
Historical Regional Survey (Summary)

1 Theological Heritage

In order to understand contextualising theologies as these have developed in the countries of Southeast Asia in the past two centuries, it is necessary to recognise their beginnings and their diverse contributions in previous centuries also. The theological heritage of Christians throughout Asia is in fact much vaster than is usually recognised and brief surveys for this are provided below for the periods 7th-15th centuries, 16th-18th centuries, and the 19th century. For fuller outlines see: *Groundwork for Asian Christian Theologies* I and II (chapters 1 and 2 of volume 1), and country chapters throughout.

In each country of Southeast Asia pioneering work prior to the 19th century has provided groundwork for contextual theological reflection, in linguistic, historical and anthropological studies, as well as in theological and inter-faith studies. As the basis for understanding later theological developments, selected examples of this groundwork are outlined in chapter 2 of this volume below. For the period since 1800, country chapters given in this volume give the fuller treatment for authors, movements and sources.

1.1 Theological Heritage Before 1500

(See *"Groundwork for Asian Christian Theologies I"*, volume I, chapter 1.)

In the manuscripts from writers of Turkestan and west China, from the 7th to 11th centuries, Christian scriptures and teaching are found not only in the Syriac of the parent 'Oriental Orthodox' tradition, but also in the Sogdian, Uighur and Chinese vernaculars. They utilize imagery, terminology and literary forms then current in Central Asian communities, especially those of Buddhist tradition.

Along with many translations of liturgical and ecclesiastical texts, the sutras and fragments thus far translated present a Christian faith which preserves orthodox doctrine - as in the *Nestorian Motwa Hymn: Honouring the Majestic Three*, and the *Credo of Rabban bar Sauma*, and also interprets the Gospels contextually - as in The *Lord of the Universe's Discourse on Almsgiving*. Some stress simplicity of life-style and compassionate service - as in the *Sianfu* (Xi'anfu) *Stele inscription* (sometimes called the *Nestorian Monument*) and many reflect a sympathetic dialogue with those of other living faiths - as in the sutras of Alopen such as *The Discourse on the Oneness of the Universe*, *Parable Part II* and the *Jesus Messiah Sutra*.

These and other writings are outlined in the books below, and additional texts are still being discovered and translated. Together these offer a growing body of Christian literature that has been significantly shaped by its context, and which has abiding significance for Christian life and mission in the region.

Selected References:
> See Supplementary Bibliography, Chap. 3, Vol. I: Moffatt 1992; England 1998; Philip 1998.
> Gillman, Ian and Hans-Joachim Klimkeit. *Christians in Asia before 1500*. Richmond: Curzon, 1999.
> Kitagawa, Joseph Mitsuo. *The Christian Tradition: Beyond its European Captivity*. Philadelphia: Trinity Press International, 1992.
> Palmer, Martin. *The Jesus Sutras. Rediscovering the Lost Scrolls of Taoist Christianity*. New York: Ballantyne, forthcoming.
> Saeki, Paul Yoshiro. *The Nestorian Documents and Relics in China*. Tokyo: Maruzen, 1951.
> Standaert, Nicholas. *Handbook of Christianity in China. Vol.1: 635-1800*. Leiden: Brill, forthcoming.
> van der Ploeg, J.P.M. *Syriac Manuscripts of St. Thomas Christians*. Bangalore: Dharmaram, 1983.
> See also the journals *Harp* (Kottayam); *Numen* (Leiden); *SOAS Bulletin* (London); and those listed in Gillman and Klimkeit (1999).

1.2 Theological Heritage 1500-1800

(See also *Groundwork for Theologies II*, volume I, chapter 2; and *Southeast Asia 16th-18th Centuries*, chapter 2 below.)

Christian writings of the 16th to 18th centuries - most of which have yet to receive serious study - include many confessional, historical and apologetic documents, many of which translate or imitate European models. Although these often reveal the imagery and thought of indigenous translators, there are also, however, extensive writings which openly draw on indigenous tradition and display contextualising insight. And these come both from the hands of 'local' clergy, lay-women and men, and from 'foreign' lay men and women and clergy.

Treatises and narratives modify or reject western teaching (see for example Chong Yak Jong in Korea, Lu Y Doan in Vietnam and Fukansai Fabian in Japan); indigenous poetry and drama reshapes Christian thought (see for example Paul Yoho-ken in Japan and Aquino de Belen in the Philippines); dialogues and treatises restore local religious tradition (see for example Yang Ting Yun, China, and the Christ Veda writers in India). There is also sometimes a complete integration of vocation, life-style, and writing in the lives of some authors, notably women (see for example, Candida Hsu (Xu) in China and Gracia Hosokawa in Japan).

Fully traditional literary or art forms are also often employed: those such as encyclopaedia (Korea and India), *babad* (East Indies), *pasyon* (Philippines), and *Maria-Kannon* (Japan).

Selected References:

Ba, Vivian. *The Early Catholic Missionaries in Burma*. A collected series of articles from *Guardian Monthly*, Rangoon, c. 1957-1964. Rangoon Reprint 1997.

Baago, K. *A Bibliography. Library of Indian Christian Theology*. Madras: Christian Literature Society, 1969.

Cho Kwong. *A Historical Study of Catholicism in the Late Chosun Dynasty* (in Korean). Seoul: 1988.

England, John C. "Bamboo Groves in Winds from the West: Indigenous Faith and Westernization in Asian Christian Writings of 16th - 18th Centuries." In *Christen und Gewürze*, edited by Klaus Koschorke. Göttingen: Vandenhoeck & Ruprecht, 1998.

Laures, Johannes. *Kirishitan Bunko: A Manual of Books and Documents on the Early Christian Mission in Japan*. Tokyo: Sophia University, 1957.

Lumbera, Bienvenido L. *Tagalog Poetry 1570-1898: Tradition and Influences in its Development*. Quezon City: Ateneo de Manila University Press, 1986.

Nguyen Van Truong et al. *Ve Sach Bao cua Tac Gia Cong Ciao: The Ky XVII-XIX* (Books and Newspapers by Catholic Authors - Vietnam 17th-19th Centuries). Ho Chi Minh City: University of Ho Chi Minh, Literature Department, 1993.

Pieris, Edmund. *Studies Historical and Cultural*. Colombo, 1978.

Standaert, Nicholas. *Handbook of Christianity in China*. Vol.1: *635-1800*. Leiden: Brill, forthcoming.

Streit, R. and J.Dindinger, eds. *Bibliotheca Missionum*. Rome: Herder, 1963: Vols. 4-8.

1.3 Theological Heritage 1800 - 1900

(See also Country chapters, volumes I, II, III.)

Despite continuing proscription of Christianity in many countries of the region in this period, the number of theological writings which recognise the historical and indigenous, inter-church and inter-faith dimensions of Christian faith and practice, steadily increase in this century. This is largely because of the growth of the 'modern missionary movement' throughout the region, but it also drew on continuing and renewed sources of reflection and writing within the Christian traditions of particular peoples.

In India, for example, theological and contextual writing was greatly stimulated by a cultural and religious renaissance from the 1820s on, by nationalist movements, and by inter-faith encounter. (See Volume I). In the Philippines, the traditions of the *pasyon*, folk-poetry, and narrative, often as vehicles for subversive Christian insight, continued to develop, along with strongly nationalist theology and advocacy. (See Volume II).

In China, study of the Chinese culture and classics remained central for many, often placed in the context of social and educational reform, or of ecumenical co-operation. In Japan, many

Contextual Christian Theology in Asia

Kakure Kirishitan communities continued their traditions of accommodation even after the return of Catholic missionaries, while by the late 19th century, Japanese theology and identity-within-culture are being clearly expressed. (See Volume III)

In Korea and Vietnam, confessional literature arose from continuing persecution which, however, eases by mid century, to be later followed by a growing body of nationalist and reformist writing. (See Volumes II and III). In Sri Lanka, Malaya, Burma, and the East Indies, the circumstances of colonial domination largely restricted the growth of indigenous writing. Nevertheless there are many examples in each place of sustained contextual study and reflection which are now being recovered.

Selected References:

Bays, Daniel H., ed. *Christianity in China: From the Eighteenth Century to the Present.* Stanford: Stanford University Press, 1996.

Boyd, Robin H.S. *An Introduction to Indian Christian Theology.* Madras: Christian Literature Society, 1969, 1975.

Deats, Richard L. *Nationalism and Christianity in the Philippines.* Dallas: Southern Methodist University Press, 1967.

Furuya, Yasuo, ed. *A History of Japanese Theology.* Grand Rapids: Eerdmans, 1997.

Germany, Charles H. *Protestant Theologies in Modern Japan*: A History of Dominant Theological Currents from 1920-1960. Tokyo: IISR Press, 1965.

Handbook of Christianity in China. Vol.2: 1800-2000. Leiden: Brill, forthcoming.

Hoekema, Alle Gabe, *Deken in dynamisch evenwicht: de wordingsgeschiedenis van de nationale protestantse theologie in Indonesie (ca. 1860-1960).* Goudstratt: Uitgeverij Boekencentrum, B.V., 1984.

Lam, Wing-hung. *Chinese Theology in Construction.* Pasadena: William Carey Library, 1983.

Nguyen Van Truong et al. *Ve Sach Bao cua Tac Gia Cong Ciao: The Ky XVII-XIX.* (Books and Newspapers by Catholic Authors, 17th-19th Centuries.) Ho Chi Minh Ville: University of Ho Chi Minh Ville, 1993.

Ryu Dong Shik. *A History of Korean Theological Thought* (in Korean). Seoul: Jun Mang Sa, 1982.

Scheiner, Irwin. *Christian Converts and Social Protest in Meiji Japan.* Berkeley & Los Angeles: University of California Press, 1970.
Schumacher, John N. *Revolutionary Clergy: The Filipino Clergy and the Nationalist Movement, 1850-1903.* Quezon City: Ateneo de Manila University Press, 1981.
Thomas, George. *Christian Indians and Indian Nationalism 1885-1950: An Interpretation in Historical and Theological Perspectives.* Frankfurt a.M: Lang, 1979.
Thomas, M.M. *The Acknowledged Christ of the Indian Renaissance.* Confessing the Faith in India 5. Madras: C.L.S. 1970.

1.4 Asian Regional and Ecumenical Theologies (19th-20th Centuries).

For a full treatment see *Asian Regional and Ecumenical Theologies* (volume I, chapter 3).

In the last two centuries theology in the Asian region has been greatly stimulated and nourished by regional and ecumenical movements in mission, study and reflection. These have emerged in rich interaction between Christian faith and the shared realities of history and culture, and have often exercised strong influence upon the development of both national and Christian identity in witness, action and theology. Churches and communities across the region have "found each other in mission", developed a wide range of networks and associations which further their common mission and produced many volumes of contextual theology.

Key movements here have been the Asia-wide council of churches - the Christian Conference of Asia (formerly the East Asia Christian Conference, 1957-) and its forerunners since the mid-19th century, and the Federation of Asian Bishops' Conferences (1970-). Both organizations operate a range of commissions and study programmes, and provide focus for many tributary institutions, centres and scholars. Both publish regular bulletins and journals addressing the theologies and practice of mission, church and society concerns, international affairs, theological formation and inter-religious life and dialogue.

Contextual Christian Theology in Asia

From these and similar movements - Roman Catholic, Protestant and Orthodox - has come a stream of creative theological reflection, writing and collaboration. (See especially the *FABC Papers*, and *CTC Bulletin*, along with *In God's Image, East Asia Pastoral Review* and *Asia Journal of Theology*). Notable here is the role of multiplying movements and associations of women in ministry and theology, as well as of lay centres and movements and of those active in a wide variety of frontier and social ministries.

Selected References

Alangaram, A. *Christ of the Asian Peoples: Towards an Asian Contextual Christology Based on the Documents of the FABC.* Bangalore: Asian Trading Corporation, 1999.

Christian Conference of Asia and Federation of Asian Bishops' Conferences. *Living and Working Together With Sisters and Brothers of Other Faiths in Asia. An Ecumenical Consultation, Singapore, 1987.* Hong Kong: CCA & FABC, 1987. Also published as FABC Paper 49.

Christian Conference of Asia. *Colombo to Tomohon: Christian Conference of Asia 1995-2000.* Hong Kong: CCA, forthcoming.

Chung Hyun-kyung. *Struggle to be the Sun Again: Introducing Asian Women's Theology.* Maryknoll, NY: Orbis Books, 1991.

England, John C. and Archie C.C. Lee, eds. *Doing Theology with Asian Resources: Ten Years in the Formation of Living Theology in Asia.* Auckland: Pace Publishing (for the Programme for Theology & Cultures in Asia), 1993.

Fabella, Virginia and Sun Ai Lee Park. *We Dare to Dream. Doing Theology as Asian Women.* Hong Kong: Asian Women's Resource Centre for Culture and Theology, 1989.

Kwok Pui-lan. *Introducing Asian Feminist Theology.* Sheffield: Sheffield Academic Press, 2000.

Philip, T.V. *Ecumenism in Asia.* Delhi: ISPCK & CSS, 1994.

Rosales, Gaudencio, C.G. Arevalo and Eilers, F.J. eds. *For All the Peoples of Asia.* 2 vols. Federation of Asian Bishops' Conferences Documents from 1970-1997. Manila: Claretian, 1992; Maryknoll, NY: Orbis Books, 1995 and 1997.

Sugirtharajah, R.S., ed. *Frontiers in Asian Christian Theology: Emerging Trends.* Maryknoll, NY: Orbis Books, 1994.

Weber, Hans-Ruedi. *Asia and the Ecumenical Movement 1895-1961.* London: SCM Press, 1966: Chap. 3.

Yap Kim Hao. *From Prapat to Colombo. History of the Christian Conference of Asia 1957-1995.* Hong Kong: CCA, 1995.

2 Groundwork for Asian Christian Theologies : Southeast Asia
A Selection from Christian Writings of the 16th to 18th Centuries - an Annotated Bibliography

1 Indochina, Siam, Burma

Many writings from these countries in this period are extant only in anonymous form (see Introduction above), and consistent research upon sources and for further examples has yet to be carried out. Those selected below evince in diverse ways the intention to own, and interpret, aspects of indigenous culture and religion.

1.1 Extant Letters and Lives (Indochina) include:

[Statements or letters of those imprisoned or killed during persecution in Annam or Tonkin. These remain as Vietnamese statements of faith and although many of these are anonymous, known authors include Peter Dang (d. 1661), Thomas Lucy Ki (d. 1665), Paul Kien (d. 1698) and Luke Thu (d. 1723). (Shortland 1875, Selected References following 1.9.3.)]

Letters and confessions of faith are also extant for the martyrs Gil de Federich (1702-1745), Mathieu Liciniana (1702-1745), Hyacinth Castagneda (1743-1773) and Vincent Liem (1732-1773).

The biographies of fifty-three native priests in Tonkin, are given in Mgr Neez, *Documents sur le Clergé Tonkinois aux XVIIe & XVIIIe siecles* (1754-61), reprinted Paris, 1925. (See also Nguyen Huu Trong, 1959, Selected References following 1.9.3.)

Ordonnez de Cevallos records in his *Historia y Viage del Mondo* (1615) the legendary life of the Christian princess and convent superior Mai Hoa (16th cent.), for which additional discoveries in Thanh Hoa province now suggest a historical core.

1.2 Writings in part theological, by **Alexandre de Rhodes** and his Vietnamese colleagues, including the former Buddhist monk Joachim, and the scholarly catechist Ignatius, include:

Dictionarium annamiticum, lusitanum, et latinum ... (1651);
Relation des progrez de la Foy au Royaume de la Cochinchine ... (1652);
Divers voyages et missions du P. Alexandre de Rhodes en la Chine ... (1653);
Relation de la Mission des Pères de la Compagnie de Jesus ... (1659). (For these see Phan 1998: 206f., Selected References following 1.9.3.)
"The Three Fathers" (Ba Cha) -in which God is *High Father*, the king of one's country *medium father*, and one's blood father is *low father* - and which was to form a basis for much later contextual reflection - appears first in de Rhodes' book *Phep giang tam ngay* (Catechism explained in Eight days) of 1651, last reprinted Ho Chi Minh Ville: Tu Sach Dai Ket, 1993.

The theology of Three Fathers (Ba Cha) was also embodied in the long anonymous poem from the late 17th century entitled, *Alexu,* and would become a central tradition in later Catholic thought in Vietnam. (See for example Dang Duc Tuan and Nguyen Truong To in Volume II, chapter 9).

1.3 Other Catechetical or Apologetic Works (Indochina, Siam) in which contextualising elements are easily recognised, include.

Sam Truyen ca (To teach repentance), a catechism in verse (1670) by Lu Y Doan, utilises Confucian and Buddhist imagery. It was rejected by missionary priests but widely used by Vietnamese Christians 'underground' until 1810. Translated into Quoc Ngu by Phan Van Can 1816. (Nguyen Van Trung 1993: 53-71, Selected References following 1.9.3.)
Lu Y Doan also wrote many paraphrases of biblical passages in Nom. (Nguyen Van Trung 1993: 72f., Selected References following 1.9.3.)
Salut des Infidèles et baptême. (ca 1675). Annoté par Jean-Paul Lenfant. *Documents Interéglises.* Paris: Missions Etrangères de Paris, 1988.
"Instructions pour ceux qui iront fonder une mission dans les royaumes du Laos et d'autres pays (1682)." *Epiphanie*

(Bulletin de documentation des Missions Etrangères de Paris) 24 (1965).

La Divinisation par Jésus-Christ (1693). Traduit du Latin par Jean-Paul Lenfant. Paris: Missions Etrangères de Paris, 1987.

1.4 Other Writings by Annamese or Tonkinese include:

Bento Thien *Lich Sur Nuoc Annam* (History of Annam) 1659. (Taylor & Whitmore 1995: 131, Selected References following 1.9.3.) Reprinted Saigon, 1972.

Philippe Phan Van Minh. *Phi nang thi tap* (Poetry of strong spirit) c.1760.

Philipe de Rosario Binh (c.1758-1832). Amongst 23 volumes of his writing are:

Ngat Trinh Kim Thu Khat Chinh Chua Giao (Chronicle of all events of the Catholic Church). It includes also letters and poems by Binh. *Borgiani Tonchinesi* (Manuscript volumes) 7 volumes. Vatican library, 1793-1826.

Tua Truyen Ong Thanh Phanchico Xavier (a Life of the Holy Francis Xavier). Includes also lives of Annamese martyrs of the 18th century and a history of the mission in Annam. Borg. Tonch. 6. Printed Lisbon, 1818.

The book of poems by Catherine (Man Tai) c.1635, covered "the entire sacred history from the creation to ... the ascension of our Lord" and included the coming of de Rhodes' mission to Tonkin. No copy now seems to be extant.

1.5 Other anonymous volumes include:

Chuyen Duc chua Thu (History of our Lord) in Nom dialect is believed to date from the early 18th century.

Hoi Dong Tu Giao (c.1790). Also anonymous, this work however presents a summary of exchanges by leaders of four religious traditions (Confucian, Buddhist, Christian and Taoist), in part upon the relation of filial piety to the Christian faith. Fourteenth edition printed Ho Chi Minh Ville, 1959.

1.6 Many writings by indigenous authors in this region are still to be identified, because of the wide-spread practices of anonymity, of using only such initials as JMJ (Jesus, Mary, Joseph) or AMDG (Ad Majoram Dei Gloriam), or of attribution to missionary authors (sometimes to protect nationals from persecution). Other writings by the authors named above, or by other nationals such as Joseph

Trang (fl. 1685) or Vincent le Paz Liem (1731-1773), are yet to be identified.

1.7 Amongst the **earliest writings of Burmese Christians** in this period are the poems of Nat-shin-naung ('Mahadhammraja', 1578-?1613), prince of Taung-ngu. Before his baptism (c.1610) he was a warrior and Theravadin scholar taking a metaphysical and mystical approach to Buddhism. His poetry however includes many '*yadu*' (love-poems tracing the seasons), 35 '*motaw*' (verses on the rain) along with *sapyaing* and *kye-se* verses. Much of his poetry takes its subject from nature and includes philosophical reflection. (Kyaw Dun, 1953 & Maung Thu Ta, 1966, Selected References following 1.9.3.)

1.8 Other writings by Burmese include:
> Letters by John of Yedana (fl. 1765) are extant, notably one on palm-leaf written to Pope Pious VI. He was also the co-author with J.M. Percoto, of the *Dialogue between a Phongyi and a Christian* (1776).
> Gian Maria Zau (b. 1720) was co-author with Mantegazza of the *Burmese Catechism* of 1785, and the *Dialogues between a Chin and a Siamese* (?1789), although this is only extant in Italian.

1.9 Narrative and Linguistic works, which were written by expatriates and which study indigenous history and culture include the following:

1.9.1. For Burma:
> Gaetano Mantegazza (1745-1794) published in 1784 his *History of the Kingdoms of Ava and Pegu (*reprinted Rome,1950*)* which includes Burmese literature, geography, politics and religion; and in 1787 his *Alphabetum Bramanorum seu Regni Avensis*, on Burmese language and literature.
> Joseph d'Amato (ca. 1756-1832) wrote Burmese verse and also works on the natural history of Burma, on Buddhist cosmogony and geography.

1.9.2. For Siam:
> Francoise de Choisy. *Journal ou Suite du Voyage de Siam en forme de Lettres familieres, fait en 1685-6 par M.L.D.C.* Amsterdam,

Pierre Morhier, 1687. Choisy's journal of his voyage appeared in the same year in Paris, and a new edition in 1930.

Mgr Laneau, who succeeded Bp Lambert de la Motte in 1679, spoke Thai and Pali, studied Thai culture and encouraged an indigenised mission practice. His writings include 26 volumes in Thai on various aspects of Christianity.

Marcel Le Blanc. *Histoire de la Revolution de Royaume de Siam Arrivé en l'année 1688*. Lyon: Horace Molin, 1692.

1.9.3. For Tonkin, Annam and Cochinchina:

Saccano, Metello. *Relation de progrez de la Foy au Royaume de la Cochinchine*. Paris: printed by S. Cramoisy, 1653.

Alexandre de Rhodes. *Sommaire des divers voyages et missions apostolique du P.P. Alexandre de Rhodes de la Compagnie de Jésus, a la Chine et autres royaumes de l'Orient.. Depuis l'année 1618 jusques a l'année 1653*. Paris: 1653.

de Marini, Jean Phillipe. *Relation Nouvelle et Curieuse des Royaumes de Tunquin et de Lao*. Paris: Gervais Crouzier, 1666.

Borri, Christoforo. *Relation de la Nouvelle Mission ... au Royaume de la Cochinchine*. Reprinted Saigon: 1931.

Selected References

Ba, Vivian. *The Early Catholic Missionaries in Burma*. A collected series of articles from *Guardian Magazine* (Monthly). Rangoon: c.1957-1964.

Ba Thein, U. "A Dictionary of Burmese Authors." *Journal of Burma Royal Asiatic Society* X,iii (1920).

de Bèze, P. sj. *Memoir*. Trans. and ed. as *1688 Revolution in Siam*, by E.W. Hutchinson. Hong Kong: Hong Kong University, 1968.

Bigandet, Paul Ambroise. *An Outline of the History of the Catholic Burmese Mission*. Rangoon: Hanthawaddy Press, 1887; Bangkok: White Orchard, 1996.

Hoang Gia Khanh. "Three Hundred Years of Catholic Writing in Vietnam." *Thuyen Tap Then Hoc* (Selected theological writings) April, 1993.

—. "Filial Piety and Christian Faith". In *Filial Piety and Christian Faith. Papers Delivered at the Seminar held in Hue, November 1999*. (In Vietnamese). Ho Chi Minh Ville: Institute for the Study of Religion, 2000.

Hutchinson, E.W., trans. *Adventurers in Siam in the Seventeenth Century*. Bangkok: Royal Asiatic Society, 1940.

Kyaw Dun, U., ed. *Anthology of Burmese Literature*. 2 vols. Rangoon: Government Printer, 1953.

Larqué, Victor mep. *History of the Catholic Church in Thailand*. (In Thai). Bangkok: 1967.

Launay, Adrien. *Histoire de la Mission de Cochinchine 1658-1823: Documents Historiques*. 3 vols. Paris: Tequi, 1923-1925.

—. *Histoire de la Mission du Siam (1662-1811). Documents Historiques*. Paris: Tequi, 1927.

—. *Histoire de la Mission du Tonkin: Documents Historiques*. Volume 1, 1658-1717. Paris: Libraire Orientale, 1927.

Maung Htin Aung. *A History of Burma*. New York: Columbia University Press, 1967.

Maung Thu Ta. *Sawsodawinya Atokpatti* (Biographies of writers). 2d rev. ed. Rangoon: Hathawaddy Press, 1966.

Nguyen Huu Trong. *Les Origines du Clergé Vietnamien. Le clergé national dans la fondation de l'église au vietnam*. Saigon: Grope Littéaire Tinh-Viet, 1959.

Nguyen Van Trung et al. *Books and Newspapers by Catholic Authors - Vietnam 17th -19th Centuries* (in Vietnamese). Ho Chi Minh Ville: University of Ho Chi Minh, 1993.

Pallu, Francois. *Histoire de l'éstablissement du Christianisme dans les Indes Orientales par les éveques francais at autres missionnaires apostoliques*. Paris: 1803.

Phan, Peter C. *Mission and Catechesis: Alexandre de Rhodes & Inculturation in Seventeenth-Century Vietnam*. Faith and Cultures Series. Maryknoll, NY: Orbis Books, 1998.

Shortland, John R. *The Persecutions of Annam: A History of Christianity in Cochin China and Tonking*. London: Burns & Oates, 1875.

Schurhammer, Georg. "Annamitische Xavieriusliteratur." In *Gesammelte Studen II (Orientalia)*. Rome and Lisbon: 1963.

Schmidlin, Joseph. *Catholic Mission History*. Translated and edited by Matthias Braun. Techny, Illinois: SVD Mission Press, 1933.

Taylor, K.W. and John K. Whitmore, eds. *Essays into Vietnamese Pasts*. Studies on Southeast Asia. Ithaca, NY: Cornell University, Southeast Asia Program, 1995.

Tran Anh Dung, Lm. *The Catholic Church - Vietnam: A Brief Bibliography of Sources in Vietnamese*. Paris: Lm. Tran Anh Dung, 1992.

2 Malay Peninsula and Archipelago
2.1 Sixteenth and Seventeenth centuries

Christian presence in modern times in both Peninsular and Archipelago Malaya dates from the first decades of the 16th century. Amongst a wide variety of Christian writing only a few contain contextual elements. For example:

2.1.1. Possibly the earliest recorded words of a 'Malay' Christian (in the colonial period) is the speech of Manuel, chief of Hatiwi, and a disciple of Xavier. The exhortation to his fellow Christian chiefs in Ambon c.1546, is given in a letter of Nicolo Nunes. (Jacobs 1981: I. 363; Selected References following 2.2.4.) The extensive letters of Nunes himself provide also reflections on Christian mission in the Moluccas.

2.1.2. Writings of the few Portuguese or Dutch administrators and Ministers of this period, who also actively promoted policies of inter-religious reconciliation or supported Christian initiatives, include the letters and reports of Antonio Galvao (1536-1540), Admiral van der Haghen (c.1600), Vlaming van Outshoorn (fl. 1650, analysed in de Graaf, 1977), and others such as members of the group of scholars and landowners around Governor-General Johannes Camphuys (1684-1691) in Batavia. (Vlekke, 1965: 421; Selected References following 2.2.4.)

2.1.3. Narratives and histories. The more significant examples include:

> Antonio Galvao (in Malukus 1536-1539) *A Treatise on the Moluccas* (c.1544). Available only in the preliminary version, edited by Hubert Jacobs (Rome: Jesuit Historical Institute, 1970).
> Gabriel Rebello (in Ternate 1543-1544 and 1556-1570). *Informacao das Cousas de Maluco ...* (1569). The "fullest description of the Spice Islands ... from a Portuguese", printed in Lisbon 1856 and 1955.
> S. Dankaets (Minister in Ambon 1617-1621). *Historisch ende grondich verhael van de standt des christendoms int quartier van Amboina* (1621, reprinted by Nijhoff, 's-Gravenhage, 1859). Concentrates on religious life and the development of the Christian mission.

2.1.4. Poetry written in Dutch in the Indies included some works on Christian or religious themes, notably those of
> Jacob Steendam (b. 1616, superintendent of a Batavian orphanage), such as his didactic poem 'For the Youth of Batavia' (1671).
> see *Jacob Steendam, noch water: Memoir of the First Poet in New Netherland.* New York: Dodd Mead, 1908 (1861).
> Also Pieter van Hoorn who discussed Confucianism in poetic works (c.1700). (See Murphy 1970; Vlekke 1965; Selected References following 2.2.4.)

After 1770, poetry was included in publications from government presses, as were several plays by Dirk van Bogendorp (for example his *Berigt,* 1799), advocating a radical reform of all aspects of the political and economic structures of the Indies and opposing all forced systems of cultivation and production along with distinction between Indonesian and European peoples.

2.1.5. A significant integration of the Christian faith within the *adat* of the lesser Sunda Islands occurred in Flores in the 16th and 17th centuries. The Old Catholics of Laruntuka so preserved the regalia, artefacts and practices of the Confreria de Rosario diaconate from the 1590s to the mid-19th century, that these became enshrined in local *adat*, to be rediscovered in 1853. (Webb 1986: 12ff.; Selected References following 2.2.4.)

2.2 Eighteenth century

Few writings of theological import are extant by Christians for whom Malay was their mother tongue, although their assistance in preparation of biblical and scientific texts is well attested.

2.2.1. The later rich development of **Rotinese prayers,** chants and sermons in which an indigenous theological language was developed is prefigured in the writings of Rotinese Christian rulers from 1729 on. These included letters written to officials of the VOC, but also early forms of chants and prayers utilizing both high Malay and Rotinese in a parallelism echoing Biblical patterns. (Fox 1991: 30ff., Selected References following 2.2.4.)

2.2.2. The Batavian Society of Arts and Sciences (founded 1778) issued its *Transactions* (Verhandelingen) as four detailed studies of the history and culture of Sumatra. These comprised J.C.M. Radermacher, *Beschryving van het eiland Sumatra,* (1778), Charles Miller, *"An Account of the Islands of Sumatra"* (1781), Eschels-kroon *Beschreibung der Insel Sumatra* (1783) and William Marsden, *History of Sumatra* (1784) (Kuala Lumpur: O.U.P. 1975).

2.2.3. From this period also come the letters of Jan Frederick Gobius, (from 1717 on) giving favourable views of pre-Islamic customs; the Malay prayers and catechisms of P. Gernault (in Penang from 1786); and the letters of P.C. Hoynck van Papendrecht (in Malacca 1778-1788), later published as "Some old Private Papers from the Cape, Batavia and Malacca". (JMBRAS 2.1, 1924).

2.2.4. Chronicles (*Babad*) and books (*Serat*). These form an important part of classical Javanese literature, and sometimes include extended references to biblical figures, to Christians or to Christian belief.

Serat Sekonder (The book of Kasendar) is a collection of stories from the 17th and 18th centuries depicting in mythical form the relationships of the Dutch "rightful rulers of West Java", to Mataram and the Kraton at Yogyakarta. With both Islamic and Christian (Spanish-Dutch) ancestors, Kasendar gives his life leading Christian forces against Muslims, yet is revived to rule as the Dutch 'baron' in West Java. Apparently written by the Surakarta poet Ngabei Judasarta, the fullest version is held in the British Museum. (Add. MS 12289, c. 1810).

A sequel is given in the *Serat Surja Radja* (Ricklefs 1974, in Selected References below).

Selected References

Andaya, Barbara. *To Live as Brothers - S.E. Sumatra in the 17th and 18th Centuries.* Honolulu: University of Hawaii, 1993.

Cardon, Rene Edouard mep. *Catholicism in the East and the Diocese of Malacca: 1511-1888*. Reprinted from *Malaya Catholic Leader*, Dec. 1938.

Chew, Maureen K.C. ip. *The Journey of the Catholic Church in Malaysia 1511-1996*. Kuala Lumpur: Catholic Research Centre, 2000.

de Graaf, H.J., ed. *De Gescheidenis van Ambon en de Zuid-Molukken*. Treneker: Wever B.V., 1977.

de Sa, Artur Basilio. *Documentacao para a historia das missoes ...* 5 vols. Lisbon: 1954-1958.

Fox, James. "Bound to the Core, Held Locked in all our Hearts - Prayers and Invocations among the Rotinese." *Canberra Anthropology* 14.2 (1991).

Gallop, Annabel Teh. *Early Malay Printing 1603-1900: An Exhibition in the British Library 20th January to 4th June 1989*. London: British Library Board, 1990.

—. "Early Malay Printing - an Introduction to the British Library Collections." *JMBRAS* 63.1 (1990).

Jacobs, Hubert, ed. *Documenta Malucensia*. 3 vols, 1542-1682. Rome: Jesuit Historical Institute, 1975-1984.

Kumar, Ann, ed. *Surapati: Man and Legend: A Study of Three Babad Traditions*. Amsterdam: Brill, 1976.

Murphy, Henry C., ed. *Anthology of New Netherland*. New York: Garrett Press, 1970 (1865).

Ricklefs, M. *A History of Modern Indonesia c.1300 to the Present*. London: Macmillan, 1981.

—. *Jogjakarta under Sultan Mangkubumi 1749-1792. A History of the Division of Jawa*. London: OUP, 1974.

Roxborogh, John. "The Roman Catholic Church." In *Christianity in Malaysia: A Denominational History*, edited by Robert Hunt, Lee Kam Hing and John Roxborogh. Petaling Jaya: Pelanduk Publications, 1992.

Schurhammer, Georg Otto sj. *Zeitgenossichen Quellen ... zur Zeit des hl. Franz Xavier 1538-1552*. Rome: 1962.

—. *Francis Xavier: His life, His Times*. Vol. III. Rome: Jesuit Historical Institute, 1973.

Vlekke, B.H.M. *Nusantara: A History of Indonesia*. Leiden and the Hague: van Hoere, 1965.

Webb, R.A.F. Paul. *Palms and the Cross: Socio-economic Development in Nusatenggara 1930-1975*. Townsville: Centre for Southeast Asian Studies, James Cook University of North Queensland, 1986.

3 The Philippines
3.1 Engravings
From the Philippines in the late 16th century, extensive church records and memoranda in Spanish are extant, but the earliest works we have from Filipino hands are the engravings from the early 17th century by generations of Filipino printers and artists.

Along with individual prints, maps, or santos, illustrations were engraved for sermons, biographies, prayer-books, calendars and historical works. Although often copied from European originals, most display Filipino perceptions and stylistic changes, along with persisting 'folk' elements. They have been judged to be often of better artistic quality than the originals.

Notable amongst these artists are the printer and writer Tomas Pinpin (d. c.1680 - see below, 9.2.; 9.3.), the sangley (Filipino Chinese) Juan de Vera (d. c.1607), the engravers Juan Correa (active 1701-1724) and his son Jeronimo Correa de Castro (active 1729-1752), Luis Suarez (active 1737-1760), Laureano Atlas (active 1743-1771), Nicholas de la Cruz Bagay (d. c.1770), and Philipe Sevilla (active 1749-1794). (Jose 1991: 131ff., Selected References following 3.8.).

3.2 Linguistic Works
Pinpin (see 3.1 above and 3.3 below) was also the author of *Librong Pagaaralan nang manga Tagalog nang uicang Castila* (The book with which Tagalogs can learn Castilian), Manila: 1610. Probably the earliest book written and published by a Filipino, this presents language as the "inside" of all things Spanish and in the course of teaching the Spanish language, includes many *awit* (songs) and other distinctively Filipino features of style, imagery and thought.

3.3 Early History
The earliest historical writing by a Filipino so far discovered is the *Narrative of Juan Masolang, first Christian of Lilio, Laguna, and of the Founding of the Town in 1572*. An 18th century manuscript of this was translated and annotated, with a transcript of the original Tagalog text, by C. Quirino and M. Garcia (Manila, 1958).

Pinpin's (see 3.1 and 3.2 above) last work was the *Relacion de lo que asta agora se a sabido de la vida, y Martyrio del mila grato padre Marcelo Francisco Mastrili S.J.* (A Narrative of the learning, life and martyrdom of the gracious Father Francisco Mastrili sj) 1639.

See also Spanish writings below (3.8.).

3.4 Domingo de Salazar and social criticism

One of the earliest, and probably most important, of writings by Spaniards in the Philippines were the reports and memorials of Domingo de Salazar, first Bishop of Manila. Many of these protested against the abuses and cruelties inflicted on Filipinos by Spanish settlers, and strongly advocated specific policies for correcting these. Chief among these are the letters to Felipe II of Spain, of June 20, 1582, June 27, 1588 and June 24, 1590; along with the documents

Affaires in the Philipinas Islands (1583),
Relacion de las cosas de las Filipinas (1583), and
Relation of the Philippine Islands (1588). (Gutierrez 1979; Selected References following 3.8.)

Another strong demand for the elimination of obligatory service and other forms of oppression of the Filipino is fully argued by Gomez de Espinosa (d. c.1658), a High Court Judge of Manila, in his *Discurso Parenetico* (Admonitory address), published in Manila in 1657.

Cf. The detailed letters of Basilio Sancho de S. Justa Y Rufina (Archbishop of Manila 1767-1787) urging his Filipino priests to adapt church practices and community development suited to the situation of their people. (Coronel 1998: 103f., Selected References following 3.8.)

3.5 Poetry

Much of the Christian writing we have in the Philippines for this period is poetry which dealt extensively with Christian themes and drew on the rich oral tradition of vernacular languages like Tagalog and Visayan. (Lumbera 1986: chaps. 1 & 2. See also Selected References following 3.8. below.)

Epic poetry by Pedro Bukaneg (1590-1626), and the poems of ladino writers (bilingual in Spanish and native language), fused native traditions with new content and forms. Prominent among these are Fernando Bagongbanta (fl. 1605), and Pedro Ossorio (fl. 1625), whose work shows the influence of folk poetry as does the fine anonymous allegory, *May Bagyo Ma't May Rilim* (Though it is stormy and dark). (Lumbera, 1986: 39ff.,150f., Selected References following 3.8.)

A collection of Tagalog poetry was published by San Augustin in the *Compendio de la lengua tagala*. (Manila: 1703.)

3.6 Early Women Religious

A number of Spanish and Hispanized women pioneered religious life for women in the Philippines, often in the face of determined male opposition. Among those whose writings must be mentioned are the following:

Jeronima de la Asuncion (b.ca.1557; Poor Clare) has left letters of forthright defence to local Superiors, and of petition to Philip IV and the Royal Audiencia, presenting clearly her theology of the religious life, the right of women religious to independence from male control and to self-support through labour, and in particular their right to accept any women in the colony regardless of race as being capable of religious life. (See her letters to King Felipe IV, of August 1, 1623, and July 31, 1626, given in Ruano 1991, and cited in Cruz, 2000. Selected References following 3.8.)

Others who similarly strove for independence and for a "way of life [which was] both a critique and solution for colonial policies towards mestizas and indias", included Ignacio del Espirito Santo (fl. 1685, Compania de Jesus); and Francisca Fuentes (fl. 1690; Dominican), in letters to the Archbishop of Manila. (Refer de Santo Domingo, 1996; Agda, 1998; Cruz, 2000, Selected References following 3.8.)

3.7 Pasyon (see also 1.4, chapter 7)

The *Pasyon* is a dramatic and metrical account of events in the Passion of Christ drawing on Spanish and Philippine traditions of folk-poetry and performed during Holy Week.

The first known narrative poem in Tagalog, and a classic model for the *pasyon* genre is Gaspar Aquino de Belen's (fl. 1710) *Mahal na Pasiong ni Jesu Christong Panginoon Natin na Tola* (The story of our Lord Jesus Christ's priceless suffering) 1704; five editions by 1760. This is widely regarded as the seminal work in what became a rich Filipino tradition of contextualising, and often revolutionary, Christian drama that continued well into the 20th century. De Belen's drama places the Passion in Filipino setting, portrays Filipino characters, and stresses the humanity of Jesus, within the context of the events of Holy Week. (Lumbera 1986: and Ileto 1979: passim; also Selected References following 3.8.)

A similar early narrative is by Felipe de Jesus (fl. 1715); *Dalit na Pamucao sa Balang Babasa Nitong Libro* (Poem meant to arouse the piety of every reader of this book). Manila: 1712. A Tagalog version of the legend of Barlaam and Josaphat.

3.8 Amongst the many **Spanish writers working in the Philippines** in this period who have left studies on Filipino history, languages and culture, are:

Diego de Bobadilla (1590-1648) who wrote an account of the customs and social organisation of Visayans, as well as a narrative of Philippine history.

Francisco Colin (1592-1660) also wrote *India sacra, hoc est, suppetiae sacrae ex utraque India in Europam* (Madrid 1666), presenting 'new light' on the Old Testament, through knowledge acquired in the 'far east' and the 'new world'.

Francisco Combes (1620-1665) also left a *Disertacion en defensa de la libertad de los indios* (Manila 1657) to make public the practices of extortion and oppression suffered by Filipinos.

Francisco Encina (1715-1760) wrote *Arte de lenga zebuana* (printed in 1801 and 1836), and a number of other manuscripts.

Mateo Perez (1771-1842) compiled a collection of maxims, amongst other writings, probably the first literary work in Cebuano. (Mojares 1975: 24ff., Selected References following 3.8.)

Selected References

Agda, Maria Corazon D. "The Shaping of the Ignacion Community". MA Thesis, Maryhill School of Theology, 1998.

Coronel, Hernando M. *Boatmen for Christ: The Early Filipino Priests.* Manila: Catholic Book Center, 1998.

Cummins, J.S. *Jesuit and Friar in the Spanish Expansion to the East.* London: Variorum, 1986.

Cruz, Reginald D. "Con el Sudor de su Rostro: Incipient Religious Communities for Women established in Colonial Philippines until 1750 as Spaces of Co-optation and Defiance". *Religious Life Asia* (Oct.-Dec., 2000).

de la Costa, Horatio. *The Jesuits in the Philippines 1581-1768.* Cambridge: Harvard University Press, 1961.

de Santo Domingo, Juan. *Beaterio de Santa Catalina: The Cradle Years of the Dominican Sisters in the Philippines,* edited by Fidel Villaroel. Quezon City: Congregation of Dominican Sisters, 1996.

Doctrina Christiana: The First Book printed in the Philippines, Manila, 1593. A Facsimile of the copy in The Lessing J. Rosenwald Collection, Library of Congress, Washington, with an introductory essay by Edwin Wolf 2nd. Washington: Library of Congress, 1947.

Gutierrez, Lucio. "Domingo de Salazar's Struggle for Justice and Humanization in the Conquest of the Philippines (1579-1594)." *Philippiniana Sacra* 14.41 (1979).

Ileto, Reynaldo Clemena. *Pasyon and Revolution: Popular Movements in the Philippines, 1840-1910.* Quezon City: Ateneo de Manila University, 1979.

Javellana, Rene B., ed. & trans. *Casaysayan nang Pasiong Mahal ni Jesucristong Panginoon Natin ...* Quezon City: Ateneo de Manila University Press, 1988.

—. *Mahal Na Passion Ni Jesu Christong Panginoon Natin Na Tola Ni Gaspar Aquino De Belen* Quezon City: University of Ateneo, 1990.

Jose, R.T. *Simbahan - Church Art in Colonial Philippines 1565-1898.* Manila: Ayala Museum, 1991.

Lumbera, Bienvenido L. *Tagalog Poetry 1570-1898: Tradition and Influences in its Development.* Quezon City: Ateneo de Manila University Press, 1986.

Mojares, Resil B. *Cebuano Literature: A Survey and Bio-Biography with Finding List.* Cebu City: University of San Carlos, 1975.

—. *Origins and Rise of the Filipino Novel: A Generic Study of the Novel until 1940.* Quezon City: University of the Philippines Press, 1983.

Rafael, Vincente L. *Contracting Colonialism: Tradition and Christian Conversion in Tagalog Society under Early Spanish Rule*. Quezon City: Ateneo de Manila University, 1988.

Ruano, Pedro. *Jeronima de la Asuncion: the Poor Clares First Woman Missionary to the Philippines*. Quezon City: Monasterio de Santa Clara, 1991.

Santiago, Luciano P.R. *The Hidden Years: The First Filipino Priests*. Quezon City: New Day Publishers, 1987.

Schumacher, John N. *Readings in Philippine Church History*. 2nd ed. Quezon City: Loyola School of Theology, 1987.

— J.C.E.

3 Contextual Theology in Burma / Myanmar 1800-2000

(See also *"Groundwork for Asian Christian Theologies - Southeast Asia"*, chapter 2 above.)

1   Theological Foundations 1800-ca. 1950
   1.1 Introduction
   1.2 Catholic Scholars and Writers 1
   1.3 Protestant Burmese and Karen Writings 1
   1.4 Women Doing Theology - Early Writings by or about Women
   1.5 Christian Periodicals
   1.6 Protestant Scholars and Writers (Expatriate)
   1.7 Protestant Burmese and Karen Writings 2
   1.8 Catholic Scholars and Writers 2
   1.9 Supplementary Bibliography 1

2   **Contextual Theology in Burma /Myanmar 1950 - 2000**
   2.1 Historical Context
   2.2 Roman Catholic Presence
   2.3 Christian Theology in Post-war Burma/Myanmar
   2.4 A Note on Sources for Burmese Christian Writing
   2.5 Theologians, Scholars, Animators
       2.5.1. Women Doing Theology; **2.5.2.** U Pe Maung Tin (1888-1973); **2.5.3.** U Hla Bu (1897-1970); **2.5.4.** George Appleton (1902- ?); **2.5.5.** Francis Ah Mya, Archbishop (1904-1999); **2.5.6.** Mrs Ba Maung Chain (Claribel Irene Po, 1905-1994); **2.5.7.** U Ba Hmyin (1912-1982); **2.5.8.** U Kyaw Than (1923-); **2.5.9.** Paul Clasper (ca.1925-); **2.5.10.** U Pe Thwin (1929-1996); **2.5.11.** Victor Sanlone (1930-1985); **2.5.12.** U Khin Maung Din (1931-1987); **2.5.13.** U Tun Aung Chain (1933-); **2.5.14.** Arthur Ko Lay (1935-); **2.5.15.** Eh Wah (1938-); **2.5.16.** Ba Thann Win (Kanbawza Win) (ca.1940-); **2.5.17.** Edmund Za Bik

(1940-); **2.5.18.** Mary Dun (1941-); **2.5.19.** Anna May Say Pa (1942-); **2.5.20.** Lahpai Zau Lat (1943 -); **2.5.21.** Simon Pau Khan En (1944-); **2.5.22.** Mar Gay Gyi (1945-); **2.5.23.** Alan Saw U (1949-); **2.5.24.** David Laisum (1954 -); **2.5.25.** Samuel Ngun Ling (1956 -); **2.5.26.** Cung Lian Hup (ca. 1960-)

2.6 Other Theologians, Scholars, Writers 1 - 1950- ca.1975
2.7 Other Theologians and Scholars 2 - ca.1975-2000
2.8 Catholic Writers and Theologians
    2.8.1. Catholic Writers and Theologians 1 - Sources, Journals, Theses; **2.8.2.** Catholic Writers and Theologians 2 - Bishops and scholars; **2.8.3.** Catholic Bishops' Conference
2.9 Supplementary Bibliography 2

1 Theological Foundations 1800-ca. 1950

The groundwork for contextual theology in Burma is found both in writings of the 16th-18th centuries (see above) and in the work of both nationals and expatriates of the 19th and early 20th centuries.

1.1 Introduction

There is evidence for Oriental Christian presence in areas of present-day Myanmar, from at least the 11th century in both mid- and north Burma (see England 1998). Roman Catholic presence dates from 1550, with Franciscans in Pegu and Jesuits in Bassein, and by 1600 Dominicans had also arrived. In the early 17th century, Franciscans and Jesuits were active in Syriam, and there is evidence of Christians, including Armenian communities, also in Arakan.

Burma has a tradition of Christian writing dating from at least the 16th century, with Burmese amongst the earliest authors. (See "Groundwork for Asian Christian Theologies - Southeast Asia", chapter 1 above). In the period from 1800 on, extant writings which contained contextual elements came mainly from members of major religious congregations: the Barnabites, members of the Propaganda Fide, the Mission d'Etrangère de Paris (1855), the Christian Brothers (1859) and the Milan Foreign Mission Society, and later the Columbans (1936). By the 1880s, women's orders included Sisters of the Convent of the Good Shepherd, Oblates of Mary, and the local order of Sisters of St Francis Xavier, later to be followed by Sisters of St. Joseph of the Apparition, the Little Sisters of the Poor and the Missionaries of Mary. Principal Protestant societies included the American Baptist Foreign Mission (from 1813), which commenced the earliest Protestant press, the Society for the Propagation of the Gospel (1854), the Methodist Episcopal Mission (1879) and the British Methodists (1885). The latest mainline church to establish congregations was the Presbyterian (1956).

Although the first Karen priest was ordained in 1882, almost all writers would be expatriates until late in this period. Indigenous pastors and lay leaders were prominent in all aspects of Protestant church life from the 1820s on, in part because of the thorough system of graded Bible Schools and seminaries which developed for several language groups, but extant writings are rare. Protestant writers for which we now have materials worked chiefly under the auspices of the American Baptist Foreign Mission, the Society for the Propagation of the Gospel and the Methodist Episcopal Mission.

From early in the 20th century, many such leaders were also participants in ecumenical conferences and movements, although at first still listed under Indian initiatives or deputations. From some, often those who were active in one or more ecumenical associations (YMCA and YWCA from ca. 1900, the SCM from 1912, and the Burma Christian Council from 1914), there are articles of theological reflection. These movements, along with participation by Burmese in all the major ecumenical conferences from 1910 to 1948, contributed strongly to the development of Christian identity in Burma and fostered many levels of Christian mission and secular ministry. Amongst publications of the Burma Press of the Christian Literature Society, Madras, (from 1907), and from the CLS Burma (from 1948), would come ecumenical writings, as well articles in early periodicals. (See 1.5.)

Churches in Burma throughout this period display a high diversity of peoples and cultures, with the largest Christian communities being comprised of Karen, Kachin, Chin and Lahu members. In the 1930s and 1940s, the impact both of colonial administration and church development led to increased ethnic divisions and to distance between their cultural and theological endeavours. Yet occasions when members of many ethnic and religious groupings met in conference on shared concerns were then possible, as is seen in the gatherings reported by West and Atwool (1933). The Burma Christian Council was already active in rural reconstruction with programmes especially for mountain farmers of various ethnic groupings in both the north and the south. The focus was upon the development of health and community development through education, agricultural aid and cottage industries.

From the mid-1930s, also, many Christian associations supported nationalist causes, although this was true of only a few church leaders such as U Maw Naw. Despite growing nationalist and anti-colonial movements, some Christian leaders remained sympathetic to British administrators and suspicious of pan-Burmese independence. Although Burman and Buddhist nationalists came to resent such attitudes, and Christianity would appear subversive to successive regimes, Buddhist Karens would later join in rejecting the Burmese state. At the same time many Christians would seek to reconcile a growing Burmese, or Karen, identity with a still largely westernised understanding of Christian faith. Similar tensions would develop amongst the Chin and Kachin peoples. In each case disaffection with national political policies was largely caused by early failures of the Union government to fulfil promises of plebiscites on such decisions as possible federation. In the half century from 1948, this would bring continuing division and conflict - along with economic hardship and socio-religious restriction - to be the context for much of the churches' life, witness and theological reflection. (See 2.1.)

Selected References

Ba, Vivian. *Early Catholic Missionaries in Burma.* Rangoon: Reprint, from *The Guardian* monthly, Rangoon, 1957-1964. (Last reprinted in 1997.)

Bailey, Faith C. *Adoniram Judson: Missionary To Burma 1813-1850*. Chicago: Moody Press, 1955.

Catholic Major Seminary. *History of the Catholic Church in Myanmar*. Yangon: Catholic Major Seminary, 2000.

Clasper, Paul. "The Church Amid the Pagodas." In *Christ and Crisis in Southeast Asia*, edited by Gerald H. Anderson. New York: Friendship Press, 1966.

England, J.C. *The Hidden History of Christianity in Asia: The Churches of the East before the Year 1500*. 2nd rev ed. Delhi: ISPCK; Hong Kong: CCA, 1998.

Kyaw Than, U. "Burma: Theologizing for Selfhood and Service." In *Asian Voices in Christian Theology*, edited by Gerald H. Anderson. Maryknoll, NY: Orbis Books, 1976.

Parker, E.H. *The Missions Etrangères. History of the Churches of India, Burma, Siam, The Malay Peninsula, Cambodia, Entrusted to the Society of the 'Missions Etrangères'*. Kiungchow: printed privately?, 1893. (Originally printed in the *China Review*.)

Purser, W.C.B. *Christian Missions in Burma*. 2d ed. Westminster: Society for the Propagation of the Gospel in Foreign Parts, 1913.

Shwe Wa, G. and E. Sowards. *Burma Baptist Chronicle*. Rangoon: BBC, 1963: chapters 10, 20, 21.

Smith, Donald Eugene. *Religion and Politics in Burma*. Princeton: Princeton University Press, 1965.

Trager, H.G. *Burma Through Alien Eyes: Missionary Views of the Burmese in the Nineteenth Century*. London: Asia Publishing House, 1966.

von der Mehden, Fred R. *Religion and Nationalism in Southeast Asia: Burma, Indonesia, the Philippines*. Madison: University of Wisconsin Press, 1963: chapters. IX & X.

West, G.A. and D.C. Atwool. *Jungle Folk*. Westminster: SPG, 1933.

1.2 Roman Catholic Scholars and Writers 1

Amongst laymen and priests (Barnabite, MEP and Oblate), expatriate and Burmese, there are many in the 19th century who have left linguistic, historical and theological writings. Of these, a number of them provide pioneering studies of Burmese natural history, language, history and culture (though sometimes using unverified generalisations). Others have left collections of homilies, prayer-books, meditations and commentaries. Amongst those writings which study or reflect a specifically Burmese context are included:

> Joseph d'Amato (c1756-1832) - *Natural History of Burma with Drawings and Explanations* (ca. 1820); *Drawings and notes on Buddhist Cosmogony and Geography* (ca. 1830).
>
> Ignatius de Brito (d.1832) - composed a *Collection of Religious Hymns*, and published also a *Volume of Sermons*, and a *Burmese Pharmacology*.
>
> Vincenzo Sangermano (1758-1819) - *A Description of the Burmese Empire, Compiled Chiefly from Native Documents* (1833); *Short History of the Burmese Mission* (1808). Other manuscripts of his are in the Barnabite Archive in Rome.
>
> F. Bertelli (1806-1856) - *Burmese Meditations* (1847); *Hymns in Burmese Verse* (ca.1850).
>
> Luigi Gallo (fl.1845) - *Early Catholic Missionaries in Burma* (3 vols., 1862).
>
> Jean-Piere Barbe (d.1861) - *Habits and Customs of the Kooke Tribe - Chittagong* (1844); *Some Account of the Hill Tribes in the Interior of the District of Chittagong* (?1846).
>
> P. Abbona (d.1874) - *A Geographical Treatise in Burmese made at King Mindon's Request* (1845).
>
> J. Simeon (fl.1870) - *Book of Religious Proverbs* (1873); *An Outline of the History of Burma* (1876); a series of *Anglo-Vernacular Readers* (from 1879).
>
> Paul Ambrose Bigandet (1813-1894) - *Thirty-one States of Being According to Buddhism* (1842); *The Life or Legend of Gaudama the Buddha of the Burmese* (1858); *Memoire sur les Phongies ou religieux Bouddhistes appelés aussi Talapoins* (1865); *An Outline of the History of the Burmese Catholic Mission from the year 1720 to 1887* (1887). Many papers appeared first in *Journal of the Indian Archipelago and Eastern Asia* (from 1847; see vols. 4,6,7,8,9,11).

Selected References (Additional)

> Ba, Vivian. *Early Catholic Missionaries in Burma.*
>
> Bigandet, Paul Ambroise. *An Outline of the History of The Catholic Burmese Mission from the Year 1720 to 1887.* Originally published Rangoon, 1887. Reprint Bangkok: White Orchid Press, 1996.
>
> Catholic Major Seminary. *History of the Catholic Church in Myanmar.* Yangon: Catholic Major Seminary, 2000.

Hosten, H. *Jesuit Letters and Allied Papers on Mogor, Tibet, Bengal and Burma*. Calcutta: Baptist Mission Press,1916.

—. *Varia List of publications by Catholic Missionaries of Burma: from 1776 to 1913* (Extract). Rangoon: British Burma Press, 1913. "Supplement to *The Voice*, October 1913.

—, and E. Luce. *Bibliotheca Catholica Birmana*. Rangoon: British Burma Press, 1915. (Enlarged version of *Bibliographical Notes on Catholic Missionaries in Burma*. Rangoon: British Burma Press, 1914.)

Maung Latt, Johnny. "A Summary of the History of the Roman Catholic Church in Burma" *(1365-1965)*. Thesis, Burma Divinity School, 1966.

Sauzerman, P. *Religione del regno Birmano, translated* by Cardinal Wiseman. London: Asiatic Society, n.d.

Streit, R. and J. Dindinger, comps. *Bibliotheca Missionum*. Rome: 1916-1974: Vol. VIII.

1.3 Protestant Burmese and Karen Writings 1

Only a small number of these have yet been discovered and much research awaits scholars on other writings which may be extant from Burmese Christians. Examples of those so far known are in the form of memoirs, letters, hymns, reports and confessional statements, and are to be compared with those writings extant from the 16th - 18th centuries (chapter 2 above) in their often tacit inclusion of indigenous theological understanding. Oral tradition preserved by for example the Karens, includes both monotheist beliefs of a Creator God and prophecies of the return of "the Lost Book" by the "younger white brother", believed to be fulfilled in the bringing of the Bible to Burma by Christian missionaries. (See *The Golden Book*, and *Sayings About God*, below).

Amongst memoirs or biographical fragments extant are those for early converts such as Ko Thah-Byu of Tavoy (fl.1830-1840), Saw Quala of Toungoo (fl.1840-1850) and Saya Shia Kyaw ("first convert in the Haka Area", M.Div. thesis, MIT, David Shwe, 1993), Pau Suan and his wife Kham Ciang, Thuam Hang and his wife Dim Khaw Cing (Robert G. Johnson, 1988). We also have biographies for later leaders such as the "Kayin missionaries of Chin Land Before the First World War", (Go Lian Thang, M. Div. thesis, MIT, 1993), the profile of the early Karen evangelists in

Burma (Hay Moo, M. Div. Thesis 1992), the Christian widow Tailum Jan (A.T. Houghton, 1930), and another group of five women (Arey, 1943). See Refs. to 1.4.

An outstanding indigenous theological work is that of Theodore Thanbyah (1842-1920). He studied at Bassein, Rangoon and Rochester University (USA), was an accomplished linguist and was also devoted to the welfare and development of his people, founding, in 1881, the *Dawkalu* association (later the inter-religious Karen Central Organization) for these purposes. Amongst the 25 books which he wrote (in Karen) between 1884 and 1920 are volumes on Karen history, customs and ceremonies; on the life of Christ on earth; on Christian ethics; and in biblical studies. Although a convinced Baptist, he was knowledgeable in both Protestant and Roman Catholic teachings. Ecumenical faith for him meant the fullest ecumenical collaboration in urgent human tasks.

Mission reports are extant from a number of evangelists and teachers. Maung Coompany of Bassein (fl.1860-1870) was one of the Karen lay leaders who produced dictionaries and hymnbooks. Fragments of the teaching of prophets such as the Lahu, A-Teh-Pu-Cu (ca. 1890), and of leaders of Christian-Animist sects like Ko Pai San (fl.1895) and Thomas Pellako (fl. 1898), are also recorded. Some of the letters transcribed by missionaries or travellers such as Howard Malcom (1839), J.A. Colbeck (1878-), C.H. Carpenter (1883), and Arthur Knight (1910) contain contextual elements.

Selected References
    Aung Mo. *Church History*. Rangoon: Burma Union Press, 1948.
    Brumberg, Joan Jacobs. *Mission for Life: the Judson family and American Evangelical Culture*. New York: New York University Press, 1984.
    Chit Lwin. *Maung Naw: The First Burmese National Christian*. (In Burmese) Rangoon: Burma Baptist Churches Union, 1919.
    Day, Saw Christopher. "Biographical Sketches of Noted Karen Leaders." M.Div. thesis, MIT, 2000.
    The Golden Book, collected by Thra Htoo Hla E. Rangoon: KBC, 1955.

Hovemyr, A. *In Search of the Karen King*. Uppsala: University of Uppsala, 1989.
Hta Htoo Hla Ywa (Sayings About God). Collected by Thra San Maung. Yangon: KBC, 1992.
Kyaw Dwe, Clifford. *The Life of Poo Tha Byu*. (In Karen). Rangoon, KBC, 1990.
Maung Latt, J. *The Baptists in Burma*. Thesis, SEAGST, Rangoon: 1977.
Maung Shwe Wa, G. and E. Sowards. *Burma Baptist Chronicle*. Rangoon: BBC, 1963: chapters 10, 20, 21.
Purser, W.C.B. *Christian Missions in Burma*. London: SPG, 1913.
Thanbyah, Theodore. *The Karens and Their Progress*. Rangoon: ABM Press, 1913.
Yaba Tolo, *The Biography of Saw Ko Tha Byu*. (In Karen). Rangoon: Go Forward Press, 1980.
Walker Frank Deaville. *The Land of the Gold Pagoda. The Story of the Burma Mission of the Methodist Missionary Society.* London: Cargate Press, 1939.

1.4 Women doing Theology - Early Writings by or about Women

The history and bibliography of reflection and writing by Christian women in Burma is yet to be given any systematic study. And although they have played essential roles in almost all levels of church life in Burma, few women of any ethnic grouping have been able to publish writings. Glimpses of their theological beliefs and reflections do occasionally appear in the documents of particular congregations, which in this period included Sisters of the Convent of the Good Shepherd, the Oblates of Mary, the local order of Sisters of St Francis Xavier, Sisters of St. Joseph of the Apparition, the Little Sisters of the Poor, and the Missionaries of Mary. An Anglican community of women was also established in 1909. Writing from these congregations, as from early Protestant women converts and lay workers, catechists and missionaries are often in letter form, but also sometimes appear in the periodicals and newsletters which proliferated in the 19th century. (See below 1.5.)

Larger studies were produced by a number of women missionaries, most often in biographical or autobiographical form, but these seldom included theological reflection which specifically recognised the Burmese context. It is, however, necessary to recognise the portrayals of faith lived out in demanding Burmese circumstances by an Ann Judson or a Tailun Jan (see references below), or the study of Burmese culture and religion, and the narratives of people stories, which are often included by such writers as Mrs Maclead Wylie, Leslie B. Arey and Honore Morrow. Later in the period ecumenical figures such as Katherine Khin Khin (Meh Kha Khway,1909- ?) and Rebecca Shwee (1912-) would provide fuller writings that arose from their many-sided ministries (see 2.5.1.). Some relevant writings were to come from the All Burma Baptist Women's Society, founded in 1923 for educational and evangelistic work and presided over in following decades by Daw Win Mya, Daw Thaung Tin, Daw Htwa Yee, Daw Aye Tin, Daw Tee Tee Luce, Daw Hla Shein, Rev'd Daw Mi Mi, Daw Htu Raw, Daw Cecilia Sar Yee, Daw Nellie Mya Yee, Daw May Si and Daw Saw Tint.

The writings of some of the many women teaching Christian subjects and the humanities in colleges, Bible Schools and high schools by the 1940s are yet to be collected. Amongst nationals in teaching ministries were Eleanor San Tay, Thramu E. Byu, Thramu Laura, Thramu Naw Paw, Thramu Pyu May, Sramu Luella San Gyaw, Sramu Alice, Daw Ohn Mya, Daw Kai, and Daw Than.

Selected References

    Arey, Leslie B. *Five women of Burma*. Philadelphia: Judson Press, 1943.

    Carson, Laura H. *Pioneer, Trails, Trials and Triumphs*. New York: Baptist Board of Publications, 1927.

    Hall, Gordon Langley. *Golden Boats from Burma: The Life of Ann Hasseltine Judson, The First American Woman in Burma*. Philadelphia: McRae Smith Co., 1956.

    Houghton, A.T. *Tailun Jan: Christian Widow in the Wild Mountains of Upper Burma*. London: Marshall, Morgan and Scott, 1930.

    Judson, Ann H. *An Account of the American Baptist Mission in the Burman Empire*. London: Printed for J. Butterworth & Son, 1823.

Judson, Emily Chubbock. *Memoir of Sarah B. Judson*. New York: 1848.

Katherine, Sr. *Towards the Land of the Rising Sun.* London: Society for Promoting Christian Knowledge, 1900.

Mason, Mrs Francis. *Civilizing Mountain Men.* London: James Nisbet & Co., 1862.

Milne, Mrs. Leslie. *Shans at Home.* London: 1910.

Morrow, Honore W. *The Splendor of God.* New York: Grosset and Dunlap, 1929.

Stewart, Arabella. *The Lives of Mrs Ann Judson, and Mrs Sarah B. Judson, with a Biographical Sketch of Mrs Emily C. Judson, Missionaries to Burma.* Buffalo and New York: 1854.

Wilson, Elizabeth. *The Story of Fifty Years of the Young Women's Christian Association of India, Burma and Ceylon.* Foreword by Mrs. Sinclair Stevenson. Calcutta: YMCA Association Press, 1925.

Wylie, Mrs Macleod. *The Gospel in Burmah.* Calcutta: G.C. Hay; London: W.H. Dalton, 1859.

1.5 Christian Periodicals

Christian periodicals issued during this period include reports, reflections and articles which remain important for the study of Burma's contextual theology and church history. In view of the difficulties faced in Christian publishing throughout this period (which continued in the later period also, see 2.5.), periodicals and journals hold special importance as sources for theological study. Although few complete sets of these periodicals are as yet available, some collections are to be found in such libraries as those of the MIT, Insein, the Major Theological Seminary (Catholic), Rangoon; and Yale University, New Haven. Amongst the most valuable periodicals for this period are the following:

Burma Baptist Mission Magazine. Rangoon: A.B.M. Press 1803-1909; *Hsar Tu Gaw* (Morning Star). Sgaw Karen Newspaper, from 1843; *The Young men of India, Burma and Ceylon*. National Council, Young Men's Christian Associations of India, Burma and Ceylon. Continued as *Young Men of India* (from 1925), superseded by: *Association Men; The Young Women of India, Burma and Ceylon*, Bombay. Continued by *Women's Outlook in India* (from 1916); *NCC India, Burma and Ceylon Review* 1925-1931; *Burma*

Catholic News (formerly Indo-Burma Catholic News) 1890-1895; *Rangoon Diocesan Magazine*. Toungoo, quarterly 1897-1927; *Burma Mission Herald*. (Methodist Episcopal Church) Semi-annual from 1901; *Journal of the Burma Research Society*. Rangoon: The Society, 1911-1981; *Burma News*. Rangoon Diocesan Association 1928-1970?; *The Student Outlook*. Madras: 1928-1954. Continued as *Student Movement Review; Church Union News and Views.* (India, Burma and Ceylon.) Madras: Christian Literature Society for India. July 1930-Nov. 1947. For women's writing see also: *Toe-Teh-Ye* (Advance), *Myanmar Ah Swe* (Burma Friend), *Shu-mu-wa* (Ever Lovely), *Taing Yin May* (Nation's Women).

1.6 Protestant Scholars and Writers (Expatriate)
From the middle of the 19th century on, a number of (mainly expatriate) Protestant scholars studied and wrote on aspects of Burmese culture, language, history and religion. These were often undertaken to provide the necessary framework for traditional mission work, and sometimes also included unverified and unflattering generalizations (see Traeger 1966, Selected References 1.1). The Burma Bible and Tract Society, Rangoon, also issued a number of apologetic writings and texts in translation: see *A Brief History of the Church of Christ*, by Christian G. Barth (1878), and *The Christian Religion. A message sent to the Buddhists of Burma by the English Bishop of Rangoon* (1879). Figures like Samuel F. Smith were writers, editors and poets in the period 1830-1900, although only fragments of their writings can be termed contextual.

The best however contain careful scholarship which, along with Roman Catholic works, pioneered Burmese historical, ethnological, linguistic and religious studies which are still essential for contextual theology. This was of course only possible with the full assistance of many Christian nationals. This had been the case of all Burmese studies since those of Judson, for whom seven Burmese colleagues are known by name, along with the Shan assistants of Henderson at Mongnai. Volumes by Hanson (1913), Halliday (1917), Marshall (1923), Cochrane (1915) and Furnivall (1929) - to mention only a few - are amongst those now considered standard

Contextual Theology in Burma/Myanmar 1800-2000 37

works. Hymns, letters, dictionaries, tracts and treatises are also extant from many of these scholars.

In the first half of the 20th century, they would be followed by Bishops Arthur Knight (see Purser, 1.1 above) and George West (volumes in 1937 and 1943 below), and by a series of writings, in for example, the *International Review of Mission* and in the *Burma Christian Council Annual*, by such scholars as A.C. Hanna, G.P. Charles and George Appleton. Amongst other writers, J. Herbert Cope produced 35 text-books in Chin dialects before 1940 and J. Russell Andrus wrote on rural reconstruction in Burma (1936), on Burmese economic life (1953), and with others on contemporary East Asia (1941).

Many such scholars were active, along with Burmese colleagues in ecumenical associations such as the YMCA and the SCM, and played, with them, important roles in the NCC of India, Burma and Ceylon and in the development of the Burma Christian Council (later Burma/Myanmar Council of Churches). From these bodies would come an increasing number of writings which included contextual theological reflection. (See 2.1, 2.3). By the 1940s also there was further recognition by some theologians of the nobility in Buddhist ethics and way of life and its capacity for reform as a "real dynamic in the daily lives of the people". (Appleton, ?1946, 1960).

Selected References

  Andrus, Russell. *Rural Reconstruction in Burma*. Bombay: Oxford University Press, 1936.
  Appleton, George. *On the Eight-fold Path: Christian Presence Among Buddhism*. London: SCM Press, 1960.
  Burma Christian Council Executive Committee. *Records of the Burma Christian Council, 1927-1961*. Archive Folder, Library of Yale Divinity School.
  Carpenter, C.H. *Self-Support Illustrated in the Bassein Karen Mission 1880-1890*. Boston: 1883.
  Cochrane, W.W. *The Shans*. Rangoon: Govt Printing Office, 1915.
  Furnivall, J.S. *Christianity and Buddhism in Burma: An address to the Rangoon Diocesan Council, August 1929*. Rangoon: People's Literature Committee and House, 1960.

Halliday, R. *The Talaings*. Rangoon: Govt. Printing Office, 1917. Reprinted, Bangkok: Orchard Press, 1999.

Hanson, Ola. *The Kachins; Their Customs and Traditions*. Rangoon: ABM Press, 1913.

Marks, John E. *Forty Years in Burma*. London: Hutchinson, 1917.

Marshall, Harry Ignatius. *The Karen People of Burma: a study in anthropology and ethnology*. Columbus OH: The University, c1922.

Mason, Francis. *Burma its People and Natural Products*. Rangoon: Ranney, 1860.

Paton William. *Work and Significance of the National Christian Council of India, Burma and Ceylon*. n.p.: NCC India, 1926.

Philip, P.O. *Report on a Survey of Indigenous Christian Efforts in India, Burma & Ceylon*. Poona: 1928.

St. John, Wallace. *The Literatures of Burma*. Rangoon: 1911.

Tilbye, H.H. *Pali Buddhism*. Rangoon: American Baptist Mission Press, 1900.

Tyndale-Biscoe, John. *For God Alone: the Life of George West Bishop of Rangoon*. Oxford: Amate Press, 1984.

Weber, Hans-Ruedi. *Asia and the Ecumenical Movement*. London: SCM Press, 1966.

Wesleyan Methodist Society Archive. 9 vols. 1886-1944. Zug: Mikrofiche-Ausg, Interdocumentation.

West, George. *The World that Works*. Bombay: Thacker, 1943.

1.7 Protestant Burmese and Karen Writings 2

The impact of Christian presence upon nationalist movements in Burma was both positive - in fostering self-hood and organization, and negative - in provoking reaction against a faith which was seemingly "foreign", favoured and divisive. Some Christian leaders like Dr San C. Po (see below), speaking for another nationalism, wrote that his people, the Karen, spoke of the missionaries as their 'Mother' and the British government as their 'Father', and did not hesitate to advocate separate self-government for the Karens. However only a minority of Christians attempted to understand social and religious changes about them or to explore relationships with either sister churches or Buddhist compatriots.

However in the early decades of the 20th century a growing number of Christian nationals became known for their scholarship, their writing or their theological reflection. Saya Thun Aung was one of many who collaborated in the production of linguistic works. Amongst many who participated in ecumenical gatherings and programmes, one of the speakers at the Tambaram IMC Conference (1938) was Thra Chit Maung, later Principal of BIT (formerly Burma Divinity School) and a long-time theological teacher deeply concerned with the development of an authentic Karen Church. (See "The Karen Church in Burma in the Growing Church", 1939).

Despite ethnic divisions, and the growth of nationalist movements in the decades before World War II, a group of Burmese Christian scholars from central, southern and eastern Burma, were active both in discourses and debates with Buddhist monks and thinkers, and also in preaching and writing in the context of Buddhist resurgence and national transitions. The thrust of their work was in the main apologetic and they were at home both in Christian interpretation and in Buddhist scholarship. Their work would help to form "the basis of theological literature for the period" (Kyaw Than, 1976), and established Burmese sources and approaches for its articulation.

Saya U Tha Din, of Prome, (fl.1940) was trained in Buddhist priestly scholarship and was also a prominent ecumenical leader of the Burmese churches. Active in the Public Relations Committee of the Burma Christian Council of Churches, he was also Chairman of Burma Baptist Council. Volumes of his sermons and historical writings have been published, but his most important work was the *Comparative Study of Buddhist and Christian Scriptures* (1936/ 1953).

Thra Ba Tay, of Taunggyi (fl. 1950), was also trained in Buddhism and interested in comparative religious studies. See his *Barthantara beida dipani. Ko kwe thaw bartha a yat yat ko hnaing shin yei tha thaw sar ok* (An outline study of comparative religion; based on the writings of the Rev. William Paton, 1954).

A third Christian scholar in Buddhism in this period was U Pan Yi: see his *Commentary on the Tripitakas*, published in Rangoon, circa 1950.

A number of eminent Karen leaders have contributed in this period to social witness, theological teaching and writing:

San Crombie Po (1870-1946) studied at Bassein and at Colgate Academy and Albany Medical College(USA), during which time the freedom and liberty of his own country became important to him. Following the first years of innovative medical practice (1894-1912), San C. Po became politically active as a municipal and Karen leader, a Member of Legislative Assembly (later Senator), as well as being a peacemaker during ethnic hostilities and also continuing his dispensary. In his principal book, which retains its importance for Burmese studies, *Burma and the Karens*, he presents the traditions and aspirations of the Karen, the life of Karen women, social reforms both for Burma and for the Karen people, and proposals both for home-rule for Burma and for a "Karen country". For these goals, the leaders he pictures will possess the highest practical ability and training along with the "beautiful characteristics of an inward Christian life."

Thra Mooler Teh (1905-1991) studied and taught at the Burma Divinity School (now MIT). Later he was lecturer and vice-principal of Karen Theological Seminary, Insein. He was the most eminent Karen evangelist and worked not only amongst Karen but also amongst the Naga, Wa, Lisu, Lahta, Lahu and Moken peoples. His lectures, sermons and writings are always simply biblical and evangelical, but show sensitive awareness of the particular situation of his peoples. His reflections, *Thra Mooler Theh: Events in His Life* were collected only near the end of his life.

Other Karen leaders who wrote and worked for both the faith and the social welfare of their people include Thra Tha Hto (1902-1993), Saw San Po Tin (1903-1983), Smith Dun (1906-1979), Mrs Ba Maung Chain (see 2.5.6.) and Dr Ba Than Chain (1890-1968).

By the late 1940s, increasing numbers of other writings that included localised theological reflection began to emerge from Burmese Christians. Amongst those for whom writings are extant are U Hla Bu, U Pe Maung Tin, U On Kin, U Chit Pe, Daw Win Mya, Francis Ah Mya, U Ba Hmyin, U Kyaw Than, U Pe Thwin, Paul Clasper, and William Winn. (For all these see Contextual Theology in Burma/Myanmar 1950-2000, below).

Selected References:

Bunker, Alonzo. *Soo Thah: A Tale of The Making of the Karen Nation*. Edinburgh: Oliphant, Anderson and Ferrier, 1902.

Chit Lwin, U. *Maung Naw, the First Burmese National Christian*. (In Burmese). Burma Baptists Churches Union. Rangoon: Thirithati Press, 1969.

Chit Maung, U. "The Karen Church of Burma." In *The Growing Church. IMC Meeting at Tambaram, Madras, December 1938*. Vol II. London: Oxford University,1939.

Day, Saw Christopher. "Biographical Sketches of Noted Karen Leaders." M.Div. thesis, MIT, 2000.

Kyaw Than, U. "Theologising for Selfhood and Service." In *Asian Voices in Christian Theology*, edited by G.H. Anderson. Maryknoll NY: Orbis Books, 1976.

Mooler Theh, Thra. *Thra Mooler Theh: Events in His life*. Translated by Saw Ba Saw Khin. Rangoon: KBC of Burma, 1988.

—, and Thara Doh. *Handbook for Christians*. Rangoon: Baptist Board of Publications, 1950 (1941).

Peh Paleh. *Dr Chit Maung: His Life and Achievements*. Thesis, MIT, 1992.

Po Pin Lay. *Go Forward*. Rangoon: Karen Press, 1938.

Po, San Crombie. *Burma and The Karens*. London: Elliot Stock, 1928. Reprint 1998.

Smith, Donald E. *Religion and Politics in Burma*. Princeton NJ: Princeton University Press, 1965: chap 2.

Tha Din, U. *Comparative Study of Buddhism and Christian Scriptures*. 3rd ed., rev. and enl. Rangoon: American Baptist Mission, 1936; CLS, 1953.

—. *Shay phyit haung auk may bwe wuthtu* (Story of early Christianity in Burma). Rangoon: BBC, 1954.

Tha Hto, Saya. *The Way of Independence*. (In Burmese). Rangoon: K.N.U. Press, 1948.

—. *Karen Political Problems*. Rangoon: K.N.U. Press, 1948.

Thama nadi nat min wathtu (The king of the golden river). Rangoon: Burma CLS, 1954. (Notes romanized.)

Weber, Hans-Ruedi. *Asia and the Ecumenical Movement*. London: SCM Press, 1966.

1.8 Catholic Scholars and Writers 2

Catholic expatriate writers working in the first half of the century included linguists, historians and ethnologists. Prominent among these was Charles Gilhodes (c.1870-1946), missionary pastor, scholar, teacher and agriculturalist. His writings would eventually include publications on Kachin language, culture and rural development. Most famous among these is his full ethnological study, *The Kachins: Religion and Customs* (1922). This is now regarded as a standard work on Kachin culture, providing essential empirical data for later studies. In it he also discusses his findings with the specialists in the Kachin religion, the *Jaiwa*, who are the ritual bards or reciters of the myths being studied. In this innovative work he thus anchors his study and writing in indigenous tradition.

Amongst other scholars, Charles Duroiselle completed two works on the Pali language (published in Rangoon in 1906, 1911); Bishop Albert Falière (b.1889) wrote a history of the mission as the sequel to that of Bishop Ambrois Bigandet (1887); and Monsignor Patrick Usher (1899 -1958) left a ms. at his death, "History of the Catholic Church in Burma." Thomas Rillstone wrote on the church in wartime Burma (c.1946) and the Burmese lay scholar Vivian Ba commenced in 1948 his series of carefully researched articles on writings of *The Early Catholic Missionaries*, using Latin, Italian, Portuguese, and French sources.

By the 1950s similar changes in Christian attitudes to those noted in 1.7 above were beginning to emerge in Catholic communities, later to be characterised by Fr. Kelleher (1972) as a more "outgoing, spiritual attitude", more identified with the people and with changed attitudes to non-Christians and Buddhists. (Fischer, 1980). See period 1950-2000 below.

Selected References
 Ba, Vivian. *Early Catholic Missionaries in Burma.*
 Baretto, W.L. *Heroes of Burma.* Rangoon: 1935.
 Catholic Directory of India, Ceylon and Burma. (ca.1912-1948).
  Madras: Catholic Supply Society. Madras Catholic directory
  and annual general register.
 Duroiselle, Charles. *A Practical Grammar of the Pali Language.*
  Rangoon, 1906.
 —. *Pali Reader.* Rangoon: 1911.

Fischer, Edward. *Mission in Burma. The Columban Fathers' Forty-three years in Kachin Country.* New York: Seabury Press, 1980.

Gilhodes, Charles. *The Kachins: Religion and Customs.* Calcutta: The Catholic Orphan Press, 1922. Last reprint Bangkok: White Lotus Press, 1996.

Hosten, H. and Luce, E. *Bibliotheca Catholica Birmana.* Madras: Indian Office Library, 1915.

Mondini, Livio. *La citta felice. Aventura missionaria in Birmania.* Bologna: Edizione Di Missione Italiana, 1989.

Usher, Patrick. *History of the Catholic Church in Burma.* MS, Typewritten, ca. 1956.

1.9 Supplementary Bibliography 1

A Brief History of the Burman Theological Seminary. (In Burmese) Rangoon: Thudamma Press, 1951.

An account of the Catholic Mission of Southern Burma and of the Cathedral of the Immaculate Conception, Rangoon... Edited from materials supplied by E. Luce. London: Burns & Oates, 1909.

Anderson, Courtney. *To The Golden Shore: The Life of Adoniram Judson.* Valley Forge: Judson Press, 1987 (1954).

Annual Reports of the Burma Baptist Convention. Rangoon: 1866.

Annual Reports, American Baptist Foreign Missionary Society. Valley Forge: 1814-.

Aung Hla. *The Karen History.* Bassein: Karen Magazine Press, n.d.

Ba Tay, Thra. *An outline study of comparative religion ; based on the writings of the Rev. William Paton* (In Burmese). Rangoon: Burma CLS, 1954.

Church of England. *Book of Jubilee of the Rangoon Diocese, 1877-1927.* Rangoon: ca.1928.

Colbeck, J.A. *Letters from Mandalay (1878-1892).* n.p., 1892.

Crittendon, Mark. "The Effect of the Missionary Movement among the Burmese Karen 1913-1949." Diss., University of Kent at Canterbury, 1983.

Fisher, Joseph. *Research Bibliography of Books, Documents and Pamphlets on Burma.* Rangoon: Hopkins Centre for SEA Studies, 1953.

Griffin, Andrew, comp. *A brief guide to the sources for the study of Burma in the India Office records.* London: India Office Library & Records, 1979.

Hanna, A.C. "Literature. in Burma." *IRM* 7 (1931).

History of Shan Baptist Mission. Namkham: Shan Bible Centenary Jubilee, 1985.

Holt, A.E. *A Study of the YMCA of India, Burma and Ceylon...*Calcutta: National Council YMCA, 1933.

Hkum Paw Lu, N. *God in the Traditional Life of the Kachins.* Thesis, MIT, 1993.

Johnson, Robert G. *History of the American Baptist Chin Mission... 1899 to 1966.* Valley Forge, Pa: 1988.

Kaung, U. "A Survey of the History of Education in Burma before the British Conquest and After." *Journal of the Burma Research Society.* Vol. XlVI, Rangoon, 1963.

Kyi, U. *Essential Burmese History.* (In Burmese) Rangoon: Shwe Pyi Thar Press, 1960.

Lewis, James Lee. "Self-supporting Karen Churches in Burma: A Historical Study of the Development of Karen Stewardship." Th.D. Dissertation, Central Baptist Theological Seminary, 1946.

Loo Shwe, Thra (Saw). "The Karen People of Thailand and Christianity." Rangoon: Typescript, n.p., 1962.

McLeish, Alexander. *Burma, Christian Progress to the Invasion.* London, New York, etc.: World Dominion Press, 1942.

Mason, Francis. *The Karen apostle, or, Memoir of Ko Thah-Byu: the first Karen convert: with notices concerning his nation.* Tavoy: 1843, Rangoon: ABM Press, 1928; Microfilm, Interdocumentation, Zug, 1986.

—. "Saw Quala, the Second Karen Convert." *Baptist Missionary Magazine,* XXXVI.

Meersman, P.I. "The Franciscans in the Burmese Kingdoms of Ava and Pegu 1557-1818." MS. (Typewritten).

Myint Lay. *History of Eastern Shan State Mission.* Rangoon: BBC, 1920.

Nason, Ann M. "The Adoption and Diffusion of Christianity amongst the Khumi-Chin people of the Upper Kaladan River ... 1900-1966." Thesis M.A., University of Warwick, 1988.

Our Baptist Heritage. Rangoon: Baptist Convention, 1963.

Phinney, F.D. *The American Baptist Mission Press: historical, descriptive, 1816-1916.* Rangoon: American Baptist Mission Press, 1917.

Po Tun. *The Lahus.* Tavoy: Shepherd Press, 1926.

SCM India, Burma and Ceylon. *Records of the Student Christian Movement of India, Burma, and Ceylon, 1920-1966 (inclusive).* Yale University.

Scott, James George (Shwe Yoe). *Burma, As it was, As it is, and As it will be.* London: 1886.
Shulman, F.J. *Burma: an Annotated Bibliographical Guide to International Doctoral Dissertation Research, 1898-1985.* Lanham NY: University Press of America, 1986.
St. John, Wallace. *Josiah N. Cushing, Missionary and Scholar.* Rangoon: A.B.M. Press, 1912.
Tegenfelt, Herman G. *A Century of Growth. The Kachin Baptist Church of Burma.* Pasadena: William Carey Press, 1974.
Vincent, Stanley. *Out of great tribulation: the story of Methodism in Burma, 1942-5.* London: Cargate Press, 1946.
Wayland, Francis. *A Memoir of the Life and Labours of the Reverend A. Judson.* 2 vols. London: James Nisbeth, 1853.
Webb, Willis B. *Incidents and Trials in the Life of E. Kincaid, the Hero Missionary to Burma.* Kansas: Monitor Pub. House, 1890.
Win, Henderson. "Christian Mission Among the Pa-O," BRE thesis, MIT, 1971.

2 Contextual Theology in Burma /Myanmar 1950 - 2000
2.1 Historical Context
(See 1.1 Introduction.)

Burma has been an independent nation since 1948, living under a socialist constitution and initially possessing parliamentary rule. Insurrections commenced almost immediately, in part because although Burma was at first nominally Federal with partial autonomy for each state, power was concentrated in the Prime Minister and Cabinet and the right for some states to later secede from the Union was never honoured. This would lead to protracted civil conflict throughout this period. A Buddhist religious revival, which was also firmly nationalist, developed in the 1950s and led to Buddhism being declared the state religion in 1961. A coup by the army, which had been strengthened through the civil conflict, ushered in military rule (1962), which immediately introduced land, health and education reforms. Many rights were then legally protected, but growing restrictions were placed on Christian activities and also on foreign exchanges. By 1966 all expatriate missionaries other than those who had come to Burma before independence had to leave. In the decades since, the army, and from 1988 SLORC (the State Law and Order Restoration Council, later the State Peace and Democracy Council - SPDC), has assumed more ideological and totalitarian policies, with a rejection of all democratic processes including the landmark election of 1990. Throughout this period, nationalist, religious and ethnic movements have continued, including those of Buddhist resurgence and democratic protest; student and other movements for democracy; and ethnic campaigns for recognition or autonomy.

Today, the population of Burma (officially named Myanmar) is 41.7 million. Burma remains ruled by military junta as a state-ownership society with key industries controlled by the military, with widespread corruption and an extensive black-market economy. Burman dominance over Karen, Shan, Rakhine, Mon, Chin, Kachin and other minorities continues to fuel tension and sporadic conflict, causing large settlements of refugees in border territories. The leader of the government elected in 1990 and Nobel Peace Prize winner, Aung San Suu Kyi, has been under house-arrest since then, and many democratic leaders have been imprisoned. The military "have been accused of gross human rights abuses, including the forcible relocation of civilians and the widespread use of forced labour, which includes children." (BBC, London). Severe poverty is widespread, and all civil rights are restricted. There are few non-government or independent social organizations. According to the 1996 Report on Human Rights, Buddhists are currently more favoured by the government which has been attempting in this way to gain popular legitimacy.

Diverse ministries of the Christian churches have been continued and reshaped in these decades, retaining a measure of independence for many pastoral activities, despite the loss (from 1965) of schools, hospitals, lands and publications (see 2.4). The national council of churches (BCC) continued in this period its full involvement in community development through a series of programmes and agencies. These included a relief and rehabilitation committee (since1948); a National Church Loan Fund (1959); and the Christian Service Board for emergency and integrated development (from 1966; from 1994, the Service and Development Unit). The Training Institute for Christian Participation in Development (1977) led to the formation of the CPDSK (1980) for both training and development in the Shan, Kayah and Karen states. Such work as this, and that of the Myanmar Baptist rural development committee, thereafter came under increasing government restriction.

Member churches of the MCC and the Myanmar Catholic Bishops' Conference have more recently been registered by the government, but much of their work cannot be openly carried out, especially if related to ethnic minorities. This applies to the translation or circulation of materials in indigenous languages, the building of new churches, the maintenance of cemeteries and even the provision of emergency relief. Expatriate church workers are allowed visas for only some weeks, although numbers of these do visit for special events or programmes.

Ecumenical and denominational associations and seminaries are, however, able to continue a variety of educational and service activities along with the private circulation of periodicals and booklets (see 2.4). Baptist churches, which form by far the largest proportion of Christian communities, maintain national conventions, 27 seminaries and Bible Colleges, along with 'publications', and have more than 1,000 men and women in the active ministry. Amongst many of those who have provided key leadership from Baptist churches in this period (apart from those mentioned individually below) are such people as U Aung Khin, U Chit Maung, U Mynt Hla, Saw Lader, John Thetgyi, Daw Myat Yan, Dorothy Tin Tin Hla, Thra Mooler, Stephen Hre Kio and George Po Ba. Anglican and (episcopal) Methodist churches, although smaller, are also vigorous in ministerial training for lay people and clergy. Amongst their leaders to be noted in these years are, in addition to those below, such figures as Archbishop John Aung Hla and Archbishop Ah Mya, Andrew Mya Han, Canon San Hoo, U Dun, David Htin Ya, George Kyaw Mya, U Ba Aye, Bishop Peter Ba Mau and Bishop Daniel Hoi Kyin. (See also below 2.7, 2.8).

Selected References
a) History and Society

Aung San Suu Kyi. *The Voice of Hope: Conversations with Alan Clements with contributions by U Kyi Maung and U Tin U.* London: Penguin, 1997.

Ba Than. *Burmese History.* (In Burmese). Mandalay: Pidakat Press, 1964.

Becka, Jan. *Historical Dictionary of Myanmar.* Asian Historical Dictionaries 15. Metuchen: Scarecrow Press, 1995.

Carey, Peter, ed. *Burma: The Challenge of Change in a Divided Society.* Houndsmills: Macmillan, 1997.

Casino, E.S. *Burma and the Burmese: A Historical Perspective.* Honolulu: University of Hawaii Press, 1997.

Clements, Alan, and Kean, Leslie. *Burma's Revolution of the Spirit: The Struggle for Democratic Freedom and Dignity.* New York: Aperture, 1994.

Donkers, Jan and Nijhuis, Minka, eds. *Burma Behind the Mask.* Translated by P.J. van de Paverd. Amsterdam: Burma Centrum Nederland 1996.

Keyes, Charles F. *The Golden Peninsula: Culture and Adaptation in Mainland South East Asia.* Honolulu: University of Hawaii Press, 1995.

Kyaw Thet. *History of the Union of Burma.* (In Burmese). Rangoon: Ava House Press, 1962.

Ni Ni Myint. *Burma's Struggle Against British Imperialism.* Rangoon: The Universities Press, 1983.

Rotberg, R.I., ed. *Burma: Prospects for a Democratic Future.* Washington: Brookings Institution Press, 1998.

Smith, D.E. *Religion and Politics in Burma.* Princeton: Princeton University Press, 1965.

Smith, Martin. *Burma: Insurgency and the Politics of Ethnicity.* New York: St Martin's Press, 1999. 2nd. ed. London: Zed Books 1999.

Steinberg, David I. *Burma: A Socialist Nation of Southeast Asia.* Boulder CO: Westview Press, 1982.

Tun Tin, Frankie. *Through Myanmar Eyes.* Singapore: Viscom Editions, 1997.

b) Religion and Church

Bawla, L.R. *History of the Presbyterian Church of Burma.* (In Burmese). Rev. ed. Burma Presbyterian Church; n.d.

Burma Christian Council Constitution. Rangoon: BCC, 1969.
Burmese Literature and Translation Society. *Survey of Religions in Burma*. Rangoon: Mimeographed, 1969-1970.
Ko Ko Naing. "Church History of Myanmar". *MIT Magazine* 1998-99.
Kyaw Dwe, Clifford. *History of the Karen Baptist Convention 1913-1991*. (In Karen). 2 vols. Rangoon: KBC, 1992.
Kyaw Nyunt, ed. *Burma SCM Diamond Jubilee 1912-1987*. Rangoon: Burma Christian Council, 1987.
Lay, William. "History of the YMCA: Life and Work and Mission". Thesis, BDS, Insein, 1973.
Mackley, Dorothy Emma. *Methodism in Burma*. Halifax : S.A. Ashton, 1986.
Maung Latt, J. "A History of the Burma Divinity School." B.Th. Thesis, BDS, 1964.
—. "The Baptists in Burma." M.Th. Thesis, SEAGST, Rangoon, 1977.
Shwe Wa, Maung. *Burma Baptist Chronicle*. Edited by Genevieve Sowards and Erville Sowards. Rangoon: Board of Publications, BBC, 1963.
Tuan Khaw Kham Ngaihte. *Christianity in Myanmar and its Progress*. Yangon: Tedim Baptist Church, 1998.

2.2 Roman Catholic Presence

(See also Burma 1800-1945, 1.2 and 1.8, above.)

In this period the Roman Catholic Church established work amongst all eight major racial groupings of which the Burmese population is composed - Bamar, Kachin, Chin, Shan, Mon, Kaya, Rakhine and Kayin - and now has nine dioceses in the Archdioceses of Yangon, Mandalay and Taunggyi. The first Burmese national to be consecrated bishop was Joseph U Win (1954), active in spreading Catholic literature, who became Archbishop of Mandalay in 1961. There are now 16 Bishops and 19 Religious Orders, many of which are directly involved in catechetics, theological teaching, conduct of courses and seminars, and the preparation for the sacraments. Theological study and writing had virtually ceased during the 1940s, but the foundation of the National Major Seminary in Rangoon was laid in February 1956, originally offering courses in philosophy as well as theology. A separate Major Seminary was later established for the students of philosophy, close to the National

Major Seminary, soon to be transferred to Maymyo in the Archdiocese of Mandalay. In 1984-85 the "Institute of Theology" commenced teaching "a wide and solid teaching in the sacred sciences, together with a general culture appropriate to the needs of our time in the country".

Unlike the leaders of Protestant churches and of the Burma Christian Council, the Roman Catholic hierarchy had not opposed the moves to make Buddhism Burma's national religion in 1961, although many Kachin faithful joined the mass protests. Following the commencement of military rule in 1962, Catholics also suffered increasing restrictions that led to the departure of all but 11 expatriate nuns and priests by 1966. In 1965 the Government had nationalised all Catholic (and Protestant) schools, hospitals, dispensaries and social institutions. The radical change marked by handing over diocesan control to the indigenous clergy and faithful during the next ten years brought both a local articulation of the Church's mission and the emergence of local leadership. "... We have learned [from the missionaries] not to sneer and rage, but to be light-hearted and joyful even when we suffer in earnest. They gave us the wisdom of acceptance, the will and resilience to push on" declared Marie Nyun in 1972 (Fischer 1980, 150f.). In that year, Bishop Howe, who envisioned 'prayer leaders' for every village who would "teach the people how to live", convened a first diocesan synod in Myitkyina to develop local leadership and here Paul Grawng was consecrated Bishop and two Kachin priests were ordained.

Many more local bishops were consecrated in other districts in 1975, and vocations to the priesthood and to the religious life increased annually. Laity Councils which had first been formed in 1946, spread to almost all dioceses, and Sodalities and lay movements such as the Youth Apostolate also developed in this period. In the 40 years since 1936, formerly isolated Catholic communities had become less "colonial" or "triumphalistic" in attitude and more open to their neighbours of whatever faith, according to Fr. Jeremiah Kelleher in 1972. Churches also grew steadily in this period.

In 1992 Mgr. Charles Maung Bo, president of the Conference of Bishops in Burma, founded a Centre for Pastoral and Religious Studies, and himself led in establishing courses for spiritual formation. Catholic Relief Services, which were aimed at strengthening the dioceses in their work for social justice and democratic processes, began, with the assistance of Caritas Philippines and the Catholic Council of Thailand for Development. In 1998, six of the twelve dioceses participated in strategic planning workshops where bishops, priests, and lay leaders formulated their mission statements and prepared programmes concerning the issues confronting the people of Burma. Similar exercises were conducted in the remaining dioceses in 1999. (See also 2.3 and 2.8.1-3 below.)

Selected References

Carmignani, R. "Le Fonti storiche in lingua italiana per una storia generale della Birmania". *Barnabiti Studi*, (Rome), 1985.
Catholic Directory of India, Ceylon and Burma. (ca.1912 - 1948). Madras: Catholic Supply Society, ?1948.
Catholic Life. "Burma an Almost Completely Indigenous Church." *Catholic Life* 27 (1980).
Evans, Eddie. "Birmania." 4 parts. *Messis* (Napoli) 38, 39 (1987).
Fischer, Edward. *Mission in Burma. Columban Fathers' Forty-three Years in Kachin Country*. New York: Seabury Press, 1980.
Metta ron khrann Kaksalac maggajan (Catholic Magazine). Rangoon: Rvhe Rup Lvha Cape, 1992.
Morland, David. "Suu Kyi's Call to Catholics." *The Tablet* (London) 1276 (1998).
Myo Kye Thu (The Sower). National Catholic Monthly.
Mondini, Livio. *La citta felice avventura missionaria in Birmania*. Bologna: Editrice Missionaria Italiana, 1989.
Peitz, Marietta. "Kirche im Sozialistischen Birma. Ein Besuch Nach funf Jahran." *Die Katholischen Mission* 94 (1975).
Pyin Pye Ye Let Swe (Development Workers' Handbook). Yangon: Searsolin Alumni Association of Myanmar, 2000.
Smith, D.E. *Religion and Politics in Burma*. Princeton: Princeton University Press, 1965.
Sotero Phamo (Thein Myint). *Loikaw: Ten Years' Sojourn*. Loikaw: Pastoral Centre, 2000.

2.3 Christian Theology in Post-war Burma/Myanmar
(See also above 1.7, 1.8)

Burmese theological reflection in the second half of the 20th century has come to concentrate more and more on the issues of indigenous leadership and ministry; on Christian presence in Buddhist society, and within the cultures of particular ethnic groupings; on appropriate patterns of evangelism, stewardship and social witness; and on the development in particular, of contextual Christology, eschatology, ecclesiology and hermeneutics. The major Protestant communities have notably remained firmly rooted in both evangelical and ecumenical traditions and have made significant contributions to both, despite the vicissitudes and restrictions of life and witness in Burmese society. The growth of more localised theology has also been stimulated both by the removal of expatriate personnel as well as by movements of nationalism, socialism and wider ecumenical encounter. This has in part been true also for Catholic theology, although major changes would only come with the increasing influence of the documents of Vatican II and later from the work of the FABC.

As in the earlier period, much Burmese theology has been "formulated and communicated orally as pulpit" or training-course theology, but the formerly confrontational patterns of theology have been replaced for many by those of co-operation and dialogue. Earlier triumphalist or wholly exclusive understandings of the Gospel have been further replaced for many by a more open ecclesiology, a recognition of the truths in other living faiths, and by a witness in life and writing to the God who is present and to be served everywhere in Burmese life. Here the emphasis is sometimes upon Jesus Christ as both the fulfilment of Dhamma in all religions and also as a historical figure; and sometimes upon "God as transcendent reality", creating and preserving, rather than a Person within one religious tradition only. Within diverse ethnic groupings, theology has included discernment of Gospel elements within both primal and "meta-cosmic" religio-cultures, and within the daily life of Myanmar society. It became true in this half-century that Christians in whatever branch of the Christian church, were sharing in the struggles and suffering of their compatriots for livelihood, community survival and for the establishment of democracy. An overall trend has therefore been towards a Burmese theology which is incarnational and indigenous, confessing, transformative and people-centred.

Significant theological movements in which individual theologians or groups that are mentioned below, have participated, have somewhat different characteristics depending upon denominational and ecumenical contexts. Theological colleges such as the Burma Divinity School (later MIT) and Holy Cross College would also play important roles as would the Study Documents and activities of the Burma Christian Council. The SCM, with strong theological tradition, had been especially active at Rangoon University, and by the 1950s strong branches had developed also at Myitkyina, Bassein, Moulmein and Mandalay.

Along with the growth of regional and world-wide ecumenical theologies such movements had, by 1960, produced writings by figures of international importance such as U Hla Bu, U Ba Hmyin, Francis Ah Mya and U Kyaw Than (see 2.5.3., 2.5.7., 2.5.5., 2.5.8.). From the early 1960s would come the early graduates from the Burma Divinity School BRE programme including William Lay, Esther Byu, Grace Hla, Arthur Ko Lay, Anna May Say Pa, U Pe Thwin and Johnny Maung Lat (see e.g. 2.6, 2.7, 2.5.14., 2.5.19., 2.5.10.). These and younger generations of Baptist theologians would continue work in coming years in studies of Bible, ecumenics, mission and evangelism, other faiths and wholistic spirituality, and would include such theologians as U Khin Maung Din, Victor Sanlone, Edmund Za Bik, Simon Pau Khan En, Mary Dun, David Laisum, Lahpai Zau Lat and Alan Saw U. (See 2.5.12., 2.5.11., 2.5.17., 2.5.21., 2.5.18., 2.5.24., 2.5.20., 2.5.23.).

Catholic theologians and teachers in this period were closely watching the discussions at Vatican II, and were soon to be engaged in new programmes of Bible translation, and the writing of catechetics. In the years 1980-2000, increasing numbers of students were able to complete post-graduate studies. Biblical translation and research, doctrinal studies, along with catechetical reflection remained important, as did Catholic social teaching in Myanmar;

participation in community development, and the review and dedication of Jubilee 2000. (See 2.8 below).

For Anglican theologians and scholars there were movements from the late 1950s on, towards indigenous leadership; the study of Burmese history, culture and Buddhist context (see Pe Maung Tin, 2.5.2.); the development of "disciplined Christian living for laity and ordinands"; and the moves towards a three-self church from 1966 (See Ah Mya, 2.5.5.). In 1976-1986 came the Samuel Project for educational training of pastors and teachers, to be followed by fuller ecumenical programmes (see below). Lay and clergy leaders such as Paul Chen and San Si Tay contributed to both ecumenical and Anglican programmes and writing.

Ecumenical themes and movements in which much creative theological reflection arose in this period include, in the 1950s, those to foster Christian diakonia, Christian communication and Church unity. By the 1970s, there were significant movements to develop partnership in mission, spiritual and 'secular' formation of the laity, interfaith study, training for participation in human development and for peace-making. To these in the next decades would be added the recovery of wholistic stewardship, church growth and integrated mission. The Bi-Annual Symposia of Theological Faculties has produced papers in all the major sections of theological study in preparation for writing of theological textbooks in the Burmese context. From 1994 the MCC programme "Reading the Bible with New Eyes" has been of growing significance, with its focus also upon groups of suffering people in Myanmar and the causes of such suffering. In 1997 was formed the Ecumenical Fellowship of Theologians, concerned especially to work further on the development of a Myanmar theology. In conjunction with this has been the Ecumenical Seminar Series "The Concept of God in the Burmese Context" held at Holy Cross College since 1999.

From these movements, as well as from theologians active in each of them, have come many writings of which selections will be mentioned below.

Selected References

Ano, Stephen. "The Context of Missionary Activity in Contemporary Myanmar." Lic.S.Theol, Thesis, University Santo Tomas, Manila, 1995.

Charles, G.P., ed. *Buddhism in Burma*. Rangoon: Commission on Buddhism of the Burma Christian Council, 1955.

Doh Say. "Missio - Contextual Theology." *Thamar Alin* 2.2 (1996).

Khin Maung Din. "Some Problems and Possibilities for Burmese Christian Theology Today". *IRM* (April 1976). Also in *What Asian Christians are Thinking: A Theological Source Book*, edited by Douglas J. Elwood. Quezon City: New Day Publishers, 1976.

Kyaw Than, U. "Burma: Theologizing for Selfhood and Service". In *Asian Voices in Christian Theology*, edited by Gerald H. Anderson. Maryknoll, NY: Orbis Books, 1976.

Laisum, David. "Maranatha or Pro morafinis. Hope and Hermeneutics (Myanmar Context)." *Annual Magazine MIT*: 1995-1996.

Maran Yaw. *The Church is Central*. Rangoon: BBC, 1986.

MCC Workbook of Bible Studies for Peace. Yangon: MCC, 2000.

Ngulh Za Thawng, Smith. "The Ecumenical Movement in Burma: ...." Mimeo'd. Bossey: Ecumenical Institute Graduate School, 1984.

Ngun Ling, Samuel. "Towards a Theology of Myanmar: A Study of the Myanmar Situation in the Light of Her Encounter with the Christian Mission and Theology." *Rays. MIT Journal of Theology* 1.1 (2000).

Pau Khan En, Simon. "Myanmar Theology." In *Dictionary of Third World Theologies*, edited by Virginia Fabella and R.S. Sugirtharajah. Maryknoll NY: Orbis Books, 2000.

PIM Sar Dan (Partnership in Mission). Rangoon: Anglican Provincial Office, 1988.

Tint Lwin. "Reflections on Contextualization." *Thamar Alin* 4 (1999).

Yang Joshua. "Towards an Indigenous Church." *Journal of Theology for Myanmar* (1995).

2.4 A Note on Sources for Burmese Christian Writing

Although in the period following the end of the Pacific war, there was, until 1962, comparative freedom for the publication of Christian writings, the life of the churches and their educational and publishing work in particular, were soon subject to the severe restrictions of civil conflict, military rule and economic hardship. These conditions still continue despite periodic and partial relaxation. In the 1960s, when almost all expatriate church personnel had to leave, stimulating the growth of a more self-reliant and indigenous church, contextual Burmese theology came to develop more fully.

Although churches had lost all other educational institutions, theological seminaries still possessed freedom to teach and to publish - at least privately. They therefore assumed a growing importance not only in training the ordained ministry but also in laity formation, in publication, and latterly even in general education. Publication departments of the churches have also been allowed to publish for private circulation, and such materials have included Christian education materials, theological textbooks, sermon collections, periodicals and materials for ecumenical and community development programmes.

A large amount of theological writing, apart from the contents of journals remains however in mimeo'd or even typewritten form in such libraries as those of Holy Cross College, MIT and the Major Theological Seminary (all of Rangoon). Any adequately representative collection or survey of such diverse sources is yet to be made, although a selection will be included in the entries below. In rare cases theological works have been published outside of Burma (most often in English), or Burmese theologians have contributed to publications in western countries. An increasing number of theses and dissertations by Burmese studying overseas are held in the libraries of other countries. A selection from all these sources has been included below. It has also been necessary to recognise theological writing in a wide range of formats, wherever they are held, and whether formally published or not, for the alternative would be only to arbitrarily truncate the rich story of Burma's contextual theological reflection.

Periodicals and Theological Journals include:

Annual Magazine Student Christian Movement, Rangoon; *Burma Christian Council Annual / BCC Half Yearly Activity Report;*

Myanmar Faman (Burmese Messenger), Burmese Christian Union; *Myo Kye Thu* (The Sower) - Catholic Monthly; *Myitta Faman* (Messenger of Love), monthly, Myanmar Baptist Convention; *Rays of the BIT* (Annual magazine of Burma Institute of Theology, in Burmese and English - later published as *Myanmar Institute of Theology Annual Magazine*); *Rays MIT Journal of Theology.* - begun in 2000 as faculty publication of MIT; *SCM Womens' Concern Magazine* (from ca. 1995); S*halom.* Annual Magazine of Holy Cross College; *The South East Asia Journal of Theology - Special Burma Issues.* Vol. 3. 1 (1961); Vol. 7. 4 (1966); *Ta Ding Hlwa* (Newsletter of Anglican Province) since 1966; *Thamar Alin*, Baptist theological Journal. See also *In God's Image,* Special Issue 19.2 (2000).

Other periodicals including elements of contextual Christian reflection, include:

Annual Magazine. Catholic Major Seminary. Rangoon - since 1957; *Burma News.* (Valley Forge); *Dhamma let Yone* (Christian life). Christian Literature Society Monthly Notes: "Organ of the churches in Burma." - from 1948; *Endeavour Magazine.* (Karen Baptist Convention) - from 1955; *The Guardian.* Monthly since 1953. Rangoon, Guardian Press; *Jinghpaw Kasa* (Kachin Messenger) - from 1956; *Lehsu Hsu Nya* (Go Forward). Karen Baptist Convention; *Life style today.* (In Burmese) Rangoon: Sa Thvan, Today Publishing. House, 1997- ; *Lone-ma-lay* (Young Woman). Monthly, includes many Buddhist contributors; *Myat Paleh* (Honoured Pearl). National monthly - includes 'secular' writers; *Myitta Yaung Chi* (Catholic Magazine). Rangoon, 1992-; *NBCM newsletter* (North Burma Christian Mission - Irregular from 1991? *Pashee Paghaw* (Home Magazine); *Zomi Christian* - Monthly; *Empowering Women of Burma* - Annual from 1993.

2.5 Theologians, Scholars, Animators
2.5.1. Women Doing Theology

Women continued in this period to play indispensable roles in the churches of Burma in every dimension of their life and witness. Ordained ministry has been open to Baptist and Methodist women since1968, but although women have graduated with degrees in theology since 1979 from Holy Cross (Anglican) College, none have yet been ordained to the priesthood. As with many ordained sisters, their work remains chiefly in religious education, women's ministry, teaching or administrative work. Roman Catholic religious women similarly continue in their traditional ministries. And although many women have taught in seminaries, institutes and schools, and also preached or led in the church's congregations and associations, the writings of only a few have been published or recorded in periodicals or documents. Individual entries are given below for Mrs Ba Maung Chain (2.5.6.), Eh Wah (2.5.15.), Esther Byu (2.7), Anna May Say Pa (2.5.19.) and Mary Dun (2.5.18.), but a selection of the many others must also be included.

Katherine Khin Khin (Meh Kha Khway,1909-1995) was a writer and educator, Deputy Director of the Ministry of Information (1945-1946), Director of Education for the Diocese of Rangoon and Editor for the Christian Literature Society (1941-1942). She was also active in the Women's Literature League, the Women's Literature Council and the Burma Christian Council (1948-1992). The theology which sustained her many works was both ecumenical and world-oriented, with particular concern for the role of women in literature and in education. Her many writings as journalist and Christian educator appeared in such journals as *Toe-tet-ye* (Advance), *Myanmar Ah Swe* (Burma Friend), *Shu-ma-wa* (Ever Lovely) and *Lone-ma-lay* (Young Woman).

Rebecca Shwee (1912-1991, B.Theol. 1940, BDS) was teacher, evangelist, mid-wife and Director of KBC Women Leadership Training. In 1958, with Thra Sein Pe and Thra Po Nyo, she founded a Bible School at Meh Nyah Harday, near Chiangmai in Thailand. In 1978 she was the first woman to be ordained by the Karen Baptist Convention, and was also the first Baptist national to be so ordained. Strongly committed to the total ministry of the church and to improved status for women, her whole-hearted devotion and zealous activity became a model for many. Her few published writings are found in Church reports and newsletters, and in her autobiography (1986).

Since the 1960s women writers on Christian life, thought and mission in Burma have included Rosie Tin Tin Win, Tin May, Daw

Win Mya, Lin Lin Shwee, Lilian Hka Nau, Esther Lwin, Naw Grace, Rosalind Bwa, Sr. Patricia Mary Ma Rita and Esther Tun Hlaing (along with Mrs Ba Maung Chain, Eh Wah, Esther Byu, Greeta Din, Anna May Say Pa and Mary Dun, mentioned elsewhere). Tin May graduated from BDS (1958) to become a lecturer, preacher, composer and writer (in Mon), especially on Mon Church and mission history. Like Katherine Khin Khin, Rosie Tin Tin Win (December Moon) has gained a name as the author of Christian novels. Daw Win Mya and Lin Lin Shwee are examples of those whose sermons have been collected and published in recent years. Lilian Hka Nau has been a YWCA and ecumenical leader whose articles have appeared in national periodicals and also in those of the Asian Church Women's Conference and the WSCF (Asia-Pacific). Ma Lay Lone has also written many novels amongst which *Theint* has been filmed. She also published a women's magazine *Lone-ma-lay* (Young Woman).

Amongst the writings of many other women who have been teachers, animators and authors, articles which are yet to be studied are extant for Daw Thaung Tin, Sara Zau Yaw, M.K. Lwin, Mrs William Winn, Daw Hla Shein, and Daw Nyein Tha. Younger women now writing in national theological journals include Mu Mu Kyu, Yin Yin Maw, C. Htu Ra, Kyin Nang, Su Mo Mo Win, Huai Man Cing, Cho Cho Win, Tin Hla Kyi, Esther Khaing Oo, Grace Aye Maung, Laivet Mami, Moo Paw, Nyunt Nyunt Thein, Khaing Thiri and Marcheta Thein.

Selected References

Bible Study for Women. (In Karen). Rangoon: Women's Dept, KBC, ca. 1985.

Grace, Naw. "Ecumenical Decade for Churches in Solidarity with Women 1988-1998." MIT Thesis 1993.

Harley, Rosemary K. "The Impact of Feminist Theology on the Mission of the Church in Myanmar ...." M.Theol. Thesis, University of South Africa, forthcoming.

Hla Shein, Daw. "The Healing of the Nations." *Baptist World Alliance* (1955).

Holy Cross Theological College Golden Jubilee Magazine 1985.

Htu Ra, C. "The Situation of Myanmar Women." *Journal of Theology for Myanmar* (1995).
Huai Man Cing. "Jesus' Attitude to Women in the Gospels." *In God's Image* 19.2 (2000).
Khaing Oo, Esther. "The Woman who Touched Jesus' Cloak." *SCM Women Concern Magazine*, 1998.
Lin Lin Shwee (Gold Flower). *Tayar Haw Chef* (Sermons). Rangoon: Women's Dept, MBC, 1993.
Lwin, M.K. "The Role of Women in Burmese Society." *Asia Focus* (EACC/CCA) 7.3 (1972).
Moo Paw. "Radical faithfulness." *In God's Image* 19.2 (2000).
Nyo Kwee Tha. "Rev. Rebecca Shee. The First Ordained Woman of Sgaw-Kayin Baptist Church." MIT Research Paper, Mimeo'd, 1994.
Procter, M. *The World My Country: the Story of Daw Nyein Tha of Burma.* London: Grosvenor, 1976.
Soe Soe Mar. "Women in the New Testament: Collaborators in Jesus' Ministry." *SCM Women Concern Magazine*, 1998.
Su Mo Mo Win. "The Concept of Hesed in Ruth 1.1-22." *In God's Image* 19.2 (2000).
Win Mya, Daw. *Kyay Zu Daw Chee Mwan Tayar Haw Chet* (Sermons of thanksgiving). 2nd Ed. Rangoon: Women's Dept, MBC, 1991.
Yin Yin Maw. "Women and Men in God's Creation." *In God's Image* 19.2 (2000).

2.5.2. U Pe Maung Tin (1888-1973)

Pe Maung Tin studied in Rangoon, the University of Calcutta (MA 1911) and at Oxford University. He then became Professor of Pali and Burmese at Rangoon University and was its first Rector. Later he also became Professor of Oriental Studies, established the Burmese Literature Department at the University of Rangoon, and was a visiting professor at the University of Chicago. He received many academic awards, edited the *Journal of the Burma Research Society* (1913-1920, 1923-1936) and was later Chairman of the Burma Historical Commission. His contributions to the churches of Burma and to national and regional ecumenical movements were many.

He has been recognised for his eminence in linguistic, epigraphical and historical scholarship in Burma, and as a pioneer educator there, as well as for his studies of Buddhism, along with his reflections as a Christian upon Buddhism in Burma. In all his writing he stressed the importance of careful scholarship, and his translations into English of two of Ledi Sayadaw's treatises - *Atthasalini Kyan* under the title *The Expositor* (1920-21) and *Visuddhi Magga* under the title *The Path of Purity* (1923-31) earned him international fame, as have his articles and books on Pagan inscriptions, Burmese literature, and Burmese folk-songs.

In theology, missiology and inter-faith dialogue his detailed study of terms and images in both biblical and Buddhist sources, along with his interpretation of parallel teachings and insights in Christianity and Buddhism remain of lasting significance. Apart from many similarities between particular Buddhist and New Testament texts, more important parallels included for him the ideas of selflessness in both faiths; the role of faith in Christianity and of grace in Buddhism; the parallels of prayer in Christian tradition and Buddhist meditation; Buddhist metta and Christian charity; the human being in both traditions; and the relationship of Nirvana to the Kingdom of Heaven. Yet more important to him was the re-establishment of full Buddhist-Christian relationships, and the demonstration by Christians of full Burmese identity, through "the way Christians live" rather than through teaching or debate. This is seen for instance in the series of lectures "Christian Faith and Buddhism in Asia", given at the EACC Assembly, 1957, Kuala Lumpur, Malaysia. Apart from his own prolific work he actively promoted the writings of others through the CLS of Burma.

Selected References
Works by Pe Maung Tin

Dhammapada. Rangoon: British Burma Press, 1914.
Prayer and Meditation. Rangoon: Burma Christian Council, 1960.
Buddhist Prayers. Rangoon: The Study Centre on Buddhism, Burma Christian Council, 1960.
Prayer and Meditation. Rangoon: Burma Christian Council, 1960.
Buddhist-Christian Parallels. Yangon: The Study Centre on Buddhism, Burma Christian Council, 1961.
Buddhist Devotion and Meditation; An Objective Description and Study. London: SPCK, 1964.

The Path of Purity. Being translation of Buddhaghosa's Visuddhi Magga. London: Luzac, for the Pali Text Society, 1971.

"Women in the Inscriptions of Pagan". *Journal of the Burma Research Society* 25 (1935). Also in *Burma Research Society 50th Anniversary Publication* 2 (1960).

"Revival of Buddhism in Burma". In *Let God Speak. Burma Christian Council Annual 1953.* Rangoon: BCC, 1953.

"The Study of Buddhism in Burma". *SEAJT* 1.3 (1960).

"Christianity in Independent Burma." *Church and Society* (EACC) 1 (Sept. 1960).

"Resurgence of Buddhism and the Search for New Foundations". *In Witnesses together,* edited by Kyaw Than. Rangoon: EACC, 1962.

"Certain Factors in the Buddhist-Christian Encounter". SEAJT 3.2 (1961). Also Myanmar CLS, 1998.

Life and Work of Professor Pe Maung Tin. Papers from the SOAS Symposium, Nov. 1999. (In Burmese and English) Contains a full bibliography. London: 2000?

Ma Lay Lon. *Maung Tin tho-mahok Ba Thet-shei* (Pe Maung Tin or Father Longlife). Vols I & II. Rangoon: Thit-sa sa-pei, 1975.

Takkasuil mya "Samuin", Sutesana Thana. *Pe Maung Tin - a Tribute.* Yangon: Universities Historical Research Centre, 1999.

U Pe Maung Tin 111 Hnit Pyi Gone Pyu Sar Dan Mya (Essays in honour of Pe Maung Tin's 111th birthday), edited by Maung Pauk Si, Maung Swan Yi and Yar Pyi U Soe Nyunt. Yangon: Lawka Sa Pay, 1999.

2.5.3. U Hla Bu (1897-1970)

Hla Bu was the first principal of Judson College, Rangoon, and was later professor of philosophy and also Vice-Rector in the University of Rangoon, as well as visiting professor at Union Theological Seminary, New York. He was the son of the Rev'd Tha Din (of Prome). From student days he was active in the SCM and the WSCF and became a leading figure in most ecumenical movements in Burma, as president of the national YMCA, the national SCM and the national Council of Churches. His philosophical and sociological writings included volumes on the role and development of voluntary movements (1934), on psychoanalysis (1938), and on practical psychology (1948), as well as on the processes of secularization and the interaction of Communism and nationalism.

His theological and missiological thought was focused particularly upon Christian mission within the academic community and on Christian response to Buddhism in Burma. Studying the "resurgence of Buddhism" in Burma, Hla Bu recognised the challenges this brought to Christians. This meant for him that under the renewed judgement of the Gospel, Christians must divest the faith of encrusted western trappings; identify themselves with their neighbours; and think and speak in "forms natural to their own culture." Criticism of Christianity from Buddhist, from humanist or from Communist, is to be taken seriously, without self-righteousness or spiritual laziness, as guidelines for reform of life and social witness. Even though differences exist in the understanding of human nature and society, their significance and their ends, must be recognised. More important than criticism or debate is our commitment as Christians to understand the life of our society, "giving ourselves in love to the struggle for doing away social injustices and uplifting the masses of the people."

Selected References
Works by U Hla Bu
> *Evangelistic Task in the Universities & Colleges.* Rangoon: WSCF, 1951.
> "The Christian Encounter with Buddhism in Burma". *IRM* (April 1958).
> "The Nature of the Resurgence of Buddhism in Burma". *SEAJT* 3.1 (1961).
> "Forces that Challenge the Authority of the Gospel." Report *Consultation on World Mission.* Hong Kong: Baptist Alliance, 1963/1964.
>
> Thet Tun. "My Three Sayas." *The Guardian* (July 1970).

2.5.4. George Appleton (1902-?)

Following an East London curacy, George Appleton became a rural missionary in the Irrawady Delta (1927) and five years later, Warden of Holy Cross College, Rangoon. After the invasion of Burma by the Japanese he was Director of Public Relations for the Burma Government in Exile and from 1943-1946 was also Archdeacon of Rangoon. He worked as secretary of the Conference of British Missionary Societies (1950-1957) and was later Archbishop of Perth, Western Australia (1963-1968), and of Jerusalem (1969-1974).

From his early years in Burma he became deeply committed to fostering inter-faith understanding and reconciliation. He continued his study, teaching and writing for these concerns, with a particular concern for the life of prayer in the major living faiths, until 1990. The papers of Archbishop Appleton (in Parkes Library, University of Southampton) mainly relate to his work in Burma and Jerusalem and to inter-faith and Jewish dialogue concerns.

Selected References
Works by George Appleton
  John's Witness to Jesus. New York: Association Press, c1955 (1946)
  In His name, Prayers for the Church and the World; a discipline of intercession based on Bible insights. London: Edinburgh House Press, 1956.
  Burma. The War and After Series 1. London: SPG, ?1946.
  On the Eightfold Path. The Christian Presence Amidst Buddhism. London: SCM Press, 1961.
  The Christian Approach to the Buddhist. London: Edinburgh House Press. 1958.
  The Divine Strategy: Seven Studies in Mission. London: SCM, 1955.
  Glad Encounter: Jesus Christ and the Living Faiths of Men. London: SPCK,1978.
  Unfinished: George Appleton Remembers and Reflects. London: Collins Fount, 1990.
  — et al. *The Human search: with Teilhard de Chardin.* London: Fount, 1979.

2.5.5. Francis Ah Mya, Archbishop (1904-1999)

Francis Ah Mya studied at Bishop's College, Calcutta (1925-1928) and was ordained in Holy Trinity Cathedral, Rangoon (1931). During ministries at the Holy Cross College, he attended world assemblies of the Anglican Congress, Moral Re-armament and the WCC. He also ministered in villages such as Kwan Ta, Kwan Be,

Kwang Taw, and also in Maw Lam Yine and Pa-an. During the war and following years Ah Mya became a leader in Karen movements to restore their culture and in attempts to mediate in growing political conflicts. Consecrated bishop in 1949, he was sent to Pa-an to develop the *Three in One Project* (self- government, self-support and self-propagation) and initiated self-supporting projects in Kayin State including schools, printing presses, and agricultural development. In 1965 he took up duties at Holy Cross College, Rangoon, becoming Bishop there (1966) and the first national Archbishop of the Anglican Church (1970-1973).

Few writings of Francis Ah Mya are extant, but amongst his principal concerns in ministry and speaking were the improvement of inter-faith and inter-ethnic relations and for peace-making, along with the recognition of ethnic selfhood and identity. His theology was strongly ecumenical, embracing in its understanding not only diverse Christian traditions but also the creative traditions of Buddhism and of his own Karen people. He was thus strongly committed to the church's national identity; to theological and laity education; and to church renewal and unity. In these and other fields his name remains eminent throughout Burma, and many of his characteristic beliefs and sayings, such as "the only way for Christians to do anything good is to get inside society", are widely quoted.

Selected References

Works by Francis Ah Mya

Ah Mya, Francis. *Autobiography.* Rangoon: Mimeo'd, 1984.

— et al. *Pastors' Handbook on Pastoral Counselling.* Rangoon: Burma Christian Council, ?1954.

Aung Hla Tun. "Bishop Francis Ay Mya". *Home Magazine* (1994).

—. "A Personal Interview with Francis Ah Mya." *Golden Jubilee Magazine* (1985).

Day, Saw Christopher. "Biographical Sketches of Noted Karen Leaders." MDiv Thesis, MIT, 2000.

Omu Paw. "Biography of Francis Ay Mya: First National Archbishop of the Church of the Province of Burma." B.Th. thesis, Holy Cross College, Yangon, 1999.

Tun Tun. "The Retired Archbishop Francis Ah-Mya." *Immanuel Annual Magazine* (1997).

2.5.6. Mrs Ba Maung Chain (Claribel Irene Po, 1905-1994)

Claribel Irene Po graduated from Judson College and taught at secondary schools 1927-1935. She served in attempts toward mediation during conflicts in 1949/1950 and was a cabinet minister 1952-1953. Committed to ecumenical education and welfare work, especially for Burma's women and girls, she was the first national president for the YWCA, first woman to be elected president of the Burma Council of Churches, and was elected the vice-president of the world YWCA (1955-1959). In her tasks of organising, liaison and teaching Ba Maung Chain gave fully to the work of YWCAs and other ecumenical networks, in such endeavours as raising the status of women, in citizenship education, in refugee work and in mutual community service.

In Burma she was also strongly concerned for mass education for farmers and peasants, as well as for the political and ideological education of Christians so that they could "relate in a constructive manner what they have learned as Christians to what they ought to do as voters" in the new independent Burma. She envisioned a pioneer role for Christians in the building of just and democratic societies, on the basis of a theology of social welfare, of public service and of wide toleration. This would be embodied in multiplying programmes of village (and church) education, in agricultural training and in rural health centres. She remained deeply committed in animation and speaking, to peace-making and to the service of all deprived of education, health and livelihood.

Selected References

Ba Maung Chain. "Christian Service in Burma's New Setting." *Church and Society.* (EACC) 2 (Mar. 1961).

Biographies of Outstanding Christian Women. (In Burmese) Vol 1. Yangon: MCC Gender Committee, forthcoming.

Day, Saw Christopher. "Biographical Sketches of Noted Karen Leaders." MDiv Thesis, MIT, 2000.

Saw Mong Nyin (Ayee). *Burmese Ladies.* Toungoo: Tin Shwee Press, 1998.

2.5.7. U Ba Hmyin, (1912-1982)

Teacher, pastor, church administrator and pioneer of ecumenical and youth movements in Myanmar, Ba Hmyin studied at Burma Divinity School, Rangoon, and Yale Divinity School, New Haven. He returned to be pastor to the Judson Chapel of the University of Rangoon, and later pastored churches at Lanmadaw and at Kemmendin. In 1947, with colleagues, he organised the All Burma Christian Youth League to increase the role of nationals in Christian leadership. He was also one of the leaders who organised the first post-war Christian Youth Conference (1946). He later became General Secretary of the Baptist Churches Union (1952-1956) and of the BBC (1970-1973).

In his few writings he affirmed that the ecumenical movement in Asia had grown rapidly because Christians in most diverse situations and traditions had "come to see that in Christ they belong to each other, and that there is a sufficiency and finality in Christ for the whole world" and for each distinct people and culture. Such a realisation brings them both re-assessment and re-direction through a recognition of God's presence in the world. It makes possible an ecumenical and local theology which is related to the "oriental mind", through a break with purely western ways of thought and the substitution of Asian forms for Hellenic.

But such a theology only arises from the implications of living out the Gospel in Asia and from a sharing in the spiritual struggles of those in other living faiths, Ba Hmyin believed. It would grow in recognition of the total relationship of the Being of men and women to God's Being, rather than in just the processes of reason and knowledge, and by recognising the contribution of oriental insights into meditation and yogic discipline, along with the mystic awareness such as we see in Jesus himself. He also declared that this living theology would only grow from churches which have their own identity, self-support, and inter-church mutuality - both nationally and internationally. Such churches are to be "close to poor, humiliated people"; places where "the meaning of human existence is made plain", living, creative, and free of all static forms and traditions.

Selected References
Works by U Ba Hmyin
>Interview. *One World* 9 (1975).
>Sermon given at New Delhi Assembly WCC, 1961. In *The New Delhi Report: The Third Assembly of the World Council of Churches, 1961.* New York: Association Press, 1962.
>"Each in His Own Native Tongue." *Church and Society* (EACC) 4 (1962)
>*Reports of the Public Relations Committee, BCC.* Rangoon: ca.1950s.
>"New Patterns of Mission." Report *Consultation on World Mission.*" Hong Kong: Baptist Alliance, 1963/1964.
>—, with Maung Shwe Wa. "The Church Among Burmese-Speaking People". In *Burma Baptist Chronicle,* 1963.

2.5.8. U Kyaw Than (1923-)

Kyaw Than graduated with honours from the University of Rangoon and also lectured in history there. He was Associate General Secretary of the WSCF (1950-1956), and Associate General Secretary - later General Secretary - of the EACC (1957-1974). In these positions he was closely associated with D.T. Niles (see Vol. 1, chapter 8, 6.3) in the organisation and development of Asia-wide ecumenical programmes in every aspect of Christian mission. He then served as visiting professor at the Yale Divinity School (1974-1976), the University of Vancouver, and at Selly Oak Colleges, Birmingham. He taught in the theological seminaries of Insein and directed the Training Institute of the MCC for Christian Participation in Development (1978-1984), and has since been senior professor of World Religions at Mahidol University, Bangkok. Kyaw Than co-ordinated the publishing of many ecumenical volumes during his work with the WSCF and the EACC and also chaired the history working group of the WSCF for the production of five centenary volumes (1992-1997).

In his own thought and writings Kyaw Than has been strongly influenced by the theology of D.T. Niles. His prime concerns have been the vocation and witness of Christians in the university and in secular occupations; the contribution of ecumenical history to present missionary tasks in Asia; the theology, purposes and strategies for mission in unity; the theological and missiological challenges of Asian Christians to western churches; and Christian understanding of, and partnership with, Buddhist neighbours. Central to his understanding of integrated Christian mission is a recognition that Christians are enlisted in God's design for the redemption and transformation of this world in all its levels of human endeavour. This presents us with resources and visions for human life in our communities which are comprehensive, localised, world-oriented and evangelical. They are possible through the infilling of the Holy Spirit when the people of God collaborate in each place and in ever-widening circles: in diakonia to fulfil human needs, in dialogue and communication of the gospel, for prophetic witness in the secular world, and in theological reflection upon these dimensions of presence and engagement.

Selected References:
Works by U Kyaw Than
> *Joint Labourers in Hope.* Bangkok: EACC, 1973.
> "The Christian Mission in Asia Today." In *The Ghana Assembly*, edited by R.K. Orchard. London: Edinburgh House Press, 1958.
> "Man in Buddhism and Christianity." *SEAJT* 3.1 (1961).
> "Christian Laity in Asia." *SEAJT* 3.3 (1962).
> "The Ear, The Eye and the Head." *IRM* 62.248 (1973).
> "The Context of Mission." *Conversations* (Graymoor) Fall (1974).
> "Burma: Theologising for Selfhood and Service." In *Asian Voices in Christian Theology,* edited by G.H. Anderson. Maryknoll NY: Orbis Books, 1976.
> "The Obligation of the church to Share." *Ecumenical Review* 36.1 (1984)
> "What Mission Is. Our Understanding of Mission as a Factor for Unity or Division." *Missiology* 18.4 (1990).
> "Christianity on the Threshold of the 21st Century." *Rays. MIT Journal of Theology* 1.1 (2000).
> "A Blessed Military-Missionary Encounter: A Historical Essay on a Contemporary Congregation." *Rays, MIT Journal of Theology.* Forthcoming.
> —, ed. *Witnesses Together. Inaugural Assembly of the East Asia Christian Conference.* Rangoon: EACC, 1959.

—, ed. *Proclaiming Christ in Asia*. Rangoon: EACC, ?1962.
—, ed. *Christian Action in the Asian Struggle*. Singapore: CCA, 1973.

2.5.9. Paul Clasper (ca.1925 -)

Paul Clasper studied at Southern Baptist Seminary, Louisville, KY, and Union Theological Seminary, NY (Ph.D.) and came to Burma as a Baptist missionary in 1952. He was there assigned to train Christian pastors for engagement in Christian-Buddhist dialogue. He taught until 1964 at BDS, and when forced to leave Burma, taught Ecumenical Theology and Asian Religions at Drew University, NJ, the Graduate Theological Union, CA, and at the Chinese University of Hong Kong. He frequently returned to Burma for short-term teaching assignments under the SEAGST and was later Anglican Dean of Hong Kong.

Seeing himself as "an academic with pastoral concerns", Clasper has combined in his study and teaching, the traditions of Asian religions, both Indian and Chinese; psychology and pastoral counselling; and Christian traditions of prayer and spirituality. He has been particularly interested in the cosmic and inter-religious dimensions of faith, and "the hope of Christian faith finding Asian, as well as western, forms of expression." Clasper has persistently sought to live and reflect on "the frontiers" of Christian thought and life, in "patient and sensitive identification" with those of other cultural and religious milieux, learning the other's language, "re-looking at our own faith" and interpreting it "in the idioms and metaphors of the other's faith." He writes that the mark of those who see Jesus Christ in cosmic terms is "to be concerned with *both* the Christian faith in its Asian expression *and* the appreciation of Asian wisdom for the expansion of western understanding."

Selected References
Works by Paul Clasper
> "The Buddhist-Christian Encounter in Burma." *Burma News* (1959); *Practical Anthropology* Nov.-Dec. (1959).
> *The Dhammapada, an Introduction*. Rangoon: BBC, 1960.
> "Buddhism and Christianity in the Light of God's Revelation in the Christ." *SEAJT* 3.1 (1961).

The Evangel and the Evangelist. Rangoon: BBC, 1961.
New Life in Christ, a study of Paul's theology for today. World Christian books 9, 2nd series. New York: Association Press, 1962.
The Yogi, the Commissar, and the Third-world Church. Valley Forge: Judson Press, 1972.
Eastern Paths and the Christian Way. Maryknoll, NY: Orbis Books, c1980.
Theological Ferment: personal reflections. Quezon City: New Day Publishers, c1982.

2.5.10. U Pe Thwin (1929-1996)

Pe thwin grew up in Syriam, studied at Rangoon University and was commissioned in the Burma Navy in 1950. He was later chief instructor in the Burma Navy Training School and Staff Officer to the Chief of Naval Staff. In 1967 he became Chief Editor and Executive Secretary of the Burma Christian Literature Society and continued in these positions until retirement in 1995. He graduated BRE (1970) and M.Theol. (SEAGST 1977), and in 1993 was ordained to the pastoral ministry. Concerned for theological education, he taught theology at both the MIT and the MICT, as well as in night classes for lay people.

Known throughout Myanmar as a writer, Pe Thwin's articles and short stories number more than 200, along with 12 Christian novels, and scores of Bible commentaries, devotional books, works on contemporary theology and theology textbooks. In many plays he presents stories in which theological reflection upon nationalism is included. His articles appeared in periodicals such as *Myawaddy, Shumuwa, Thwe Thauk* and *Lone Ma Lay,* in which novels of his were often serialised. He described his own writing as being based on particular events or characters, to which he gave imaginative form in order to portray the nature of faith (not proof) and love in actual human life. "You cannot find people who are 100% saints or sinners" he has said, but in the story of this thief, that good person or this young couple in love, he believed it possible to present the choices which the Christian gospel offers. In this way he would explore the contemporary meaning of central Christian beliefs in ways which ordinary Burmese could understand.

Selected References
Works by U Pe Thwin

Pan kalay mya ma nwan say chin (So flowers may not wither). Rangoon: CLS, 1969.

Ah Mone Than Thayar (Circle of hatred). Rangoon: CLS, 1982.

Thanthaya Hnalonetha (The doubtful heart). Rangoon: CLS, 1986.

Into the World. (In Burmese). Rangoon: CLS, 1972.

Collected Sermons. (In Burmese). Rangoon: CLS, n.d.

"A Buddhist View of Man and Nature". In *Theology and Ministry,* edited by Yeow Choo Lak. Singapore: ATESEA, 1978.

Say Pa, Anna May. "U Pe Thwin: Christian Writer and Theologian." *Thamar Alin* 2.2 (1996).

Thomas, Winburn T. and Rajah B. Manikam. *The Church in Southeast Asia.* New York: Friendship Press, 1956.

2.5.11. Victor Sanlone (1930-1985)

Victor Sanlone studied at Rangoon University (BA 1955), Kayin Theological Seminary and Burma Divinity School (BRE 1974), later completing the M.Theol. with the SEAGST (1977). He taught at the Karen Baptist Theological Institute and at the BIT where he also became president. He was General Secretary BBC (1974-), convenor for Faith and Witness of the MCC and later President of the Council. A most respected ecumenical leader, Sanlone was regularly chosen to represent Burma at world ecumenical meetings (1978-1984), was later vice president of the Baptist World Alliance, and president of the CCA.

In his writings on mission in Burma, he stressed the close relationship between ecumenism and evangelism, and between both of these and the Burmese society and nation. Witness for him was always a "witnessing together and witnessing through involvement in the country's life", as pictured in Jeremiah's message to exiles (Jeremiah 29: 4-8). Along with a basis in biblical and Baptist traditions, his theology had been shaped by the thought of earlier Karen Christian leaders, in which strong evangelical faith was intimately linked with able political leadership; and in whom personal commitment to Jesus Christ was lived out in selfless service to the Burmese peoples. He is remembered for his leadership in theological education, in wide-ranging ecumenical activities and for his understanding and work for wholistic mission in unity for the Burmese people.

Selected References
Works by Victor Sanlone
"Saw San C. Po: Apologist for the Karens." BRE thesis, BIT, 1964.
"Response to Yeow Choo Lak". In *Theology and Ministry*, edited by Yeow Choo Lak. Singapore: ATESEA, 1978.
"Mission in Burma." *Journal of Theology for Burma* 1 (1985).

2.5.12. U Khin Maung Din (1931-1987)

Khin Maung Din was born in Thaton, Mon State, and is widely revered as one of Burma's most creative theologians. He graduated in Philosophy at Rangoon University in 1957, being by then assistant lecturer in Philosophy, and became successively lecturer in 1963, and professor in 1981. He was an admired teacher of many branches of philosophy, believing that the 'magic' of communication depends on "how much one has endured ... how much one has practised." Of modern philosophical movements therefore, only existentialism was for him "pro-humanic". Khin Maung Din studied theology and also Buddhism extensively, was strongly ecumenical and active in the SCM, and in laity and theological education. Along with study papers and articles in philosophy, theology and inter-faith understanding, he became widely known for his many plays, written largely for students, which addressed theological and social issues. These were privately printed in Burmese and include: *That's Our Country; The Saviour They Expected; The Kingdom of Love; Calvary; Go to the End of the World; From the Past and On;* and *Just do Believe, My Love.*

Khin Maung Din advocated in all his Christian writing and teaching the free creativity of the human person, the centrality of Jesus' life and teaching, and the coming of God's realm for all people. This required both dialogue and partnership with all and also the "human-centred qualitative maturity of churches." He was therefore both a devoted educator and courageous animator in Christian groups and in movements for "human survival ... social justice" and mutual dialogue. For all these tasks the Gospel was to be understood in a Burmese way, so that the Burmese understanding of humanity, nature and the ultimate reality is included in the overall content of the Gospel. Bringing together the "I am that I am" of Exodus and the insights of Yin-Yang dialectic, he affirmed the oriental, and biblical, understanding of God, to be "the ultimately silent One", both person and not person, both being and becoming. Such understanding he believed to be more comprehensive and more faithful to the Gospel.

The Christ event he interpreted kairologically, uniting the historical relativity of Jesus with the universal availability of Christ. Yet he declared that we require more Christologies than one - for Jesus is man, yet not just so. In him God has spoken "a human language for concrete humanity", while also being beyond us and all relative terms. But this also brings the theological task of discovering "in what manner the living Christ has already come to our people even before the arrival of Christianity". The priorities of Christian faith he believed, depend first on shared humanity, on existential decisions rather than metaphysical beliefs, and on prophetic witness in society. In his later writings he presented the biblical and theological foundations for much fuller Buddhist-Christian mutual acceptance, through a "dialogical evangelism" which makes possible the formation of Buddhist-Christian Communities. For the final test for both Buddhists and for Christians is not their knowledge of God, but "their concrete love for human persons."

Selected References
Works by Khin Maung Din
> "The Creed Today", and "New Thought upon Evangelism." Study Papers. Insein: BIT, ca.1974-1976.??
> "Some Problems and Possibilities for Burmese Christian Theology Today". *IRM* April (1976). Also in *What Asian Christians are Thinking: A Theological Source Book,* ed. by Douglas J. Elwood. Quezon City: New Day Publishers, 1976.
> "Models for Today". In *Christianity and Religions of the East,* ed. by R.W. Rousseau. Scranton: Ridge Row Press, 1982.

"Called to be Servant" *Judson Chapel Jubilee Magazine* Rangoon, Judson Church (1983).

"Can Buddhists be Buddhist-Christian." BBC Seminar on Evangelism, November, 1986. *Thamar Alin* 3 (1997).

"Towards Unity." In *Burma SCM Diamond Jubilee 1912-1987*, ed. by Kyaw Nyunt. Rangoon: Burma Council of Churches, 1987.

"Asleep in Jesus, Professor Khin Maung Din." *Myanma Taman Magazine,* October-November (1987).

"The Reggie I know." *Myanma Taman Magazine,* January (1988).

Kam Sian Thang. "Arc of Archives: U Khin Maung Din, Man of the Century". M.Div. thesis MIT, 1995.

See also *The Burman Messenger* (Oct/Nov 1987, Jan 1988).

2.5.13. U Tun Aung Chain (1933-)

U Tun Aung Chain is a lay theologian of the Burmese Baptist Church and taught as professor of history at the University of Arts and Sciences, Rangoon, for many years until 1996. His many writings cover the fields of church history, linguistics, peace and politics in Burma, Burmese intellectual life, and women's concerns in Burma. He has contributed to many seminars on these subjects and is a regular contributor to theological journals. His central concerns include the recognition of the cultural resources of Burma, understanding of creative aspects of Burma's mission history, restoration of influence for the people's faith and values, and the foundations of democracy and international peace. In considering the writings of Barnabite missionaries he concludes that despite their frequent lack of appreciation for Burmese culture they reveal a sympathy and understanding for the people of Burma and in particular for the beginning of their sufferings as a colonised people. In detailed studies of the work of Judson in translation he concludes that Judson, by living fully "in two worlds" did form an effective bridge between the culture of the Bible and that of Burma. Recognising that in contemporary Asian history many states are authoritarian and highly elitist, Tun Aung Chain reaffirms the place of religious faith and values in the lives of their peoples, and "in the political market place", and for this they are to be further empowered.

Selected References
Works by Tun Aung Chain
"Judson, Hough and the Early Mission Press." *Rays of BIT* (1985-86).
"The Intellectual in Burmese Society." In *Burma SCM Diamond Jubilee 1912-1987*, ed. by Kyaw Nyunt. Rangoon: Burma Christian Council, 1987.
"Jonathan Price and the Inwa Baptist Mission." *Annual Magazine MIT* (1990-91).
"Women of Myanmar." Rangoon: Mimeo'd, n.d.
"Between two Cultures: Judson's Translation of the Bible." Rangoon: Mimeo'd, 1992.
"Religion, Politics and State." *Thamar Alin* 1.1 (1995).
"Barnabite Missionary Accounts of Myanmar: Mantegazza and Sangermano." Rangoon: ATEM Historical Commission. Mimeo'd, 1996.
"Peace a Perspective from the International System." MCC Seminar of Peace. Rangoon: Mimeo'd, 1998.

2.5.14. Arthur Ko Lay (1935-)

Arthur Ko Lay studied political science at Mandalay University and law at Rangoon University, later studying theology at the BDS (BRE) and with the SEAGST (M.Theol.). Amongst many duties as Baptist minister, he has been pastor to students, and writer of study materials for ecumenical programmes. He has chaired the units on Faith and Witness and on Mission for the MCC, with particular concerns for urban-rural mission and has undertaken leadership in the ten-year programme for Spiritual Renewal of the Myanmar Baptist Convention (1990-2000) aiming at the recovery of prayer-life, wholistic mission, and a theology of life.

The resurgence of Buddhism in Burma, he believes, calls for a much fuller Christian response, and for this there must be both closer association with para-church and Pentecostal groups and also with Buddhist colleagues. The dialogue with Burmese culture, although essentially with Buddhism, is in his thought not just religious but includes the social and political dimensions of national reconstruction for which partnership with Buddhists is essential. Within the church fuller dialogue is also necessary, he believes, in order to bridge the gaps between widely diverse groups so that theology becomes both biblical and integrated, socially concerned and evangelical. Ko Lay has written extensively since the 1970s on these concerns, in particular on biblical studies and contextual theology - as in the paper "Holistic Mission in its Contextual Situation" - especially in order to provide manuals and resources for theological and lay education.

Selected References
Works by Arthur Ko Lay
"Salvation in Isaiah." Thesis, MIT, 1972.
Oth-Thone-Satee-Worship (Holistic stewardship). Rangoon: BBC, c.1991.
Four Bible Studies for Mission. Rangoon: Myanmar Christian Council, 1993.
Sinye Thar Dot Atwe Thadin Gaung (Good news to the poor). Rangoon: BBC, c.1994.
Effective Leadership and Church Renewal. Rangoon: BBC, c.1994.
Christian Mission from a Holistic Perspective. (In Burmese). Yangon: CLS. Forthcoming.
"Biblical reflection on Mission". Study Paper. MIT, ca. 1983.
"The Goal of Human Development." *Thamar Alin*. Forthcoming.
—, ed. *AD 2000 Baptist Publications.* (21 Booklets on Holistic Mission and Renewal.) Rangoon: BBC, 1990-1993.

2.5.15. Eh Wah (1938-)

Eh Wah studied at the University of Rangoon (BA 1957), and Colgate Rochester Divinity School (M.Div.1962) and received the DD from Judson College, Illinois, 1998. A lecturer at Burma Divinity School from 1962, she was later Vice-Principal (1978-1988) and Principal (1988-1998). She also chaired the Theological Education Department of MBC and also the Higher Education Committee of the ATEM.

Amongst her chief theological concerns have been the establishment of New Testament scholarship in Burma, the promotion of theological education and lay training - especially for women - and the wider fostering of spiritual and theological formation. Apart from her many lectures in both formal and non-formal settings, her few writings reflect on the place and potential of women in theological education and ministry, and also on the larger issues of independent life and witness for churches in Burma in the decades since all missionaries left. Missionary spirit, she writes, has increased since the mid-1980s despite severe economic and political constraints upon the church, but now there are increased opportunities to be taken for theological and lay education, in particular, if the people of God are to be formed for their present service and mission.

Selected References
Works by Eh Wah
"The Word of God." *SEAJT* 7.4 (1966).
"Women in Theological Education: Country Report from Myanmar." Workshop on Women in Theological Education. Hong Kong: ATESEA, 1993.
"A Personal Perspective: Thirty Years after the Western Missionary Era in Myanmar". *American Baptist Quarterly* 15.2 (1996).
"Tribute to my Father." *Thamar Alin*. Forthcoming.
—, and Anna May Say Pa. *The Personality of Jesus in the Eyes of Women*. Yangon: Alin Ein (forthcoming).

2.5.16. Ba Thann Win (Kanbawza Win) (ca. 1940-)
Ba Thann Win holds degrees in political science and international relations from Rangoon University (M.A., 1970), Seoul University (Ph.D., 1979) and Washington International University (Ph.D., 1999). He has taught history and international studies in Burma (1969-1974), Thailand and Canada (1997-), been Secretary of Foreign Affairs to the Prime Minister of the then Socialist Republic of Burma (1977-1981) and co-ordinated the Christian Participation in Development (CPDSK) of the Shan, Kayah and Karen Sate Communities, Burma (1980-1986). He has also edited the *Newsletter of the Asian Conference on Religion and Peace*, the *New Era Journal*, and the *Burma Research Journals*. Strongly committed to both the causes of democratic change and of ethnic welfare, he and his wife Rosie have also provided leadership in both denominational and ecumenical ministries in a number of countries.

In his theological writings Ba Thann Win has reflected upon the history of Christianity in Burma, Christian identity and response to current events in Burma and southeast Asia, and the relation of liberation theology to human development and international relations. He has also written a theology of the *Thingyan* (Burmese Water Festival), taking this as a basis for a contextual theology. In all his writings Ba Thann Win is concerned to hold together the evangelical goals of personal renewal with the goals of re-structured and just societies, declaring that Jesus himself demanded both of these. Development Studies therefore necessarily include the study of liberative theologies in which the processes of colonialisation and oppression are analysed and the resources of the Gospel for personal and social transformation are provided. In studying the *Thingyan*, he finds there the symbolisms and practices of life-giving and reconciliation which can provide resources for Christian action to resolve the differences in Burmese society: between Christian and Buddhist, between wealthy and destitute, and between governed and government.

Selected References
Works by Ba Thann Win
> *Daw Aung San Su Kyi: the Nobel Laureate.* Bangkok: CPDSK Publications, 1992.
> *Comparative Study of Two Military Juntas.* Bangkok: CPDSK Publications, 1994.
> *Burmese Water Theology.* Winnipeg: Privately Circulated, 1999.
> *An Introduction to Development Studies.* Winnipeg: CPDSK Publications, 1999.
> "A Christian in Southeast Asia Peninsula. (A Burmese Perspective)." *Asian Journal of Theology* 1 (1987).
> "Colonialism, Nationalism and Christianity in Burma." *Asian Journal of Theology* 2.2 (1988).
> "Refugees, Human Rights and the Christian Response in Southeast Asia." *Asian Journal of Theology* 6.1 (1992).

2.5.17. Edmund Za Bik (1940 -)

Edmund Za Bik is professor of systematic theology, Christian ethics, philosophy and contemporary theology, at the MIT, Rangoon. Strongly grounded in Protestant Reformed theology, his writings include studies in biblical exposition, in historical theology and in contextualisation, as well as re-interpretations of key Christian doctrines.

In writing of contextualisation Za Bik draws on the thought of Shoki Coe, Kosuke Koyama and Gustavo Gutierrez, amongst others, and describes "contextuality as the method and principle which 'seeks to press beyond' ... [with the] advantage of missiological discernment of the signs of our time" in which God is calling us to participate. As revelation and event the Word of God is to be "done" in Myanmar today by articulating the ways in which "the saving Word speaks, critiques, judges and saves the people of God in Myanmar today." Such a theology includes critical reflection on such questions in Myanmar as the extremes of wealth and poverty, economic self-sufficiency, moral decadence, religious discrimination, the growth of para-churches, and other socio-cultural realities of the context. He terms this a "Theology of Realism" which holds together academic reflection and concrete involvement. In a full study of Christian interpretations of "universal salvation" Za Bik presents "the validating factor for salvation" as being the way of life of Jesus Christ, rather than religious structures, rituals, dogmas or labels. Hence inter-faith dialogue is "a must for our healing." It is to be integral to mission and service and theo-centric, and to be "a forum to promote love, understanding ... and the creation of joint programs to combat common evils ..." which Za Bik also proposes. Here will be found a liberating mission which in partnership with those of other faiths helps to make and keep life human, establishes equality between women and men, and serves the needs of the afflicted and the victims of injustice.

Selected References
Works of Edmjund Za Bik
"Faith of the Church for a New Humanity". *Rays of the BIT* (1984-85).
"The Word of God in Myanmar Today". *Asia Journal of Theology* 9.2 (1995).
"The Future of Reformed Theology". *Thamar Alin* (1995).

"The Three Philosophers of Life (Luke 10:25-37)". *MIT Annual Magazine* (1996).
"The Challenge to Reformed Theology - A Perspective from Myanmar." In *Toward the Future of Reformed Theology - Tasks, Topics, Tradition*, ed. by David Willis and Michael Welker. Grand Rapids: Eerdmans, 1999.
"Universal Salvation". *Rays. MIT Journal of Theology* 1.1 (2000).
"Liberation Now. Luke 4.18-19". *Rays. MIT Journal of Theology* 2 (2000).

2.5.18. Mary Dun (1941-)

Mary Dun studied at the University of Arts and Sciences, Rangoon, at the MIT and with the SEAGST (M.Theol. 1984; D.Th. 1996). She has been lecturer at MICT for the years 1968-1997 and is now Principal there. In early writings she was concerned to build a theology of Christian mission which is relevant to Asian contexts; one that addresses the whole person in the present world to which God's reign comes. Salvation is then a liberation of human beings in community made possible through informed participation in social service and nation-building. For this, theological and political education is required, along with dialogue with those of other living faiths.

Studying biblical and theological issues raised by religious pluralism, Dun is concerned to clarify processes of dialogue in which Christian identity is held together with a "reconstructed inclusive theology of pluralism." But this requires that theology be reconstructed for Myanmar if it is to be authentic for Burmese Christians. Here it must recognise God's saving power beyond the limits of the Christian church, embracing all women and men, as well as nature. For this it will draw on biblical understandings of God's dealings with the nations other than Israel and with the "Gentiles". Also important are theocentric perspectives of creaturely relatedness, and Christ-centric perspectives of the cosmic Christ, present through the Holy Spirit in all truly salvific traditions and actions. The purpose here is to discern God's larger work and presence, Dun believes, in order to "live in appreciation of the Buddhist faith" and in co-operation with Buddhist neighbours "for peace and justice in Burma."

Selected References
Works by Mary Dun
>"Christian Mission in Asian Contexts". M.Theol. Thesis, SEAGST, 1984.
>"Interfaith Dialogue. Christian Initiative for Dialogue with Buddhists in Myanmar". D.Th Thesis, SEAGST, 1996.
>"The Concept of God in Myanmar Context." Mimeo'd (ca. 1996).
>"The Image of Women in Myanmar Culture". *In God's Image* 19.2 (2000).
>"Women Empowerment". *Thamar Alin.* Forthcoming.

2.5.19. Anna May Say Pa (1942-)

Anna May Say Pa has worked as Programme Secretary, Student Christian Centre, Rangoon (1962-1964); lecturer in biblical studies and Dean of Studies (1964-1979), and later as Vice-Principal and Principal (1989-) of MIT, Rangoon. She holds degrees in biblical studies from SEAGST (M.Theol.1977), and from Princeton Theological Seminary (M.Theol.1980, Ph.D., 1989). She has also chaired the Women's Department and the Leadership Development and Scholarship Committee, MBC, been active in regional and world ecumenical committees for theological education and for lay participation, as well as editing the *Myanmar Journal of Theology* and *Rays MIT Journal of Theology*.

Anna May Say Pa has worked to expound the Hebrew prophetic literature in relation to Yahweh's concern for the nations, and also for justice and restoration of the oppressed. Along with academic studies she has therefore read the Bible along with 'ordinary' people who suffer oppression: women, the poor, uneducated youth and members of ethnic minorities. And this is in a context where young people have never known peace or democracy, free access to education or to choice of career. Say Pa has given particular attention to Asian feminist theology, as she works to develop a feminist theology for Myanmar. This, she believes, must address Burmese patriarchal culture which is largely shaped by Buddhism, as well as the issues of violence, peace and reconciliation, and of human value, in Burmese society. Sources for such theology include the biblical images of God as female and the role of the Holy Spirit, the female principle of God, as witnessed to in other faiths in Burma, along with the work of other woman theologians in Asia and elsewhere. A new ecumenical hermeneutic is also required, in which diverse interpretations are included in dialogical perspective so that women, the destitute, Karen, Kachin, Shan and Chin can contribute, and receive wholeness and healing.

Selected References
Works by Anna May Say Pa

"The Name of the Covenant God - Significance for the Church Today." Rangoon: Mimeo'd, 1975.

God of the Exodus. An Old Testament Theology Reader for Myanmar. Yangon: Privately Printed, 1993.

"In God's Image (Gen. 1:26-28)." *MIT Annual Magazine* (1991/1992).

"The Confessing Community." *Mya Pale*, July (1993).

"Women in Jeopardy: Sara and Sita in the Harem." *YMCA Golden Jubilee Magazine*, 1994.

"Women Liberators of the Exodus Story: A Feminist Reading." *Thamar Alin* 1 (1995).

"Yahweh and the Chaos Dragon." *Journal of Theology for Myanmar* (1995).

"Towards Wholeness Amidst Brokenness: Ecumenical Hermeneutics and the Journey Towards Unity in Myanmar." *Rays MIT Journal of Theology* 1.1 (2000).

"The Feminine Image of God." *In God's Image* 19.2 (2000). Also Guest Editor.

"Militarism and Violence Against Women. A Study of Judges 19-21. *Rays MIT Journal of Theology* 2 (2000).

— with Eh Wah. *The Personality of Jesus in the Eyes of Women.* Yangon: Alin Ein. Forthcoming.

2.5.20. Lahpai Zau Lat (1943 -)

In studying at Insein, then with the SEAGST and later at the Graduate Theological Union, Berkeley, Zau Lat gained the degrees Th.M., M.Theol. and D.Min. He now teaches courses at the MIT, with particular reference to Old Testament studies in Myanmar, which integrate lectures with field experience and practical service, along with continuing theological reflection. In early study papers he wrote on Bonhoeffer's thought, on Asian theology, the development of lay ministry, and a theology of people movements in Myanmar, along with studies of the Hebrew Bible.

Amongst his main concerns have been the recovery of the liberative elements of the Hebrew Bible, and of the gospels, within the sociological context both of the Hebrew prophets and of today's Myanmar. Here he concludes that biblical writings portray a wholistic and participatory liberation for all people in which human identity and selfhood is of supreme value. The church in her mission is therefore "to be identified with the ordinary people ... [to] share their burden as they struggle for survival." Zau Lat also recognises that the liberative presence of God can already be found in many people's movements that work for human welfare, for justice and for human dignity. "Human dignity, from the biblical perspective," he writes, "is as important as one's life. It is God-given dignity (glory and honour) and should be respected and protected in our full capacity. It is not only a passive abstention from doing injustices, but active action to free and help other creatures as a representative of God on earth." He now also contributes these insights in the project to "Read the Bible through a Burmese Lens" in which alternative interpretations of scripture are yielding new directions for faith understanding and for the churches in Myanmar.

Selected References
Works by Lahpai Zau Lat

"Exegesis of the Priestly Creation Story." M.Theol. Thesis, SEAGST, ?1984.

"Looking at People's Movements in Burma - From a Christian Perspective." In *Doing Theology and People's Movements in Asia,* ed. by Yeow Choo Lak and John C. England. ATESEA Occasional Papers 3. Singapore: ATESEA, 1986.

"Reading the Hebrew Bible from Asian Liberation Perspective, Burma in Particular." D.Min. Thesis, Graduate Theological Union, Berkeley.

"Hope of reconciliation." Paper presented to the Anglican Peace and Justice Network, Edinburgh, October 1994. Mimeo'd.

"Human Dignity (Biblical Perspective)." Rangoon: BBC Theological Education Forum. Mimeo'd, 2000.

"To Greater Heights." *Rays. MIT Journal of Theology* 1.1 (2000).

2.5.21. Simon Pau Khan En (1944-)

Following studies at Burma Divinity School (B.Th. 1968; BRE 1973) Pau Khan En gained the degrees of B.D. from Serampore College (1980), STM from Union Theological Seminary, NY (1971) and Ph.D. from the University of Birmingham (1995). During these years he was successively lecturer and principal at the Zomi Theological Seminary, Falam; General Secretary of ZBC (1983-1986); professor of theology, teaching contextual theology, and church and society at MIT; and Associate General Secretary (later General Secretary) of MBC (1986-1990). He is now General Secretary of the MCC. From 1977-1986 he also fulfilled pastoral ministries.

In his many articles on theology in the Burmese context he has been particularly concerned with the development of Christology. In response to the question Who is Jesus Christ in Myanmar? he writes that he will be a Christ of the religions, in dialogue; and Christ as the truth in all. He will be Christ the liberator (of people from *samsara*), a kenotic and serving Christ; a Christ who is both high priest and victim (within a background of Nat worship). Pau Khan En sees the religious culture of the people to be the locus for theology and although western theology can be supportive, a constructive theology of Jesus Christ for Myanmar must be first for Myanmar people. Rather than an abstract contextualization, it is to focus on the transformation of the actual life of the people. It will draw on the largely oral theology of Christians in Burma, respond to the conditions of society and culture there and be actively non-violent for peace. This may lead to a Burmese Christianity which has the features of "Christian Buddhism" for the essential work of Christ in Myanmar is "not to be too Christian". His writings include volumes and articles on Christian ethics, introduction to the New Testament, New Testament Christology, basic concepts of pastoral counselling as well as particular biblical studies.

Selected References
Works by Simon Pau Khan En
> "New Testament Christology." BTh Thesis, Burma Divinity School 1968.

"Nat Worship: A Paradigm for Doing Contextual Theology." Ph.D. Thesis, University of Birmingham, 1995. Summary version in *Asia Journal of Theology* 8.1 (1994).
"Sycretism: A Friend or a Foe." *Annual Magazine MIT* (1996).
"The Quest for a Relevant Hermeneutics: A Liberative Reading of the Book of Esther for Today." *Thamar Alin*, II.2 (1996).
"Who is Jesus Christ? A Theological Exercise for Doing Contextual Theology in Myanmar." *Annual Magazine MIT* (1998).
"A Dialogical Soteriology on Liberation: Christian Soteriology and the Theravad Concept of Nibban." *Rays MIT Journal of Theology*, 1.1 (2000).

2.5.22. Mar Gay Gyi (1945-)

Mar Gay Gyi attended Mandalay University gaining the degree of Bachelor of Agriculture. Later he attended MICT and graduated with the BD. He was active in development work as Assistant Director of Christian Service Board, MCC, and as Director of Evangelism and Mission in the MCC. He was the General Secretary of the MBC from 1992-1999 and at present is the General Secretary of the Myanmar Bible Society. He plays a key role in the churches' relationship with the state and also in peace negotiations with the Karen National Organisation.

Mar Gay Gyi was one of those initiating the Myanmar Baptist Church's mission advance under the theme of "Christ for Myanmar." He emphasises wholistic mission, especially in rural development, for the uplift of the people in rural areas. His zeal for evangelism is evident in his sermons and writings in magazines such as *Myitta Tamman* and *Myanma Tamman*. He has become a key leader in the understanding and operation of "AD2000 Mission" in Myanmar, working closely with such colleagues as Victor Sanlone and Arthur Ko Lay.

Selected References
Works by Mar Gay Gyi
"Christian Service." B.D. thesis, MICT, 1986.
Doing the Best in Your Life. Yangon: MBC, 1999.
Ko Lay, Arthur, ed. *AD 2000 Baptist Publications*. (21 Booklets on Holistic Mission and Renewal.) Rangoon: BBC, 1990-1993.

2.5.23. Alan Saw U (1949-)

Saw U studied at the Rangoon Institute of Technology and received the B.E. degree in the year 1972. He joined the Christian ministry as support staff (1972-75); as Executive Secretary of Urban Rural Mission Desk (1976-81); and later as Executive Secretary of the Education and Communication Programme Unit (1981-88) of the MCC. After taking a sabbatical leave to do research at Chulalongkorn University, Bangkok (1989-92), he returned to serve as Personal Secretary to the Anglican Archbishop of Myanmar (1992-1994). At present he is serving as Executive Secretary of the Myanmar CLS (1995-).

Saw U's early theological writings explored faith and discipleship issues within socialist Burma, where Christians, he declared, were called to new forms of "justing love". He was also concerned to provide theological undergirding for programmes of Urban Rural Mission in Burma, as well as for ecumenical and inter-faith dialogue. Since his service as lecturer in ecumenics, and church and society at the MIT (1979-84), his chief concern has been: "mobilising and enabling the local congregation members, especially those who are involved in secular vocations, to become theological practitioners through in-depth and contextual reading of the Bible." He has held seminars, taught and written - in articles such as "A Leaven in a Loaf", and "The Social Side of Being Spiritual" - to these ends, both locally and abroad. He has written on the work of Pe Maung Tin (see above 2.5.2) and republished selected writings by him and U Hla Bu (see above 2.5.3). Most recently his theological writing has focused upon Karen interpretation of the Bible and upon the works of reconciliation and peace-making, through the Anglican Peace and Justice Network.

Selected References
Works by Alan Saw U

"Christian Mission Within the Socialist System." In *Towards a Theology of People*, ed. by Oh Jae Shik. Tokyo: CCA Urban Rural Mission, 1977.

"Pe Maung Tin: A Christian Life and Teaching of Buddhism." In *Life and Work of Professor Pe Maung Tin. Papers from the SOAS Symposium*, Nov. 1999. London: 2000.

"Salting Within the System." Situation Report, CCA-URM 1979 Committee Meeting, February 1979, Yangon, Myanmar. In *Minutes, National Reports, Biblical Reflections*. Hong Kong: CCA-URM, 1979.

"The Travails of Unity Dialogue in Burma." *CCA News* Dec. (1984). Also in *Impact Magazine* 20.2-3 (1985).

"Mobilizing the Karen People for the Future Development of Myanmar." A Position Paper, Mimeo'd. June 2000.

"Reading the Bible Through the Eyes of the Karen: A Personal Reflection." International Gathering of the Karen for Bible Study, Chiang Mai. Forthcoming.

—, and Hsa Mu Htaw. "The Voice of God in the Cries of the People (Discerning God's Purpose in People's Movement for Democracy as a Starting-point for Doing Theology in Burma)." Hong Kong: Mimeo'd, 1989.

2.5.24. David Laisum (1954-)

David Laisum studied at the MIT, Insein, and at the University of Chicago, and is now lecturer in systematic theology and world religions at MIT. His early studies focussed on those aspects of Chin culture and religion in which religious truth and aspects of the nature of God can be discerned. Later he addressed the issues of Christian identity and witness in the larger context of Burma as a whole with particular concern to relate a contextual theology to the concrete hopes and choices of Christians in Myanmar. A key question for him is "Does one wait for the end, or build and confirm now?" A comprehensive hope for Christians, he believes, will include both hope for the coming of the Lord as judge and hope for the preservation and betterment of life in the present. This he defines as "hope for the coming kingdom which is something ultimate in the present", offering "corrective transformations" of society, culture and ideologies. In considering the relationship of Christianity to state polity, Laisum makes a full study of political options in Myanmar history and context. He concludes that interpretation of the religious symbol for ruler and nation must allow the choice of "a political system which is creatively inclusive to embrace all the people". Once again Christian hope is centred upon the rule of justice and love, which begins now in the concrete context of life and relationships in Myanmar.

Selected References
Works by David Laisum
"God's Revelation in Chin Tradition." BD Thesis, MIT, Insein, 1988.
"Naming God in Burma Today." D.Min Thesis, University of Chicago, 1994.
"Maranatha or Pro morafinis. Hope and Hermeneutics (Myanmar Context)." *Annual Magazine MIT, 1995-1996.*
"Religious Symbols and Political Options (A Myanmar Context)." *Thamar Alin* II (1996).
"Jesus the Cosmocrator: The Quest for a Relevant Theology in Myanmar." *Thamar Alin* IV (1999).

2.5.25. Samuel Ngun Ling (1956-)

Following B.Th. and B.D. studies at the MIT, Samuel Ngun Ling gained a Th.M. at Princeton Theological Seminary (1991) and his Ph.D. in comparative culture from International Christian University, Tokyo. He has taught systematic theology, and also theology of religions, and Gospel and culture at MIT, since 1998. He now edits *Rays MIT Journal of Theology.*

Ngun Ling has studied the encounter of Christianity and Buddhism in Burma from a historical and theological perspective in order to clarify the obstacles to both political relationship and religious communication between them. He evaluates theologically earlier Christian responses to Buddhism and concludes that Christian understandings of mission are to be reformulated in a more inclusive way, through both study of other religions in Burma and inclusion of their truths as "part of our own theological enquiry". Inculturation is here seen as a function of dialogue, following some of the guidelines of Lynn de Silva (see Vol. I, chap. 8, 6.5.). In considering the development of theology in Myanmar, Ngun Ling proposes certain requirements: Myanmar is to be "the object of Christian theology"; there is to be a "critical integration of text and context"; and Myanmar theology must be both contextual and trans-contextual, indigenous and global-oriented. Regarding the communication and living of Christian truth in a Burman Buddhist context, Ngun Ling recognises the particular issues of patriotism, of dogma and western image, and advocates a "living and acting like Christ" rather than dogmatic evangelism. This may then lead to a presentation of Christianity in "Bama (Burman) Buddhist ways and terms".

Selected References
Works by Samuel Ngun Ling
"The Meeting of Christianity and Buddhism in Burma: Its Past, Present and Future Perspectives." Ph.D. dissertation, International Christian University Graduate School, Tokyo, 1998.
"The Gospel Encounters the Chin Culture." In *Thinking about Christianity and the Chins in Myanmar,* ed. by Cung Lian Hup. Yangon: Cung Lian Hup, 1999.
"Dialogue and Inculturation." *MIT Annual Magazine* (1999-2000).
"Towards a Theology of Myanmar: A Study of the Myanmar Situation in the Light of Her Encounter with the Christian Mission and Theology." *Rays. MIT Journal of Theology* 1.1 (2000).
"Doing Theology Under the Bo Tree: Communicating the Christian Gospel in the Bama Buddhist Context." *Rays. MIT Journal of Theology* 2 (2000).

2.5.26. Cung Lian Hup (ca. 1960-)

Cung Lian Hup studied at Mandalay University and the MIT. Believing that charismatic movements in the Chin Hills had led many to misunderstand the meaning of the work of the Holy Spirit, his early studies concentrate on pneumatology. He later analysed and interpreted the work of the missionaries in the Chin Hills, and has written on mission, culture and liberation theology in Myanmar.

Cung Lian Hup believes that the mission of God (*missio Dei*) is not just a project or a plan, but a lifelong commitment for the work of God in this world. It cannot be evaluated only through figures and statistics, but through the presence of love and charity among all believers. Many scholars, missionaries and missiologists have emphasised the size and numbers of Christian churches to awaken their missionary conscience, but "disunity and disintegration have been conspicuous among the ethnic groups, [and these] were inherited from overseas missionaries." The abrupt separation of the local people and the missionaries in 1966 made the Christians in Myanmar unable to see the strong and weak points of the missionaries, but led them to remember the missionaries in a largely idealised way. Therefore, "seeing a more balanced picture of the work of the missionaries may help us to evaluate our own present and future missions in Myanmar." Looking back critically to our history is one of the most important theological tasks that we should carry on for the present and future mission in Myanmar, he believes.

Selected References
Works by Cung Lian Hup

"The Work of the Holy Spirit." M.Div. thesis, MIT Insein, 1984.
"A Critical Look at the Work of the Missionaries in the Chin Hills." Ph.D. diss., Lutheran School of Theology at Chicago, 1993.
"Formal Education and Christianity in the Chin Hills." *Annual Magazine of Chin Student Fellowship.* 1999-2000.
"Christians and Liberation Theology in Myanmar." *Annual Magazine of Chin Student Fellowship.* Forthcoming.
—, ed. *Thinking about Christianity and the Chins in Myanmar.* Yangon: Chin Evangel Centenary, 1999.

2.6 Other Theologians, Scholars, Writers, 1: 1950-ca.1975

Any full study of theological reflection during these years is yet to be attempted but the outline below gives a selection of those whose work makes important contributions to this.

U On Kin (fl.1950) was active in ecumenical networks, reflected upon Burma's experience of Japanese invasion (1947) and also upon interfaith understanding. In his main book (1956) he provides a bird's eye view of the inner conflicts in post-war independent Burma and the shape of things to come, if and when we will them, along with the Christian role in doing this.

P'do Ba Tun Tin (1900-1969) was educated at Judson College (B.A. 1922), was educator and Inspector of Schools and became Assistant Director of Education. He was also secretary of the KBC and wrote some scores of books and booklets. Along with many on education and personal relationships, eight of these were in theology or church history, and included teaching for pastoral and preaching ministries.

Aye Myat Kyaw (1915-) was principal of the Pwo Karen Bible School, Rangoon, a staff member of the WCC, Geneva (1962-1967) and General Secretary of both the BBC and the Pwo Karen Conference (1969-1995). In his many booklets, lecture notes and commentaries he evinces deep concern for theological education, the communication of the Gospel and for ecumenical mission and co-operation.

Victor G. Shearburn was Anglican Bishop of Rangoon (ca. 1960), influenced both Burmese and expatriate scholars such as Trevor Ling, and contributed to the work and publications of the Burma Christian Council. A particular concern for him was the recovery of Christian traditions of spirituality in the light of partially similar Buddhist traditions.

William Winn taught theology in the 1960s at the Burma Divinity School, Insein (as did Mrs Win), and contributed articles and book reviews in historical and systematic theology to a number of journals. Chief among these were his writings that related traditional doctrines, and the works of western theologians to the tasks of contemporary theology in Burma.

William Lay (1934-1977) was Director of the Student Centre (SCM), University of Rangoon (1960-1970), and General Secretary of the Burmese YMCA (1970-1977). In his writings and work, Lay was deeply interested in the ecumenical mission of the Christian Church, and in the development of leadership for it. A close colleague of Arthur Ko Lay and Anna May Say Pa, he also wrote on wholistic forms of Christian life and on what could be the Christian learnings from Buddhism, including meditation practice, the nature of charity and intimacy with culture.

Other writers of relevant articles in this period include Hla Thwin, U Chit Pe and U Mynt Hla. Theological textbooks were written by Thra Asa Htoo Tha, Kler Taw and D. Admund, amongst others. Poets and writers of Christian novels and short stories included Thra Tu Saw, Saw Taw, Thaw Tu, Kyer Baw Nai and Ma Lay Lone.

Selected References

Ba Tun Tin, P'do. *The History of Christianity in Burma.* Rangoon: KBC, n.d.

—. *Foundation of Christian Faith.* Rangoon: KBC, n.d.

Day, Saw Christopher. "Biographical Sketches of Noted Karen Leaders." M.Div. Thesis, MIT, 2000.

Hla Thwin. "The Christian Strategy in the Changing Times - A Layman's Point of View." *Church and Society* (EACC) 2.3-4 (1965).

Khin, Robert. *Prophetic Understanding of God in Relation to Karen Animists.* B.Theol. Thesis, Burma Divinity School, 1960.

Lay, William. "Buddhism in Burma." Rangoon: Mimeo'd, n.d.

—. "Wholistic Freedom." Rangoon: Mimeo'd, 1971.

On Kin, U. *Cruising Down the Irrawaddy.* Rangoon: Thudhama Press, 1956.

—. "The Psychological Approach to Buddhism". In *Burma Christian Council Annual,* 1953.

Shearburn, Vicor G. "Spirituality: Buddhist and Christian." *SEAJT* 7.4 (1966).

Taw, Saw, comp. *Anthology of Poetry.* (In Karen.) 2 vols. Insein: Baho Press, n.d.

Tu Saw, Thra. *Dog's-Crooked-Tail-Turns-Straight.* Rangoon: KBC, ca. 1954.

Win, William. "F.D. Maurice and Contemporary theology". *SEAJT* 2.2 (1960).

—. "The Doctrine of Creation." *SEAJT* 7.4 (1966).

2.7 Other Theologians and Scholars 2: ca.1975-2000

These years would see a steady growth in the number of lay people and clergy, women and men, who were taking post-graduate courses in theology, both within and outside Burma, along with increased writings by Burmese of every ethnic origin in contextual Burmese theology. It will only be possible to briefly outline some of the many other writers of theological reflection not yet mentioned, in what follows. The theses and research papers of the MIT in particular form a rich resource for all areas of Burmese theological study. (See selection below).

U Di Aung Yi (b. 1930) for example, is a lay theologian and writer who has developed cell-houses and congregations, and lectured widely on Christian living, Bible study, prayer and spiritual welfare. In 1995 , along with colleagues such as Arthur Ko Lay (see 2.5.14.), he promoted wholistic mission as part of the "Coming of the AD2000 Great Revival" and worked to promote a more integrated understanding and practice of Christian mission.

Esther Byu (1939-) taught at BIT/MIT, following masters' and doctoral studies (SEAGST and Andover Theological School) and later co-ordinated CCA Women's Concerns (1988-1996), and the International Committee for the Fellowship of the Least Coin (ICFLC). Byu's theological concerns, fostered in local and international workshops and consultations, include inclusive leadership from biblical, theological and feminist perspectives; gender awareness and sensitivity training; and partnership between women and men in mission. This, she writes, "is a relationship grounded in mutual understanding ... in the sharing of space, equal rights and responsibility for the benefit of the whole community."

Chum Awi studied in Myanmar and with SEAGST, and has written on Haka Chin customary law (1976); on liberation theology; on Chin culture, ethics and biblical interpretation; and on ecumenical mission (1999). He has also recently outlined a "theology of reality" for Myanmar peoples in their historical context.

Do Sian Thang has provided theological leadership for Chin peoples also and has written on inculturated theology, spirituality and mission for their particular contexts. His doctoral thesis was on "Theology of the Water Festival" (SEAGST, Singapore, 1993) and he has continued to study such contextual issues, in relation both to early Israelite festivals (1995) and to the present social situation of ethnic groupings in Myanmar (1999). He has also written on the movement "from proclamation to penetration of the Gospel" amongst these peoples (1998-1999).

Amongst those who have also lectured and written as seminary teachers in different areas of Myanmar, are U Chit Maung (theology, ecumenics, pastoralia), Paul Chen (church history), Tint Lwin (biblical studies, contextualization), Ko Ko Naing (Buddhism, church history), Maung Maung Yin (dialogue, systematics), Mark

Maung Doe (pastoral theology, ecumenics), Yaha Laylayla (systematic and pastoral theology, ecumenics), and Simon Be Bin Htu (spirituality in Myanmar, lay ministry).

Other ecumenical authors have included Bishop U Aung Khin, Tun Meh, San Si Htay, Smith Ngulh Za Thawng and Peter Joseph of the MCC, as well as writers of articles and study papers including Than Tun, N-Gan Tang Gun, Seng Kyaw, L Hkan Naw, Lung No, Naw Hosanna, Maran Yaw and Augustus Spurgeon.

Other writers on contextual Christian theology for Myanmar include, Myint Maung, Doh Say, Ngai Gam, Joshua Yang, Salai Hla Aung, K. Hting Nan, Hsi Ya Da, Nang Ngaih Pau, Dingrin La Seng, Van Kung, Mike Zung Ceu, San Min Tun and L. Naw Ming.

Further writers on aspects of theology within particular Burmese cultures include - amongst many others - Sing Khaw Khai, Lian Sakhong, Khen Cham, Za Theh Lo, Nawl Uk and Pum Suan Pau (Chin culture and church); Naw Kyin Nang, N. Hkum Paw Lu, J.Z. Vung Za Thang, Nhkum Pau Tu, Nhkum Lying Nang, Seng Bu (Kachin society and tradition); Saw Lar Ba, James K. Ban, Hsar Min Htaw, Glar Taw, Saw Laban and Joseph Aung Khin (Karen culture and literature); along with Tint Lwin, Maung Maung Yin, Aye Aye Thein, Ko Ko Naing, Naw Eh Tar Gay, Van Lal Vena, and Augurlion.

Amongst writers who have reflected on human issues in Myanmar society or upon on social and national questions in relation to Gospel insights are Tun Myat Aye, Nyi Win Hman, U Mya Than Tint, San Si Tay, L. Hkawn Aung, Nilar Win, Zaw Min Tun, K.D. Naw San Dee, Eh Wah Hpaw, Tin Maung Shwe and Naw Hosanna.

Others who have written on a range of educational, devotional, ecumenical, pastoral and mission issues include U Ba Ohn, U Ba Aye and Bishop Mawia, Peter Aye, David Htin Ya, Wilfred Aung Hla Tun (also a playwright), Archbishop Andrew Mya Han (also writing for secular magazines), John Maung Pe, Lazuk dau Hkawng, Lal Rawng Bawla, Honor Nyo, Sang Awr, Kyaw Htun Lin and Hlaing Bwa.

Selected References

Aye Aye Thein, Li Esther. "Christ in Lisu Culture." B.D. Thesis, MIT, 1998.

Be Bin Htu, Simon. "Ministry of the Laity in the Church of the Province of Myanmar." Thesis, SEAGST, Trinity Theological College, Singapore, 1998.

Byu Esther. "Women in Asia" *Link* (CCA) 1992.

Chum, Awi. "Theology of Reality." *Journal of Theology for Myanmar* (1995).

—. "Thinking about the Unity of the Chin." In *Thinking about Christianity and the Chins in Myanmar*, ed. by Cung Lian Hup. Yangon: Cung Lian Hup, 1999.

Di Aung Yi. *Coming of the "AD2000 Great Revival."* Compilation with application to Myanmar. Rangoon: Privately Printed, ca.1991.

—. *Christian Maturity for Christian Service.* Collected Lectures and Articles. Rangoon: Privately Printed, n.d.

Do Sian Thang. "A Theology of Redemption in the Light of the Israelite New Year Festival with Special reference to the Myanmar *Thinkyan* (Water Festival)." Part I, *Thamar Alin* 1.1 (1995); Part II, *Thamar Alin* 4 (1999).

—. "Faithfulness as a Chin Spirituality." In *Thinking about Christianity and the Chins in Myanmar*, ed. by Cung Lian Hup. Yangon: Cung Lian Hup, 1999.

Hla Aung, Salai. "Relational Trinity and its Conceptual Implications for Asian Community." *Asian Journal of Theology* 14.1 (2000).

Joseph, Peter. "Report of the Workshop on Integration of Communication Studies in Theological Education, sponsored by the BCC and WACC." *Asia Journal of Theology* 3 (1989).

Lar Ba, Saw. "The Concept of Salvation in the Oral Tradition of the Karen and its Significance for Mission." M.Min. Thesis, Trinity Theological College, Singapore, 1992.

Lian Sakhong, H. *Religion and Politics among the Chinese People in Burma (1896-1949).* Sudia Missionalia Uppsaliensis 80. Uppsala: Uppsala University, 2000.

Mang Khan Suum. "Critical Reflection on Christology in Chin Community." M.Div. Thesis, MIT, 2000.

Maung Doe, Mark. "Keeping the Word of God Alive in Myanmar." Thesis, Berkeley, 1994.

Maung Maung Yin. "Dialogue and Diversity." *MIT Annual Magazine* (1993-1994).
N-Gan Tang Gun. "Historical Study of Theological Turning Points of the CCA and their Relevance ... to the Role of Urban Mission." Diss., SEAGST, Union Theological Seminary, Das Marinas (Manila), 2000.
San Si Htay. "Gospel and Social Change in Burma." Bossey Paper, Mimeo'd, 1990.
Sing Khaw Khai. "The Theological Concept of Zo in Chin Tradition and Culture." Thesis, SEAGST, Rangoon, 1984.
Za Theh Lo. "Jesus Zahuup. The Image of God in Ngawn Chin." *MIT Annual Magazine* (1994-1995).

2.8 Catholic Writers and Theologians
(See 1.2, 1.8, and 2.2 above).

2.8.1. Sources, Journals, Theses

Catholic writings in Burma in this period were initially included in publications of the Church for India, Burma and Ceylon and must be sought in periodicals such as *The Catholic Educational Review*, which had commenced in 1920, to be followed by other Catholic periodicals which included writings from Burma in later decades. Catholic writers such as U Maung Kaung had contributed to the *Journal of the Burma Research Society* (founded in 1911) for many years, and Vivian Ba's article series on Mission and Church history were re-issued in the 1960s (in the *Guardian*), and last reprinted in 1997. One of the first Catholic periodicals to be published in Burma, *Jinghpaw Kasa* (Kachin Messenger) was established by Fr Bernard Way in 1956, and in following years he also published catechisms, Bible histories and collections, and Handbooks. The *Annual Magazine* (Catholic Major Seminary, Rangoon) has been issued since 1957. Other journals would be founded in the decades after, including the Catholic magazines, *Metta ron khrann Kaksalac maggajan*, from 1992, and *Myo Kye Thu* (The Sower).

Biographies of long-serving expatriate staff have also been published since 1970, including those for Pasquale Ziello, Mario Vergara, Clement Vismara, Paolo Manna and Pietro Manghisi. Since 1976 there have of necessity been few further writings by expatriate scholars. Most publishing in this period has been concentrated upon training or catechetical materials and pastoral documents, along with study guides for particular diocesan or national programmes. There are in addition a growing number of dissertations and treatises written by graduate scholars, most often during studies overseas, yet often dealing with issues which are significant for Myanmar theology. A number of these interpret issues of contextualisation, especially in regard to the documents of Vatican II, the context of Buddhism, and the requirements of education and catechesis (See selected listing below).

Few writings have yet been published by women, apart from those contained in the documents of some women's congregations. Gender issues also receive little discussion or publication, although the contribution of women in church consultations or conferences - and even more noticeably in any decision-making bodies - is minimal and yet to be recognised. Their writings, apart from those appearing in *Myo Kye Thu* remain almost entirely unpublished.

The monthly *Myo Kye Thu* (The Sower) is now published regularly by the Catholic Literature Service, Yangon, and includes pastoral concerns, and stories of faith in life, as well as reflections on the faith. Saw Michael (Thar Do Thon Kyaing) is editor and has amongst many other articles on pastoral issues, written on "Literature in the Catholic Church in Myanmar". A series of articles on key festivals in Myanmar's life has been written by William Aung Soe Myint. Other regular writers include Sr Mary Trinity rndm, Philip Lian, Sr Patricia Sue sja, Sr. Patricia Mary Ma Rita and Eugene Ge Gui Shing. Myanmar Bishops such as Sotero Phamo have recently encouraged clergy and faithful to write on issues of spirituality and mission for *Myo Kye Thu*.

Selected References

    Ba, Vivian. *Early Catholic Missionaries in Burma.* Rangoon: Reprint, from *The Guardian* monthly, Rangoon, 1957-1964.

    Eikhein, Henry. "Quel Monachisme Chrétien pour l'Eglise de Birmanie en Pays Buddhiste?" Mémoire L.C.Th., Université de l'Ouest d'Angers, 1991.

    Htun Latt, Noel. "The Call to Catechise the People of the Church in Burma in the Light of Post-Vatican II." Thesis Lic.S.Theol, University Santo Tomas, Manila, 1994.

Htun Maung, Germano. "Missionary Contextualization: in Respect to Theravada Buddhism in Myanmar". Diss., Univ. Urbaniana. Roma, 1995.
Jangma Pawlu. "Catholic Mission to Kachins." B.Th. Thesis, BDS, 1972.
Khu, Anthony Kudovico. "The Catholic Church in Myanmar and in Taunggyi Diocese." Taunggyi, Diocesan Office, 1995.
"Petite minorité animée d'esprit missionnaire: Une église en croissance regulière (1948-1989)". *Agence Internationale Fides Informations* 3867, 1995.
See also:
Journal of the Burma Research Society. Rangoon: The Society, 1911-1981.
Metta ron khrann Kaksalac maggajan (Catholic Magazine). Rangoon: Rvhe Rup Lvha Cape, 1992.
Myo Kye Thu (The Sower). Yangon: Catholic Literature Centre.

2.8.2. Bishops and scholars

The first Kachin to be consecrated bishop, Paul Z. Grawng, was also the first national to write a study of the church's mission in Myanmar (1961). U Ba Yin, Stephen (1903-1987) was a Catholic catechist, religious instructor and music master, and also editor of the Catholic monthly *Sower* from 1949. He taught at the Major Seminary, Rangoon, and in his published tracts and books, was chiefly concerned to teach the faith and communicate the Gospel to contemporary Burma through effective journalism. A number of other Catholic scholars and writers have contributed to Myanmar theology in recent decades. These have included, in biblical studies and translation: Fr John Aye Kyaw (Mandalay), and Fr Soosai (Mawlamyine) who has also written an introduction to the Bible for Myanmar and issued a collection of sermons. On the Church's social teaching Fr Joseph Maung Win (Rangoon) has taught and conducted seminars (see below 2.8.3.) and the Searsolin Alumni Association has issued a guide for Christian development workers. Booklets and articles on catechetics and also theological reflection have come from Fr John Hsane Hgi (Sapran Seminary, Bangkok), Fr Justine Min Thide (Pyin Oo Lwin Seminary) and Fr Mark Tin Win (Mandalay). Mgr Charles Maung Bo has initiated a number of innovative training programmes in ministry and theology.

Bishop Sotero Phamo (Thein Myint) is president for the Catholic Literature Society (see 2.8.1.) and believes that the study of Burmese cultures is of central importance for Myanmar theology. He recognises the pioneering work of many Catholic missionaries in such studies and encourages its continuance. Christianity is to become part of Myanmar culture, he believes, integrated with other faiths and showing "the people of Burma that they can be Buddhist and also 'serve Christ'." In doing theology in Myanmar, the culture of the people is to be preserved wherever possible. Along with the preparation of manuals and liturgies in Kayah style, Bishop Sotero Phamo has contributed his concerns in documents of the FABC, in comments upon the *Lineamenta* document for the Asian Synod (1998), and in columns for national (secular) newspapers. Along with many pastoral writings, he has written articles to foster the study of other faiths, written reflections on episcopal ministry and a manual for the Jubilee 2000.

Stephen Ano, of the Diocese of Kyine Tong, holds a doctorate in Canon Law and is currently Dean of studies at the Major Seminary, Yangon. His writings have included contextual and post-conciliar studies, concerning both the forms of missionary activity for Myanmar today and such issues as inter-faith relationships, as well as collegiality in its particular application to churches in Myanmar.

Maurice Nyunt Wai of Pathein, has researched and written on the five precepts (pañcasila) of Buddhism in comparison to the corresponding Christian precepts and virtues. In both traditions he believes that these precepts are seen as expressions of love, generosity, self-control, truthfulness and watchfulness. They are therefore also expressions of spiritual experience and a basis for inter-religious dialogue between Buddhists and Catholics that leads to common action of building a just society.

Amongst other theological works, Fr John Saw Yaw Han has published a volume on Christian evangelism in Myanmar. Bishop Joseph Thaung Shwee of Pyay has promoted the replacement of western liturgical customs by the incorporation of Burmese practices, and has written on the basis and aims for this. A number of scholars have written especially for the 2000 millennial studies and celebrations. These include Professor Marco who has written a guide to the pilgrimage of faith; Joseph Kung En Hmung who has written devotional and pastoral works, and Basilio Ai Theik writing on the Jubilee itself.

Selected References

Ai Theik, Basilio. *Hta Ma Ta Yan Pan Yeik Mya.* (For Jubilee 2000). Yangon: 2000.

Ano Stephen. "The Context of Missionary Activity in Contemporary Myanmar." Thesis Lic.S.Theol, University Santo Tomas, Manila, 1995.

—. "The Mutual Relationship Between Diocesan Bishops and Religious in the Light of Conciliar and Post-conciliar Teachings: Its Application to the Context of Myanmar." Doct. Diss., University Santo Tomas, Manila, 1996.

Grawng, Paul Z., Bishop. *Jinghpaw Mungdaw Kahtawlik Nawku Hpung a Labau.* (Kachin Catholic Church history). Toungoo: Catholic Press, 1961.

Htun Maung, Germano. "Missionary Contextualization: in Respect to Theravada Buddhism in Myanmar". Diss., Univ. Urbaniana. Roma, 1995.

Kung En Hmung, Joseph. *Searching for the Will of God.* (In Burmese.) Pathein: 2000.

Marco, Professor. *The Journey of Man to Find God.* (In Burmese.) Yangon: 2000.

Nyunt Wai, Maurice. *Pañcasila and Catholic Moral Teaching. Moral Principles as Expression of Spiritual Experience in Theravada Buddhism and Christianity.* Forthcoming.

Pyin Pye Ye Let Swe (Development Workers' Handbook). Yangon: Searsolin Alumni Association of Myanmar, 2000.

Soosai, Fr. *Understanding the Bible in Myanmar.* Mawlamyine: ca. 1995.

Sotero Phamo, Bishop. *Loikaw: Ten Years' Sojourn.* Loikaw: Pastoral Centre, 2000.

—. *Guidelines for the Celebration of the 2000 Jubilee year.* Loikaw: Pastoral Centre, 2000.

Tai, Michael Cheng Teh. *In Search of Justice: The Development of the Social Teachings in Asian Churches.* Chilliwank BC: Griffith Institute, 1985.

Yaw Han, Fr John. *Sit Hman Thaw Christian That Tha* (Christianity and evangelism in Myanmar). Yangon: Catholic Major Seminary, 2000.

2.8.3. Catholic Bishops' Conference

The Catholic Bishops' Conference Myanmar was established in 1954 and is now formed of 12 Bishops (see above 2.2). Its pastoral, educational and administrative functions are carried out by constituent commissions. These include: Commissions for Liturgy, Social Communication, Ecumenism, Major Seminaries, Peace and Justice, Youth, Laity, Promotion of Family Life, Migration and Tourism, Inter-Religious Dialogue, Religious Superiors, and for Biblical Studies. The conference has occasionally issued Pastoral Letters in recent years, and also formulated through the Episcopal Commission for Dialogue, guidelines for the nurture of spirituality and priesthood (*The Trinitarian Multibillionarian Spirituality and the Catholic Priesthood*, 1985). In 22 short chapters this gives selected biblical passages concerning every aspect of priesthood, followed by guides to reflection and application. Bishops have also issued reports from the series of strategic planning workshops held in many dioceses in the 1990s.

In a Lenten Pastoral Letter (1998), the Catholic Bishops' Conference of Myanmar (CBCM) called on the country's Catholics to a renewal of faith and life that emphasises "solicitude towards the poor" and justice for all. They also asked Myanmarese Catholics to "actively 'suffer with' those who are poor and experience inadequacy." The letter spoke both of those who lack adequate shelter, food, employment, primary education or health care; and those who "lack spiritual nourishment and undergo grave sufferings of the soul." "Let us then go to our brethren," the bishops exhorted, "listen to them, be reconciled with them and help them in any way we can." Referring to Pope John Paul II's message for World Peace Day 1998, and to the Universal Declaration of Human Rights, they declared: there is "a special obligation to defend the dignity of every human being ... because we believe in God the Creator and because Jesus invites us to hunger for justice ... Are we just with our neighbour and with the community in which we live? Do we justify our injustice by blaming our corrupt surroundings?" Amongst those who have worked in the light of such statements, Fr Joseph Maung Win of the CBCM staff has developed seminar programmes on the Social Encyclicals, on strategic planning and on social animation and relief in Myanmar, but full reports and reflection for these are still in preparation.

Selected References

> David, Edwin et al., comp. *Archdiocesan Youth Apostolate and University Students' Apostolate (1978-1991)*. Yangon: Private Circulation, ca.1992.
> Diocese of Laikaw. *Manual for the Catholic Faithful of Loikaw Diocese*. Loikaw: Pastoral Centre, 2000.
> Episcopal Commission for Dialogue. *The Trinitarian Multibillionarian Spirituality and the Catholic Priesthood*. Yangon: St Xavier Printing Press, 1985.
> Grawng, Paul Z., Bishop. *Jinghpaw Mungdaw Kahtawlik Nawku Hpung a Labau*. (Kachin Catholic Church History). Toungoo, Burma: Catholic Press, 1961.
> Lashio Diocese. *First Diocesan Synod of Lashio. August 10-15, 1992*. Lashio: Diocesan Office, 1992.
> Myanmar Catholic Bishops' Conference. *Lenten Pastoral Letter*. Yangon: Catholic Bishops' Conference Myanmar, 1998.
> *Directory of Myanmar*. Yangoon: Catholic Bishops' Conference of Myanmar, 2000.
> Sotero Phamo, Bishop. *Guidelines for the Celebration of the 2000 Jubilee year*. Loikaw: Pastoral Centre, 2000.

2.9 Supplementary Bibliography 2

Aung Hla. *The Karen History*. Bassein: Karen Magazine Press, n.d.

Aung San Suu Kyi. *Freedom from Fear and other writings*. 2nd. ed. with an introd. by Michael Aris. Harmondsworth: Penguin, 1995.

—. *Letters from Burma*. Introd. by Fergal Keane. Harmondsworth: Penguin, 1997.

Aye Kyaw. *The Voice of Young Burma*. Southeast Asia Program 12. Ithaca: Cornell University, 1993.

Bama thamaing hinlay. Studies in Burmese History by the Colleagues of Dr. Than Tun. Mandalay: History Department, Mandalay University, 1982.

Ba Shin. *The History of the Union of Burma.* (In Burmese.) Rangoon: Pyithualin Press, 1950.

Ba Te, Thra. An Outline Study of Comparative Religion; based on the writings of the Rev. William Paton. (In Burmese). Rangoon: Burma CLS, 1954.

Brandon, J.J., ed. *Burma/Myanmar Towards the Twenty-First Century: Dynamics of Continuity and Change.* Bangkok: Chulalongkorn University, 1997.

Buddhist-Christian Encounter Booklet Series. Myanmar CLS, 1998.

"Burma Catholic, Protestant leaders discuss Christian unity." *UCA News.* 351, 28.05.1986.

Burma: Voices of Women in the Struggle. Bangkok: Alternative Asean Network on Burma, 1998.

Camps, Arnulf ofm. *Asien; Burma; Laos.* Gütersloh and Mohn: Benziger, 1988.

Carey, Peter. *From Burma to Myanmar: Military Rule and the Struggle for Democracy.* London: Research Institute for the Study of Conflict and Terrorism, 1997.

Christian Institute of Buddhist Studies. *Consultation on Buddhist-Christian Encounter Burma, Thailand, Ceylon.* Colombo: Christian Institute of Buddhist Studies, 1961.

Dispossessed: Forced Relocation and Extra-Judicial Killings in Shan State. Chiang Mai: Shan Human Rights Foundation, 1998.

Daw Say. "Toward a New Missionary Impulse of the Karen Baptist Church of Myanmar." D. Min. thesis, Fuller Theological Seminary, 1993.

Falla, Jonathan. *True Love and Batholomew: Rebels on the Burmese Border.* New York: Cambridge University Press, 1991.

Forgotten Victims of a Hidden War: Internally Displaced Karen in Burma. Chiang Mai: Burma Ethnic Research Group and Friedrich Naumann Foundation, 1998.

Gern, Wolfgang. *Burma: Texte und Fragen.* Hamburg: Missionshilfe Verlag, 1979.

Gheddo, Piero. "P. Clement Vismara: 61 années en Birmanie". *Monde et Missione* 114 (1985), and in *Le Christ au Monde* 31 (1986).

—. "Ritorno in Birmania." *Mondo e Missione* 122 (1993).

Human Rights Yearbook: Burma 1998-99. Bangkok: National Coalition Government of the Union of Burma, 1999.

Khai, Chin Khua. "Dynamics of Renewal: a historical movement among the Zomi (Chin) in Myanmar." Microform. Ph.D.Thesis Fuller Theological Seminary, 1999.

Kyi, U. *Essentials of Burmese History*. (In Burmese.) Rangoon: Shwepyetan Press, 1960.

Labang La. *To God I Confess - A Scrap from My Diary*. Edited by Arthur Ko Lay. Myitkyina: 1984.

Lating, Sumlut. "Ministry of the Laity and Mission of the Kachin Churches in Myanmar." Diss. Fuller Theological Seminary, 1997. (In Burmese).

Lintner, Bertil. *Land of Jade*. Edinburgh: Kiscadale; Bangkok: White Lotus, 1990.

Matthews, Bruce, ed. *Religion, Culture and Political Economy in Burma*. Vancouver, BC: Institute of Asian Research, University of British Columbia, 1993.

Maung Maung. "The Church in Burma. 25 Years in Isolation." *Touchstone* 3 (1989).

Mi Mi, Kaung. *Burmese Family*. Bombay: Orient Longmans 1956.

—. *The World of Burmese Women*. London: Zed Press, 1985.

Mirante, Edith. "Ethnic Minorities of Burma Frontiers and Their Resistance Groups." In *Southeast Asian Tribal Groups and Ethnic Minorities: Prospects for the Eighties and Beyond*. Cultural Survival Report 22. Cambridge, MA: Cultural Survival, Inc., 1987.

Morse, Ronald. A. et al., eds. *Burma: A Study Guide*. Washington: John Hopkins University Press, 1988.

O'Shannassy, Teresa. *Burma's Excluded Majority: Women, Dictatorship and the Democracy Movement*. London: CIIR, 2000.

Pan Po, Emerson E. "The History of the Karen Bible Schools and Seminaries." B. Min. Thesis, Burman Theological Seminary, 1976.

Pedersen, M.B., Emily Rudland and R.J. May, eds. *Burma-Myanmar: Strong Regime, Weak State?* Bathurst: Crawford House, 2000.

Phonphimon Trichot. The Burmese Government and the Ethnic Minority Groups. (In Burmese). Krung Thep: Samnakng an Kongthun Sanapsanun Kanwichai, 1999.

Pulpit Messages. (In Karen.) Yangon: Minister Dept., KBC, 1999.

Sarkisyanz, E. *Buddhist Backgrounds of the Burmese Revolution.* Hague: M. Nijhoff, 1965.

Shwe, Matthias U., ed. *Story of a Pilgrim Church.* Taunggyi: Taunggyi Diocese, 1986.

Smith, B.L., ed. *Religion and Legitimation of Power in Thailand, Laos and Burma.* Chambersburg PA: Anima Books, 1978.

Smith, Martin, in collaboration with Annie Allsebrook. *Ethnic Groups in Burma: Development, Democracy and Human Rights.* London: Anti-Slavery International, 1994.

Steinberg, D.I. *Burma: Prospects for Political and Economic Reconstruction.* WPF Reports 15. Cambridge: World Peace Foundation, 1997.

—. *The Future of Burma: Crisis and Choice in Myanmar.* Asian Agenda Report 14. Lanham: Asia Society and University Press of America, 1990.

Strengthening Civil Society in Burma: Possibilities and Dilemmas for International NGOs, edited by Burma Centre Netherlands and Transnational Institute. Chiang Mai: Silkworm Books, 1999.

Tadaw, Hanson. "The Karens of Burma: A Study in Human Geography." M.A Thesis, University of London, 1958.

The 1947 Constitution and the Nationalities, Vol.1. Rangoon: Universities Historical Research Centre, 1999.

Thein Pe Myint. *Sweet and Sour: Burmese Short Stories.* Translated by Usha Narayanan. New Delhi: Sterling, 1999.

Thein Shwe, Saw. *The Need for Renewal and Mission in the Karen Baptist Church of Burma.* Mikrofiche-Ausg. 1993. Ann Arbor, Mich: UMI, 1994.

Traditions in Current Perspective: Proceedings of the Conference on Myanmar and Southeast Asian Studies, 15-17 November 1995. Rangoon: Universities Historical Research Centre, 1996.

Trager, Helen G. *We the Burmese: Voices from Burma.* New York: Praeger, 1969.

Upa Piangzathang, comp. *The Paite Christians in Indo-Burma.* Churachandpur, Manipur: Piangzathang, 1984.

Voices of '88: Burma's Struggle for Democracy. New York: Open Society Institute, 1998.

Weller, Marc, ed. *Democracy and Politics in Burma: A Collection of Documents.* Manerplaw: National Coalition Government of the Union of Burma, 1993.

JCE with AMSP, AP, PJ.

4 A note on Contextual Theology in Cambodia and Laos

1 **Cambodia**
  1.1 Context and Christian Presence
  1.2 Writing and Theological Reflection
2 **Laos**
  2.1 Context and Christian Presence
  2.2 Writing and Theological Reflection

1 Cambodia
1.1 Context and Christian Presence

After centuries of Thai and Vietnamese domination a French protectorate was established in 1863 and French colonial administration followed from 1887 until 1953. From 1954 until 1979 Cambodia was ruled by Prince Sihanouk (1954-1970), and from 1967 until 1978, suffered coups d'état, insurrections and the brutal Khmer Rouge regime. The populist People's Republic of Kampuchea was imposed by Vietnam in 1979, to be followed by a further 12 years of civil war. Through the efforts of the United Nations Transitional Authority, elections were held in 1993 and the Kingdom of Cambodia was established. The population amounts to approximately 9.5 million, 85% of whom are Khmers, approximately 5% each of Chinese and Vietnamese and 3% Cham or Aboriginal. Religious affiliation numbers 87% of people to be Buddhist, 3% Muslim, 2.8% Animist, 0.2% Christian and 7% other groupings.

Christianity had been introduced into Cambodia by Roman Catholic missionaries in the 16th century, and despite many difficulties Catholics numbered over 100,000 by 1950, although this would be halved by 1970. In earlier periods the churches had received leadership from many orders including the Society of

Jesus, the Franciscans, the Missions Etrangères de Paris and the Order of Mary Immaculate. In 1952 a Benedictine monastery had been established in Kampot province and in 1957 the first Khmer priest was ordained, with six more following in the next 16 years. The Apostolic Vicariate of Phnom Penh was subdivided in 1968 and in 1970 a Catholic commission to aid victims of war was organised. In the rapidly increasing conflict the commission developed to become Caritas Cambodge. In 1975 the vicariate was re-organised and Mgr Joseph Chhmar Salas was made Bishop Coadjutor of Phnom Penh. Both he and Mgr Paul Tep Im Sotha, as well as all Khmer priests, religious and a great number of Khmer Catholics were killed in the next three years. With only a few exceptions, churches, although not convents, were destroyed but 'under-ground' churches continued. Government permission to worship freely only returned in 1990, and a major seminary has since been established at Battambang, with consequent ordination of Cambodian priests. The Apostolic Vicariate of Phnom Penh currently comprises Phnom Penh city, Sihanoukville, the provinces of Kandal, Takeo, Kampot, Kompong Speu and Koh-Kong. The Prefecture of Battambang covers eight provinces, and the Prefecture of Kompong Cham seven provinces. Catholics now number approximately 15,000, both Cambodian and Vietnamese.

Protestant work was begun by the Christian and Missionary Alliance in 1923 and by 1962 members numbered approximately 2,000. A Bible School was founded at Battambang in 1925 by the Rev'd and Mrs David Ellison. By 1933 the New Testament had been translated by the Rev'd and Mrs Arthur Hammond, and the whole Bible by 1953. By then also the Cambodian Church had become self-supporting. At that time a Unitarian mission also maintained a teacher-training school in Phnom Penh, and Baptist missions functioned in Battambang and Siemreab provinces. The Khmer Evangelical Church was established in 1964. Following five years of restrictions on Christian work and the return of expatriate missionaries in 1970, churches would flourish and grow until the Khmer Rouge took control in 1975. Protestant Christians then suffered a similar decimation through massacre and migration, with only three of the 14 national pastors escaping death. During these years ecumenical solidarity between churches and Christians had grown, simply to assist human and Christian survival. Observers report in 1980 that "there were more registered Khmer Christians among the refugees in camps in Thailand than in all of Cambodia before 1970", and in those camps Theological Education by Extension (TEE) was continued. There were also reports that in 1982 "three Christian villages existed in Cambodia."

Emergency relief, aid and service agencies such as Asian Christian Service and the Mennonites continued their work in these decades, to be joined later by other groups such as the Maryknoll missioners, Jesuit Service Cambodia and WSCF Frontier Interns. (See also chapter 9, section 5.) These, along with Southeast Outreach (formerly Cambodia for Christ), have followed a largely holistic and church-based approach to work in relief, literacy and agriculture. Christian activity has steadily increased since the 1980s despite occasional harassment, with the Overseas Missionary Fellowship, Anglican, Reformed and Methodist churches also now active. Other influences from outside Cambodia however continue to foster denominational division. But following a number of ecumenical initiatives, a Kampuchea Christian Council, uniting six groupings of churches, was formed in August 1998. Most service and aid agencies were already collaborating closely as Cambodian Christian Services.

Since 1990 ministries in education, arts and music, and in community development have been started by these and other churches, with dialogue and development workshops also initiated by the YMCA of Chiangmai, and involving staff of many NGOs. Student Christian Movements have been recently reconstituted and include both Bible study and programmes on social justice and human rights. In 1994 the Cambodian Christian Women's Association (CCWA) was formed by Yos Em Sithan, who had formerly led her own underground (non-denominational) church in Phnom Penh, along with Kei Serey Vuthi. The CCWA is registered as an NGO and programmes include Bible study, prayer, gender awareness training, vocational education, literacy training and credit schemes.

Selected References
i) History and Culture

Chandler, David. *A History of Cambodia*. London: Allen and Unwin, 1993.

—. *Facing the Cambodian Past*. Chiangmai: Silkworm Books, 1996.

Chou Ta-Kuan (Zhou Daguan). *The Customs of Cambodia*. Trans. from French version by Paul Pelliot of Chou's Chinese original by J.Gilman d'Arcy Paul. 3rd. ed. Bangkok: Siam Society, 1993.

Ebihara, May M. et al. *Cambodian Culture since 1975: Homeland and Exile*. Ithaca: Cornell University, 1994.

Heininger, Janet Elaine. *Peacekeeping in Transition: the United Nations in Cambodia*. New York: Twentieth Century Fund Press, 1994.

Gheddo, Piero. *Vietnam Cambogia: non stiamo a guardare*. Giacomo Girardi. 2nd. ed. Bologna: EMI, 1980.

Hildebrand, George C. and Gareth Porter. *Cambodia (Starvation & Revolution)*. New York; London: Monthly Review Press, 1976.

Khing Hoc Dy. *Ecrivains et Expression Litteraires du Camboge au XXme Siecle*. Paris: n.p. 1993.

Kiernan, Ben and Chanthou Boua, eds. *Peasants and Politics in Kampuchea 1942-1981*. London: Zed Press; Armonk, NY: M.E. Sharpe, 1982.

Lyons, Adrian. *Voices, Stories, Hopes: Cambodia and Vietnam: Refugees and Volunteers*. Melbourne: Collins Dove, 1993.

Muscat, Robert J., and Jonathan Stromseth. *Cambodia: Post-Settlement Reconstruction and Development*. New York: Columbia University, 1989.

Mysliwiec, Eva. *Punishing the Poor (The International Isolation of Kampuchea)*. Oxford: Oxfam, 1988.

Osborne, Milton. *The Mekong: Turbulent Past, Uncertain Future*. NY: Atlantic Monthly Press, 2000.

Report of the Fact-Finding Commission to Cambodia 28th March-2nd April 1994. Hong Kong: Asian Human Rights Commission and CCA, 1994.

Skidmore, Monique. "In the Shade of the Bo Tree: Dhammayietra and the Re-awakening of Community in Cambodia." *Crossroads* 10.1 (1993).

ii) Church History and Theology

Amalanathan, M. Antony. "La Experiencia de Jesuitas en un Campo Camboyano." *Centrum Ignatianum Spiritualitatis* 14 (1983).

Cochinchina et Cambodia (vicariato apostolico). Sinodi, 1841 Synodus Vicariatus Cochinchinensis Cambodiensis ... anno 1841. Hong Kong: Societas Missionum ad Exteros, 1893.

Burke, Todd and DeAnn. *Annointed for Burial.* Plainfield NJ: Logos International, 1977.

Cormack, Don. *Killing fields, Living fields: an Unfinished Portrait of the Cambodian Church - the Church that Would Not Die.* 2nd edited London: Monarch Books; Singapore: OMF International, 2000.

Coueron, Raymond. "Activités du Bureau pour la Promotion l'Apostolat parmi les Khmers (BPAC)." *Echos de la Rue du Bac (1985).*

De Roeck, René. "Vietnam, Cambodia and Laos: The Church at the Crossroads of Chaos." In *Christ and Crisis in Southeast Asia*, edited by G.H. Anderson. New York: Friendship Press, 1968.

Ellison, Paul. *A Short History of the Cambodian Evangelical Church.* Mimeo'd. San Jose: Cambodian Christian Services Conference, 1991.

Haughey, John C. "Church and State in Cambodia." *America* 125 (1971).

Indochina Dialogue. Report of Meeting held in Phnom Penh, Cambodia, December 1992. Chiangmai: YMCA for Northern Development Foundation, n.d.

Irwin, E.F. *With Christ in Indochina. The Story of Alliance Missions in French Indochina and Eastern Siam.* Harrisburg: Christian Publications, 1936.

Lockerbie Jeanette. *When Blood Flows, the Heart Grows Softer.* Harrisburg: Christian Publications, 1976.

Mathews George Chunakara, ed. *Indochina Today: A Consultation on Emerging Trends.* Hong Kong: CCA-WCC Indochina Programme, 1994.

—, ed. *Ecumenical Response to Indo-China.* Hong Kong: CCA, 1995.

Penfold, Helen. *Remember Cambodia.* Sevenoaks: OMF Books, 1980.

Politi, Giancarlo. "Cambogia, Rinascita al Rallentatore." *Mondo e Missione* 125 (1996).

Ponchaud, Francois. *Cambodia Year Zero.* Trans. from the French by Nancy Amphoux. London: Allen Lane, 1978.

A note on Contextual Theology in Cambodia and Laos 113

—. *La cathédrale de la Rizière: 450 ans d'Histoire de l'Eglise au Cambodge* (Cathedral of the Rice Paddy: 450 Years of the Church in Cambodia). Paris: Le Sarment: Fayard, c1990.

—. "La Vie Quotidienne a Phnom Penh et au Cambodge." *Echos de la Rue du Bac* (1986).

—. "Religion und Politik in Kambodscha." *Die Katholischen Missionen* 109 (1990).

Ramousse, Yves. "Les Chrétiens du Cambodge." *Mission de l'Eglise* 30 (1976).

—. "The Church in Cambodia: Interview with Yves Ramousse, Apostolic Vicar of Phnom Penh." *Catholic International* 4 (1993).

1.2 Writing and Theological Reflection

Literature arising from the turbulent history of Cambodian Christians and appearing in journal articles or monographs, has until recently been mainly in the form of church histories, biographies, mission chronicles, studies of religious life and customs, or collected addresses, testimonies or hymns. Most have been written by expatriates, often in the French or English languages. The earliest example in Khmer may be the catechism written by Levasseur in 1770. Many more recent studies have focused upon church-state relationships in the last 150 years or upon the often tragic vicissitudes of Christian communities during that time. Amongst the writers of these have been the Catholics Raymond Coueron, Jean Pihan, Giancarlo Politi, Francois Ponchaud, P. Rondineaux, Yves Ramousse and Adrian Lyons. Amongst Protestant writers are E.F. Irwin, J. Paul Ellison, Jill Perkins, Sam Isaacs, Helen Penfold, Jeannette Lockerbie, Todd and DeAnn Burke, Don Cormack and Mathews George Chunakara.

Amongst expatriate women active in education and cultural programmes, Alice Compain and Gwynneth Squires of the OMF have written and composed local lyrics. Since 1945 a growing number of Khmer and western scholars in anthropology, linguistics, literature, history and ethnomusicology - amongst them Christians - have worked to recover and record aspects of the rich Cambodian culture.In contextual Christian art, Paul Tep Im Sotha, apostolic prefect of Battambang (1968-1975) had, before his execution, installed there paintings of the life of Jesus in the style of pagoda representations of the Buddha.

Regarding vernacular writing, the New Testament had appeared in Khmer in 1933, and this would be followed by a number of pamphlets and tracts in local languages. Roman Catholic publications appeared in Cambodian script only in the 1960s through the work of Fathers Rondineaux and Ponchaud. Few Cambodians have been able to write or publish material in the decades since but some remarkable testimonies of faith amidst suffering have been published. Some of these appear in volumes such as those of Jeannette Lockerbie, Todd and DeAnn Burke and Don Cormack, as well as in various periodicals and the bulletins of some mission or development agencies.

There is now, however, a bilingual Khmer-English theological journal (*Honeycomb*) which makes possible the regular publishing of Cambodian writing, in what promises to be a new era for theological work in Cambodia. *Honeycomb* commenced in the year 2000 and is published by Training of Timothys, Phnom Penh. In early issues, Arun Sok Nhep and Uon Seila are national writers who have already written on the subjects of indigenisation and contextualisation. Arun Sok Nhep writes that indigenisation requires more than self-support, self- government and self propagation. "It requires" he says, "a deep reflection on and evaluation of the cultural identity of a national church", which he here begins. He also outlines the basis for a "critical contextualization" of theology and of church structures. Uon Seila uses the imagery of the bamboo in prose and verse to illustrate the role of resilience and humility, of mutual support and unity in the life of the church and of the Christian. Other authors in initial issues include Christopher LaPel, Francois Ponchaud, Ravi Jayakaran, Debbi Maher, Glenn Miles, Margaret Street, Russell Bowers and Neal Youngquist.

Selected References

Antone, Hope, Yong Ting Jin and Esther Byu. "VLC (Vietnam, Laos, Cambodia) - Sense of Hunger, a Note of Promise: Reflections on the Consultation of Indochinese Women." *In God's Image* 15.3 (1996).

Arun Sok Nhep. "Indigenization of a National Church - A Reflection on a National Church Structure" *Honeycomb* 1.1 (2000).
Burke, Todd and DeAnn. *Annointed for Burial.*
Cormack, Don. *Killing fields, Living fields.*
Fenton, James, ed. *Cambodian Witness. The Autobiography of Someth May.* Bangkok: White Lotus, 1998 (New York, 1986).
Garcia, Sarah, FMA. "Cambodia: A sharing of a minority Church in difficult situations." *Religious Life Asia* I. 1 (1999).
Keeping doors open: a CCA team in Vietnam and Kampuchea. Singapore: CCA, 1982.
"La Renaissanc d'une Eglise bilan d'une pastorale. Document du Conseil de Mission de l'Eglise du Cambodge." *Weltkirche* (1996).
Leslie, Emma. "Post Communist Cambodia: Christian Women Speaking and Acting Boldly." *In God's Image* 17.4 (1998).
Lockerbie Jeanette. *When Blood Flows, the Heart Grows Softer.*
Maher, Debbi. "Biography: Yos em Sithan." *Honeycomb* 1.1. (2000).
Perkins, Jill. *Fragments of War: Asian Christian Service at Work in Vietnam and Laos.* S.l.: Chinese Christian Literature Council for Central Committee of the Fellowship of the Least Coin, Asian Church Women's Conference, 1970.
Pihan, Jean. "Rèflexions a l'Occasion du Retour de Missionnaires du Cambodge et du Vietnam." *Présence et Dialogue* (18 Sept. 1975).
Reformed Church: A Documentation. Compiled by Lukas Vischer and Jean-Jacques Bauswein, 1991-1999. Geneva: WCC Archives.
Uon Seila: "Bamboo" and "Biography: Christopher LaPel." *Honeycomb* 2.2 (forthcoming)
Yap Kim Hao, et al. *Nurturing an Asian Christian Presence in Indochina.* Singapore: CCA, 1983.

2 Laos
2.1 Context and Christian Presence

The Lao monarchy had governed from 1353 until the French colonial period began in 1893. Independence movements brought freedom from France in 1953 and the Lao People's Revolutionary Party, formed in 1955, had gained complete control of the country by 1975. Laos has since been a one-party republic. The population of Laos numbers approximately 5.5 million, 80% of whom live in rural areas. One-hundred-nineteen different ethno-linguistic groups comprise the socio-cultural categories of Highland Lao (14%), Midland Lao (36%) and Lowland Lao (50%). Christians form 1.5 % of the population and Muslims 1 %, while the vast majority are Buddhist (58%) and Animist (33%). Emphasis by the Laotian government upon nationalism and upon Lao Buddhist values, along with acceptance of private enterprise, have now replaced earlier moves towards a fully socialist state.

Freedom of religious belief is given in the Lao constitution yet Christians have been continually harassed: churches closed or converted into schools, members imprisoned without trial, and sharing of religious beliefs prohibited. The government has declared (1999) that Christians are the "number one enemy of the State", and have labelled Christianity as an "imperialist foreign religion." Although Laotian Christians have long suffered persecution by successive governments, this has become much more aggressive, and even extreme, in recent years. Christians have since early 2000 been required to sign a "Voluntary resignation from a foreign religion ..."declaration. This acknowledges: 1) regret for actions (belief in and practice of Christianity); 2) the goodness of the (Communist) Party; 3) a resignation from foreign religion; 4) that they do not believe and will no longer participate in the foreign religion; 5) their promise to work for the initiatives of the Party; and 6) if found exercising the foreign religion, their acceptance of the consequences (like imprisonment or other serious infringements on basic human rights, e.g. loss of job, loss of right to education, loss of land). Signing of this is enforced by Security Police who travel throughout the country and also conduct 're-education'.

Roman Catholic contacts date from Jesuit work in the 16th century, although permanent presence began only in the 19th century with missioners sent from Cambodia in 1858. In the 1870s and 1880s, Jean-Louis Vey as apostolic vicar in Siam and, with the support of the MEP, was able to oversee the growth of churches amongst Laotians both in Siam and Laos. Missioners strongly opposed the slave trade in these areas, and despite the martyrdom of 17 priests by 1890, the mission slowly grew, though still part of the Siam vicariate. Laos became a separate vicariate in 1898 although for much of the 20th century Bangkok remained an important centre for Roman Catholic work there. By 1970 Catholics numbered almost 30,000, with 8 ordained priests, and operated 30

A note on Contextual Theology in Cambodia and Laos

schools. Despite the restrictions and harassments since 1975, the church has slowly grown and now has three bishops, 16 priests and approximately 35,000 members. Central issues remain those of religious freedom and of formation for the laity.

Early Protestant contacts were established by the Presbyterian Daniel McGilvary of Chiangmai (from 1872), Gabriel Contesse and his wife of the Swiss Brethren (from 1902) and G. Edward Rofe of the Christian and Missionary Alliance (from 1929). By 1939 there were communities formed in southern Laos as well as at Luang Prabang, Vientiane and Xieng Khouang. Churches were strengthened by OMF and other ex-China staff after 1950 and relatively peaceful life and work was possible following the Geneva Agreement of 1954. By 1970 there were 65 churches, 26 national and 45 expatriate workers, and almost 10,000 members and adherents. By then also co-operation between the Evangelical Church in Laos, the Church of Christ in Thailand, and the East Asia Christian Conference was developing, with plans for joint work in education, leadership training and health services.

Despite the persecution that soon followed, significant numbers are entering the churches in some districts, with numbers growing from approximately 17,000 in 1975, to twice that today. There are however urgent needs for trained clergy and lay leaders. Although some freedom of movement and work has been allowed to church leaders, since 1998 Christians have suffered from government efforts to close all house churches while retaining official churches to give foreigners the impression that there is religious freedom in the country. In the last months of 2000, more scores of people have been imprisoned for their Christian beliefs.

Selected References
i) History and Culture

> Backus, Mary. *Siam and Laos, as Seen by Our American Missionaries.* Philadelphia: Presbyterian Board of Publication, 1884.
>
> Bountavy Sisouphanthong. *Atlas of Laos : the spatial structures of economic and social development of the Lao People's Democratic Republic.* Copenhagen, Denmark: NIAS; Chiang Mai, Thailand: Silkworm books, 2000.

Butler-Diaz, Jacqueline, ed. *New Laos, New Challenges*. Tempe: Arizona State University, 1998.
Cordell, Helen. *Laos*. [Bibliography]. Oxford: Oxford University Press, 1991.
Evans, Grant. *Lao Peasants under Socialism and Post-Socialism*. Chiang Mai: Silkworm Books, 1995.
—, ed. *Laos: Culture and Society*. Chiang Mai: Silkworm Books 1999. Contains full bibliography.
Lafont, Pierre-Bernard. *Bibliographie du Laos. Tome II seul. (1962-1975)*. Paris?: Editions de l'Ecole Française d'Extrême-Orient, 1978.
LeBar, Frank M. and Adrienne Suddard, eds. *Laos: its People, its Society, its Culture*. New Haven: HRAF Press, 1960.
McClellan, Monique. "Laos Revisited." *Church and Society*, May-June (1976).
Manich, M.L. *History of Laos*. Bangkok: Chalermnit, 1967.
Ratnam, Perala, ed. *Laos and its Culture*. New Delhi: Tulsi Publishing House, 1982; Bangkok: White Lotus, 1994.
Stuart-Fox, Martin. *A History of Laos*. Cambridge: University Press, 1997.
—. *Historical Dictionary of Laos*. Lanham, MD: Scarecrow Press, 2000.

ii) Church History and Theology

Bayet, Claudius. *"Une Lumière s'est levée. Historique de l'evangelisation au Nord-est de la Thailande et au Laos*. Bangkok: Chamras Karnphim, 1985.
Berthéas, M. *La mission du Laos: Notice Historique*. Lyon: Poncet, 1909.
Bordo, Vicenzo. "Mission O.M.I. au Laos." *Le Christ au Monde* 30 (1985).
Decorvet, Jeanne et Georges Rochat. *L'Appel du Laos*. Yverdon (Suisse): H. Cornaz, 1946.
De Roeck, René. "Vietnam, Cambodia and Laos: The Church at the Crossroads of Chaos." In *Christ and Crisis in Southeast Asia*, edited by G.H. Anderson. New York: Friendship Press, 1968.
Karat, G.R. and Franz Tumiwa. "The Church in Laos and Vietnam." *National Christian Council Review* 101 (1981).
Loosdregt, E. "Laos. Catéchistes dans la Tourmente." *Lumen Vitae* 27 (1972).

Mathews George Chunakara, ed. *Indochina Today: A Consultation on Emerging Trends*. Hong Kong: CCA-WCC Indochina Programme, 1994.

—. ed. *Ecumenical Response to Indo-China*. Hong Kong: CCA, 1995.

Menger, J. Matt. *Slowly Climbs the Sun*. New York: Twin Circle Publishing, 1973.

—. *In the valley of the Mekong; an American in Laos*. (Dr Thomas Dooley.) Paterson, NJ: St. Anthony Guild Press, 1970.

Reformed Church: A Documentation, comp. by Lukas Vischer and Jean-Jacques Bauswein, 1991-1999. Geneva: WCC Archives.

Wilson, J., and others. *The Laos hymnal*. Chiengmai: American Presbyterian Mission, 1914.

Zago, Marcel. *Rites et Cérémonies en Milieu Bouddhiste Lao*. Documenta Missionalia 6. Rome: Universita Gregoriana Editrice, 1972.

—. "Missionary Pastoral Practice in a Laotian Buddhist Milieu." *Teaching All Nations* 9 (1972).

2.2 Writing and Theological Reflection

In Laos, literature has traditionally served the Buddhist temple by supporting the acceptance of inherited roles in society and religion. Under the French this meant the acceptance of a colonial subjectivity where France was the cultural and political centre. Lack of publishing agencies or technology have also greatly hindered publication of any writings. Until the mid-20th century, the primary method of reproducing a manuscript was "the centuries-old practice of transcribing text onto strips of palm leaves with a stylus." (Koret, 1999). By the 1950s a few monthly magazines began to appear, along with writers such as Pa Nai, Douang Champa and Dok Ket. These were all students of Maha Sila Viravong, the eminent scholar of Lao history, culture and literature. Since the 1950s, Lao revolutionary literature has been largely written in traditional poetic forms, most often serving only current government policies. Since 1975 groups of prose-writers have also emerged, some producing revolutionary writings, some such as Outhine Bounyavong writing for the new Lao society, and some post-revolutionary writers such as Bounthanong Somsaiphon and Viset Savengseuksa. In recent years writers of all kinds have been forced to avoid political comment because of severe government control.

Such conditions also continue to inhibit most would-be Christian writers in Laos.

Little work has been done to assemble or study the writings of national or expatriate Christians in Laos, although such materials are extant. These range from the letters and reports of Jean-Louis Vey (from 1872) and other missioners, to reflective articles by nationals such as Jean Khamsé Vithavong or Nakhon Sawan; from books or articles by expatriate missioners to the occasional Pastoral Letters from the Laotian Bishops, as part of the Laos-Cambodia Catholic Bishops' Conference, or statements issued by the Laos Evangelical Church. Reflections arising from the life and witness of nationals have appeared in these pastoral letters and statements and in such articles as those by Khamsé Vithavong, Nakhon Sawan, a number of anonymous writers, and in collections such as those by Jill Perkins and J. Wilson. Histories and narratives of the church form the largest proportion of the books and articles published, by writers such as René De Roeck, Rosemary A. Watson, Claudius Bayet, J. Matt Menger, Jeanne Decorvet and Georges Rochat. Important cultural studies have come from such scholars as Marcel Zago, Perala Ratnam and Grant Evans. The many vernacular tracts that continue to be published (by for example Chick Publications) contain few contextual elements.

Selected References

"Avec les Plus Pauvres du Laos." *Pole et Tropiques* 4 (1972).

"Evangélisation et Dévelopement sous la Menace Rouge au Laos." *Le Christ au Monde* 17 (1972).

Khamsé Vithavong, Jean. "La Iglesia de Laos: una Iglesia que lucha por Sobrevivir." *Misiones Extranjeras* (1994).

Koret, Peter. "Contemporary Lao Literature." In *Mother's Beloved: Stories from Laos* by Outhine Bounyavong. Chiangmai: Silkworm Books, 1999.

Le divin chez les peuples du Laos. [prefazione di Marcello Zago]. S.l.: s.n., 1974.

Nakhon Sawan. *Life after Liberation: the Church in the Lao People's Democratic Republic*. Chiangmai: Lao Christian Service, c1987.

"Pastoral Letters" of the Laos-Cambodia Catholic Bishops' Conference. See e.g. "Pastoral Letter from Laotian Bishops." *CCAN* 15.4.1976.

"Peace Comes to Laos." Statement of Laos Evangelical Church. *CCA News* (May 15, 1974).

Perkins, Jill. *Fragments of war: Asian Christian Service at Work in Vietnam and Laos*. S.l.: Chinese Christian Literature Council for Central Committee of the Fellowship of the Least Coin, Asian Church Women's Conference, 1970.

Pitt, Jan, and Dan Wooding. *Laos: No Turning Back: the Story of Lungh Singh*. The Church in Areas of Conflict. Basingstoke: Marshalls, 1985.

Watson, Rosemary A. *As the Rock Flower Blooms*. Sevenoaks : OMF, 1984.

5 Contextual Theological Reflection in Indonesia 1800-2000

For Christian reflection in Indonesia prior to 1800 see chap. 2 above.

1 **General Characteristics**
   1.1 Brief Overview of the Cultural Context
   1.2 Brief Overview of the Authors
   1.3 Women Authors
      1.3.1. Women's Organisations
   1.4 Ecumenical and Professional Contacts
      1.4.1. International; **1.4.2.** The Communion of Churches in Indonesia (DGI/PGI); **1.4.3.** The Association of Theological Schools in Indonesia (Persetia); **1.4.4.** Indonesian Conference of Bishops (MAWI, KWI); **1.4.5.** The Indonesian Religious Leadership Conference (KOPTARI, formerly MASRI)
   1.5 Journals and Commemorative Volumes
   1.6 Periods

2 **The Emergence of Written Theological Reflection in Indonesia ca 1860-1945**
   2.1 Early Echoes: 1860-1910
      2.1.1. C.L. Coolen (1775-?1873); **2.1.2.** Paulus Tosari (1813-82); **2.1.3.** Asa Kiman (died 1892); **2.1.4.** Ibrahim Tunggul Wulung (ca. 1800-85); **2.1.5.** Sadrach Surapranata (1835-1924); **2.1.6.** Distanced from Islam; **2.1.7.** Francis George Joseph Van Lith sj (1863-1926)

   2.2 The Impact of National Awakening and Independence 1910-45
      2.2.1. Clearing the Deck: 1911-42; **2.2.2.** Japanese Occupation - A Defining Experience: 1942-45; **2.2.3.** Amir Sjarifoeddin (1907-48)

Contextual Theological Reflection in Indonesia 1800-2000 123

3 **Indonesian Thinkers Find their Voice ca. 1945-65**
   3.1 Establishing a Modern Nation: 1945-65
   3.2 Opening Horizons: Lay Thinkers Take Centre Stage
   3.2.1. T.S.G. Moelia (1896-1966); **3.2.2.** Johannes Leimena (1905-66); **3.2.3.** Tahi Bonar Simatupang (1920-90)
   3.3 Professional Scholars Take Up the Challenge
   3.3.1. Harun Hadiwijono (1915-85); **3.3.2.** Johannes L. Ch. Abineno (1917-95); **3.3.3.** Peter D. Latuihamallo (1918-); **3.3.4.** Nicolaus Driyarkara sj (1913-67)

4 **Towards More Systematic Contextual Theologies ca. 1965-2000**
   4.1 Robert Hardawiryana sj (1926-); **4.2** Ihromi (1928-); **4.3** Yusuf Bilyarta Mangunwijaya (1929-99); **4.4** Tom Jacobs sj (1929-); **4.5** Fridolin Ukur (1930-); **4.6.** I. Wayan Mastra (1931-); **4.7** Victor Immanuel Tanja (1936-98); **4.8.** Franz Magnis-Suseno sj (1936-); **4.9** Judowibowo Poerwowidagdo (1942-); **4.10** Agustina Lumentut (1937-); **4.11** Eka Darmaputera (1942-); **4.12** Agustina Nunuk Prasetyo Murniati (1943-); **4.13** Henriette Marianne Katoppo (1943-); **4.14** Th. Sumartana (1944-); **4.15** Andreas Anangguru Yewangoe (1945-); **4.16** Johanes Baptista Banawiratma (1946-); **4.17** John Mansford Prior svd (1946-); **4.18** Sientje Merentek-Abram (1947-); **4.19** Karel Phil Erari (1947-); **4.20** Emanuel Gerrit Singgih (1949-); **4.21** Gabriel Possenti Sindhunata sj (1952-); **4.22** Henriette Tabita Hutabarat-Lebang (1952-); **4.23** Septemmy Eucharistia Lakawa (1970-); **4.24** Other Contributions to Contextual Theology

5 **Supplementary Bibliography**
   5.1 Bibliographies
   5.2 Introductory Listing for 1860-1910
   5.3 Introductory Listing for 1911-1950
   5.4 Histories and Historical Sources
   5.5 Overviews

1 General Characteristics

Indonesia is an archipelago of over 13,000 islands scattered across the equator, of which 73 are larger than 500 square kilometres. Java, with the smaller island of Madura, is the habitat for 60% of the population of 203 million (2000 census). With 87% of the people adhering to Islam, Indonesia possesses the largest Muslim community anywhere. With 10% of the population belonging to one of the Christian churches - just over 6% Protestant, and roughly 4% Catholic - Indonesia also has one of the larger Christian minorities of any Muslim country. With a Hindu and Buddhist past which still shapes the cultural ethos of the Javanese majority, and with some 350 languages and over 30 major cultural domains, Indonesia has chosen an apt and accurate national motto: *bhinneka tunggal ika* - unity in diversity. This rich diversity was suppressed during more than 30 years of military rule (1965/66-98). The long, hard road to a civil democracy is straining this diverse ethnic and religious patchwork to the limits.

Archaeological excavations at Baros in the 1990s confirm documentary evidence of Christian communities on the west coast of Sumatra in the 7th century. There was also a Franciscan mission in the 12th century (Muskens 1972:19-40). However, present-day Indonesian Christian churches date back to the Catholic and Protestant missions of the 16th and 17th centuries, and more particularly the missionary outreach of the 19th and early 20th centuries. The early Catholic evangelists were Portuguese, the later ones Dutch. Protestant evangelists came from the Netherlands and Germany. Catholic and Protestant Churches in Indonesia had little contact with each other until the 1960s; theological collaboration commenced only in the last two decades of the 20th century.

Selected References

Cribb, Robert. *Historical Atlas of Indonesia*. Richmond: Curzon, 2000. Detailed maps - Landscape & Environment, Peoples, States & Politics until 1800, The Netherlands Indies 1800-1942, War, Revolution & Political Transformation, 1942-2000.

End, Th. van den and J. Weitjens. *Ragi Carita: Sejarah Gereja di Indonesia, I th.1500-1860an* (The leaven of love: history of the Church in Indonesia I, 1500-1860s). Jakarta: BPK Gunung Mulia, 1996.

— *Ragi Carita II. th. 1860an - sekarang* (The leaven of love: II, 1860s to contemporary times). Jakarta: BPK Gunung Mulia, 1993. A revised edition is being prepared of this two-volume work.

Muskens, M., ed. *Sejarah Gereja Katolik Indonesia* (History of the Catholic Church in Indonesia) Vol. I, *Umat Katolik Perintis* (Pioneering Catholic communities, ca.645-1500), by Arnoldus Ende. See, Y. Bakker, "Umat Katolik Perintis di Indonesia" 19-40. Jakarta: KWI (Catholic Bishops' Conference)1972.

Steenbrink, Karel. *Catholics in Indonesia 1808-1942. A Documented History.* Vol. I: *A Modest Recovery 1808-1903.* Leiden: KITLV Press, forthcoming. See Chapter I "Indonesian Conversions to World Religions prior to 1800". Includes extensive primary sources (almost half the text).

1.1 Brief Overview of the Cultural Context

Similar to other regions of Southeast Asia, Indonesia has an absorbent culture. The past, including colonial history, is rarely rejected; it is taken on board on Indonesian terms. Accepting whatever seems useful or appropriate, the resultant symbiotic culture - and therefore theology - consists of an ongoing synthesis. If the term does not repel, it is a living syncretism. This socio-cultural context is at the root of the earliest indigenous theologising in the 19th century. However, since political independence, traditional culture has often been viewed as an obstacle to modernity and national development. Thus, 20th century Protestant theological thinkers spoke of development (Leimena, 3.2.2.), of the *Pancasila*, or State Ideology (Darmaputera, 4.11) and of relations with Islam (Tanja, 4.7; Sumartana, 4.14). However, the whole question of complex cultural identities re-emerged on the national scene during the increasingly centralised Soeharto regime (1966-98) and with the onslaught of globalisation. And so cultural rather than purely economic issues form the fertile soil for Catholic moderate liberationists as diverse as van Lith at the opening of the 20th century and Mangunwijaya (4.3) and Banawiratma (4.16) in its closing decades. The Catholic contextual philosophers Driyarkara (3.3.4.), Magnis-Suseno (4.8) and Sindhunata (4.21) also work within a (Javanese) cultural frame.

The cultures of Java and Bali have a literary tradition, while the numerous ethnic cultures of the other islands are oral. Precisely among these ethnic groups we find the largest Christian congregations - among the Bataks of North Sumatra, the Timorese, Florenese and Sumbanese of Nusa Tenggara, and the peoples of the Moluccas, Halmahera and Papua-land (Irian Jaya). Among these churches theology is also dominantly oral, that is, lived-out and passed-down in similar vein to the local culture. So far, virtually none of these oral, lived-out theologies of the ethnic churches has been studied, despite the fact that missionary linguists, ethnologists and anthropologists researched many of the languages and cultural domains early in the 20th century. Most Christians belong to non-Javanese ethnic groups. This is very much a question of power: The centre (Jakarta) versus the periphery (the outer islands). The dramatic centralisation of the state under the ageing Soekarno (1959-65) and throughout the Soeharto era (1965/66-98) marginalised local cultures and identities. Indonesian theologies voice these tensions between the oral periphery and the literary centre as well as between regional and national concerns.

Selected References

    Banawiratma, J.B. and T. Jacobs. "Doing Theology with Local Resources." *EAPR*, 1 (1989). Outlines the joint Catholic-Protestant "project-approach" of the theological faculties in Yogyakarta.

    Latuihamallo, P.D. S.W. Wahono, and F. Ukur, eds. *Tabah Melangkah* (Stepping forward patiently). Book to Commemorate the 50th Anniversary of the Jakarta School of Theology. Jakarta: STT, 1984. Fairly comprehensive reflection of ecumenical Protestant theology at the beginning of the 1980s.

    Pramudianto and Martin Sinaga, eds. *Pergulatan dan Kontekstualisasi Pemikiran Protestan Indonesia* (The wrestle and contextualisation of Protestant thinking in Indonesia). 17 Dies Natalis orations from the Jakarta School of Theology to celebrate their 65th Anniversary. Jakarta: STT, 1999. An overview of ecumenical Protestant theology 15 years after *Tabah Melangkah* (see above).

1.2 Brief Overview of the Authors

Of the hundreds of hard-working teachers of theology, some of whom have published a sizeable corpus, little mention is found in this study. This survey is limited to those who are doing theology creatively, conscious of the Indonesian context in all its complexity. Often enough the more interesting writers are not professional theologians. Creative probing in the 19th century came from "untrained" first-generation laity (e.g. Sadrach). In mid 20th century contextual theologising emerged from public figures such as Moelia 3.2.1.), Leimena (3.2.2.) and Simatupang (3.2.3.), and during the last three decades from novelists such as Katoppo (4.13) and Mangunwijaya (4.3). Simatupang is one of the more creative Protestant theological thinkers to date, while Mangunwijaya is one of the more imaginative Catholic thinkers.

Working among the literati or on the political stage, these scholars prevented the seminaries from simply servicing churches for whom faith was primarily a private matter. This survey thus records the painful move from pietist/devotional churches preoccupied with building up self-reliant but inward-looking congregations, to socially-engaged churches that became active, even 'moderately prophetic' witnesses in society. If Indonesian theology is late on the world stage, this is partly due to the fact that seminaries for too long interpreted their task as passing-on scientific theology in the western university tradition. Theology as praxis (systematic reflection upon ongoing involvement) still sits uneasily in most seminary syllabi. However, in the mid-1970s the Sekolah Tinggi Teoloji (Graduate School of Theology) in Jakarta initiated a *Hidup Berteologi* programme of "theology in action" which systematically related fieldwork with critical reflection. Since the 1980s the Protestant and Catholic Faculties of Theology in Yogyakarta have collaborated in producing more praxis-oriented courses in theology (Banawiratma, 1989). In 1982 the Association of Protestant Schools of Theology (*Persetia*) prepared a moderately contextual course for consideration and use by its members; a postgraduate syllabus was completed in 2000. In 2000 *Perwati* published a course in feminist theology for use in theological syllabi (see below). Catholics and Protestants plan to meet in mid-2002 to discuss the challenge of contextualising theological syllabi further. In 1994 Yogyakarta prepared the official undergraduate course of Catholic theology accredited by the government.

Unsurprisingly, contextual theologians have been publishing in the national and regional press, unconfined by congregational strictures. Many of the more creative theological works consist of collections of such newspaper columns (e.g. Darmaputera 1977, Mangunwijaya 1999). Here a more everyday idiom and even trans-Christian discourse have replaced the theological language of the classroom. These are not the pious comments of a bystander or ivory tower academic, but the considered reflections of persons involved in the common struggle for dignity and freedom.

Virtually all professional theologians are involved in congregational or wider forms of church leadership. And so, their theology surfaces not in large scientific tomes but as ongoing series of reflective responses to the felt and underlying needs of the congregation and of society at large. This theologising is very much a collective activity; writings are often the outcome of seminars, workshops and study-projects. This is especially the case for women doing theology (Prasetyo Murniati 1990, Lumentut 1997 and Lakawa 2000).

Twenty-five of those surveyed below are Protestants, ten are Catholic. The Protestant theological thinkers hail from the whole spectrum of the Indonesian archipelago, from Papua-land, Ambon, Sulawesi, Timor, Sawu, Sumba, Bali, Kalimantan and Sumatra as well as from Java; they include both a Papuan and a Chinese-Indonesian. Most of them are associated in some way with the Jakarta and Yogyakarta Schools/Faculties of Theology. Most are married, although one of the women and one of the men have chosen a celibate life-way. There are just six women, including five Protestants, two of whom are active as congregational leaders, one in the Christian Conference of Asia for over a decade while the other is a free-lance novelist; the Catholic is a university lecturer, married and active in women's empowerment. Seven of the ten Catholics are Jesuits and all but two are based in Yogyakarta, central Java. Seven of the Protestants are lay persons, while the Catholic entrants are ordained and therefore male celibates - except for the married woman. Catholic contextual theology has yet to make its mark outside Java.

1.3 Women Authors

Women have needed to struggle long and hard against the patriarchal culture of both Indonesian church and society to gain a toehold on the theological landscape of the churches. Tine Fransz and Lieke Simanjuntak pioneered ecumenical educational and women's programmes from the 1950s on and a number of Protestant women gained degrees in theology. In 1989 Nieke Atmadja-Hadinoto was the first Indonesian woman to receive a doctorate in theology (from Kampen, The Netherlands). Women are collaborative writers working through professional and practical associations (see below). Perhaps this is why few names have emerged so far in the Protestant churches and just one in the Catholic Church. Women theological thinkers also seem to be "too busy" as pastors with little expectation, time or encouragement for academic theologising. Many are engaged in advocacy and human rights networks as well as carrying out family responsibilities.

Selected References

Atmadja-Hadinoto, Nieke. "De vrouw als partner in de kerk - stemmen uit Indonesia," *Allerwegen* 12.3 (1986). Report on a consultation of Indonesian women theologians at Sukabumi in 1983.

Katoppo, Marianne. "Kedudukan Wanita di Indonesia di Masa Sekarang" (The position of women in Indonesia today). *Peninjau* 5 (1978). Survey of the origin and growth of women's movements in Indonesia. Summary of MA thesis (see below).

Orteza, Edna J., ed. *Common Roots Common vision - Report of the ARF Women Consultation-Workshop, Wisma oikoumene, Sukabumi.* Jakarta: PGI, 1987.

Tan, Mely G., ed. *Perempuan Indonesia Pemimpin Masa Depan?* (Indonesian women leaders for the future?). Jakarta: Sinar Harapan, 1991.

Woro, D.E. Palupi, Maria Ginting and Noor Cahyathio. *Wanita Indonesia: Bibliografi Beranotasi* (Indonesian women: annotated bibliography). Jakarta: Pusat Informasi Wanita, 1990. A good, general survey; not specifically theological.

1.3.1. Women's Organisations

Grassroots women's movements, initially established during colonial times in 1928, were disbanded by the military after their 1965/66 putsch. For over 30 years women had to join official government organisations under the wives of local officials, led nationally by the wife of the Minister for Home Affairs. Women were herded back into domestic health programmes and support for the regime. Only in the 1990s have women's grassroots NGOs re-emerged with active participation by Christians.

Christian women's associations are ecumenical, with full Catholic participation, such as the *Kelompok Perempuan Sadar* (KPS - Association for Women's Awareness) established in Yogyakarta in 1993 with A. Nunuk Prasetyo Murniati (4.12) as its first chairperson. KPS meets for regular consultations. It networks with the women's commission of EATWOT and many Indonesian NGOs, few of which are Christian. Awareness programmes include a deconstruction of the myths, symbols, political jargon and violence of the Soeharto regime as well as the pietistic spirituality that was unable to empower oppressed women. KPS is also developing Christian and inter-faith symbols that free and empower. (Address: KPS, Jl. Simanjuntuk 8, (belakang Apotek), Yogyakarta, Indonesia).

Jaringan Mitra Perempuan (JMP - Women's Partnership Network) was established during a 1995 Gender Workshop run by the Social Research Unit of the Catholic Bishops' Conference (LPPS-KWI; known internationally as Missio). JMP has eleven regional networks. Its national secretariat is located at the office of the Bishops' Conference in Jakarta. Workshops and publications focus upon gender injustice and solidarity in integral humanity. JMP is also involved in advocacy and in more practical support of gender victimisation through its local networks. JMP is developing a moderately feminist theology as framework and motivation for its work. (Address: JMP, Jl. Cut Mutiah 10, Jakarta Pusat, Indonesia. E-mail: <jmpnas@jmp.famili.com>.

Persekutuan Wanita Berpendidikan Teologi di Indonesia (*Perwati* - Communion of Women with Theological Education in Indonesia) was born in Tomohon in 1995. In 2000 *Perwati* had 15 branches covering most parts of Indonesia, with a couple of hundred individual members. *Perwati* holds four-yearly assemblies and occasional Study Institutes. Together with the Women's Office of the National Communion of Churches (PGI) and the National Association of Theological Colleges (*Persetia*) it held a major seminar-workshop on feminist theology in 1999. In 2000 it published a course in feminist theology for use in theological syllabi. Since March 2000 *Perwati* has published its own triennial journal *Sophia: Jurnal Berteologi Perempuan Indonesia* (Sophia: An Indonesian Women's Theological Journal). *Sophia* is edited by Septemmy E. Lakawa, who has been General Secretary of *Perwati* since its National Congress in 1998. (Address: Perwati, Jl. Proklamasi 27, Jakarta Pusat 10320. E-mail: <perwatijkt@hotmail.com>).

Selected References

    Damai. "Solidarity Movements of Women." *Rohani.* 39.5 (1992).
    Doeka-Souk, Bendalina and Stephen Suleeman, eds. *Bentangkanlah Sayapmu* (Spread your wings wide). Proceedings of the Seminar and Workshop on Feminist Theology, Kaliurang, July 1997. Jakarta: Persetia, 1999.
    Hardaputranta, ed. *Gender dan Pembangunan I* (Gender and development I). Jakarta: Seri Forum LPPS-KWI 30, 1995. Workshop proceedings.
    KPS, ed. *Kekerasan terhadap Perempuan dalam Gereja* (Violence towards women in the Church). Yogyakarta, 1995. This book caused the temporary dismissal of Ibu Nunuk as lecturer at the Catholic faculty in Yogyakarta.
    Toba-Sarumpaet, Riris K. *Perempuan di Rumah Tuhan* (A woman in the Lord's house. Biography of Julia Sarumpaet-Hutabarat by her daughter). Jakarta: Persetia, 1998.

1.4. Ecumenical and Professional Contacts
1.4.1. International

Together with the World Council of Churches (WCC) the Christian Conference of Asia (CCA) has enormously influenced the development of Protestant theology in Indonesia. Outside contacts were one decisive way in which otherwise widely-scattered ethnic church enclaves were opened up to developments elsewhere, and so local and national issues have always had to be thought through within a worldwide ecumenical frame. But for periodic bouts of tension between the CCA and Communion of Churches in Indonesia (PGI), a more representative selection of Indonesian theology would surely be available in English.

Distance learning through the Southeast Asia Graduate School of Theology (SEAGST) led to a considerable number of Masters' and Doctor of Ministry dissertations being written in practical and contextual theology in English by Protestants (see Erari, 4.19).

Beginning with the impact of the Second Vatican Council (1962-65) and continuing with the ongoing work of the Federation of Asian Bishops' Conferences (FABC) since 1970, and through the regular interchange of personnel within international religious orders, Catholic theologians have been exposed to trends and movements throughout the region and the wider world.

Selected References

> Alangaram, A. *Christ of the Asian Peoples: Towards an Asian Contextual Christology Based on the Documents of the FABC*. Bangalore: Asian Trading Corporation, 1999. With index. The first analysis of an "emerging" Christology among the leadership of Asian Catholic Churches.
>
> FABC Office of Theological Concerns. *Methodology: Asian Christian Theology. Doing Theology in Asia Today*. Hong Kong: FABC Papers 96. A carefully worked-out theological methodology to support the contextualising of Asian Catholic Churches.
>
> Quatra, Miguel Marcelo. *At the Side of the Multitudes: The Kingdom of God and the Mission of the Church in the FABC Documents*. Manila: Claretian Publications, 2000. The

"implicit" mission theology of Asian Catholic bishops and theologians.

Siwu, Richard. *Misi dalam Pandangan Ekumenikal dan Evangelikal Asia 1910-1961* (Ecumenical and evangelical views of mission in Asia 1910-1961). Jakarta: BPK Gunung Mulia, 1996. Compares mainstream and evangelical approaches.

Tan, Jonathan. "Missio ad Gentes in Asia: A Comparative Study of the Missiology of John Paul II and the Federation of Asian Bishops' Conferences (FABC)." Ph.D. Dissertation, Catholic University of America (2002). Available from UMI.

Weber, H.R. *Asia and the Ecumenical Movement 1895-1916*. London: SCM Press, 1964.

Yap Kim Hao *From Prapat to Colombo. History of the Christian Conference of Asia (1957-95)*. Hong Kong: CCA, 1995. An overview by those involved.

1.4.2. The Communion of Churches in Indonesia (DGI/PGI)

Among the Protestant Churches, the Council of Churches in Indonesia (DGI) played, and continues to play, a pivotal role. At the Ambon Assembly in 1984 DGI was renamed the Communion of Churches in Indonesia or PGI. At its inception in 1950 there were 29 member churches, in 2000 the total had reached 70. Many of the Protestant scholars in this study held, or still hold, positions in the PGI central executive. They include T.S.G. Moelia (3.2.1.), T.B. Simatupang (3.2.3.), Fridolin Ukur (4.5), Agustina Lumentut (4.10), Marianne Katoppo (4.13), Th. Sumartana (4.14), Andreas A. Yewangoe (4.15) and Karel Phil Erari (4.19). The research unit of PGI (Balitbang) holds regular theological seminars and publishes the proceedings. The DGI/PGI has regularly published the journal *Berita Oikumene,* and also statements and reports of its Assemblies and consultations and an earlier overview of these appears in Cooley (1981). See also Nababan references (4 below).

Website: <http://www.pgi.or.id/balitbang/bai_06.html>.

Selected References

Simatupang, T.B. *Dua Puluh Lima Tahun DGI 1950-1975* (Twenty-five years with the Council of Churches). Jakarta: BPK Gunung Mulia, 1975. An upbeat account by one of the prime movers.

Cooley, F.L. "Bagaimana Terbentuknya DGI" (How the National Council of Churches was formed). *Peninjau* 2.1 (1975). Frank Cooley was involved with DGI from the beginning.

—. *The Growing Seed. The Christian Church in Indonesia*. Jakarta: BPK Gunung Mulia, 1981.

1.4.3. The Association of Theological Schools in Indonesia (Persetia)

Until the latter half of the 20th century, there was no regular forum for theological discussion apart from synods and other ecclesial meetings. Unsurprisingly, until recently few theologians quoted each other. Given the dominance of Javanese culture which prizes "harmony" over other values, few theologians have been willing to debate in public. In a minority church unity is more important than theological dissension, prudence more central than the search for truth.

To meet this need *Perhimpunan Sekolah Teologi Indonesia* (Persetia) - Association of Theological Schools in Indonesia - was established by the Council of Churches in Indonesia (since 1984 PGI) in Sukabumi on 27th October 1963. *Persetia* - the brainchild of Professor Ihromi - is an independent, ecumenical Protestant professional body which works to promote, "critical Indonesian contextual theology," "spiritually and ecumenically committed Indonesian Christian leaders" and "dialogical relationships with all faith communities". To these ends *Persetia* has published a house journal, *Setia*, since 1971 (relaunched by Hadiwijono (3.3.1.) in 1976), and has hosted an annual Study Institute since 1980, while also raising funds for faculty development. Beginning with 17 members in the 1960s, *Persetia* listed 32 member schools on its website in 2000. Though having no organisational link with the Communion of Churches in Indonesia (PGI), in practice *Persetia* is PGI's professional theological partner. Through its regular Study Institutes *Persetia* encourages professionalism, undertakes upgrading and inspires the growth of a more contextual theology among its members. *Persetia* publishes the proceedings of its study institutes and theological symposia (which are not, however, available through bookshops).

Contextual Theological Reflection in Indonesia 1800-2000 135

In 1982 *Persetia* drew up a proposed undergraduate syllabus for its members, which was accepted as an accredited course by the Indonesian government in the 1990s. Since 1996 nine schools have collaborated in drawing up a graduate syllabus (1999-2000).

Persetia E-mail: <persetia@bit.net.id> and <persetia@yahoo.com>

Persetia Website: <http://www.geocities.com/asinths/persetia.html>. The website lists school members, addresses, executive committee, aims and purpose, brief history, journal contents (*Setia*), list of publications, and exchange of views on contemporary projects (syllabus etc.) in both Indonesian and English.

Selected References

Proceedings of the regular Study Institutes are available, such as Church History (1993), Teaching-Learning Workshop (1989 & 1993), Missiology (1992), Communication (1991), Pastoral (1990), Ecclesiology (1988), Spiritual Direction (1984 & 1983), Dogmatics (1983), Islamology (1982), Contextual Exegesis (1980). All in Indonesian.

Women's Biography Series includes:
Rambe Hanna and Margareth Dharma-Angkuw. *Dua Permata Nusantara: Yos Masdani dan Margareth Dharma-Angkuw* (Two national Gems: Yos Masdani and Margaret Dharma-Angkuw). Jakarta: Persetia/PGI, 1999. Two theological biographies.
Solaiman, Antie. *Pelayan Tuhan di Kaki Merapi* (The Lord's servant at the foot of Merapi volcano). Jakarta: Persetia/PGI, 1998. A theological biography.
(See also 1.3. Women Authors.)

1.4.4. Indonesian Conference of Bishops (MAWI, KWI)

In 1924 the Catholic bishops of Indonesia held their first meeting (at Muntilan), the second a year later (at Girisonta). Meetings were held at five-year intervals until 1939. Not until 1955 did the bishops establish a National Conference (MAWI, renamed KWI in 1987). Pope John XXIII officially established the Indonesian hierarchy on 3rd January 1961. Since 1970 the bishops have met annually in Jakarta. Theologians in this study associated with the bishops' conference are Robert Hardawiryana (4.1), Tom Jacobs (4.4), Franz Magnis-Suseno (4.8), J.B. Banawiratma (4.16) and John Prior (4.17).

Catholic biblical theologians have met biannually since the 1980s under the aegis of Lembaga Biblica Indonesia (National Biblical Association), which body also co-ordinates grass-roots practitioners in the biblical apostolate. Philosophers and ethical thinkers have also met regularly. The Commission for Seminaries has arranged occasional conferences for various academic fields. However it was only in the early 1990s that a Theological Commission was established by the Catholic Bishops' Conference (KWI) to assist the bishops in their theological reflection upon current issues. The Commission, together with the Commission for Seminaries, established an association of Catholic theologians, which met for the first time in 1998. The association has been tasked with developing contextual theologies, but is proving slow to get going. The Commission serves the bishops' conference, while the Association is a professional body for its members.

Selected References

Banawiratma, ed. *Gereja Indonesia, Quo Vadis? Hidup Menggereja Kontekstual* (Quo vadis the Indonesian Church? Living as a contextual Church). Yogyakarta: Kanisius, 2000. Most contributions from members of the Bishops' Theological Commission; two are fairly critical, see chapters by Banawiratma and Prior.

Hadiwikato, J., ed. *Himpunan Keputasan Keputasan Mawi*. (Collection of statements 1924-1980. Jakarta: National Conference of Indonesian Bishops Office, ?1981.

Hasto Rosariyanto, F. ed. *Bercermin pada wajah-wajah Keuskupan Gereja Katolik Indonesia* (Mirroring the diocesan faces of the Indonesian Catholic Church). Yogyakarta: Kanisius, 2000. Bulky reports by diocesan secretaries of planning meetings and synods from over a dozen Catholic dioceses.

MAWI. *Indonesian Catholics in the Pancasila State*. Information Series 2. Jakarta: National Conference of Indonesian Bishops Office, 1975.

Penerbit, ed. *Gereja Indonesia Pasca-Vatikan II* (The Post-Vatican II Indonesian Church), Yogyakarta: Kanisius, 1997. Wide-ranging reflections on the past 40 years of developments in the Indonesian Catholic Church.

MAWI. "The Evangelization of the Modern World - A Theological Evaluation." *Teaching All Nations* 12.4 (1975).

1.4.5. The Indonesian Religious Leadership Conference (KOPTARI, formerly MASRI)

All Catholic orders of sisters, brothers and priests belong to KOPTARI, which has been responsible for the publication of 28 books on contextual spirituality for their members. Since 1974 they have published 17 books in the *Sumber Hidup* (Source of Life) series (mostly translations), some eight in the *Hidup dalam Roh* (Life in the Spirit) series (Indonesian originals) and a further three in the *Hidup Baru* (New Life) series (Indonesian originals). More recently they have published volumes on "para-normal" phenomena and are preparing a volume on a dialogical-inclusive spirituality.

Selected References

Harjawiyata. *Bentuk-Bentuk Hidup Religius* (Forms of religious life). Yogyakarta: Kanisius, 1979.

—. *Arah Baru Hidup Religius* (New direction in religious life). Yogyakarta: Kanisius, 1993.

Ladjar, Leo. *Inti Hidup Religius* (The core of religious life). Yogyakarta: Kanisius, 1981.

1.5 Journals and Commemorative Volumes

Seri Pastoralia. Founded as a bi-monthly journal in 1937 *Pastoralia* developed into a book series in 1984. Practical and popular theology from Nusa Tenggara, Eastern Indonesia. Edited from Ledalero Seminary, Maumere 86152, Flores-NTT. Since 1989 published by Nusa Indah. Address: Pastoralia, Penerbit Nusa Indah, Jl. El Tari, Ende 86318, Flores-NTT, Indonesia.

Basis since 1951. A bi-monthly cultural journal edited since mid-1950s by Dick Hartoko sj and edited by Sindhunata sj since late 1990s. Not strictly theological but excellent for cultural and ethical context. Address: Majalah Basis, Jl. Cempaka 9, Deresan, Kotak Pos 1299, Yogyakarta 55281, Indonesia. E-mail: <basis@yogya.wasantara.net.id>.

Rohani since 1963. Monthly of spiritual and popular theology edited by the Jesuits. Address: Majalah Rohani, Jl. Cempaka 9, Deresan, Kotak Pos 1125, Yogyakarta 55011, Indonesia. E-mail: <office@kanisius.co.id> Home page: <www.kanisius.co.id>.

Umat Baru since 1967. Bi-monthly of practical theology edited by Catechetical Centre, Yogyakarta. Address: Majalah Umat Baru, PusKat, Jln. Ahmad Jazuli 2, Yogyakarta 55224, Indonesia.

Orientasi began as a theological journal in 1969 and became an annual in 1987 (renamed *Orientasi Baru*). Edited by the Jesuits in Yogyakarta. Address: Orientasi Baru, Jl. Cempaka 9, Deresan, Kotak Pos 1299, Yogyakarta 55281, Indonesia.

Gema Duta Wacana since 1970. Biennial from the Faculty of Theology Duta Wacana University. Address: Gema Duta Wacana, Fak. Theologia UnKris Duta Wacana, Jln. Dr. Wahidin 5, Yogyakarta 55224, Indonesia.

Spektrum since 1971. Quarterly journal of the Documentation Department of the Catholic Bishops' Conference. Contains reports, proceedings and some background theological material. Address: DokPen KWI, Jl. Cut Mutia 10, Jakarta 10340, Indonesia. E-mail: <dokpen10@ub.net.id>.

Setia since 1971. Relaunched in 1976. (Fairly) regular house journal of *Persetia* - the Association of Theological Schools in Indonesia. Address: Setia, Jalan Proklamasi 27, Jakarta 10320, Indonesia. E-mail: <persetia@bit.net.id>. Website: <http://www.geocities.com/asinths/persetia.html>.

Peninjau since 1974. Theological quarterly edited by the Research Unit of the Communion of Churches in Indonesia (Lembaga Penelitian dan Studi PGI). Address: PGI, Jl. Salemba Raya 10, Jakarta Pusat, Indonesia.

Forum Biblika since 1991. Biblical theological biennial (not overtly contextual). Edited by the Indonesian Bible Society (LAI). Address: Forum Biblika, Jl. A. Yani 90, Bogor 16161, Jawa Barat, Indonesia. E-mail: <forum@alkitab.org>.

Penuntun since Oct.-Dec. 1994. Theological quarterly edited by the Synod of the Protestant Church of West Java (GKIJB). Address: Jl. Tanjung Duren Raya 4, Blok E, Lantai IV, Jakarta 11740, Indonesia.

Sophia: Jurnal Berteologi Perempuan Indonesia (Sophia: an Indonesian women's theological journal). Launched in March 2000 by *Perwati* (Association of Women with Theological

Education). Three times a year; edited by Septemmy E. Lakawa from the Jakarta School of Theology. Address: Jurnal Sophia, Jl. Proklamasi 27, Jakarta Pusat 10320, Indonesia. E-mail: <perwatijkt@hotmail.com>.

From 2000 a spate of new journals are planned, such as *Discursus* from Driyarkara, Jakarta and *Jurnal Ledalero* from Maumere, Flores. Apart from journals, most Protestant theologians are honoured with one or more *Festschrifte*, some of considerable length. Most published by BPK Gunung Mulia or directly by *Persetia*.

1.6 Periods

We can divide theological development in Indonesia into four periods with some 20th century authors spanning more than one. Key social and political issues as well as parallel changes in the evangelical and ecumenical landscape define each period. The first phase runs from 1860 to 1910 (first generation religious-cultural synthesis in a colonial state); the second from 1911-45 (the impact of national awakening upon Christian self-awareness); the third from 1946-65 (beginning the task of doing theology in a newly independent nation in increasingly poly-centric churches), and the fourth from 1966 to the end of the 20th century (towards systematic, contextual theologies amidst the tensions and opportunities of religious pluralism and economic globalization). While the earlier periods have been recorded only through the lenses of expatriate missioners, the latter periods are defined by the emergence of local and national writers who take their more important themes from the national ecclesial and social context.

The translation of the gospel of St. Matthew into Malay in 1629 by Cornelius Ruyl, an agent of the Dutch East India Company (VOC), is probably the first Scripture publication in a non-Semitic Asian language. (Refer chap. 2, above). However, the theology of the 19th century was spoken in Javanese and recorded in Dutch. Twentieth century theology is written largely in Indonesian with some Dutch. Gradually, a corpus of work is appearing in English language publications, initially through thesis writing and then through international colloquia. Thus, a bibliography confined to

English and Dutch would not be representative of Indonesian theology. However, acknowledging the accessibility of the English language, wherever possible selected references at the end of each section refer to English language publications. Those with a grasp of the Indonesian language should consult the more comprehensive Indonesian bibliography prepared by the author.

Selected References

Cooley, Frank. *The Growing Seed: The Christian Church in Indonesia.* Ende: Nusa Indah; Jakarta: BPK Gunung Mulia, 1982.

— and Fridolin Ukur, eds. *Benih yang Tumbuh* (The growing seed). Jakarta: Lembaga Penelitian dan Studi (LPS) DGI (Council of Churches). 1975-77. 23-volume study of the churches in Indonesia edited by the research unit of the Council of Churches (then DGI now PGI). The first major effort of Indonesian Protestants to rediscover their history and publish it in popular form.

End, Th. van den and J. Weitjens. *Ragi Carita: Sejarah Gereja di Indonesia, II. th. 1860an - sekarang* (History of the Church in Indonesia II, 1860s to contemporary times). Jakarta: BPK Gunung Mulia, 1993. Protestant and Catholic histories parallelled.

Fenn, Eric. "The Bible and the Missionary". In *The Cambridge History of the Bible*, edited by S.L. Greenslade, 283-407. Cambridge: University Press, 1978.

Steenbrink, Karel, *Catholics in Indonesia 1808-1942. A Documented History* I: A Modest Recovery 1808-1903; Vol II: 1903-42. Leiden: KITLV Press, forthcoming. Includes extensive primary sources. By far the most detailed and analytic history to date.

2. The Emergence of Written Theological Reflection in Indonesia, ca 1860-1945

Theological reflection before 1945 comes from Christians without formal theological training. While little of the theological reflections extant during the first sixty years (1860-1920) was published - or published only many years later - it was nevertheless influential in giving a basic direction to the theological assumptions of both the Protestant and Catholic Churches until independence (proclaimed in 1945, legal settlement in 1949). The first professional voices in theology are heard only in the latter half of the 20th century. During the 1980s and 1990s there was a renewed interest in the 19th century.

2.1 Early Echoes: 1860-1910

This was a turbulent period. There were continual revolts against the Dutch colonisers - Diponegoro (1825-30) in Java; the Padri revolt in West Sumatra (1834-37); guerrilla campaigns in Aceh from 1870 onwards; Batak revolts in Sumatra (1880-1907); and the pacification of Flores (1906-12).

The so-called "ethical policy" of the Dutch government of 1901 led to the "modernisation" of the colony of Indonesia. Large-scale infra-structural projects disrupted village equilibrium, while the advent of schooling opened up local cultures. In 1920 a mere 7.4% of the population was literate. However, in the mission churches there was little indication of the national awakening already irrupting in Muslim circles. Co-operation between the various Protestant Churches is already apparent. There was little emphasis upon confessional creeds.

Written sources for the 19th century consist of diaries, letters and reports from expatriates. In these are found sermons and traditional *tembang* (sung or recited Javanese poetry) in fragmentary form (Hoekema 1994/97:40-42). These in turn were incorporated into biographical or autobiographical sketches. In the 20th century these sources are supplemented with the emergence of pamphlets (tracts) and (more or less) regular journals. This development assisted the transition from oral (contextual) theology to written "confessional" (western) theology.

Selected References

> Kartodirdjo, Sartono. *Religious Movements of Java in the 19th and 20th Centuries.* Yogyakarta: Universitas Islam Indonesia, 1970. A re-appropriation of the 19th century.
> Hoekema, Alle Gabe, *Deken in dynamisch evenwicht: de wordingsgeschiedenis van de nationale protestantse theologie in Indonesie (ca. 1860-1960).* Goudstratt: Uitgeverij

Boekencentrum, B.V. 1984. Extensive bibliography. Indonesian translation without bibliography Jakarta: BPK Gunung Mulia, 1997. A thorough study climaxing many years of meticulous research. PhD thesis.

—. "Developments in the Education of Preachers in the Indonesian Mennonite Churches". *Mennonite Quarterly Review* 59.4 (1985).

In the Protestant Churches five remarkable first-generation evangelists made creative attempts at spreading the Word in East and Central Java. None of their work was published during their lifetime. They were concerned with Javanese mysticism (*kebatinan*), mythology and literary forms. Their teaching was both eschatological and moralistic. Catholics were not yet theologising; they were busy recommencing their mission work after a 300-year ban.

2.1.1. C.L. Coolen (1775-?1873)

Coolen was born in Semarang to a noble Javanese mother and a Russian father. After work as a draughtsman and then as government forester in Modjoagung, an ancient centre of Javanese culture, he settled at Ngoro with his family. With colleagues he commenced clearing land where Coolen established a Christian community, the first of a series of communities that he founded. Coolen formed churches in complete identification with the rural peoples employing their traditional patterns of agriculture, despite opposition from both colonial government and missionary bodies. He insisted upon generous labour and leasing conditions and the villages prospered. By 1844 there were 986 people living in 12 Christian hamlets. Muslims were welcome to join any of these while maintaining their faith. For the majority, he established patterns of Christian and ethical instruction and church order quite independent of the Dutch missionaries.

Coolen's vision was not only one of independent and self-supporting villages, but also one of a Christian community rooted in Java's religious heritage and in the traditional life of rice-cultivators. Thus his preaching and teaching integrated Javanese culture with the Christian Gospel in self-reliant agrarian communities aligned to the ongoing processes and festivals of rural Java. He used vernacular Javanese terms, traditional music and himself drew a series of large teaching pictures. His effective biblical expositions drew freely on Javanese Hinduism, which he knew well, while his prayers invoked also the power of land, labour and harvest. He valued *wayang* (traditional shadow puppet plays) and *selametan* (traditional religious meals) but avoided baptism as divisive. His summary of the creed, which he set to Javanese melody, was Muslim in form, declaring that "I believe that Allah is One. There is no God but Allah. Jesus Christ and the Spirit of Allah have power over everything..." Coolen's influence would continue in pioneers like Paulus Tosari (see 2.1.2. below) who long continued to use this creed.

Selected References

> Coolen, C.L. Prayers, letters and the creed of Coolen are given in *Sri and Christ* by P. van Akkeren (see below).
> Bruckner, G.W. "Letter to the Baptist Missionary Society." *Missionary Herald*, 1842.
> Harthoorn, S.E. *De Evangelische Zensing in Oost-Java*. Haarlem: A.C. Kruseman, 1863.
> Poensen, C. Letters in *Mededelingen vanwege het Nederlansch Zendeling-genootschap* (MNZG); *tijdschrift voor zendingswetenschap* 24 (1880).
> van Akkeren, Philip. *Sri and Christ. A Study of the Indigenous Church of East Java*. London: Lutterworth Press, 1970.

2.1.2. Paulus Tosari (1813-82), East Java

Tosari was born in Kedung-Turi near Surabaya, East Java. After his baptism in 1844 he went to live in the Christian community of Mojowarno - an eerie place of ghosts and spirits; the ideal spot for a mystic. Tosari was above all a catechist who spent his life teaching elders and new disciples through reciting or singing his mystical-ethical poems (*tembang*) in the style of the Muslim *santri* a century earlier. His wisdom poems take up biblical figures, mostly from the Old Testament, as stepping-stones to illuminate the characteristics and attitudes of a person of faith. His most famous poem-song is *Rasa Sedjati* (the most real and deepest meaning of life) probably composed in 1872 but published only in 1925 some 43 years after his death. (Last published in 1953 - some 22 songs, probably only half of the original total). Tosari takes up Islamic mystical thought from East Java and also pre-Islamic thought from the ancient Javanese-Hindu literature such as the *Sang Hyang Widi* (The Highest Divinity that ensures the unity of the entire cosmos). He seems to have avoided specifically Christian terms, even referring to churches as "mosques". Jesus was rarely mentioned by name, but was revealed as *djanma sampurna* "the perfect human". While pietism was dominant among the small first generation Christian community (brought by the Dutch and German missioners), Tosari insisted that the mystic was to live an ethical life. Madja Sir (1967) claims that these wisdom poems breathe an authentic biblical faith and admirably translate Gospel morals into the nineteenth century religious culture of East Java.

Selected References

Tosari, Paulus. "Ngelingake marang wong kang padha kaul, kanthi tembang asmaradana." (no date) UB Leiden, L Or 11.648, 4p. (Javanese)

— *Rasa Sedjati Pethikan saking Serat Rasa Sedjati, karanganipun Swargi Kyai Paulus, ing Tosari. Mendhet saking babon kini kanthi karesikaken.* Probably composed in 1872. (1953) Jakarta: Taman Pustaka Kristen. (Javanese)

Mardja Sir. *Kiayi Paulus Tosari (Pelopor Geredja Kristen Djawi di Djawa Timur)* (Kiayi Paul Tosari: Pioneer of the Protestant Church in East Java) (1967). Jakarta: BPK Gunung Mulia. First of the "re-discoveries" of Tosari.

Wieringa, Edwin P. "Het christendom als het ware inzicht. Hendrik Kraemers uitgave van Paulus Tosari's Rasa Sejati', in Molen, W. van der & Arps, B., eds., *Woord en schrift in de Oost* (2000). Leiden, 56-88. A comparison of the 19th century indigenous evangelist with one of the most prominent 20th century mission thinkers.

van Akkeren, Philip. *Sri and Christ. A Study of the Indigenous Church of East Java.* London: Lutterworth Press, 1970.

2.1.3. Asa Kiman (died 1892), East and Central Java

In 1851 Asa Kiman went to Mojowarno where he worked for a few years with Paulus Tosari (2.1.2.). About 1864 he moved to

Contextual Theological Reflection in Indonesia 1800-2000 145

Semarang in central Java and died in 1892. Unlike Tosari he wore western clothes and his western ways were blamed for the people's resistance to Christianity. Later partly incapacitated, he spent his time writing Javanese wisdom poems for recitation/singing. Only one such poem *Panggugh* is extant (Legatum Warneranum, Leiden). Through his verses Asa invited his fellow Javanese to live wisely. Gradually, verse by verse, hearers are brought to the person of Christ who is presented as *nabi panutan* (the prophet to be emulated). Christ's name is mentioned for the first time only in the fourth verse. Asa is thus much more didactic than Tosari. He finds a place in the tree of history for Islamic and Hindu branches. If Tosari catechised his elders and disciples, Asa was evangelising the non-baptised. While Tosari sung the results of his own Javanese-Christian mystical experience, Asa translated the message of the Western evangelists into Javanese recitative poems.

Selected Reference

Hoekema, Alle Gabe. *Deken in dynamisch evenwicht: de wordingsgeschiedenis van de nationale protestantse theoogie in Indonesie (ca. 1860-1960)*. Goudstratt: Uitgeverij Boekencentrum, B.V., 1994. Indonesian translation without extensive bibliography (1997) Jakarta: BPK Gunung Mulia, 400pp.

2.1.4. Ibrahim Tunggul Wulung (ca. 1800-85), Central Java

Ibrahim Tunggul Wulung was probably born on the north coast of central Java. He hailed from the ranks of the upper caste (*priayi*). For some years he lived as an ascetic on the slopes of Mount Kelud in East Java where he had a mystical conversion to Christianity. In 1853 he went to Mojowarno to live with Tosari (2.1.2.) and Asa (2.1.3.), and a year later was baptised. Although some western evangelists were concerned with his lack of formal instruction in Christianity, Tunggul Wulung travelled the island of Java as a wandering evangelist, finally setting up his abode at Bondo, near the north coast, a sacred spot full of ghosts and spirits. There he practised his mystical science (*ngilmu*) among a congregation of disciples. They anticipated the coming of the *Ratu Adil* (mythical Just Ruler to end corruption and usher in an era of peace). The disciples became convinced that Tunggul Wulung himself would establish a kingdom at Bondo and so refused to take part in the forced-work projects of the colonial government. In his sixties Tunggul Wulung still walked from village to village and from town to town proclaiming the Gospel without receiving income from any source. (The walk from Batavia in the West to Semarang in the centre took a good 25 days). His teaching was given in the form of prayers. The Ten Commandments, the Lord's Prayer, the Apostles' Creed and other prayers were recited as "living mantras". He interpreted the Gospel eschatologically - "How blessed are the meek (dispossessed) for you will inherit the earth." He was convinced that Javanese Christians would obtain self-autonomy. He gathered disciples into an eschatological community awaiting the coming of the *Ratu Adil* (the just ruler) while acknowledging the whole of humanity as the People of God.

The core of his evangelism was little different from the mysticism that he had taught on the slopes of Mount Kelud before his baptism: "don't murder, or steal, or commit adultery, that is, love your neighbour." He did not look upon biblical stories, including the birth, death and resurrection of Jesus, as history so much as wisdom literature with hidden meanings that open up their treasure through ascetical practices. Thus, he had little problem in integrating Javanese mysticism and Islam into his new-found faith. He claimed that every nation that became Christian must have its own acknowledged leaders. It was wrong for the Javanese to join with the European evangelists; they should become Javanese Christians and seek out their own Christ.

Tunggul's church can be understood as a nineteenth-century social protest movement, an expression of the social frustration and national hope of the colonised Javanese. Thus, he combined within himself the stillness of the mystic and the dynamism of the social activist. Unfortunately, only fragments of his writings survive, largely in the letters, reports and diaries of his Dutch evangelists (adversaries).

Selected References

Hoekema, A.G. "Kyai Ibrahim Tunggul Wulung (c.1800-85), 'een Javaanse Apollos'". *NthT* 33.2 (1979) 89-110.

Sindhunata, G.P. "Hoffen auf den Ratu-Adil: das eschatologische Motiv des 'Gerechten Koenigs' im Bauernprotest auf Java waehrend des 19. und zu Beginn des 20. Jahrhunderts" Hamburg: Kovac, 1992. A PhD thesis that analyses the links between 19th century Javanese popular religion and political protest.

Yoder, Lawrence M. *The Introduction and Expression of Islam and Christianity in the Cultural Context of North Central Java.* Ann Arbor: University Microfilms International. 1987. (See, ch.5, especially "The Muria Javanese Christian Movement", 281-345).

2.1.5. Sadrach Surapranata (1835-1924), Central Java

Born to a noble family, Sadrach has received some attention by scholars. Coming from the north coast of central Java, he studied Islamic law and became a *santri* (teacher). Through contacts with Mojowarno he met with Asa Kiman (2.1.3.) and later went to Bondo to meet Tunggul Wulung (2.1.4.). He stayed with Tunggul Wulung for some years before going his own way. Baptised in the Indische Kerk (1867), he afterwards met Paulus Tosari (2.1.2.) in Mojowarno. In 1870 he decided to establish his own congregation at Karangjoso - a sacred, eerie site.

As a former *santri* he evangelised by engaging traditional Islamic teachers (*kiyai*) in debate. Such poetic dialogues were a key way of doing theology in the nineteenth century. Social unrest, including the then recent revolt of Diponegoro (1825-30), led to a rapid increase in his congregation and within a short time he had built up self-governing, self-financing and self-propagating congregations, decades before that became general policy. In old age, tired of continual conflicts with the Gereformeerd Church, he joined the Apostolic Church in which he was accepted as an apostle (Sumartana 1994:60-69).

Not a single writing survives from this remarkable evangelist. Sadrach almost certainly wrote a book on church order, composed his own book of worship, prayers for private and congregational use, and a summary of Christian law and discipline. He paraphrased parts of the Gospel (eg Mat 22:37-40) in *tembang* - song-poems. We know of his work only through the writings of European evangelists. He called churches "mosques" and installed a wooden *bedug* to call people to worship and used the term *imam* for official ministers. He was convinced there was no need to imitate European congregational order. The term *guru* was at the heart of Sadrach's Christology (Sutarman Partonadi (1988:224). Jesus was the holy *guru*, who obeyed Allah's law to death. He healed the sick and expelled devils. We follow Jesus as *guru* and *panutan* (exemplar), the perfect one. Sadrach embraced wisdom from Javanese culture, law from Islam while doctrinal content came from the Gospel.

The first expatriate missioner to appreciate the Protestant Sadrach was the Jesuit van Lith (2.1.7.) (1924). Only in recent years are Tosari and Sadrach being acknowledged as the pioneers of a truly contextualised Christianity (Simatupang 1976:92-93).

Sadrach was the last of the great nineteenth century evangelists who preached in an indigenous way. Rapid economic development at the turn of the century and the national awakening from 1908 onwards - which emphasised the pivotal importance of formal education - side-lined the lifestyle and evangelical methods of these mystics. Ironically enough, when much later European evangelists finally began to speak of indigenisation, Indonesian evangelists had already become modern (western). The modernisation and later independence of Indonesia entailed leaving aside the "burden of tradition."

Selected References

Cuillot, C. *L'Affaire Sadrach, Un Esai de Christianisation a Java au XIX Siecle*. Paris: Archipel, 1981. (Indonesian trans. *Kiai Sadrach. Riwayat Kristenisasi di Jawa*, Jakarta: Grafiti Press, 1985.)

Lith, F. van. *Kjahi Sadrach. Eene les voor ons uit de Protestantische Zending van Midden-Java*. (Kyai Sadrach: A Lesson for us from the Protestant Mission in Central Java). From writings 1921-22, 1924. (Translated into Indonesian by Weitjens SJ in 1974). As much a critique of fellow Jesuits as an appreciation of Sadrach.

Partonadi, Soetarman S. *Sadrach's Community and its Contextual Roots. A Nineteenth Century Javanese Expression of Christianity*. Amsterdam: Rodopi, 1990. Amsterdam: Vrije

Universitetit, PhD dissertation 1988. Indonesian trans. *Komunitas Sadrach dan Akar Kontekstualnya*. Jakarta: BPK Gunung Mulia, 2001. A positive appreciation.

Rullmann, J.A.C. "De Sadrach Christenen. Hun beekenis voor vandaag." *Seri Allerwegen* 2.3 (1971).

Simatupang, T.B. "Dynamics for Creative Maturity," in G.H. Anderson, ed., *Asian Voices in Christian Theology*. Maryknoll, NY: Orbis Books, 1976.

Sumartana, Th. "The End of a Conflict: Sadrach and the Gereformeerde Mission," in *Mission at the Crossroads: Indigenous Churches, European Missionaries, Islamic Association and Socio-Religious Change in Java 1812-1936*. Jakarta: BPK Gunung Mulia, 1994. A nuanced, yet positive, appreciation.

2.1.6. Distanced from Islam

Much of the oral theology in Java during the second half of the 19th century was didactic and moralistic. It had an immediate impact on daily life without causing dissension while leaving wider questions of religion to one side. The main partner in religious debate was Javanese mysticism rather than Islam. Those outside Java had little direct contact with Muslims. Also, the colonial government censured anything that might give rise to inter-religious tension. European evangelists were paid government employees. The ecumenical seminary at Depok received its intake from ethnic areas where Islam was not dominant. Similarly, the journals *Bentara Hindia*, *Djahaja Sijang* and *Penhentar* (Ambon) had no Islamic background.

This oral "declamatory theology" was authentically Javanese - in form, content and expression. It was an initial - later disbanded - effort by first-generation Protestant Christians to forge a local Christian identity. After 1910 Christian mission shifted from village to town, from traditional leadership to schools and formal teaching.

From the fragmentary evidence available, it seems clear that little, if anything, of the social turmoil of the times is reflected in these writings. No evangelist other than coolen, proposed concrete social programmes in response to economic hardship or political repression.

Ecumenical co-operation (without Catholic participation) was more advanced in Indonesia than in the sending churches themselves - all the major evangelists knew each other and regularly communicated with each other. The seminary at Depok was ecumenical and the writings, tracts and journal it produced were free of denominational allegiance.

As the 21st century commences, the contemplative life and the need for cosmic harmony are still in line with the cultural philosophy of Java. Another 19th century theme - the Gospel and local customary law - is still a live issue with the ordinary believer, particularly outside Java.

Selected References

Aritonang, Jan S. "Sejarah Perjumpaan Gereja dan Islam di Indonesia" (History of the meeting of the Church and Islam in Indonesia). In *Agama dalam Dialog. Punjung Tulis 60 Tahun Prof. Dr. Olaf Herbert Schumann*, 179-201. Jakarta: BPK Gunung Mulia, 1999. An analysis by an Indonesian historian.

Azra, Azyumardi. "The race between Islam and Christianity theory revisited. Islamisation and Christianisation in the Malay-Indonesian archipelago 1530-1670." *Docmentatieblad voor de Geschiedenis van de Nederlandse Zending in Oorzeese Kerken.* 2 (2000). An appreciation of the decisive period that still influences Christian-Muslim relations by the Rector of the Muslim University in Jakarta (IAIN).

Hoekema, Alle. "Indonesische christenen over de Islam". *Kerk en Theologie*, 49.1.

Steenbrink, Karel. *Dutch Colonialism and Indonesian Islam - Contacts and Conflicts 1596-1950*. Amsterdam, 1993. An "objective" reappraisal by a Christian student of Islam.

—. "The Rehabilitation of Indigenous Teachers. A Survey of Recent Research on the History of Christianity in Indonesia." *Exchange* 22 (1993). Shifting attention from incoming missioners to indigenous evangelists.

Yoder, Lawrence M. *The Introduction and Expression of Islam and Christianity in the Cultural Context of North Central Java*. Ann Arbor: University Microfilms International, 1987. A comparison of 19th century mission by Muslims and Christians from an evangelical perspective.

2.1.7. Francis George Joseph Van Lith sj (1863-1926), Netherlands and Central Java

Towards the end of this period the Catholic Church was re-founded in Central Java by Francis van Lith, who arrived in Indonesia in 1896. In contemporary "mythologised" history, the Catholic Church was "re-born" when van Lith baptised four village leaders on 20th May and 168 others at the ancient sacred spring of Sendangsono on 15th December 1904. Sendangsono has since become the main pilgrimage centre for Javanese Catholics. This Marian shrine was rebuilt in the 1980s and 1990s by the political-mystic, novelist-architect Mangunwijaya (4.3). A "van Lith Centre" is being established in Muntilan where van Lith spent the greater part of his ministry and is buried. Until his arrival, the Jesuit mission had not been successful (J. Weitjens, 1974:843-60).

Aware that evangelisation depends upon a solid grasp of language - previously Jesuits relied upon catechist-translators - van Lith settled in the village of Muntilan, joining in the villagers' daily life, working in the fields by day and watching shadow puppet shows (*wayang*) at night. He learned each level of the complex Javanese language from everyday conversation to the wisdom of the then neglected ancient literature. Above all he learned to love the people; "*mamanggul*" (become one with them), defending the rights of small-scale farmers, buying back their mortgaged fields, often representing the oppressed villagers to the colonial administrators and high caste Javanese *ningrat*.

Only towards the end of his life, did van Lith put his mission method into writing "*mlebu ing omahe marasake sing loro lan ngandani keratoning Allah ono ing kowe*" - "enter their houses, heal the sick and announce that God's Reign has come", that is, "enter the lives, the culture and the hearts of the people; share their concerns by lessening the burden of sickness and the weight of suffering while sharing the people's joy and harmony". The Javanese could commit themselves to Christ without in any way diminishing their cultural personality or national aspirations. Van Lith - and after him most Christians until recently - held that the *Priyayi* (upper caste) and *Abangan* (lower caste) were not "book

Muslims", for their lives were much influenced by Javanese mysticism and thus open to Christianity.

In 1904 van Lith moved to Muntilan itself and opened the first teachers' training school and educated future leaders who had opinions of their own and the ability to mobilise others. This marked a break with his previous "Javanese" immersion; the school taught in Dutch and produced the first generations of Catholic intellectuals who later appeared on the national stage. He founded and edited the journal "*Jawi Seroja*" from 1914.

Contemporary admirers say that van Lith emancipated culture through formal education, politics through siding with the Javanese, and religion by presenting Christian faith as the fulfilment of Javanese religious experience.

Van Lith pressured the Jesuits into opening the first seminary, which they did in Yogyakarta (1922). He had a considerable influence on the first generation of indigenous recruits, including Sugijapranata, first Archbishop of Semarang, and Leo Soekoto, a former Archbishop of Jakarta. He initiated the policy of sending student missioners to Java to learn Javanese Indonesian and study for the priesthood among the people they would later serve. The last generation of this policy is still at work (Tom Jacobs (4.4), Franz Magnis-Suseno (4.8)).

In contemporary Catholic terms, van Lith was both an (elite) inculturationist and a (moderate) liberationist in his lived-out theological praxis.

Selected References
Works by Francis van Lith

Kjahi Sadrach. *Eene les voor ons uit de Protestantische Zending van Midden-Java.* (Kyai Sadrach: A Lesson for us from the Protestant Mission in Central Java) (1924). From writings 1921-22. (Translated into Indonesian by Weitjens sj in 1974.) Van Lith's critique of the Jesuit mission to date via an appreciation of Sadrach.

"De politiek van Nederland ten opzichte van Nederlandswch-Indie." *Studien. Tijdschrift voor godsdienst, wetenschap en letteren.*

54 (1922). Van Lith's political position four years after his appointment to the Volksraad (People's Council).

Hasto Rosaniyanto Floribertus. *Father Franciscus van Lith, SJ (1863-1926): Turning Point of the Catholic Church's Approach in the Pluralistic Indonesian Society.* Extract of Doctoral Dissertation. Rome: Pontifical Gregorian University, 1997. Includes 3 pages of manuscript sources from Indonesia, The Netherlands and Rome, one page of printed sources in The Netherlands and Rome and 26 pages of bibliography (pp.110-135). (Complete dissertation contains 363 pages of text.) Descriptive rather than analytical.

Klinken, Gerry van. "Power, Symbol and the Catholic Mission in Java: The Biography of Frans van Lith S.J.." *Docmentatieblad geschiedenis Nederlandse Zending en Overszeese Kerken,* 4.1 (1997). Well researched, very critical.

Muskens, M.P.M. *Partner in Nation Building: The Catholic Church in Indonesia.* Aachen: Missio Aktuell Verlag, 1979. Especially "Father van Lith and the foundation of the Perkumpulan Politik katolik di Djawa", 133-140. Underlines van Lith's pro-Javanese credentials.

Rijckevorsel, L. van. *Pastoor F. van Lith S.J., De Stichter van de Missie in Midden-Java; 1863-1926.* Nijmegen,Stichting St. Claverbond etc, 1952. A hagiographical study.

2.2 The Impact of National Awakening and Independence 1910-45

2.2.1. Clearing the Deck: 1911-42

As with the rest of Asia during the first half of the 20th century, Indonesia underwent a national awakening with seismic shifts in the social, cultural, educational and political fields. The political movement for independence crystalised with the proclamation of independence in 1945, the war to retain independence (1945-49), and the international acknowledgement of Indonesia's independent political existence in December 1949.

Both Protestants and Catholics were somewhat ambiguous towards nationalist aspirations right up until the Japanese defeated the Dutch in 1942. Apart from the pietist and individualistic spirituality of the sending churches, which had little concern with societal issues, Indonesian Protestants felt a conflict of loyalties between the wider Christian (western) world, including the Dutch colonisers, and the nationalist sentiments mobilised by both secular and Muslim organisations. In the towns of Java the membership of congregations, both Protestant and Catholic, was usually dominated by western expatriates and the Chinese-Indonesian minority. The latter kept out of politics while working for the rulers in trade and finance. The Dutch policy of dividing the islands and ethnic groups between different denominations, led to the growth of ethnic churches with local rather than national concerns, for instance, the Batak churches in Sumatra, the Timorese, Florenese and Sumbanese churches in Nusa Tenggara and the churches of Halmahera, Ambon and North Sulawesi. Regional seminaries taught along denominational lines with local issues in mind.

However, a slow opening-up was taking place. Local ethnic-based churches began the process of regular contact and mutual influence. The Indonesian Protestant Churches entered the wider ecumenical movement, while Catholic dioceses were serviced by expatriates, priests, Sisters and Brothers, who maintained continuous contact with their international missionary orders. It has to be noted that the ecumenical and national voices of the graduates from the Depok Seminary were heard only after the Dutch were defeated in 1942.

Theology was still largely western. No Indonesian graduate theologians were heard during this period. A clear Indonesian identity had yet to surface. While much oral theology continued at the grass-roots level, little has been investigated to date. There were no overt polemics, either narrowly denominational, anti-Protestant/Catholic or anti-Muslim. The Protestant emphasis was upon replacing the dependent missions with self-sufficient churches led by local personnel, while Catholics were busy baptising new members and building up a local clergy. At mid-20th century with a population of half a million, the island of Flores was baptised between 1920 and 1960 - except for a significant Muslim presence on the coast and in the towns. In the Protestant Churches there was the first organised attempt to publish theology in the Indonesian language by the *Komisi Lektur* in the 1920s. Paulus Tosari's work was published but not that of Sadrach.

Contextual Theological Reflection in Indonesia 1800-2000 155

Perhaps due to the ethnic base of most churches in this vast archipelago, and because of language problems (Dutch, many local languages and Malay/Indonesian), the Protestant Churches of Indonesia were late on the wider ecumenical stage. However, they proved themselves more ecumenical and less denominational than their partners in the Netherlands and Germany. Ecumenical involvement began with the visit of John Mott to Indonesia in 1926 and the subsequent presence of T.S.G. Moelia (3.2.1.) at Jerusalem in 1928. Theologians struggled with problems about local customary law, with the first generation of ordained Indonesian presbyters, and with the history of confessional churches (the emerging question of identity). Some Indonesians were already taking more positive stances towards customary law than their expatriate colleagues. Catholics studied the local languages, producing dictionaries and ethnological accounts of the peoples with whom they worked. Although they brought with them the neo-scholastic theology prevalent in Catholic Europe, nevertheless cultural understanding led to much unofficial adaptation. All churches retained a deafening silence on Islam, the religion of over 80% of Indonesians. Regular Protestant-Catholic contact began only in the mid-1960s.

Selected References

Kraemer, H. *From Mission Field to Independent Church*. The Hague, 1958. A seminal work from a controversial figure regarded as a centennial giant by some, a paternalist by others.

Steenbrink, Karel. *Catholics in Indonesia. Vol. II: 1904-42*. Leiden: KITLV Press, forthcoming. Including extensive primary documentation. The most comprehensive text available.

Weitjens, J.A. Th. *De vrijheid der katholieke prediking in Nederlands-Indie van 1900 tot 1940*. Rome/Jakarta: Gregorian University, 1969. Extract from PhD thesis. A meticulous piece of research.

2.2.2. Japanese Occupation - A Defining Experience: 1942-45

In March 1942 Japan invaded Indonesia and within a short time occupied the islands, some of which had been colonised informally by the VOC and, since 1702, more formally by the Dutch.

Understandably, many local church leaders collaborated with the Japanese occupiers. However, many teachers, presbyters and church members showed their mettle.

For all churches, the three-year occupation marked a short, sharp transition to adulthood. In 1939 all the German Protestant and Catholic evangelists were interned. In 1942, with the coming of the Japanese, it was the turn of the Dutch. While the Protestant Churches already had elders and councils and synods in place, the Catholic Churches only now allowed lay village catechists and primary school teachers to take over the (temporary) running of the parishes. The churches - without much preparation - were on their own. A few Japanese clergy, both Protestant and Catholic, were brought in by the occupiers. While no theology was published during this period, the experience of having to stand on one's own feet was a major contribution to the later maturing of theology in an independent Indonesia. Sermon notes, diaries and reports from the villages and congregational leaders have yet to be collected, organised and made available to research. Emergent leaders at the local level together with the young graduates began to "do theology" on their own for the first time.

Since the outbreak of war in Europe in 1939, the Protestant Churches in Indonesia had been accelerating their self-reliant policy. School boards and church bodies still in Dutch hands were handed over. Overnight, finance had to be found locally. There was also help from the International Missionary Council. No such policy existed in the Catholic Church at that time.

During the war of independence (1945-49) a few key nationalist figures were Christians - in the revolutionary army (Simatupang, 3.2.3.), air force (Adisucipto) and the provisional government (prime minister Sjarifoeddin, 2.2.3.).

Theological reflections on the Japanese occupation have been done by T.B. Simatupang (1972) and Fridolin Ukur (1982). Protestant Christians in Indonesia were forced to shift from a self-understanding of themselves as objects of mission to one of adult subjects in partner churches. Regional co-operation between different denominations was forced. However, without a strong theological foundation, this somewhat forced ecumenism discontinued after independence, and denominations once again took centre stage. On the Catholic side, expatriate missioners with the first generation of Indonesian clergy once again took over the leadership of local congregations from the hands of the lay catechists and teachers. Experience of self-reliance during the Japanese occupation had to be stored in the archives of popular memory until after the Second Vatican Council (1962-65) when the clerical hierarchical church began to move in a more inclusive and synodical direction. Thus, two decades later this "emergency" experience was seen as valuable.

Selected References

> Bank, Jan. *Katholieken en de Indonesische Revolutie*. Uitgeverij Ambo, 1983. Indonesian translation: *Katolik di Masa Revolusi Indonesia* (Catholics at the Time of the Indonesian Revolution). Jakarta: Grasindo, 1999. Extensive bibliography, 819-860.
> Muskens, M., ed. *Sejarah Gereja Katolik Indonesia* (History of the Catholic Church in Indonesia). Ende: Arnoldus, 1974. Vol. IIIa (Sumatra, Kalimantan, Sulawesi-Maluku, Irian Jaya), & Vol. IIIb (Java, Nusa Tenggara). Largely anecdotal with church archive perspective.
> Pandeirot-Langkong, Beatrix. "The Protestant Churches and the Missionary Fields during the Japanese Occupation in Indonesia 1942-1945 in the Japanese Controlled Areas. A Bibliographical Survey". Jakarta, 1996. Unpublished SEAGST thesis.
> Simatupang, T.B. *Report from Banaran: Experiences during the People's War*. Ithaca, NY, 1972. By the most prominent Protestant nationalist - chief of the armed forces.
> Tan Tiat-Han. "The Attitude of Dutch Protestant Missions toward Indonesian Nationalism 1945-49". Ann Arbor, Mich., 1967. Princeton University PhD thesis.
> Ukur, Fridolin. "A Brief History of the Churches in Indonesia." *CTC-Bulletin* 3.2 (1982).

2.2.3. Amir Sjarifoeddin (1907-48), North Sumatra, Java

Born into a prominent Muslim family, Amir Sjarifoeddin converted to Christianity, which event led his mother to commit suicide. A brilliant intellectual, Sjarifoeddin studied law and was fluent in eight languages. He was an outstanding leader who combined fervent nationalism, romantic socialism and prophetic Christianity. Imprisoned by both the Dutch and the Japanese, he was briefly a member of various cabinets in 1946-47. Soekarno appointed him prime minister in July 1947. However, feeling betrayed after negotiating a peace deal with the Dutch, he resigned in January 1948. Joining forces with the opposition he sided with the Madiun "revolt" in September the same year and so was executed as a communist by more moderate nationalists.

Simatupang (3.2.3.) describes Sjarifoeddin as "a prototypical political Christian". He accused the pietist churches' leaders of not preaching the socio-political role of the prophets. His fiery political speeches were redolent with biblical quotes. His faith was a source of personal empowerment and gave him an open, future-oriented form of social solidarity well beyond his Batak ethnic roots and personal Christian commitment. In retrospect, Sjarifoeddin can be described as a prophetic liberationist decades before the advent of liberation theology.

Selected References
Works by Amir Sjarifoeddin
"Het Rassenprobleem in Ned. Indie". In *Mirabile Lectu. Orgaan van het Haarlemsch Gymnasium* 4 (1928).
"Soesoenan Masjarakat dan Perang" (The ordering of society and war). *Semangat Baroe*, 1 (1941).
"Di mana tempat pemuda kita?" (Where is the place of our youth?). *Semangat Baroe*, 24 May (1941). Christian basis for nationalist politics.
"Menoedjoe kedjemaat Indonesia asli" (Towards an indigenous Indonesian congregation). In *Boekoe Peringatan Hari Djadi Isa Al-Maseh* (Book to commemorate the birth of Jesus the Messiah). 1942.
Klinken, Geert Arend van. "Migrant Moralities: Christians and Nationalist Politics in Emerging Indonesia, A Biographical Approach." Brisbane: Griffith University, PhD dissertation, 1996. Especially 189-239; 292-318. Broadly sympathetic.

Willem, Frederik. *Mr. Amir Sjarifoeddin, tempatnya dalam Kekristenan dan dalam perjuangan Kemerdekaan Indonesia* (Amir Sjarifoeddin, his place in Christianity and in the struggle for an independent Indonesia). Jakarta, 1982.

3 Indonesian Thinkers Discover their Voice, ca. 1945-65
3.1 Establishing a Modern Nation: 1945-65

Independence was proclaimed on 17th August 1945. The ecumenical seminary in Jakarta reopened in 1946 and in 1954 was officially accepted by the Council of Churches. A narrowly biblical and ecclesial syllabus still obtained. Only in the 1960s did the seminary become an accredited Graduate School of Theology with clear entrance requirements. In the 1940s and 50s various Protestant Churches opened regional schools of theology, in Macassar (South Sulawesi), Kupang (Timor), Tomohon (North Sulawesi), Pematang Siantar (Sumatra) and Abepura (Papua-land). The Catholic Church also established regional seminaries to complement Kentungan seminary at Yogyakarta in Central Java (1925/36) and Ledalero Seminary in Flores (1937). Catholic seminaries were opened at Malang, East Java (1942/47), Peneleng (Sulawesi, 1954), Pematang Siantar (Sumatra, 1956/67), Bandung (West Java, 1957/69) and Jakarta (1969). Abepura (Papua-land) followed in 1965/69. More recently Kupang (Timor) was established in the 1980s and Pontianak (West Kalimantan) in 1999. In the late 1960s and early 70s both Protestant and Catholic Seminaries became Graduate Schools accredited to the Education Department of the Government. Many have since become faculties in Protestant or Catholic Universities.

There was a great increase in publications. Since the 1920s the Catholic publishers Kanisius (Java, 1922) and Arnoldus-Nusa Indah (Flores, 1926) have produced a large range of popular theology, the content of which has become increasingly biblical from the late 1950s onwards. In 1950 an Emergency Committee led to the founding of Badan Penerbit Kristen (the name of "Gunung Mulia" was added to BPK in 1967) in Jakarta. This ecumenical-Reformed Church publisher produced between 17 and 41 books and pamphlets a year between 1950-60, each edition with between 3,000 and

10,000 copies. The Protestant Indonesian Bible Society (LAI) was founded in 1954, the Catholic Biblical Institute (LBI) a decade later. A new, ecumenical translation of the Bible was instigated and published in 1963 and later accepted by the Catholic Church. By the 1960s all these bodies were in Indonesian hands and published not only translations, but also an increasing number of original works. Protestant, Catholic and more recently Ecumenical Commentaries on the New Testament were published from 1960 onwards; and books on the Old Testament since 1963. Theology began to emerge as a professional discipline.

Nine Protestant Indonesians received doctorates between 1945-60, all overseas; seven of them graduates of the Jakarta School of Theology. Three were on ecclesial subjects, one on the local religious situation, two on religious freedom with the state Pancasila ideology as background, and two on church and society. The national ideology of *Pancasila* was a central focus. The unity of the church is linked to the unity of the nation (then in the process of consolidation with separatist movements still active in Sumatra and Sulawesi, while West Papua was still under the Dutch). Customary law, Javanese mysticism and the Bible all get theological attention. There was still very little on Islam. However, the first systematic theology was finally emerging.

The first generation of Protestant theological writers (until ca.1965) achieved prominence and facility in theology through becoming outstanding church leaders - not through accredited schools. The second generation is more in tune with the need for a thoroughly academic grasp, method and approach (from ca.1965 onwards). Catholic contextual theology has built upon the pioneering breakthrough of educators such as van Lith (2.1.7.) and the groundbreaking work of contextualised philosophers such as Driyarkara (3.3.4.). More recently women have become articulate theologically through exposure to other women's suffering and engagement in women's advocacy and empowerment.

Selected References

Cooley, F.L. "Bagaimana Terbentuknya DGI" (How the National Council of Churches was formed). *Peninjau* 2.1 (1975).

Hoekema, Alle Gabe. "Dissertations by Protestant Theologians in Indonesia - a Short Bibliographical Review." *Exchange* 42 (1985). (Of the 41 theses, 12 were completed before 1965.) First such survey in English.

Muskens, M., ed. *Sejarah Gereja Katolik Indonesia* (History of the Catholic Church in Indonesia). Ende: Arnoldus, 1974. Vol. IIIb. Cf. "Majelis Agung Waligereja Indonesia" (The Bishops' Conference of Indonesia), 1433-1518.

Pattiasina and Sairin, eds. *Gerakan Oikoumene: Tegar Mekar di Bumi Pancasila* (The ecumenical movement: convincing expansion in the land of Pancasila. Commemorating 40 years of the establishment of the National Communion of Churches). Jakarta: BPK Gunung Mulia, 1990. 3rd printing, 1997.

3.2 Opening Horizons: Lay Thinkers take Centre Stage

Three lay writers active during the colonial period played central roles in the Protestant Churches during the first decades of Indonesia's independence.

3.2.1. T.S.G. Moelia (1896-1966), North Sumatra and Jakarta

Born at Padangsidempuan in the Batak Angkela region of North Sumatra, Todung Soetan Goenoeng Moelia was one of the first Protestants to outline a necessary role for Christians in the rapidly developing nationalist movement(s). A quiet, energetic and creative person, he trained as a teacher in Indonesia and the Netherlands (1919-22). Later studying law, geography and anthropology (1929-34), he obtained his doctorate in the latter science in 1933. A voracious reader, he became extremely versatile in mission theology, politics and economics. Moelia's encyclopaedic knowledge resulted in his co-editing the three-volume *Ensiklopedia Indonesia* after independence (1954-56). A member of the Peoples' Assembly during Dutch times (1921-29; 1935-42), he can be described as a cautious nationalist, ready to work with the Dutch for increasing autonomy and eventual independence. Uncomfortable with the revolution (1945-49), Moelia withdrew from politics after independence was achieved.

In his anthropological dissertation in Leiden, *Het primitieve denken in de moderne wetenschap* (1933), opposing the then popular theory of L. Levy-Bruhl, Moelia claimed that the Indonesian "inductive-realistic" way of thinking was equally capable of intellectual achievement as any other nation, given the necessary knowledge and experience. This, among others, was the task of the churches and their schools.

Moelia was the first Indonesian to participate in the wider ecumenical movement, attending Jerusalem in 1928 and, with other Indonesians, Tambaram in 1938. For almost two years he edited the journal *Zaman Baroe* (New Times). In his writings before the Japanese occupation Moelia introduced fellow Protestants to developments taking place in other Asian churches. An educationalist himself, he wrote that absence of such developments in Indonesia was caused by lack of leadership. He was convinced that leadership should be handed over to Indonesians in the shortest possible time. This in turn necessitated collaboration between all local (ethnic) churches for which he struggled on returning from Jerusalem 1928. Moelia wrote extremely cautiously in the field of social justice. On this issue and on the question of colonialism, his cautious stand received no backing from the western leadership in the Protestant Churches.

Never formally trained in theology, he greatly influenced the development of Protestant theology as an academic science. He was the prime mover behind the upgrading of the Jakarta School of Theology (1948), in the founding of the National Bible Society (LAI, 1953) and the Christian University in 1954. He was largely instrumental in the formation of the Council of Churches in Indonesia (DGI) (1948-50) and was its president for the first six years (1950-56), playing a decisive role during the National Assembly of 1956, speaking on stewardship. He himself received a doctorate *honoris causa* from Vrijie Universeit Amsterdam in October 1966 just a month before his death in the same city. The major Protestant publisher BPK added the name "Gunung Mulia" to its title in 1967 in his honour. A dozen of Moelia's publications are available, eight in Dutch and four in Indonesian.

Contextual Theological Reflection in Indonesia 1800-2000   163

Selected References
Works by T.S.G. Moelia

"Perhoeboengan Geredja Lama dan Geredja Baroe" (The relationship between the old and the new Church). *Zaman Baroe* 11.46 (1928).

"Het primitieve denken in de moderne wetenschap." Doctoral thesis, Leiden, 1933.

"Kristen Indonesia dan Masjarkat Indonesia" (Indonesian Christians and Indonesian Society). *Jakin*, 1.3 (1939).

"Utjapan Ketua Badan Pengurus LPTTH pada Hari Peringatan tanggal 27 September 1959" (Speech of the Chair of the Governing Board of the Theological Academy, 27th September 1959). In *Djedjak Langkah Pertama. 25 Tahun Perguruan Tinggi Theologia*. Jakarta: BPK, 1960.

— with K.A.H. Hidding, eds. *Ensiklopedia Indonesia* (Encyclopaedia Indonesia) 3 vols. Bandung, The Hague: Van Hoeve, 1954-56.

Abineno, J.L. Ch., ed. *Oikumene, Geredja dan Masjarakat di Indonesia: Karangan-karangan selaku Penghormatan kepada T.S.G. Mulia* (Ecumenism, Church and society in Indonesia: writings to honour T.S.G. Mulia). Jakarta: BPK, 1965.

Klinken, Geert Arend van. "Migrant Moralities: Christians and Nationalist Politics in Emerging Indonesia, A Biographical Approach." Brisbane: Griffith University, PhD thesis 1996. See Ch. 4 "Kasimo and Mulia Welcome the Modern State" 96-147; also Ch. 9 "Gemeinschaft and Gesellschaft", 330-335. A very critical evaluation.

3.2.2. Johannes Leimena (1905-66), Ambon and Jakarta

Hailing from Ambon, Johannes Leimena was raised in the capital, Jakarta. Active in the WSCF, he helped found the Indonesian SCM. He participated at Tambaram in 1938. Leimena worked as a medical doctor in West Java (1930-41; doctorate 1939). After internment by the Japanese for six months (1942), he worked with the underground. He took part in the International Round Table Discussion at the Hague, which achieved constitutional acknowledgement of Indonesia's independence (1949).

Leimena wrote on the conditions of workers (in *Zaman Baroe*, 1927). He also wrote on the health of the nation and medical ethics, viewing the alleviation of injustice and sickness as the announcement of the grace and love of God. He worked tirelessly for ecumenism among the Protestant Churches and in the nation as a whole (where hundreds of ethnic groups were uniting into a single nation) and internationally (breaking down walls of misunderstanding). He was against an ecumenical "monolithic" church, but envisioned a future federal church between, for instance, the Dutch, Chinese and Indonesian churches.

Leimena was President of the Christian Political Party (*Parkindo*) and a member of most cabinets during 1946-56. The main theme of his life was social justice. He threw himself into the nationalist movement, but with a clear Christian identity. The (ecumenical) churches are the place where the best could be drawn out from each cultural and national grouping. Some years before Barth (1946), Leimena spoke of the (creative) tension between the supra-nationalism of Christianity and nationalist aspirations.

After independence he wrote against *Darul Islam*, communism and separatism (*daerahisme* - literally "localism"). He worked for self-reliant churches that would be an activating yeast in village community development. Promoting co-operatives, he also concerned himself with local culture, especially music. He worked tirelessly to open up narrow horizons. His theology is laid out in his book *Kewarganegaraan jang Bertanggungdjawab* (1955). While others maintained a deafening silence, Leimena concerned himself with the treatment of suspected communist detainees after the Soeharto coup (1965/66). If the church refused to read the signs of the times, it would be vomited out of the mouth of God. Though he had no formal theological training, Leimena worked for the Jakarta School of Theology.

Leimena was the only person to speak of church and state at the inauguration of the Council of Churches in 1950, of which body he became President in 1956. Leimena and others wrote against communism and were fearful of secularism. He has published eight books and a dozen articles of which five are in Indonesian, five in Dutch and two in English.

Selected References
Works by Johannes Leimena

"Nationalistische stroomingen in Nederlands Indie." *Eltheto* 90.6 (1935).

"De Ontmoeting der rassen in de Kerk." *De opwekker* 87.12 (1941).

Kewarganegaraan yang Bertanggungdjawab (Responsible citizenship). Jakarta: BPK, 1955. Expanded and republished, 1980.

"Gereja di tengah-tengah krisis dunia dan krisis di Indonesia" (The Church in the midst of the world crisis and the crisis in Indonesia. Talk at the 1955 Maluku Synod). In *Bentuk Negara jang kita Kehendaki* (The type of state to which we aspire), 1956.

"Church in Mainstream." *Church and Society* (EACC) 2.1 (1964).

"The Task of Restoring Fellowship in the Church and in the Indonesian Nation." *SEAJT* 9.3 (1968).

Panitia, Buku Kenangan (Book Commemoration Committee) and Dr J. Leimena, eds. *Kewarganegaraan yang Bertanggungjawab: Mengenang Dr J Leimena* (Responsible citizenship: In remembrance of Dr J Leimena). Jakarta: BPK Gunung Mulia, 1995. A greatly expanded version of the editions of 1955 and 1980 with full documentation on Leimena's life and work.

3.2.3. Tahi Bonar Simatupang (1920-90), North Sumatra and Jakarta

Hailing from the Toba Batak region of North Sumatra, home to the largest regional Lutheran Church in Indonesia, Simatupang joined the Dutch colonial army and graduated from the Military Academy of Bandung in 1942. Captured by the Japanese as they invaded later that year, Simatupang subsequently joined the Indonesian nationalists. After independence was proclaimed in 1945, the Indonesians fought a revolutionary war against the returning Dutch. Simatupang was made responsible for the development of a single army from the disparate guerrilla groups divided ethnically and ideologically. He succeeded. Soekarno appointed Simatupang Chief of Staff of the Armed Forces in 1951. Disagreements with the President led to his demotion in 1954; five years later he was pensioned off.

His career at an end at the age of 39, Simatupang threw the experience gained in war and government into work for the churches. In the process he became one of the more original theological thinkers of his generation.

Simatupang wrote extensively on national development founded upon the Pancasila with all its ethical, inter-religious and ecumenical implications. Active in the church and society division of the WCC, he chaired its 1966 conference and was appointed a member of the central and executive committees at Uppsala in 1968. A President of the Council of Churches in Indonesia, he also served on the board of the Christian University, and was a consultant to CCA, becoming its Chairperson and President in 1973.

Ideological tensions were ever present from 1950-65 due to the twin poles of communism and militant Islam. Simatupang claimed that the church needed to become ecumenical in order to counter the ethnic composition of most local Protestant Churches. If not, then the ethnic churches would enter their individual, static, silent ghettos. Thus the "double wrestle" that the church must engage in is with God and culture (society).

Simatupang felt it vital that the churches move from a position of weakness and isolation to the centre of society. To this end he worked for 30 years. His key phrase was that the churches should engage in society, "positively, creatively, critically and realistically" - which terms were adopted by the first church and society conference in 1962 and by the fifth assembly of the Council of Churches two years later. For Simatupang salvation history encompasses both the church and nation; and the two histories are already converging. The churches need to reread their history using both theo-centric and Indonesia-centric paradigms. Simatupang has published 18 books and booklets, including two in English and one in German and some 40 articles of which ten are in English and two in German.

Selected References
Works by T.B. Simatupang

Tugas Kristen Dalam Revolusi. (Christian task in the revolution). Jakarta: BPK Gunung Mulia, 1967.

Iman Kristen dan Pancasila (Christian faith and the Pancasila). Jakarta: BPK Gunung Mulia, 1984. Underlines congruence between Christian faith and the state ideology.

Gelebte Theologie in Indonesien. Zur gesellschaftlichen Verantwortung der Christen. Mit Geleitwort von Olaf Schumann. Goettingen, 1992.

The Fallacy of a Myth: Tracing the Experiential Significance of an Army Officer belonging to the Generation of Liberators for the Future of Indonesia (English translation of "Membuktikan ketidakbenaran suatu mitos..."). Jakarta: Pustaka Sinar Harapan, 1996.

"The Situation and Challenge of the Christian Mission in Indonesia Today." *SEAJT* 10.4 (1969).

"Christian Presence in War, Revolution and Development: The Indonesian Case." *The Ecumenical Review* 37 (1985). Also in *Church and Society: Ecumenical Perspectives, Essays in Honour of Paul Abrecht,* edited by Roger L. Shinn. Geneva: WCC.

"The East-West Tension, the North-South Imbalance - and JPIC?" *The Ecumenical Review* 40.3 (1988).

Cooley, Frank L. "In Memoriam: T.B. Simatupang 1920-1990." *Indonesia* 49 (1990).

Rae, Simon. "A Brief Introduction to the Theology of T.B. Simatupang." *PTCA Bulletin* 5.2 (1992). Includes Select Bibliography.

3.3. Professional Scholars Take Up the Challenge

3.3.1. Harun Hadiwijono (1915-85), Yogyakarta, Central Java

Born in Bandung, central Java, Harun Hadiwijono was the second of four children. While at a Dutch-medium high school in Yogyakarta (1934-37), Hadiwijono experienced a faith crisis accompanied by severe sickness. This led to his baptism into the Protestant Church in 1936, the first of his family to become Christian. He then took up theological studies in Yogyakarta (1937-41), a member of the first class to obtain a recognised certificate. This allowed him to continue theology at Vreij Universiteit in Amsterdam where he graduated in 1952. Some years later he successfully defended his doctoral thesis there (1967).

During the Japanese occupation Hadiwijono was an evangelist at Betsaida Protestant Hospital, Yogyakarta (1941-45). At this time he married Suwartini from Klaten (1943); they had three children. Ordained at the end of 1945 he was pastor for 10 months before commencing his life-long career as teacher at what has now become Duta Wacana Faculty of Theology (1946-85). During this time he became rector four times for a total of 12 years, in 1962-64, 1968-72, 1974-77 and 1977-80. For 13 years he was visiting lecturer in mysticism, dogmatics and philosophy at Satya Wacana University, Salatiga (1956-62; 1967-74).

Hadiwijono's doctoral thesis *Man in the Present Javanese Mysticism* (1967) signalled a new interest in the subject. He studied both the Hindu-Javanese and Sumatran-Islamic mystical traditions. He is one of the first Indonesian theologians to attempt a systematic dogmatic theology. Ever cautious, he relates the dogmas of the Christian faith to similar religious concepts in both Islam and Hinduism. Not quite espousing contextual theology, he places "western" dogmatic theology alongside the Javanese religious and cultural context.

Iman Kristen (Christian Faith, 1973) is a work clearly influenced by the theo-centrism of Islam, with long pieces on Javanese mysticism. He attempts to stimulate a theological discussion by suggesting an "openly traditional" way forward. He asks: Should Indonesian theology be solidly dogmatic or more of a wisdom literature? Both Hadiwijono's approach, and his tone, reflect the cosmic balance of Javanese culture. Unusual in Protestant circles at the time, he published many books on the history of philosophy and religious thought.

In 1954 Hadiwijono founded, and until 1961 edited, the journal *Penjadar* (Awareness) where chapters of his future books were first published. He placed priority on unity in faith rather than upon organisational unity. Always acknowledging the high values of pluriformity, he was nevertheless aware that some church order is nearer to God's will than some others. Thus, pluriformity is not just a cultural but also a theological issue. He elaborated the non-theological factors that prevent or endanger unity and hold back the *missio Dei*. Hadiwijono authored 19 books and booklets and a further 59 articles of which two are in English. He also translated

14 books and booklets into Indonesian. His main works in dogmatics and on mysticism have been continually available, the more recent editions coming out from 2000 on.

Selected References
Works by Harun Hadiwijono
> *Man in Present Javanese Mysticism.* Amsterdam: Vrije Universiteit, 1967. Published by Baarn, Bosch & Keuning.
> *Iman Kristen* (Christian Faith). Jakarta: BPK Gunung Mulia, 1973. Rev. ed, 1979.
> "Influence of Christianity on Javanese Mysticism." *SEAJT* 9 (Jan. 1968).
> "Theology in Asia Today." *SEAJT* 12 (Sept. 1971).
> Yusri Panggabean, et al. *Penabur Benih Mazhab Teologi: Menuju Manusia Baru* (Sowing the seeds of a theological school: towards a new humanity). Jakarta: BPK Gunung Mulia, 2000. Contains biography, complete bibliography of Hadiwijono's publications and posthumous Festschrift.

3.3.2. Johannes L. Ch. Abineno (1917-95), Timor and Jakarta

Born in Timor, Johannes Abineno studied the history of liturgy for his doctorate (Utrecht 1956). When under the Dutch East Indies Company, the Indonesian churches had to follow their Dutch "mother" church. Achieving independence from the sending churches in 1935, the Indonesian churches were finally free to arrange their liturgy without government oversight. However, liturgical change after 1945 closely followed changes taking place in the Netherlands where there was a return to the classical patterns of the "apostolic" church.

According to Abineno, the church in Timor needed to learn as much from fellow Asian churches as from the past. He viewed liturgical renewal as an attempt to free worship for mission (e.g. worship in the family/family groups, two-way sermons, openness of worship to the apostolate). His thesis was published in Indonesian as a series of pamphlets and short books, all of which concern living issues in Indonesia.

His hopes that the Reformed Church in Timor (GMIT) would put aside its Dutch heritage and work out Timorese patterns of liturgy was not realised; church members were afraid of change. Abineno came to realise that liturgical change had to come from the grassroots. In the 1980s the new hymnal *Kidung Jemaat* (1986) contained 100 Indonesian hymns out of a total of 478.

Abineno moved to Jakarta to work with the Council of Churches, becoming its President. From then on, he taught at the Jakarta Graduate School of Theology. He is the most productive Indonesian theologian to date, writing books and pamphlets on virtually every aspect of congregational life. He is an important practical theologian, providing the Graduate Schools and congregational leaders with handy guides to every aspect of their work. Abineno is kerygmatic and strong on history, although for him western models of research and theology are still the norm. He is an important transitional theologian, placing an open-ended western practical theology in the hands of the Reformed Churches, providing some of the biblical and historical tools for a later church to take up in a more clearly Indonesian manner. Most church leaders needed small, concise practical booklets; these Abineno supplied in abundance - Bible commentaries, a church history, guides to congregational worship and leadership, writing on all aspects of practical theology.

Abineno's is a biblically-based theology of witnessing, which accepted the *Pancasila* as the meeting point for all Indonesians in the political sphere. A prolific writer, Abineno has published 72 books and booklets as well as numerous articles, which apart from his thesis are all in Indonesian.

Selected References
Works by Johannes L. Ch. Abineno

> *Liturgische vormen en patronen in de Evangelische Kerk op Timor.* Proefschrift Utrecht, 1956.
> "Patterns of Liturgy." *SEAJT* 6 (1964). (Translation of booklet, 1963).
> *Sekitar Theologia Praktika* (On practical theology). 2 vols. Jakarta: BPK, 1968.
> *Roh Kudus dan PekerjaanNya* (The Holy Spirit and his work). Jakarta: BPK Gunung Mulia, 1975.

Apa Kata Alkitab? (What Says the Bible?). Seri Gereja dan Teologia, 5 vols. Jakarta: BPK Gunung Mulia, 1981.

Apostole, Pengutusan. Kumpulan Karangan dalam rangka memperingati hari Ulang Tuhan ke-70 Prof. Dr. J.L.Ch. Abineno (Apostle, Commission. Festschrift to commemorate the 70th Birthday of Prof. Dr. J.L.Ch. Abineno), Jakarta: BPK Gunung Mulia, 1987. For bibliography of Abineno's publications until 1987 see 311-316.

3.3.3. Peter D. Latuihamallo (1918-), Jakarta

Born in Mamasa, Toraja, Sulawesi, Peter D. Latuihamallo graduated from the Jakarta School of Theology in 1948. Latuihamallo was active in public life as a member of parliament in the 1950s. With a doctorate from Union Theological Seminary, New York (1959), he was appointed rector of the Jakarta Graduate School of Theology where he taught ethics for 40 years and where he was still working with post-graduate students in 2000. In the 1980s, he served as President of the Communion of Churches in Indonesia.

As Indonesia embarked upon independence, Latuihamallo formulated three major theological challenges: The necessity of understanding Islam in the light of God's will; the courage needed to reformulate faith in times of rapid change; and the total renewal of the church required by the encounter with Islam and the reformulation of their faith.

Latuihamallo was the first Indonesian to discuss the work of Kraemer critically (1959). More positive than Kraemer about nineteenth century Christian writings in Indonesia, he regarded them as first attempts to explain the core of the Christian faith. He discusses mysticism, magic and syncretism, and the penetration of western ways into the cultures of Indonesia. While he generally follows Kraemer in his theology of religions, he brings out the role of the Holy Spirit more, thus opening up Kraemer's closed Christocentrism.

Latuihamallo has surmised that Asian religions are tolerant only in their opinions; they are usually intolerant as social institutions when public roles are given religious motivation. Christian tolerance is motivated by the biblical patience of God.

Christ Himself is the final authority; all confessions of faith and ecclesial traditions are secondary. On both biblical and pragmatic grounds (the pluralistic situation in Indonesia), we need a strong, united Christian church; only then will others change their attitude towards Christians. The proclamation of the Word is primary, and all church institutions serve this end and can, and should, change. Church disunity is due to non-theological factors, in particular to the existence of ethnic churches with strong local linguistic and cultural identities as well as to the different (denominational) sending churches. For too long these ethnic/denominational churches were geographically isolated. However, he was sure that non-theological factors could also contribute to church unity, in particular nationalism and the status of Christians as a minority. Latuihamallo emphasises that spiritual unity in Christ already exists; what is needed is unity in organisation. He has published three books and over 20 articles, including seven in English and one in Dutch.

Selected References
Works by Peter D. Latuihamallo

> *Church and World: a Critical Study about the Relation of Church and World in the Writings of Hendrik Kraemer.* New York, 1959. The first Indonesian to critique Kraemer.
>
> *Theological Education Come-of-Age in Southeast Asia - Percakapan dengan Kosuke Koyama* (A conversation with Kosuke Koyama). Jakarta: STT (Theological Academy), 1974.
>
> "Missiology and Politics: Christian Alertness in Indonesia." *SEAJT* 10.2-3 (1963).
>
> "Methodological Significance of Context: Illuminating it from sociological, historical, cultural, economic, political and theological perspectives in Asia." *SEAJT* 21 (1980).
>
> "God in a Developing Plural Society: The Indonesian Experience." *SEAJT* 23 (1982).
>
> Borrong, Robert, ed. *Berakar di dalam Dia dan Dibangun di atas Dia* (Rooted in Him and built upon Him). (Book to Honour Prof. Dr. P.D. Latuihamallo on his 80th Birthday). Jakarta: BPK Gunung Mulia, 1998.

3.3.4. Nicolaus Driyarkara sj (1913-67), Yogyakarta, Central Java

If van Lith (2.1.7.) (re-)founded the Jesuit mission in Central Java according to clear cultural and educational principles (1896-1926), then Driyarkara - one of the first generation influenced by van Lith's approach - worked out a humanist philosophy that laid down the groundwork for the later growth of contextual theologies in the Indonesian Catholic Church.

Deeply immersed in Javanese literature and culture, Driyarkara was equally at home with ancient Greek philosophy and contemporary western philosophies, in particular existentialism and phenomenology (with which school he can be associated). His illustrations are taken from Javanese literature and everyday proverbs. He used classics such as *Serat Wulang Reh*, *Wedatama*, *Suluk Wudjil Djawa* and *Serat Tjentini*. His central concerns were the philosophy of the person, social ethics and the development of the state philosophy of *Pancasila* as a framework for living together as a multi-cultural and multi-religious society. He started with lived experience, within which local culture and religiosity were embedded.

Driyarkara wrote clearly and carefully, going to the root of each problem and clarifying little considered issues. His philosophical method has been described as "phenomenological circles" (Verhaak, 1988:21) or "the unspooling of coils" (Mudji Sutrisno, 1988:43) where one idea leads onto the next. His original, deep philosophical considerations were centred upon the critical function of philosophy and upon the human person as the active, creative subject of history.

Driyarkara taught philosophy while active in the administration of the Educational Academy of Sanata Darma in Yogyakarta. Education is a process of humanisation (1980a). Thus, in his philosophy he was forever asking who we are. His answer: we must face the world, the Divine and ourselves consciously. The human person is a dynamic personality, a conscious subject, an aware self who acts freely (1980b). This active presence proclaims who we are in this world. As conscious subjects (*persona*) we create a world of culture (1980c). One such product of this manufacturing process is the state. Given that Driyarkara taught philosophy during the first two tumultuous decades of Indonesia's independence in the 1950s and 1960s, he was concerned with the ethics of power and the problem of freedom and governance (1980d). He philosophised upon the human ability to arrange and humanise the system of power in order to live as *homo homini socius* - we are friends and colleagues to each and every one.

At a time when slogans defined public truth, Driyarkara's social ethics, through his careful use of words and deep philosophical analysis, gave lie to the ideologization of power that justifies "false truths". When schooling was being heavily ideologised for political ends, he developed a philosophy of education as a process of humanisation. When political culture was moulding a mass culture, he spoke of the dignity of human persons as conscious actors of their own development.

Two elements link Driyarkara, to the mission pioneer van Lith and to later Christian humanists such as Mangunwijaya (4.3) and to contemporary Catholic thinkers such as Banawiratma (4.16) and Sindhunata (4.21). The first is a living, creative appropriation of the heart of Javanese culture; the second is a carefully thought-through involvement in public affairs during a time of political turmoil. He was a deep, serene thinker who, like van Lith, willingly allowed himself to be appointed to public bodies, and even became a nimble supporter of the students' movement during the social revolution of 1965-66, which brought down the government of President Soekarno. In his quiet way, Driyarkara thought and lived out his Christian humanist philosophy in the classroom and in journals, in governmental bodies and finally in the students' movement. (He did not live long enough to see that Soeharto's New Order was much worse than Soekarno's Guided Democracy.) This "refined, thoughtful involvement" has helped to give an emergent Javanese Catholic theology one of its defining characters. He has published ten books and half a dozen articles, not including those later published as book collections.

Selected References
Works by Nicolaus Driyarkara
  Driyarkara tentang Pendidikan. Kumpulan Karangan Driyarkara (A collection of articles by Driyarkara on education). Yogyakarta: Kanisius, 1980.
  Driyarkara tentang Manusia. Kumpulan Karangan Driyarkara (A collection of articles by Driyarkara on the person). Yogyakarta: Kanisius, 1980.
  Driyarkara tentang Kebudayaan. Kumpulan Karangan Driyarkara (A collection of articles by Driyarkara on culture). Yogyakarta: Kanisius, 1980.
  Driyarkara tentang Negara dan Bangsa. Kumpulan Karangan Driyarkara (A collection of articles by Driyarkara on country and nation). Yogyakarta: Kanisius, 1980.

4 Towards More Systematic Contextual Theologies, ca. 1965-2000

During the four sessions of the Second Vatican Council (1962-65) the Catholic Church embraced a renewed vision of itself as a collegial or synodical people on pilgrimage (*Lumen gentium*, 1963), and concluded its assembly with a positive statement on involvement in the world (*Gaudium et spes*, 1965). *Gaudium et spes* employed a practical methodology and encouraged a similar shift among Catholic theologians: insertion, social and cultural analysis followed by theological reflection and practical response (action). In Yogyakarta the key persons who translated this conciliar vision into Indonesian terms were Robert Hardawiryana (4.1) and Tom Jacobs (4.4). Both are prodigious writers.

Through most of this period the Batak S.A.E. Nababan (b. 1933) was highly influential as general secretary (1967-84) and then chairperson (1984-89) of the Communion of Churches in Indonesia (DGI, since 1984 PGI). In these positions, and through his work with CCA and WCC, Nababan had great influence on ecumenical Protestants as a practical theologian though he wrote little himself. He opposed both the pietist culture of the churches and the individualist and consumerist culture of society.

Regional bodies had an increasing influence throughout this period - the Christian Conference of Asia (CCA) among ecumenical

Protestants and the Federation of Catholic Bishops' Conferences (FABC) among Catholics. There is active co-operation between these two bodies. The Programme for Theology and Cultures in Asia (PTCA), through its twice annual bulletin and annual workshop-seminars, helped to re-orient seminary teaching. The Ecumenical Association of Third-World Theologians (EATWOT) has successfully exposed its membership, and the readership of its journal *Voices from the Third World*, to developments in Asia, South America and Africa.

Notwithstanding notable advances in seminaries and faculties of theology, contextual theological reflection has also come from a number of movements and centres, active in laity formation, social welfare, community organisation, urban-rural mission, ecumenical education, communication and practical theological reflection. In Java these include Akademie Leimena, Driyarkara Institute and Bina Warga Lay and Leadership Training Centre (all in Jakarta); Yayasan Bina Darma (Salatiga - publishes the journal *Bina Darma*); the Institute of Theological Education (Malang); Balai Budaya Sindhuharjo Media Centre (formerly "Puskat", Yogyakarta, with considerable media output: books, art, videos/CVDs, TV productions, street theatre); and the Social Welfare Guidance Council (Solo - publishes the journal *Refleksi*). In Bali there is Dhyana Pura (near Denpasar); while in Flores, Candraditya Research Centre (Maumere). Commissions and Departments of the Indonesian Bishops' Conference (formerly MAWI, now KWI) and of the Communion (formerly Council) of Churches (DGI/PGI), have a considerable output in publications through regular study projects and workshops (see above 1.4.2.). Catholic (PMRI) and Protestant (CMKI) Student Movements, have also made a significant contribution in developing creative theological thinking.

The professionalisation and Indonesianisation of theological education continued apace. Most seminaries, Catholic and Protestant, received upgraded accreditation, most becoming faculties at universities. The Jakarta Graduate School of Theology established its doctoral programme in 1970. In 1979 the "Doctor of Pastoral Studies" programme commenced at Duta Wacana University, Yogyakarta, in association with SEAGST with its secretariat in Singapore. Forty theses were completed between

1979-85, albeit none by women. This theological extension programme was discontinued in the 1990s. From 1985-95 a total of 56 theses were researched by Indonesian Protestant theologians, a majority completed in Indonesia, and therefore in the Indonesian language, 14 at the Jakarta Graduate School, and another 14 with SEAGST (Hoekema 1996). Less than a fifth of the theses were completed at European universities. At a doctoral level, all Catholic theologians continued to study overseas. The topics indicate a renewed interest in local issues (cultural identity, centre-periphery struggle) as well as the perennial *Pancasila*.

Selected References

Aritonang, Jan S. "Perkembangan Pemikiran Teologis di Indonesia 1960-1990an" (The development of theological thinking in Indonesia 1960-1990). In *Bergumul dalam Pengharapan* (Struggling in hope), edited by Ferdinand Suleeman, et al, 261-285. Jakarta: BPK Gunung Mulia, 1999. An historian looks at the development of theology in Indonesia since the 1960s.

Balasundaram, Franklyn J. *EATWOT in Asia: Towards a Relevant Theology*. Bangalore: Asian Trading Corporation, 1993. Somewhat strident.

Cairns, Ian J. *Perjanjian lama dan Indonesia yang sedang membangun* (The role of the Old Testament in developing nations [with special reference to Indonesia]). Burns Lectures 1978. Jakarta, BPK Gunung Mulia, 1985. (In Indonesian).

England, John C. and Archie C.C. Lee, eds. *Doing Theology with Asian Resources. Ten Years in the Formation of Living Theology in Asia*. Auckland: PTCA & Pace Publishing, 1993. Excellent overview of the first decade of PTCA's work.

Hoekema, Alle Gabe. "Dissertations by Protestant Theologians in Indonesia - A Short Bibliographical Review." *Exchange* 14 (1985).

— "Dissertations by Protestant Theologians in Indonesia 1985-95." *Exchange* 25 (1996). Hoekema's second - and final - comprehensive survey.

Nababan, Soritua, ed. *Christ the Life*. Jakarta: BPK Gunung Mulia, 1966.

—, ed. *Lord Send Me*. Jakarta: BPK Gunung Mulia, 1977.

Penerbit, ed. *Gereja Indonesia Pasca-Vatikan II: Refleksi dan Tantangan* (The Indonesian Church after the Second Vatican Council: reflections and challenges). Yogyakarta: Kanisius, 1997. Wide-ranging, in-depth collection of reflections.

Steenbrink, Karel. "Indonesian Churches 1978-84: Main Trends, Issues and Problems." *Exchange* 39 (1984).

Thomson, Alan, C. "Churches of Java in Aftermath of 30th Sept. Movement." *SEAJT* 9.1 (1968).

4.1 Robert Hardawiryana sj (1926-), Yogyakarta, Central Java

Born in Ambarawa, Central Java, Robert Hardawiryana entered the Jesuits in 1945. After philosophy in Yogyakarta (1948-51), he studied theology in Maastricht, Netherlands (1953-57), and at the Pontifical Gregorian University, Rome (1957-61). For 30 years Romo Hardo ("Father Hardo"), as he is known, taught theology at the Wedabhakti Theological Faculty, Yogyakarta (1961-91).

Hardawiryana is rooted in the classical, Catholic theological tradition of Europe. He completed his doctoral studies (1961) immediately prior to the Second Vatican Council (1962-65). As theological advisor of both the Indonesian Catholic Episcopal Conference (early 1960s until 1998) and a member of the Theological Advisory Board of the Federation of Asian Bishops' Conferences (1986-98), the theological work of Hardawiryana reflects the Asian Catholic Church's appropriation of the Second Vatican Council. He has been seeking out a more appropriate church model for Asia, how the church can live as a small, scattered minority and how the church needs to communicate the faith as, "a drop in the oceans of the other great religions". He has been concerned that the church move out of its enclosure and become a "church-for-others"; a key term that became more and more central in Hardawiryana's theology is *dialogue*.

Hardawiryana's theology has had considerable influence upon Catholic ecclesial documents both in Indonesia and in the Asian Catholic Church (FABC). He is an excellent example of a transitional theologian in his selection and interpretation of the documents of the Second Vatican Council for a Catholic Church in the process of opening itself up to the multi-religious and multi-cultural contexts of Indonesia and Asia as a whole. His ability to compile and order myriad sources is unparalleled. A prolific writer, from the mid-1950s until the end of 2000 Hardawiryana had produced over 700 articles, reports, translations and manuscripts including 17 books and booklets of which four are in English and around 40 major articles including nine in English and one in French.

Selected References
Works by Robert Hardawiryana
> *Building the Church of Christ in a Pluri-cultural Situation. A Pastoral Primer on Christian Inculturation.* FABC Papers 41 (1986).
> *The Involvement of the Laity in Politics: The Church in Indonesia,* FABC Papers 58 (1990).
> "Contextual Theology in Indonesia: A Pastoral Approach." *Philippiniana Sacra* 14.1 (1979).
> "Asia and Indonesia." In *Mission in Dialogue*, edited by M. Motte and J.R. Lang, 34-72. Maryknoll, NY: Orbis, 1982.
> "Theology of Liberation in the Context of Recent Theologies." *Umat Baru* 17.98 (1984).
> "Theological Perspectives on Mission in Asia." *Verbum SVD* 36 (1995).

4.2 Ihromi (1928-)

Born at Garut in West Java, Ihromi was the eighth of 14 children. With a blind mother and his own poor eyesight, since childhood Ihromi has focused his life and study upon those pushed to the edge of society. He served the Pasundan Protestant Church (GKP) while studying at the Graduate School of Theology in Jakarta (1948-54). These were revolutionary times (1945-49), as The Netherlands fought to retain hold of Indonesia which had proclaimed independence. Due to the strained relations between The Netherlands and Indonesia after independence was acknowledged by treaty in 1949, but without West Papua (Irian Jaya), Ihromi could not continue his theological studies at Leiden and so studied Arabic and Sundanese at the National University in Jakarta (1955-57). He then studied Semitic languages and the Old Testament at Harvard (1957-62) and wrote his doctoral thesis at Mainz, Germany (1969-72). Since becoming a student in 1948, his working life has revolved around the Jakarta Graduate School of Theology, where he taught from 1963 until his retirement in 1998, elected rector from 1974-88. His wife since 1959, Tapi Omas Ihromi-Simatupang, was professor of law at the National University where he himself taught in the Faculty of Literature from 1963.

In his painstakingly detailed exegetical study of the use of the term *anawim* and *amm ani wadal* in the Book of Zephaniah (Zeph 3:11-12), Ihromi concluded that the *anawim* are the Hebrew poor who are oppressed and disempowered (which he calls an "objective" interpretation), rather than simply the "humble of heart" (which he calls a "subjective" interpretation).

Ihromi himself has spent much of his life theologically empowering fellow pastors. Active in the Student Christian Movement in Indonesia during the 1950s (GMKI was founded in 1950 in the house of Leimena (3.2.2.), he was chosen as its General Secretary (1954-56). As secretary he established Bible Study groups disseminating study material from the WSCF. He sent cadres overseas and organised a conference for young pastors - he himself being ordained in 1955. Meanwhile he worked for LAI - the National Bible Association (1955-57). In 1957 he helped established the Association of Theological Schools in Southeast Asia (now ATESEA) which through long-distance education has upgraded the faculties of many Asian graduate schools. In 1968 Ihromi launched the Study Institute for teachers of theology in Indonesia - *Persetia*.

Selected References
Works by Ihromi

"Amm ani wadal nach dem Propheten Zephanja." Johannes Gutenberg Faculty, Mainz University, 1972. Doctoral thesis. Chapter Four has been translated into Indonesian and published under the title "The Poor, Oppressed and Disempowered Nation according to Zephaniah." See Festschrift below.

"Respect for the Integrity of Another's Religion." *SEAJOT*, 14.2 (1973). (Indonesian original 1972.)

"Have the Poor a Role in God's Design?" *Ecumenical Review* 32 (1980).

"Studying Living Religions within a National Community." In Proceedings of Indonesian-Dutch Seminar. Yogyakarta, 1990.

Erari, Karel Phil, et al. *Keadilan bagi Kaum Lemah* (Justice for the weak). Book to Honour M.A. Ihromi. Jakarta: BPK Gunung Mulia, 1995. Festschrift.

4.3 Yusuf Bilyarta Mangunwijaya (1929-99), Yogyakarta, Central Java

Y.B. Mangunwijaya is the Javanese-liberationist-educator that van Lith struggled to be at the beginning of the 20th century. Born at Ambarawa, central Java, Romo Mangun ("Father Mangun" as everyone called him) was the eldest of 12 children. He joined a "student-soldier" brigade during the revolution (1945-48), becoming a section commander. Witnessing the suffering of the villagers during the war, he decided to spend the remainder of his life, "repaying my debt to the people."

After ordination (1959) Mangun was sent by Archbishop Soegijapranata to Aachen, Germany (1960-66), to study architecture as part of a diocesan plan to Javanise the church (others were sent to study music, dancing, literature, philosophy). From 1967-80 he was visiting lecturer in architecture at Gadjah Mada University, Yogyakarta. His own designs combined traditional Javanese feeling with contemporary technical skills. His design for the pilgrimage centre at Sendangsono focuses upon popular religiosity and the natural beauty of the surroundings rather than upon formal liturgy or large-scale buildings. He often used discarded material. Retiring from grand designs he turned to "people's architecture". His re-design of the squatters' camp by the Code River in Yogyakarta (1980-86) won the Aga Khan Award (1992) and the Erskine Fellowship Award, Stockholm, Sweden (1995).

From 1968 Romo Mangun began writing an occasional column in *Kompas*, the largest Jakarta daily, and afterwards in many newspapers and journals, secular, Muslim and Christian, in both tabloids and broadsheets. In 1981 he published the first of eleven novels, soon recognised as a contemporary classic. Most of his novels are historical, where he re-reads Indonesian history from the perspective of the poor. His protagonists are usually rural women; the unacknowledged yet strongest members of society who hand down the deepest human values. Mangun has published 26 books on architecture, politics, social and cultural issues, literature, theology and church renewal apart from the numerous collections of his newspaper columns and novels.

A brilliant person of letters, thoroughly versed in all levels of Javanese culture, a mystic-poet, at home in modern and post-modern technology, a political activist, Romo Mangun quietly worked away at alternative forms of education in a run-down primary school at the edge of town. A personal friend of the poor, he was feared but consulted by the powers-that-be. When Soeharto commanded that he be eliminated for supporting the villagers fighting the World Bank Kedungombo dam project (1986-94), the commander refused to carry out the President's orders.

In his novels and newspaper articles, in his essays, buildings and TV videos, Mangunwijaya is perhaps the most creative theological thinker to have emerged from the Indonesian Catholic Church over the past 150 years. He died on the shoulder of a friend, the Muslim intellectual Mohamad Sobary during an inter-faith seminar in Jakarta. His funeral was attended by thousands: pedicab drivers, squatters and street children, many of whom he knew personally, even the Muslim Sultan of Yogyakarta. Within a hundred days of his death Kanisius published ten large volumes, Erlangga University another two, and Kompas a further volume. A final posthumous novel was published in December 1999 and a collection of short stories in 2000.

In contrast to the utterly simple life he lived in his self-designed wooden hut, Mangun's writings are dense and complex, moving on many levels simultaneously, full of allusions to Javanese myth and contemporary Indonesian politics. Thoroughly immersed in Javanese culture, he attacked its feudal-patriarchal values from within. Whatever his topic - church, society, technology, culture - his perspective was singular: that of the marginalised and discarded. In his theology Romo Mangun avoided Christian language, choosing both contemporary and Islamic terms. Mangunwijaya has published 28 books of non-fiction as well as 11 novels, one of which is also in English (1981/91). Of his countless articles just one is in English (1993).

Selected References
Works by Y.B. Mangunwijaya
> *The Weaver Birds*. Jakarta: The Lontar Foundation, 1991. Indonesian original, *Burung-burung Manyar: Sebuah Roman* (The

weaver birds: a novel). Jakarta, 1st ed. Pustaka Kuntara, 1981; 2nd ed. Djambatan, 1993. In 1983 won the Southeast Asia Write Award. Mangun's most accessible novel; a modern classic.

Sastra dan Religiositas (Literature and religiosity). Jakarta, Sinar Harapan, 1982. 2nd printing, Yogyakarta: Kanisius, 1988. A superb treatment of the religiosity of contemporary Indonesian literature.

Gereja Diaspora (A diaspora church). Yogyakarta: Kanisius, 1999. Has become a handbook for Base Communities in the post-1998 turmoil.

"Good News through Story Telling." *EAPR* 30 (1993).

Bodden, Michael. "Woman as Nation in Mangunwijaya's *Durga Umayi*." *Indonesia* 62 (1996). Indonesian translation in *Menjadi Generasi Pasca-Indonesia* (On becoming the post-Indonesian generation), edited by Sindhunata, 53-82. Yogyakarta: Kanisius, 1999.

Rahmanto, B. *Y.B. Mangunwijaya: Karya dan Dunianya* (Y.B. Mangunwijaya: his work and world). Jakarta: Grasindo, forthcoming. An appreciation of Mangun's novels by the professor of literature at Gadjah Mada University.

Steenbrink, Karel. "Mangunwijaya als romanschrijver van de koloniale tijd." *Wereld en Zending* 26 (1997).

—. "Y.B. Mangunwijaya's Blueprint for a Diaspora Church in Indonesia." *Exchange* 27.1 (1998). Indonesian translation in *Tinjauan Kritis atas Gereja Diaspora Romo Mangunwijaya*, edited by Sudiarja, 33-67. Yogyakarta, 1999.

4.4 Tom Jacobs sj (1929-), The Netherlands and Yogyakarta, Central Java

Tom Jacobs was born in Zevenbergen, The Netherlands. Continuing the policy advocated by van Lith in the 1920s, he came to Indonesia as a student in 1949. He taught dogmatic and biblical theology at the Faculty of Theology at the University of Sanata Dharma, Yogyakarta, from 1961 until retirement in 1994, with a break for doctoral studies in biblical theology at the Gregorian University, Rome (1966). Tom Jacobs was largely responsible for both translating key Second Vatican Council (1962-65) documents into Indonesian and for supplying insightful theological commentaries (1969, 1970/73). A biblical theologian (1982, 1983), he taught systematic theology, turning vital Conciliar breakthroughs into the common currency of theological discourse in Indonesian Catholic circles. He helped pioneer the "Theological Project" approach at the Wedabhakti Faculty of Theology in Yogyakarta. This theological method takes the pastoral experience of the student-participants as its starting-point (1989).

A prolific writer, Jacobs' theological contribution to the Indonesian Catholic Church formally culminated with the publishing of the Bishops' Official Reference Book on the Catholic faith *Iman Katolik*, which he drafted (1996). Active ecumenically, he has taught regularly at the Protestant university of Duta Wacana and has developed his theology in close contact with the Protestant tradition and in dialogue with Islam. A diligent and meticulous scholar, Jacobs has aided other scholars through his involvement in the computerisation of the Kolsani Library in Yogyakarta (both books and articles). Living out the Jesuit tradition, he is in wide demand as a first-class preacher, retreat giver and spiritual director. In recent years he has been translating important classical theological texts from the Greek and Latin originals into Indonesian. In 2000 he was briefly academic dean of the newly established major seminary in Dili, Timor Leste.

Jacobs has over 29 books and booklets to his name and another 23 unpublished manuscripts; he has edited a further half dozen books and is author of over 180 articles. He has now synthesised the fruit of his 40-year theological journey through a re-interpretation of the early Conciliar dogmas via the prism of New Testament Christologies. This theological autobiography is at once broadly ecumenical while being acutely sensitive to Muslim sensibilities (2000).

Selected References
Works by Tom Jacobs

> *Konstitusi Dogmatis Dei Verbum tentang Wahju Ilahi* (The dogmatic constitution Dei Verbum on divine revelation. Translation, introduction and commentary). Yogyakarta: Kanisius, 1969. A classic commentary of great impact during the 1980s.

Konstitusi Dogmatis Lumen Gentium mengenai Geredja (The dogmatic constitution Lumen Gentium on the Church. Translation, introduction and commentary). Yogyakarta: Kanisius, 1970-73. 3 vols. Seminal insights from Vatican II entered the Indonesian Catholic Church through this book.

Siapa Yesus Kristus menurut Perjanjian Baru (Who Jesus Christ is according to the New Testament). Yogyakarta: Kanisius, 1982.

Paulus: Hidup, Karya dan Teologinya (Paul: his life, work and theology). Yogyakarta: Kanisius, 1983. Perhaps the best of Jacobs' works.

—*Imanuel: Perubahan dalam Perumusan Iman akan Yesus Kristus* (Immanuel: changes in faith formulations in Jesus Christ). Yogyakarta: Kanisius, 2000. Jacob's "final" work bringing together NT and patristic scholarship.

—, with J.B. Banawiratma. "Doing Theology with Local Resources. An Indonesian Experiment." *East Asian Pastoral Review* 26 (1989). Outlines the ecumenical theology project of the Wedabhakti and Duta Wacana Faculties in Jogja.

4.5 Fridolin Ukur (1930-), Kalimantan and Jakarta

Born in Tamianglayang, Fridolin Ukur is a member of the Evangelical Church of Kalimantan. He studied at the Graduate School of Theology, Jakarta, and the Faculty of Theology at Basel University, Switzerland, obtaining a doctorate in church history (1971). He has directed the Research and Study Institute of the Council of Churches in Indonesia (1972-80), editing many books including the 12-volume history of Protestant Christianity in Indonesia, *Benih yang Tumbuh* (The growing seed). Ukur has been General Secretary of the Council of Churches in Indonesia (1984-89). Since 1981 he has been an advisor to the Synod of the Evangelical Church in Kalimantan (GKE).

The churches have made no single response to the question of the relationship between *adat* (cultural law) and religion. In his writings, Ukur - in Barthian style - separated the two (e.g. 1999). In writing of the mission of the church in Indonesia he stresses mission, unity and renewal as characteristics of the church and as the foundation for a functional ecclesiology in the Indonesian context. Apart from his writings, Ukur is well known for his radio broadcasts. He has published six books and booklets, edited a further six and authored over 20 articles.

Selected References
Works by Fridolin Ukur

"Tantang-Jawab Suku Dayak. Suatu Penyelidikan tentang Unsur-unsur yang menyekitari Penolakan dan Penerimaan Injil di kalangan Suku-Dayak dalam rangka sejarah Gereja di Kalimantan 1835-1945" (Challenge and response of the Dayak people. A study of the elements concerning the rejection and acceptance of the Gospel among the Dayak people as part of the history of the Church in Kalimantan 1835-1945.) STT Jakarta Doctoral thesis. Jakarta: BPK Gunung Mulia, 1971.

Tuaiannya Sungguh Banyak: Sejarah Gereja Kalimantan Evangelis Sejak Tahun 1835 (The harvest is indeed great. History of the Evangelical Church of Kalimantan since 1835). Jakarta: BPK Gunung Mulia, 2000. New edition of the author's 1960 book with additional 40-page chapter on developments since 1960.

"Pengkajian Kembali Sejarah Gereja di Indonesia" (Re-analysing Church history in Indonesia). In *Theo-Doron: Pemberian Allah* (Theo-Doron: gift of God), edited by M.A. Ihromi and S.Wismoady Wahono, 39-93. Jakarta: BPK Gunung Mulia, 1979.

"A Theology of the Underprivileged." *Peninjau* 8.1 (1982).

"The Mission of the Church in Indonesia." *Peninjau* 9.2 - 10.1 (1982/1983).

"Bersikap Injili dalam konteks Kebudayaan (Daerah) (To have a Gospel attitude in a (local) cultural context). In *Agama dalam Dialog: Pencerahan, Pendamaian dan Masa Depan* (Religions in dialogue: enlightenment, peace and the future), edited by Panitia, 425-442. Jakarta: BPK Gunung Mulia, 1999. 2 pages of photos.

4.6. I. Wayan Mastra (1931-), Bali

Due both to Dutch colonial policy and the imperviousness of Balinese culture, the Protestant and Catholic Churches were born in Bali only in the early 1930s. Hailing from the mountain village of Sebetan, Karangasem, East Bali, Mastra took up a yearlong Christian catechumenate in Surabaya, and was baptised in 1952.

Contextual Theological Reflection in Indonesia 1800-2000 187

Returning to Bali in 1953 as a teacher, he later went on to study at the Jakarta School of Theology (1956-60) and was commissioned as a pastor. Mastra worked in Singaraja on the Balinese north coast starting with a single Christian, his wife Ketut. Five years later he left five small congregations in the north, personally baptising some 350 people.

Narrowly escaping the massacre of September 1965, Mastra undertook doctoral studies at Dubuque Seminary, USA (PhD 1970). Returning to Bali, he chaired the watershed Synod of the Reformed Church (1972) that left behind the culture-denying policy of the hard-line past and adopted a culture-affirming stance. Abrahamic-like, the church now aimed at becoming a blessing for the majority community. The church accepted Balinese painting, singing, percussion orchestras and even some sacred dancing into its worship. Wood and soapstone carvings now decorate its buildings and shadow plays communicate the biblical message. At the 1972 Synod Mastra was elected Moderator (Bishop) of the Protestant Church in Bali (GKPB) which position he held until 2000 with just a five-year break (1988-92).

Moderator Mastra, together with the church Synod, has systematically contextualised the life of their church since 1972. He had worked out the theological foundation for this shift in his doctoral thesis. Rejecting Hendrik Kraemer's (and therefore Karl Barth's) theology of religions, he describes the church as a *pars pro toto*, a minority at the service of the majority. Mastra leans heavily upon the theology of Karl Rahner and Yves Congar. Rejecting both a tolerance that might lead to syncretism and the inherited intolerance that led to rejection, Mastra aims for a third way, namely a critical appreciation of Balinese religion by a dedicated Christian. This approach is essentially pragmatic, even "opportunistic": Mastra makes use of what works in spreading the gospel without working out the relationship between the uniqueness of Jesus and continuity and discontinuity with other religious experience. (Sugden, 1997:105).

In his unpublished manuscript "A Catechism" (1982), Mastra outlines his practical mission theology in the form of a dialogue between a father and his son and daughter. The outward form is Balinese, the inner soul is Reformed Church. Appropriate Old Testament verses are attached to the ubiquitous three-fold symbolism of Balinese culture and religion, while Christians - mostly from the lowest caste - are exhorted to "simple living, thrift and high thinking". There is an equal emphasis upon cultural appropriation and social economic engagement. The latter has brought the Balinese church and Mastra personally into the hotel business and tourist trade through his directorship of Dhyana Pura Hotel and Tourism Training Centre. From one of the poorest and most backward of the Indonesian churches, the Balinese church is now one of the richest and strongest. *Widya Wahana* Reference library at Tuka, Dalung (Post Box 3046, Denpasar 80030) has most of Wayan's publications and manuscripts among its 20,000 volumes.

Selected References
Works by Wayan Mastra

    Contextualisation of the Church in Bali: Case Study from Indonesia. Pasadena, California: William Carey Library, 1979.

    "Christianity and Culture in Bali." *International Review of Mission* 62.251 (1974).

    "The Salvation of Non-Believers, A Missiological Critique to Hendrik Kraemer and the Need for a New Alternative." Iowa: Dubuque University, 1970. Unpublished PhD thesis. Another Indonesian who broke away from the "Kraemer" grip.

    McKenzie, D.G. *The Mango Tree Church: The Story of the Protestant Christian Church in Bali.* Brisbane: Boolarang Publications, 1988. Written in association with I. Wayan Mastra. Informative but somewhat hagiographical.

    Sugden, Chris. *Seeking the Asian Face of Jesus. The Practice and Theology of Christian Social Witness in Indonesia and India 1974-1996.* Oxford: Regnum, 1997. First part doctoral thesis of 1988 (pp.1-314), second part updated to 1996 (pp.317-452). Chapters 1-4 on the theology and mission practice of I. Wayan Mastra; Chapters 8 & 9 compare Wayan with Vinay Samuel. Good detail, gently critical.

4.7 Victor Immanuel Tanja (1936-98), Sawu and Java

Victor Tanja was born on the small island of Sawu in East Nusa Tenggara. He obtained an M.Th at the Graduate School of Theology,

Jakarta (1964), and another at the Christian Theological Seminary, Indianapolis, USA (1974). He wrote his doctorate at Hartford (1979) on the modernist Islamic students' movement (*Himpuan Mahasiswa Islam*). Tanja taught at, and later became Dean of, the Faculty of Theology *Satya Wacana* Christian University in Salatiga, Central Java. Returning to Jakarta he ministered to the *Effatha* Congregation while teaching the Phenomenology of Religion and Islamic Studies at the Jakarta School of Theology. He was a member of the World Conference on Religion and Peace for Indonesia.

For Tanja, the ethical basis for collaboration in nation building is the state ideology of *Pancasila,* while the practical context is co-operation with the Muslim majority, particularly with its progressive mode; that is, with the modernist HMI Islamic students' movement and the *Muhammadiyah* educational foundation (1986). Theologically Tanja endeavoured to open up a pietistic Reformation tradition to inter-faith dialogue, where each religion becomes a partner in building up a more just society (1994). He rejected the ideologisation and manipulation of religion to legitimise group interests. He claimed that the western emphasis upon basic human rights has to be balanced by an equal emphasis upon basic human obligations. He views religion as the soul of the body of the nation (1998). His talks, articles, speeches, sermons and later collections, honed in upon the role of the church in the face of modernisation, secularisation and inter-religious relations.

What makes Tanja controversial is not so much the text as the context of his theological and political enterprise. He put his ecumenical theology to work in practical politics, translating inter-religious dialogue into co-operation with the ruling elite. He taught at the military police academy in Jakarta, advising both the Ministry of Security and the Ministry of Education. He was a member of the working group that wrote one of the National Guidelines for a government five-year plan. After the 1997 general election he entered the National Consultative Assembly as a representative of the "functional groups" and was one of the spiritual guides of Soeharto's ruling Golkar party. Seeking to end the temptation of the church to concentrate upon defending its position in a pluralistic society, Tanja veered towards a defence of the fascist military regime in the name of inter-faith collaboration. A month after Soeharto was forced from office, Victor Tanja died in Jakarta on 26th June 1998. He has authored seven books and over a dozen articles, one of which is in English.

Selected References
Works by Victor Tanja
> *Pemikiran HMI dan Relevansinya dengan Sejarah Perjuangan Bangsa Indonesia* (The thought of the Moslem Student Association and its relevance in the history of struggle of the Indonesian people). Jakarta: Integrita Dinamika Press, 1986. The first positive evaluation of the HMI by a Christian.
> *Spiritualitas, Pluralitas, dan Pembangunan di Indonesia* (Spirituality, plurality and development in Indonesia). Jakarta: BPK Gunung Mulia, 1994.
> *Pluralisme Agama dan Problema Sosial* (The plurality of religion and social problems). Jakarta: Cidesindo, 1998.

4.8. Franz Magnis-Suseno sj (1936-), Germany and Jakarta

Franz von Magnis was born in Eckersdorf, Germany, and studied philosophy, theology and political theory at Pullach, Yogyakarta and Munich (doctorate in philosophy 1973). He was one of the last generation of Jesuits to come to Indonesia as a student (1961) following the policy advocated by van Lith in the 1920s. Since 1969 he has been professor of ethics at Driyarkara Institute of Philosophy in the capital, Jakarta, and its rector (1988-97). A well-known speaker on radio and TV, he frequently participates in inter-faith seminars on social and political ethics. A cosmopolitan intellectual, he maintains his simple religious life-style and readily allots time for the spiritual direction of others. Magnis-Suseno is close to both the moderate village-based Nahdlatul Ulama (NU) and the more exclusivist-modernist Muhammadiyah. He was often consulted by students during their demonstrations that toppled Soeharto in 1998.

Recognised nationally as a distinguished intellectual, Magnis-Suseno's many books on philosophical and political ethics are very accessible, the result of ongoing discussions with the intelligentsia, both Christian and Muslim. He is much concerned with the moral values that lie behind social policy, whether in his thesis on the young Marx (published in German only, 1975), Javanese ethics (1981/84), or contemporary political issues (1999).

For forty years Magnis-Suseno has been undertaking both an academic and a living dialogue between the Western and the *Abangan* or popular Javanese ethical traditions. Without ever deciding which is the more legitimate or superior, Magnis-Suseno compares the western philosophy of life (an ethics of obligation) with the Javanese practical wisdom (an ethics of accommodation). In Javanese cosmic culture whoever and whatever is in their appropriate place is ethical. Humans and everything else need to accommodate themselves to the cosmic order, accepting their assigned place. Magnis-Suseno appreciates this practical wisdom in small-scale society, but is scathing about its manipulation by the nation state, especially under the fascist-military regime of Soeharto (e.g. 1999).

As a philosopher trained in the western tradition and equally at home in Javanese language and culture, Magnis-Suseno's writing is trans-denominational, indeed trans-religious (e.g. 1981). This work is published by "secular" newspapers, journals and book publishers. When writing on the theology of ethics, he is comfortable using Catholic language, and indeed these books are published by the diocesan (formerly Jesuit) publisher, Kanisius (e.g. 1993). By mid-2000 Magnis-Suseno had published 24 books of which three are in German and one in English and has authored over 120 articles and book chapters of which 12 are in German and three in English.

Selected References
Works by Franz Magnis-Suseno

"Normative Voraussetzungen im Denken des jungen Marx (1843-48)." PhD thesis, Universitas Muechen, 1973. Muenchen: Alber, 1975.

Beriman dalam Masyarakat: Butir-butir Teologi Kontekstual (Living faith in society: elements of a contextual theology). Yogyakarta: Kanisius, Pustaka Teologi 40, (1993). A collection of articles.

Javanese Ethics and World-View. The Javanese Idea of the Good Life. Jakarta: Gramedia Pustaka Utama, 1997. (English version of 1981 German original; Indonesian edition 1984). Magnis' classic work on contextual ethics.

"Membangun Kembali sebuah Budaya Politik Indonesia" (Rebuilding a political culture in Indonesia). In *Pergulatan Intelektual dalam Era Kegelisahan* (Intellectual struggle in a time of uncertainty), edited by Sindhunata, 49-64. Yogyakarta: Kanisius, 1999.

4.9 Judowibowo Poerwowidagdo (1942-), Yogyakarta, Central Java

Judowibowo, or Pak Judo, as he is usually known, studied at the Graduate School of Theology, Jakarta, graduating in 1964. He commenced studies in law at Cendrawasih University, Abepura, Papua-land (1965-66), San Francisco Theological Seminary, (MA in education, 1969), and the University of Pittsburgh (PhD in education, 1972). He has been lecturer (1973-1990) and university president (1985-90) at Duta Wacana Christian University, Yogyakarta and Duta Wacana's Research Institute (PPIP, 1975-90), is one of many foundations he has founded and/or directed in the fields of communication, research and reconciliation. Pak Judo has been secretary of ATESEA (1981-85), and executive secretary for Asia and the Pacific of the WCC's Theological Education Programme in Geneva (1992-98).

In his doctoral thesis, and later as administrator of Duta Wacana University and then as associate director at the Ecumenical Institute, Bossey, Pak Judo was concerned that Faculties of Theology were simply parts of the established structure of the economic, political and cultural system of the surrounding secular society. He clearly distinguished between old and new paradigms of theological education. The old paradigm simply trained (generally male) presbyters according to a fixed syllabus, centred upon the lecture hall, using a "banking system"; the course was overtly academic emphasising knowledge; it was dogmatic and confessional in orientation. All these characteristics were aimed at producing ordained ministers loyal to a particular tradition. The new paradigm is geared to all church ministers, lay and ordained, consciously balancing women and men participants; it employs a flexible module system centred simultaneously upon campus, the local congregation and the surrounding society; it uses a group-work approach where academic excellence includes practical competence; it is ecumenical whereby the tradition is received critically (1994). Pak Judo speaks of the "glocal" context for theological education: equally considering the local and the global.

Together with his artist wife Timur I. Poerwowidagdo, Pak Judo has established a dance troupe that acts out Scriptural narratives in Javanese style. He is president of the Asian Christian Art Association (ACAA, see chap. 3 vol 1) and currently also editor of ACAA's quarterly, *Image: Christ in Art in Asia*.. The Association has held numerous art exhibitions at international venues and holds periodic conferences to discuss the role of Christian art in today's Asia. Since 2000 Pak Judo has been president of Krida Wacana Christian University, Jakarta.

Thus, Judowibowo has taught theology in a large institution, has co-ordinated theological education funding internationally and promoted the development of non-verbal forms of Christian communication through art. He has published several books and dozens of articles of which many are in English and one in German.

Selected References
Works by Judowibowo Poerwowidagdo

"An Inquiry into the Logical Relationship of Teaching and Learning, based on the Linguistic Analysis of the Concept of Knowing" PhD thesis, Pittsburgh University, 1972.

Towards the 21st Century: Challenges and Opportunities for Theological Education. Geneva: WCC, Unit I: Unity and Renewal, 1994. Indonesian translation, Yogyakarta: Duta Wacana University Press, 1994. A challenge to relocate theological education in mainstream academia.

"The Church, Globalisation and Theological Education." *Asia Journal of Theology* 8.1 (1994).

PGI Bureau of Information, *Many Voices of Christian Art in Indonesia*. Jakarta: PGI, 1993.

4.10 Agustina Lumentut (1937-), Central Sulawesi and Jakarta

Agustina Lumentut's theology is writ in her life-story. She is the daughter of a hard-working mother and a poorly paid primary school teacher-cum-evangelist father who established congregations while opening village schools in the interior of Central Sulawesi. Her family endured the harsh Japanese occupation (1942-45), the political chaos and separatist movement that followed independence, and then the later upheavals when Dutch missionaries were asked to withdraw by the local Synod. After three-year's lower secondary school she went to Macassar in South Sulawesi to study theology (1954-59), one of the first women to do so. She returned to the interior to serve congregations. Surviving gender discrimination, she was appointed to a town congregation in 1960. Military skirmishes and death-threats were common in the early 1960s. In 1963 she was appointed secretary to the Synod. Apart from administration, she visited the far-flung congregations. A year in Australia opened up international contacts (1964-65).

Returning to Sulawesi, Lumentut pioneered awareness-building programmes in the interior, combining biblical instruction and community development through discussion and practical projects. Struggles with a pietistic tradition and opposition from jealous government leaders led Ibu Tina, "Mother Tina" as she is universally known, to develop a theology of development and to stand for truth over expediency. In 1973 she visited India to study community development en route to a General Assembly of the Netherlands Reformed Church in Holland. On sabbatical (1974-78) she upgraded her degree at her alma mater and then went to Trinity College, Singapore, for an MA in theology, becoming the most academically qualified pastor in her church. She returned to community development with an even greater gender sensitivity and verve. This brought her into the struggle of the indigenous people for their land rights in the face of migrants from Java and Bali and their rubber plantations. Thus when an opportunity arose in Jakarta for Lumentut to work with the Communion of Churches, her local church was content to see her go. Integrity costs everything.

Ibu Tina moved to Jakarta and worked as vice-General Secretary of the Communion of Churches in Indonesia from 1988. Living simply, married to her work and ideals, she became a well-known broadcaster on radio and television. Her Central Sulawesi church recalled her as its moderator (1989-97). Lumentut was the first woman to become a moderator of any church in Indonesia. She was an ecumenical delegate representing the CCA at the Episcopal Synod for Asia held in the Vatican in 1998. Since 1999 Ibu Tina has been in the thick of the ethnic-religious conflict that has engulfed Poso, Central Sulawesi.

Selected References
Works by Agustina Lumentut
"Membaharui, Membangun dan Mempersatukan Gereja" (Renewing, building up and uniting the Church). Address at General Assembly of the Council of Churches in Indonesia, Tomohon, July, 1980.
"Synod Intervention." *East Asian Pastoral Review* 37 (2000). Her call for the church to walk with women.
Kirk, Margaret. *Let Justice Flow: An Asian Woman works creatively for the Liberation of Her People*. Biography of Agustina Lumentut. New Delhi: ISPCK, 1997.

4.11 Eka Darmaputera (1942-), Central Java and Jakarta

Eka Darmaputera was born in Magelang, central Java, and obtained his BD (Graduate School of Theology, Jakarta 1966), during which time he was active in the student movement, becoming president of the union. He acquired his PhD in Religion and Society from Boston College in 1982. Throughout his active life he has combined leading a local congregation in East Jakarta with teaching ethics at the Jakarta Graduate School of Theology, "Not doing theology," he disclaims, "but theology by doing", that is, responding to ethical, political and dogmatic questions as they arose. A well-known preacher and newspaper columnist, both his selected sermons and columns have been published in numerous collections over the years (e.g. 1977). He has been Moderator of the Synod of the Christian Church of West Java and has held numerous posts in the Communion of Churches in Indonesia (PGI) from 1976-2000. He has also been an advisor to a number of government commissions.

Careful in his writings, he never tries to force his viewpoint but is ever willing to offer incisive points, practical possibilities and clear choices. From the beginning he has been active in the inter-religious foundation *Interfidei* headed by Sumartana, chairing the founding body. After the fall of Soeharto (1998) he joined the Democratic Party of Struggle (PDIP) under Megawati Soekarnoputri in order to practise what he had been writing about. His "naïve" hopes and idealism were quickly disillusioned: "I am no politician but a pastor." Since May 1998, like many colleagues, he has become more openly critical in his writings of both the national scene and of the lethargy of the churches (1999). In his address to the National Catholic Jubilee Congress in 2000, Eka described the churches as, "internally irrelevant, socially insignificant". Early retirement due to ill health was marked by the publication of a 904-page Festschrift (1999) with contributions by 50 fellow theologians of different religions - a remarkable tribute. A second volume, edited by colleagues, is an 890-page "Eka Darmaputera Reader."

Darmaputera is one of many Indonesian theologians who have studied the State ideology of *Pancasila*, in his case from the perspective of Javanese culture and ethics (1982). Outwardly, Javanese culture is perceived to be governed by a totalising and hierarchical world-view. However, in the ancient mythologies acted out in the *wayang* (puppet plays), the Javanese experience a deep sense of oneness beyond all difference. For Eka the *Pancasila* is an attempt to enable traditional culture to cope with contemporary problems. For the Javanese a "both-and"- more accurately a "neither-nor" - world-view leads to an ethical perception oriented towards acceptance; not of good over evil and right over wrong, but of what is appropriate (*cocok*), what fits in, what is in accord with one's feeling and intuition (*rasa*). Eka believes that this traditional Javanese world-view is fertile soil in which to grow the idea of basic human rights. Where universal human rights and the *Pancasila* do not seem to fit, then the *Pancasila* needs reinterpreting.

Darmaputera is one of those who have returned to Javanese mystical culture in the 1980s as the locus for doing theology, rather than, for instance, holding a direct dialogue with Islam, or by openly confronting the systemic injustice of the military regime. His extensive writings in ethics can be described as both evangelical and ecumenical in his inimitable, forever inclusive, Indonesian way. In "retirement" since October 2000, Eka hopes to continue his series of books on ethics "for the layperson". He has authored 13 books and booklets and over 400 articles and manuscripts of which at least seven are in English, one in German and another in Dutch.

Selected References
Works by Eka Darmaputera
> *Berbeda tapi Bersatu. Bacaan Praktis Pimpinan dan Warga Jemaat mengenai Oikumene* (Different yet united. Practical readings for congregational leaders and members on ecumenism). Jakarta: BPK Gunung Mulia, 1974.
> *Tuhan dari Poci dan Panci* (God of teapot and enamelware - from the author's column in *Sinar Harapan*). Jakarta: BPK Gunung Mulia, 1977. Republished as *Firman Hidup 29* (The Living Word 29). Jakarta: BPK Gunung Mulia, 1982.
> *Pancasila and the Search for Identity and Modernity in Indonesian Society. A Cultural and Ethical Analysis.* Leiden: E.J. Brill, 1988. Indonesian translation. Jakarta: BPK Gunung Mulia, 1987.
> "Mengevaluasi Kehadiran Gereja di Tengah-tengah Tuntutan Reformasi" (Evaluating the presence of the Church in the midst of the demands of (national) reformation). In *Gereja dan Reformasi: Pembaruan Gereja menuju Indonesia Baru* (Church and Reform: The Renewal of the Church as we approach a New Indonesia), edited by Victor Silaen, 3-15. Jakarta: Yakoma-PGI, 1999.
> *Pergulatan Kehadiran Kristen di Indonesia* (The struggle of the Christian presence in Indonesia). Jakarta: BPK Gunung Mulia, forthcoming. An 890-page edited selection of Eka's writings with 35-page annotated bibliography of Darmaputera's writings which have been made available to the Jakarta Graduate School of Theology library.

—, with Lukas Hendrata. *AIDS: Kutukan Tuhan? Beberapa Catatan Medis, Teologis dan Etis* (AIDS? God's curse? Medical, theological and ethical notes). Jakarta: BPK Gunung Mulia, 1995.

Suleeman, Ferdinand, et al., eds. *Bergumul dalam Pengharapan* (Struggling in hope). Jakarta: BPK Gunung Mulia, 1999. Festschrift, 904pp. Largest festschrift to date.

4.12 Agustina Nunuk Prasetyo Murniati (1943-), Yogyakarta.

A. Nunuk Prasetyo Murniati was born during the Japanese occupation when her self-effacing mother, daughter of a Javanese ascetic, quietly cooked meals for the freedom fighters. Ibu Nunuk - "Mother Nunuk" as she is usually known - herself studied economics and sociology at *Gajah Mada* University in Yogyakarta, when she was Chairperson of the Catholic Youth Organisation, graduating in 1968. Ibu Nunuk then taught at the *Tarakanita* Social Welfare Academy for 30 years, where she was Director for 15. She was team-teaching on pastoral work with the family at *Wedabhakti* Faculty of Theology when publication of her book on violence towards women in the church (1995) brought that to an end. Sidelined by Catholics, she was in constant demand in Protestant and Islamic women's groups. Three years later her teaching at the *Wedabhakti* Faculty was resumed, this time in feminist theology in the Post-graduate School (20 sessions). Married to a civil servant and with three, now married, children, Ibu Nunuk has been a family counsellor for 25 years.

Ibu Nunuk was initially active in the Laity Commission of the Semarang Archdiocese which she found too introverted and restricting. A friend and collaborator of Mangunwijaya (4.3), she moved to non-governmental organisations and inter-faith networks in 1976. Starting as an economist, Ibu Nunuk's work with women's cooperatives led her to widen her knowledge and she studied cultural anthropology and social psychology. To avoid being appointed Rector of *Atma Jaya* University, Ibu Nunuk applied for a sabbatical, taking a diploma in pastoral counselling at the Maryknoll School in New York (1982) and so "accidentally" discovered theology. Ibu Nunuk is the first Catholic Indonesian

Contextual Theological Reflection in Indonesia 1800-2000

woman to study theology at the Master's level (Maryknoll 1984). Feminist theology brought on a faith-crisis as the pious Jesus of her upbringing was challenged by the biblical Jesus of feminist research. Giving up her devotional Jesus, she rooted her liberationist Christ into the life-witness of her independent parents and ascetic grandparents. Feminist theology provided a theoretical frame for her empowerment work with women.

For Ibu Nunuk theology is conversation - an ongoing questioning process by groups of involved women (1998:36-45). Theology is a truly collaborative exercise (c.f. 1986, 1990). Before theology can liberate, the Bible and church dogma have to be liberated from masculine culture and from narrow androcentric interpretations. In contrast to women's movements in the West, she experiences no dichotomy between extremes - between the peace and pro-life movements, for instance. Her support for natural family planning is rooted in indigenous spirituality, in the effectiveness of traditional herbal contraceptives and in her opposition to the hegemony of capitalist, pharmaceutical TNCs. Her approach is not one-sidedly cerebral; words are not the only theological language. Theology is personal, birthed by the heart in music, movement, painting, architecture, meditation and asceticism.

Ibu Nunuk is a member of the National Commission on Women (established after the military-organised mass rape of Chinese-descent women in May 1998), and so divides her time between Jakarta and Yogyakarta. In 1993 she founded *Kelompok Perempuan Sadar* (Group of Aware Women) of which she is Chairperson (see 1.3. above). She runs gender-awareness workshops throughout Indonesia, more particularly in violent trouble spots. She was General Chairperson of the *Perserikatan Solidaritas Perempuan* (Union of Solidarity with Women - 1998-). From 1995-2000 she was EATWOT co-ordinator for Indonesia.

Retiring from teaching early (2000), Ibu Nunuk is devoting the remainder of her active life in justice movements and inter-faith gender networks which were banned for most of her adult life (1966-98). Meanwhile she is working on her SEAGST doctorate on the right to reproduction - a feminist theology of life.

Selected References
Works by A. Nunuk Prasetyo Murniati

Gerakan Anti-Kekerasan terhadap Perempuan (Movement against violence towards women). Yogyakarta: Kelompok Perempuan Sadar, 1995. Expanded ed., Yogyakarta: Kanisius, 1998. The book that led to Ibu Nunuk's temporary removal as visiting lecturer at Wedabhakti Faculty of Theology.

"Rediscovering the Indonesian Women's Potential." EATWOT Asian Feminist Theology Meeting. Madras, 15-20 December, 1990. Typescript.

"An Indonesian Contribution to a Spirituality of Liberation: Two Perspectives. An Approach from the Javanese World View" In *Asian Spirituality Reclaiming Traditions*, edited by Fabella, Lee, and Kwang-sun Suh. Maryknoll, NY: Orbis Books, 1992.

"Perempuan Indonesia dan Pola Ketergantungan" (Indonesian women and the model of dependence). In *Citra Wanita dan Kekuasaan (Jawa)*. Yogyakarta: Kanisius & Lembaga Studi Realino, 1992.

"Peran Perempuan dalam Gereja" (The role of women in the Church), *Gender dan Pembangunan I*, Jakarta: Seri LPPS 30 (1995).

"An Expanded Vision of Pastoral Work in Indonesia." New York: Maryknoll School of Theology. MA thesis, 1984. Bibliography. Typescript.

4.13 Henriette Marianne Katoppo (1943-), Tomohon and Jakarta

The theology of Marianne Katoppo, recorded in her many writings, finds its most apt embodiment in her own life struggle. She is the youngest of ten siblings, a member of a prominent Dutch-speaking Protestant family and has been an energetic participant in international ecumenical networks. She was born in Tomohon, North Sulawesi, but brought up in Jakarta, obtained her BA from Graduate School of Theology, Jakarta (1963) and then studied in Japan (1964-65). Work followed with the British and Foreign Bible Society in London (1966-69), and Sweden (1970-74), with later post-graduate studies in Jakarta (MA, 1976) and at the Ecumenical Institute at Bossey, Switzerland, writing *Compassionate and Free*

(1979). Continuing her peripatetic lifestyle she was appointed visiting lecturer at Selly Oak Colleges, Birmingham, UK (1985-86). Since 1983 she has lived as a free-lance theologian, novelist, journalist and translator. Katoppo is a founder member of, and was the first Indonesian co-ordinator for, the Ecumenical Association of Third World Theologians (EATWOT). She is a founding-member of the journal *In God's Image* and was a contributing editor to the same (1983-97); she has also been a contributing editor to *Mission Studies*. She has been a member of the Executive Committee of the Communion of Churches in Indonesia (PGI), seeing to woman's concerns (1984-89).

Intelligent, independent, forthright, conversant in a dozen Asian and European languages, Katoppo embodies the ambiguities and brokenness of those who do not fit into any single category - socially, culturally, religiously. Her most successful and most explicitly Christian novel is *Raumanen* (1977) where a love affair across ethnic lines tragically ends with the suicide of the protagonist. However, her other female protagonists are not defeated, as, for instance, in *Terbangnya Punai* (A pigeon's flight, 1978) and in *Rumah di atas Jembatan* (House on the bridge, 1981). Also, *Dunia Tak Bermusim* (World without seasons, 1974), her most clearly "autobiographical" novel, is an opened-ended story. Her theological articles and WCC book spring partly from personal experience (disappointment, even bitterness) and partly from social critique, taking up themes of justice (option for the poor and gender issues). Living with her two-dozen cats, she most admires *Prapanca* who has become the feline subject of a short story on the difficulty of finding a place to breathe in Indonesia. By mid-2000 she had authored five novels, a few short stories, one theological work and over 20 articles, of which ten are in English.

Selected References
Works by Marianne Katoppo

>*Raumanen*. Jakarta: Gaya Favorit Press, 1977. (Won the Arts Council Award (Jakarta, 1975) and the Southeast Asian Write Award of 1982.) Marianne's best novel by far.

Compassionate and Free: An Asian Woman's Theology. Geneva: World Council of Churches, 1979; Maryknoll, NY: 1980 & 1981. Also available in Dutch, German and Swedish editions, but no Indonesian translation. Marianne's classic work.

"Asian Theology: An Asian Woman's Perspective." *WCC Exchange* 3 (1979) Reprinted in *Asia's Struggle for Full Humanity*, edited by Virginia Fabella, 140-151. Maryknoll, NY: Orbis Books, 1980; *Logos* 20.1 (1981).

"The Concept of God and the Spirit from the Feminist Perspective." In *Feminist theology from the Third World*, edited by Ursula King, 244-250. London: SPCK, 1994.

"Marianne Katoppo" (Interview with commentary) In *Pribadi-pribadi Pemuka Cakrawala: Tokoh Seni dan Profesional* (Individuals who Opened Horizons: Artists and Professionals), edited by Frans M. Parera, 107-118. Jakarta: Kompas, 2000.

Mantik, Maria Josephine. "Kesetaraan dan Keadilan: Raih dan Perjuangkan! Renungan Awal Novel 'Anggrek Tak Pernah Berdusta' Karya Marianne Katoppo" (Equality and justice: grasp and struggle! A preliminary reflection on the novel 'Orchids Don't Lie' by Marianne Katoppo). In *Perempuan dan Pemberdayaan*, edited by Surita Notosusanto and E. Kristi Poerwandari, 325-341. Jakarta: Obor, 1997.

Steenbrink, Karel. "Ecumenical Adventures of Marianne Katoppo." In *Changing Partnership of Missionary and Ecumenical Movements*, edited by Leny Lagerwerf, Karel Steenbrink, and Frans Verstraelen, 212-225. Leiden-Utrecht: Inter-university Institute for Missiological and Ecumenical Research, 1995. A critical yet sympathetic profile.

4.14 Th. Sumartana (1944-), Central Java and Jakarta

Th. Sumartana was born at Karangkobar, Banjarnegara, Central Java, and studied at the Graduate School of Theology, Jakarta, later continuing with missiology at Vrije Universiteit, The Netherlands (doctorate 1991). He has worked as theological editor at BPK Gunung Mulia Publishers and part-time at the Research and Study Unit of the Communion of Churches (Balitbang-PGI). Sumartana has been post-graduate lecturer in religion and society at Satya Wacana (Protestant) University in Salatiga and post-graduate lecturer in religion and culture at Sanata Dharma (Catholic) University in Yogyakarta.

In his youth Sumartana was close to HMI (Modernist Muslim Student Association). Wishing to break out of the constricting dogmatic identity of the Protestant Church, he has endeavoured to work for justice in society with people of other faith traditions. In his theology Sumartana articulates a biblical basis for such inter-faith involvement. He discovered the theological tools he needed when studying at Bossey Institute (1972). He describes Hendrik Kraemer's "conquest" mission paradigm as imperial-colonial and Karl Barth, on whom Kraemer depended, as a religious fascist (only Christianity is true). In his doctorate (published in 1994), Sumartana undertook a study of the theological paradigms used by missioners who established the Indonesian Protestant Church and underlined the need for a new inter-faith theological framework.

Sumartana is Director of *Interfidei*, the Institute for Inter-faith Dialogue that he co-founded in 1992. This institute is not tied to any institutional religion although it has good working relationships with religious leaders. Its personnel are Muslim, Christian, Hindu and Buddhist. *Interfidei* has gradually extended its regular study days, workshops and training sessions, scientific research and publications from the city of Yogyakarta to the whole of Java and now works on a national scale, particularly in trouble spots. The institute has over a dozen substantial books on its list.

Since the break-down of the Soeharto regime (1998), Sumartana has involved himself in practical politics, becoming one of the Chairpersons of *Partai Amanat Nasional* (PAN - National Party). PAN is headed by Amien Rais, the former Director of the modernist educational Muslim association *Muhammadiyah*. Thus, Sumartana dialogues with Muslim leaders who oppose the corrupt elite in contrast to Victor Tanja (4.7) who conversed with the Muslims who ran the Soeharto regime. He sees his controversial involvement in politics as a practical application of his theology. As PAN became more overtly Islamist (and opportunist), so Sumartana and other Christians resigned.

Sumartana continues to combine academic research with practical involvement. He has authored one book, edited a further half dozen and written numerous articles. In mid-2000 he was writing a comprehensive work on dialogue based largely on his experience at *Interfidei* during its first decade.

Selected References
Works by Th. Sumartana

> *Mission at the Crossroads: Indigenous Churches, European Missionaries, Islamic Association and Socio-Religious Change in Java 1812-1936.* Jakarta: BPK Gunung Mulia, 1994. (PhD thesis, Vrije Universiteit, 1991). The most critical evaluation of Kraemer to date.
>
> "Sinkretisme Agama: Penyakit atau Obat?" (Religious syncretism: illness or medicine?). In *Atas Nama Agama* (In the name of religion), edited by Andito, 87-91. Bandung: Pustaka Hidayah, 1998.
>
> "Theologia Religionum" (Theology of religions). In *Meretas Jalan Teologi Agama-agama di Indonesia* (Opening up the way for a theology of religions in Indonesia), by Tim Balitbang PGI (research unit of the Communion of Churches), 17-39. Jakarta: BPK Gunung Mulia, 1999.

4.15 Andreas Ananggguru Yewangoe (1945-), Sumba and Kupang

Andreas A. Yewangoe was born at Mamboru in Sumba, obtained his MA from the Graduate School of Theology, Jakarta (1969), and both his Masters and Doctorate in theology (1987) from Vrije Universiteit in Amsterdam. Since the opening of the Graduate School of Theology in Kupang, Timor (1971), Yewangoe was appointed lecturer, twice combining teaching with rectorship (1972-76; 1980-84) and later took the Presidency of the newly-established Artha Wacana University (1988-98) of which the Graduate School became a Faculty. Yewangoe has penned a fortnightly column in the regional daily newspaper *Pos Kupang* since its inception in 1992. In the tradition of Darmaputera (4.11), he makes lively and incisive comments in accessible language on local, national and global affairs. He has been one of the co-Chairpersons of the

Communion of Churches in Indonesia (1989-94) and has been re-elected for the 2000-2005 term.

Until the 1980s, Indonesian theologians were either very Indonesian or very western. Through his doctoral research and subsequent teaching, writing and administration, Yewangoe has introduced other Asian theologies into mainstream church discourse and some seminary syllabi. If the wider Asian context is finally entering the theological debate, it is his achievement in no mean measure. He has been carefully prising theology away from the pietist congregation where classroom theology remained for too long.

Yewangoe, from the Reformed tradition, has taken up the liberationist frame of Sri Lankan Jesuit Aloysius Pieris through which to analyse emerging theologies in Asia (1987). Quietly, yet persistently, in newspapers and at seminars, Yewangoe reflects upon current affairs through his moderately radical liberationist prism. And this he did when the value of harmony was masking the centralising of political and economic power in Indonesia under Soeharto and in the world at large through the "inevitable" process of economic globalisation. More recently Yewangoe (1999) has been reflecting upon the multiple crises (economic, political, cultural, educational, legal and moral) that have burst forth at the end of the 32-year long Soeharto regime.

Yewangoe began with a theological reflection on reconciliation that came out of his own Eastern Indonesian Sumbanese culture (1983). With his ever broadening perspective over the years, like Mangunwijaya (4.3) and Banawiratma (4.16), he is showing that the more creative thought is deriving from those who have drunk at their own cultural wells and then thrown themselves into the struggle for a more just and democratic society. Apart from his more than 200 newspaper columns, Yewangoe has authored nine books, of which one is in English, and 40 articles.

Selected References
Works by Andreas A, Yewangoe

Pendamaian: Suatu Studi tentang Pemulihan Relasi antara Allah, Manusia dan Alam-semesta (Reconciliation: a study of the restoration of the relationship between God, people and creation). Jakarta: BPK Gunung Mulia, 1983.

Theologia Crucis in Asia: Asian Christian Views on Suffering in the Face of Overwhelming Poverty and Multifaceted Religiosity in Asia. Amsterdam: RODOPI, 1987. (PhD thesis, Vrije Universiteit). One of the first theological conversations with fellow Asian theologians.

Agama dan Kerukunan (Religion and harmony). Jakarta: BPK Gunung Mulia, forthcoming. Collection of papers on contemporary issues.

"Gereja di Era Reformasi" (The Church in a time of reform). In *Gereja dan Reformasi: Pembaruan Gereja menuju Indonesia Baru* (Church and reform: the renewal of the Church as we approach a new Indonesia), edited by Victor Silaen, 16-35. Jakarta: Yakoma-PGI, 1999.

4.16 Johanes Baptista Banawiratma (1946-), Yogyakarta, Central Java

Born in Yogyakarta, central Java, J.B. Banawiratma obtained his doctorate from Innsbruck (1981) and became professor of systematic theology at the Theology Faculty of Sanata Dharma University, Yogyakarta. Romo Bono - or "Father Bono" as he has been universally known - has been a member of the Theological Commission of the Bishops' Conference since its inception in 1992 becoming its secretary (1998-). He has regularly participated in meetings of the FABC, the CCA and the Jesuit Asian Regency. He is a member of the Theological Commission of EATWOT. He has long cultivated contacts with Protestant colleagues and Muslim intellectuals both locally and nationally. He has engaged with the women's movement and actively supported the students who swept Soeharto from power (1998). Later Romo Bono left the Jesuits and married Judith Lim and was appointed to the Graduate School of Theology (STT), Jakarta.

In his MA thesis (1977) Romo Bono compares the relationship between teacher and disciple in both the elitist and popular cultural traditions of Java with that obtaining in the Gospel of John. His emphasis is not so much upon the content of the Javanese teachings as upon the cultural dynamics at work: dialogue, question-answer, riddles, sayings, parables, symbols, paradoxes, which step by step open up the heart of the disciple. The great themes of John are very much part of the psyche of the Javanese: light, life, water of life, darkness. Romo Bono distinguishes between the rich spiritual tradition of Java that remains meaningful today and the demands of the Gospel which forever challenge. A natural symbiosis has already taken place in the lives of Javanese Christians.

Refreshed in the wells of his Javanese culture, Banawiratma immersed himself in contemporary culture while evolving a more contextual methodology for researching and teaching theology (1989). For part of the course at Sanata Dharma University, students research particular themes or projects (hope, salvation, work etc.). After engaging in case studies with a local community, course participants reflect upon the issues that emerged theologically, calling in professors from a number of disciplines (1993, German edition 1995, English 1999).

This contextual theological praxis is an example of how the Second Vatican Council (1962-65) is being received by the most important Faculty of Theology for Catholics in Indonesia. The approach is "moderately liberative". It aims at getting students thinking rather than providing them with ready answers. As the collaborative effort of a university faculty, it necessarily compromises method (partly practical, partly classic) and content (the demands of a Catholic seminary versus the demands of contextual theology). Both in these thematic projects and as editor of dozens of collections of theological writings, Banawiratma shows how doing theology in Indonesia is very much a collective enterprise.

Christology has remained one of Romo Bono's constant theological preoccupations. His 1977 MA reflected upon an encounter between one culture and one gospel writing. In the 1980s he looked at images of Jesus at various historical periods - in colonial times, during Soeharto's regime, in a pluralistic society (1986). Towards the end of the 1990s the Gospel-culture encounter had become a multi-dimensional, critical, transforming dialogue (1999a). His turn-of-century Christology is a "liberative, inter-contextual" theology. His Christology now begins with the experience of the believing congregation. The marginalised poor are not just context; theirs is the perspective through which the entire Trinitarian Christology needs to be viewed. Culture is no longer simply cosmic-holistic, but also secular. Feminism deconstructs both the feudal patriarchalism of local culture and of the dogmatic tradition. A two-way dialogue with the majority Muslim community translates faith in Christ into Islamic terms while inviting Muslim experience of their encounter with God to enrich our Christology.

Banawiratma does theology as a liberationist firmly rooted in his Javanese culture while open to national, regional and global contexts. He continues to reflect upon the little tradition of criticism and the great tradition of oppression (1999b). Human dignity, the right to participate, and even the need to revolt are embedded in the cosmic-holistic culture of the powerless, while feudal patriarchalism shapes the hierarchical culture of the powerful. Banawiratma has authored five books of which one has appeared in German (1995) and English (1999) translations; he has edited a further 14 volumes and published over 70 articles, of which 13 are in English and one in German.

Selected References
Works by J.B. Banawiratma

    Yesus Sang Guru: Pertemuan Kejawen dengan Injil (Jesus the teacher: an encounter between Javanese culture and the Gospel). MA thesis. Yogyakarta: Kanisius, 1977. An interplay between the "great" and "little" traditions of Java and the Gospel.

    "Yesus Kristus dan keterlibatan Sosial Gereja (Jesus Christ and the social involvement of the Church). *Orientasi* 18 (1986).

    "Kebudayaan Jawa dan Teologi Pembebasan" (Javanese culture and the theology of liberation). In *Bergumul dalam Pengharapan* (Struggling in hope), (1999a). Jakarta: BPK Gunung Mulia, 1999a. Twenty years after "Yesus Sang Guru", Bana has opened out his Javanese perspective to a broad inter-contextual one.

    "Kristologi Trinitaris dengan Pendekatan Kontekstual" (1999b). Yogyakarta: Sanata Dharma. Manuscript, forthcoming.

—, with J. Mueller. *Berteologi Sosial Lintas Ilmu: Kemiskinan sebagai Tantangan Hidup Beriman* (Doing an interdisciplinary social theology: poverty as a challenge to the life of the faithful). Yogyakarta, Kanisius, 1993. Rev. ed., 1995. German translation *Kontextuelle Sozial Theologie: Eine Indonesisches Modell.* Freiburg: Herder, 1995. English translation "Contextual Social Theology: An Indonesian Model", *EAPR* 36.1-2 (1999). A classic text in use in most faculties.

4.17 John Mansford Prior svd (1946-), UK and Flores

Hailing from Ipswich, UK, John Prior has been working in Flores since 1973. Prior's post-graduate diploma (Cambridge 1973) found practical expression in his ongoing work with the biblical apostolate. Meanwhile involvement in building base communities in town on the north coast (1973-81) and in the hinterland (1981-87) led to his awareness of a "split-level church" which found articulation in his doctorate (Birmingham 1987). In the latter he took up the question of marriage, where he sensed a key dislocation between the lived "popular" theology of the people and the theology (canonical norms) of the official church. The official church survives through a "working misunderstanding" with the people. After 14 years at Ledalero Seminary (1987-2001), John returned to Maumere to recently become secretary of Candraditya Research Centre.

A member of two Commissions of the Indonesian Bishops' Conference - Theology (since 1994) and Justice and Peace (since 1997) - Prior has reached out nationally from his local base in Flores. Coordinating missiological education and research for the Society of the Divine Word (SVD) in Asia-Pacific (1994-99) and working with the FABC Offices for Evangelisation (since 1991) and for Ecumenical and Inter-religious Affairs (since 1997) John has gained Asia-wide experience. Liaison with the press during the Episcopal Synod for Asia at the Vatican (1998) led to critical observations on the differing approaches to mission from Rome (dogmatic-didactic) and Asia (dialogical-experiential).

Prior's writings combine a sensitivity to the liberative heart of the culture of the tribal-marginalised and the role of grassroots Bible sharing in establishing a more compassionate and just society.

He has published four books (three in Indonesian), edited over 30 others (just one in English), and published over 80 articles and book chapters in Indonesian, of which 30 have also been published in other Asian (Mandarin, Urdu) or Western (English, French, German, Polish and Hispanic) languages.

Selected References
Works by John Mansford Prior

> *Church and Marriage in an Indonesian Village: A Study of Customary and Church Marriage among the* Ata Lio *of Central Flores Indonesia, as a Paradigm of the Ecclesial Inter-relationship between Village and Institutional Catholicism.* Frankfurt: Peter Lang, 1987. PhD thesis.
>
> *Bejana Tanah Nan Indah: Refleksi Sosio-Cultural atas Jemaat-jemaat Basis Nusa Tenggara sebagai Wujud Evangelisasi Baru.* (Earthenware pots, fragile but beautiful: a socio-cultural reflection on the basic communities of Nusa Tenggara as vessels of the new evangelization). Ende: Nusa Indah, 1993.
>
> *Daya Hening, Upaya Juang: Menoleh kepada Agama dan Budaya Kaum Tersisih.* (Potent silence, strength in struggle: passing-over to the religion and culture of the marginalised). Jakarta: BPK Gunung Mulia, 1999. Collection of missiological papers.
>
> "From Head-hunting to the Return of the Child: Mission at the Encounter with Cosmic Religion." *Pacifica*, 7.2 (1994). Also in French *Spiritus* 34.133 (1993); and Indonesian, *Vox*, 38.4 (1994) and *Sawi* 10 (1995). Social dislocation explained through a popular scare story.
>
> "Towards a New Evangelization Among the Nusa Tenggara Peoples of Eastern Indonesia." *Asia Journal of Theology*, 10.2 (1996). Also in Indonesian, *Seri Pastoral* 319. Yogyakarta: Pusat Pastoral. A critical evaluation of mission.
>
> "A Tale of Two Synods: Observations on the Special Assembly for Asia." *Sedos* 30.8-9 (1998) and *Vidyajyoti*, 62.09 (1998). Indonesian version with additional footnotes, *Sawi* 13 (1998) and *Penyalur* 15.05 (1998). Also published in Urdu (Multan, Pakistan).
>
> "Portraying the Face of the Nazarene in Contemporary Indonesia: Literature as Frontier-Expanding Mission." *Pacifica*, 14.2 (forthcoming).
>
> "Dialogue and Culture: Reflections of a Temporary Sojourner." *EAPR* 39.4. Indonesian version, *Sawi* 16.

4.18 Sientje Merentek-Abram (1947-), Sulawesi

Sientje Merentek-Abram comes from Bowongkulu, Sangihe, North Sulawesi. In 1980 she obtained her MTh from Western Theological Seminary, Holland, Michigan, and her doctorate from the Southeast Asia Graduate School of Theology (1996), a study of the Joseph narratives in Genesis 37-50. Ordained in the Protestant Church of Minahasa (GMIM) in 1981, Sientje has been a member of the theological department of the Christian University at Tomohon (UKIT) since 1974, lecturing in such subjects as the prophetical books, NT hermeneutics, narrative hermeneutics and feminist theology. She was Dean of the Faculty (1981-84) and has been a long term advisor to the Cultural Council of Sangihe Talaud, Manado.

Active in regional and international gatherings, Sientje was a member of the Programme on Theological Education (PTE) of the WCC (1984-89). In 2000 she was Chairperson of the Association of Theological Schools in Southeast Asia, Area Dean in Eastern Indonesia for the Southeast Asia Graduate School of Theology (SEAGST) and Assistant Chairperson of the Programme on Theology and Culture in Asia (PTCA). Nationally, Sientje chairs the Association of Women with Theological Education in Indonesia (PERWATI), while more locally, she is Chairperson of the General Synod of the churches of North and Central Sulawesi. Since 1985 Sientje has published over a dozen articles written for national and international gatherings, on biblical, missiological and theological subjects. Her doctoral dissertation is being prepared for publication in Indonesian. She is now Dean of SEAGST.

Selected References
Works by Sientje Merentek-Abram

"Narasi Yusuf dan Kenabian" (The Joseph narrative and prophecy). In *Keadilan Bagi Yang Lemah* (Justice for the Weak), edited by Ph. K. Erari, al. Jakarta: Persetia 1985.

"Management and Accountability in Theological Education: A Response to Dr. C.S. Song's Key Note Address." In *ATESEA Occasional Papers*. Singapore: ATESEA, 1985.

"Penggunaan Alkitab" (Using the Bible). In *Persebaran Firman Di Sepanjang Zaman* (Spreading the word in every age), edited by Weinata Sairin et al. Jakarta: BPK Gunung Mulia, 1994.

"Kemitraan dalam Kristus di Tengah Dunia yang Cepat Berubah" (Equality in Christ in a fast changing world). In *Berikanlah Aku Air Hidup Itu* (Give me that living water), edited by Bendalina Doeka and Stephen Suleeman. Jakarta: Persetia, 1997.

"Teologi Feminis dan Sumbangannya dalam Gereja dan Masyarakat" (Feminist theology and its contribution in the Church and world). In *Bentangkanlah Sayapmu* (Spread wide your wings), edited by Stephen Suleeman et al. Jakarta: Persetia, 1999.

"Doing Theology in The New Millennium.." In *PTCA Bulletin*, edited by Martinez, Salvador. Chiang Mai: Glang Vieng Printing Co., 2000.

4.19 Karel Phil Erari (1947-), Makimi and Jakarta

Karel Phil Erari was born in Makimi, Papua-land (then Dutch New Guinea). With great difficulty and personal hardship he completed his primary and lower secondary schooling, winning a scholarship to the high school on the island of Biak, graduating in 1966. Moving to Jakarta, Karel Erari undertook both undergraduate and graduate studies in theology. His master's thesis, published in 1994, explored the work of PGI members in tackling poverty during the 1960s and 70s. Interest in ecological questions led him to participate in the Rio de Janeiro Conference of 1992 and to research environmental ethics, in particular the question of land, for his doctoral thesis (SEAGST, 1996). He concluded that the peoples of Papua have components within their cultures that could lay the foundations for a contextual eco-theology (see 1999).

Karel Erari has taught ethics and ecumenical missiology at Kijne Graduate School of Theology (1973-88). He was secretary to the Synod of the Protestant Church in Irian Jaya (GKI, 1984-92) and since 1998 has directed the Research Unit of the Communion of Churches in Jakarta (Balitbang PGI). In the latter capacity Erari has edited many collections of theology, himself contributing articles on questions of environmental ethics.

Selected References
Works by Karel Phil Erari
Supaya Engkau Membuka Belenggu Kemiskinan. (So that you open the chains of poverty). Jakarta: BPK Gunung Mulia, 1994.
Tanah Kita, Hidup Kita. (Our land, our life). Jakarta: Sinar Harapan, 1999.
—, et al., eds. *Keadilan bagi Kaum Lemah* (Justice for the weak). Book to honour M.A. Ihromi. Jakarta: BPK Gunung Mulia, 1995.

4.20 Emanuel Gerrit Singgih (1949-), Macassar and Yogyakarta

E. Gerrit Singgih was born in Jakarta of a Javanese father and a mother of Indo-Dutch-Macassar descent. As with his genealogy, Singgih's theology manifests multi-cultural perspectives in a pluralistic society. He obtained a BSc in economics from Macassar (1971) and completed his Master's at the Duta Wacana Faculty of Theology (1977). His doctoral research in Old Testament Studies was undertaken at Glasgow University, Scotland (PhD 1982). Ordained in 1983, he ministered in the GPIB Reformed Church in Macassar, South Sulawesi, while teaching part-time at the local Theological College. Since 1985 he has been teaching theology at his alma mater in Yogyakarta. He has been Dean of the Faculty of Theology (1993-99) and is presently Dean of Post-graduate Studies.

Singgih is an Old Testament scholar who struggles with how to develop distinctly Indonesian interpretations of the Bible. Most of his writings are not exclusively biblical, but bring together an interpretation of Indonesian society (a hermeneutics of life) with critical, biblical reflections (an hermeneutics of the text). His hermeneutical keys are outlined in his first book where he moves away from exclusively confessional or western models (1982). The Indonesian cultural and political context helps in his choice and use of hermeneutical tools both for interpreting present reality and the biblical text (1997). Confronting key issues that challenge the theory and practice of Christianity in Indonesia, Singgih's intellectual scope has become ever wider, taking in contemporary western philosophy (2000). Nevertheless, throughout the past 20 years his aim has been consistent: To help develop communities of faith who are socially aware through a biblical theology at once distinctively local and broadly ecumenical - the latter including the wider ecumenism of inter-faith action and reflection. Rigorous in his biblical analysis, he openly accepts a variety of Javanese approaches, seeing the socio-cultural context as primary, rather than, say, an exclusively socio-economic one. His detailed exegesis of Ecclesiastes expounds the text verse by verse, balancing historical with literary criticism. The treatment is "Javanese" in its balanced interpretations, in its moderate emphases, in its illustrations from Javanese popular culture, in its inviting the reader to consider varying readings and in its placing of the biblical text in the context of daily life.

Singgih is a trans-denominational, socially committed biblical theologian with a personable and bold writing style, rooted in inter-faith praxis. His is a local theology working for a global coherence where all parties contribute from what they have. A Taize-inspired celibate life-style enables Singgih to live simply in communion with theological students and local congregations. By mid-2000 he had authored nine books and over 50 articles.

Selected References
Works by E. Gerrit Singgih

Dari Israel ke Asia (From Israel to Asia). Jakarta: BPK Gunung Mulia, 1982.

Reformasi dan Transformasi Pelayanan Gereja Menyongsong Abad ke-21 (The reformation and the transformation of the Church's ministry as we welcome the 21st century). Yogyakarta: Kanisius, 1997. Collection of practical theological papers.

Iman dan Politik dalam Era Reformasi di Indonesia (Faith and politics in the Reformation era in Indonesia). Jakarta: BPK Gunung Mulia, 2000.

Berteologi dalam Konteks: Pemikiran-pemikiran mengenai Kontekstualisasi Teologi di Indonesia (Doing theology in context: thoughts on the contextualisation of theology in Indonesia). Yogyakarta: Kanisius, 2000.

Dunia yang Bermakna (A world with meaning). Jakarta: Persetia, 2000.

Hidup di bawah Bayang-bayang Maut: Sebuah Tafsir Kitab Pengkhotbah (Living under the shadows of death: an exegesis of the Book of Ecclesiastes). BPK Gunung Mulia, forthcoming.

4.21 Gabriel Possenti Sindhunata sj (1952-), East Java and Yogyakarta

Coming from Batu, East Java, Sindhunata was a journalist with the largest circulation national daily *Kompas,* for which paper he still writes a column on world soccer fixtures. After joining the Jesuits (ordained 1983), Sindhu, as he is generally known, spent his first two years as a pastor at Pakem to the north of Yogyakarta - the location of much of his later narrative writing. He researched his PhD at the Jesuit Philosophical Institute in Munich (1986-92) taking up the theme of Javanese peasant messianic movements from 1850 to 1940. Since then stationed in Yogyakarta, he is a full-time writer of columns, articles (2000), short stories (1996) and novels in both Indonesian and Javanese. He also edits the cultural and religious monthly *Basis* previously edited by Dick Hartoko.

Sindhu comes from, and is actively developing, the Javanese syncretistic tradition at its prophetic best. With scarcely a footnote, devoid of any explicit reference to Christian or Muslim sources, Sindhu gives voice to the victims of oppressive politics and rapacious economic development. His is a universal humanism, open to the Spirit, in the language of Javanese popular culture. He interweaves powerful and popular images from the culture of the oppressed with sharp humour accompanied by a devastating critique of the formal culture of the governing elite. In the convention of the traditional and prophetic puppet plays of the villagers, Sindhu is blithely unconcerned whether his sources are Muslim, Christian or Javanese, as long as they give voice to and strengthen the cultural renewal needed to empower the marginalised of Java. His writings articulate the practical, everyday wisdom through which the poor refuse to be defeated and by which they survive and on occasion thrive. As such Sindhu writes in the tradition of Mangunwijaya (4.3). However, unlike Mangun, Sindhu makes little reference to the official church and writes a considerable amount in Javanese as well as Indonesian. The prophetic syncretism of Sindhunata is an interesting phenomenon at the turn of the century when the politicisation of religion is drawing ever-sharper demarcations between religious institutions.

Sindhu is yet another example of Indonesian theologising by someone who is not a professional theologian. Like other creative theological thinkers, he has sided with the victims of society while writing in the language of popular culture. Growing from a lively, oral tradition Sindhu's popular writings (as with those of Mangunwijaya) would need a host of academic footnotes to make them accessible in English translation. At the beginning of 2001 Sindhunata had published 11 books, two of which are in Javanese and one in German, and had edited a further dozen volumes and written three dozen articles.

Selected References
Works by Gabriel Possenti Sindhunata

Dilema Usaha Manusia Rasional. Kritik Masyarakat Modern oleh Max Horkheimer dalam rangka Sekolah Frankfurt (The dilemma of the rational being. The critique of modern society by Max Horkheimer in the Frankfurt School). Jakarta: Gramedia, 1982.

Air Penghidupan: Peziarahan Mencari Diri (Water of life: journey to find oneself). Yogyakarta: Kanisius, 1988.

Ndherek Sang Dewi ing ereng-erenging redi Merapi (Following the goddess on the slopes of Mount Merapi). Yogyakarta: Kanisius, 1995. Javanese. Indonesian version published under the title *Mata Air Bulan* (Water source of the moon). Yogyakarta: Kanisius, 1998.

Semar Mencari Raga (Semar seeks a body). Yogyakarta: Kanisius & Basis, 1996.

Sakitnya Melahirkan Demokrasi (The pain of giving birth to democracy). Yogyakarta: Kanisius, 2000.

4.22 Henriette Tabita Hutabarat-Lebang (1952-), Macassar, Jakarta, Hong Kong

Born in the city of Macassar, South Sulawesi, Henriette Hutabarat-Lebang is an ordained pastor (1992) of the Protestant Church in Toraja. She undertook undergraduate and graduate studies at the Jakarta School of Theology (BTh. 1975; MDiv. 1977). She later

Contextual Theological Reflection in Indonesia 1800-2000 217

completed her doctoral research at the Presbyterian school of Christian Education, Richmond, Virginia, on the theme of contextualisation and the role of metaphor (1991). She married Ralph Donald Manahara Hutabarat in 1980.

Hutabarat was a member of the staff of the Centre for Leadership Training of Toraja church (1978-80) moving to Jakarta in 1984 to head the women's desk of the Communion of Churches in Indonesia (PGI) for two years. She moved to Hong Kong in 1991 where she was Associate General Secretary for Programme Co-ordination of the Christian Conference of Asia (CCA) and later Associate General Secretary for Relationships and Communications. These positions have involved her in many WCC meetings and projects.

Thus at local, national and Asia-wide levels, Hutabarat has initiated numerous programmes that enhance mutual understanding between the Asian churches. In particular she has been involved in programmes for women's leadership development and adult education, as well as for migrant workers, refugees and internally displaced communities in Asia. In all her ecumenical positions Hutabarat has brought both administrative ability and an enquiring theological mind. Her presentations encompass areas such as Asian spirituality, education for peace with justice in Asia, pluralism, women and tourism, as well as many Bible studies with congregations. Like other women theologians, her work has been developed with teams of colleagues and published jointly as the fruit of workshops. Hutabarat is probably the most influential Indonesian woman theological thinker during the last decade of the 20th century.

Selected References
Works by Henriette Hutabarat-Lebang
 "Pendidikan bagi Perdamaian serta Keadilan di Asia" (Education for justice with peace in Asia). In *Terbit Sepucuk Taruk: Teologi Kehidupan* (An opening shoot: a theology of life). Jakarta: BPK Gunung Mulia, 1993.
 "Pilihlah Kehidupan: Peranan Kenabian Wanita Asia" (Choose life: prophetic roles of Asian women). In *Keadilan bagi yang*

Lemah (Justice for the weak), edited by Karel Phil Erari et al, 214-226. Jakarta: BPK Gunung Mulia, 1995.

"Teologi Feminis yang Relevan di Indonesia" (A relevant feminist theology in Indonesia). In *Bentangkanlah Sayapmu* (Open wide your wings), edited by Bendalina Doeka-Souk and Stephen Suleeman. Seminar-Workshop on Feminist Theology by the PGI Office of Women's Concerns, Perwati & Persetia. Kaliurang, 28-30 July 1999. Jakarta: Persetia, 1999.

"Is an Inclusive Community Possible?" In *Do Justice, Love Mercy*, edited by John and Bridget Newbury. Geneva: Frontier Internship in Mission, 2000.

co-editor. *Mission of God in the Midst of Asian Plurality*. Hong Kong: CCA 1994.

co-author. *Becoming the Church of the Stranger*. Hong Kong: CCA 1997.

4.23 Septemmy Eucharistia Lakawa (1970-), Central Sulawesi and Jakarta

In Septemmy Eucharistia Lakawa we meet with the new generation of women theologians. Born in Kendari, Central Sulawesi, she began studying theology at the Jakarta School of Theology in 1989, graduating in 1994. Temmy - as she is known - then obtained an MA from Austin Presbyterian Seminary (1996) followed by an MTh from Jakarta (1998). Her latter thesis is entitled: "A Missiology of Compassion: Missiology according to an Indonesian Christian Woman."

While doing her masters course in Austin, Temmy found her faith questioned by her theological investigations for the first time. Lectures in feminist theology led to tears and prayer. She finally decided to continue with feminist theologies in order to engage a lifelong wrestle with the key questions: who is the God whom we know in Indonesia? Who and where is Christ in Indonesian realities? How should the church participate in God's mission of justice, peace and truth in Indonesia? She describes her Indonesian feminist theology as "brave like Hagar, honest like the Samaritan woman, risk-taking like Rahab, visionary like Mary of the Magnificat; a theology able to rest in silence like Saul's concubine Rizpah, weep bitterly like Tamar and dance joyfully like Miriam". Orthodoxy has to be questioned by orthopraxis. For Temmy theology is a collaborative effort, ever inclusive, beginning with women's stories born in an "epistemology from the broken body". Major influences on her theology include Chung Hyun Kyung, Mercy Amba-Oduyoye, Elisabeth Schuessler-Fiorenza and Elisabeth Johnson.

In 1996 Temmy was ordained. After a brief period serving her church in Central Sulawesi she returned to Jakarta in 1998 to teach at her alma mater (missiology, ecumenism, reading the Bible with new eyes and modern theology). Her theology has been developing in concert with a community of activists, probers and scholars. She joined *PERWATI* (see 1.3. above). During *PERWATI*'s National Congress in 1998, where she delivered a paper, Temmy was elected general secretary. She is also the first editor of *Sophia*, the journal of *PERWATI*, founded in March 2000 (cf. 1.5. above). Involved in the Christian Conference of Asia, Temmy has been preparing and presenting studies in the CCA programme "Reading the Bible with New Eyes" for Gender-Awareness workshops throughout Asia (e.g. Mt. 26:26-28; Jg. 19:1-30; 2 Sam. 13:1-39). Participating in the Harare General Assembly of the WCC in 1998, Temmy Lakawa was elected to its Executive Committee.

Selected References
Works by Septemmy Eucharistia Lakawa
> "God Who Sees: An Indonesian Christian Woman Reading the Story of Hagar in Searching a Liberating Spirituality for Indonesian (Christian-Muslim) Women Co-operating in Praxis." In *Berakar di dalam Dia dan Dibangun di atas Dia* (Rooted in Him and built upon Him), edited by Robert Borrong, 195-210. Jakarta: BPK Gunung Mulia, 1998. Reprinted 2000.
> "Pengkajian Kritis terhadap Teologi kaum Feminis. Suatu Pendekatan Metodologis" (A critical study of the theology of feminists. A methodological approach). In *Bentangkanlah Sayapmu* (Open Wide your Wings). Seminar-Workshop on Feminist Theology by the PGI Office of Women's Concerns, Perwati & Persetia. Kaliurang, 28-30 July, 1999. edited by Bendalina Doeka Souk and Stephen Suleemam. Jakarta: Persetia, 1999.

"Keheningan dan Kekerasan: Perjalanan Perempuan Mencari Kebenaran demi Rekonsiliasi" (Silence and violence: the journey of women seeking the truth for the sake of reconciliation,). *Sophia* 1.1 (2000).

4.24 Other Contributions to Contextual Theology

Many other theologians and writers have contributed to theology in Indonesia. Their writings have appeared in such Indonesian journals as *Peninjau, Basis, Prisma, Rohani, Gema Duta Wacana, Umat Baru, Orientasi Baru, Spektrum* and *Refleksi*, as well as in international journals such as the *Southeast/East Asia/Asia Journal of Theology, International Review of Mission, Asia Focus* and *Exchange*. (For Indonesian journals see 1.5 above.)

Among these authors are priests and ministers, theological teachers and lay leaders, writers and activists each of whom has played, or is playing, a role in theological development. A selection of these authors is given below along with examples of their published work.

Abednego, Benjamin Agustinus. (1934-): From the city of Bandung in west Java, Abednego taught at the *Seminari Alkitab Asia Tenggara* (Southeast Asian Bible Seminary) in Malang, east Java. Doctorate in Pastoral Studies from SEAGST. He has written a series of theological books and many articles mainly on ecclesiology.

> *Jabatan Gereja dan Kharisma I* (Church ministries and charisms). Jakarta: BPK Gunung Mulia 1984.
>
> "Selayang Pandang Sejarah Awal 'Gereja Kristen Indonesia Jawa Timur'" (A Short look at the early history of the East Java Protestant Church). *Peninjau* 11.1-2 (1984).
>
> "The Call to be Servants of God." *International Review of Mission* 63.251 (1974).
>
> "Perjalanan Penyatuan Gereja Kristen Indonesia" (The Ecumenical road of the Christian Church in Indonesia). In *Jalan Menuju Kesatuan* (The Path towards unity). Ed. Henky C. Wijaya etc. Jakarta: BPK Gunung Mulia, 1996.
>
> with Piet Go o.carm *Mengenal Gereja-gereja Kristen Protestan* (An Introduction to the Protestant Churches). Malang: Analekta 1988.

Aritonang, Jan S. (1953-): A Batak from Sibolga in Northwest Sumatra. A Lutheran, Aritonang is a church historian at the Jakarta Graduate School of Theology (STT) where he has been rector. He obtained his doctorate from SEAGST and is now area Dean of SEAGST for western Indonesia. Co-editor with Karel Steenbrink (Utrecht) of a major two-volume ecumenical history of Christianity in Indonesia (forthcoming).

> *Apa dan Bagaimana Gereja?* (What and how is the Church?) Jakarta: BPK Gunung Mulia 1989. A short church history.
>
> *Sejarah Pendidikan Kristen di tanah Batak: suatu Telaah Historis-teologis atas Perjumpaan orang Batak dengan Zending (khususnya RMG) di bidang Pendidikan, 1861-1940* (History of Christian education in Batakland: An Historical-theological analysis of the meeting between the Bataks with the Reinland Mission Society (RMG) 1861-1940). Jakarta: BPK Gunung Mulia 1988. Doctoral thesis. English edition *Mission Schools in Batakland (Indonesia) 1861-1940*. (translated by R. Beohlke) Amsterdam 1994.
>
> *Berbagai Aliran di dalam dan di sekitar Gereja.* (Some currents within and around the church). Jakarta: BPK Gunung Mulia 1995.

Borrong, Robert Patannang. (1954-): From Mamuju in south Sulawesi, Borrong began his theological studies in Rantepao, Sulawesi, completing his first degree at STT Jakarta (1980). He obtained both his Masters (1983) and Doctorate (1996) from SEAGST. After teaching in Macassar, south Sulawesi (1984-87), Borrong became secretary of the education unit of the Council of Churches in Jakarta (1987-92). Since 1996 Borrong has been teaching environmental ethics, philosophy and modern theology at the Jakarta Graduate School of Theology (STT).

> *Etika Bumi Baru: Akses Etika dalam Pengelolaan Lingkungan Hidup* (A New ethics for the earth: An ethical access in managing the environment). Jakarta: BPK Gunung Mulia, 1999.
>
> "Peranan Gereja dalam Penyelenggaraan sekolah Kristen di Indonesia" (The role of the Church in running Christian schools in Indonesia). *Peninjau* 15.2 (1990).
>
> "Etika Lingkungan dan Gereja: Ekologi dan Ekumene" (Environmental ethics and the Church: ecology and

ecumenism). In Robert Borrong, ed., *Berakar di dalam Dia dan Dibangun di atas Dia*. (Rooted in Him and built on Him: 80 years with Prof. Dr. P.D. Latuihamallo). Jakarta BPK Gunung Mulia, 2000, 124-141.

"The role of Humankind in the Environmental Crisis." In Robert Borrong, ed., *Berakar di dalam Dia dan Dibangun di atas Dia*. (Rooted in Him and built on Him: 80 years with Prof. Dr. P.D. Latuihamallo). Jakarta BPK Gunung Mulia, 2000, 156-16.

Chang, William ofm.cap (1962-): A Chinese-Indonesian from West Kalimantan. Rector of the post-graduate Seminary at Pontianak which prepares ordinands for pastoral work in the dioceses of Kalimantan. Specialises in social and environmental ethics. Chang writes regularly in the Jakarta dailies *Kompas* and *The Jakarta Post*, the weekly *Mingguan Hidup* and also in *Asia Focus* (Hong Kong).

"Jesus' Commandment of Love and Confucian Jen: An Ethical Comparative Study." Rome: Pontifical Gregorian University, 1994. Licentiate thesis.

The Dignity of the Human Person in Pancasila and the Church's Social Doctrine: An Ethical Comparative Study. Quezon City: Claretian Publications, 1997. Doctoral thesis.

Moral Lingkungan Hidup (Environmental Ethics). Yogyakarta: Kanisius, forthcoming.

Menggali Butir-butir Keutamaan (Uncovering Elements of the Virtues). Yogyakarta: Kanisius, forthcoming.

Kerikil-kerikil di Jalan Reformasi: Catatan-cataan Etika Sosial (Pebbles on the Road of the Indonesian Reformation: Notes on social ethics). Jakarta: Penerbit Buku Kompas, forthcoming.

Danuwinata, Francis Xavier sj: taught at Wedabakti theology faculty, Sanata Dharma University, Yogyakarta. He was rector in the 1980s when Sanata Dharma had not yet become a recognised university. He has been concerned with both contextualisation and the role of Christianity in human development.

"Indonesianisasi dan Imamat" (Indonesianisation and the priesthood). *Spektrum* 1.4 (1970).

"Indonesianisation - A Summary of pre-Synod Discussions." *Exchange* 5 (1973).

"Konsientiasasi Gereja Indonesia" (The conscientisation of the church in Indonesia). *Rohani* 34 (1987).

Hartono, Christophorus Thoekoel (1939-): Chris Hartono is a Chinese-Indonesian from Klaten, central Java whose father came from mainland China and his mother from the foot of Mount Merapi in central Java. Hartono obtained his Masters in 1979 and teaches at *Duta Wacana* Christian University, Yogyakarta. Author of many books and articles on church and mission history, in particular regarding Chinese-Indonesian Christian communities.

Ketionghoaan dan Kekristenan: Latar Belakang dan Panggilan Gereja-gereja yang berasal Tionghoa di Indonesia (Being Chinese, Being Christian: The background and vocation of Chinese-origin Churches in Indonesia). Jakarta: BPK Gunung Muia 1974.

Pietisme di Eropa dan Pengaruhnya di Indonesia (Pietism in Europe and its influence in Indonesia). Jakarta: BPK Gunung Mulia, 1974.

Memahami dan Menghayati Kehidupan Jemaat Sekuler (Understanding and living in a secular congregation). Jakarta: BPK Gunung Mulia, 1974/77.

Gerakan Ekumenis di Indonesia (The ecumenical movement in Indonesia). Yogyakarta: PPIP Duta Wacana, 1984.

Orang Tionghoa dan Pekabaran Injil: Suatu Studi tentang Pekabaran Injil kepada Orang-orang Tionghoa di Jawa Barat pada Masa Pemerintahan Hindia Belanda (The Chinese and the proclamation of the gospel: A study of the evangelisation of the Chinese in West Java during Dutch colonial times). Yogyakarta: Taman Pustaka Kristen, 1996.

"Kehadiran Zending di Zaman Kolonial Belanda: Suatu tinjauan historis-teologis" (The presence of protestant mission societies in Dutch colonial times: an historical-theological analysis). In *Tahun Rahmat dan Pemerdekaan* (A Year of grace and liberation), ed. F. W. Raintung et al. Surakarta: YBKS, 1995.

Hartoko, Dick sj (1922-2000): born in East Java from a Dutch father and Javanese mother, Hartoko was professor of history at Sanata Dharma University and long-time editor of the cultural-intellectual journal *Basis* (See above 1.5). Not a professional theologian, Hartoko has nurtured Christian humanism in cultural and intellectual circles.

Saksi Budaya (Cultural witness). Jakarta: Pustaka Jaya, 1975. Collection from articles in *Basis* 1958-72.

Tonggak Perjalanan Budaya: sebuah antologi (Markers in the journey of culture: An Anthology of articles). Yogyakarta: Kanisius, 1986.

Mencari Bulir-bulir Gandum. Kumpulan renungan singkat (Looking for ears of corn. A collection of short reflections). Yogyakarta: Yayasan Andi, 1999.

Rahmanto, B. ed., *Dari Maliho O Borok sampai Seni Sono: Pilihan Tanda-tanda Zaman* (From Maliho O Borok to Seni Sono: A Selection from the monthly column "Signs of the Times" by Dick Hartoko in *Basis*). Jakarta: Gramedia, 1992.

Moedjanto, G. et alia (ed.), *Tantangan Kemanusiaan Universal: Antologi Filsafat, Budaya, Sejarah-Politik dan Sastra pada 70thn Dick Hartoko* (The Challenge of Universal Humanism: An anthology of philosophy, culture, political history and literature on the 70th birthday of Dick Hartoko). Yogyakarta: Kanisius, 1992.

Sindhunata, G.P. *Melik Nggendong Lali: Pameran Lukisan 50 Tahun Basis* (Record of the exhibition at Bentara Budaya Yogyakarta 24 November - 1 December 2001 on the 50th anniversary of the journal *Basis*). Published by the Exhibition committee.

Kieser, Bernard sj (1938-): German-born, Kieser has taught at Wedabakti Faculty of Theology at Sanata Dharma University since ordination. He graduated from Innsbruck University. A prolific writer in moral theology with 9 books and over 30 articles published between 1979-2000. Librarian of the computerised Jesuit Kolsani library in Yogyakarta.

"Moraltheologische Fragen des menschlichen Sterbens ein Beitrag zum Gespraech zwischen Humanwissenschaften und Moraltheologie." Innsbruck: University of Innsbruck, Faculty of Theology. 2 Vols. 1973. Doctoral thesis.

Ikut Menderita, Ikut Percaya: Pastoral Orang sakit (Suffering together, believing together: the pastoral care of the sick). Yogyakarta: Kanisius, 1984.

Moral Sosial: Keterlibatan Umat dalam Hidup Bermasyarakat (Social ethics: the involvement of believers in social life). Yogyakarta: Kanisius, 1987.

Solidaritas 100 Tahun Ajaran Sosial Gereja (Solidarity: 100

Years of the church's social teaching). Yogyakarta, Kanisius, 1992.

Liem Khiem Yang: Liem is a Chinese-Indonesian from central Java. Now retired, he has taught theology and New Testament studies at the Graduate School of Theology Jakarta (STT) where he became professor in 1973 and where he has also been rector. Liem has also taught at the National University of Indonesia (UI). He was active in EACC-CCA.

"Geredja dalam Revolusi Indonesia" (The church in the Indonesian Revolution). In *Partisipasi Kristen dalam Pembangunan* (Christian Participation in Indonesian Nation-Building). ed. W.L. Sidjabat. Jakarta: BPK Gunung Mulia, 1968.

Memberlakukan yang dilakukan Allah: suatu tinjauan ke dalam segi utama dari hidup dan pemberitaan Yesus dan Paulus (Enacting the Acts of God: a reflection on the most important element in the life and proclamation of Jesus and Paul). Jakarta: BPK Gunung Mulia, 1974. Shortened English version in *SEAJT* 14.2 (1973).

Mardiatmadja, Bernhard S. sj (1943-): From Yogyakarta, Romo Mardi, as he is known, studied in both Germany and Australia. He taught theology at Sanata Dharma University, Yogya, and then at the Driyarkara Philosophy Institute, Jakarta, before becoming apostolic vicar for specialised ministries in the Jakarta Archdiocese. Author of a series of books on faith/belief and other volumes and articles on ecclesiology.

Beriman dengan Taqwa (Believing with devotion), *Beriman dengan Bertanggung Jawab* (Believing responsibly), *Beriman dengan Radikal* (Believing radically), *Beriman dengan Sadar* (Believing with awareness), *Beriman dengan Tanggap* (Believing appropriately). Yogyakarta: Kanisius. The whole series published in 1985.

Putranta, C.B. sj (1951-): Putranta has now returned to teaching theology in Yogyakarta after a term as congregational leader of the Jesuits in Indonesia. He has been engaged in teaching catechists and writes popular, contextual ecclesiology.

"The Idea of the Church in the Documents of the Federation of Asian Bishops' Conferences (FABC) 1970-1982." Roma: Gregorian University 1985. Doctoral thesis.

Pewarta Kerajaan Allah: Sebuah Pengantar Ekklesiologi (The herald of the reign of God: an introduction to ecclesiology). Yogyakarta: Puskat, 1998.

"Kesadaran Misioner: Landasan bagi Pembaharuan Pelayanan Gerjeani" (Mission awareness: the base for the renewal of the church's ministry). *Orientasi Baru* 1.

Sidjabat, W.B.: Sidjabat obtained his doctorate at Princeton Theological Seminary, USA, in 1960 and taught at the Jakarta Graduate School of Theology (STT) for many years. He has written or edited books and articles on theology, religious tolerance and political participation.

Religious Tolerance and the Christian Faith. Jakarta: BPK Gunung Mulia, 1965. Sidjabat's doctoral thesis of 1960 published in English. Original title: "Religious Tolerance and the Christian Faith; A Study Concerning the Concept of Divine Omnipotence in the Indonesian Constitution in the Light of Islam and Christianity."

—, ed. *Christian Participation in Indonesian Nation-Building.* Jakarta: BPK Gunung Mulia, 1968.

"The Turbulence that South East Asians are Facing", *SEAJT* 23 (1982).

Sitompul, Adelbert Agustin (1932-): Hailing from Medan, north Sumatra, Sitompul did his undergraduate studies at the Batak seminary in Pematang Siantar (1954-59) and his post-graduate studies at Johanes Gutenburg University, Mainz (1961-64) and at Leiden (1965-66) obtaining his doctorate in 1967. From 1959-1979 he taught Old Testament at the Pematang Siantar Seminary where he also became rector and director of the seminary's Research Unit (1971-79). He was also secretary for Theological Education for the Lutheran World Federation (1975-79) in which capacity he has written and edited books. Since 1979 until his death Sitompul worked in the central offices of the Protestant Batak Church (HKBP).

Serving and Witnessing. Jakarta: BPK Gunung Mulia, 1973. Doctoral thesis. O.T. in relation to Batak culture (proverbs etc.) Original thesis: "Weisheitssprueche und prophetische Mahnrede im hintergrund der Mahnungeninder Toba-Batak auf Sumatera." Mainz, 1967.

Theological Education within the Whole People of God: International Consultation on Theological Education, held at the Ecumenical Institute Chateau Rossey 21-27 September 1975. Geneva: LWF, 1976.

Gereja Modern Mau Kemana? (Where is the modern church going?). Bandung: Yabina, 1995.

"Nature and the Natural in Asian Thinking. Asian Animism and Primal Religion." *East Asia Journal of Theology* 1.1 (1983).

—, ed. *Current Asian Theological Thinking: Progress reports and papers from seminars conducted by Asia Programme for Advanced Studies 1977*. Geneva: LWF, 1977.

—, ed. *Perintis Kekristenan di Sumatera bagian Utara* (Pioneer of Christianity in Northern Sumatra). Jakarta: Gunung Muia, 1986.

Ketika Aku di dalam Penjara, Harapan dalam Keterasingan: buku kenangan 50 tahun pdt. Dr. A.A. Sitompul (When I was in prison, hope in exile. Book to commemorate 50 years of Dr. A.A. Sitompul) . Pematang Siantar: Grafina, 1986.

Soejatno, Ardi: Coming from East Java, Soejatno is a former Director of the Institute of Theological Education, Malang. He has been prominent in lay and ecumenical education; now retired in Yogyakarta.

"Decision-making in East Java." *Asia Focus* 4.3 (1969).

"The Church as a Dynamic Instrument." *International Review of Mission* 63.3 (1974).

—, ed. *Sepuluh Amanat Kesatuan Gereja: sebuah uraian tentang bagaimana kita secara kongkrit harus mewujudkan keesaan gereja Tuhan di Indonesia* (Ten Instructions on the unity of the church: an explanation of how we can concretely achieve unity in the Lord's Church in Indonesia). Jakarta: DGI, 1978.

Thomson, Alan: taught theology and church history in Indonesia and was secretary for the Foundation for Theological Education.

"Churches in Java in the Aftermath of the 30th September Movement." *SEAJT* 9.3 (1968).

"Faith and Politics: the Indonesian Contribution." *SEAJT* 11.1 (1970).

Titaley, John: Hailing from Ambon, Maluku, John Titaley is a long-time staff member of the theological faculty at the Christian University of Salatiga (UKSW). He publishes in Indonesian, English and Dutch. With a brother killed in the Moluccan clashes since

1999, Titaley has been much involved "on the Christian side" though earlier writings were concerned with inter-faith relations.

"Membentuk Sikap Inklusif" (Forming an inclusive attitude). In *Pendidikan Agama dalam Perspektif Agama-agama* (Religious education from an inter-religious perspective). Ed. M. Quraish Shihab & Mastuhu. Jakarta: 1995.

"Future Possibilities within the Field of Religious Studie." *Gema Duta Wacana* 52 (1997).

"Theological Education in the Pancasila Society of Indonesia." *Studies in World Christianity* 3 (1997).

"De ene kerk in Indonesie." *Wereld en Zending* 28 (1999).

Widyatmadja, Josef P.: Widyatada obtained his MTh from Edinburgh in 1992. He taught at the Lay Training Centre in Malang, East Java before moving to STT Jakarta. He is a former secretary of *Persetia* Board (network of Protestant Theological Schools) and for 25 years Executive Secretary of the Social Welfare Guidance Council (YBKS) Solo, central Java, from where he edited the centre's journal *Refleksi* in which he wrote regularly. He has also been secretary for Urban-Rural Mission for the CCA.

"Incarnation as Subversion." In *Towards a Theology of People*, ed. Oh Jae Shik. Tokyo: CCA-URM, 1977.

Yesus Orang Desa (Jesus the Villager). *Refleksi* 4 (1979).

"Tahun Yobel dan Kemitraan untuk Pembebasan Hutang: suatu perspektip sejarah" (The jubilee year and partnership in cancelling debt: an nistorical perspective). In *Tahun Rahmat dan Pemerdekaan* (Year of grace and liberation) ed. Raintung, F.W. et al. Surakarta: YBKS, 1995.

Hidup dalam Kristus bersama Rakyat: antara Bethlehem dan Golgota (Living in Christ with the people: between bethlehem and golgotha). Surakarta: YBKS. n.d.

—, ed. *Bunga Rampai: Refleksi edisi HUT 25 Hidup bersama di dalam Kemajemukan dan Keadilan* (Collection on the occasion of 25th anniversary of YBKS. Living together in pluralism and justice.) Surakarta: YBKS, 1999.

Wismoady, Wahono S.: Wismoady taught at the Seminari Alkitab Asia Tenggara (Southeast Asian Bible Seminary) at Malang, east Java and at the Graduate School of Theology Jakarta (STT). Author and editor of numerous books and articles.

"Messianism in Peasant Revolt: A Reflection from the Christian Side". *Prisma* (Jan. 1977).

Di Sini Kutemukan (I find it here). Guidance to studying and teaching the Bible. Jakarta: BPK Gunung Mulia, 1986.

"Beberapa Thema Kontemporer Theologis" *Setia* 1, 3-9 (1987).

"Curriculum Construction: The *Persetia* Experience" *East Asian Journal of Theology* 1.2 (1983).

"Christian Involvement and Solidarity with People's Struggles", *Asia Journal of Theology* 4 (1990).

"Christian Mission in Asia: The Colonial Past and Challenges for Today" *International Review of Mission* 87 (1998).

5 Supplementary Bibliography
5.1 Bibliographies

Evers, Georg. *Bibliography on Local Church in Asia*. Theology in Context Supplements 3. Aachen: Missio, 1989.

—. *Bibliography on Interreligious Dialogue*. Theology in Context Supplements 7. Aachen: Missio, 1992.

—. *Directory of Christian University Libraries in Indonesia*. Surabaya: Library Automation Project for Christian Higher Education in Indonesia, 1998.

—. *Annotated Bibliography on Inculturation*. Theology in Context Supplements 9. Aachen: Missio, 1994.

Hoekema, Alle Gabe. "Dissertations by Protestant Theologians in Indonesia - a Short Bibliographical Review." *Exchange* 42 (1985).

—. "Protestant Dissertations in Indonesia 1985-1995." *Exchange* 25 (1996).

Janssen, Hermann and Gerhardt Angrit. *Annotated Bibliography on Ministries in the Church in Asia-Pacific*. Theology in Context Supplements 4. Aachen: Missio, 1989.

—. *Bibliography on Christology in Africa, Asia-Pacific and Latin America*. Theology in Context Supplements 5. Aachen: Missio, 1990.

Jongeneel, Jan A.B. *Daftar Buku-buku Dogmatika Kristen di Indonesia* (List of books in Christian dogmatics in Indonesia). Macassar: Sekolah Tinggi Theologia. (Early 70s?)

—. *Bibliografi Ilmu Agama dan Theologia Kristen dalam Bahasa Indonesia* (Bibliography of the scientific study of religions and

Christian theology in the Indonesian language). Jakarta: BPK Gunung Mulia. Vol. I, 1975; Vol II, 1976.

—. *Protestant Missionary Periodicals from the Nineteenth and Twentieth Centuries in the Netherlands East Indies and Dutch West Indies: A Bibliographical Catalogue with Introduction.* Leiden: IIMO, 1990.

Karmito. *Theology and Culture in Indonesia: A List of Selected Bibliographical Resources.* Yogyakarta: Universitas Kristen Duta Wacana, c.1994. Mimeo'd.

Kemp, Herman C. *Annotated Bibliography of Bibliographies on Indonesia.* Leiden: KITLV, 1990. (Lists 1649 titles in all languages in three sections-general, regional and subject bibliographies.

Kratz, Ernst Ulrich. *Bibliografi Karya Sastra Indonesia dalam Majalah Drama, Prosa, Puisi* (A bibliography of Indonesian literature in drama, prose and poetry journals). Yogyakarta: Gajah Mada University Press; London: School of Oriental and African Studies, 1989.

Losher, D. Jay. *Bibliografi Agama dan Masyarakat* (Bibliography on religion and society). Jakarta: BPK Gunung Mulia, 1994.

Retnowinarti, et al. *Hendrik Kraemer Bibliografie en Archief.* IIMO Research Publication 22. Leiden/Utrecht: IIMO, 1988.

Bibliographical Journal

Theology in Context: An Annotated Bibliography of Theological Journals from Africa, Asia, Oceania and Latin America. Aachen: Missio. Twice a year since 1984. ca. 250pp a year. Books and articles. Section on Asia includes Indonesia. Institute of Missiology, Missio, Bergriesch 27, D-5100 Aachen, Germany. E-mail: <mwi@missio-aachen.de>.

5.2 INTRODUCTORY LISTING FOR 1860-1910
Theses

Hartono, Chr. Th., "Teologi Etis dan Pekabaran Injil. Suatu Studi tentang Pengaruh Teologi Etis Belanda atas Pekabaran Injil Belanda yang Bekerja di Hindia Belanda pada 1900-1925."

Dissertation at Southeast Asian Graduate School of Theology, 1989.

Hutagalung, S.M. "The Problem of Religious Freedom in Indonesia, 1800 to the present." Yale University PhD thesis, 1958.

Soetopo, C, "Kyai Sadrach." Yogyakarta: Duta Wacana Graduate School of Theology. MTh, 1975.

Books & Pamphlets

Adriaanse, L., *Sadrach's Kring*. (Sadrach's circle - a substantial book). Leiden: 1899.

Albers, C. *Hikajat Garedja*. Rotterdam. (Apart from two paragraphs a history of the Western Church.) 1892.

Amorie van der Hoevan, H.A. des, *Het Streven der Indisch-radicalen. Een woord aan de Nederlandsche Christenen*. Amsterdam: 1869.

Arps, B. *Tembang in Two Traditions, Performance and Interpretation of Javanese Literature*. 1992.

Catalogus van de Maleische, Javaansche en Soendaneesche Colportage Lectuur (10 biblical poems for singing/recitation with gamelan in Sudanese (West Jawa). 1924.

Cuillot, C. *L'Affaire Sadrach, Un Esai de Christianisation a Java au XIX Siecle*, Paris: Archipel, 1981. Indonesian trans. *Kiai Sadrach. Riwayat Kristenisasi di Jawa*, Jakarta: Grafiti Press, 1985.

End, Th. van den. *De Nederlandse Zendingsvereniging in West-Java 1858-1963 een bronnenpublicatie*. Oesgstgeest, 1991.

Enklaar, I.H. *Joseph Kam, "Rasul Maluku"*, 1960.

Giay, Benny. *Zakheus Pakage and his Communities. Indigenous Religious Discourse, Socio-political Resistance and Ethnography of the Me of Irian Jaya*. Amsterdam: Free University Press, 1995.

Hadiwijono, Harun. *Kebatinan Islam Abad XVI*. Jakarta: BPK Gunung Mulia, n.d.

—. *Kebatinan dan Injil*. Jakarta: BPK Gunung Mulia, n.d.

Hale, Leonard. *Jujur Terhadap Pietisme: Menilai Kembali Reputasi Pietisme dalam Gereja-gereja Indonesia*. Jakarta: BPK Gunung Mulia, 1993.

Hardjoprakoso, Sumantri. *Indonesisch Mensbeeld als basis ener psychoteherapie.* 1956.

Ichticar Hikajat Gredja. Penghentar bagei moerid-moerid Seminarie die Depok. 1885?

Kipp, Rita Smith. *The Early Years of a Dutch Colonial Mission. The Karo Field.* Ann Arbor: University of Michigan Press, 1990.

Meersman, A. *The Franciscans in the Indonesian Archipelago 1300-1775.* Leuven. 1967.

"Menggali Teologi GKJW.Bahan Pembinaan Teologi Warga Gereja" (Uncovering the theology of the Protestant Church in Java. Material for theological formation of Church members). Malang, 1994.

Mulders, A. *De missie in tropisch Nederland.* Missiewetenschappelijke bijdragen 2. Den Bosch, 1930.

Muskens, M.P.M. *Indonesie. Een strijd om nationale identiteit. Nationalisten, Islamieten, Katholieken.* Bussum, 1969.

Partonadi, Sutarman S. *Sadrach's Community and its Contextual Roots. A Nineteenth Century Javanese Expression of Christianity.* Amsterdam: Rodopi, 1990. Amsterdam: Vrije Universitetit, PhD dissertation, 1988.

Pedersen, P.B. *Batak Soul and Protestant Soul. The Development of National Batak Churches in North Sumtra.* Grand Rapids: Eerdmans, 1970.

Prawiratirta, M. *Kabaripoen Malehekat dateng angger Menoengsa.* n.d. (19th c.?).

Proceedings of the Seventh IAHA conference 22-26 August 1977. Bangkok, 2 vols. Includes A.B. Lapian, "Tjahaja Sijang its Significance for the History of the Indonesian Local Press, II:910-923. (Tjahaja Sijang was published in Minahasa from 1868 onward.) 1977.

Rae, Simon. Breath Becomes the Wind. Old & New in Karo Religion. Dunedin: University of Otago, 1994.

Rullmann, J.A.C. De Sadrach Christenen. Hun beekenis voor vandaag. *Seri Allerwegen* 2.3 (1971).

Rumainum, F.J.S. *Guru Petrus Kafiar (1872-1926), Putera Irian Barat yang pertama mendjadi Pembawa Suluh Kristus.* 1959.

Soetikno, M. *Ngelmoe Oerip* Edisi Komite Pakabaran Injil. n.d. (19th c.?).

Sumanto, W.P. *Kyai Sadrach, Seorang Pencari Kebenaran, Sebabak Sejarah Pekabaran Injil di Jawa Tengah* (Kyai Sadrach, A searcher for truth, an historical phase in the preaching of the word in Central Jawa). Jakarta: BPK Gunung Mulia, 1974.

Sumartana, Th. *Mission at the Crossroads: Indigenous Churches, European Missionaries, Islamic Association and Socio-Religious Change in Java 1812-1936.* Jakarta: BPK Gunung Mulia, 1994.

Tosari, Paulus. "Ngelingake marang wong kang padha kaul, kanthi tembang asmaradana." UB Leiden, *L Or* 11.648. (Jawanese), n.d.

—. *Rasa Sedjati. Pethikan saking Serat Rasa Sedjati, karanganipun Swargi Kyai Paulus, ing Tosari. Mendhet saking babon kini kanthi karesikaken.* Reprinted in Jakarta in 1953 by Taman Pustaka Kristen. 1972.

Van Akkeren. *Dewi Sri dan Kristus.* Jakarta: BPK Gunung Mulia, n.d. English version: *Sri and Christ.* London: Lutterworth, 1970.

van Randwijck, S.C. Graaf. *Oegstgeest. Kebijaksanaan "Lembaga-lembaga Pekabaran Injil yang Bekerja Sama" 1897-1942.* Jakarta: BPK Gunung Mulia, 1989.

Velden, A.J.H. van der. *De Roomsch-Katholieke Missie in Nederlandsch Oost-Indie 1808-1908. Eene historische schets.* Nijmegen: 1908.

Wieringa, Edwin P. "Een gelofte aan God is geen koehandel: Een christelijk traktaatje in moslims gewaad van de Javaanse 'prototheoloog' Paulus Tosari over geloften." *Nederlands Theologisch Tijdschrift*, 50.4 (1996).

—. "Het christendom als het ware inzicht. Hendrik Kraemers uitgave van Paulus tosari's Rasa Sejati'. In *Woord en schrift in de Oost*, edited by W. van der Molen and B. Arps, 56-88. Leiden: 2000.

Witlox, J.H.J.M. *De staatkundige emancipatie van Nederlands katholieken 1848-1870*. Vol. III of *De Katholieke Staatspartij in haar oorsprong en ontwikkeling geschetst*. Ingeleid door L.J. Rogier en verzorgd door F. Pikkemaat-Meyer. Bussum, 1969.

Articles & Book Chapters

1883	Poensen, C. "Paulus To-sari" *MNZG* 27, 283-316, 333-360.
1903	Bodde, J. "Ferdinand Rantoeng" *MNZG* 3, 195-214.
1912	"Was die Pandita Batak aus ihrer Arbeit zu berichten haben" (Apa yang diberitakan para Pendeta Batak mengenai Pekerjaan mereka) *Bverichte der RMG* 69, 53-55.
1942-46	Nortier, C.W. "Paulus Tosari, Predikant te Modjowarno, 1848-1882." *Serie Lichtstralen op den Akker der Wereld* 47.3.
1967	Mardja, Sir. *Kiayi Paulus Tosari (Pelopor Geredja Kristen Djawi di Djawa Timur.*
1972	Rullmann, J.A.C. "De Sadrach Christenen: hun betekenis voor vandaag", *Allerwegen*, II, 2:1-22.
1974	Weitjens, J. "Pastur van Lith mengenai Kyahi Sadrach", *Orientasi*, VI. Yogyakarta: Kanisius, 183-202.
1979	Guilloot, Claude. "Karangjoso revisite: aux origines du Christianisme a Java central" *Archipel* 17, 115-133.
1979	Hoekema, A.G. "Kyai Ibrahim Tunggul Wulung (c.1800-85), 'een Javaanse Apollos'", *Nederlandse Theologisch Tijdschrift* 33.2, 89-110.
1981	Quarles van Ufford, Ph. "'Why don't you sit down?' Sadrach and the Struggle for religious Independence in the Earliest Phase of the Church of Central Java (1861-1899)." In *Man, Meaning and History*, edited by R. Schefold, 204-229.
1985	Hoekema, A.G. "Developments in the Education of Preachers in the Indonesian Mennonite Churches." *Mennonite Quarterly Review* 59.4, 398-409.
1985/6	Hartono, Chr. Th. "Sekitar Pietisme di Indonesia" *Setia*, 2.

1990	End, Th. van den. "Riwayat Pertobatan Ang Boeng Swi: Permulaan Agama Kristen di Indramayu", an edited version of the autobiography of Ang Boeng Swi (1811-1864). In *Masihkah Benih tersimpan...? Kumpulan Karangan dalam Rangka 50 Tahun GKI Jabar* (Is the seed still being stored? Collection of articles to celebrate the 50th anniversary of the Protestant Church of West Jawa), edited by F. Suleeman and Ioanes Rakhmat, 83-93. Jakarta.
1990	Heru Hendarto, Yohanes. "Frans van Lith, SJ, Pembaharu Karya Missi Gereja di Jawa Tengah." *Rohani*, 37, 214-220.
1993	Steenbrink, Karel. "The Rehabilitation of Indigenous Teachers. A Survey of Recent Research on the History of Christianity in Indonesia." *Exchange*, 22, 25-263.
2000	Singgih, Emanuel Gerrit. "Mengkaji Ulang Makna Sinkretisme: Suatu Tinjauan Historis" (A new study of the meaning of syncretism: an historical appraisal)., Chapter Five of *Berteologi dalam Konteks* (Doing theology in context). Yogyakarta: Kanisius.

Manuscripts

1970	Kartodirdjo, Sartono. "Religious Movements of Java in the 19th and 20th Centuries." Yogyakarta: Universitas Islam Indonesia.
1984	Suryohatmodjo. "Tembang kristen kanggo ngaluhurake Asmane Allah" (Poems for singing to praise the name of God). Blora, Mimeo'd.

5.3 INTRODUCTORY LISTING FOR 1911-1950

(Note: More extensive bibliographies for individual theologians are available from the author.)

Theses

1961	Cooley, F.L. "Altar and Throne in Central Moluccan Societies." New Haven: Yale University.
1967	Tan, Tiat-Han. "The Attitude of Dutch Protestant Missions toward Indonesian nationalism 1945-49." Princeton University PhD thesis.

1978	Webb, Paul. "Indonesian Christians and their Political Parties 1923-1966. The Role of the Partai Kristen Indonesia and the Partai Katolik." Townsville: James Cook University PhD Thesis.
1990	Nyhus, E. "An Indonesian Church in the Midst of Social Change: The Batak Protestant Christian Church, 1942-57." PhD University of Wisconsin-Madison, 1987.

Books

1915	Rijckevorsel, L. van. *Missie en misse-actie. Aan de Indische Vereeniging van Nederlandsche Katholieken.* Nijmegen.
1932	*Jaarboek van de katholieke missie in Nderlandsch Oost-Indie.* Batavia.
1945	Rijckevorsel, L. van. *Naar Indie? Beseffen wij, Katholieken, onze verantwoordelijkheid voor Indie?* Maastricht.
1945	Veraart, J.A. *De zending en het Indonesisch nationalisme.* Amsterdam.
1952	Rijckevorsel, L. van. *Pastoor F. van Lith SJ. De stichter van de missie in Midden-Java 1863-1926.* Nijmegen: Stichting St. Claverbond etc.
1957	*Buku Peringatan Sekolah Theologia Yogyakarta 1906-56* (Book to commemorate the Jakarta School of Theology 1906-56).
1957	Tennien, M. and T. Sato. *I Remember Flores.* New York. (Reflections of the Japanese commander in Flores 1942-45).
1958	Kraemer, H. *From Missionfield to Independent Church.* The Hague.
1964	Piskaty, K. *Die katholische Missionsschule in Nusa Tenggara (Suedost-Indonesien). Ihre geschifchtliche Entfaltung und ihre Bedeutung fuer die Missionsarbeit.* Steyl.
1969	Muskens, M.P.M. *Indonesie Een strijd om nationale identiteit Nationalisten, Islamieten, Katholieken.* Bussum: Paul Barnat. 1969. Indonesian translation under the title *Sejarah Gereja Katolik Indonesia* (History of the Catholic

Church in Indonesia). Published as volume IV of the History of the Catholic Church in Indonesia. Jakarta: DokPen KWI. 1973. Includes appendices.

1969 Weitjens, J.A. Th. *De vrijheid der katholieke prediking in Nederlands-Indie van 1900 tot 1940.* Rome/Jakarta: Gregorian University. Extract from PhD thesis.

1974 Panjaitan, J.Th. (ed.) *Panggilan dan Suruhan Allah. 75 Tahun Pekabaran Injil HKBP 1899-1974.* Pematang Siantar.

1974 Hartono, Chr. *Pietisme di Eropa dan Pengaruhnya di Indonesia* (European pietism and its influence in Indonesia). Jakarta: BPK Gunung Mulia.

1975 Moeryantini, M.H. *Mgr. Albertus Soegijapranata SJ.* Ende: Nusa Indah.

1983 Bank, Jan. *Katholieken en de Indonesische Revolutie.* Uitgeverij Ambo bv 1983. Indonesian translation: *Katolik di Masa Revolusi Indonesia* (Catholics at the time of the Indonesian revolution). Jakarta: Grasindo, 1999. Extensive bibliography 819-860.

1989 van Randwijck, S.C. Graaf. *Oegstgeest. Kebijaksanaan "Lembaga-lembaga Pekabaran Injil yang Bekerja Sama" 1897-1942* Jakarta: BPK Gunung Mulia.

1990 Jongeneel, J.A.B. *Protestantse Zendingsperiodieken uit de negentiende en twintigste eeuw.* Leiden: IIMO Research Publication 30.

1992 Steenbrink, Karel. *Dutch Colonialism and Islam: Contacts and Conflicts in Southeast Asia 1596-1950.* Amsterdam and Atlanta.

1998 Hayward, Douglas J. *Vernacular Christianity among the Mulia Dani. An Ethnography of Religious Belief among the Western Dani of Irian Jaya, Indonesia.* Lanham: University Press of America.

Articles & Book Chapters

1928 Sjarifoeddin, Amir. "Het Rassenprobleem in Ned. Indie." In *Mirabile Lectu. Orgaan van het Haarlemsch Gymnasium* 4.1-2.

1941	—. "Soesoenan Masjarakat dan Perang." (The ordering of society and war). *Semangat Baroe*, 1.28, 29, 30.
1942	—. "Menoedjoe kedjemaat Indonesia asli" (Towards an indigenous Indonesian congregation). In *Boekoe Peringatan Hari Djadi Isa Al-Maseh* (Book to commemorate the Birth of Jesus the Messiah), 6-8.
1957	"Pertemuan diantara Orang Kristen dan Orang Muslimin" (The encounter between Christians and Muslims). In *Buku Peringatan Sekolah Theologia Yogyakarta 1906-56* (Book commemorating the Yogyakarta School of Theology 1906-56), 26-29.
1957	Pos, A. "Theologia Indonesia." *Buku Peringatan Sekolah Theologia Yogyakarta 1906-56*. (Book commemorating the Yogyakarta School of Theology 1906-56). 19-22.
1968	Thomson, Alan, C. "Churches of Java in Aftermath of 30th Sept. Movement." *Southeast Asian Journal of Theology* 9.1.

Manuscript

1981	Wismoady, Wahono. "Kegiatan Theologia di dalam Pembaharuan Gereja" (Theological activity in the renewal of the Church). Presentation at the 50th Anniversary of the General Synod of the Wetan Mojowarno Protestant Church. Mimeo'd.

5.4 Histories and Historical Sources
Books and Pamphlets

?	Jongeneel, Jan. "Dutch-language mission-periodicals."
1958	*Kitab Peringatan 100 Tahun Geredja Kristen Indonesia Indramaju 1858- 13 Dessember - 1958* (Book commemorating 100 years of the Indonesian Protestant Church of Indramaju, 1858-1958).
1960	*Djedjak Langkah Pertama. 25 Tahun Perguruan Tinggi Theologia.* (First steps: 25 years of the Graduate School of Theology Jakarta). Jakarta.
1972	*50 Tahun Kanisius 1922-1972: Percetakan Penerbitan Kanisius sebagai Karya Gereja* (50 years of Kanisius:

Contextual Theological Reflection in Indonesia 1800-2000

printing and publishing as a work of the Church). Yogyakarta: Kanisius.

1972-74 Muskens, M., ed. *Sejarah Gereja Katolik Indonesia*. Ende: Arnoldus. I *Umat Katolik Perintis* (Pioneering Catholic communities, ca.645-1500). Photos; II *Wilayah tunggal Prefektur-Vikariat* (The Single Prefecture-Vicariate, 19th & 20th Centuries); III *Wilayah-wilayah Keuskupan dan Majelis Agung Waligereja Indonesia* (The dioceses and the Conference of Bishops in the 20th Century). IIIa pp.1-714, IIIb pp.719-1593; IV *Pengintegrasian di Alam Indonesia* (Integration into the Indonesian context).

1974 "Notulen Pertemuan Konsultasi tentang 25 Tahun Dewan gereja-gereja di Indonesia 15-21 November 1974 (Minutes of the Consultation on the 25th Anniversary of the Council of Churches in Indonesia). Jakarta.

1980 End, Th. van den. *Ragi Carita: Sejarah Gereja di Indonesia 1 th. 1500 - 1860an.* Jakarta: BPK Gunung Mulia. Reprinted 1996.

1981 Haire, James. *The Character and Theological Struggle of the Church in Halmahera, Indonesia, 1941-79*. Frankfurt am Main/Bern: Peter Lang.

1985 End, Th. van den. *De Gereformeerde Zendingsbond 1901-1961, Nederland-Tanah Toraja, een bronnenpublicatie*. Oegstgeets/Leusden/Zeist. Indonesian translation under the title *Sumber-sumber Zending tentang Sejarah Gereja Toraja 1901-1961*. Jakarta: BPK Gunung Mulia, 1994. 13 photos.

1987 End, Th. van den. *Gereformeerde Zending op Sumba. een bronnenpublicatie*. Oegstgeest. Indonesian translation under the title, *Sumber-sumber Zending Tentang Sejarah Gereja Kristen Sumba 1859-1972* (Sources of the Protestant mission on the history of the Christian Church of Sumba 1859-1972). Jakarta: BPK Gunung Mulia, 1996. 13 photos.

1988 Aritonang, J.S. "Sejarah Pendidikan Kristen di Tanah Batak"." SEAGSTh thesis. Published in English as

Mission Schools in Batakland (Indonesia) 1861-1940. Leiden: 1994.

1989 Randwijck, S.C. Graaf van. *Oegstgeest: Kebijaksanaan "Lembaga-lembaga Pekabaran Injil yang Bekerjasama" 1897-1942* (The policies of the United Bible Societies 1897-1942). Jakarta: BPK Gunung Mulia.

1991 End, Th. van den. *De Nederlandse Zendingsvereniging in West-Java 1858-1963 een bronnenpublicatie.* Oesgstgeest.

1993 End, Th. van den, and J. Weitjens. *Ragi Carita: Sejarah Gereja di Indonesia, II. th. 1860an - sekarang* (History of the Church in Indonesia II, 1860s to contemporary times). Jakarta: BPK Gunung Mulia.

1996 de Jong, Chris G.F., *"Ilalang Arenna...": Sejarah Zending Belanda di Antara Umat Bugis dan Makassar Sulawesi Selatan* (In the name of ... A history of the Dutch mission among the Bugis and Macassar peoples of South Sulawesi). Jakarta: BPK Gunung Mulia.

1999 Archdiocese of Merauke. *Sejarah Gereja Katolik di Irian Selatan* (History of the Catholic Church in South Irian). Merauke, 1999.

2000 Laan, Peter. *Sejarah Gereja Katolik di Timor* (History of the Catholic Church in Timor). Printed privately in Ende, Flores, by Heinz Neuhaus. Indonesian translation by Herman Embuiru of the Dutch primary sources collected by Peter Laan. Vol. I 1-439; Vol. II 440-914; Vol. III 915-1310. Dutch originals available in Utrecht.

Forthcoming: Steenbrink, Karel. *Catholics in Indonesia 1808-1942. A Documented History* I: A Modest Recovery 1808-1903; Vol II: 1903-42. Leiden: KITLV Press. Includes extensive primary sources.

Articles

1963 Thomson, Alan, C. "Indonesia." In *Prospects for Christianity Throughout the World*, edited by Bates.

1968 —. "Churches of Java in Aftermath of 30th Sept. Movement." *SEAJT* 9.3.

1975	Cooley, F.L. "Bagaimana Terbentuknya DGI" (How the National Council of Churches was formed). *Peninjau* 2.1.
1979	End, Th. van den. "Overzicht van de Literatuur op het gebiewd van de kerkgeschiedenis in de bahasa Indonesia." *W & Z* 8.1.
1986	—. "Historische Inleiding." In *Indonesische Geloofsbelijdenissen*, by Th. van den End, J.A.B. Jongeneel and M.R. Spindler, 13-35. Leiden/Utrecht: IIMO Research Pamphlet 20.

Resource in Progress

A major, two-volume writing project *History of Christianity in Indonesia* has been in progress since 1999, co-ordinated by Jan Aritonang (Jakarta) and Karel Steenbrink (Utrecht). Team of authors including Azra, Steenbrink & Heuken (The First Christians: until 1800); Van den End, Ngelow, Aritonang, Prior, Ipenburg, Giesen, Tapilatu, Parengkaun, Ukur, Brevoort, Rae, Daulay, Kipp & Hartono (Chronological and Regional Surveys: 1800-2000); Hoekema, Prior, Ngelow, Aritonang, Hartono, Azra, Schumann, Steenbrink, Kuester & Rosariyanto (Special Subjects). Information from IIMO, Heidelberglaan 2, 3584 CS Utrecht, The Netherlands. E-mail: <ksteenbrink@theo.uu.nl >. Due in 2003.

5.5 Overviews
Books

1971	Nababan, ed. *Pergumulan Rangkap. Laporan Konsultasi Theologia* (A double wrestle. Report of a theological consultation). Sukabumi 23-28 November 1970. Jakarta: BPK Gunung Mulia.
1975	*Dua Puluh Lima Tahun DGI* (Twenty-five years of the Council of Churches in Indonesia). Jakarta: BPK Gunung Mulia.
1979	Muskens, M.P.M. *Partner in Nation Building. The Catholic Church in Indonesia*. Aachen: Missio aktuell Verlag.
1981	Cooley, F.L. *The Growing Seed. The Christian Church in Indonesia*. New York: Wuppertal-Barmen; Jakarta: BPK Gunung Mulia.

1984	Hartono, Chr. Th. *Gerakan Ekumenis di Indonesia* (The Ecumenical Movement in Indonesia).
1992	Cribb, Robert. *Historical Dictionary of Indonesia*. Asian Historical Dictionaries 9. New York: The Scarecrow Press.
1994	Hoekema, Alle Gabe. *Deken in dynamisch evenwicht. De wordingsgeschiedenis van de nationale protestantse theologie in Indonesie (ca. 1860-1960)*. Goudstratt: Uitgeverij Boekencentrum, B.V. 35 page list of Indonesian theological works until 1960/65, with a separate list of Indonesian language periodicals. Indonesian translation without this extensive bibliography, *Perfikir dalam Keseimbangan*. Jakarta: BPK Gunung Mulia 1997.

Articles

1972	Jongeneel, J.A.B. "Christelijke Dogmatiek in Indonesie." *K&Th* 23.
1973	Widjaja, Albert. "Beggarly Theology: A Search for a Perspective Toward Indigenous Theology." *SEAJT* 14.2.
1975	Jongeneel, J.A.B. "Christelijke literatuur in de Indonesische taal." *W&Z* 4.4.
1983	Abednego, B.A. "Sekilas Sejarah Perkembangan Pergumulan Theologia di Asia." (A glance at the history of the development of theological struggle in Asia). *Gema Duta Wacana*, 23.
1985	Hutauruk, J.R. "Towards Church History in Indonesia." In *Asia and Christianity*, edited by M.D. David. Bombay: Himmalaya Publishing House.
1988	Hartono, Chr. Th. "Teologi Etis dan Relevansinya" (Ethics and its relevance). In *Konteks Berteologi di Indonesia*, edited by Eka Darmaputera, 301-323. Jakarta: BPK Gunung Mulia.
1989	Banawiratma, J.B. and T. Jacobs. "Doing Theology with Local Resources." *East Asian Pastoral Review*, 1.
1989	Steenbrink, Karel. "Towards a Pancasila Society. The Indonesian Debate on Secularization, Liberation and Development, 1969-1989." *Exchange*, 54.

Manuscript

1974   Ihromi. "Promosi Para Ahli Teologia Warga Negara" (The promotion of theological experts who are nationals). Jakarta. Mimeo'd.

Internet Source

Sularso Sopater. *The Third World Theology: World Mission Policy Indonesia. Understanding Mission in an Eastern Pluralistic Society.* URL:-<peacenet.or.kr/ccas/miss7.htm>. In March 1999, material from ca. 1995. *Indonesian Christian Universities Virtual Library.* Online Catalogue and Documentation. <http://incuvl.petra.ac.id>

— JMP

6 Contextual Theology in Malaysia and Singapore 1800-2000

For Christian writing and reflection in Malaya prior to 1800 see chapter 2 above.

1 **Introduction**
   1.1 Historical and Religious Context
   1.2 The Christian Story

2 **Peninsular Malaya and Singapore 1800-1945**
   2.1 Christian Writings and Theology
   2.2 Groundwork for Contextual Theology
      2.2.1. William Milne (1785-1822); **2.2.2.** Abdullah bin Abdul-Kadir (1796-1854) and colleagues; **2.2.3.** Catholic Scholars and Writers; **2.2.4.** Sophia Blackmore (1857-1943); **2.2.5.** William Shellabear (ca.1863-1947); **2.2.6.** Ministers and 'Nationalists'; **2.2.7.** Robert Blasdell (fl. 1920-1940); **2.2.8.** Ecumenical Movements and their Theology: The Beginnings; **2.2.9.** Writings in Malay, Chinese, English
         2.2.9.1. Letters and Journals; **2.2.9.2.** Memoirs and Biographies; **2.2.9.3.** Histories

3 **Malaysia and Singapore 1945-2000**
   3.1 Context and Christian Response
   3.2 Ecumenical Theology and Mission 1950-2000
      3.2.1. Ecumenical Movements and Writing; **3.2.2.** Theology and Society 1970-2000
   3.3 Women Doing Theology
   3.4 Catholic Church 1950 - 2000
      3.4.1. From Institutional Enclave to Social Presence

4 **Theologians and Scholars**
   4.1 Roman Catholic Episcopal Leaders; **4.2** Tan Sri Roland Koh Peck Chiang (1908-1972); **4.3** John Robb Fleming (1910-

1999); **4.4** K. Jambunathan (1931-); **4.5** Ray Nyce and the Institute for Study of Religions and Society; **4.6** Dulcie Abraham (1931-); **4.7** Yap Kim Hao (ca.1932-); **4.8** Theresa Ee Chooi (1938-); **4.9** Yeow Choo Lak (1938-); **4.10** Angeline Bones-Fernandez (1939-); **4.11** Huang Hsing Peng (ca. 1940-); **4.12** Paul Tan Chee Ing sj (1940-); **4.13** Denison Jayasooria (ca.1940-); **4.14** Cecil Rajendra (ca.1940-); **4.15** Thu En Yu (1945-); **4.16** Batumalai, Satayandy (1946-); **4.17** Hwa Yung (1948-); **4.18** Anthony Rogers (1949-); **4.19** Lee Tzu Pheng (ca. 1950-); **4.20** Albert Sundararaj Walters (1952-); **4.21** Yong Ting Jin (1953-); **4.22** Ng Kam Weng (1953-); **4.23** Yeoh Seng Guan (1958-); **4.24** Patricia Martinez (1960-); **4.25** Edmund Kee Fook Chia (1962-); **4.26** Fung Jojo M., sj (b. 1964); **4.27** Roland Chia (ca. 1965-); **4.28** Jonathan Tan (1969-)

5 Other Theological Writers, Scholars and Activists
  5.1 Contextual Theological Reflection
  5.2 Regarding Malaysian Church History
  5.3 Social Ethics and Culture
  5.4 Theological Education and Indigenisation
  5.5 Biblical and Missiological Studies
  5.6 Graduates' Christian Fellowship

6 Periodicals for Research

7 Supplementary Bibliography
  7.1 Malaysia.
  7.2 Singapore

1 Introduction
1.1 Historical and Religious Context
The Buddhist Srivijaya Empire, centred in Sumatra (present-day Indonesia), ruled most of the Malay Peninsula from the 9th to the 13th centuries, and was followed by the Javanese Majapahit Empire. During the 14th century most of the population was converted to Islam under a Muslim Malay State ruled from Malacca on the west coast of the Peninsula. In 1511 Malacca was taken by the Portuguese and in 1641 passed on to the Dutch. The British East India Company

was established in Penang in 1592, although the British acquired Penang only in 1786; in 1795 they conquered Malacca. Gradually British influence spread; in 1867 Penang, Malacca and Singapore became colonies and in 1888 Sabah, Sarawak and Brunei became protectorates. The colony of the Federated Malay States was established in 1895.

Malaysia is the southernmost nation of mainland Southeast Asia. The country consists of two parts (West and East Malaysia) separated by more than 650 km of the South China Sea. Most of Malaysia occupies the southern tip of the Malay Peninsula, south of Thailand, where over 80% of the population lives. East Malaysia, constituting the two states of Sabah and Sarawak, occupies the northern portion of the island of Borneo, the larger part of which consists of Indonesian Kalimantan. In 2000 the population reached 20 million and the principal languages used are Malay (official), English, Chinese dialects, Tamil, Telugu, and Malayalam. Malaysia is a multi-racial and multi-cultural society composed of Malays (over 50%), Chinese (32%) and Indians (about 8%); the latter two being descendants of late 19th and early 20th century immigrants. Primarily urban dwellers, the Chinese have traditionally dominated the economy. Non-Malay indigenous ethnic groups such as the Dayak, Iban and Kadazan peoples of East Malaysia represent 8% of the population.

Religion closely follows racial lines where 53% of the population - virtually all the Malays - are Muslims, 17% are Buddhists (mainly Chinese), 7% Hindus (Indian), with just 6.5% Christians (almost all Chinese and Indian Malaysians). Taoists, Confucians and adherents of other traditional Chinese and folk religions approximate 15% of the population (Chinese), with a small number of Sikhs. In Sabah, Christians form 27% of the population. Although a minority, Christianity throughout Malaysia has a potentially catalytic role as the only multi-racial religious group (Batumalai, 1991). Emerging concerns for Malaysian peoples have been identified to include the preservation of unity across ethnic boundaries; movements for and against Islamicisation; preservation of human rights, including freedom of religion, for all citizens;

reduction of undue concentrations of political and economic power, and of corruption in finance and government.

In Singapore, the principal languages are similarly Malay, Mandarin Chinese, English and Tamil, and the major religions are Taoism and Buddhism - and traditional blends of these faiths - along with Islam and Christianity. The population numbers approximately 3.5 million. In practice government has been in the hands of one party, the People's Action Party, since independence was declared, and strong controls on social, political and religious life have been maintained. This has included restriction of democratic processes, imposition of censorship and control of media and community organisations. These measures have meant that concerns for ethnic identity, social justice and human rights, have necessarily been muted. Since the mid-1990s there has been some relaxation of government controls and a growing advocacy for more democratisation.

Selected References

Ackerman, Susan E. and Raymond L.M. Lee. *Heaven in Transition. Non-Muslim Religious Innovation and Ethnic Identity in Malaysia.* Honolulu: University of Hawaii Press, 1988.

Amin, Mohamed and Malcolm Caldwell, eds. *Malaya: the Making of a Neo-colony.* Nottingham: Spokesman Books, 1977.

Buchanan, Iain. *Singapore in Southeast Asia.* London: G. Bell and Sons, 1972.

Emerson, Rupert. *Malaysia. A Study in Direct and Indirect Rule.* Kuala Lumpur: University of Malaya Press, 1970.

Gulick, J.M. *Malay Society in the Late Nineteenth Century.* Singapore: Oxford University Press, 1989.

Lee, Raymond L.M. and Susan E. Ackerman. *Sacred Tensions: Modernity and Religious Transformation in Malaysia.* Columbia, SC: University of South Carolina, 1997.

Muzaffar, Chandra. *Freedom in Fetters. An Analysis of the State of Democracy in Malaysia.* Penang: Aliran, 1986.

Ooi Keat Gin. *Malaysia.* World Bibliographical Series. Rev. ed. Oxford: Clio, 1999.

Roff, William R. *The Origins of Malay Nationalism.* Kuala Lumpur: University of Malaya Press, 1967.

Tan Hwi Choon, Eugene and Kwa Chong Guan. *The Singapore Story: a learning nation: a select bibliography.* Singapore: National Reference Library, National Library Board, 1998.

Tow, Timothy. *Nation-State, Identity and Religion in Southeast Asia.* Singapore: Singapore Society of Asian Studies, 1998.

Tremewan, Christopher. *The Political Economy of Social Control in Singapore.* New York: St. Martin's Press in association with St. Antony's College, Oxford, 1994.

Turnbull, C. Mary. *A Short History of Malaysia, Singapore and Brunei.* Singapore: Graham Brash, 1981.

—. A History of Singapore 1819-1975. Singapore: Oxford University Press, 1977.

Unity in Diversity. 10th Anniversary Souvenir Programme of the Malaysian Consultative Council for Buddhism, Christianity, Hinduism and Sikhism. Kuala Lumpur, Feb. 1994.

1.2 The Christian Story

Early Christian presence can be traced to Nestorians in the centre of the Peninsula and to traders in Malacca. Roman Catholicism arrived with the Portuguese in 1511 and Presbyterianism with the Dutch in 1641. Catholic priests from Thailand established a major seminary in Penang in 1810 and the London Missionary Society (LMS) was based in Malacca and Penang from 1815. Catholic leadership was divided between the Portuguese and French. In Sarawak, the rule of Rajah Brooke included support for an Anglican ministry from 1847; Catholics were later admitted. In 1828 the Australian Borneo Evangelical Mission began work with modest resources. Open Brethren ministry dates from 1860, and the Methodist mission, which engaged in education, publishing and evangelism, dates from 1885. Presbyterianism grew through Chinese churches in Johore and expatriate congregations in Penang, Ipoh and Kuala Lumpur. Mission to Sengoi indigenous people began in 1932.

Chinese and Indian immigration was an important factor in church growth. In Sabah, the Basel Mission began work among migrant Hakka Chinese in 1882, many of whom were already Christian. Tamil migrants to Malaya included Catholics, Lutherans, Anglicans and Methodists. Migration increased after the Boxer Rebellion (China 1890s), particularly to Sitiawan and Sibu, still strong Chinese Methodist centres. Mar Thoma and Syrian Orthodox Churches were established in the 1930s following migration from the Kerala Coast of India.

The Pacific War (1942-1945) saw the removal of expatriate leadership and a path toward an indigenous church was more clearly set. The Malayan Christian Council (MCC), founded in 1947 (on the basis of movements since 1913), coordinated mission groups during the Malayan Emergency. Chinese inhabitants, relocated into "New Villages", were served by missionaries, sometimes ex-China hands, who worked alongside local Christians in social and medical work. However, many churches would remain over-dependent on expatriates even after independence was obtained in 1957. By mid-century there was some basis laid in the studies, thought and ministries of a small number of both nationals and expatriates for the later development of more contextual understandings of the faith.

In Singapore, British and American Protestants, and French and Portuguese Catholic missionaries were active from the 1820s, followed by the Armenians (1835), Christian Brethren (1864) and Methodists (1885). Most Protestant missionaries left for China after 1842, nevertheless European, Eurasian, Chinese and Indian Christian communities developed through the 19th century. Many more denominations arrived in the 20th century and other missionary, ecumenical and also charismatic movements or institutions developed. Amongst these were the YMCA, the YWCA (late 19th century), the Student Christian Movement (c.1920), the Malayan Christian Council (1947, later divided), Trinity Theological College (1948), Overseas Missionary Fellowship (1951), Intervarsity Christian Fellowship (1952), Graduates' Christian Fellowship (1955), Catholic Students Society, the Association for Theological Schools in Southeast Asia (1959, later ATESEA) and the Christian Conference of Asia (1973).

The political climate in Singapore since 1963 has more readily fostered movements which avoid social, cultural or political concerns, while those engaged in such ministries have been often restricted or closed down (See 3.2.2 below.) This circumstance has greatly limited both the writing and publishing of contextualising theology, despite the multiplicity now of Bible Colleges, seminaries and Christian publishing houses. Evangelistic and charismatic movements have flourished and since 1970 both Catholic and Protestant churches have grown substantially, so that in 1990 12.5% of Singaporeans were recorded as being Christians.

Selected References

> Batumalai, S. *An Introduction to Asian Theology*. Delhi, ISPCK, 1991. Chap. 12.
> Browne, L.E. *Christianity and the Malays*. London: SPG, 1936.
> Chew, Maureen K.C. *The Journey of the Catholic Church in Malaysia 1511-1996*. Kuala Lumpur: Catholic Research Centre, 2000.
> Ho, Daniel. "Malaysia." In *Church in Asia Today Challenges and Opportunities*, edited by Saphir Athyal. Singapore: Lausanne Committee for World Evangelisation, 1996: 266-298.
> Hunt, Robert, Lee Kam Hing and John Roxborogh, eds. *Christianity in Malaysia. A Denominational History*. Petaling Jaya: Pelanduk Publications, 1992.
> Lee Kam Hing, ed. *History of Christianity in Malaysia*. Petaling Jaya: Pelanduk Publications, 1988.
> Roxborogh, John W. *A Bibliography of Christianity in Malaysia*. Malaysian Church History Series 2. Kuala Lumpur: STM and Catholic Research Centre, 1990.
> Russell, A. Sue. *Conversion, Identity and Power: the impact of Christianity on power relationships and social exchanges*. Lanham, MD: University Press of America, 1999.
> Sng, Bobby E.K. *In His Good Time. The Story of the Church in Singapore 1819-1978*. 2nd ed. Singapore: GCF, 1993.
> Voon Choon Khing, comp. "Bibliographies of Malaysian Christian Literature: Monographs, Periodicals, Theses, Articles." Petaling Jaya: STM, Mimeo'd, 1997.

2 Peninsular Malaya and Singapore 1800-1945
2.1 Christian Writings and Theology

There has been a long and rich tradition of Malay religious writings from the 16th century (see above bibliographies and chapter 2 above), even though Roman Catholic writings from the early 19th century - chiefly letters, prayers and catechisms - show little awareness of this tradition. There is, however, discussion of the training of an indigenous ministry found in the correspondence of such M.E.P. Fathers as Colivier and Letondal (1807-) and that of Bishops Courvezy (1845-) and Olcomendy (1875-). The records of the College General, Penang (from 1810), also contain materials that place importance upon native priesthood and its training, which is always a necessary step in contextualization.

In the 19th century Christian writing in the Malay language became focused on Penang (from 1810), Malacca (from 1818) and Singapore (from 1843). The lithograph press, begun by Benjamin Keasberry (Singapore 1843), printed, among other works, Malay Christian materials including those of Abdullah (See 2.2.2.). In the next one hundred years Christian publishing included Bible translations, Malay dictionaries, Gospel tracts, letters and articles, lyrics and memoirs, historical works, versions of Malay and Arabic classical texts, and treatises in traditional *Sha'ir* (Syair) form. Much of this material is found in monographs such as Keasberry's publications at Singapore, or in such periodicals as the *Chinese Monthly Magazine* (1815-1821), *The Indo-Chinese Gleaner* (1817-1822), *Malay Message* (1892-1947), *Bintang Timor* (Morning Star, 1894-), *Journal of the Malay Branch Royal Asiatic Society* (JMBRAS, from 1923), *Journal of the Singapore Branch Royal Asiatic Society* (JSBRAS, 1878-1922), *Muslim World* (c.1905-?) and *International Review of Missions*.

A small proportion only of these writings shows recognition of the culture, language or religious sensitivity of Malay or Chinese, or contains insights relevant to contextual theology. The exceptions to this would be found in parts of Milne's work in the first quarter of the 19th century (2.2.1) and the later work of Shellabear (2.2.5.) and his colleagues. It must be added that Malaysia has a unique cultural, political and religious history, with now fully multi-religious societies, where Western theological pre-occupations are not always relevant.

Selected References
    Bird, Isabella. "Missionary Printing in Malacca 1815-1843." *Libri* 32.3 (1982).
    Byrd, Cecil K. *Early Printing in the Straits Settlements 1806-1858 - a Preliminary Enquiry.* Singapore: National Library, 1970.

Chew, Maureen K.C. *The Journey of the Catholic Church in Malaysia 1511-1996.*

Gallop, Annabel Teh. *Early Malay Printing 1603-1900: An Exhibition in the British Library 20th January to 4th June 1989.* London: British Library Board, 1990.

Hunt, Robert, Lee Kam Hing and John Roxborogh, eds. *Christianity in Malaysia: A Denominational History.*

Proudfoot, I. *Early Malay Printed Books: A Provisional Account of Materials in the Singapore-Malay Area up to 1920.* Kuala Lumpur: University of Malaya and Academy of Malay Studies, 1993.

Roxborogh, John. *A Bibliography of Christianity in Malaysia.*

Tomlin, Jacob. *Missionary Journals and Letters* (Malacca and Singapore). London: 1844.

Voon Choon Khing, comp. "Bibliographies of Malaysian Christian Literature."

2.2 Groundwork for Contextual Theology
2.2.1. William Milne (1785-1822) - Scholar and missionary, Malacca.

In addition to historical writings in Chinese and English, Bible translations and the editing of two periodicals - on *Sacred History* (1819) and *Kingdoms of the World* (1821) - Milne wrote in English *A Retrospect of the First Ten Years of Protestant Mission* (1820). Milne was co-translator with Robert Morrison of the Old Testament into Chinese, edited Chinese and English periodicals and completed five biblical/theological works in Chinese: *Exposition of the Lord's Prayer* (1818, 1820); *The Two Friends* (c.1918 ? 17 editions by 1906); *Commentary on the New Testament; an Essay on the Immortality of the Soul*; and *Practical Exposition of the Epistle to the Ephesians.*

The Two Friends (Liang-yu hsiang-lun) presents an extended dialogue between two Chinese friends over some weeks, one of the friends being a Christian. Written in an easy literary style (*'wenli'*) and set informally in a Chinese garden, the tract presents mainstream Christian doctrines of the 19th century in ways sympathetic to Chinese understanding. Ancient Chinese sages are respected and a majority of crucial terms used come from the corpus of Mahayana Buddhist writings in Chinese (c.f. Daniel Bays in Barnett and Fairbank, 1985).

Milne showed in his writings "an attitude of informed, if restrained, admiration ... toward the Chinese social and cultural tradition" (Harrison 1979). This was a similar approach to that of earlier Jesuits in China and would be developed later in the century in the Straits Settlements for Malay culture by W. Shellabear (1862-1948) (2.2.5) and R. Blasdell (fl. 1920-1940) (see 2.2.7.).

Selected References

> Barnett, Susan Wilson and John King Fairbank, eds. *Christianity in China: Early Protestant Missionary Writings*. Harvard Studies in American-East Asian Relations 9. Cambridge, Mass; London: Harvard University Press, 1985.
> Bays, Daniel H. "Christian Tracts: The Two Friends." In *Christianity in China: Early Protestant Missionary Writings*, edited by Susan Wilson Barnett and John King Fairbank. Cambridge, Mass. and London: Harvard University Press, 1985.
> Box, E. "Morrison, Milne and Medhurst." In *Chinese Recorder and Missionary Journal* (1904)..
> Gallop, Annabel Teh. *Early Malay Printing 1603-1900: An Exhibition in the British Library 20th January to 4th June 1989.*
> Haines, Joseph H. "A History of Protestant Missions in Malaya during the Nineteenth Century, 1815-1881." Unpub. thesis, Princeton, NJ, 1962.
> Harrison, Brian. *Waiting for China: The Anglo-Chinese College at Malacca, 1818-1843, and Early Nineteenth-Century Missions*. Hong Kong: Hong Kong University Press, 1979.
> Philip, Robert. *The Life and Opinions of the Rev. William Milne, D.D., Missionary to China ...* London: John Snow, 1840.

2.2.2. Abdu'llah bin 'Abdu'l-Kadir (1796-1854) and colleagues

Abdu'llah bin 'Abdu'l-Kadir, pre-eminent Malay writer of the 19th century, was an instructor and librarian in the Anglo-Chinese College in Malacca up until 1840, after which he worked in Singapore with Benjamin Keasberry. Though remaining a practising Muslim, he collaborated in many Christian publications and sometimes attended Christian worship.

Along with editions of *The Pancatantra, Sejarah Malayu* or other Malay classics, and *The Hikayat Abdullah* (1843) for which he is chiefly remembered, he wrote, with Milne, Thomson and Keasberry, biblical commentaries, translations of the Book of Acts and the Gospels, *The Birth of Christ*, and books of moral instruction. He was a master of colloquial Malay style and a model for all later Malay work. He was also a master of realistic description, a social critic and a prophet of enlightenment.

Of the graduates of the Anglo-Chinese College in Malacca, Shaou Tih, a Roman Catholic, is known for his work as a translator and later Imperial interpreter in Penang, Malacca, Peking and Canton.

John Henry Moor (1802-1843; died Macao) was student tutor, later founder and editor of *Malacca Observer*, editor of *Singapore Chronicle* and later of *Singapore Free Press*. He wrote also *Notices of the Indian Archipelago* (Singapore, 1837).

Ho Fuk Tong (c.1820-1871) studied here from 1840-1843, was ordained in 1846 and became a prominent Hong Kong pastor, financier and close colleague of James Legge (See volume 3, Hong Kong). He has left letters and articles (in for example, the *Missionary Magazine* 1840s and 1850s).

Selected References

Abdullah bin Abdul-Kadir. *The Hikayat Abdullah: The Autobiography of Abdullah bin Abdul Kadir (1797-1854)*. An annotated translation by A.H. Hill. Singapore: Oxford University Press, 1969.

Harrison, Brian. *Waiting for China: The Anglo-Chinese College at Malacca, 1818-1843, and Early Nineteenth-Century Missions.*

—. "The Anglo-Chinese College and Early Modern Education." In *Melaka: the transformation of a Malay Capital, c.1400-1980*, edited by Kernial Singh Sandhu and Paul Wheatley. Kuala Lumpur: Oxford University Press, c.1981.

2.2.3. Catholic Scholars and Writers

The innovative missionary Don Carlos Cuarteron (fl. 1850), later Prefect of Labuan and Borneo, wrote, in 1852, a detailed Memorial concerning "missions to the Far East" to the Propaganda Fide. The *Quadri*, as this report was named, was published by the Congregation in 1855. Central concerns of Cuarteron included the proclamation of the Gospel throughout Borneo and beyond, the gathering of redeemed slaves into self-supporting communities and the development of partnership between mission work and commerce in growing communities.

The Pastoral Letters of J.P. Hillary M. Courvezy (d.1857), Bishop of the Malay Peninsula until 1845, included in his teaching on worship and prayer modifications regarding the feasts and fasts of the church due to different conditions of life and climate in Malaya.

Experience and insight from three decades of life and work with the Orang Mantra (aboriginal peoples) is recorded by Pièrre Borie in his *La Presqu'ile de Malacca* (Paris, c.1872). Borie was also notable for his ecumenical relations with Protestants.

A number of competent Malay scholars like Bishop Garnault, Bishop Le Turdu (fl. 1870) and Fr Le Tessier (fl. 1905) were active in writing and translating many works on doctrine and spirituality but these seldom recognised the life or context of Malaya. H.L. Emil Luering (1863-1937) had studied at the universities of Zurich and Strassberg and became expert in many languages of the Malay Peninsula. He also carefully studied the local cultures, in particular that of the Orang Asli in Perak.

Selected References

Cardon, R. *Catholicism in the East and the Diocese of Malacca (1511-1888)*. Reprinted from the *Malaya Catholic Leader*, Dec, 1938. Singapore: 1939.

Chew, Maureen K.C. *The Journey of the Catholic Church in Malaysia 1511-1996*.

Lee, Felix George. *The Catholic Church in Malaya*. Singapore: Eastern University Press, 1963.

Lüring, H.L. Emil. *Wundersame Wege* (Marvellous road): *Erlebnisse aus der Missionsarbeit im Fernen Osten*. Nurenburg: Zeitbücherverlag, 1922.

Rooney, John. *Khabar Gembira: A History of the Catholic Church in East Malaysia and Brunei, 1880-1976.* London & Kota Kinabalu: Burns and Oates, 1981.

Schreike, Bertram, ed. *The Effect of Western Influence on Native Civilizations in the Malay Archipelago.* Batavia: 1927.

Williams, Kenneth M. "The Church in W. Malaysia and Singapore. A Study of the Catholic Church regarding her Situation as an Indigenous Church." Doct. Dissertation, Katholieke Universiteit de Leuven, 1976.

2.2.4. Sophia Blackmore (1857-1943)

Sophia Blackmore is remembered chiefly for her work over many decades dedicated to the nurture of women leaders in Malaya and Singapore, her opposition to the exploitation of women, and the development of many institutions for an educated womanhood who would have ideals, "for which they have courage to stand in the community". Originally a Methodist from Australia, her life was a model of lived faith and compassion for generations of Singaporeans. Primarily concerned for the education and evangelisation of confined Baba Chinese women, she also pioneered a Tamil Girls' School in Singapore (1887), followed by other schools aimed in part at the rescue of young girls from prostitution and slavery. She inaugurated training courses for Bible Women (1890s) and undertook extensive work with women's groups in education, evangelism and women's refuges.

Blackmore wrote frequently in *The Malay Messenger* including personal stories of the life of Nyonya women, and in these articles shows both a search "for all Christ has" for her, and for "the abundant life" Christ intends for all.

Note also the Anglican educator, activist and YWCA leader Sophia Cooke.

Selected References

Works by Sophia Blackmore

Record of Woman's Work in Malaya, 1887-1927. Singapore: Methodist Archives, ca. 1928.

"Looking Backward." *Malaysia Message*, Dec. (1918).

Doraisamy, T.R. *Forever Beginning. One Hundred Years of Methodism in Singapore. Volume I.* Singapore: Methodist Church in Singapore, 1985.

—, ed. *Sophia Blackmore of Singapore*. Singapore: Methodist Church Bookroom, 1987.

Sng, Bobby E.K. *In His Good Time. The Story of the Church in Singapore 1819-1978.*

Walker, E.A. *Sophia Cooke: Or Forty-two Years' Work in Singapore.* London: Elliot Stock, 1899.

"A Report on Fifty Years of W.F.M.S. work in Malaya." Manuscript, United Methodist Archives, Madison, NJ, ca. 1930.

2.2.5. William Shellabear (ca.1863-1947)

William Shellabear was a scholar of Malay and of Islam, a translator, publisher, missionary and writer of book-length *syairs* (prose-poems). He produced dictionaries, grammars and translations of the Malay classics, used traditional Malay forms and idiom to present biblical and theological teaching and wrote many articles on Islam in the *Journal of the Singapore Branch Royal Asiatic Society*, the *Malay Message* and the *Muslim World*. For the last two he long served as editor. Although many of his hopes for Christian-Muslim encounter were not then fulfilled, his work was continued by Blasdell (2.2.7.) and still provides a basis for contemporary dialogue.

Shellabear held friendly discussions on Islam and Christianity and came to recognise major truths of belief in Islam regarding such concepts as that of *tawhid* (the unity of God), valuing particularly Islamic traditions of mysticism. To overcome misunderstanding by Christians of Islam and of Malay culture, and by Muslims of the Christian Gospel, he stressed the history of early Muslim recognition of Jewish and Christian beliefs and the significant convergences in Christian and Muslim beliefs. He also advocated utilising Qu'ranic texts to clarify Christian terms and to find shared perspectives - all as a necessary beginning for Christian-Muslim encounter. Close colleagues of Shellabear included Pang Yan Whatt and Sulaiman bin Muhammad Nur (see below).

Selected References
Works by William Shellabear

The Influence of Islam on The Malays, an essay presented to the Straits Philosophical Society. Singapore: Methodist Publishing House, 1913.

Mohammedanism as Revealed in its Literature. Singapore: Methodist Publishing House, 1915.

Islam's Challenge to Methodism. New York: Board of Foreign Missions, 1919.

Sha'ir Nabi Yang Berpengasehan (Verses on the living prophet). (In Jawi.) Romanised version of the first edition which appeared in the *Methodist Message* Malay Supplement, 1932-1934.

Sha'ir Kerajaan Allah (Verses on the Kingdom of God), parts 1-5. (In Jawi.) Singapore: Methodist Mission, 1933.

Al Nabi M'asum (The sinless prophet). (In Jawi.) Singapore: Methodist Mission, 1948.

Chjerita Yang Sempurna (The perfect story). (In Jawi.) Singapore: Methodist Mission, 1949.

— with Sulaiman bin Muhammad Nur. *Kitab Kiliran Budi* (A whetstone for wit). Singapore: Methodist Publishing House, 1909.

Hunt, Robert. *William Shellabear: A Biography.* Kuala Lumpur: University of Malaya Press, 1996.

Dodsworth, Marmaduke. "The Assimilation of Christianity by the Malays of the Malay Peninsular." MA Thesis, University of Chicago, 1928.

Note: Sulaiman bin Muhammad Nur (1870-1928) was Shellabear's close associate and co-worker (until 1918). He became proficient in Arabic, Persian and Malay, a master of Malay verse, a student of Sufism and a teacher at the Malay Teachers' College, Malacca. With Shellabear he prepared a collection of Malay Proverbs: *Kitab Kiliran Budi* (A whetstone for wit), published by the Mission Press in 1906 in their Malay Literature Series (Methodist Publishing House, 1909). His own *Kitab Gemela Hikmat* (The gem of wisdom - a collection of poetry and riddles) followed in 1907.

2.2.6. Ministers and 'Nationalists'

William Henry Gomes of Ceylon (1827-1902) pioneered work amongst the Iban of Sarawak and later superintended Anglican work in Singapore. Active in training catechists and evangelists, he was also a gifted linguist who has left Malay translations of liturgies, hymns and a life of Christ.

J.S. Yasudian (fl. 1910-1950) was appointed to Tamil work in Kuala Lumpur (1914) and began a Tamil Christian association aimed at, "creating an active interest on the part of Tamil Christians in the church's work and to improve the social and spiritual standards of the Tamil Christians themselves" (*Singapore Diocesan Magazine*, November 1914). He also organised a team of catechists, evangelists and lay readers to work in thirty estates and two mines. With Gnanamani Poniah he called for recognition of Asian sentiments and identity and of the relevance of nationalist sentiments in the (Anglican) Church, thus pioneering important elements for a contextual theology.

Ho Seng Ong (fl. 1920-1940) was especially notable for his work in education (see *Methodist Schools in Malaysia: Their Record and History*. Petaling Jaya: Malaya Annual Conference, 1964). Ho regularly promoted indigenous leadership, declaring in 1937 that "almost every Annual Conference had its calls for indigenous leadership with little action to show for it ... Do we ... really want Asiatic leadership ... or is it simply good politics ...?" (*Malaysia Message*, September 1937).

Other nationals who have left indigenous writings include:

Gnanamani Poniah who began the indigenisation of Indian worship using Tamil lyrics and music; M.R. Doraisamy (d. 1933) who initiated indigenous forms of teaching in his *Kalachepans* or lyrical lectures; S.S. Pakianathan who was appointed for the Perak Tamil District (1931) and also commenced a small Tamil (Methodist) seminary. The possibility of a church in Malaya having its own voice and theology was raised by all these forerunners.

Selected References

Bryan, J.N. Lewis. *The Churches of the Captivity in Malaya*. London: Society for Promoting Christian Knowledge, 1946.

Ho Seng Ong. *Education for Unity in Malaya. An Evaluation of the Educational System of Malaya with Special Reference to the Need for Unity in its Plural Society*. Penang: Malayan Teachers' Union, 1952.

Hunt, Robert, Lee Kam Hing and John Roxborogh, eds. *Christianity in Malaysia: A Denominational History*.

Hunt, Robert. *William Shellabear: A Biography*.

2.2.7. Robert A. Blasdell (fl. 1920-1940)

Blasdell arrived in Malaya c.1920, and was to continue aspects of William Shellabear's work (2.2.5 above). After further studies at Hartford, he undertook a *Descriptive Bibliography of Malay Muslim Religious Literature* (Hartford Seminary, Masters' Thesis, 1930). In Malaya he initiated the monthly newsletter *Perkhabara Melayu* (1931-) to foster "respect and understanding for Islam and Malay culture". Later he translated al Ghazali's treatise on repentance into Malay and wrote a series of articles on Islam and on Christian mission in Malaya. (*International Review of Missions* 1945-1952).

In the novel *Sa Biji Beneh*, he presents the aspirations of a Malay girl born in the 1930s, whose "people were very much marginalised in the governing of their own country. Many were poor because they did not know their rights and no one wanted to help them obtain their rights". But she wished to study in order "to help her people rise up and take their proper place as people with a right to govern their own country." Put in fictional form, the book nonetheless strongly affirms a theology of national identity, of selfhood and of human rights to be restored.

Selected References
Works by Robert A. Blasdell

    Sa Biji Beneh, translated by RAH. Singapore: Methodist Publishing House, 1954.
    "How Islam came to the Malay Peninsula." *Moslem World* 32.2 (1942).
    "Renaissance in Malaya." *International Review of Missions* 41.161 (1952).
    "High Tide in Malaya." *International Review of Missions* 43.170 (1954).
    Hunt, Robert. *William Shellabear: A Biography*.

2.2.8. Ecumenical Movements and their Theology: The Beginnings

Ecumenical movements can be traced to just prior to the First World War (1914-1918) with often cordial cooperation and regular inter-church meetings during the following decades. Ecumenical beginnings can be seen in the co-operation of nationals and missionaries in social work, education and evangelism in the previous century. Other patterns of ecumenical work had begun with the Chinese Educational Institute established in Singapore by Archibald Lamont (1891-1897), pioneering adult education for Chinese working men. Ecumenical movements continued to slowly grow in the pre-war decades.

More established patterns of co-operation became possible with the formation of the MCC in January 1947 with H.B. Amstutz as first secretary, followed in 1952 by John R. Fleming. Among those who had provided leadership in this movement, and in "moves towards Malayanisation" were R.D. Whitehorn, T. Campbell Gibson, Bp. Leonard Wilson, S.M. Thevathasan, Bp H.W. Baines and D.D. Chelliah. Strongly ecumenical theology is found in their extensive correspondence (IMC and CBMS Archives) and in the extant writings of Chelliah, Baines, Wilson and H.A. Wittenbach. Baines in particular worked both for institutional ecumenical collaboration and for religious freedom, along with greater participation by Christians in their community and society.

In the following years, ecumenical programmes which would be developed included those for theological education, education and social services in the New Villages, evangelism, literature, home and family life, student work, social concern and urban mission. Central to these movements was a theology of mission in unity which was also to be embodied by some lay people and clergy, in 'worldly' ministries at the frontiers of community life. By the 1930s and 1940s the concerns of home, of social issues, for urban workers and rural settlements became more recognised as part of such ecumenical mission and the experiences of war and emergency would only sharpen this understanding. Trinity Theological College, Singapore, commenced as an ecumenical foundation for Methodists, Anglicans and Presbyterians in 1948 and would soon become a regional centre for theological education and, with the Southeast Asia Graduate School of Theology, for publication. (See Asia Regional and Ecumenical Theologies, vol.1, chap.3.)

Selected References

Baines, H.W. "The Church in Malaya." *East and West Review* 19 (1953).

—. "The Church in Singapore and Malaya 1949-1960." *East and West Review* 26 (1960).

Bryan, J.N.L. *The Churches of the Captivity in Malaya.* London: Society for Promoting Christian Knowledge, 1946.

Chelliah, D.D. "The Growth of Unity among the Churches in Malaya." *International Review of Missions* 37.148 (1948).

McKay, Roy. *John Leonard Wilson, Confessor of the Faith.* London: Hodder, 1973.

"Malayan Christian Council Correspondence 1941-1949." IMC Archives (IMC 26.5.115.7), WCC, Geneva.

"Records of a Conference held at Singapore, on January 21st, 22nd, & 23rd, 1913, together with the papers presented at the conference." Edinburgh: Continuation Committee of the World Missionary Conference, 1910.

Roxborogh, John. *A Common Voice: A History of the Ecumenical Movement in Malaysia.* Ecumenism in Malaysia I. Petaling Jaya: CCM, 1991.

—. "The Story of Ecumenism." In *Christianity in Malaysia: A Denominational History*, edited by Robert Hunt, Lee Kam Hing and John Roxborogh. Petaling Jaya: Pelanduk Publications, 1992.

Wittenbach, H A. *Working together IV, Malaya.* London: Highway Press, 1957.

2.2.9. Writings in Malay, Chinese, English

Other writings from the period, which in some cases feature the beginnings of localised reflection, include:

2.2.9.1. Letters and Journals: Jacob Tomlin (b. ca.1898), *Missionary Journals and Letters* (1844); Harriette McDougall, *Letters from Sarawak* (1854); J.A.B. Cook (to the Presbyterian Church in England in the 1880s), reporting - inter alia - moves towards a "Three-Self Church" in Singapore).

2.2.9.2. Memoirs and Biographies: "Life of Fr John Tschu." (*Singapore Free Press*, 1848); Harriette McDougall, *Sketches of Our Life at Sarawak* (1882); Royopen Balavendrum (ordained 1877), *A Short History of the Life of ...* (c.1895); E.A.Walker, *Sophia*

Cooke: or Forty-Two Year's Work in Singapore (1899); Goh Hood Keng (fl. 1930) *Memoirs of Goh Hood Keng* (c.1950); J.C. Wilson, *Confessor for the Faith* (1943); A.F. Sharp, *The Wings of the Morning* (1954); Eiichi Kamiya, "The Story of Dr Eiichi Kamiya" (?1990); A. Talaivasingham, *Malayan Notes and Sketches* (1924); F.A.Mouton, "Eerwaarde Archibald Lamont - Kampvegter Vir die Minderbevoorregte" (*Historia* 34.1,1989).

2.2.9.3. Histories: Jean Marie Beurel mep, *Annals of the Catholic Mission at Singapore* (c.1870); C.E Ferguson-Davie, *In Rubber Lands* (1921); R. Cardon, *Catholicism in the East and the Diocese of Malacca* (1938); P. Browning, *A Short History of the Chaplaincy of Taiping and North Perak* (1929); R.S. Muthuswami, *Report of the North Circle, Tamil Evangelical Church in Malaya* (1934); Song Ong Siang, *One hundred years of the Chinese in Singapore* (1923); Brian Taylor, "The First Hundred Years: A History of the Anglican Church in Sarawak" (?1963); Archibald Lamont and Tan Teck Soon co-authored the novel *Bright Celestials* (1894).

Selected References

Bunce, Thirza. "A Study of Moral and Religious Education in British Malaya." Thesis, University of Indianapolis, 1932.

Chan, Lean Choi Lily. "Christian Missions and the Iban of Sarawak during the Brooke Rule (1840s to 1940s)." Thesis, Australian National University, 1975.

Cornwall, Nigel E. *Borneo, Past, Present and Future*. London: SPG, 1953.

Dodsworth, Marmaduke. "The Assimilation of Christianity by the Malays of the Malay Peninsular."

Ferguson-Davie, C.E. *In Rubber Lands: An Account of the Work of the Church in Malaya*. London: SPCK, 1921.

Heron, A.C. "A History of the Protestant Christian Churches in West Malaysia and Singapore." Unpublished manuscript, 1977.

Hunt, Robert, Lee Kam Hing and John Roxborogh, eds. *Christianity in Malaysia: A Denominational History*.

McKay, Roy. *John Leonard Wilson: Confessor of the Faith*.

Muntung, Jonathan Jelanding. "History of the Iban Church in Sarawak." Research Paper, Trinity Theological College, Singapore, 1979.

Roxborogh, John. "Colonial Expansion in South East Asia and Christianity." In *Western Colonialism in Asia and Christianity*, edited by M.D. David. Bombay: Himalaya Publishing, 1988.
—. *A Bibliography of Christianity in Malaysia*.
Williams, K.M. "The Church in West Malaysia and Singapore: A Study of the Catholic Church in West Malaysia and Singapore Regarding her Situation as an Indigenous Church."
Voon Choon Khing, comp. "Bibliographies of Malaysian Christian Literature."

3 Malaysia and Singapore 1945-2000
3.1 Context and Christian Response

After the Japanese occupation (1942-1945), British rule continued for 12 years, although a guerrilla insurrection known as the Emergency lasted until 1960. The Federation of Malaya attained independence (1957), and in 1963 the Federation of Malaysia was founded, incorporating Malaya, Singapore, Sarawak and Sabah. In 1965 Singapore seceded to become an independent state, ensuring that Malays formed 50% of the remaining population. The Federation of Malaysia is a constitutional monarchy, the head of state being one of nine sultans on a rotating basis and the head of government a prime minister. In 1969 rioting between Malays and Chinese threatened political stability, as did sporadic Chinese-Malay tensions which in 1987 and 1996 led the government of Mahathir Mohammed to imprison alleged proponents of unrest.

Principal political parties are the *Barisan National* (National Front) - the ruling alliance - comprised of twelve parties of which the Malaysian Indian Congress (MIC, founded 1945), the United Malay National Organisation (UMNO, 1946), and the Malaysian Chinese Association (MCA, 1949), are the more prominent. The *Barisan National* (read UMNO) has increasingly centralised power in its own hands since 1965 through constitutional amendments, the expulsion of judges and the imposition of over-riding legislation for internal security and censorship, along with the allocation of resources to key electoral groups. Twenty-two other parties, grouped (since 1998) largely in two alliances, comprise the opposition.

Policies of Islamisation, declared by the Barisan in 1981, led to the formation (1983) of the Malaysian Consultative Council for

Buddhism, Christianity, Hinduism and Sikhism (MCCBCHS), for which MIRO (Malaysian Inter-Religious Organisation), was the forerunner in the 1970s. Aims of the MCCBCHS include the promotion of understanding, mutual respect and co-operation; studying and resolving inter-religious problems; and making representations to government when necessary. Since 1983 also, the National Evangelical Christian Fellowship (NECF) has provided a focus for evangelical and independent congregations. The Sabah Council of Churches and Association of Churches of Sarawak fulfil similar functions in East Malaysia. All Christian communities are represented on the MCCBCHS by the Christian Federation of Malaysia (formed in 1985), consisting of the Catholic Church in Malaysia, the Council of Churches of Malaysia (CCM) and the NECF. Prime objectives include the extension through dialogue and consultation, of the common areas of agreement between Christian groups; representation of the Christian community upon such matters as religious freedom and constitutional rights; and co-operation with government and non-government bodies on all matters of common concern. Recent growth in independent churches is another sign of a desire to establish a Malaysian Christian identity.

Christian commitment to education has been strong in Malaysia through Anglican, Catholic and Methodist schools, which are now part of the government education system. Social concern has been expressed through medical work, projects of urban, industrial and rural mission, through students' and graduates' associations, the Kairos Research Centre, Catholic Research Centres, and through organisations such as the CCM and Malaysian CARE. The Salvation Army and YMCA/YWCAs also make distinctive contributions and lay leadership has developed strongly in most churches. Although there are many challenges through changing political and economic circumstances, like the country as a whole, the churches are beginning to see that they have a contribution to make on a larger stage.

Expatriate missionaries had early used Singapore as a centre for outreach to the region and in this period, following restrictions to Christian work in mainland China, it became a regional centre both for theological education and publication, and for mission outreach. There was steady growth in both the Catholic Church and older Protestant denominations, with rapid growth in younger and charismatic churches and in many non-denominational associations. Singaporean culture finds some Christian values, especially those with evangelical and Pentecostal emphases, congenial, and social ministries have been limited. Community service programmes and in particular social criticism in any form are restricted. (For social ministries and reflection see 3.2.1, 3.2.2 below.)

Ecumenical leadership had been associated more with expatriates during the colonial era, although a number of Chinese and Indian church leaders maintained ecumenical ministries then, and also since. In a few cases also theological writing has come from these leaders. But ecumenical ministries or collaboration have flourished only periodically since independence, due partly to government restrictions and to the more parochial understandings of faith and witness that these reinforced. Theological reflection upon the issues of human life and society in Singapore however has become more diverse in recent years, as will be seen below.

Selected References

Ackerman, Susan E. and Raymond L.M. Lee. *Heaven in Transition. Non-Muslim Religious Innovation and Ethnic Identity in Malaysia*. Honolulu: University of Hawaii Press, 1988.

"Development of Interreligious Dialogue in Malaysia." *Bulletin Ponteficium Consilium pro Daialogo inter Religiones* 24 (1989).

Hoekema, Alle. "Kirche und Theologie in Malaysia: Neuere Etwickklungen." *Zeitschrift fur Mission* (2000).

Howes, Peter. "Why Some of the Best People aren't Christian." *Sarawak Museum Journal* 9.15-16 (1960).

Hunt, Robert, Lee Kam Hing and John Roxborogh, eds. *Christianity in Malaysia. A Denominational History*.

Khoo Yoke Kuan, ed. *One God, Many Paths. Essays on the Social relevance of religion in Malaysia from Islamic, Buddhist, Christian, Hindu and Philosophical Perspectives*. Penang: Aliran, 1980.

Lau Chee Wai "The Cross and the Crescent: a Study of Christianity and Malay Nationalism in Peninsular Malaysia." Thesis, St Barnabas Theological College, Adelaide, 1988.
Roxborogh, John W., ed. *A Bibliography of Christianity in Malaysia*.
Sng, Bobby E.K. *In His Good Time. The Story of the Church in Singapore 1819-1978*.
Thiangaraja, R. "Inter-Religious Council: MCCBCHS Clarifies". *Aliran Monthly* 18.7 (1998).
Voon Choon Khing, comp. "Bibliographies of Malaysian Christian Literature."

3.2 Ecumenical Theology and Mission 1950-2000
3.2.1. Ecumenical Movements and Writing

By 1947 the Malayan Christian Council (MCC) was in formation, on the basis of earlier negotiation and co-operation. Largely through the leadership of Bishop J.L. Wilson, Bishop Hobart Amstutz, Archdeacon D.D. Chelliah and the Rev'd L.C. Gibson, it was inaugurated on the 9th January 1948. The MCC was an unprecedented act of faith of the churches on Malaysian soil to stay and grow together through ecumenical co-operation. Following the establishment of the Council, and that of Trinity College soon after, many joint projects were undertaken in education, social service and in social witness. Ministries by all the churches were greatly extended during the years of "emergency" as their programmes of outreach and service grew to meet the needs of the "New Villages" formed. Not only social service, but the issues arising from ministry amidst rapid change and conflict, now had to be included in the understandings and practice of mission. Reports on Social Issues and Programmes of Social Service were published by the MCC along with surveys of inter-church ventures.

Student Christian Centres were formed at the Universities of Malaya and Singapore, ca.1953. The Youth Movement of the MCC was formed in 1954, with ecumenical work-camps, retreats and conferences following. In these programmes as well as in student movements, key figures at that time were K.C. Peoh, P.D. Thomas, K. Jambunathan (see 4.4.), Peter Chew and Samuel Jesudason. From the 1960s there was an SCM chaplaincy established for "frontier ministries" in tertiary education, later led in Singapore by such theologian-activists as Huang Hsing Peng (4.11), Biem Lap and James Sutton. Students and some faculty members, along with YMCA and YWCA groups were active in social service and community advocacy. SCMs were active in both Malaysia and Singapore despite periodic restrictions, in activities of study, community welfare and sometimes social protest.

In 1965 the MCC formed two national bodies following the separation of Singapore, and later in Malaysia it became the CCM (1975), able to play a larger role with government for national reconstruction following the conflict of May 1969. Staff members for the activities of the Council in these years were John R. Fleming (4.3), Chung Chi-an, Wong Hoon-hee and James Sutton, along with such leaders as Bishop Roland Koh Peck Chiang (4.2.), Bishop Hobart Amstutz and the Rev'd Denis Dutton. At the 40th anniversary of the founding of the MCC, the history of the Council was reviewed, and the changing multi-ethnic and multi-religious context was addressed, along with the dual calling to Christian witness and active citizenship. Changes in the Council's future activities were also planned. Similar concerns appear in the volume from the 50th anniversary (1997), under the theme of "Unity in Christ" and "Service to the Nation". Here the moral and ethical issues raised in a rapidly developing industrial society were highlighted.

From conferences and programmes of the MCC/CCM have come a series of publications both on the issues of church unity and faith, and on inter-church action for mission and service. Amongst these have been documents on joint social ministries; doctrinal and inter-faith issues, on Islamisation and religious freedom. These include *Christian Approach to those of Other Faiths; Christian Approach to Social Issues*; *Trends and Challenges in Social Service Today*; *Baptism, Eucharist and Ministry;* and a series of booklets *Reading the Bible with New Eyes*. Reports and articles have also appeared in *MCC News* (Kuala Lumpur), *Southeast Asia Journal of Theology / East Asia Journal of Theology* (Singapore); *IDOC Bulletin* (Rome); and the *Church Labour Letter* (Kyoto).

Beginnings in theological education for Malaysia were made by Bishop Roland Koh Peck Chiang (4.2) in the theological centre he established at Sungei Buloh near Kuala Lumpur in 1972, and in which K. Jambunathan for example, lectured, (4.4). The ecumenical Seminari Theoloji Malaysia was established in 1976 with Denis Dutton as Principal. It was to become a lively centre not only for theological teaching but also for writings and publications in Malaysian theology. (See individual entries below.)

At the time of the formation of the MCCBCHS (see 3.1; 3.3), the Christian Federation of Malaysia (CFM, Persekutuan Kristian Malaysia) was also finally formed (1985). This had grown from the National Christian Conferences which had been held in 1979 and 1982, and had as its aims a greater unity of Christians through dialogue and consultation. This was to be directed to preserve religious freedom, to represent the Christian community of Malaysia, and to work with governmental and non-governmental organizations on all matters of common concern. The CCM is a constituent member of the CFM as the CFM is of the MCCBCHS.

For Graduates' Christian Fellowship see 5.6.

Selected References

A Survey of the New Villages in Malaya. Rev. ed. Singapore(?): MCC, 1959.

CCM. *Reading the Bible with New Eyes.* Kuala Lumpur: CCM, n.d.

Christian Federation of Malaysia. *The Malaysian Church in the 1990s: Addresses, Papers, Homilies and Recommendations of the Fourth National Conference.* Kuala Lumpur: CFM, 1992.

Growing in Unity with Christ, Council of Churches in Malaysia 40th Anniversary General Assembly 13-16 February 1987. Kuala Lumpur: MCC, 1987.

Denison Jayasooria, ed. *Trends and Challenges in Social Service Today.* Petaling Jaya: CCM, 1992.

Lim Chin Chin, Theresa. "The Council of Churches of Malaysia 1947-1987." In *Growing in Unity with Christ, CCM 40th Anniversary General Assembly 13-16 February 1987.* Kuala Lumpur: CCM, 1987: 35-42.

Lindbeck, George A. "The Present Ecumenical and Church Situation in West Malaysia and Singapore." *SEAJT* 11 (1969).

Malay Christian Council. *Unity in the Faith: The Churches Working Together.* Kuala Lumpur: MCC, 1960.

—. *The Churches Working Together; Reports Presented to the General Council.* Kuala Lumpur: MCC, 1964.

—, and Christian Federation of Malaysia. "Response to the Government White Paper 14 Tahun 1988." *Tugon* 8.3 (1988).

Roxborogh, John. "The Story of Ecumenism." In *Christianity in Malaysia: A Denominational History*, edited by Robert Hunt, Lee Kam Hing and John Roxborogh. Petaling Jaya: Pelanduk Publications, 1992.

Shastri, Hermen et al. *United in Christ, Serving the Nation. Celebrating 50 Years of United Witness and Service.* Kuala Lumpur: CCM, 1997.

"Survey of Church Union Negotiations 1979-1981, Malaysia." *Ecumenical Review* 34 (1982), reprinted from *Faith and Order Paper* 115, WCC, Geneva. References are also given to the *Ecumenical Review* (1968); (1970); (1972); (1974); (1976); (1978).

The Malaysian Church in the 90s. Addresses, papers, homilies and recommendations of the Fourth National Christian Conference. Kuala Lumpur: CFM, ?1991.

Yeoh Seng Guan, ed. *Baptism, Eucharist, Ministry - A Malaysian Contribution.* Ecumenism in Malaysia 2. Kuala Lumpur: CCM, 1992.

3.2.2. Theology and Society 1970-2000

On the foundation of earlier social and ecumenical ministries, the Selangor UIM (COMSUIM), was formed in 1969, with leadership from such ministers and laymen as David Eichner, Sebil John, Ron Fujiyoshi, Ahmed bin Hussein Shah, James Lee, Victor Oorjitham, and Clabon Allen. Projects for Community Organization followed in the 1970s - sometimes in collaboration with Muslim social workers - along with training and exposure programmes such as the Theology in Action Workshop of 1974. The Bukit Lan Rural Life Centre, led by Ing Hua and Ricky Ling, and the Petaling Jaya Christian Fellowship conducted programmes and courses for such groups as plantation workers led by Martha Ratnam and others. Laity training programmes were held at St Mark's Centre by John

Savarimuthu - later Bishop - and in Lutheran Churches by Dwain Vierow. Others active in similar ministries included Lionel Muthiah, members of the Mill Hill Missionaries, and Samuel Ho (later of Asian Human Rights, Hong Kong).

In Singapore many churches, student and worker movements, were active in ecumenical, social and industrial studies and missions - in for example the Jurong Industrial Mission (JIM). Those providing leadership in urban mission there included Edwin Chan, Stephen Tan, Michael Wong, Chew Beng Lan (Ms) and James Wong. These activities however were subject to severe government censure by the early 1970s, with "clear and distinct lines between church (religion) and the labour movement (politics)" imposed. The Institute for Study of Religions and Society in Singapore and Malaysia was directed by Ray Nyce from the early 1970s and conducted many studies and consultations from which a series of volumes were issued (see 4.5.). The Friends Service Committee - including Stewart Meachem, Grace Brewster and Merv Henkel - initiated international seminar programmes on major social issues. Government harassment led to the eventual closing of the Jurong Industrial Mission by 1972, along with other rice-roots organisations by the mid-1970s, including the SCM and the Catholic Students' Society.

In the same years the *Aggiornamento* commences in Malaysia for Roman Catholic Churches. Basic Christian Communities are formed, and Young Christian Workers and student work grows, led by Irene Fernandez and Frs. Lim and Florimond. The Catholic Welfare agency becomes the Office for Human Development and amongst its newsletters some feature Catholic social teaching regarding social justice. By 1980, Urban Clergy and Church Workers in Malaysia were addressing issues of religious freedom and urban mission. The Catholic Welfare Service, YCW, the Catholic Student Society, SCM members, and former UIM workers, were co-operating with the MCC in training and advocacy programmes on behalf of such communities as fisher villagers, aboriginal peoples, and plantation workers. Catholic Welfare services moved from palliative services to address the root-causes of poverty and injustice, and the Peninsular Consultation on Church and Development (July,1983) affirmed that authentic human development should take into account structural changes in society in order to meet the basic needs of human beings in Malaysia.

From these frontier ministries came reflections, newsletters and reports based in a theology of human community and social justice, and which offered compassion and solidarity for deprived and exploited communities in Malaysia. (See for example, publications of the MCC/CCM, CFM, CARE, PMV and Graduate Students' Fellowship in Refs. below.) The Society of Christian Service based in Sibu, Sarawak, has been engaged in such work from the early 1970s under the guidance of theologically trained leaders such as Wong Meng Chow, and in its regular newsletter (*SCSNEWS*) has also published writings on contextual theology. Such ministries would also lead in early 1988 to opposition from sensitive government agencies and to the eventual imprisonment in Malaysia and in Singapore, of Christian activists such as Vincent Cheng, Theresa Lim Chin Chin, Anthony Rogers, V. David, Sebil John, Patricia Lourdes, Cecilia Ng and Jamaluddin Othman. But from this experience also would come Christian reflection, in the letters from prison of lay ministers like Theresa Lim Chin Chin and others.

In response to government white papers and the detention of social workers in the late 1980s, the Christian Federation of Malaysia - formed in 1985 and including the Roman Catholic Church, the CCM and the NECF (3.1) - issued a number of documents concerning Christian witness in political and cultural matters. Here they present clearly the social concerns of Christians as loyal citizens, as well as presenting a theology of dissent and diversity, of Christ-like ministry for the poor, true religious freedom and the legitimacy of cultural adaptation of the Gospel. They also correct misunderstandings of liberation theology and of Christian indigenisation. Christian "theology and practices", they declare, "must be embodied in the local cultures". Catholic Pastoral Letters also criticised, in 1987 for example, the use of the draconian Internal Security Act (ISA) which allows detention without trial.

Theological teachers such as Liong Yuk Chong in Sarawak, Francis Danil in Sabah, and Albert Walters in West Malaysia (see

4.20), have also sought in their work to liberate Christian thought from the bondage of ethnic or religious segregation, and to foster a theology which is in dialogue with other religious traditions and responsive to the contemporary movements and issues of Malaysian society. (See also below Thu En Yu, Cecil Rajendra, Yong Ting Jin, Satayandy Batumalai, Denison Jayasooriya, Hwa Yung, Angeline Bones-Fernandez, Ng Kam Weng, Yeoh Seng-guan, Paul Tan Chee Ing, Anthony Rogers, Edmund Chia, Fung Jojo M., and Patricia Martinez).

In the same years such issues as religious freedom and race relations were dealt with fully in the *Christianity in Malaysia* Series of the Graduates Christian Fellowship. Their more recent publications have concerned the ethics and theology of the marketplace. (See 5.6). In the 1990s, the theology enunciated by the Federation in 1988 has undergirded many activities of both the CCM, and of Malaysian CARE in relation to the larger ethical and moral issues of Malaysia's rapidly changing society. Malaysian CARE has also published materials both for devotion and on pastoral and social concerns. Many concerns for social justice and a humane community have also been advocated by the Aliran institute led by Chandra Muzaffar and, especially in regard to religious freedom, by the MCCBCHS. The series of conferences of the Bishops' Institute for Social Action (BISA, III-VII) also provided impetus and understanding for the churches' social ministries. Publications of the Catholic Research Institute (Kuala Lumpur: Paul Tan Chee Ing sj and Theresa Ee Chooi), the Kairos Centre (Kuala Lumpur: Ng Kam Weng) and the later Church and Society group (Trinity Theological College, Singapore: Tan Kim Huat and Roland Chia) have also regularly dealt with issues of religious freedom and of social ethics and concern. (For these see entries below. For the work of ATESEA and AWRCCT see chapter 3, volume 1.)

Along with those already mentioned, other Malaysian or Singaporean theologians who have written on these and related issues since the 1980s include Choong Chee-pang, Stephen Tan, Hermen Shastri, Dulcie Abraham, Victor Oorjitham and Goh Keat Peng. (For these see below.)

Selected References

"A call for responsible and critical voting in the general election." Kuala Lumpur: CCM, August, 1999.

Chelladurai, I.R. "Church and Society in Malaysia." MA dissertation. Department of Theology, University of Birmingham, 1973.

Cheng, Elizabeth. "To be a Christian is to be Radical." *New Q* (Singapore SCM) 2 (Jan. 1972). Also *SCC Reprint* (Hong Kong).

Chew, Maureen K.C. *The Journey of the Catholic Church in Malaysia 1511-1996.* Kuala Lumpur: Catholic Research Centre, 2000.

Chin Chin, Theresa Lim. "Letters." Taiping Detention Centre: Mimeo'd, 1988.

Dutton, Denis C. "Reflexions." In *Growing in Unity with Christ: Council of Churches of Malaysia 40th Anniversary, General Assembly 13-16 February, 1987.* Kuala Lumpur: MCC, 1987.

England, John C., ed. *Theology in Action 2.* Kuala Lumpur: CCA, 1974.

MCCBCHS. "Freedom of Religion and Belief. Declaration of the Malaysian Consultative Council for Buddhism, Christianity, Hinduism and Sikhism." *Weltkirche* (1989)

Institute for Contextual Theology. "Whose Theology?" *SCS News* 18 (1985).

Jayasooria, Denison. *Update on Detention of Christians and the Christian Response in Malaysia.* S.l.: Malaysian CARE, Nov. 1988.

Lau, Sabrina King Lang. "Malaysian Christians' Attitudes towards Christian Social Responsibility." Thesis, STM, 1986.

Lee Soo Ann. "On Being a Christian Economist." *Church and Society* (EACC) 2.8 (1968).

Lim, Daniel. "The Role of Christians in the Liberation Process." Singapore: Mimeo'd, 1974.

Lim Mah Hui. "Malaysia: Race Relations and Economics." In *Southeast Asians Speak Out,* edited by Barbara and Leon Howell. New York: Friendship Press, 1975.

Loh Soon Choy. *In Search of a Responsible Society: A Responsible Church in a Sensitive Asian Society.* Klang, Malaysia: Malaysia Bible Seminary, 1990.

Malaysian Consultative Council for Buddhism, Christianity, Hinduism and Sikhism. *Contemporary Issues on Malaysian Religions.* Petaling Jaya: Pelanduk Publications, 1984.

Moey, Michael et al., eds. *The Christian and Race Relations in Malaysia*. The Christian in Malaysia Series 1. Kuala Lumpur: Graduate Students' Fellowship, 1986.

Nyce, Ray. *The Kingdom and the Country: a Study of Church and Society in Singapore.* Singapore: Institute for Study of Religions and Society 1972 (see also 4.5).

"Pastoral Letter of the Bishops of Peninsular Malaysia." and "Analysis of the White Paper." *Tugon* 8.3 (1988).

"Peninsular Consultation on Church and Development." *National Office on Human Development Bulletin* (July-August, 1983).

PMV Dossier. *The Malay Dilemma*. Asia-Australasia Dossier 28 (1984).

"Report of the Urban Clergy and Church Workers' Conference July 1980, Port Dickson." In *STM Archives*, Seremban.

Shastri, Hermen et al. *United in Christ, Serving the Nation. Celebrating 50 Years of United Witness and Service.* Kuala Lumpur: CCM, 1997.

Thiangaraja, R. "Inter-Religious Council: MCCBCHS Clarifies."

Yeow, Patrick C.S. "Lee Pak Sook in Asian Suffering and Hope." In *Asian Theological Reflections on Suffering and Hope*, edited by Yap Kim Hao. Singapore: CCA, 1977.

Yeoh Seng Guan, ed. *Baptism, Eucharist and Ministry. A Malaysian Contribution.* Kuala Lumpur: CCM, 1992.

3.3 Women Doing Theology

In the life and work of churches in Malaysia and Singapore women have long been leaders, despite continuing discrimination against their recognition, their opportunities for publication, and even against the recording of their names. From some, however, have come writings, in various forms, which include elements of contextual theological reflection. Amongst those in the period 1800-1945, are Sophia Blackmore (see 2.2.4.) and Sophia Cooke. In the following period national organisations which have worked to combat discrimination, and in which Christian women have contributed, include the National Council of Women's Organisations (1963), the Women's Aid Association (ca.1975), the Women's Committee of the Malaysian Trade Union Congress, the Joint Action Group Against Violence Against Women (1984), the All Women's Action Movement and the Women's Development Collective. Women were also active both in industrial mission projects (in for example, Kuala Lumpur and in Jurong, Singapore) as well as in Catholic welfare programmes, in the YCW and in the SCM. Amongst these were Irene Fernandez, Elizabeth Cheng and Chew Beng Lan. In these years also a growing number of women have gained recognition in other church-related work, as lay and ecumenical leaders, as journalists, theological teachers, animators, and writers. Those to be mentioned include Ivy Chou, Theresa Ee Chooi, Angela Fernandes, Dulcie Abraham, Lee Tzu Pheng, Patricia Martinez and Yong Ting Jin, all of which appear in entries below.

Malaysian Women in Ministry & Theology (MWMT) have met periodically since May 1986, holding seminars and workshops with the objectives of both studying and articulating the situation of women in Church and society and also women's perspectives on the Bible and theology. They also have the aims of enhancing the theological participation and ministries of women, along with dialogue and work with women of other faiths in promoting women's status, role and image. Articles from the movement have appeared in their bi-annual newsletter and in *In God's Image*. A booklet containing new ecumenical feminist/women's liturgies has also been published.

Women's Voice was founded in 2000 and is an independent ecumenical group the majority of whom are Catholics. Members are active in women's NGOs, and in regular meetings reflect, question and respond to the many issues facing both women's movements and women in the church. They have also conducted seminars on "the role women have and are playing in society, the church and the bible" and seek particularly to be a voice for women's issues in the Catholic Church. Group papers are now being prepared and writings by members are available. (See those by Cecilia Ing, and Yong Ting Jin below.)

Amongst others who have contributed to contextual theology in Malaysia and Singapore in this period are the following:

Maureen K.C. Chew ij has undertaken thorough study of the history of the Catholic Church in Malaysia, culminating in her volume *The Journey of the Catholic Church in Malaysia 1511-1996* (2000). In this she traces also the theological journey of the church and includes careful reflection upon the processes of indigenisation begun and required, concluding that in theology and education there must now be "mutual spiritual empowerment" and also mutual theological enrichment", with full attention to reconciliation and conflict management as well as to collegial decision-making.

Aileen Khoo (BTh, MA) is Christian Education Director, Trinity Methodist Church, Petaling Jaya. She has been active for many years in both Christian and musical education, in theological teaching and in national and regional theological organisations. In teaching and writing she stresses the unity of belief and feeling, the role of Christians as co-creators with God, the recognition of the arts and music as sources of creativity and spontaneity, and the means of both participatory learning and enriched "human relationships, together with God".

Yeow-Teo Giok Lian (MEd) has taught at Trinity Theological College, Singapore, over some years and contributed to national and regional programmes for theologically-trained women. She has also written on these programmes and on Christian education subjects in the *Asia Journal of Theology.*

Voon Choon Khing (MTh, DMin) is librarian at Seminari Theoloji Malaysia and has compiled full bibliographies of *Malaysian Christian Literature* (1997). She has also studied and written on the subjects of Christian Spirituality, Spiritual Direction and Theological/Biblical Anthropology.

Pang Ken Phin (ThD) is an ordained minister of the Basel Christian Church of Malaysia in Sabah and is a full time faculty member of Sabah Theological Seminary. She is also a secretary for the Office for Ecumenical Affairs of the Lutheran World Federation and has recently been elected Assistant Bishop. She has contributed chapters to collaborative volumes as well as articles to such journals as *LWF Women's Magazine*, *In God's Image* and *Zeitschrift fur Mission Writings.*

Other books or theses have come from Nathalie Means, Lee Bee-teik and Sabrina Lau King Lang (West Malaysia), and Sylvia M. Jeanes, Jessica Aliah Umbukun, Chung Song Mee and Alice

M. Shea (Sabah), amongst others. Articles in such journals as *MCC News, ACISCA Bulletin, Great Commission Magazine, Asia Journal of Theology,* and *In God's Image,* have come from, amongst others, Martha Ratnam, Marilyn Lim, Rinnie Lau, Cecilia Ing, Swinnie Shum, Tan Yak Hwee, Pang Ken Phin, Jessica Aliah Umbukan and Girija Nair. In journals such as *Catholic Asia News, Catholic News, Herald, Glory,* and *East Asia Pastoral Review,* we have articles by Patricia Pereira, Marie Turner, Sharon A. Bong, Maria Yan, Bernadette Teh, Victorine, Irene Xavier, Fernando, Anne D'Oliviero, Grace Chia, Elaine Morais and Dianne Bargent. In Singapore Christiane Santhau fdcc, Grace Chia ij and Jacinta Cardoza ij have also written on women's search for an egalitarian spirituality and community in a patriarchal ecclesia.

Selected References

Chew, Maureen K.C. "Women in the Church in Malaysia." *EAPR* 26 (1989).

Chia Nyoke Lin. "Women in Ministry in Malaysia." In *Theological Education for Women.* ATESEA Occasional Papers 1. Singapore: ATESEA, 1983.

Diocesan Women's Board. *Not Alone Along Life's Pathways.* Singapore: Anglican Diocese, 1995.

Doraisamy, Theodore R. "Women Pioneers of Methodism in Singapore and Malaysia: Messengers of Love." *Asia Journal of Theology* 4 (1990).

Ing, Cecilia. "Women in Malaysia: Problems and Issues." *In God's Image* (December 1986).

—. "Towards a Gender-Friendly Information Technology." *In God's Image* 19.1 (2000).

Khoo, Aileen. "Arts and Music as a Means in Christian Education." *Great Commission Magazine* 131 (n.d.)

—. "Love Nation and Love Church." *In God's Image* 10.3 (1991).

Lau, Sabrina King Lang. "Malaysian Christians' Attitudes towards Christian Social Responsibility." Thesis, STM, 1986.

Lee Bee-teik. *Deepening Joy. A Reflection on God's Grace by a Malaysian Christian.* Petaling Jaya: SUFES, 1993.

—. *Friends of the Bridegroom.* Kuala Lumpur: Reconre, 1999.

Malaysian Women in Theology. "Statement and Objectives." *In God's Image* (December 1986).

Pang Ken Phin. "Women and Ministry." In *Towards a Chinese Feminist Theology*, edited by Winnie Ho. Hong Kong: Taosheng Publishing House, 1988.

—. "The Decade as the Great Commission." In *In Search of a Round Table: Gender, Theology & Church Leadership*, edited by Musimbi R.A. Kanyoro. Geneva: WCC Publications, 1997.

—. "Towards Greater Participation in the National Development by Women of the Malaysian Churches." In *Christian Reflections within an Emerging Industrialised Society*, edited by Thu En Yu, David R. Burfield et al. Sabah: Seminari Teologi Sabah, 1998.

Sin Ho-chee. "Women's Work and Leadership in the Methodist Church, Singapore." *Asia Journal of Theology* 1 (1987).

Voon Choon Khing. *Body Theology - Where is the Body in Christian Anthropology?: a quest for somatic spirituality that promotes life-giving faith formation*. MTh thesis, Divinity School of Duke University, 1996.

—. *Spiritual Direction - Spiritual Direction in a Malaysian Context: in search of a viable way ahead*. DMin thesis, Graduate Theological Foundation, Donaldson, Indiana, 1999.

Woman Community Worker. "A Personal Experience in Jurong Industrial Mission." *Church Labor Letter* 136 (August 1976).

Women in the Methodist Church of Malaysia, 1885-1984. Kuala Lumpur: Women's Society of Christian Service, ca. 1986.

Xavier, Irene. "Gender and Women's Concerns: An Asian Perspective." *In God's Image* 19.1 (2000).

Yeoh Seng Guan. "Writing about Women and Building Partnership." *In God's Image* 13.3 (1994).

Yeow-Teo Giok Lian. "Filial Piety in Contemporary Society." *SEAJT* 22.2 (1981).

3.4 Catholic Church 1950 - 2000
3.4.1. From Institutional Enclave to Social Presence

Until the mid-1970s the Catholic Church remained institution-centred, with an authority-centred hierarchy, a foreign image, and an insignificant role for the laity. Internally its congregations were divided into separate racial, cultural and linguistic groupings; externally there was little ecumenical or inter-religious dialogue. Isolated ethnically, Catholics also tended to be identified with the middle and upper-middle classes. This period experienced also a considerable exodus from the priesthood and religious Sisterhoods and Brotherhoods.

Towards a Participatory Church. The watershed for Malaysia came in 1976 when the sacramental church "shut down" for August as the whole presbyterium of Peninsular Malaysia gathered in Penang for a month-long *Aggiornamento* (renewal) to re-vision the church's mission. Final statements emphasised the building of Christ-centred Base Communities, lay formation, dialogue with other Christians and other faith traditions, and integral human development of the poor (Chew 2000). Inspired by John XXIII's Council and by the East Asian Pastoral Institute in Manila, this was however still a priest-led and priest-centred initiative and so was its follow-up.

Muslim resurgence in Malaysia also urged ongoing renewal. Catholic Pastoral Conventions have been held from 1986, the first issuing the statement, "Ongoing Formation, Unity within the Church, Dialogue with other Christians and People of other Faiths, Integral Human Development and Ministry for Youth" (*Report of PMPC 1986*. Kuala Lumpur). A Peninsular Malaysia Pastoral Council (PMPC) Study Guide was prepared, followed by Study-Days and Assemblies, 1994-5, and the PMPC II, 1996. This added to the concerns of PMPC I: "Inculturation, Pastoral Care of Families, and Social Communication". The Mission Statement of the Pastoral Convention was "rooted in the Communion of the Trinity" and, "the solidarity of the whole Human Family" and had the vision of developing human communities through Base Communities, through dialogue with other cultures and religions and with the poor, and in these ways finding new ways of being Church. (Chew 2000). Malaysian bishops joined their colleagues throughout Asia at the special assembly for Asia of the Synod of Bishops (April/May 1998) in calling for fuller freedom for the Asian churches to express the faith according to their own categories and cultures. By the year 2000, some groups in the Church's hierarchy were fostering parish-led Base Communities in order to buttress Catholic identity, while more radical elements had moved away into extra-parochial inter-faith networks.

In Sabah, the period of periodic persecution (from 1970), during which national leadership developed through Parish Councils and the Sabah Catholic Association, was followed in the 1980s by full freedom under political parties led by Catholics. Education and publication again flourished, including the monthly *Catholic Sabah* (editions in three languages), and ecumenical co-operation led to the formation of the Sabah Council of Churches. In Sarawak, inter-racial and inter-religious tensions have at times been raised in periods such as the late 1980s, by fundamentalist groups in all religions. A small Catholic press operates, although there has been less social or political involvement than in Sabah. Catholics and Protestants work together through the Association of Churches in Sarawak.

In Singapore the Centre Zhonglian de Singapour, led by Jean Charbonnier (1981-1992), has been able to continue studies and publications on the life of the Catholic Church in China since the late 1970s. The Centre's publications have included the newsletter *Zhonglian* and five editions of the *Guide to the Catholic Church in China*, most recently issued in 2000. Catholic Welfare Services (CWS) have been active in Singapore in these decades despite periodic suppression, and in Malaysia have initiated a number of constructive programmes through its later organisational form of the Office for Human Development (see 3.3).

The Catholic Research Centre was founded in 1977 in Kuala Lumpur as an integrating centre for research, reflection, information and formation, "concentrating on raising the awareness of our people to the realities of the Malaysian situation". It also aims to foster participation in society in its socio-political, economic and religious context; and to help people of different faiths to understand one another, "upholding in love the principles of truth, justice, equality and freedom." The Institute conducts research, seminars and dialogues, has developed a library and documentation centre, facilitates dialogue between people of different faiths and publishes *Catholic Asia News* (*CANews*), occasionally the journal *Information &Formation*, and also books.

New understandings of lay ministry, Basic Ecclesial Communities (BEC) and collegiality have begun to develop in this period, and in Malaysia in particular these have issued in new programmes of education and ministry. The Empowerment Programme for the Theological Education of the Laity at the parish of St. Francis Xavier in Petaling Jaya is led by Angeline Bones-Fernandez (see 4.9). The Empowerment Programme is birthing a group of budding lay theologians through the many theology courses it offers. Emerging from that programme are persons like Dr. Robert Penafort, Sharon Cahill, Caroline Lopez Caballero (Ph.D), now a visiting Research Fellow at the Institute of Malaysian and International Studies, Universiti Kebangsaan Malaysia, and Cheryl Lee, now studying at the East Asian Pastoral Institute, Manila. Wider Catholic-Protestant co-operation is also developing, in joint programmes in formation and publication, and through an ecumenical committee of Catholics and Protestants convened by the Council of Churches in Malaysia (1998) to prepare prayers and liturgical materials, which have been distributed by the Vatican to local churches worldwide.

Selected References

Aruldas, Arokianathan. "Mission of the Catholic Church in Malaysia." *Indian Missiological Review* 16.1 (1994).

Chew, Maureen K.C. *The Journey of the Catholic Church in Malaysia 1511-1996.*

Chan, Francis. "Incorporating Traditional Values in Church Celebrations." *Today's Catholic* (1990).

Chan, James. "Rekindling the Spirit of Aggiornamento." *Herald*, July 30 (1995).

Charbonnier, Jean. "Chronique de Centre Zhonglian de Singapour." *Echos de la Rue du Bac* (1986).

—. "Singapour 1975: Pragmatique de la Modernisation et Ambiguites Chrétiennes." *Exchange France-Asie* (Oct. 1975).

Conference of Bishops Peninsular Malaysia. "Pastoral Letter." (Re Government White Paper 1988). *Tugon* 8.3 (1988).

Fernandes, Anthony Soter. "Vers une Église de Participation." *Spiritus* 30 (1989).

Focus upon Malaysian Realities. Kuala Lumpur: National Office of Human Development, n.d.

Lee, Felix George. *The Catholic Church in Malaya.* Singapore: Eastern University Press, 1963.

Pereira, Patricia. "Equal Responsibility after PMPC?" *Herald*, February 23 (1997).
Pinto, Aloysius Francis. "Signs of Hope: PMPC II - The Plentong Experience." *Catholic Asia News*, Oct. (1996).
—. *Towards a New Way of Being Church in Malaysia*. PMPC Study-Guide. Kuala Lumpur: 1996, 1997.
"Present Situation of the Church in Malaysia." *EAPR* 4 (1984).
Our Journey as the Church in Peninsular Malaysia. Kuala Lumpur: 1996. (Also in *Catholic Asia News*, July 1996).
Rogers, Anthony, ed. *Report on the Peninsular Malaysia Pastoral Convention 1986*. Kuala Lumpur: 1987.
—, ed. *Towards a Common Understanding of the Church as Communion*. Kuala Lumpur: National Office for Human Development, 1994.
—, "Moving Towards a Church of the Future in Malaysia." *Herald*. (Oct. 6, 1996).
Rooney, John. *Khabar gembira: The Good News: a History of the Catholic Church in East Malaysia and Brunei, 1880-1976*. London and Kota Kinabalu: Burns & Oates and Mill Hill Missionaries, 1981.
Yong, Gregory. "The Hopes and Concerns of a Growing Church". *Catholic International* 1.1 (1990).

4 Theologians and Scholars
4.1 Roman Catholic Episcopal Leaders

Writings of theological import have come both from individual bishops in this period as well as from the conferences of Bishops and their agencies in Malaysia and Singapore (See above 3.4.1.). The Conference of Bishops in Peninsular Malaysia as well as the Malaysia-Singapore-Brunei Bishops' Conference, have issued occasional pastoral letters or statements, as well as contributing to the statements of Pastoral Conventions and participating fully in the work of the MCCBCHS. Amongst those bishops who have provided significant leadership are the following:

Dominic Vendargon (b.1909, ordained priest 1934) served in parishes in Singapore and Peninsular Malaysia and taught at seminaries in Singapore and Penang. As Archbishop of Kuala Lumpur (1973) he initiated Lay Ministry Training and fostered the gifts and charismas of "religious and lay people ... to transform the local church into a more visible sign and effective instrument of God's kingdom" (Archbishop Gregory Yong). He emphasised involvement of the church in ecumenical affairs, particularly in the CFM. He was the first President of MCCBCHS, where he showed a commitment to human rights and religious freedom.

Peter Chung Hoan Ting (b. 1928), Bishop of Sabah, Vicar Apostolic and later Archbishop of Kuching, was the first President of *Persatuan Agama Katolik Sabah* (Sabah Catholic Union), founded the Major Seminary for East Malaysia at Kuching (St Peter's College), and initiated the training of the laity in Theology, Canon Law and Religious Studies. He also revived the Archdiocesan Pastoral Council to make possible fuller lay participation and instituted Sarawak's 'Bible Years'. Bishop Chung's writings include articles in *Catholic Asia News*, *Today's Catholic* and the *Herald*, along with Pastoral Letters.

Cornelius Piong (later Bishop in Sabah) was a competent musical composer and advocated ecclesial localisation. Piong has promoted Summer Courses on "The Sacraments and Inculturation", stressing that the New Testament must be used for the Church's spiritual nurture but also that "the local church cannot remain cut off from our culture." He has also strongly advocated care for the environment, and "short term profits through extensive logging, (especially) in water catchment areas must be stopped". See his articles in *Today's Catholic* and regular articles also in *Catholic Asia News*.

Other bishops who have later initiated pastoral and publishing programmes include Bishop Francis Chan, and Bishop James Chan Soon Seong.

Selected References

> *1934-94 Sacerdotal Diamond Jubilee Souvenir Programme of Archbishop Emeritus Tan Sri Dominic Vendargon.* Kuala Lumpur: n.p., 1994.
> Chung Hoan Ting, Peter. "Our Task and Our Responsibility." Kuching: Pastoral Letter, 1977.
> —. "Association of Churches in Sarawak." *Catholic Asia News*, July (1988).
> Conference of Bishops Peninsular Malaysia. "Pastoral Letter." (Re Government White Paper 1988). *Tugon* 8.3 (1988).

Fernandes, Anthony Soter. "Vers une Église de Participation." *Spiritus* 30 (1989).
Piong, Cornelius. "The Church Must be Rooted in Local Culture." *Today's Catholic* 6 (1990).
"To Be New In Christ. Malaysia-Singapore-Brunei Bishops' response to the Linneamenta ..." *Catholic International* 9 (1998). Also published as "Malaisie, Singapour, Brunei: Résponse de la Conférence Episcopale aux 'Lineamenta'." *Églises d'Asie Supplément* 257 (1998).
Thy will be Done. Pictorial Essay on Life and Times of Archbishop Dominic Vendargon. Kuala Lumpur: n.p., 1995.

4.2 Tan Sri Roland Koh Peck Chiang (1908-1972)

Koh Peck Chiang studied theology in China, England and the United States, later receiving both the DD and LLD degrees. Following ministries in Hong Kong and Kuala Lumpur, he became Assistant Bishop of Kuala Lumpur (1958), Bishop of Sabah (1965) and Bishop of West Malaysia (1970). He was thus the first Chinese Anglican Bishop in Malaya or Singapore. In the 15 years following the declaration of independence for Malaysia, he was "active in forging a national identity for the church", in providing a "vital focus in the period before and after Merdeka", and also in fostering inter-racial understanding in times of tension.

As part of his commitment to develop autonomy for the Malaysian churches he inaugurated a theological centre - the St Mark's Training Centre for lay people and clergy - at Sungei Buloh near Kuala Lumpur in 1972. This later became the Kolej Theoloi Malaysia, soon to be part of the ecumenical Seminari Theoloji Malaysia (1976) with full inter-church participation. Koh remained a scholar in New Testament studies, and was also active in national and regional ecumenical councils. In pastoral letters he advocated self-support and independence for the church, the development of indigenous leadership, and co-operation and understanding between those of different faiths.

Selected References

Works by Roland Koh

The Writings of St Luke. Hong Kong: Diocesan Literature Committee, 1953.

Hoh Wai Ying. "Written Notes of Roland Koh." Trinity Theological College Singapore (in Chinese). Library of Trinity Theological College.

Hunt, Robert, Lee Kam Hing and John Roxborogh, eds. *Christianity in Malaysia. A Denominational History.*

Morgan, D.I. "A Life of Roland Koh, first Chinese Anglican Bishop in Singapore and Malaysia." In Morgan, D.I. *They became Anglicans.* London: Mowbray, 1959, 74-83.

The Anglican News 1 (April 1970).

4.3 John Robb Fleming (1910-1999)

John Fleming came to Malaysia and Singapore following missionary work in Manchuria (ca. 1952) and completed doctoral studies at Union Theological Seminary, New York, in 1962. Secretary to the MCC during the 1950s, he also became Secretary for Life, Message and Unity for the EACC from 1959. He was later Director of the newly-formed SEA Association of Theological Schools and editor of the *Southeast Asia Journal of Theology*. As director of SEAATS he also initiated the series of Annual Theological Study Institutes for theological teachers around the region, and as EACC staff member was responsible for organising and documenting major programmes of theological consultation and study.

Although Fleming's chief theological concerns were for "faith and order" and for the ecumenical movement amongst the churches of Malaysia and Asia, he also made significant contributions to the theology of mission as well as to theological education, in Malaysia and throughout the Asian region. His early writings concerned doctrinal discussions in Malaya, and mission practice in Malaysia's "new villages". Later, in recounting the development of "confessing theology" in Asian churches, he would stress the need to combine the "confession of life" with a theological understanding of what a "common confession of Jesus Christ means"; a study and sympathetic understanding of other faiths in their contemporary forms; and recognition of the actual life-situations of people where they are. He went on to write of "situational theology": the theology of men and women taking seriously the word of God, as they grapple with their existential situation. A living theology, he declared, could only come from such situational obedience.

Selected References
Works by John R. Fleming

The New Villages in Malaya. Kuala Lumpur: MCC, 1958.

Faith and Order discussions in Malaya 1951-1960. Memorandum ... for the first meeting of the Negotiating Committee for Church Union in Malaya. Mimeo'd, Oct. 1960.

"The Growth of the Chinese Church in the New Villages of the State of Johore, Malaysia, 1950-60: A Study in the Communication of the Gospel to Chinese Converts." ThD Thesis. New York: Union Theological Seminary, 1962.

—, ed. *One People One Mission. The Situational Conferences of the EACC, 1963.* Singapore: EACC, 1963.

with Kenyon Wright. *Structures for a Missionary Congregation.* Singapore: EACC, 1964.

—, ed. *This We Believe.* Hong Kong: Taosheng, 1968.

Some notes on the history and development of the Malayan Christian Council. Mimeo'd, Council of Churches of Malaysia and Singapore, December 1966.

"'Then and Now' in Theological Education in S.E. Asia." *SEAJT* 6.4 & 7.1 (1965).

"Confessions, Confessionalism and the Confessing Church in Asia Today." In *Confessing the Faith in Asia Today,* edited by John Fleming. *SEAJT* 8.1&2 (1966).

4.4 K. Jambunathan (1931-)

Jambunathan studied in Singapore and Kolkata (Calcutta, BD). He was active in the university student ministry through WSCF/SCM programmes and following ministry in Ipoh, he was appointed the first Asian Warden for the Anglican Kolej Theoloji Malaysia which was based in the Parish of St. Barnabas, Klang, and its social ministries. KTM later became Seminari Theoloji Malaysia. Along with D. Chelliah, John Savarimuthu and others Jambunathan was early advocating stronger identification of the Church with its Malaysian context, through an indigenisation of theology, of architecture, of leadership and the development of social ministries. He also insisted that theological students should be properly exposed to other faiths and taught by experts of that faith rather than Christian 'non-believers'. Reverting to full-time parish work he developed patterns of Christian service by parishioners among those of other faiths, including assistance in claiming national rights, head-start education for indigent children, student hostel facilities and a residential centre for drug addicts and destitutes - all these being staffed and manned by trained personnel and the resident seminarians on a full-time basis so that the seminary was set within a microcosm of a community at large.

The roots of Jambunathan's formulation of a "Banana Theology" lay in his deep desire to understand the Hindu/Indian culture of prominently using banana trees in all their festivals and celebrations, including funerals. Finding that this ancient tree has stood for some very fundamental values of life which have inspired many peoples and been noted by scholars, Jambunathan later sees in it powerful indigenous imagery both for the Christian life, and in particular, for the life of Jesus. Here are symbolisms of complete utility, abundant flow of love in action, fruitfulness which always involves pain and loss so that others may thrive, along with the offering of one's total life for the generation of new life. Here are down-to-earth sacraments of "the beauty and fullness of life - such a life that the person of Jesus, and all religions, have offered to men and women." By the mid-1970s other indigenous symbolisms multiplied by which to express the Jesus Event: including the 'Dulang' washer, who stands in the rushing river to painstakingly scoop up and filter out the heavy metal of tin dust for later making tin and pewter. Here is an indigenous way of describing the process of our separation and identity, to be finally made into useful vessels - a redemption that does not mean being just freed from sin, but a fashioning and restoration to fullness of life.

Selected References

Jambunathan, K. *The Banana Tree - at all times and especially Christmas*. Mimeo'd. Klang: 1999.

Northcott, Michael S. "Two hundred Years of Anglican Mission." In *Christianity in Malaysia. A Denominational History*, edited by Robert Hunt, Lee Kam Hing and John Roxborogh. Petaling Jaya: Pendaluk Publications, 1992.

Walters, Albert Sundararaj. *We Believe in One God?* Delhi: ISPCK, 2000. ch. 6.

4.5 Ray Nyce and the Institute for Study of Religions and Society

Ray Nyce was a Lutheran missionary based in Singapore in the 1970s, who developed the programmes of the Institute for Study of

Religions and Society in Singapore and Malaysia. In this he collaborated closely with colleagues in churches, universities, government departments, social service councils, and lay movements. On the basis of the Institute's programmes of research and consultation, Nyce wrote or edited a series of volumes which studied church life and societal issues, the 'new villages', Chinese folk religion, and processes of racial and religious harmony in both Malaysia and Singapore. In these he sought to clarify the role of the church within the populations, social structures and issues of Singapore and Malaysia. The volumes include social scientific surveys, church history and bibliographies. Nyce was also concerned to delineate future forms of service and congregational life, along with the resources necessary for these new directions.

Selected References
Works by Ray Nyce
> *Lift Up Your Heads ...: a research project dealing with church life and work in towns and villages in West Malaysia.* Singapore: Institute for Study of Religions and Society in Singapore and Malaysia, 1971.
> *The Kingdom and the Country: a study of church and society in Singapore.* Singapore: Institute for Study of Religions and Society in Singapore and Malaysia, 1972.
> —, ed. *Racial Integration as a Process of Development: report of a seminar held in Singapore 14th - 20th March, 1972.* Singapore: Institute for study of Religions and Society in Singapore and Malaysia, 1972.
> —, ed. *The Value of the Human Person: an inter-religious "get-together".* Singapore: Inter-Religious Organisation, Institute for Study of Religions and Society in Singapore and Malaysia and Trinity Theological College, 1973.
> *Chinese New Villages in Malaya: a community study,* ed. by Shirley Gordon. Singapore: Malaysian Sociological Research Institute, 1973.
> *Into a New Age; a Study of Church and Society in Kuala Lumpur, Malaysia.* Singapore: Institute for Study of Religions and Society in Singapore and Malaysia,1973.
> "Chinese Folk Religion in Malaysia and Singapore." *SEAJT* 12 (1971).

4.6 Dulcie Abraham (1931-)

Dulcie Abraham is an Anglican deaconess and theologian, and was a founding - later Co-ordinating -member of the AWRCCT. She also taught at the Seminari Theoloji Malaysia. She has been active both in study and ministry to rectify abuses against women as well as to develop support and resource networks for Malaysian and Asian women theologians.

For Abraham the aim of doing/studying theology and culture "has been to critique both traditional theology and culture, because one reinforces the other in its discrimination against women". She sees Malaysian women experiencing a double oppression when cultural prejudices, discriminatory practices and the abuse of power over them are supposedly justified by teachings and practices of the church. Authentic theology will therefore challenge the validity of male-biased theology and teaching and correct the church's age-long misunderstanding of the meaning of the new creation inaugurated by Jesus, for this offers to Asian women and to all, a full freedom and joy in full exercise of their thought, ministry and leadership. She expounds this meaning in studies of the Hebrew Scriptures and of the Gospels, and of the writings of Paul, followed by a critique of later writers and church leaders.

But in her work and writing Abraham has been concerned also to correct partial understandings of deity and the Trinity which have been confined to the masculine. This means for her the recovery of the maternal traits of God. In this journey, she declares, it has been important "to discover for ourselves the gentle, inclusive womanly face of God. And for this women are rereading the Bible through women's eyes". There will be here a unique and feminine "interplay of reason and emotion, of heart, mind and spirit ... an authentic way of knowing." Her writings on this have included expressive poetry on those "whose spirits burn with God's eternal fire..."

Selected References
Works by Dulcie Abraham
> "Jesus the New Creation: Christology in the Malaysian Context." In *Asian Women Doing Theology: Report from Singapore*

Conference, November 20-29, 1987, edited by Dulcie Abraham et al. Kowloon, Hong Kong: AWRCCT, 1989: 189-194.

"Feminine Images of God." *In God's Image* (June 1989).

"Christian Women's Contribution to Inter-religious Dialogue." *Newsletter of the AWRCCT* 2.1 (January 1997).

"Journeying Ahead Together - Journeying with Malaysian Women." Paper delivered at the symposium entitled *Journeying Ahead Together*, December 5, 1999, Petaling Jaya.

"They do not Die." *In God's Image* 18.3 (1999).

—, ed. with Sun Ai Lee Park and Yvonne Dahlin. *Faith Renewed. A Report on the First Asian Women's Consultation on Interfaith Dialogue*. Hong Kong: AWRCCT, 1989.

4.7 Yap Kim Hao (ca.1932 -)

Yap Kim Hao studied at Trinity Theological College, Baker University and Boston School of Theology (ThD 1969). He was the first Asian bishop of the Methodist Church in Malaysia and Singapore (1968-1973) and General Secretary of the CCA (1973-1985). He later taught at Perkins School of Theology, Texas, Vancouver School of Theology, Boston School of Theology and Trinity Theological College, Singapore. He continues to write and preach in Singapore.

From early concerns for the mission of Methodism in Malaysia and Singapore, and being deeply influenced by D.T. Niles (see Vol 1, Chapter 8), Yap Kim Hao came increasingly to study and write of the history and present nature of ecumenical issues of ecclesiology and mission there and in neighbouring countries. By 1969 he was active in the committees of the EACC, with concern for Christian education and lay training, and later, for a wide range of ecumenical undertakings in the life and mission of Asian churches at the cutting edges of society. In this he regularly related " to people who are engaged in local action or development, justice and peace." Along with the writing of popular ecumenical history and consultation documents, Yap Kim Hao has written fully on the tasks of contextual theology: the principles, personal location, sources and sociology of local theologies. He stresses the nature of theology as praxis, holding a dialectic relationship with both theory and with the realities of pluralistic societies. He goes on to spell out the processes of contextualisation in regard to religious diversity, political affairs, and environmental issues. In all these his basic assumptions are those of participation, relationship, mutuality and communality.

Selected References
Works by Yap Kim Hao
"Church Structure Issues in Asian Ecumenical Thought with Particular Reference to Malaysia and Singapore." ThD, Boston University School of Theology, 1969.
Doing Theology in A Pluralist World. Singapore: Methodist Book Room, 1990.
From Prapat to Colombo. History of the Christian Conference of Asia 1957-1995. Hong Kong: CCA, 1995.
"Partnership in Mission in the 1980s." *CTC Bulletin* 4.1 (1983).
—, ed. *Asian Theological Reflections on Suffering and Hope.* Singapore: CCA, 1977.
—, ed. *Report of an Asia Ecumenical Consultation on Development: Priorities and Guidelines.* Singapore: CCA, 1974.
—, ed. *Islam's Challenge for Asian Churches. Papers from a Consultation.* Singapore: Millbond, 1980.
—, ed. *Living in Christ with People: A Call to Vulnerable Discipleship.* Singapore: CCA 1981.
—, et al., eds. *Methodism at the Crossroads.* Kuala Lumpur: Union Press, 1966.

4.8 Theresa Ee Chooi (1938-)

Theresa Ee Chooi was born in Singapore and studied there and overseas. She is an eminent Catholic laywoman and a journalist of international reputation. She has been a president of the League of the Women Catholics of Malaysia and is active in the International Apostolate Movement which links lay Catholics who are active in the secular world. In 1977 she was the co-founder of the Catholic Research Centre (Kuala Lumpur, see 3.4.1.) and of *Catholic Asian News*; the widely distributed Christian periodical that includes national and regional reports and theological articles. She also assists with the management of the Asia-wide *Union Catholic Asian News*. Ee Chooi participated in the Synod for Laity (Rome, 1987), is member of the Pontifical Council for Laity and of the Pontifical Council for Communication, and is currently president of the International Union of Catholic Journalists.

In much of her writing and teaching, Theresa Ee Chooi is deeply concerned for the spiritual life of lay people in daily life, as well as to foster inter-faith collaboration for a better world, where deep divisions, inequalities and conflicts obstruct this. She also recognises and opposes the abuse of religion, along with ideological and absolutist distortions of it by those who would dominate and oppress. She has co-edited the theological journal *Information and Formation*, published occasionally by the Catholic Research Centre, with particular concerns both to interpret Christian beliefs for contemporary Malaysians and to apply the faith to the Malaysian inter-religious and social context. She has also written on the spirituality of tertiaries, regarding its identity, situation, inculturation, and practice. Ee Chooi has led courses in inter-religious dialogue and contributed to the foundation of the CFM and of the MCCBCHS Advisory Council of Malaysia (For these see 3.2.1)

Selected References
Works by Theresa Ee Chooi
>"The Multi-Ethnic Complexity of Malaysia." *Inter-Religio* 6 (1984).
>"The World Consultation at Rocca de Papa - Address to the Synod." *EAPR* 24.2 (1987).
>"The Co-Responsibility of the Secular Carmelite in the Spiritual Apostolate." Mimeo'd, Sept 2000.
>—, ed. *Formation and Information*. Kuala Lumpur: Catholic Research Centre, 1979, 1980, 1981, 1994.

4.9 Yeow Choo Lak (1938-)

Yeow Choo Lak grew up in Singapore and has been for more than 20 years a key figure in the development of theology and theological education in the Asian region. Following studies in Singapore, Europe, and the USA (PhD), he pastored churches in Malaysia and came to teach at Trinity Theological College, Singapore. He has since been Dean at Trinity, Director of ATESEA and Dean of SEAGST (since1981). He also edited the *East Asia Journal of*

Theology (now *Asia Journal of Theology*) until 1995, and has been a co-organiser in innovative programmes of faculty training - especially for women and graduate students - and in the publication of Asian theological writing.

His own writings have sometimes been in the areas of philosophical and systematic theology in the Asian context, apologetics and methodology in theological education, and in doing theology. For Yeow Choo Lak, contextual theology means doing theology "where people are", alongside people in urban and rural areas, taking seriously their religions, cultures and spirituality, and also the socio-political circumstances of their daily life. Here the interaction of "the two stories" of Christian identity and cultural heritage gives the locus for doing theology, and a contextual theology will grow from both praxis and spirituality. Yeow Choo Lak has also related such understandings to the church's practices in Christian education, contextual preaching, and in socio-political witness.

Selected references
Works by Yeow Choo Lak
> *To God be The Glory*. Singapore: Trinity Theological College, 1981.
> *Church and Theology*. Singapore: Yeow Choo-lak, 1985.
> *Time for Action*. Singapore: ATESEA, 1988.
> *Bent Over No More: A Meditation on Luke 13:10-17*. Singapore, ?ATESEA, 1997.
> "Philosophy and Theology." *SEAJT* 9.4 and 10.1 (1968).
> "Christ and Cultures." In *Lux Mundi. 30th Anniversary of Trinity Theological College*, edited by John Hamlin. Singapore: Trinity Theological College, 1978.
> "Theology's Long March Against Corruption." *East Asia Journal of Theology* 3.2 (1985).
> —, ed. *Theology and Ministry in S.E .Asia*. Singapore: Trinity Theological College, 1978.

4.10 Angeline Bones-Fernandez (1939-)

May Angeline Bones-Fernandez studied in Kuala Lumpur and in Liverpool, UK(1956-58), at the University of Malaya (TESL,1977-78) and later at Loyola University, USA (MPS, 1996-97). Fernandez has taught in urban and rural areas (1959-85), was appointed a coordinator at the MARA Institute of Technology (1985-88) and later was Lecturer in Linguistics at Western Michigan University, twinned with Sunway College, Malaysia. Dialogue and support groups which she has founded or co-founded include DAWN (1994) and FIRE - a parish group for Fostering Inter-Religious Encounter and to ease away from a parish-model; and INSAF ("Inter-faith Spiritual Fellowship"), a Hindu-based, though non-institutional, inter-religious group (1997-99).

Fernandez is best known for her practical theological work in Petaling Jaya (See 3.4.1.). From 1979-95 she was involved in the restructuring of St. Francis Xavier Parish to form a network of base communities. She has been a member of the Parish Renewal Team to train lay leaders, co-ordinating and facilitating leadership courses and weekend programmes on spiritual growth. She also has been on the planning team for "Presence" and "Response" - courses on practical theology. Since 1999 Fernandez has been coordinator of "Empowerment" - a parish-based group responsible for creating and conducting theological courses for the laity. In such theological animation and in her writings, she is deeply concerned for Church renewal and spirituality, for inter-religious understanding and co-operation, and for the nurture of lay ministry. She sees herself as a practical theologian who is "doing alternative theology" by discerning the needs of her community and responding to these. Regarding the Malaysian context, she has written that, "when we promote solidarity with peoples of other faiths, we become a healing community even though we are imperfect."

Selected References

Angeline Fernandez has published school text-books for language teaching - study workbooks, teacher's guide books and readers, such as "Fireflies" (1988), "Tales of Wisdom" (1989) and "The Green Door" (1990). As she is fully occupied in doing practical theology with fellow laity, her theological programmes have yet to be published. Further information from abonesf@pc.jaring.my <mailto:abonesf@pc.jaring.my>.

4.11 Huang Hsing Peng (ca. 1940-)

Huang Hsing Peng studied at the University of Singapore and Trinity Theological College, Singapore, and returned to Nanyang University as a lecturer and a minister in frontier mission, affiliated to the SCM and the WSCF Frontier Mission Programme. He there pioneered forms of non-institutional Christian presence within academia, which included not only pastoral ministry, but also innovative patterns of spirituality and theological reflection. He later worked with the Ecumenical Institute.

In his writing as in his ministry, he was sensitive alike to the demands of suffering and the often solitary journey of faith within that; to the power of vulnerable personal courage and witness; as well as to the absurdities and ambiguities of the human situation. Yet he also wrote movingly of the consciousness of transcendence within human life, and of the transfiguring mystery of the Trinity - "the triune symbolisation of the Way Life Is" - known through the love of mother Church. In the poem "Yet", he concludes that "If the then mystics and purifying saints learn contemplation, the mind of Christ, We should now, activists and ambiguous secularists, do cruciformity, the style of Christ ..."

Although writing in theological journals on critical aspects of Christian witness within society, his creative writing is also expressed in meditative prayer-poetry, which drew on both reflections on daily experience and the traditions of Christianity and of other faiths. This he described as "prayer engaged, utterly religious, utterly secular" and the "intensification of the poetry of politics". In this he sought to hold together radical secular involvements, the practice of Christian disciplines and a deepening contemplation. Theology, as also Christian life, was therefore for him the attempt

> "to do a prayer, a preliminary tryst to enchant and mold doubt;
> an holy office of radical open integrity, at once the secular-religious ...
> to walk upon the waters of depth engagement,
> as of friend paulos, petros and laotze, gautama and mohammad,
> to transmute matter into spirit".

Selected References
Works by Huang Hsing-peng
  Montaged Contemplation. Singapore: Mimeo'd, 1974.
  "Power and Justice." *SEAJT* 7.4 (1966).
  "Presence on a Frontier in Nanyang University, Singapore." *Student World* 59.2 (1966).
  "Catching up with God, the Radically Unfamiliar." *Presbyterian Messenger* (Combined Edition 1971-74).
  "The Death of a 20th Century Churchman - Goh Kee Siang, One Life, One Death." Singapore: Mimeo'd, 1975.

4.12 Paul Tan Chee Ing sj (1940-)

Paul Tan was born in Johor, grew up in Singapore, and studied in Hong Kong and the Philippines (MA,1965). Two years of pastoral formation in Taipei, Taiwan (1966-1968) were followed by studies in Ireland (LicTh) and in Paris where he obtained his doctorate in Chinese History from *École des Hautes Études*. At the request of the then Archbishop of Kuala Lumpur, Tan Sri Dominic Vendargon (see 4.1.), and together with a lay couple, Paul Tan started the Catholic Research Centre in Kuala Lumpur (see 3.4.1.). Paul Tan Chee Ing was one of the founding members of the CFM, and of the MCCBCHS, in which he was active until 1992. He was called to Rome to work as Assistant to the Jesuit Superior General for East Asia and Oceania in 1993.

In his theological writings Tan Chee Ing has edited *Catholic Asia News - Malaysia* from 1980 until 1992, writing all the editorials until 1992. He also edited *IF (Information and Formation)*, writing regular articles in the journal. These have expounded issues of interfaith dialogue, Christian devotion, challenges to the religious life and the theology of liberation and of salvation. Along with books of apologetics, he has also written many articles that deal directly with the contemporary social, political and religious context in Malaysia. In contextual theology, the discussions and documents of the Second Vatican Council provide for Tan essential foundations for not only the coming shape of the church, but also for Christian response to both religious and societal realities in Malaysia. The continuing task of inculturation is therefore to be based on theologies of "creation, salvation, incarnation, death and resurrection" which he presents with the aim of making possible the "bridge between faith and culture". Central here will be the understandings that, regarding the Malaysian people, all "who sincerely seek truth and practice love" can experience salvation; and regarding the Christian community, that it is to be "endowed with the riches of its own nation's culture [and] deeply rooted in the people." This will involve the church and theology in political issues, for all religion is to assist in building a society having justice, peace, truth and love, and also to oppose any evils "introduced into a nation by the ruling government."

Selected References
Works by Paul Tan Chee Ing
> *Straight to Catholics: Why I Believe in what I Believe.* Kuala Lumpur: Catholic Research Centre, 1984.
> *Islamic State?* Kuala Lumpur: Archdiocese of Kuala Lumpur, 1986.
> *In Defence of* .... Kuala Lumpur: Catholic Research Centre, 1991. (Also in Malaysian.)
> "Liberation - Salvation." *Information & Formation* (1981).
> "Inculturation." *Information & Formation* (1979).
> "Human Rights, Freedom of Expression and Belief." In *Human Rights in Malaysia.* Kuala Lumpur: Catholic Research Centre, 1986.
> "The Mediation of the Church in the Context of Inter-religious Dialogue." *Pro Dialogo.* Pontificum Consilium pro Dialogo Inter-religiones, Bulletin 85-86.1 (1994).
> "Muslim-Christian Relations in Peninsular Malaysia." *Islamochristiana,* Pontificio Istituto di Studi Arabi e d'Islamistica, Roma 1993.
> —, and Selvaraju Selvam. "Church and Politics." *Information & Formation* (1994).

4.13 Denison Jayasooria (ca.1940-)

Denison Jayasooria has produced a series of theological writings arising directly from his ministries in social welfare. Following doctoral studies, he has held a number of positions, including those of Assistant Director for Malaysian CARE, Director for Community Study (Pusat Kajian Masyarakat), Executive Director of Yayasan

Strategik, and Social Consultation Secretary for 'Word, Kingdom and Spirit'. He has also been active in the Centre for Community Studies, and the Foundation for Community Studies & Development, both of Kuala Lumpur, and has undertaken advocacy on a wide variety of social problems, with particular concern to analyse and interpret the causes of crime, violence and alcoholism, which lie in poverty. For this he advocates agencies to implement comprehensive social intervention programmes addressing issues like housing, public facilities, education and economic well-being.

In his work and writings Jayasooria reflects a theologically and biblically-based advocacy on behalf of the oppressed, and a thorough professionalism in social work, along with commitments to inter-faith and inter-church co-operation in a multi-racial and multi-religious society. In his theological study of social transformation he bases this in biblical visions of creation, fall and transformation. After considering the obstacles and misunderstandings which paralyse theology as well as Christian action, Jayasooria outlines a "strategy for social transformation which includes the teaching, prophetic, pastoral, intercessory and incarnational roles of the church. Although writing primarily with evangelical colleagues in mind, Jayasooria presents here and in other writings a unity of theological reflection with people's concrete experience and socio-religious context.

Selected references
Works by Denison Jayasooria
> *Community Caring: A Strategy for Meeting Needs in Your Community.* Petaling Jaya: Malaysian CARE, 1987.
> *Training the Whole Church.* Kuala Lumpur: Academe Art & Printing Services, 1982.
> —, ed. *Trends and Challenges in Social Services Today.* Kuala Lumpur: Resource, Research and Communication Unit CCM, 1988.
> *Update on Detention of Christians and the Christian Response in Malaysia.* s.l.: Malaysian CARE, Nov. 1988.
> *Social Transformation: Theology and Action.* Kuala Lumpur: CARE, 1990.

4.14 Cecil Rajendra (ca.1940-)

Cecil Rajendra studied at St Xavier's Institution, Penang, at the universities of Singapore and London, and practices as a lawyer in a free legal centre at Penang. Also a newspaper columnist, his poetry has been published and translated in many Asian and European countries. He does not however believe in "pure poetry" for he is not a "disinterested artist". He describes his poetry as "public statements on the times we live in" for he is committed to the building of a more human and humane society, as well as to awakening people to such evils as social injustice, the arms trade, community conflict, inhuman development and totalitarian oppression. His poems thus show a deep compassion for the victims of violence, hunger and exploitation, along with sharp rejection of the structures and attitudes which cause them. Any contemporary event can be his subject and his vivid contrasts provide sharp images for a contextual theological reflection: the heedless celebration of Christmas and the "continents of hunger"; an "over-ripe metaphor" to fill a child's belly; the miracle of human love and the insane compulsion to drop more bombs.

Selected References
Works by Cecil Rajendra
> *Embryo.* s.l. Regency P, 1965.
> *Bones and Feathers.* Hong Kong: Heinneman, 1978.
> *Refugees and Other Despairs.* Singapore: Choice Books, 1980.
> *Hour of Assassins and other Poems.* London: Bogle-l'Ouverture Publications, 1983.
> *Songs for the Unsung.* Risk Book Series. Geneva: WCC, 1983.
> *Dove on Fire: Poems on Peace, Justice and Ecology.* Geneva: WCC Publications, 1987.
> *Bibliography & Selected Profiles Reviews Essays.* London: Bogle-l'Ouverture, c1989.
> *Lovers, Lunatics and Lallang.* London: Bogle-l'Ouverture Publications, 1990.
> *Broken Buds.* Mapusa: Other India Press. 1994.

4.15 Thu En Yu (1945-)

Thu En Yu was ordained in November 1972 in the Basel Christian Church of Malaysia, obtaining his BD (1972) and M Theol (1977) from the Chinese University of Hong Kong. He furthered his studies at Birmingham, UK, and San Francisco Theological Seminary, USA (ThD,1995). More recently Thu En Yu has undertaken research at his alma mater in Hong Kong on "Christian Church in the Asian Context". Thu has worked in Sabah as Director of Theological Education by Extension with indigenous people (1972-1981), Bishop of Basel Christian Church of Malaysia (1981-1995) and Principal of Sabah Theological Seminary.

In his writings, Thu En Yu has regularly advocated the development of an Asian theology which is grounded in the concrete situations and life of Asian people, their divisions, and aspirations. "The Church must recognize", he affirms, " ... and face squarely the realities of Asian life and culture while continuously reflecting on the message and task of the gospel. An Asian theology embracing a strong sense of community infused with the spirit of humility and openness is a possible starting point to break down traditional barriers. Thus, there is a need to re-examine our Christian concepts of ecclesiology and missiology." He seeks this in his writing and ministry, both in relation to the traditional life of his people and in the encounter with industrial society and social conflict. Thu En Yu, like the patristic theologians in the early Church, combines careful congregational oversight with theological reflection. But he feels that the church is still far from ready to address a world divided by race, religion and politics and must begin to break down barriers both in thought and action throughout the community.

Selected References
Works by Thu En Yu

"The Christian Encounter with Animism: The Christian Mission among the Rungus People of Sabah." MTh thesis. Hong Kong: Chung Chi College, 1977.

"Christmas a Message of Hope." *CCM News* (December 1984).

"'Muhibbah': The Christian's Ministry of Reconciliation in the Pluralistic Society of Malaysia." STD dissertation. Berkeley: San Francisco Theological Seminary, 1995.

Christian Reflections within an Emerging Industrialised Society. Kota Kinabalu: Sabah Theological Seminary, 1998.

"Paradigm Shift of the Theology of Mission towards a Reconciliation of Society." LWF-DMD reports, 1999.

"The Experience of Violence and the Call to Mission - A Malaysian Perspective." EMW reports, 2000.

—, et al., eds. *Christian Reflections within an Emerging Industrial Society*. Kota Kinabalu: Sabah Theological Seminary, 1998.

4.16 Batumalai, Satayandy (1946-)

Batumalai Satayandy was born in Perak. Formerly teaching at the Seminari Theologi Malaysia, he has been vicar of the Church of St John the Divine, Ipoh, and also vicar at Malacca. Following studies in Singapore, Manila and Madurai, he gained his doctorate at the University of Birmingham with a dissertation on Christian Prophecy and Intercession in the Malaysian Context. He has been active in the Diocesan Standing Committee, the Malaysian Theological Fellowship and the Theological Commission of the Anglican Christian Council of East Asia. He has written extensively on the content and method of contextual Malaysian theology and also of Asian theology.

The task of theology for Batumalai is to discern the divine in the human, in locality, society and neighbour. This is to discern gratefully the inner working of the Spirit in our community and the faiths of others, all of which are being renewed by God, and so to discern also "the re-creational grace of God in bringing something new to Malaysia". The method of contextualisation, by which he believes theology is to be done in Malaysia, involves encounter with the languages, thought-forms and life of Malaysians; recognition of the presence and power of Malay, Chinese and Indian cultural heritages; joint religious and political study, and also co-operative action, by those of different faiths. Batumalai sees the large contribution of lay people in mass communications in defence of human rights as an important part of contextual theology, and throws the net wide in identifying the resources available from churches, libraries, periodicals and in the mass media. In his theologies of "neighbourology' and of "*muhibbah*" (goodwill) he advocates study of and response to the needs and the quests of sister and brother Malaysians - Muslim, Hindu, Buddhist and Sikh - along with the recasting of Christian language and imagery.

Theology would then present the Christian message in Islamic categories, to prepare "to offer a Malaysian Gospel - the 5th Gospel" of the everyday life of Christians in their world.

Selected References
Works by Satayandy Batumalai
> "Christian Prophecy and Intercession: the Bible, Barth and Koyama in Relation to Contemporary Malaysia." Dissertation, University of Birmingham, 1984.
> *A Prophetic Christology for Neighbourology. A Theology for Prophetic Living.* Kuala Lumpur: STM, 1986.
> *A Malaysian Theology of Muhibbah.* Kuala Lumpur: Batumalai, 1990.
> *An Introduction to Asian Theology.* Delhi: ISPCK, 1991.
> *Islamic Resurgence and Islamization in Malaysia: A Malaysian Christian Response.* Ipoh:, Batumalai, 1996.
> —, ed. *A Christian Response to Vision 2020: Theoloji Wawasan 2020.* Petaling Jaya: Batumalai, 1992.
> "A prophetic way of life in Malaysia." *Asian Theological Search* 23 (1986).
> "The Task of Malaysian theology." *Inter Religio* 13 (1988).
> "An Understanding of Malaysian Theology." *Asia Journal of Theology* 4 (1990).
> "Malaysian Islamic Situation and a Response from a Malaysian Christian Perspective." *CTC Bulletin* 12.1 (1994).
> "Learning the Faith of my Neighbour from a Malaysian Perspective." *Asia Journal of Theology* 9.1 (1995).

4.17 Hwa Yung (1948-)

Hwa Yung obtained his BD amd MTh from the University of London (1979, 1980), and his doctorate in missiology at Asbury Theological Seminary, Kentucky, (1995). A minister in the Methodist Church, Hwa Yung has been principal of Seminari Theoloji Malaysia at Seremban, Negeri Sembilan and is now Director of the Centre for the Study of Christianity in Asia at Trinity Theological College, Singapore. He is active in the International Association of Mission Studies (since 1992), the International Fellowship of Evangelical Mission Theologians (since 1999), and a director of the Oxford Centre for Mission Studies (since 1999).

Hwa Yung has authored three books and monographs and 15 articles, all in English. He has also been working on a textbook on systematic theology from an Asian perspective. In his principal work he argues that truly indigenous Asian Christian theology is still to appear, for the domination of western dualism and Enlightenment thought still continues. He thus finds the work of many (Protestant) Asian theologians either too relativistic or dualistic, too accommodating, or missiologically or socio-politically weak. He therefore proposes four criteria by which to assess Asian theologies: ability to address diverse socio-political Asian contexts; empowerment they bring to evangelistic and pastoral ministry; their ways of inculturating the Gospel; and their faithfulness to Christian tradition. These he feels will enable Asian theologies to break a cultural captivity to the West which he discerns in both "ecumenical' and "evangelical" Asian theologians, although he also wishes to limit the acceptance of eastern world-views and spiritualities. For him authentic contextualisation "demands a dual recovery of confidence, both in the gospel and in one's own culture and history".

Selected References

Works by Hwa Yung

Christian Thinking on Emigration. Petaling Jaya: Graduate Student Fellowship, 1987/1988.

Mangoes or Bananas? The Quest for an Authentic Asian Christian Theology. Oxford: Regnum Books, 1997.

Beyond AD 2000. A Call for Evangelical Faithfulness. Petaling Jaya: Kairos Research Centre, 1999.

Kingdom Identity and Christian Mission. Fifth David Adeney Memorial Lecture. Singapore: Discipleship training Centre, 2001.

"Christian Ethical Thinking in the Asian Context." In *Christian Reflections within an Emerging Industrialised Society*, edited by Thu En Yu et al. Kota Kinabalu: Sabah Theological Seminary, 1998: 153-180.

"Church and State in Islamic Context." *Trinity Theological Journal,* 6 (1997).

"Towards an Evangelical Approach to Religions and Cultures." *Transformation. An International Evangelical Dialogue on Mission and Ethics*, 17.3 (2000).

Yong, Amos. "Mangoes or Bananas? The Quest for an Authentic Asian Christian Theology. Book Review." *Asia Journal of Pentecostal Studies* 2.1 (1999).

4.18 Anthony Rogers (1949-)

Born on Pulau Pinang, Anthony Rogers is a member of the De La Salle Brothers (fsc). He has degrees in Education, English and Economics (University of Malaya), and an MA in Pastoral Sociology (Asian Social Institute, Manila). Originally active in social justice concerns for the Catholic Church in Malaysia, where he is still National Director of the Office for Human Development in Kuala Lumpur, Rogers is the long-standing executive secretary of the Office for Human Development of the Federation of Asian Bishops' Conferences (FABC-OHD). As a member of the Pontifical Council for Justice and Peace, Rome, since 1989, Rogers serves the cause of social-justice at national, Asia-wide and global levels. His work with the FABC-OHD has led him to run numerous national and international workshops and colloquia for Asia's Catholic Bishops, including 17 major conferences since 1990. He has contributed papers to each of these as well as edited the proceedings.

Once imprisoned by the government for his work for racial justice, Rogers has also had to learn to walk the tightrope between frequent hierarchical timidity and the justice issues he tries to keep alive. He has been patiently developing a praxis for a contextual kingdom-centred theology, so to prevent the ritualistic church of ethnic minorities from withdrawing from the national scene and becoming socially-insignificant enclaves. Believing that "involvement in the area of social justice is part and parcel of living the Christian faith", while many Catholics are unaware of the social dimensions of the Gospel, Rogers questions why these should be so regularly omitted from Catholic teaching and preaching. Changes in the church since Vatican II, in liturgy, lifestyle, participation and architecture, may be only superficial unless the "consciousness and spirit of Vatican II" are integral within the total life of the church, he affirms.

Selected References
Works by Anthony Rogers
>*Integral Human Development and Justice for Peace at the Service of Life in the Context of Asia.* FABC Paper 72m. Hong Kong: FABC 1995.
>*Discovering the Face of Jesus in Asia Today.* FABC Paper 84. Hong Kong: FABC, 1999. Also published from Manila: FABC-OHD 1999.
>*A Church in Universal Harmony and Solidarity through Justice and Peace.* FABC Paper 92c. Hong Kong: FABC 2000.
>"The Asian Bishops' Dream: Towards a New World in Asia." *National Office on Human Development Bulletin* (July-August 1983).
>"The Church in Asia Towards the Twenty-First Century." *Sedos Bulletin* 26.2 (1994).
>—, ed. *Report on the Peninsular Malaysia Pastoral Convention 1986.* Kuala Lumpur, 1987.
>—, ed. *Colloquium on the Social Doctrine of the Church in the Context of Asia.* Manila: FABC-OHD, 1993.
>—, ed. *Colloquium on Church in Asia in the Twenty-First Century.* Manila: FABC-OHD, 1997.
>—, ed. *Human Promotion and Human Rights in the Third Millennium.* Manila: FABC-OHD, 1999.

4.19 Lee Tzu Pheng (ca. 1950-)

Lee Tzu Pheng is a Catholic lay woman who was educated at Raffles' School and the University of Singapore, where she is a Senior Lecturer in the English Department. Her poetry has appeared in many journals and she has contributed to many anthologies. She assisted in preparing the "Report on Literary Arts in Singapore" (1988) and was the first woman to receive the South East Asia WRITE award, for poetry and contributions to literature. She became a Roman Catholic in 1989.

Her writings since 1988 in particular, have included reflection upon such themes as the religious quest and its mystery, the discernment of divinity within human life, the life experience of women and the larger dimensions of risking love. She finds in her own experience "security in the constancies making us whole", when there is found in our stories "a certainty that points us, surely, to the gateways leading forth ..."

Yet the "blight of our knowing" hinders the advent of mystery and must be replaced by love which is "wrung of compassion, born from the blood, yet better than wine, joyfully good."

The summons here is to be called forth from each "closed confessional",

> "to the true safety
> of a genuine distress
> which we must bear to
> risk for more, not less."

Selected References
Works by Lee Tzu Pheng

> *Prospect of a Drowning.* Singapore: Heinemann Educational Books (Asia), 1980.
> *Against the Next Wave.* Singapore: Times Books International, 1988.
> *The Brink of an Amen.* Singapore: Times Books International, 1991.
> *Lambada by Galilee & Other Surprises.* Singapore: Times Books International, c1997.
> "My Country and My People." *Asia Bureau Australia Newsletter* 27 (1976).

4.20 Albert Sundararaj Walters (1952-)

Born at Butterworth, Albert Walters gained his BD from Bishop's College, Calcutta, India (1986), his MTh from the Presbyterian Theological College, Seoul, South Korea (1989), and his PhD in Islamic Studies from the University of Birmingham, UK (2000). An ordained priest in the Anglican Church, Walters has been a social worker with the destitute and drug dependent (1980-1982; 1986-1988), and has been organiser for community development with the YMCA in Klang. This was followed by terms as lecturer at St. Mark's Anglican Theological College, Dar es Salaam, Tanzania, then as lecturer at the STM, Petaling Jaya and Seremban since 1992.

As a theologian, Walters has grappled with Christian-Muslim relations, inter-religious dialogue and issues of Church and society. He is concerned that Christians must move from an "insular, potted-plant complacency ... to an active involvement in serving the community" which will include responsible citizenship at all levels of the society. The challenge of the socio-political and religious (especially Islamic) context, and Christian action within that, he believes, is the chief stimulus for indigenous theology. And the faith and spirituality that resonates with local sensibilities and struggles, in Malaysia and other religiously pluralistic situations, is to be tapped and expressed in ways that retain Christian identity. He also finds Malaysian contextual theology emerging in "incarnational" reflections within a multi-cultural society, in critical reflection upon social involvement, from women's reflections in an Islamic context and from the voices of the people as they express religious insight, commitment to human rights, and concerns for injustice. For Walters, theology in Malaysia must become more pro-active rather than reactionary, more socially engaged and more participatory in the inclusion of lay people in emerging theological tasks.

Selected References
Works by Albert Sundararaj Walters
> *We Believe in One God?* Delhi: ISPCK, 2000.
> "The Challenge of Vision 2020 and the Christian Family." In *Vision 2020: A Malaysian Christian Response*, ed. by S Batumalai. Kuala Lumpur: Batumalai, 1992.
> "Islam in Malaysia." In *Religious Fundamentalism: An Asian Perspective*, edited by John S Augustine. Bangalore: South Asia Theological Research Institute, 1993.
> "Malaysian Theology." In *Dictionary of Third World Theologies*, edited by Virginia Fabella and R. S. Sugirtharajah. Maryknoll, NY: Orbis Books, 2000.
> "Contemporary Presentations of the Trinity in an Islamic Context: A Malaysian Case Study." Unpublished PhD Thesis, University of Birmingham, UK, 2000.

4.21 Yong Ting Jin (1953-)

Following studies in Kuala Lumpur where she was active in SCM leadership, Yong Ting Jin worked as a church worker/pastor of the Basel Christian Church of Malaysia (BCCM) in Sabah (1978-1980), and later as Regional Secretary, Asia-Pacific Region of World Student Christian Federation (WSCF A-P, 1986-1993), based in Hong Kong. In 1994-1995 she was Organising Secretary for the Asian Women's Resource Centre for Culture and Theology, and since 1996 has been AWRC Co-ordinator. Over 20 years, Ting Jin has been a leader in many leadership formation and theological programmes for college or university students and young women; and in programmes for the WSCF, CCA and WCC, including Christian women's programmes. She is also a member of Malaysian Women in Ministry and Theology, and of the WCC Asia Regional Group.

Apart from the books and periodicals she has edited (notably *In God's Image*), Yong Ting Jin's own writings include biblical studies, and articles upon the roles and resources of women in theology in Asia. In these as in her ministries, she has concentrated mainly upon the promotion and resourcing of women's theology which is grounded in women's experience and in their biblical interpretation, as well as being socially and religiously critical. For this there must be, she believes, both an awareness in women of their key roles in social and religious renewal, and the establishment of adequate space for Christian women and others in which transformative thought and action is possible. She has therefore been concerned to firmly relate women's theology in Malaysia and other Asian countries to "new ways of being Church", to new lifestyles and forms of community, and to innovative forms of theological reflection. These in turn are for her seen in the perspective of God's kingdom and the new creation of love, justice and peace which God brings.

Selected References
Works by Yong Ting Jin

"Theological Reflections on Women in the Church - A Protestant Perspective." In *We Dare to Dream. Doing Theology as Asian Women*, edited by Virginia Fabella and Sun Ai Lee Park. Hong Kong: AWRCCT, 1989.

"Bible Study: Jesus calls her 'Woman'." *In God's Image* 15.3 (1996).

"Bible Study: Women Reclaiming Their Place at the Table." *In God's Image* 17.4 (1998).

"Jesus and Women in the Context of Re-Positioning Church Mission in Asia." In *The Asian Church in the New Millennium*, edited by Raul Fernandez-Calienes. Delhi & Sydney: ISPCK & Centre for Millennial Studies, 2000: 102-115.

"On Being Church: Asian Women's Voices and Visions." *The Ecumenical Review* 53.1 (forthcoming).
—, with Hope S. Antone, eds. *Re-Living Our Faith Today: A Bible Study Resource Book*. WSCF-Asia-Pacific, 1992.
—, with Hope S. Antone, eds. *Our Stories, Our Faith*. WSCF-Asia-Pacific, 1992.

4.22 Ng Kam Weng (1953-)

Ng Kam Weng is Research Director/Resident Scholar of Kairos Research Centre, Petaling Jaya, and has produced many writings in contextual theology in response to life and events in Malaysian society. His doctoral thesis (1996) researched the social thought of Albrecht Ritschl, Karl Barth and Jurgen Moltmann. His writings focus upon developing more realistic attitudes among Christians toward Islamization, along with strategies for social engagement in society, and in church-state relations. Thus he interprets mission and nation-building with a special emphasis upon a revitalisation of civil society. Present interests revolve around the issues of public theology and civil society, especially upon the ways that churches can contribute towards building civil society as a foundation for democracy in a pluralistic nation. He is also working on a comparative spirituality in Christianity and Buddhism, as well as on the issues of political theology and nation building, with special reference to Malaysia and Singapore. He is deeply concerned both for Christian intellectual witness in society and for the development of the social and political tools and resources by which Christians can be active reconcilers, democratic citizens and responsive theologians.

Ng Kam Weng has published five books, a further eight numbers in the *Occasional Papers* from Kairos Research Centre and over a dozen articles.

Selected References
Works by Ng Kam Weng
> *Doing Responsive Theology in a Developing Nation*. Petaling Jaya: Kairos/Pustaka SU, 1994.
> *Bridge-building in a pluralistic Society: A Christian Contribution*. Petaling Jaya: Kairos/Pustaka SU, 1994.

Tools for Developing Intellectual Witness. Petaling Jaya: Kairos Research Centre, 1996.

"Christian Order and Civil Order." *Readings in Malaysian Church and Mission* (1992).

"Dialogue and Constructive Social Engagement: Problems and Prospects for the Malaysian Church." *Trinity Theological Journal* 5 (1995).

—, ed. *Doing Responsive Theology. Theological readings and Resources. Vol 1: Modernity in Malaysia - Christian Perspectives*. Petaling Jaya: Kairos Research Centre, 1998.

—, ed. *Modernity in Malaysia: Christian Perspective*. Petaling Jaya: Kairos Research Centre, 1998.

4.23 Yeoh Seng Guan (1958-)

Yeoh Seng Guan studied at Wolfson College, Cambridge, and in Edinburgh (1998-9), and is the Co-ordinator for the Resource, Research and Communications Unit of the CCM. His writings explore the place of knowledge (in ritual, theologies, literature) and practices (in pilgrimages, festivals, rallies), in the political contexts of urban space and identity (ethnicity, gender, kinship) in Malaysia. He looks particularly at ways in which Malaysians of different religious and non-religious persuasions negotiate and construct their sense of place in the face of globalisation, (post) modernity and multi-cultural forces. In his theological writing he critiques the politics of western epistemology in post-colonial social ethical discourse and sees this being replaced by 'local' liberation and contextual theologies. In these, hegemonic theories and alliances are being rejected, and other voices are being retrieved.

The new task of theology, Yeoh believes, is that of "'doing theology' in creative tension between the 'micro' and the 'macro', between 'local knowledge' and 'global knowledge' ...". It will be distinct from other disciplines because, through the eyes of faith, 'local' aspirations, struggles and insight become the content for theology. These will include hopes for freedom from exploitation, the praxis of community resistance, and the interaction of "self/ community contradictions ... with the normative sacred texts". In this context he has studied and written much on the concrete realities of post-colonial urban life and religiosity in Malaysia, with particular concern for urban squatters, the partnership of women and men, urban geography and public culture.

Selected References
Works by Yeoh Seng Guan
"Women and Theology in Asia." STM student dissertation, 1987.
"Women and Human Rights in Asia. The Religio-cultural Dimension." *Praxis* 1-2 (1989).
"Between Three Worlds: Notes on a methodology for a contextual theology in Malaysia." Unpublished MTh thesis, University of Edinburgh, 1992.
"Dismantling the Master's House: The Pursuit of Modernity and Third World Theological Discourse." *Asia Journal of Theology* 7.2 (1993).
"Writing about Women and Building Partnership." *In God's Image* 13.3 (1994).
"In whom do we trust? Religion in a Changing World." *Anthropology Today* 13.4 (1997).
"Pioneers, Squatters and Flat-dwellers." *Aliran Monthly* 20 (2000).
"Powerful Landscapes: Squatting, Space and Religiosity in Urban Malaysia." Unpublished PhD thesis, University of Edinburgh, 1997.
"Producing Locality: Space, houses and public culture in an urban Hindu festival." *Contributions to Indian Sociology* (Forthcoming).
"Creolised Urban Utopias: Squatter Colonies and the Postcolonial Malaysian city." *Sojourners* (in press).

4.24 Patricia Martinez (1960-)

Patricia A. Martinez obtained her PhD in religion with specialisation in Islam from Temple University, USA (2000). This forms the culmination of 20 years in higher education which included English studies (BA, 1982 University of Malaya), theology (MA, 1994, Christian Theology, Maryknoll), comparative religion (MA, 1997, Temple University), and Arabic (Diploma, 1998, Al-al bayt University, Jordan). Her work experience has ranged from Foreign Investment Promotion to Customer Relations and most recently a UNICEF consultancy in the "Whole Child Education Project" which is pioneering educational initiatives that aim to overcome cleavages of religion and race in Indonesia (Sumatra).

Working at the Asia-Europe Institute of the University of Malaya and resident in Petaling Jaya, Martinez is controversial - a Catholic, non-Malay woman researching Islam in a Muslim State. With the revivification and politicisation of religion in Southeast Asia, boundaries between religions have sharpened and the theological conversation across ethno-religious borders that Martinez is undertaking is found by many to be unacceptable. Yet she is maintaining both professional and scholarly work of quality, along with writings which provide full studies of political and Islamic processes in Malaysia and the roles of women within these.

Selected References
Works by Patricia A. Martinez
"Women and Fundamentalism: Negotiating Sacred Terrain." In *Women in Action*. (Sept. 2000). Publication of Isis Women of the Netherlands and the Philippines.
"Theorizing Muslim Women's Political Participation: from Activism on the Margins to Political Power at the Center." Electronic Conference and Journal Women's Organisations and the Building of Civil Society in the 21st Century. December 12-22 2000. Website: <http://www.philanthropy.org/GN/KEN/gntext/index.html>.
"The Islamic State or the State of Islam in Malaysia." *Contemporary Southeast Asia: A Journal of International and Strategic Affairs* 23.3 (forthcoming).
"Complex Configurations: The Women's Agenda for Change and the Women's Candidacy Initiative." In *From Moral Communities to NGOs in Malaysia*, edited by Meredith Weiss and Saliha Hassan. London: Curzon Press, forthcoming.
"A Reflection on Theory in Malaysian Studies." In *Second Malaysian Studies Conference,* edited by K.S. Jomo and Modh. Hazim Shaf. Kuala Lumpur: University Kebangsaan Press, forthcoming.

4.25 Edmund Kee Fook Chia fsc (1962-)

Edmund Chia is one of two De La Salle Brothers to emerge on the practical theological scene, not just in Malaysia but also, and more crucially, Asia-wide, through work with the FABC (See Anthony Rogers, 4.18). Joining the teaching brothers in 1984, Edmund holds a degree in Psychology (BA, Lewis University, USA, 1992), and

Masters' degrees in Human Development (University of Maryland, 1994) and Religion and Religious Education (Catholic University of America, 1995). He is now doing doctoral studies in inter-cultural theology at the Catholic University of Nijmegen, Netherlands. Chia became adjunct lecturer in religion and psychology at De La Salle institutes in Kuala Lumpur (1995-), and Executive Secretary of the Office of Ecumenical and Inter-religious Affairs of the FABC (1996-).

In Chia we find the rare combination of teacher and organiser, thinker and visionary. Under his direction the FABC-OEIA has introduced, or invigorated, inter-religious dialogue as a central congregational concern. He edits and publishes *Partners: For Catholics in Asia and their Partners-in-Dialogue*, an occasional newsletter of the FABC-OEIA. From his work in some twenty major international gatherings has come the editing of one book and the publication of over 20 articles. The focus of his chief writings is upon inter-religious and cross-cultural studies, especially in relation to social identity, human rights and human development.

Selected References
Works by Edmund Kee Fook Chia

"The Effects of Stereotyping on Impression Formation: Cross-Cultural Perspective on Viewing Religious Persons." *The Journal of Psychology* 128.5 (1994).

"Turning 20, Embracing Dialogue: New Way of Being Church." *Inter-Religio* 35 (1999).

"Inter-religious Dialogue for Human Promotion and Human Rights." In *Consultation on Human Promotion and Human Rights in the Third Millennium*, edited by Anthony Rogers. Manila: FABC-OHD, 1999.

"Inter-religious Dialogue in Pursuit of Fullness of Life in Asia." Seventh Plenary Assembly Workshop Discussion Guide. *FABC Papers* 92k. Hong Kong: FABC, 2000.

"Of Fork and Spoons or Fingers and Chopsticks: Inter-religious Dialogue in *Ecclesia in Asia*." *East Asian Pastoral Review* 37.3 (2000). Also *Sedos Bulletin* 32.7 (2000). See also, "Inter-religious Dialogue in 'Ecclesia in Asia'." *Jeevadhara* 30 (2000).

"FABC's 'Response' to *Dominus Iesus.*" *Jeevadhara* 31 183, 229-233 and also *EAPR* 38.3. (Forthcoming.)

—, ed. *Dialogue? Resource Manual for Catholics in Asia.* Bangkok: FABC-OEIA, forthcoming.

4.26 Fung Jojo M. sj (1964)

Joseph Matthew Fung Jee Vui (Jojo Fung) was born in Sabah, and studied at the Loyola School of Theology, Manila (1983-86). Exploring Karl Rahner's theory of anonymous Christians, he was deeply influenced by other Asian Jesuits - Francisco Claver and Carlos H. Abesamis (of the Philippines), Aloysius Pieris (of Sri Lanka), and Michael Amaladoss (of India). His doctoral studies were completed at the Catholic Theological Union, Chicago (1997). From 1997-1999, he was a Research Fellow at the Catholic Research Centre, Kuala Lumpur, working for the empowerment of the laity through practical, contextual theology, and assisting Basic Ecclesial Communities. Jojo also assisted the empowerment programme in Petaling Jaya (See 3.4.1.) through courses in a theology of solidarity, ecclesiology of communion, inter-religious dialogue and practical theology. Since 1999 Jojo has been a member of the Arrupe Jesuit Community in Taman Rinting, Johor, engaged in campus ministry while continuing his research into, and work with, indigenous people.

Jojo's passion is researching the cultural politics of agency among the indigenous peoples of Malaysia (*orang asli*). His "barefoot local theology" aims to move and motivate the local church to engage in the struggle of the *orang asli*. He is also interested in indigenous shamanism in order to facilitate an inculturating and inter-religious process between the Christian faith and indigenous cultures and struggle. His short books are in "lay" language devoid of footnotes, as aids to nurture an embryonic local theology among "ordinary" Christians. Jojo is aware of the need for a more thorough and broad-based reflection on the lived experiences of the Malaysian people, of a deeper and more scientific analysis of the socio-economic, political, cultural and religious situation, and of a more comprehensive biblical foundation to local theology. He is a frequent contributor of articles on the struggle of the *orang asli* to newspapers such as *Today's Catholic*, *Catholic*

Asian News, Herald, Glory and Catholic Sabah, as well as to the East Asian Pastoral Review.

Selected References
Works by Jojo M. Fung

Inner Whisper. Petaling Jaya: Pyramid Design and Print, 1991. A first collection of poetry.

Rainbow of Love. Petaling Jaya: Longman Malaysian Sdn. Bhd., 1992. A second collection of poetry.

Shoes off, Barefoot We Walk. Petaling Jaya: Longman Malaysian Sdn. Bhd., 1992.

"An Indigenous-Serving Missiology: Models, Methods, Mission Strategies." STL Thesis. Jesuit School of Theology, Berkeley, California, 1994.

"A Struggle with Indigenous Peoples for a Society of Equals." Doctoral Dissertation, Catholic Theological Union, Chicago, Ill., 1997.

"Glimpses of the Malaysian Jesus." *Vidyajyoti Journal* 62 (1998).

"Ongoing Dialogue on Environmental Ethic: A Basis for A General Malaysian Rainforest Ethic and Its Liturgical Practices." *EAPR* 34.4 (1997).

"Doing Practical Theology: A Malaysian Perspective." *EAPR* 36.4 (1999).

"Making a Forward Leap: Understanding Proclamation, Christ and Unity." In *The People of God among All God's People: Frontiers in Christian Mission*, edited by Philip L. Wickeri. Hong Kong: CCA; London: CWM, 2000, 215-130.

4.27 Roland Chia (ca. 1965-)

Following completion of his doctoral thesis "Revelation and Theology: The Knowledge of God in Balthasar and Barth", Roland Chia has been teaching at Trinity Theological College, Singapore, since 1995. His particular theological interests are in epistemology, confessional theology, social ethics, the theology of music and art, and contemporary theological movements in the West. His writings include studies of aesthetics, of post-modernism, the doctrines of the Incarnation and of the Trinity, John Wesley's theology, as well as of contemporary social questions. He has written a number of series of short articles on the Apostles' Creed, and of Bible studies, along with reflections upon Christian involvement in traditional

Chinese Funerals, on rock music and film, on healing and on spiritual discernment (see *Fairfield Compass* and *Methodist Message*, 1995 - 2000). He has also written on Church and culture / Church and society issues in the Singapore context. (See *Church and Society* 1998-2000).

Selected References
Works by Roland Chia

"Revisioning Our Christian Past. Scripture, Tradition & Theological Truth in the Culture of Interpretation." *Trinity Theological Journal* 7 (1998).

"Privileging the Particular. Postmodernism and the Eclipse of the Universal." *Jian Dao* 11 (1999).

"Did the Son of God Assume Sinful Human Nature in the Incarnation?" *Trinity Theological Journal* 8 (1999).

"Editorial: Secularism, Neo-Paganism and the Modern Church." *Church & Society* 2.3 (1999).

"The Shadow Our Future Throws." *Methodist Message* 101.10 (1999). Republished in *The Presbyterian Express* (Nov/Dec 1999).

4.28 Jonathan Tan (1969-)

Jonathan Tan was born in Ipoh, Perak, and was educated by the De La Salle Brothers (fsc) in Ipoh (1976-1981) and Singapore (1982-1985). As a member of a student solidarity (the Legion of Mary), his interest grew in theology. Tan's subsequent training as a lawyer (National University of Singapore, 1988-1992) laid the foundation for a rigorous analytical framework, critical thinking and paying attention to actual realities involving real people - not just abstract theories and principles. Following three years as barrister in Singapore (1993-1996) Tan left the legal profession and, "embarked on a journey into the unknown". Without church support he has completed his post-graduate research in theology through awards and scholarships (MA, Jesuit School of Theology at Berkeley, and now doctoral studies, Catholic University of America). He also lectures in religion and religious education, and is an Assistant Editor of *The New Catholic Encyclopaedia*. A lawyer and theologian, Jonathan Tan is also a fully trained musician, and as a pipe organist, was appointed to the Good Shepherd Cathedral in Singapore (1988-1996).

Tan's interests include missiology (PhD dissertation in progress), inculturation and contextualisation (MA thesis), and comparative theology, specifically focusing on Confucian-Christian dialogue but also exploring possibilities in Islam-Christian and Buddhist-Christian dialogues. He lists his areas of expertise as religious studies, systematic theology and liturgical studies. Along with his editing work for *The New Catholic Encyclopaedia,* his main research and writings are concentrated studies of the documents, theology and methodology of the Federation of Asian Bishops' Conferences (FABC). He is multilingual, working in three Chinese dialects (Mandarin, Cantonese and Hakka), Sino-Vietnamese and Modern Vietnamese, as well as bahasa Malaysia, English, French and German.

Selected References
Works by Jonathan Tan
> "Towards a Theology of '*Muhibbah*' as the Basis for Cross-cultural Liturgical Inculturation in the Malaysian Catholic Church." MA thesis, Graduate Theological Union, 1997. Unpublished.
> "The Ancestor Veneration Rites of the Contemporary Malaysian Chinese Community and Inculturation." *EAPR* 35 (1998).
> "Constructing an Asian Theology of Liturgical Inculturation from the Documents of the Federation of Asian Bishops' Conferences (FABC)." *EAPR* 36 (1999). See also, *FABC Papers* 89, Hong Kong, 1999.
> "Theologizing at the Service of Life: The Contextual Theological Methodology of the Federation of Asian Bishops' Conferences (FABC)." *Gregorianum* 81.3 (2000).
> "*Missio ad Gentes* in Asia: A Comparative Study of the Missiology of John Paul II and the Federation of Asian Bishops' Conferences." PhD dissertation in progress.

5 Other Theological Writers Scholars, and Activists
5.1 Contextual Theological Reflection
Amongst those whose writings should also be mentioned as including contextual theological reflection are:

Patrick C.S. Yeo, who contributed to the "Jesus Christ in Asian Suffering and Hope" studies of the CCA in writing of the life situation of poor Malaysian workers. See his "Lee Pak Soon in Asian Suffering and Hope." In *Asian Theological Reflections on Suffering and Hope*, edited by Yap Kim-hao. *Asia Focus* 1 (1977).

Samuel Liew wrote and arranged songs with contextual Christian relevance in the 1960s and 1970s, and some of these were recorded in a series of LP discs by the "Christones", a quartet of alumni from Trinity Theological College. See e.g. *Meet the Christones* (Singapore: Tribune, ca. 1968) and *New Songs for Asian Cities,* edited by Loh, I-To (Tainan: EACC-URM, 1972).

David Wong studied at the Seminari Theoloji Malaysia and has written on liberation theology within the Malaysian context. See his *Towards a Malaysian Liberation Theology* (Kuala Lumpur: STM, 1986).

Simon Chan teaches systematic theology at Trinity Theological College, Singapore, and has also written on hermeneutics in the Asian setting. See "Problem and Possibility of an Asian Theological Hermeneutic." *Trinity Theological Journal* 9 (2000). See also his volume *Spiritual Theology* (Downers' Grove: IVP, 1998).

5.2 Regarding Malaysian Church History

Duain W. Vierow studied the history and life of Lutheran Churches in Malaysia and Singapore, and was Director of lay training for the Evangelical Lutheran Church of Malaysia. See his *History of Lutheranism in West Malaysia and Singapore* (New York: Board of World Missions, Lutheran Church of America, 1968).

John Roxborogh taught church history at the STM (1983-1991) when he pioneered the collection, writing and interpretation of Malaysia's church history, with particular concern for bibliography and missiology. See: *A Short Introduction to Malaysian Church History* (1987), and *A Bibliography of Christianity in Malaysia* (Kuala Lumpur: STM & Catholic Research Centre, 1990); *A Common Voice: A History of the Ecumenical Movement in Malaysia* (Petaling Jaya: CCM, 1991); and as editor, with Robert Hunt and Lee Kam Hing, *Christianity in Malaysia: A Denominational History* (Petaling Jaya: Pelanduk Publications, 1992).

Robert Balhetchet has taught church history and theology in Penang and Singapore and is currently Rector of the Roman Catholic Cathedral of the Good Shepherd in Singapore. Following early studies of the Christian community in Singapore, and along with pastoral and educational duties, he has been active in seminars on local theology and inter-religious dialogue. See *Metamorphosis of a Church. A Study on the People of God in the Republic of Singapore: Analysis and Projection* (Rome: s.n., 1976). Thesis - P. Univ. a S. Thoma Aq, In Urbe.

Bobby E.K. Sng has specialised in Singapore church history and written or co-edited a series of volumes, including *In His Good Time. The Story of the Church in Singapore 1819-1978* (1980); and with Chung Chee-pang, *Church and culture: Singapore Context* (1990) both published by the Graduates' Christian Fellowship, Singapore. In the latter he also wrote on "Gospel and Culture" and "Church, Ethnicity, and Culture." (See also Supplementary Bibliography below.)

Hermen Shastri did his doctoral study on the Christian interaction with tribal peoples, and taught for a period at the STM. He has later written, as the General Secretary of the MCC, a historical outline of the MCC's history. See his *Christ in Tribal Culture: A Study of the Interaction between Christianity and Samai Society of Peninsular Malaysia in the Context of the History of the Methodist Mission (1930-1983) Mimeo'd* (ThD dissertation, Ruprecht-Karls University, Heidelberg, 1989); and "The wider Ecumenism: Ecumenical concerns in interreligious dialogue" in *CTC Bulletin* XV.2 (1998).

See also **Goh Keat Peng,** ed., *Readings in Malaysian Church and Mission* (Petaling Jaya, Pustaka SUFES, 1992).

5.3 Social Ethics and Culture

Two lay leaders who have reflected on their long involvement in politics and in education are **Thio Chan Bee** and **Tan Chee Khoon.** Thio Chan Bee became the first Asian principal of the Anglo-Chinese School (1952) and founded other colleges with the view to enhancing inter-racial goodwill and harmony amongst diverse ethnic groups in both Singapore and Malaysia. See his

Extraordinary Adventures of an Ordinary Man (London: Grosvenor Books, 1977). Tan Chee Khoon was a devout Methodist who became a leader in government opposition, widely known for his championing of the voiceless and deprived. See *Malaysia Today: Without Fear or Favour* (1985), and *From Village Boy to Mr Opposition. An Autobiography* (1991) both from Petaling Jaya: Pelanduk Publications.

Lim Mah Hui was active in SCM activities in the 1970s and came to specialise in ethnic and economic studies, along with critical analyses of inequality and social injustice in Malaysia. See "Malaysia: Race Relations and Economics," in *Southeast Asians Speak Out,* edited by Barbara and Leon Howell (New York: Friendship Press, 1975); *Ownership and Control of the 100 Largest Corporations in Malaysia* (Kuala Lumpur: Oxford University Press, 1981); and "Affirmative Action, Ethnicity and Integration: The Case of Malaysia" in *Ethnic and Racial Studies* 8.2 (1985).

Choong Chee Pang has been principal of Trinity Theological College and a Lutheran leader in theological education both in Singapore and neighbouring countries. His writings include biblical and Lutheran studies, along with co-authored works on ethnic and cultural aspects of the Christian community in Singapore. See "Working Together in Social Concern: A Biblical Basis" in *Lux Mundi. 30th Anniversary of Trinity Theological College,* edited by John Hamlin (Singapore: Trinity Theological College, 1978); and with Sng, Bobby E.K, *Church and Culture: Singapore Context* (1990).

Tan Kim Huat obtained his PhD from London University in 1993 and teaches New Testament at Trinity College Singapore. He is also co-founder of the journal *Church and Society*. His writings include articles in *Church and Society* such as "Conversion and Intrafamilial Conflict: Some New Testament Perspectives" (1998); "The Bible and Homosexuality: The Evidence and the Debate" (1998); "Biblical Perspectives on the Christian Family" (1999).

Loh Soon Choy lectures at the Malaysia Bible Seminary, and advocates an evangelical theology for social transformation, which is situationally sensitive and biblically faithful. See his *In Search* *of a Responsible Society: A Responsible Church in a Sensitive Asian Society* (Klang: Malaysia Bible Seminary, 1990).

Jeffery Choo Kee Goh is lecturer in dogmatic theology and sacramentology at St Peter's College, Kuching, Sarawak. In his major work, *Christian Tradition Today: A Postliberal Vision of Church and World* (Louvain: Peeters Press; Grand Rapids: Eerdmans, 2000) he includes a full study of "present experience [as] a category which ... a context-specific cultural-linguistic theology must seriously take account of". He then attempts a new Catholic and post-liberal methodology and ecclesiology.

Teo Bong Kwang is a practising lawyer concerned for theology in the public arena. He writes extensively on issues of justice and law from the Christian perspective, the challenge of the marginalised, and Christian involvement in the Chinese community. See *e.g., The Tripartite Relationship - A Short Analysis of the Law Relating to Religious Freedom in Malaysia* (Kuala Lumpur: Huazi Resource and Research Centre, 1990).

5.4 Theological Education and Indigenisation

Ivy Chou Su Teng was Principal of the Methodist Theological School, Sibu, Sarawak; Minister, Wesley Methodist Church, Singapore: and Staff Member, Theological Education Fund (London and Geneva). Her primary work has been in the development of new patterns of theological education. See "Planning a leadership training program for the Theological School in Sarawak, Borneo" (Doctor of Education thesis, Columbia University Teachers College, 1955). She was also active in translation.

Frank Balchin was a long-term LMS missionary stationed in Singapore and active in theological education there as well as in many concerns of ecumenical mission in Malaysia, Singapore and the Southeast Asia region. Along with many documents arising from these concerns, he also edited the *Presbyterian Messenger*. See for example, his *On China's Doorstep* (Broadway Books 4. London: Livingstone Press, 1952); and "The Next Decade," in *Presbyterian Messenger* (Combined Edition 1971-74).

Dennis Dutton has played important roles in theological education and ecumenical endeavours since the 1970s, being Secretary and later President of the CCM, and since 1987 Bishop of the Methodist Church. A co-founder of the STM, he was also active in EACC/CCA programmes. He edited *Pelita Methodist,* and also wrote in the periodical *Community Voice,* and in ecumenical periodicals.

John G. Savarimuthu, Anglican Bishop of West Malaysia from 1973, believed theological education to be crucial, and pioneered the Kolej Theology Malaysia (KTM) in 1974. He was also concerned for the indigenisation of Christianity in Malaysia. See John G. Savarimuthu, "The Guru and Disciple Relationship" (Hong Kong: Council of the Church of East Asia, Mimeo'd. 1981); and *A Man of Vision: Messages and Essays in Honour of Bishop Tan Sri J.G. Savarimuthu* (Kuala Lumpur: Diocesan Office, 1985).

Chooi Mun Sou is a Catholic layman much involved in the leadership and resourcing of the lay apostolate in Malaysia. See for example his "The Role of the Laity in the Malaysian Context," in *East Asia Pastoral Review* 22 (1985).

O.C. Lim sj is currently the Director of the Catholic Research Centre in Kuala Lumpur (see above 3.4.1.), and guides both the centre's training programmes and also the publication of its educational booklets and periodicals, including *Catholic Asia News* and *Formation Information.* See for example, his regular editorials in *Catholic Asia News.*

Stephen Tan held pastorates in Singapore and was later Principal of Trinity Theological College, Singapore. He has also been active in both urban-industrial mission and laity education. He has been particularly concerned for theology which arises from people's life and the theological education which assists this. These he has promoted in Singapore and other countries of Southeast Asia. See for example his "Christian Mission in the Modern World," in *Presbyterian Messenger* (Combined Edition 1971-74).

5.5 Biblical and Missiological Studies

Tan Jin Huat is concerned for holistic growth in the church and for study of trends in Malaysian Church History as well as for biblical study. See "Principalities and Powers in Pauline Literature" (MTh thesis University of Aberdeen, 1989).

Solomon Rajah's theological concerns include faith and culture, folk religions and Gospel communication. In writing on Folk Hinduism in Peninsular Malaysia he draws out cultural-theological implications for gospel communication. See *Folk Hinduism: A Study ... in Peninsular Malaysia from a Christian Perspective* (Manila: ATESEA, 2000).

Other Biblical studies have come from staff members of the STM and TTC: see above.

5.6 Graduates' Christian Fellowship (GCF)

The Graduates' Christian Fellowship (formerly Graduate Students Fellowship) in both Malaysia and Singapore, has been a source for many theological publications since the late 1970s. Subjects of concern have included: social ethics, religious freedom, Christian discipleship and the relation of faith to work and marketplace. The GCF has published a number of volumes on these subjects as well as on church history and missiology. (See below). Articles aimed at a popular audience are found in the *Asian Beacon* magazine, where the focus has been largely on workplace issues.

Selected References

Urbanisation and church growth in Singapore. Singapore: GCF, 1971.

Christian in the Marketplace, Vol. 1 (1995), published by GCF, covering the 3 topics - A Christian Ethical Framework, Office Politics, Being Witnesses in our Workplace.

Christian in the Marketplace Vol. 2 (1997), published by Pustaka SUFES, covering 2 topics - Christians and Investment, Sexual Harassment.

Hwa Yung. *Christian Thinking on Emigration.* Petaling Jaya: Graduate Students Fellowship, 1987.

Moey, Michael, et al., eds. *The Christian and Race Relations in Malaysia.* The Christian in Malaysia Series 1. Kuala Lumpur: Graduate Students Fellowship, 1986.

Koh, Philip, N.T. *Freedom of Religion in Malaysia; the Legal Dimension.* The Christian in Malaysia Series 1. Kuala Lumpur: Graduate Students Fellowship, 1987.

Tan Soo Inn. "An Integrated Seminar Curriculum For a Foundational Programme." Fuller Seminary DMin Seminar Paper, 1998.
—. *The Ministry of the Graduates' Christian Fellowship, Malaysia.* Fuller Seminary DMin Seminar Paper, 2000.
Marvin Wong. *Between Friends: Conversation on Christian Discipleship in the Real World.* Petaling Jaya: Pustaka SUFES. Forthcoming.

6 Periodicals for Research

A selected list of those containing theological reflection would include:

Anglican Messenger (Bi-monthly: Kuala Lumpur); *Armour of God* (Newsletter of the Church of Singapore); *Asian Beacon* (Bi-monthly: Graduate Students' Fellowship, Kuala Lumpur); *Berita CCM/CCM News* (Monthly: Christian Council Malaysia, Kuala Lumpur); *Berita NECF* (Bi-monthly: National Evangelical Christian Fellowship, Petaling Jaya); *Berita STM* (Quarterly: Seminari Theoloji Malaysia, Seremban); *The Bridge* (Bi-monthly: Persatuan Penulis Penulis Kristian Malaysia, Kuala Lumpur); *Catholic Asian News* (Monthly: Catholic Research Centre, Kuala Lumpur); *Church and Society* (Quarterly: Trinity Theological College, Singapore); *Communique* (Quarterly: Graduate Students' Fellowship, Petaling Jaya); *Diocesan Bulletin* (Diocese of Sabah, Kota Kinabulu); *Formation/Information* (Occasional: Catholic Research Centre, Kuala Lumpur); *Herald* (The Catholic Fortnightly. Petaling Jaya); *In God's Image* (Asian Women's Resource Centre for Culture and Theology); *Journal of Methodist Church Malaya/Singapore* (1940s-1950s); *Lux Mundi* (Students' Association, Trinity Theological College, Singapore, 1964-); *Macrux* (Malaysia Bible Seminari, Klang); *Malaysia Bible Seminari Newsletter* (Quarterly: Klang); *Malaysia Message* (from 1890s - see Shellabear 2.2.5.); *National Office on Human Development Bulletin* (Catholic Bishops' Conference, Kuala Lumpur); *Pelita Methodist* (Bi-monthly: Kuala Lumpur); *Presbyterian Messenger* (Singapore/Kuala Lumpur - 1970s); *SCS News* (Society of Christian Service, Kuching, Sarawak); *Singapore Bible College Journal* (Singapore); *Trinity Theological Journal* (Singapore).

7 Supplementary Bibliography
7.1 Malaysia

Banks, David J. *From Class to Culture. Social Conscience in Malay Novels since Independence.* New Haven: Yale University Southeast Asia Studies, 1987.

Bungay, Roy G.W. "The History of the Salvation Army in Singapore and Malaysia." MMin Thesis, Trinity Theological College, Singapore, 1983.

Chan Seong-foong. "Interaction of Ethnicity and Protestant Christianity in West Malaysia." Thesis, STM, 1987.

Daniel, J. Rabindra. *Indian Christians in Peninsular Malaysia.* Kuala Lumpur: Tamil Annual Conference, Methodist Church, Malaysia, 1992.

Doraisamy, T.R. *The March of Methodism 1885-1980.* Singapore: Methodist Bookroom, 1982.

Dorall, Richard F. "Inter-Religious Dialogue in Malaysia: The Christian Contribution to National Unity." Petaling Jaya: Mimeo'd, March 1986.

Fowler, J.Andrew. "Evangelism without Imperialism among the Iban." *SEAJT* 18.2 (1977).

Gabriel, Theodore P.C. *Christian-Muslim Relations: A Case-Study of Sarawak, East Malaysia.* Aldershot: Avebury Press, 1996.

Goh Keat Peng, ed. *Readings in Malaysian Church and Mission.* Petaling Jaya: Pustaka SUFES, 1992.

Haglund, Ake. *Contact and Conflict: Studies in Contemporary Religious Attitude Among Chinese People.* Lund: CWK Gleerups Bokforling, 1972.

Harcus, A. Drummond. *History of the Presbyterian Church in Malaya.* London: Presbyterian Historical Society of England, 1955.

Harris, Annette Suzanne. "The Impact of Christianity on Power Relationships and Social exchanges: A Case Study of Change among the Tagal Murut, Sabah, Malaysia." Doctoral thesis, Biola University, USA, 1955.

Ho, Daniel K. C., ed. *Renewal in the Malaysian Church. Papers of the 2nd National Evangelical Christian Fellowship Seminar 24-25 June, 1988.* Petaling Jaya: NECF, 1988.

Hwang Wei-Tjang. "A General History of Baptist Work in Malaysia." MDiv dissertation, Baptist Theological Seminary, Penang, 1981.

Jensen, Erik. *The Iban and their Religion.* Kuala Lumpur: Oxford University Press, 1974.

Kahn, Joel S. and Frances L.K. Wah, eds. *Fragmented Vision: Culture and Politics in Contemporary Malaysia.* Sydney: Asian Studies Association; Honolulu: University of Hawaii, 1992.

Khoo Yoke Kuan et al., eds. *One God, Many Paths. Essays on the Social Relevance of Religion in Malaysia from Islamic, Buddhist, Christian, Hindu and Philosophical Perspectives.* Penang: Aliran, 1980.

Kwan Lee Kun. "A Survey of the Contribution of the Christian Missionary Movement in Sabah to Education (1880-1962)." (In Malay) Thesis, University Kebangsaan Malaysia, 1988.

Lee Huck Tee. "The Cross and Liberation in the Malaysian Context." STM Thesis, 1983.

Lim, Daniel Seng Peng. "Towards a Biblical View of Humanization." STM Thesis, 1983.

Loh Keng An. *Fifty Years of the Anglican Church in Singapore Island 1909-1959.* Singapore Studies on Borneo and Malaya 4. Singapore: University of Singapore, 1963.

Means, Paul and Nathalie. *And the Seed Grew.* Kuala Lumpur: Methodist Council of Missions, 1987.

Marinan, Gérard. *The Church in the Smaller Asiatic Lands: a Study of the Catholic Church in Siam, British Malaya, Burma and French Indo-China.* New York: America Press, 1948.

Monash, Paul. *The Church and the Urban Poor: an Agenda for Action.* STM dissertation, 1986.

Newton, Brian William. "A New Dawn over Sarawak: the Church and its Mission in Sarawak, East Malaysia." MA thesis, Fuller Theological Seminary, 1988.

Ng Moon Hing. "History and Mission of the Anglican Chinese Church in West Malaysia." MDiv dissertation, STM, 1989.

Northcott, Michael S. "Christian-Muslim Relations in West Malaysia." Muslim World 81 (Jan 1991).

O'Brien, Kevin J. *Redemptorists in Singapore-Malaysia*. Singapore: Navjiwan Press, 1985.

Poh Boon Sing. *The Christian in the Chinese Culture*. Seri Kembangan: Good News Enterprises, 1989.

Poilis, William. *A Popular History of the Catholic Church in Sabah*. Kota Kinabalu: The Diocese of Kota Kinabalu, 1981.

Ponniah, M.E. *A Theology of Ministry for the Diocese of West Malaysia*. Thesis, MLitt, University of Birmingham, Dept. of Theology, 1990.

Punnoose, Matthew K. "The Theology of the St James Liturgy as used in the Mar Thoma Church and its Relevance for us today in Malaysia." Thesis, STM, 1984.

Russell, A. Sue. *Conversion, Identity, and Power: the Impact of Christianity on Power Relationships and Social Exchanges*. Lanham, Md: University Press of America, c1999.

Saunders, Graham. *Bishops and Brookes. The Anglican Mission and the Brooke Raj in Sarawak 1848-1941*. Singapore and New York: Oxford University Press, 1992.

Schwenk, Richard L. "Iban Solidarity: Structural Factors that Promote Development." *Missiology* 3 (1975).

Taie, Daniel. "Christian Faith in the Midst of Islamic Society." (In Malay). Thesis, Sabah Theological Seminary, 1990.

Tan, Jonathan Yun Ka. *Towards Asian Liturgical Inculturation*. FABC Paper 89 (1999).

Young, Betty. *Who Cares*. Kuala Lumpur: Malaysia Care, 1991.

7.2 Singapore

Alfred, Hedwig. *St Francis in Singapore*. Singapore: Franciscan Friars, 1997.

Allan, Sheila (Sheila Bruhn). *Diary of a Girl in Changi 1941-1945*. Kenthurst: Kangaroo Press, 1994.

Brown, Francis. *La Salle Brothers: Malaya and Singapore, 1852-1952*. Petaling Jaya: La Sallian Publication, 1997.

Chee, Soon Juan. *Dare to Change: an Alternative Vision for Singapore*. Singapore: Singapore Democratic Party, 1994.

Chua, Carolyne Cheng Sim. *Religion and Secularization: a Study of Christianity in Singapore*. Singapore: National University of Singapore, 1984.

Clammer, John R. *The Sociology of Singapore Religion: Studies of Christianity and Chinese Culture*. Asia Pacific Monograph 4. Singapore: Chopmen Publishers, 1991.

Clammer, John R. - *The Social Structure of Religion: a Sociological Study of Christianity in Singapore*. Singapore: University of Singapore, 1978.

Goh Peh Siong, Daniel. *Rethinking Resurgent Christianity in Singapore*. Singapore: Southeast Asian Journal of Social Science, 1999.

Kok, Wong Chan and Chuck Lowe, eds. *Ministry in Modern Singapore*. Singapore: Bible College, 1997.

Kuah, Khun Eng. "Confucian Ideology and Social Engineering in Singapore." *Journal of Contemporary Asia* 20.3 (1990).

Lim, Isaac. *The Christian Church in 21st Century Singapore*. Singapore: National Council of Churches, c2000.

Makepeace, Walter E. et al., eds. *One Hundred Years of Singapore*. Singapore: Oxford University Press, 1991. 2 vols. Reprint. Originally published in London, 1921.

Malayan Christian Council. *The Churches Working Together*. "Reports presented to the General Council ..." Microfilm. National Library of Singapore, 1976.

Michell, Brian. "Contextualization: The Continuing Missiological Challenge." *Trinity Theological Journal* 9 (2000).

O'Brien, Kevin J. *Redemptorists in Singapore-Malaysia*. Singapore: Navjiwan Press, 1985.

Our Heritage Our Future [Trinity Theological College]. Singapore: Armour Pub., c1999.

Quah, Jon Siew Tien. *Religion and religious conversion in Singapore: a review of the literature*. Singapore: Ministry of Community Development, 1989.

Singam, Constance et al. *The role of civil society in Singapore*. Singapore: Association of Muslim Professionals, 1997.

Sng, Bobby E.K. and You Poh Seng. *Religious Trends in Singapore with Special Reference to Christianity*. Singapore: GCF and FES, 1982.

—, and Choong Chee Pang. *The Spread and Development of Christianity in the Singapore Chinese Community, 1900-1940*. Singapore: GCF, 1991.

Solomon, Robert M. *Living in Two Worlds: Pastoral Responses to Possession in Singapore*. Frankfurt am Main: Peter Lang, 1994.

Teixeira, M. *The Portuguese Missions in Malacca and Singapore 1511-1958*. 3 vols. Lisboa: Agência Geral do Ultramar,1961-1963.

Tey, David Hock. *Chinese Culture and the Bible*. Singapore: Here's Life Books, 1988.

Tim Yap-fuan. *Singapore Literature: a Select Bibliography of Critical Writings*. Singapore: National University of Singapore Library, 2000.

Tong, Chee Kiong. *Religious Conversion and Revivalism: a Study of Christianity in Singapore*. Singapore: Ministry of Community Development, 1989.

Topley, Marjorie. "The Emergence and Social Function of Chinese Religious Associations in Singapore." *Comparative Studies in Society and History* 3 (1960).

Trinity Theological College 40th anniversary: Historical Journal, 1948-1988. [chief editor David Wu]. Singapore: The College, 1989?

Wingeier, Douglas E., ed. *Gereja Di-Dalam Dunia: a Study Book on the Nature and Mission of the church*. Singapore: Methodist Church in Malaysia and Singapore, 1970.

Wong, James Kok Yui. *The Urban Church in the Midst of Social Change*. Singapore: Church Growth Study Centre, 1973.

Yen, Ching Hwang. *A Social History of the Chinese in Singapore and Malaya 1800-1911*. Singapore: Oxford University Press, 1986.

— JCE with DK, FJJ, JMP

7 Contextual Theology in the Philippines 1800-2000

For Christian writing and reflection in the Philippines prior to 1800 see "Groundwork for Asian Christian Theologies: Southeast Asia," chap. 2 above.

1 **Theological Foundations 1800-1946**
   1.1 Historical and Religious Context
   1.2 Church and Theology
   1.3 Women Doing Theology 1
   1.4 The *Pasyon* Tradition
   1.5 Nationalist Clergy and Filipino theology
      1.5.1. Don Pedro Pelaez (d.1863); **1.5.2.** José Apolonio Burgos (1836-1872); **1.5.3.** Nationalist Priests, Propagandists and Writers
   1.6 Pioneers of Nationalist Thought and Theology
      1.6.1. José Rizal (1861-1896); **1.6.2.** Gregorio Aglipay (1860-1940); **1.6.3.** Isabelo de los Reyes Sr. (1864-1938); **1.6.4.** Aurelio Tolentino (1867-1915); **1.6.5.** The Iglesia Filipina Independiente Labor Apostolate
   1.7 Early Evangelical and Ecumenical Theology
      1.7.1. Heritage and Selfhood; **1.7.2.** Nationalism and Ecumenism; **1.7.3.** Asuncion Arriola Perez (1893-1967); and Josefa Jara-Martinez (1894-1987); **1.7.4.** Enrique C. Sobrepeña (1899-1978)
   1.8 Catholic Reconstruction and Social Apostolate
      1.8.1. Context and Watershed; **1.8.2.** Joseph A. Mulry sj (1889-1945) and Walter Hogan sj (fl. 1950)
   1.9 Protestant Theology and Society
   1.10 Supplementary Bibliography 1

2 Contextual Filipino Theology 1946-2000
  2.1 Historical Context
  2.2 Developments in Contextualizing Theology
  2.3 People and Themes - a Mini-Guide
  2.4 Women Doing Theology 2
  2.5 Selected Theologians, Writers, Activists
  2.5.1. Horacio de la Costa sj (1916-1977); **2.5.2.** Catalino G. Arevalo sj (1925-); **2.5.3.** Vitaliano R. Gorospe; **2.5.4.** Julio Xavier Labayen ocd (1927-); **2.5.5.** Francisco F. Claver sj (1929-); **2.5.6.** Peter G. Gowing (1930-1983); **2.5.7.** Virginia Fabella mm; **2.5.8.** Carlos Abesamis, sj (1934-); **2.5.9.** Leonardo N. Mercado svd (1935-); **2.5.10.** Lydia Nazario Niguidula; **2.5.11.** Emerito P. Nacpil; **2.5.12.** Mariano C. Apilado (1936-); **2.5.13.** Mary John Mananzan osb (1937-); **2.5.14.** Kathleen Coyle (1937-); **2.5.15.** Pedro V. Salgado op (1937-); **2.5.16.** Lode Wostyn (1937-); **2.5.17.** Hilario Gomez Jr.; **2.5.18.** Levi V. Oracion; **2.5.19.** Anscar Chupungco osb (1939-); **2.5.20.** Louie G. Hechanova cssr (1940-); **2.5.21.** Elizabeth Dominguez; **2.5.22.** Teodoro C. Bacani (1940-); **2.5.23** Julita A. Quintos rc.; **2.5.24.** Feliciano Cariño; **2.5.25.** Mary Rosario Battung rgs (1943-); **2.5.26.** Teresa Dagdag mm (1944-); **2.5.27.** Edicio de la Torre (ca. 1945-); **2.5.28.** Melba Padilla Maggay; **2.5.29.** Evelyn Miranda-Feliciano; **2.5.30.** Oscar S. Suarez; **2.5.31.** Benigno P. Beltran svd (1946-); **2.5.32.** José M. de Mesa (1946-); **2.5.33.** Karl Gaspar cssr (1947-); **2.5.34.** Dionisio Marcello Miranda svd (1947-); **2.5.35.** Melanio LaG. Aoanan; **2.5.36.** Everett L. Mendoza; **2.5.37.** Sharon Rose Joy Ruiz-Duremdes; **2.5.38.** Muriel Orevillo-Montenegro (1954-); **2.5.39.** Elizabeth Padillo-Olesen; **2.5.40.** Sophie Lizares- Bodegon (1955-); **2.5.41.** Elizabeth Tapia (1955-); **2.5.42.** Amelia Vasquez rscj (1959-); **2.5.43.** Agnes M. Brazal (1960-); **2.5.44.** Hope S. Antone, (1960-); **2.5.45.** Noriel D. Capulong; **2.5.46.** Luna Dingayan
  2.6 Other Contributions to Contextual Filipino Theology
  2.6.1. Contextual Theological Reflection and Spirituality; **2.6.2.** Regarding Philippine Church History; **2.6.3.** Filipino

History and Culture; **2.6.4.** Socio-political Theology and Concerns; **2.6.5.** Studies Pastoral and Missiological; **2.6.6.** Theological Education and Indigenization; **2.6.7.** The Contributions of Centers, Movements, Institutions
2.6.7.1. Catholic Bishops' Conference of the Philippines, Manila (CBCP 1945-); **2.6.7.2.** East Asian Pastoral Institute, Quezon City (EAPI 1961-); **2.6.7.3.** Institute for Religion and Culture, Quezon City, Cebu City, Bukidnon (IRC 1980-); **2.6.7.4.** Institute for Studies in Asian Church and Culture, Quezon City (ISACC); **2.6.7.5.** Institute of Women's Studies, St. Scholastica's College, Manila. (1988-); **2.6.7.6.** National Council of Churches in the Philippines, Quezon City (NCCP 1963-); **2.6.7.7.** Silsilah Foundation, Zamboanga; **2.6.7.8.** Socio-Pastoral Institute, Manila (SPI 1980-); **2.6.7.9.** Supreme Council of Bishops, Philippine Independent Church (Iglesia Filipinas Independiente - IFI); **2.6.7.10** United Church of Christ in the Philippines (UCCP)
2.6.8. The Contributions of Other Institutes and Associations
2.6.8.1. Association of Major Religious Superiors in the Philippines (AMRSP, 1974-); **2.6.8.2.** Association of Women in Theology (AWIT); **2.6.8.3.** Ecumenical Bishops' Forum (EBF); **2.6.8.4.** Forum for Interdisciplinary Studies and Endeavors (FIDES); **2.6.8.5.** Filipino Chapter of EATWOT; **2.6.8.6.** Igorota Foundation (IF); **2.6.8.7.** Other institutes
2.7 Supplementary Bibliography 2
2.7.1. Church History and Society; **2.7.2.** Contextual Theology; **2.7.3.** Periodicals

1 Theological Foundation 1800-1946
1.1 Historical and Religious Context
As it had done since 1565, the Philippines remained under Spanish rule in the 19th century (until 1898), becoming for the next half century a colony of the USA. In this period Filipinos would

experience vast socio-political changes that resulted from, for example, the alternating policies of monarchic and liberal governments in Spain; the dissolution, reduction or reform of religious orders; the increasing corruption and mismanagement of major primary industries; the growing grievances over land-use, livelihood and colonial exactions despite the increased material prosperity for a small minority; and the increasing consciousness of Filipino identity and aspiration which would lead to multiplying revolutionary movements and eventually to the struggles for independent nationhood. Filipinos had long participated in repeated insurrections and in millenarian movements, and in this later period came to increasingly challenge the pervasive power of Spanish religious orders. Despite the role of some exceptional Spanish administrators and local priests, the predominant response to Filipino needs and aspirations came to be more oppressive, culminating in the *Gomburza* executions (1872) and the rapid rise of movements such as the Propaganda Movement and the *Katipunan*. The successful revolution against Spain (1896-1898) was, however, tragically aborted by conquest by the United States of America, followed by both violent "pacification" programs and then by partial social, educational and land reforms.

US sovereignty was imposed in 1901, although a partially elective bicameral legislature was planned in 1902. Nationalist movements for independence were well re-established by 1907, and, despite repeated frustration, these culminated in the inauguration of the Philippine Commonwealth through a Constitutional Convention with limited powers in 1935. By the 1920s however, the rapid expansion of commercial agriculture and the introduction of a money economy had brought the rural Philippines to crisis point, with tenants reduced to virtual slavery. The Pacific war followed, with the establishment of Philippine political (though not economic) independence in 1946. But the seeds of widespread revolt and continuing disaffection had been sown in the pre-war failures of social reform and these would only be deepened by the refusal of successive governments to redress the manifest injustices to tenant, share-cropper and industrial laborer.

In culture, society and religion both Spanish and US colonization would leave a "legacy of syncretic, rather than totally destructive elements." The religiosity of pre-hispanic Filipinos was largely animistic, although many held a belief in a Supreme Being. Living under Spanish colonial rule for almost four centuries, Christians in most islands of the Philippines had experienced rapid "Christianization," along with widespread oppression and the destruction of much of their culture. The legacy of Spanish colonial rule in the Philippines was largely destructive of indigenous culture and religious practices, including native scripts and literature that might be used to foment rebellion. However slave-holding, polygamy, gambling and the drinking of alcohol were discouraged, and many Catholic practices blended well with indigenous myth, ritual and art-forms. And the best of Spain's traditions in law and scholarship, in the arts and in devotion would continue to be valuable sources for Philippine society and church. Many aspects of Filipino culture and identity would further decline in the decades of US control, despite positive advances in education, livelihood and social welfare for sections of the Filipino people. Economic exploitation and cultural domination would also continue, along with movements of renewal coming in part from the influences of western philosophy and literature (as in the 19th century), from those in Catholic social apostolates and from the beliefs and praxis of some Protestant communions. (See further below, e.g. 1.8; 2.3; 2.6.)

Selected References

Agoncillo, Teodoro A. and Oscar M. Alfonso. *History of the Filipino People*. 8th ed., Quezon City: Garotech Publishing, 1990.

Blair, E.H., and J.A. Robertson. *The Philippine Islands 1493-1898*. 55 vols. Cleveland: A.H. Clark, 1903-1909.

Cabrero, Leoncio. *Historia general de Filipinas*. Madrid: Ediciones de Cultura Hispánica, 2000.

Constantino, Renato. *The Philippines: A Past Revisited*, chapter 13. Manila: Foundation for Nationalist Studies, 1975.

de la Costa, Horacio. *Readings in Philippine History: Selected Historical Texts* Manila: Bookmark, 1965.

Friend, Theodore. *Between Two Empires*. New Haven, Conn: Yale University, 1965.

Gowing, Eric G. *Muslim-Filipinos: Heritage and Horizon.* Quezon City: New Day Publishers, 1979.
Guillermo, Artemio R. and May Kyi Win. *Historical Dictionary of the Philippines.* Asian/Oceanian Historical Dictionaries 24. Lanham, Md.; London: Scarecrow Press, 1997.
Ileto, Reynaldo Clemeña. *Pasyon and Revolution: Popular Movements in the Philippines, 1840-1910.* Quezon City: Ateneo de Manila University, 1979.
—. *Filipinos and their Revolution: Event, Discourse, and Historiography.* Centennial of the Revolution. Quezon City: Ateneo de Manila University, c1998.
Mahajani, Usha. *Philippine Nationalism: External Challenge and Filipino Response, 1565-1946,* chapter 4. St. Lucia: University of Queensland Press, 1971.
Philippiniana Sacra. "400 Years of Printing in the Philippines (1593-1993)." *Philippiniana Sacra* 29.85 (1994).
Salamanca, Bonifacio S. *The Filipino Reaction to American Rule 1901-1913.* Quezon City: New Day Publishers, 1984.
Schumacher, John N. *The Propaganda Movement: 1880-1895.* Manila: Solidaridad Publishing House, 1973.
Scott, William Henry. *Cracks in the Parchment Curtain and other Essays in Philippine History.* Quezon City: New Day Publishers, 1982.

1.2 Church and Theology

Throughout this period, the major religious forces would remain those of a largely Tridentine and sometimes resurgent Catholicism, in often uneasy relationship with "folk-Catholicism"; continuing animistic and shamanistic religious traditions; the people-oriented Catholicism of the *Iglesia Filipina Independiente* (from 1898); and also from 1898, a range of Protestant movements from the USA, often intent upon "civilizing" the Philippine people, and aware of their task to "continue the Reformation." For all these forces, the middle and later decades of the 20th century would bring a rapid deepening of indigenizing, ecumenical and society concerns in both theology and ministries.

The Roman Catholic theology inculcated in the Spanish period remained that of the Counter-Reformation, but it was a Catholicism that had come to blend elements of native animistic religion with the teachings of the catechism, and that was increasingly influenced by nationalist aspirations. With the introduction of the Catholic cult of the saints, many of the roles and functions of spirits still recognized in nature were transferred to saints, while in "folk Catholicism" the indigenous belief in a spirit world remained basically intact. Issues surrounding the role of Filipino clergy would, however, provide the seedbed both for Filipino theology and for wider nationalist aspirations (see below 1.5). Following many earlier struggles to develop an indigenous clergy, there were, by 1800, four colleges in Manila training native candidates for the priesthood and by 1810 the number of native priests and seminarians exceeded that of the regular clergy. Exceptional ones of these would produce Filipino interpretations of the Gospel within the Philippine context.

The relationship of "Catholicism that is Roman [or Spanish] to a truly indigenous Christianity" now became a central question in church leadership and faith understanding. It was in this context, and in that of the revolutionary movements that followed, that indigenous theological reflection would have its birth. The hymns and prayers of the revolutionary *Cofradia* and the letters containing the teachings of its founder and charismatic leader, Apolinario de la Cruz (1814-1841), remain important early sources for Filipino theology and imageries of the "Tagalog Christ." Similar traditions would continue in the *Katipunan* and later movements (see Ileto 1979).

Writings by missionaries in this period remained almost entirely expository, catechetical or devotional, and in some cases, ideologically anti-Filipino. There were few apologetic works apart from those of A. Lopez sj, and later, Frs. MacCarthy and J.P. Delaney. A survey of "more formal theological work" for the period until 1898 appears in Fernandez (1979).

The independent church movement at the turn of the century was part of a larger trend in the remaining Spanish empire, where faith was now being distinguished from allegiance to an arbitrary authority. Christian ideals permeated the thought and writings of nationalist and revolutionary societies such as the *Katipunan*, in their concern to "defend the oppressed" and to prevent violence against women. But despite revolution and the rejection of Spanish control, and the influx of clergy from the USA and Europe to replace the Spanish, there was little questioning of traditional doctrines in Roman Catholic communities in the following decades. Theology, apart from developments within the social apostolate, would remain in largely Tridentine form until the post-war years. The traditions of the *Pasyon*, however, developed further, often with revolutionary connotations, as did other movements of folk Catholicism and by the middle of the 20th century, the issues of Filipino and national identity would increasingly become the subjects of writings by Filipinos themselves.

In the *Iglesia Filipina Independiente* (IFI), which was born from the revolution (1896-1898), there was rejection of the (Spanish) socio-political order, though initially not of the Roman Catholic Church. The IFI's theology of "religious Filipinism" was strongly influenced by both a recovered Filipino folk-culture and by the aspirations of peasant and labor movements (see below 1.6). Some decades of isolation, but also of theological and liturgical reconstruction followed, but it would not be until 1948 that the IFI was fully welcomed by sister churches through the concordat reached with the Episcopal Church. This led to mutual theological and educational interaction along with significant localized ministries and theologies in mountain provinces and other districts of the Philippines.

Protestant churches in the Philippines, being largely the results of US missionary effort, also showed a blend of syncretic, creative and destructive elements. They often strongly reflected the characteristic beliefs, ethos and practices of churches in the West, but from early decades held to the principles of comity and cooperation in mission activity. In doctrine these churches would include emphasis upon Christ as the only savior, upon the need for no other intercessors, and upon biblical standards for ethical life. There are also denominations and local communities which have from early in the 20th century come to develop both their theology and ministries in Filipino terms and models. Notable here would be the progressive and ecumenical stance developed by the United Church of Manila, the United Church of Christ (1948 - formerly the United Evangelical Church from 1929), and by national ecumenical councils (from 1929). (For these see 1.7.2.) The theology and practice of nationalism, self-support and social justice would be central to the work of all these bodies (see 2.6.7.) as also of groupings within major Catholic congregations.

Selected References

Apilado, Mariano. *Revolutionary Spirituality.* Quezon City: New Day Publishers, 1999.

Clark, Francis X. *"Mission" and the Philippines: Past, Present, Future.* Manila: Loyola School of Theology, 1981.

Coronel, Hernando M. *Boatmen for Christ.* Manila: Reyes Publishers, 1998.

Deats, Richard L. *Nationalism and Christianity in the Philippines.* Dallas: Southern Methodist University, 1967.

Fernandez, P. *History of the Church in the Philippines (1521-1898).* Manila: National Book Store, c1979.

Ileto, Reynaldo Clemeña. *Pasyon and Revolution: Popular Movements in the Philippines, 1840-1910.*

Kwantes, Anne C., ed. *A Century of Bible Christians in the Philippines.* Manila: OMF, 1998.

Osias, Camilo and Avelina Lorenzana. *Evangelical Christianity in the Philippines.* Dayton, Ohio: The United Brethren Publishing House, c1931.

Salanga, Alfredo N. *The Aglipay Question: Literary and Historical Studies on the Life and Times of Gregorio Aglipay.* Quezon City: Communication Research Institute, 1982.

Santiago, Luciano P.R. *The Hidden Light: The First Filipino Priests.* Quezon City: New Day, 1987.

Schumacher, John N. *Readings in Philippine Church History.* 2nd. ed. Quezon City: Loyola School of Theology, 1987.

Sitoy, T. Valentino, Jr. *Several Springs, One Stream: The United Church of Christ in the Philippines* 2 Vols. Quezon City: UCCP, 1992, 1997.

Whittemore, Lewis B. *Struggle for Freedom: History of the Philippine Independent Church.* Greenwich, Conn.: Seabury Press, 1961.

1.3 Women Doing Theology 1

The ministries and wisdom of women, as religious, catechists, Bible women, evangelists and auxiliaries continued throughout this period to be essential to the life and witness of all churches. Women "distinguished themselves as patriots, poets and revolutionaries" throughout the Spanish period, although few writings are extant from the 19th century to equal those of Jeronima de la Asuncion, Ignacio del Espirito Santo and Francisca Fuentes (in the 16th and 17th centuries: see above chapter 2). However the biographies of activist saints such as Melchora Aquino (1812-1919), along with those like Si Maria, Nena, and Gabriela Silang, provide insights into their lived beliefs. Melchora Aquino's faith-understanding, for example, clearly united national aspiration, compassionate service and devoted spirituality. Among other nationalist women in leading roles in the first years of occupation by the USA, and for whom we have recorded statements, are the Aglipayans Sra. Carmen Villacampa of Negros and Sra. Vicente Sotto of Cebu, the (initially) Presbyterian Sra Polbete of Manila and others like Sra Lozano-Santander of Cebu. Juliana Lopez of Batangas, along with her family, strongly opposed the occupation by the U.S.A. and for this was targeted with special abuse during the brutal US military campaign in Batangas (1901-1902). Her letters (1904) have just been republished as *The Story of the Lopez Family* (2000).

Movements of women were to receive greater impetus in the US period and these included nationalist, suffragist, educational, labor, social welfare and religious organizations. Institutes such as the Ellinwood Training School for Girls (1907), the Young Women's Bible Training School (1910) and the ecumenical National Association of Women (from 1929) would have far-reaching influence. By the 1920s, there were also noted deaconesses and women pastors, evangelists and Bible women, along with physicians, medical superintendents and social workers. Writings from some of these which include theological reflection are found in annual church reports, in church periodicals of the period, such as *Philippine YWCA Magazine*, and in the memoirs of missionaries such as J.B. Rodgers and Frank C. Laubach, but no full collection of such sources has yet been made or interpreted. Somewhat fuller sources are available for the lived theology of such later professional women as Asuncion Arriola Perez (1893-1967) and Josefa Jara-Martinez (1894-1987). (See 1.7.3.)

Throughout the 19th and early 20th centuries the dominance in religious congregations of expatriate leadership along with the traditional anonymity of women religious had frequently prevented any written expression of faith by them. However the writings of some women religious appear in records of their congregations, and the biographies of some founders or Mother Superiors are extant. Collections of letters by religious women have also been identified in some congregations, but as with the records just mentioned, these sources are yet to be published or studied. The works of poets such as Natividad Marquez (Ana Maria Clavez, 1901-1957) and Trinidad L. Tarrosa-Subido (1912-?) include such faith reflections, as do other writers such as Linda Ty Casper and Rowena Tiempo Torrevillas.

From the mid-20th century, however, a steadily growing number of theological writings by women gain publication, in periodicals, booklets, mimeographs or in monographs. These have often arisen from the many women's movements active in this period, from teachers, activists, religious and ministers. In these they contribute to, but often also question or reject, the purposes, content and style of other writings in theology. (See further 2.4.)

Selected References

Arriola, Fe C. *Si Maria, Nena, Gabriela Atbp: Kuwentong Kasaysayen Ng Kababaihan* (Maria, Nena, Gabriela and others: stories on women in Philippine history). Manila: IWS, St. Scholastica's College, 1989.

de Guzman, J.V. et al. *Women of Distinction: Biographical Essays on Outstanding Filipina Women.* Manila: Jovita Editorial Board, c.1967.

Infante, Teresita. *The Woman in Early Philippines and Among the Cultural Minorities.* Manila: Unitas Publications, 1975.

Orrevillo-Montenegro, Muriel. "Tracing the Footsteps of the Filipina." *NCCP Magazine* 39.4 (1998).

Orteza, Edna J. *Women in the Growth of Protestantism in the Philippines.* UCCP Study Series. Quezon City: UCCP, ?1994.

Pantoja-Hidalgo, Cristina, ed. *Pinay: Autobiographical Narratives by Women Writers, 1926-1988.* Quezon City: Ateneo de Manila University Press, c2000.

Quiambao, E.C. "Asuncion Perez, Social Worker." In *Women of Distinction: Biographical Essays on Outstanding Filipina Women of the Past and the Present,* edited by Jovita Varias-De Guzman et al. n.p., c1967.

Santiago, Lilia Quindoza. *Tales of Courage & Compassion, Stories of Women in the Philippine Revolution.* Quezon City: DIWATA Foundation and HASIK Inc., ?1995.

—. *Sangalan ngina: sandaang taon ng tulang feminista sa Pilipinas, 1889-1989.* Quezon City: University of the Philippines Press, 1997.

Sitoy, T. Valentino, Jr. *Several Springs, One Stream. United Church of Christ in the Philippines.*

—. *Comity and Unity. Ardent Aspirations of Six Decades of Protestantism in the Philippines (1901-1961).* Quezon City: NCCP, 1989.

Velez, Maria Cristina, ed. *Images of the Filipina: a Bibliography.* Manila?: Ala-Ala Foundation, 1975.

1.4 The *Pasyon* Tradition

For Spanish colonizers the passion play or *sinakulo* in the rituals of Holy Week was seen as inculcating the moral virtues of resignation, perseverance in suffering and hope for the life to come. However they also came to "provide lowland Philippine society with a language for articulating its own values, ideals, and even hopes for liberation" (Ileto 1979). From the dramatization of the story of Jesus Christ Filipino writers in the 18th and 19th centuries developed a series of plays which retold the Passion in a wholly Filipino context. The classical version is that of Aquino de Belen (fl.1700-1720), which stresses the humanity of Jesus in friendship as well as in brutal suffering, and in which the characters are distinctly Filipino. Many forms of *Pasyon* were widely used throughout the 19th century, notably the *Casaysayan nang Pasiong Mahal ni Jesucristong Panginoon Natin,* first published in 1814.

Contextual Theology in the Philippines 1800-2000

Roman and Jewish authorities in the Passion story became identified in the *indio* mind with the colonial rulers and their collaborators, and Jesus, persecuted for his dream of universal *kapatiran* and equality, became the exemplar of their hopes of liberation. The gospel narratives provided "powerful images of transition from ... despair to hope, misery to salvation, death to life ... from the dishonourable age of Spanish rule to a glorious era of freedom (*kalayan*)" (Ileto). As in many other poems by Filipinos, the *Pasyons* moved thus decisively beyond the inculcation of orthodox Roman Catholic teaching - along with loyalty to Spain - to provide the images and aspirations for Filipino Christian reformers, and for the revolutionary movements and brotherhoods which formed to oppose Spanish - and later also US - domination.

In the mid-to-late 19th century this lively tradition contributed to many nationalist movements, including those for the Filipinization of the clergy, and for the establishment of Philippines independence. In the 20th century it would also later influence the development of Filipino theology. In the tradition of Apolinario de la Cruz (ca.1814-1841), leaders of revolutionary *cofradia* like Felipe Salvador (d.1912) invoked images from the *Pasyon* and of the "Tagalog Christ" in the formation and leadership of guerilla movements such as his *Santa Iglesia*. From Salvador in particular we have narratives in which the wanderings and encounters, prayer and theological reflection of the (poor and humble) leader and his disciples reflect many features of the life and sufferings of Jesus Christ. The close relationship between intense prayer and the hardships which must be endured, between the *loob* (inner self) and the struggle for new world, is especially notable and would recur in Filipino theology of the late 20th century. (See for example, de Mesa 2.5.32.)

Selected References

Aligan, Rodel. "The Biblical and Folkloric Elements of the First Tagalog Pasyon." *Philippiniana Sacra* 27.81 (1992).

Ang Bayang Kahapishapis (The deeply grieving country). Tabloid edited by Diego Mojica. San Franciso de Malabon: Katipunan, 1899.

Aquino de Belen, Gaspar. *Mahal Na Passion ni Jesu Christong Panginoon Natin Na Tola* (The story of our Lord Jesus Christ's priceless suffering). Arranged and annotated by Rene B. Javellana. Manila: Ateneo de Manila University, 1990.

Foronda, Marcelino. "The Image of Christ in the Ilocano Pasion." *Diwa* 6.1 (1981).

Francisco, Jose Mario C. *"Native Ground for Philippine and Theological Reflection."* Mimeo'd. Quezon City: Loyola House of Studies, 1981.

Ileto, Clemeña Reynaldo. *Pasyon and Revolution: Popular Movements in the Philippines, 1840-1910.*

Javellana, R.B., ed. *Casaysayan nang Pasiong Mahal ni Jesucristong Panginoon Natin* (Account of the Sacred Passion of Our Lord Jesus Christ). *Quezon* City: Ateneo de Manila University, 1988.

Litterae Annuae; and *Historiae Societatis Iesu* (The Jesuit Letters of the Mission of the Philippines). Philippine section, Central Jesuit Archives Vols. 5-14. Rome.

Lumbera, Bienvenido L. *Tagalog Poetry 1570-1898: Tradition and Influences in its Development.* Quezon City: Ateneo de Manila University, 1986.

Mojares, Resil B. *Origins and Rise of the Filipino Novel: A Generic Study of the Novel until 1940.* Quezon City: University of the Philippines, 1983.

Salvador, Felipe. "Autobiography." In *Ang Tatlong Napabantog na "Tulisan"sa Pilipinas,* by Jose P. Santos. Gerona, Tarlac: n.p. 1936.

Tiongson, Nicanor G. *Kasyasayan at Estetika ng Sinakulo at Ibang Dulang Panreihiyon sa Malalolos.* Quezon City: Ateneo de Manila University, 1975.

1.5 Nationalist Clergy and Filipino Theology
1.5.1. Don Pedro Pelaez (d.1863)

Born of Filipino-Spanish parents, Pedro Pelaez gained his STD at the University of Santo Tomas (1844) and there taught theology and philosophy to generations of Filipino priest-scholars. He was the principal leader in the movement of Filipino clergy from 1849 to rectify injustices within the church and to establish a church in which Filipino and Spaniard were equally regarded. He became secretary to the archbishop, administrator of the Manila Diocese, and later was elected acting archbishop. He was an eminent advocate for the Filipinization of the church, (along with Frs. Mariano Gomez, Agustin Mendoza, José Guevarra), and senior mentor to all nationalist priests. He also led the campaign for the secularization, in effect the Filipinization, of parishes. He opposed injustices done to Filipino clergy, especially regarding the deprivation of parishes and relegation to inferior positions, reprinting Archbishop Sancho de Santa Justa's statements on their behalf. Pelaez was deeply concerned and tireless in working for church reform, although remaining strict concerning the requirements of canon law. He also founded, with Fr. Francisco Gainza, *El Catolico Filipino* newspaper, 1862, and wrote a series of articles on behalf of Filipino clergy, in *La Generacion* (Spain).

Selected References
Works by Don Pedre Pelaez
>   *Brebes apuntes.* Memoranda, Vatican Archives.
>   *Documentos importantes para la question pendiente sobre la provision de curatos en Filipinas.* Madrid: El Clamor Publico,1863
>   Letters in Archivio Segreto Vaticano (Arch. Nunz Madrid) and Archives of the Archdiocese of Manila.
>   *Memorial to Queen of Spain* (opposing Decree of 1861). Manila: 1861.
>   Coronel, Hernando M. *Boatmen for Christ.*
>   de la Costa, Horacio and John N. Schumacher. *The Filipino Clergy: Historical Studies and Future Perspectives.* Loyola Papers 12. Manila: Loyola School of Theology, 1980.
>   Schumacher, John N. *Father José Burgos: Priest and Nationalist.* Quezon City: Ateneo de Manila University, 1972.
>   —. *Revolutionary Clergy: The Filipino Clergy and the Nationalist Movement, 1850-1903*, 7ff. Quezon City: Ateneo de Manila University, 1981.
>   —. "The Literature of Protest: Pelaez to the propagandists." In *Brown Heritage: Essays on Philippines' Cultural Tradition and Literature*, edited A.G. Manuud. Quezon City: Ateneo de Manila University, 1967.
>   Zaide, Gregorio F. *Great Filipinos in History: an Epic of Filipino Greatness in War and Peace.* Manila: Verde Book Store, 1970.

1.5.2. José Apolonio Burgos (1836-1872)

A brilliant scholar and theologian, Burgos was rector of Manila Cathedral, the protegé and successor of Pelaez, a leader in Comité de Reformadores, and finally a martyr (with Frs. Mariano Gomez and Jacinto Zamora). He remained loyal to Rome while rejecting the ethnocentric policies and theology of the Friars and advocating the Filipinization of the Church. He wrote extensively in the cause of reform and social justice, for the recognition of Filipino clergy, and for the equality of Filipino and Spaniard.

With Joachim Pardo de Tavera, he founded the journal *El Eco Filipino* (Madrid) to publish these concerns. There and elsewhere he drew on a wide knowledge of history, scientific discovery, canon law and theology to articulate a theology of national identity and Filipino Christianity in their social and political application. Writings extant include articles, letters, and manifestos.

Selected References
Works by Jose A. Burgos
> *Como se forman las religiones* 1842-1972. Manila: [s.n.] 1861.
> Cruz, Hermenegildo. *El P. Burgos, precursor de Rizal: breve ensayo acerca del gran patriota agarrotado cuyos sacrificios fueron la inspiracion del Heroe Nacional.* Con una nota prefacial del editor Guillermo Masangkay. Manila: Libreria "Manila Filatelica," 1941.
> De Ligan, Francisco. *El proceso de los padres Jose V. Burgos, Mariano Gomez y Jacinto Zamora.* Manila: Imprenta Nueva Era, 1963.
> *"Manifesto"* (defending Pelaez) and other writings are collected (Spanish and English) in *Father Jose Burgos: Priest and Nationalist,* by John N. Schumacher. Quezon City: Ateneo de Manila University, 1972.
> Schumacher, John N. *Father Jose Burgos: a Documentary History with Spanish Documents and their Translation.* Quezon City: Ateneo de Manila University, 1999.
> Villarroel, Fidel. *Address on Father Jose Burgos.* Manila: University of Santo Tomas, 1971.
> *See also:*
> de la Costa, Horacio and John N. Schumacher. *The Background of Nationalism and Other Essays,* 178ff. Manila: Solidaridad Publishing House, 1965.

Schumacher, John N. *Readings in Philippine Church History*, 221ff. 2d ed. Quezon City: Loyola School of Theology, 1987.

—. *Revolutionary Clergy: The Filipino Clergy and the Nationalist Movement, 1850-1903.*

1.5.3. Nationalist Priests, Propagandists and Writers

These were the "heirs of Burgos" and associates of revolutionaries, who distributed and wrote for "subversive" newspapers or journals. Many also reclaimed parishes from the regular clergy, and later supported nationalist forces in the nationalist revolution. Many were arrested and imprisoned by both the Spanish and the US armies.

In theology they followed closely the thought of Pelaez and Burgos, remaining loyal to Roman Catholic doctrine and faithful in their exercise of pastoral care and teaching. Until the 1890s, the larger proportion also retained loyalty to Spain, as did Burgos and Rizal.

Msgr. Mariano Sevilla, an associate of Marcello del Pilar and Rizal, worked with Jose Changco, Manuel Roxas and other nationalist priests to restore the rights of Filipino clergy while remaining loyal to Rome. In articles and memorials he affirmed the legitimacy of Filipino aspirations, criticized the friars, defended the Catholic faith, and advocated adequate clergy education.

Fr. Manuel Roxas (b. ca.1855), prebendary of Manila Cathedral, worked with Sevilla, Changco and Silvino Manalo to consolidate nationalist and loyalist clergy. He advocated the return, by delegation, of ecclesiastical authority to Filipino priests, and encouraged them both to make the administration of the sacraments their primary duty "out of love for the people" and to actively support the revolution. See his articles and letters in *La Republica Filipina*.

Other nationalist priests, active in animation, spiritual direction, in writing and in support for the Revolutionary government included: the Carlists, Lupo Capio, Jose Consunj, Vicente Garcia and Pedro Dandan, along with Teodoro de la Cruz; other priests including Manuel Crisostomo, Rafael Canlapan, Juan Gatmaitan, Toribio del Pilar and Maximo Viron; and lay leaders such as Joachim Pardo de Tavera, José Basa, Maximo Paterno, Manuel Genate and Mariano Moreno.

Among many writings in Filipino on nationalism and reform were those of Marcel del Pilar (many articles, letters to his niece, editorials in *La Solidaridad*); G. Lopez-Jaena (articles and letters); A.L. y Novicio (satires, stories, writings on Filipino customs); M. Ponce (biographies, articles, histories); and J. Panganiban (poetry and articles).

Among those prominent in supporting Gregorio Aglipay, were Frs. Pedro Brillantes, Eustaquio Gallardo and Pio Romero (Circular opposing Aglipay's excommunication) and also the laymen Felipe Buecamio and Isabelo de los Reyes. In opposition to Aglipay, Fr. Isaac Albano was one of the more eloquent advocates, along with General Manual Tinio.

A number of dramatists and poets - apart from authors of the *Pasyon* and those of the Propaganda Movement - also wrote in support of movements for nationalism and social justice, often using the life or teaching of Jesus as a central source and framework. Among these were Isabelo de los Reyes Sr. (see 1.6.3); the pioneer novelist and ethnographer Pedro Paterno (1858-1911); and the novelist, dramatist and journalist Aurelio Tolentino (see below 1.6.4). Among a number of secular Cebuano priests who were publishing writings by 1920 - devotional, literary and sometimes nationalistic-were Blas Cavada de Castro, Miguel Nellas del Carmelo, Alejandro Espina, Ismael Paras and Roque Maduro. Later novelists presenting similar themes included Juan Villagonzalo (1886-1914), Nicolas Rafols (1894-1947), Faustino Aguilar (1882-1955), Lope K. Santos (1879-1963) and (Ms) Magdalena Jalandoni (1893-1978).

Selected References

    Agtarap, Alfredo San Pedro. "A Christian Response to Philippine Liberation Movements." PhD Thesis, Fuller Theological Seminary, 1991.

    Coronel, Hernando M. *Boatmen for Christ.*

    de Achutegui, Pedro S. and Miguel A. Bernard. *Religious Revolution in the Philippines.* Vol. 4. Manila: Ateneo de Manila University, 1960-1972.

    Mojares, Resil B. *Origins and Rise of the Filipino Novel: A Generic Study of the Novel until 1940.*

Philippine Revolutionary Papers 1899-1901. Collection held in the National Library of the Philippines, Manila. Also available on microfilm.

Pons y Torres, Salvador. *El Clero secular Filipino: apuntes bibliograficos y biograficos* ... Manila: Impr. La Democracia, 1900.

Schumacher, John N. *The Propaganda Movement: 1880-1895.* Manila: Solidaridad Publishing House, 1973.

—. *Revolutionary Clergy: The Filipino Clergy and the Nationalist Movement, 1850-1903,* 36-47, 199f.

Tolentino, Aurelio. *Selected Writings,* edited by Edna Zapenta-Manlapaz. Quezon City: University of the Philippines, 1975.

For newspapers containing articles see Schumacher, John N. *Revolutionary Clergy: The Filipino Clergy and the Nationalist Movement, 1850-1903;* 287ff.

1.6 Pioneers of Nationalist Thought and Theology
1.6.1. José Rizal (1861-1896)

Brilliant physician, scientist, linguist, poet and writer, Rizal is regarded as the greatest of Filipino reformers, advocating full recognition of the rights of Filipinos, although in continued unity with Spain. He was deeply religious, though he rejected orthodox Roman Catholicism. His most influential writings were the novels *Noli me Tangere* and *El Filibusterismo,* written "to distinguish true religion from the false" which has substituted outward forms, superstition and exploitation for the consolation of the oppressed and the humiliation of the rich and powerful.

Rizal retained central Christian beliefs in one merciful God, who is knowable in nature, in history and in Jesus Christ; who is followed in respect and service for all others, in devotion for one's people and country, in a repentant heart and in good deeds. All men and women have innate dignity and worth for Rizal, and an inherent right to liberty and happiness, for God is working out God's ultimate purpose which is happiness for all and the eternal destruction of none. He quoted widely from the Bible although he did not accept it as infallible (Hessel 1983).

Note the reflection of Rizal's beliefs in the codes of revolutionary movements such as the *Katipunan* (Agoncillo and Alfonso, 1960: 190ff.)

Selected References

Refer Bibliography in Hessel (1983) and documents in Juan Collas, ed. *Rizal's Unknown Writings*. (Manila, 1953)

Rizal, José. *Diarios y memorias*. Manila: Comision Nacional del Centenario de Jos. Rizal, 1961.

Araneta, Salvador. *Rizal and His Message*. Manila: Institute of Economic Studies and Social Action, University Press, 1962.

Deats, Richard L. *Nationalism and Christianity in the Philippines*. Dallas: Southern Methodist University, 1967.

Dictionary on José Rizal's Thoughts, Teachings, Principles. Quezon City: Philippine Education, c.1979.

Diokno, José W. "Rizal's Continuing Challenge." *Solidarity* 95 (1983).

Hessel, Eugene A. *The Religious Thought of José Rizal*. Quezon City: New Day, 1961. Rev. ed. 1983.

Olaes, Rodolfo O. *A Critical Study of Rizal's Early Religious Thought from His Early Years until the End of His Period of Study in Madrid*. Microfilm. Dasmarinas, Cavite: Union Theological Seminary, 1966.

Pardo de Tavera, T.H. *The Character of Rizal and the Legacy of Obscurantism*. Manila: n.p.,?1960.

Schumacher, John N. *Revolutionary Clergy: The Filipino Clergy and the Nationalist Movement, 1850-1903*, 36ff., 47ff.

—. "Rizal and Filipino Nationalism: A New Approach." *Philippine Studies* 48.4 (2000).

Sta. Maria, Felice Prudente. *In excelsis: the mission of José P. Rizal: Humanist and Philippine National Hero*. Makati City: Studio 5 Designs, c.1996.

Zaide, Gregorio F. and Sonia M. Zaide. *José Rizal: Life, Works, and Writings of a Genius, Writer, Scientist, and National Hero*. Manila: National Bookstore, c.1984.

1.6.2. Gregorio Aglipay (1860-1940)

Aglipay studied - along with Aguinaldo, Mabini and Isabelo de los Reyes - at San Juan de Letrán. He became active in supporting the campaigns for the Filipino clergy and, as a priest in Manila, and later in Cavite he remained in contact with nationalist groups and leaders in the later revolution. In May 1898 he was appointed military vicar general by Aguinaldo, and worked closely with Mabini to establish schools, seminaries, and adequate administration for local government. As Vicar General Aglipay issued "semi-schismatic" manifestos (Oct. 1998), and was excommunicated in 1899. Following attempts to form a national (Roman) Catholic Church, he joined Isobelo de los Reyes in the establishment of the Iglesia Filipina Independiente (1902) - which quickly became a mass movement representing especially laborers, share-croppers and the poor.

In theology, his early orthodoxy was modified by the movements of nationalism, of Filipinization and for religious liberty. He came to believe that only by revolution would the friars be forced to relinquish lands and controlling power, and the Spanish hierarchy be replaced by Filipino bishops. Following the reluctant break with Rome, he was influenced by Unitarianism and, with de los Reyes, by Filipino traditions and aspects of ancient Filipino religious beliefs. These markedly diluted the Catholic character of the new church's theology (until 1948), which however remained clearly liberalizing and nationalist in its theology, with the structure of Roman Catholic doctrine.

Selected References
Works by Gregorio Aglipay
   Catecismo de la Iglesia Independiente. Manila: Impr. de Fajardo, 1905.
   Novenario de la Patria. Manila: Iglesia Independiente, 1926.
   Cátedra (sermonario) de la Iglesia filipina independiente. Manila: I. de los Reyes, 1932.
   —, with Isabelo de los Reyes and Simeon Mandac. Six Epistles. Formation and discipline of the I.F.I. Manila: 1902-1903.
de Achutegui, Pedro S. and Miguel A. Bernard. New Documents on Gregorio Aglipay: a series of papers published in Philippine Studies. Manila: Ateneo de Manila, 1959.
Rodríguez, Isacio R. Gregorio Aglipay y los orígenes de la iglesia filipina independiente (1898-1917). Madrid: Consejo Superior de Investi-gaciones Científicas, Departamento de Misionología Española, 1960.
Salanga, Alfredo Navarro. The Aglipay Question. Literary and Historical Studies on the Life and Times of Gregorio Aglipay. Quezon City: Communication Research institute for Social and Ideological Studies, 1982.

Scott, William Henry. "The Philippine Independent Church in History." *East and West Review* 28.1 (1962); *Silliman Journal* 10.3 (1963).
Whittemore, L.B. *Struggle for Freedom: the History of the Philippine Independent Church.* New York: Seabury, 1961.

1.6.3. Isabelo de los Reyes y Florentino Sr.(1864-1938)

A graduate of Vigan Seminary and University Santo Tomas, de los Reyes was an ardent nationalist and Filipinologist, and has been termed "father of Philippine folklore." He was also a vigorous labor leader and the founder and/or editor of six papers and journals including *Filipinas ante Europa* and *La Iglesia Filipinas Independiente: Revista Catolica.* He founded the Union Obrera Democratica, an early labor union, was a prominent leader in movements of workers and was jailed for labor agitating. He campaigned for the rights of Filipino clergy, was firmly anti-American and a close associate of Aglipay and Mabini. He became the key organizer, liturgist and theologian for the IFI. In later years he co-founded the Republican Party of the Philippines.

In doctrinal and liturgical formulations, de los Reyes combined elements of ancient Filipino belief in the nature deity *Bathala,* with Christian beliefs and scientific thought. In the *Oficio Divina* (1906) he rewrote the Roman Missal to express Filipino devotion and cultural heritage, and in this he departed from many traditional Christian concepts. His liturgies and prayers, however, have been judged to be "deeply sensitive" and "keenly ethical" (Deats 1967: 74ff.). He retained belief in the Incarnation, but not in the Trinity as traditionally understood, nor in a sacrificial atonement. Throughout all his writings, the central concern is for a faith and life of worship which expresses Filipino selfhood and is liberative for the Filipino people.

Selected References

Works by Isabelo de los Reyes

Ilocanadas: Articulos varios sobre Etnologie, Historias y Costumbres del Pais. Manila: 1887.
El Folk-lore Filipino. Manila: 1889.

La sensacional Memoria sobre la revolucion filipina en 1896-7, La Religion del "Katipunan," Filipinas: Independencia y Revolucion! Madrid: 1899.
La religión del "Katipúnan." 2nd. ed. Madrid: Tipolit. de J. Corrales, 1900.
Oficio divino de la Iglesis Filipina Independiente; primera parte, novisimo evangelio: secuna parte, culta eucharistio. Barcelona: I. de los Reyes, 1906. (Compare revised *Oficio Divina*, of the IFI, 1961).
Letters in IFI Archives, St. Andrews Theological Seminary, Quezon City.
Deats, Richard L. *Nationalism and Christianity in the Philippines.* Dallas: Southern Methodist University, 1967.
Schumacher, John N. *Revolutionary Clergy: The Filipino Clergy and the Nationalist Movement, 1850-1903.*
Scott, William Henry. *Cracks in the Parchment Curtain and other Essays in Philippine History*, last 3 chapters. Quezon City: New Day Publishers, 1982.

1.6.4. Aurelio Tolentino (1867-1915)

Aurelio Tolentino was born in Pampanga, studied law at Santo Tomas University and became a member of the *Katipunan* working closely with Andres Bonifacio. He was imprisoned by the Spanish, but was afterwards one of the signatories of the Declaration of Philippine Independence in Kawit, Cavite, on June 12, 1898. During the American Period, he organized the *Junta de Amigos*, a group of Katipuneros that fought against the new colonizers. He was also a playwright, writing *zarzuelas (*musical dramas), *awit* verse, commedia and novels. Some of his nationalistic plays dramatize the Filipinos' fight for independence and the drama *Kahapon, Ngayon at Bukas* (Yesterday, today and tomorrow) led to his imprisonment by the US (1903-1912).

In the three-act "drama socialista" *Bagong Cristo*, Tolentino portrays Jesus Gabiaya's mission to challenge the rich and to give poor laborers hope of a bright future. His tragedy *Tagalog Tears* was written in 1902, at the height of US-Filipino tensions, and was also considered a seditious drama. The author sets the play in the 1400s, hoping to avoid action by authorities of the time, and depicts the story of Filipinos fighting and losing a battle against Chinese invaders, an obvious parallel to conquest by the USA. Writing at a time of heightened national consciousness, Tolentino raised important issues for Filipinos, and also articulated his understanding of a Christian's concern for people and nation. Here he points to the socio-political dimension of the Christian faith, liberation from oppression, and concern for the basic human rights of people. Later novels are more quiescent in tone, but also have social content and present "... Friendship, Marriage and Family as social and metaphysical touchstones in the struggle between Good and Evil" (Mohares 1983: 248). Plays of his have been filmed and stage performances are still mounted internationally.

[Compare the later 'social novels' of Lazao Francisco (*Bayang Nagpatiwakal*, 1930); Servando de los Angeles (*Ang Huling Timawa*, 1936); and Antonio G. Sempio (*Nayong Manggagawa*, 1940).]

Selected References
Works by Aurelio Tolentino
> *Discurso pronunciado por el ciudadano.* Nueva Caceres: Impr. "La Sagrada familia." S.l.: s.n., 1898.
> *Ang Buhok ni Ester.* 3 vols. Maynila: Limbagang Noli, 1914-1915.
> *Selected Writings*, edited, and with an introduction by Edna Zapanta-Manlapaz. Diliman, Quezon City: University of the Philippines Library, 1975.
> Fernando, Felipe D. "Aurelio Tolentino: Playwright, Poet and Patriot." *Philippine Studies* 12.1 (1964).
> Mojares, Resil B. *Origins and Rise of the Filipino Novel.* Quezon City: University of the Philippines, 1983.

1.6.5. The Iglesia Filipina Independiente Labor Apostolate

Along with a theology of "religious Philippinism," the Aglipayan church understood the Gospel as a challenge to the socio-political order in which not only Spain and the Roman Catholic Church but also the USA were involved. The people's church therefore worked for the livelihood of all Filipino people. In the same years that Isabelo de los Reyes co-founded the *Iglesia Filipina Independiente* (IFI), he had already been stimulating the movements of Filipino workers by organizing, with Hermenegildo Cruz and other leading organizers of labor, the first Filipino trade union and the Union de Impresores de Filipinas (UIF). This became the Union Obrera Democratica (UOD) in 1902 and was later renamed the Union Democratica de Filipinas, with strongly nationalist and anti-imperialist aims. The UOD under Hermenegildo Cruz concentrated on transforming the craft unions (*gremios*) into fully-fledged industrial unions so that these would be the stronger basis for a new labor federation. On May 1, 1913, it became the Congreso Obrero de Filipinas with particular aims of opposing the racial and discriminatory policies of the American Federation of Labor. In all these movements members of the IFI were active, and the IFI was able in these years to enlist many Filipinos not only because of its strongly nationalist and Filipinizing principles, but also because of its close alliance with the people's movements which championed the rights of Filipino workers and peasants.

Because the church had been founded in the desire of Filipinos "for liberty - religiously, politically and socially," documents of the IFI of the earliest years, in for example *Revista Catolica* (LIFIRC), along with other journals edited by de los Reyes, clearly assert these principles and the rights of Filipino people. But because such declarations were often in opposition to the burgeoning interests of US commerce, they were not always recognized by Protestant missionaries or Catholic clergy, newly arrived from the USA. Yet despite the major losses of property and state support after 1905, and consequent declines in membership (from 25% of the population in 1903 to 7% in 1948), the IFI retained its nationalist and socialist character, and sections of it continued their work in labor movements. In the founding of the Republican Party, Aglipay and de los Reyes reaffirmed (1935) the IFI principles of national independence, livelihood for workers and farmers, land for the needy, the development and Filipinization of industry, the elimination of luxury and corruption, and Tagalog as the official language. And in this they were articulating fundamental tenets of the IFI's theology from its beginning.

Selected References
 Constantino, Renato. *The Philippines: A Past Revisited*, chapter 13. Manila: Foundation for Nationalist Studies, 1975.

de Achutegui, Pedro S. and Miguel A. Bernard. *Religious Revolution in the Philippines*, vol. 1. Manila: Ateneo de Manila University, 1960.

Deats, Richard L. *Nationalism and Christianity in the Philippines*, chapter 3. Dallas: Southern Methodist University, 1967.

Garcia, Candido Fernandez. *La doctrina de la Iglesia Filipina independiente: exposicion y critica.* Manila: University de Sto.Tomas, 1924.

Mahajani, Usha. *Philippine Nationalism: External Challenge and Filipino Response, 1565-1946*, chapter 4. St. Lucia: University of Queensland Press, 1971.

Manaligod, Ambrosio. *The Ecclesiality of the Philippine Independent Church*. Quezon City: National Priest Organization, 1988. This is the first in a 5 volume series of the IFI.

Ranche, Apolonio M. "The Iglesia Filipina Independiente (IFI): A People's Movement for National Freedom, Independence and Prosperity." *Philippiniana Sacra* 35 (2000).

Scott, William Henry. *The Union Obrera Democratica: First Filipino Labor Union.* Quezon City: New Day, 1992.

1.7 Early Evangelical and Ecumenical Theology
1.7.1. Heritage and Selfhood

Although Protestant missionary societies entered the Philippines before 1870, it was only after the declaration of US rule in 1899 that Protestant missions were officially established there. The theology they brought was essentially that of the 16th century Reformation in Europe, shaped by the evangelical revivals of the 18th and 19th centuries in the United States. This centered upon Jesus Christ as the only Mediator, a substitutionary atonement for sin and "justification by grace through faith." There was also stress upon (individualist) ethical standards, and upon medical, educational and social work. These emphases were seen by many as Gospel alternatives to Catholic "superstition" and "idolatry." For recent studies of early Protestant theology see Mendoza and Suarez (2.5.36 and 2.5.30).

Little of earlier Filipino Christian writings, or of the movements towards a Filipino church, was recognized, although some conversations occurred between Protestant missionaries and

Gregorio Aglipay and Isabelo de los Reyes. Early Protestant missions were largely dependent upon the work of Tagalog and Cebuano evangelists, including women in particular, but the lack of adequate recognition for Filipino leadership would again lead to resentment and division.

By the last decades of the 19th century a number of Protestants were active in nationalist movements and in journalism. Prominent here was Pasqual H. Poblete (1857-1921) who founded five newspapers between 1888 and 1893 and founded the National Party in 1901. Rejecting control by foreign missionaries, he later assisted in the formation of the Iglesia Filipina Independiente. By 1906, the prominent Filipino evangelist Nicolas Zamorra (1875-1914) was advocating self-determination and the proclamation of the Gospel through the "leadership of our countrymen." He also strongly criticized paternalism and foreign control. In 1909 he and colleagues formed the independent *Iglesia Evangelica Metodista en las Islas Filipinas* (IEMELIF), which however retained the doctrinal basis of the (American) Methodist Church. The self-determination of Filipino Methodists was also the issue upon which Cipriano Navarro led in the formation of the Philippine Methodist Church (1933), which later joined the United Church of Christ (1948).

Selected References

Aklat Pang-Alaala Sa Ika - 50 Anibersario ng Iglesia Evangelica Metodista en las Islas Filipinas, 1909-1959. Manila: 1959.

Anderson, Gerald H. "Providence and Politics behind Protestant Missionary Beginnings in the Philippines." In *Studies in Philippine Church History*, edited by Gerald H. Anderson, 279-300. Ithaca and London: Cornell University, 1969.

Bayot, Felix V. "The Life Story of Nicolas Zamora." Translated and condensed by Juan Nabong. *Philippine Christian Advance* 2.4 (1950).

Clymer, Kenton J. *Protestant Missionaries in the Philippines, 1898-1916: An Inquiry into the American Colonial Mentality*. Urbana and Chicago: University of Illinois, 1986.

—. "The Methodist Response to Philippine Nationalism 1899-1916." *Church History* 47 (1978).

Deats, Richard L. *Nationalism and Christianity in the Philippines.*
—. "Nicolas Zamora: Religious Nationalist." In *Studies in Philippine Church History*, edited by Gerald H. Anderson, 325-336. Ithaca and London: Cornell University, 1969.
Hibbard, D.S. *Making a Nation; the Changing Philippines.* New York: The Board of Foreign Missions of the Presbyterian Church in the USA, c1926.
Laubach, F.C. *The People of the Philippines, Their Religious Progress and Preparation for Spiritual Leadership in the Far East.* New York: George H. Doran, 1925.
Roberts, Walter N. *The Filipino Church: the Story of the Development of an Indigenous Evangelical Church in the Philippine Islands as Revealed in the Work of "the Church of the United Brethren in Christ."* Dayton: Women's Missionary Association, United Brethren in Christ, c1936.
Salamanca, Bonifacio S. *The Filipino Reaction to American Rule.* Quezon City: New Day Publishers, 1984. Chapter 6.
Sitoy, T. Valentino, Jr. "The Coming of Protestant Missions to the Philippines." *Silliman Journal* 14 (1967).
—. *Several Springs, One Stream: The United Church of Christ in the Philippines.* Vol I. *Heritage and Origins (1898-1948).*
Von Oeyen, Robert R. *Philippine Evangelical Protestant and Independent Catholic Churches: an Historical Bibliography of Church Records, Publications, and Source Material Located in the Greater Manila Area.* Quezon City: Asian Center, University of the Philippines, 1970.

1.7.2. Nationalism and Ecumenism

Indigenous leadership - in mission, theological training, self-support and union movements - developed further in the next two decades. Comity and cooperation agreements strengthened the role of the Union Theological Seminary (1914-) and later the Silliman Bible School (1920-). Although a proposed scheme of union for all Protestant mission churches was not finally ratified (1915), cooperative ventures continued to grow, and union itself now became an issue for the Philippine churches independent of the mission organizations.

An effective demonstration of ecumenical theology and mission was provided by the formation (1924) of "The United Church of Manila" (including United Brethren, Congregational and Baptist members). This was initially proposed by Senator Camilo O. Osias, and following brief ministries by Juan A. Abellera and Dr. Frank Laubach, Enrique C. Sobrepeña (1899-1978 - See 1.7.4) was minister for 27 years.

An Evangelical Union, planned earlier, was formed in 1901, with the ultimate aim of establishing a National Evangelical - and indigenous - Church on the basis of self-support, self-government and self-propagation. In the wake of the advocacy by, for example, the Philippine Youth Movement, for a "Christian interpretation of nationalism," and for a self-supported, self-propagated church (1926), the United Evangelical Church was formed in 1929. This included Presbyterians, Congregationalists, United Brethren and the United Church of Manila, and became the United Church of Christ in the Philippines (UCCP) in 1948. As "a product of Christian Fraternity and Filipino Nationalism," the UCCP affirmed both nationalist and ecumenical principles for its common life. The role of women in leadership was prominently recognized, as was the responsibility of the Church to "support the poor" and fulfill the obligations of citizenship. These aims would be taken up by the Philippine Federation of Christian Churches, later (1963) the National Christian Council of the Philippines (NCCP).

From these and allied movements in particular, would come a growing number of contextual theological writings (see further below 2.6.7.). In the same year the NCCP was also organized, replacing the earlier Evangelical Union (later to be the Philippine Federation of Evangelical Churches, 1938), of which Sobrepeña was the Executive Secretary (see 1.7.4. below). Proculo Rodriguez, later the President of Southern Christian College, had early called for church independence, and founded the Bolingsong (now Bonifacio) Farmers' Institute in Misamis Occidental. He also led in church union negotiations (1923-1948) and was recognized as "the apostle of understanding, peace and reconciliation." Other important figures in these movements included Cipriano Navarro and Bishop Benjamin Guansing, president of United Theological Seminary, Das Marinas.

Student Christian movements were also seedbeds for both nationalist sentiment and for ecumenical endeavors of many kinds.

In the Philippines a number of early periodicals featured writings in both these causes, and included: *Manila Young Men,* ca. 1921, *The Filipino Student,* ca.1934, and *Union College Script,* ca.1938.

For theological discussions see 1.9, below.

Selected References

Aoanan, M. LaG. *Ecumenical and Prophetic.* Manila: Claretian, 1998.

Articles of incorporation and constitution of the Young Men's Christian Association of the Philippine Islands. Manila: YMCA Philippines, 1911.

Golden Jubilee Book, United Church of Manila, July 1974.

Grant, Fern Babcock, Domini Torrevillas-Suarez and Leon O. Ty, eds. *Enrique C. Sobrepeña: His Life and Work.* Quezon City: The Sponsorship Committee, 1975.

Guansing, Benjamin. "Theological Seminary and Rapid Social Change." *Church and Society* (EACC) 2 (1961).

Roberts, Walter N. *The Filipino Church: the Story of the Development of an Indigenous Evangelical Church in the Philippine Islands as Revealed in the Work of the Church of the United Brethren in Christ.*

Rodriguez, A. Proculo. "The Contributions of Mindanao to the United Church of Christ in the Philippines", edited by Lloyd van Vactor. *Typescript,* 1987.

Sitoy, T. Valientino, Jr. *Comity and Unity: Ardent Aspirations of Six Decades of Protestantism in the Philippines (1901-1961).*

—. *Several Springs, One Stream: The United Church of Christ in the Philippines.* Vol. 1, *Heritage and Origins (1898-1948).*

1.7.3. Asuncion Arriola Perez (1893-1967) and Josefa Jara-Martinez (1894-1987)

Asuncion Perez studied social work in the USA, and became a university teacher in Manila. However in 1923 she left teaching to join Josefa Jara-Martinez in work for destitute and homeless in Manila. She followed Jara-Martinez as executive secretary of the Associated Charities of Manila, successfully campaigned for laws on fire safeguards, health and sanitation regulation, and initiated the organization of the National Relief Administration. She was also a member of the National Security Board to revise labor laws and became director of Public Welfare in 1941. Soon after, she was working in the Filipino guerilla forces during Japanese occupation, and eventually became a colonel. She was the first woman in the president's cabinet, and first as chairperson of UNICEF (both in 1948). She held leadership positions in the Methodist Church, including that of president of what is now Philippine Wesleyan University. A devout Christian, her writings are contained in many reports, articles, and statements for the above agencies, and they evidence the living of her faith amid lifelong dedication to her people.

Josefa Jara-Martinez worked for the Philippine Commission on Public Welfare (1921-1934) after studies in the USA. She became the first Filipino executive secretary of Associated Charities of Manila and founded national organizations for women, and for homeless children. She also founded the Women's Civic Assembly and the Philippine Council of Welfare Agencies, and was first director of the School of Social Work, Philippine Women's University. She was a United Nations social worker overseas, an ordained elder of the United Church of Manila (see 1.7.2.) and executive secretary of the Manila YWCA (1934-1946). Her unwavering commitment to service along with the faith that empowered this, is seen in all her callings and also in many writings.

Selected References

Higdon, E.K. and I.W. *From Carabao to Clipper.* New York: Friendship Press, 1941.

Quiambao, E.C. "Asuncion Perez, Social Worker." In J.V. de Guzman et al. *Women of Distinction: Biographical Essays on Outstanding Filipina Women.* Manila: Jovita Editorial Board, 1967.

Sitoy, T. Valentino, Jr. *Comity and Unity: Ardent Aspirations of Six Decades of Protestantism in the Philippines, 1901-1961.* Quezon City: NCCP, 1989.

Philippine YWCA Magazine (Jan.-Mar. 1987).

1.7.4. Enrique C. Sobrepeña (1899-1978)

Educated both in the Philippines and the USA (Macalester and Princeton), Sobrepeña was active in the YMCA and in the Student

Volunteer Movement. During his long ministry to the United Church of Manila, he became first moderator of the United Evangelical Church of the Philippines (later the United Church of Christ), a leading figure in Philippine Protestantism, and later a co-founder of the East Asia Christian Conference (EACC).

His theology was centered upon the lordship of Christ which extends not only within the church but also in the world. There could be no "separation of the Kingdom of God and the world, of church and society, of spiritual and material." Such a dichotomy "was untrue to the spirit of Jesus" (Grant et al.1975). From this came his deep social concern for the extremes of wealth and poverty, and his commitment to the cooperative movement in the Philippines. It was expressed also in his foundation of schools and colleges, and in his leadership in national and international ecumenical initiatives. As for the church itself, it could only become truly indigenous, he believed, if it became free from "any kind or shadow of outside rule, control or direction." In pastoral, political and ecumenical engagements Sobrepeña envisioned "Christ's redemptive work and influence as a mighty spiritual influence, not only for the saving of individual souls, but also for the saving of society as a whole, the beautifying of individual lives, the sweetening of social relationships .... [and] for the sanctifying of national institutions."

Selected References
Works by E.C. Sobrepeña

    A New Emphasis in Religion. Forewords by A.L. Ryan and E.K. Higdon. 2nd. ed. Manila: Church Council of the United Church of Manila, c1929.
    Decisive Moments. Manila: UCCP, 1936.
    That They May be One: A Brief Account of the United Church Movement in the Philippines. Manila: UCCP, 1954.
    Call to Moral Renewal. Manila: UCCP, 1963.
    "Christians as Citizens." *Church and Society* (EACC) 7 (1963).
    Deats, Richard L. *Nationalism and Christianity in the Philippines.*
    Grant, Fern Babcock, Domini Torrevillas-Suarez and Leon O. Ty, eds. *Enrique C. Sobrepeña: His Life and Work.*
    Sitoy, T. Valentino, Jr. *Several Springs, One Stream: The United Church of Christ in the Philippines.* Vol 1.

Yap Kim Hao. *From Prapat to Colombo. History of the Christian Conference of Asia 1957-1995*. Hong Kong: CCA, 1995.

1.8 Catholic Reconstruction and Social Apostolate
1.8.1. Context and Watershed

In the period following the US conquest, American bishops replaced Spaniards in all but four Roman Catholic dioceses (by 1917), and there was only slow growth in the number of Filipino clergy. Their exclusion from leadership throughout the next half century would lead to continuing controversy. The larger issue, however, arose from the widespread suffering of the Filipino peasantry in a society which remained feudal in structure and allowed unrestrained exploitation and abuse by landlords, money-lenders, government officials or constabulary. The Council of Manila in 1907 had recommended the foundation of sodalities of workers (*Circulos Catolicos de Obreros*), but little action or reflection resulted for some years. Movements for social justice such as the Aglipayan *Sakdalistas* (from the mid-1920s) strove for the redistribution of land and the reduction of taxes for the poor, and rejected control by both Filipino élite and American colonialist. They drew inspiration and imagery from the *Pasyon*, affirming that "the leaders of a subject country should be first in making the sacrifice and suffering the pangs of hardship."

Christian concern centered upon ways to restore real charity to class relationships when the "educated and wealthy practised only a private devotion and the uneducated and landless sought the weightier matters of ... justice and mercy ..." Based on Catholic social teaching and biblical study, Jesuits in particular pioneered in the 1920s the teaching and animation programs which would develop into national organizations working for social justice. The birth of this social apostolate, although not the first Christian challenge to injustice in Philippine society (see "Groundwork for Asian Christian Theologies: Southeast Asia", chap. 2 above), was a watershed in the development of Filipino social ethics and mission.

The first national Congress of Catholic Action was held in Manila in 1925, and affirmed that its purpose was principally social action, in the formation of workers' organizations through Catholic education, along with the formation of Catholic citizens. In the following years, members of Catholic Action associated with the Bellarmine Evidence Guild, and the Catholic weekly *The Philippines Commonweal* - see especially the series of articles in 1937 - went beyond a simple anti-communism to address the sources of unrest in the injustices of Philippine society. In 1947, the Institute of Social Order was founded to be "a clearing house on social order" and to apply the social teachings of the Catholic Church to the Philippines. Key figures here were Frs. Walter Hogan, Horacio de la Costa (see 2.5.1.), Joseph Mulry sj (1.8.2.) Pacifio Ortiz, William Nicholson and Arthur Weiss.

Selected References

Alonso, Esther. "Spanish Friar and Evangelist in the Philippines." *The Missionary Herald* XCV (1899).

Carroll, John J. "Phillipine Labour Unions." *Philippine Studies* 9.2 (1961).

Catholic Bishops' Conference of the Philippines. *Pastoral Letter of the Philippine Catholic Hierarchy on 'Social Justice.' May 21, 1949.* In *Ours to Share: An Approach to Philippine Social Problems*, by Jeremias Montemayor. Manila: Rex Bookstore, 1966.

Constantino, Renato. *The Philippines: A Past Revisited.* Chapter 17.

Deats, Richard L. *Nationalism and Christianity in the Philippines,* 52ff.

Fabros, Wilfredo. *The Church and its Social Involvements in the Philippines, 1930-1972.* Quezon City: Ateneo de Manila University, 1988. Chapter 1.

Schumacher, John N. *Readings in Philippine Church History,* 369ff.

Staunton, John A. *Industrial Catholic Mission: a Letter Addressed to the Friends of the Mission of St. Mary the Virgin, Sagada; Giving an Account of What we have Done, are Doing, and Hope Further to Do for the Igorot People.* Sagada: Igorot Press, 1920.

Tamayo, Serapio. *El amigo del parroco filipino.* Manila: Tip. Pontificia del Colegio de Sto. Tomas, 1921.

Weiss, Arthur A. "Jesuit Social Apostolate 1859-1956." *Philippine Studies* 4.2 (1956).

1.8.2. Joseph A. Mulry sj (1889-1945) and Walter Hogan sj (fl. 1950)

While Catholic Action addressed "the necessities of contemporary Philippine society" through "Catholic education" from 1925 on, it was Fr. Joseph A. Mulry sj (1889-1945), professor of humanities at Ateneo University who, along with his students, provided leadership. Mulry and his colleagues brought the social teaching of the encyclicals *Rerum Novarrum* and *Quadragesimo Anno* to their students, who were largely from land-owning gentry families. In literature classes, roundtables with citizens, and the Bellarmine Evidence Guild, Mulry inculcated the principles of social justice and compassion as alternatives to communism, to be practiced by college graduates as they returned to the land to work with landless farmers. The guild lectured in the plazas of Manila and sat down with town workers and farmers of the rice country to share their social problems and the social doctrine of the Church.

Mulry himself wrote prolifically for newspapers and journals such as *Cultura Social*, and became the mentor of Raul Manglapus and Manuel Quezon. His work would be extended by the radio dramas and publications of the "Catholic Hour," and continued in the Jesuit Institute of Social Order (from 1947), the Federation of Free Workers (1950) and the Federation of Free Farmers (from 1953), along with John Patrick Delaney sj and Walter Hogan sj and his colleagues. Horacio de la Costa sj, in particular, would articulate the principles for research, communication and action upon which this social apostolate should be based (see 2.5.1).

Walter Hogan had worked with labor unions from the late 1940s, implementing the church's social teachings, and was a key organizer of both the ISO and the FFW. He believed in the "natural rights of workers" to fair reward and to good conditions and well-being, and campaigned vigorously for these despite opposition from government officials and from the Catholic hierarchy of the time. By the 1960s, however, many of his policies and practices were adopted by the Philippine churches. (See 2.6.7.)

Selected References

> A collection of Mulry's *Letters and Articles* is held in the Lauinger Library, Georgetown University (USA).
> Carroll, John J. "The Philippine Church of the Crossroads." In *World Catholicism in Transition*, edited by Thomas Gannon. New York: Macmillan; London: Collier Macmillan, 1988.
> de la Costa, Horacio. *Asia and the Philippines*. Manila: Solidaridad Publishing House, 1967.
> Deolindis, Sr. "The Role of Religious Mission Sisters in Church Renewal Today through the Federation of Free Farmers." *Verbum* 12.4 (1971).
> Fabros, Wilfredo. *The Church and its Social Involvements in the Philippines, 1930-1972*. Quezon City: Ateneo de Manila University, 1988. Chapter 1.
> Schumacher, John N. *Readings in Philippine Church History*. 2nd. ed.
> Weiss, Arthur A. "Jesuit Social Apostolate 1859-1956."

1.9 Protestant Theology and Society

In the 1920s and 1930s, theological discussion and dispute between "liberals" and conservatives was lively. The issues concerned biblical inspiration, the correct mode of Baptism, and in particular, the question of "open membership" by which members of different denominations could be accepted to communion. The "positive preaching of the Gospel," however, was an alternative to such divisive issues, stated Stephen Corey of the United Christian Mission (Sitoy, 1992). Meantime, Presbyterians and Congregationalists agreed not to require any credal statement for use in the Union Theological Seminary, although both adhered to the content of the simplified statement drafted for Nanking Union Seminary. In 1929, the United Evangelical Church (later the United Church of Christ), affirmed a theology of unity based on allegiance to the One Lord in worship and mission, and a Confession of Faith which "represented minimum requirements."

Deep social concerns, which were included in the United Church's Constitution, were carried forward by such missionaries as Frank J. Woodward and **Frank C. Laubach.** Laubach had come to the Philippines in 1915, had seen the desperate poverty and injustice suffered by Filipinos and developed literacy programs to enable them to "solve their own problems." Prior to this he had chaired the Commission on Social Reconstruction of the Evangelical Union where he interpreted political and economic problems of health, labor conditions, legislation and the alleviation of poverty as theological and ethical issues.

"When a moral issue becomes political," Laubach asked in 1926, "does it automatically drop out of the Christian program, and is it the duty of the missionary to ignore the question and enjoin the native church to ignore it? ... Are Christians to sympathise with the insistent demand of [Americans] to 'exploit' the lands of [Filipinos]; or to sympathise with the attitude of Filipinos that the land is theirs ... ?" For Laubach the answer of a theology that is biblical stands clear, and young church leaders like Proculo Rodriguez, Donato Galia and Cirilo del Carmen agreed. The theology and action of the United Church in later decades would also witness to this.

Fidel P. Galang, Methodist District Superintendent for Pampanga, was active for some years in the *Hukbahalap* movement (originally People's Anti-Japanese Army), and presented the church as an agent in social change throughout his ministry. He also organized programs of community reconstruction, in which 25 pastors and a deaconess labored with barrio members and conducted agricultural training and evangelistic meetings. It was from this experience that he developed his theology for social action in the Philippines. Fellow Methodists who were prominent in secular ministry and writing include José Luna Castro, managing Editor of the *Manila Times*, and Cicero Calderon, Director of Philippines Labor Center and President of Silliman University.

Selected References

Galang, Fidel P. "A Theory of Protestant Social Action for the Philippines." Th.D. Dissertation, Boston: School of Theology, Boston University, 1953.

Gowing, Peter C. "The Legacy of Laubach." *International Bulletin of Missionary Research* 7 (1983).

Laubach, Frank C. *The People of the Philippines: Their Religious Progress and Preparation for Spiritual Leadership in the Far East.* New York: George H. Doran, 1925.

———. *Writings by or About Dr Frank C. Laubach.* A Bibliography held by the Texas Literacy Center, Baylor University. n.p., c.1960. Laubach's principal writings are published as The Heritage Collection.

Norton, Karen, ed. *Man of Prayer: Man of Justice and Peace* and *Teacher: the Selected Writings of a Literacy Pioneer.* Syracuse, NY: New Readers' Press, 1999.

Sitoy, T. Valentino, Jr. *Several Springs, One Stream: The United Church of Christ in the Philippines.* Vol. 1, chapter 9.

1.10 Supplementary Bibliography 1

Alipit, Ramon A. "The Position of the Philippine Independent Church." *SEAJT* 4.1 (1962).

Arcilla, José S. *Jesuit Missionary Letters from Mindanao.* Quezon City: Philippine Province Archives, 1993.

———. "Philippine Jesuit Ascetical Literature." *Landas* 10.2 (1996).

Clymer, Kenton J. *Protestant Missionaries in the Philippines, 1898-1916: An Inquiry into the American Colonial Mentality.* Urbana: University of Illinois, 1986.

de Ayala, Fernando Zobel. *Philippine Religious Imagery.* Quezon City: Ateneo de Manila, 1963.

de Leon, Avelio and Gerald Anderson. *The United Missionary Office in the Philippines: its Ecumenical Significance.* Manila: Union Theological Seminary, 1970.

Deats, Richard L. *The Story of Methodism in the Philippines.* Manila: NCCP for Union Theological Seminary, 1964.

Diaz, Jesus. "The Christianization of the Philippines in its Theological Perspective", Philippiniana Sacra 1.2 (1966).

Diaz-Perez, Nicolas. *Los Frailes de Filipinas; datos y apuntes ineditos sacados de los documentos de Nicolas Diaz-Perez y publicados por Viriato Diaz-Perez.* Madrid: Estab. Tip. de A. Perez, 1904.

Gomez, Fausto, ed. *'The Dominicans' Mission Here and Now. 1587-1987.* Quadricentennial lectures. Orientalia Dominicana Philippines 5. Manila: University of Santo Tomas, 1988.

Gutierrez, Lucio. *Historia de la Iglesia en Filipinas* (1565-1900). Coleccion Iglesia Catolica en el Nuevo Mundo 4. Madrid: Editorial Mapfre, 1992.

Higdon, E.K. *Jesus and National Aspirations and Other Addresses.* Manila: Philippines Christian Institute, c1929.

Historical Symposium on the Beginnings of Christianity in the Philippines. *Articles of the Historical Symposium on the Beginnings of Christianity in the Philippines.* Manila, Philippines Historical Committee, 1965.

Jose, Regolato Troto. *Simbahan: Church Art in the Colonial Philippines 1565-1898.* Manila. Ayala Museum, 1991.

Laubach, Frank C. *The Silent Billion Speak.* New and expanded ed. New York: Friendship Press, c1945.

Mallari, I.V. *Vanishing Dawn. Essays on the Vanishing Customs of the Christian Filipinos.* Manila: Philippine Education Co., n.d. (?1954).

Mullen, Edward G. *"Bring your Brother with You": the Episcopal Missions in the Philippines.* Hartford, Conn.: Church Missions Publishing Company, 1943.

Pastells, Pablo. *Mission to Mindanao 1859-1900.* 2 vols. Cebu City: San Carlos University, 1994- .

Rodgers, James B. *Forty Years in the Philippines: a History of the Philippine Mission of the Presbyterian Church in the United States of America, 1899-1939.* New York: The Board of Foreign Missions of the Presbyterian Church in the USA, 1940.

Rodriguez, Isacio Rodriguez y. *Gregorio Aglipay y los origenes de la Iglesia Filipina Independiente (1898-1917)* Biblioteca "Missionalia hispanica" Vol. 13. Madrid: Consejo Superior de Investigaciones Cientificas, Departamento de Misionologia Espanol, 1960.

Santos, Ruperto C. *Archdiocesan archives of Manila: a Catalogue of Archival Documents, Testaments and Holdings.* Manila: Roman Catholic Archbishop of Manila, 1994.

Sequera, Mariano. *Justicia ñg Dios: mga ilang bagay na inasal dito sa Filipinas nang mañga Fraile.* Maynila: Chofré y Comp.a, 1899.

Staunton, John A., Jr. *An Open Letter to the Rt. Rev. F.R. Graves, D.D.: Bishop of Shanghai ... From the Rev. John A. Staunton, Jr., Priest-in-Charge of the Mission of St. Mary the Virgin, Sagada, Philippine Islands.* Sagada: Igorot Press, 1919.

Thoburn, J.M. *Light in the East*. Evanston, Ill.: Thomas Craven, c1894.

Turner, E.S. *Nation Building*. (History of the Philippine YMCA). Manila, YMCA Philippines and Capitol Publishing House, 1965.

Uy, Antolin V. *The state of the Church in the Philippines 1850-1875: the Correspondence between the Bishops in the Philippines and the Nuncio in Madrid*. Studia Instituti Missiologici Societatis Verbi Divini 35. St.Augustin: Steyler, 1984.

Vilanova, José Tomas. "Letters ..." *Philippiniana Sacra* 27.79 (1992)

Wise, Francis H. *The History of the Philippine Independent Church (Iglesia Filipina Independiente)*. Quezon City: University of the Philippines, 1965.

2 Contextual Filipino Theology 1946-2000

2.1 Historical Context

In this period the Filipino people have encountered many obstacles to full independence and national unity within and beyond the archipelago, and yet increasing numbers have also striven again and again to build a society based on Filipino identity and the well-being of all Filipino people. The socio-political system obtaining since 1900 largely continued in the post-war period despite the gaining of political independence. Increasing extremes of wealth and poverty, malnutrition and homelessness for many meant that by 1955, 60% of national wealth was owned by 0.03% of the population. Attempts to legislate and enforce major changes to such extremes since then (notably in 1957, 1963, 1974, 1987) have largely failed. Highly feudal patterns of land ownership have continued, with tenants and sharecroppers often severely exploited. Poorly implemented labor laws and monopolies by local and overseas corporations have resulted in depressed wages for workers, in constantly high levels of unemployment for even well qualified workers, and the consequent loss of large numbers to be migrant workers overseas. In much of this period, extensive graft and corruption in industry, in local and national government and the military have also contributed to urban decay and rural depression, to extensive violations of human rights, to the alienation of peasant or tribal lands, as well as to vigilante movements and "involuntary disappearances." Secessionist conflict and massacres have continued in the southern Philippines despite the attempts by successive governments at resolving issues there.

During this last half-century however, educational institutions, welfare agencies and non-government organizations have multiplied exponentially, as have people's cultural, political and religious associations and networks. Filipino literature, art and music have burgeoned and achieved creative identity, and the work of Filipino scholars in many fields has received wide recognition. Christian denominations have also multiplied with regular new arrivals often of strongly conservative groups; yet the Roman Catholic Church and other 'mainline' churches have experienced many periods of resurgence and renewal. According to the census of 1990, 86% of all Filipinos are Roman Catholic (with approximately 10% of these being charismatic); 2.6% belong to the Independiente church; 2.3% to the Iglesia ni Cristo; and 5.8% to Protestant churches (more than half of which have arrived since 1945 and many of which are Pentecostal).

As in previous centuries, movements of protest, resistance and often armed revolt have continued in diverse forms from primitivist cult to labor strike, and from street drama or demonstration to violent insurrection. These greatly multiplied, as did the numbers of political detainees, during the years of martial law (1972-1986), including in their numbers peasant farmers and educators, displaced tribals and writers, church leaders and social workers. The significance of armed revolt by *Hukbahalap* and communist movements had declined by the early 1980s, but despite the apparent miracle of the 1986 people's revolution, basic causes of injustice and unrest remain and those working on these issues still suffer harassment. Social Action Centers in many dioceses, most recently the Diocese of Ilagan, still suffer surveillance and occasional violence.

Yet countless movements for social reconstruction, land reform, and human rights have also continued and the life and identity of numerous communities have often been thereby transformed. A virtually uncountable range of local or national networks, institutes, coalitions and cooperatives have been working in projects for integrated community development, for people's education and people's livelihood, as well as in programs of emergency relief, and of medical care, and in folk arts, literature and music. Sources for such endeavors have come increasingly from the renewal of Christian vision and commitment, the recovery of Philippine cultural values, and the dedication and solidarity offered by Catholic, ecumenical and 'secular' social movements in both the Philippines and the Asian region. (See further below 2.6).

Selected References

Abinales P. N. *The Revolution Falters: the Left in Philippine Politics after 1986*. Southeast Asia Program series 15. Ithaca, N.Y.: Cornell University, 1996.

Bernas, Joaquin. *Safeguarding Freedom: Church-State Relations in Public Policy Transformation*. Pulso Monograph 6. Manila: 1990.

Cannell, Fenella. *Power and Intimacy in the Christian Philippines*. Cambridge: Cambridge University, 1999.

Constantino, Renato. *The Philippines: The Continuing Past*.

Elestrio, Fernando G. *Essays on Philippine Culture*. Monograph series 7. Manila: De La Salle University, 1989.

Gomez, Fausto. *The Philippine Revolution and the Involvement of the Church*. SRC Monograph 4. Manila: The Center, c1986.

Gorospe, Vitaliano and Richard Deats, eds. *The Filipino in the Seventies*. Quezon City: New Day Publishers, 1973.

Guillermo Artemio R. and May Kyi Win. *Historical Dictionary of the Philippines*.

Kerkvliet, Benedict J. *The Huk Rebellion. A Study of Peasant Revolt in the Philippines*. Quezon City: New Day, 1979.

Obusan, Teresita B. and Angelina R. Enriquez, eds. *The Filipino Spiritual Culture*. Manila: Mamamatha, 1997.

Permanent People's Tribunal on the Philippines. *Philippines: Repression and Resistance*. n.l.: KSP Komite ng Sambayanang, 1981.

Philippine Human Rights Information Center, Manila. "Development and Human Rights." *Human Rights Forum* 3.1 (1992).

Steinberg, David Joel. *The Philippines: a Singular and a Plural Place*. 3rd. ed. Nations of the Modern World. Boulder: Westview Press, 1994.

That we may Remember. [Introduction by Rogelio Obja-an OSA]. Quezon City: Promotion of Church People's Rights, 1989.
Youngblood, Robert. *Marcos against the Church: Economic Development and Political Repression in the Philippines*. Ithaca: Cornell University, 1990.

2.2 Developments in Contextualizing Theology

This period witnessed not only recurrent movements of protest and revolutionary intent in the face of continuing inequities and government repression but also growing movements - in the arts, in literature and in nationalist scholarship - for the rediscovery and creative expression of Filipino culture and national identity. Major movements in Filipino Christian theology have included those of research-analysis-reflection in historical theology; the study and application of Vatican II thought to Filipino context; and the development of the theologies of society, struggle and liberation. The movements of nationalism and protest within Filipino society and culture deeply influenced Christian response in thought and action, so that by mid-century it was clear to many that prophetic social criticism, along with the recovery of Filipino cultural resources, were integral to theological reflection. This was to emerge especially in the work of many social centers and movements such as the Jesuit Institute of Social Order (1947, see 1.8.2.), the nation-wide activities of the Federations of Free Workers and Free Farmers (from 1953), the East Asian Pastoral Institute (from 1961 see 2.6.7.2.), Christians for National Liberation (CNL 1971), the Catholic Bishops' Conference of the Philippines (CBCP, see 2.6.7.1.), the Ecumenical Development Center (1980), the Socio-Pastoral Institute (1980, see 2.6.7.8.), and women's movements such as *Malayang Kilusan ng Bagong Kababaihan* (MAKIBAKA, Free Movement of New Women, 1970), the Ecumenical Association of Women in the Philippines (1983), and the Association of Women in Theology (AWIT, 1994). (For all these see 2.4.)

This has also been true of the ecumenical centers and movements for social education and action related to the National Council of Churches (from 1929, see 1.7.2. and 2.6.7.6.), including the *Kapatiran Kaunlaran* Foundation (1950), the Christian Institute for Ethnic Studies in Asia (1966), the Inter-Seminary Urban-Industrial Institute (from 1966), the Wednesday Forum (1973), the Ecumenical Movement for Justice and Peace (1979), the Institute for Studies in Asian Church and Culture (ISACC, 1980, see 2.6.7.4.), the Institute for Religion and Culture (IRC) (1986, see 2.6.7.3.), the Forum for Interdisciplinary Endeavors and Studies (FIDES, ca.1988), and the Integrated Church and Community Development Center. Numerous other people movements, college communities, networks and institutes - some of them active for many decades - continue to work in programs of labor education, social analysis, human rights advocacy, community organization and conscientization. From almost all of these, along with countless workshops and study-action groups, has come, along with other activities, a flow of social critique, contextual theological reflection and protest liturgy.

Contextual theology would also come from Plenary Councils and Pastoral Conferences of the Catholic Church, as well as from programs for mission and ministry of the United Church of Christ (see 1.7.2. and 2.6.7.10), of the Independiente and Episcopal Churches (in concordat from 1948), and from the Methodist Church in the Philippines, all of which developed programs of lay ministry, theological education and urban-rural mission. From these, as also from individual teachers within both Protestant and Catholic colleges, and from scholarly lay people and clergy, came significant writings despite the continuance of traditional and essentially colonial approaches to theology and mission on the part of some Protestant and Catholic leaders. (Attempts to indigenize leadership and thought in Catholic orders and institutions in the 1950s had led to censure and expulsion for some priests.)

Far-reaching stimulus for contextual theology would come however from the documents of Vatican II (1962-65), as from the activities and publications of the EACC/CCA (from 1957), from those of the FABC (from 1970), from EATWOT and ASPAMIR, as well as from other Asia-wide networks of theological schools (ATESEA, from 1957), institutes of social concern (ACISCA, from 1970), and from the Asian Women's Resource Centre (AWRC, from 1985). For all these see Vol.1, chap.3. Commentaries on Vatican II, or upon works of liberal European theology, or again on the writings of liberation theologians, made contributions here, as did study of particular Asian theologians. But the major influences remained the realities of Philippine society and the movements of Christian renewal arising within these, to discern the "signs of the times" in both reflection and action. The more contextual theological writing following mid-1960s therefore, addressed many issues which continually overlap in concern and content; and the commitments to Filipinization and church renewal, to spirituality, biblical reinterpretation and social transformation appear to a greater or lesser degree in the work of almost all theologians (see 2.5).

Selected References
a) Church Life and History

Deats, Richard L. *Nationalism and Christianity in the Philippines.*

EACC. *New Forms of Christian Service in the Philippines: Report of the Consultation called by the EACC, April 1-4, 1961 in Quezon City, Philippines.* n.l.: Committees on Interchurch Aid and Church and Society of the EACC, 1961.

Fabros, Wilfred. *The Church and its Social Involvement in the Philippines 1930-1972.*

Gabriel, Manuel G. *Inter-BCC dialogue: a Philippine Experience.* Quezon City: Lay Formation Institute, 1984.

Giordano, Pasquale T. *Awakening to Mission: The Philippine Catholic Church 1965-1981.* Quezon City: New Day Publishers, 1988.

Jocano, F. Landa. *Folk Christianity: a Preliminary Study of Conversion and Patterning of Christian Experience in the Philippines.* Quezon City: Trinity Research Institute, Trinity College of Quezon City, 1981.

Kiley, Henry, ed. *Filipino Tribal Religious Experience.* Biblical and Non-Biblical Revelation series 2. Quezon City: Giraffe Books, 1994.

Kwantes, Anne C., ed. *A Century of Bible Christians in the Philippines.* Manila: OMF, 1998.

Lim, Hilario A. *Memorial to Pope Pious 12 on the Native Religious Clergy in the Philippines.* Manila: Mimeo'd, 1957.

Maningas, Ismael Ireneo. *Filipino Christian Morality.* Metro Manila: St Pauls, 1998.

Orteza, Edna J. *Women in the Growth of Protestantism in the Philippines.* UCCP Study Series 19. Quezon City: UCCP, ?1993.

Sitoy, T. Valentino, Jr. *Comity and Unity: Ardent Aspirations of Six Decades of Protestantism in the Philippines, 1901-1961.*

Tuggy, Arthur. *The Philippine Church: Growth in a Changing Society.* Grand Rapids: Eerdmans, 1971.

Von Oeyen, Robert R. *Philippine Evangelical Protestant and Independent Catholic Churches: an Historical Bibliography of Church Records, Publications, and Source Material ...* Quezon City: Asian Center, University of the Philippines, 1970.

b) Theological Thought and Movement

Abesamis, Carlos. *Salvation - Historical and Total.* Quezon City, JMC Press, 1978.

Arevalo, Catalino G. "After Vatican II: Theological Reflection in the Church of the Philippines 1965-1987." *Landas* 2 (1988).

—. "Filipino Theology." In *Dictionary of Mission,* edited by Karl Muller et al. Maryknoll NY: Orbis Books, 1997.

Aviso, None S. et al., ed. *Currents in Philippine Theology.* Kalinangan Book Series II. Quezon City: Institute of religion and Culture, 1992.

Battung, Mary Rosario et al., eds. *Religion and Society: Towards A Theology of Struggle.* Book I. Manila: FIDES, 1988.

Bulatao, Jaime et al. *Inculturation, Faith and Christian Life.* Loyola Papers 6. Manila: Loyola House of Studies, 1978.

Fabito, Cornelia. *Philippine Liberation Theology.* Microform: an index to selected materials. BISA special projects series. Sydney: BISA, 1986.

Fernandez, Eleazar S. *Toward a Theology of Struggle.* Maryknoll, NY: Orbis Books, 1994.

"Filipino Theology for Liberation: A Working Paper." (A Group of Filipino Christians) *Journal of Radical Religion* (1976).

Gorospe, Vitaliano, ed. *Filipino Theology Today.* Budhi Papers 3. Quezon City: Ateneo de Manila Press, 1979.

Hardy, Richard P., ed. *The Philippine Bishops Speak, (1968-1983).* Quezon City: Maryhill School of Theology, 1984.

IDOC Documentation Participation Project. *An Asian theology of liberation: the Philippines*. Future of the Missionary Enterprise; Dossier 5. New York: IDOC North America, 1973.

Kroeger, James. "Signs of the Times - A Thirty-year Panorama." *EAPR* 26 (1989).

Lambino, Antonio B. *Towards "Doing Theology" in the Philippine Context*. Loyola Papers 9. Manila: Loyola School of Theology, 1977.

Selected Philippine Sermons, edited by G.H. Anderson et al. Quezon City: NCCP for Union Theological Seminary, 1967.

Tano, Rodrigo D. *Theology in the Philippine Setting: a Case Study in the Contextualization of Theology*. Quezon City: New Day, 1981.

—. "Theological Issues in the Philippine Context." *Evangelical Review of Theology* 19:4 (1995).

c) Theology and Society

Agcaoili, Leonard C. "The Social Action of the Church." *Philippine Priests' Forum* 2 (1970).

Anonymous letters by priests and lay-leaders opposing and supporting Martial Law (1973-1986). See e.g. IDOC documents 071/011 & 012 (1973).

Cariño, Feliciano V. *Church, State and People: the Philippines in the '80s*. Singapore: CCA-CTC, 1981.

Carvajal, Orlando. "The Social Action Apostolate: Total Salvation." *MSPC Communications* 18 (1975).

Cunanan, José P.M. *Jesus the Organizer. Organizing Principles and Practices Based on the Gospel of Mark*. Hong Kong: CCA-URM, 1994.

Dacayanan, Felicidad, and Lourdes V. Albarillo. *Social Action Activities of the Catholic Church in the Philippines*. Malate: Social Institute Pastoral Methods Center, 1976.

Deolindis, Sr. "The Role of Religious Mission Sisters in Church Renewal Today through the Federation of Free Farmers." *Verbum* 12.4 (1971).

Gerlock, Ed, et al., eds. *You are not Forgotten: Symbols during Martial Law*. Manila: SPI, 1988.

Legaspi, Leonardo Z. "Role of the Church in Social Transformation: 1946-1996 and Implications for the Future." *Boletin Eclesiastico de Filipinas* 72 (1996).

Mendoza, Marquita S. and Zone C. Narito, eds. *Spirituality, the Activist and Social Movements*. Bangkok: Asian Cultural Forum on Development; Manila: SPI, 1992.

Montalbo, Melchor B. *The Church on Labour and Workers*. Antipolo: Pampayanan, 1988.

Montes, Valentino. "Social Thinking of the Churches in the Philippines." *SEAJT* 4.1 (1962).

Putzel, James. *A Captive Land: The Politics of Agrarian Reform in the Philippines*. London: CIIR, 1992.

"Two Bishops Write regarding the Good News and the Church's Political Involvement." *Signs of the Times*, August 1st (1975).

UCCP. "Open Letter by Leaders of the United Church of Christ in the Philippines." *Tugon* 7 (1987).

2.3 People and Themes - a Mini-Guide

Representative examples of those who have given attention to particular fields of study and reflection are indicated below. Although some themes are clearly defined, many overlap - as do the works of the authors - in concern for pastoral issues, evangelism, national identity, theological construction and social apostolate. (Only a selection of those working in each area can be included here.)

Philippine church history: see for example Horacio de la Costa, William Henry Scott, P. de Achutegui, T. Valentino Sitoy, Jr., John Schumacher, Apolonio Ranche, John Carroll, Everett Mendoza and Mariano Apilado.

Filipino cultural values and inculturation: see for example Vitaliano Gorospe, Horacio de la Costa, Francisco Claver, Leonard Mercado, Jaime Belita, Evelyn Miranda-Feliciano, José de Mesa, Mary Hollensteiner, Kate Botengan, Ambrosio Manaligod, Lode Wostyn, Dionisio Miranda, Anscar Chupungco, Ramon Reyes, Henry Kiley, Melba Maggay, Agnes Brazal, and Mario Francisco.

For folk culture and Catholicism: see for example James Bulatao, Vitaliano Gorospe, F. Landa Jocano, Jaime Belita, Benigno Beltran and V. Marasigan.

Theology of society and human development: see for example Richard Poethig, Henry Aguilan, Edicio de la Torre,

Vitaliano Gorospe, Teresa Dagdag, Julio Labayen, Teodoro Bacani, Oscar Suarez, Elizabeth Tapia, Karl Gaspar, Melanio LaG. Aoanan, Mary Rosario Battung, Mary John Mananzan and Luna Dingayan.

Liberation and the "signs of the times": see for example Catalino Arevalo, Emerito Nacpil, Levi Oracion, Feliciano Cariño, José Maximiano, Luis Jalandoni, José Blanco, Louis Hechanova, William Henry Scott, Richard Deats, Eli Mapano, Cirillo Rigos and Valentino Montez.

Concerns for the **full recognition of women's theological voice** appear in the work of Virginia Fabella, Lily Quintos, Agnes Brazal, Hope Antone, Cora Tabing-Reyes, Mary John Mananzan, Mary Rosario Battung, Teresa Dagdag, Elizabeth Tapia, Amelia Vasquez, Luna Dingayan and Muriel Orevillo-Montenegro.

Spirituality: see for example Horacio de la Costa, Pedro Salgado, Susana Jose, Sophie Lizares-Bodegon, Kathleen Coyle, Cirilo Rigos, Mary Rosario Battung, Amelia Vasquez, Karl Gaspar, Feliciano Cariño and Elizabeth Padillo Olesen.

Theological method and hermeneutic: see for example Carlos Abesamis, Edicio de la Torre, Virginia Fabella, José de Mesa, Lode Wostyn, Antonio Lambino, Francisco Claver, Feliciano Cariño, Sharon Rose Joy Ruiz-Duremdes, Eleazar Fernandez and Dionisio Miranda.

"Theology of Struggle": see for example Edicio de la Torre, Levi Oracion, Mary Rosario Battung, Karl Gaspar, Melanio LaG. Aoanan, Oscar Suarez, Benito Dominguez, Sharon Rose Joy Ruiz-Duremdes, Everett Mendoza, Luna Dingayan.

Inter-faith issues and dialogue: see for example Lily Quintos, Hilario Gomez, Vitaliano Gorospe, Peter Cowing, Hope Antone, Mary Rosario Battung, Amelia Vasquez, Leonardo Mercado, Julio Labayen, Melanio LaG. Aoanan, and also the Silsilah Foundation.

Biblical studies: amongst many theologians, see for example Cirillo Rigos, Sharon Rose Joy Ruiz-Duremdes, Judette Gallares, Melba Maggay, Lydia Niguidula, Elizabeth Dominguez, Benito Dominquez, Noriel Capulong and Maria Lucia C. Natividad.

2.4 Women Doing Theology 2

In this half century, the theological work and writings of women in the Philippines have gained more recognition and a rapidly growing access to publication. This has been greatly stimulated by women's movements such as the National Christian Women's Association (from 1948, on basis of 1929 formation), the Association of Major Women Religious Superiors (1955, see 2.6.8.1.), the *Malayang Kilusan ng Bagong Kababaihan* (1970), the Ecumenical Association of Women in the Philippines (1983), the Igorota Foundation (IF, see 2.6.8.7), the Cordillera Women's Education and Resource Center, the Institute of Women's Studies, St. Scholastica's College, GABRIELA (the national federation of women's movements), the Women Studies and Resource Center, the Ecumenical Women's Forum and the Association of Women in Theology (AWIT see 2.6.8.2.).

Particular women theologians have provided leadership in these movements and in contextual Philippine theology and these appear in entries below. These include Virginia Fabella, Mary John Mananzan, Lydia Niguidula, Elizabeth Dominguez, Amelia Vasquez, Kathleen Coyle, Agnes Brazal, Teresa Dagdag, Hope Antone, Sophie Lizares-Bodegon, Melba Maggay, Evelyn Miranda-Feliciano, Lily Quintos, Mary Rosario Battung, Elizabeth Padillo-Olesen, Sharon Joy Ruiz-Duremdes and Elizabeth Tapia.

Many of these have contributed books or articles to the body of contextual Filipino theology arising from their particular ministries and research; others receive more brief mention below (see Selected References and 2.6 below). Their writings have appeared in publications of such groupings as the AMRSP, the NCCP, FIDES, the SPI, the OMF, EATWOT, the Institute of Women's Studies at St. Scholastica's College, and AWIT, as well as in many journals and periodicals. Amongst these are *Philippine Studies*, *DIWA*, the *MST Review*, *Boletin Eclesiastico de Filipinas*, *Tugon*, *NCCP News*, *Kalinangan* and *Humig Ugnayan*; they also appear in regional or world journals such as the *East Asian Pastoral Review*, *Asia Journal of Theology*, *Religious Life in Asia*, *In God's Image*, *Verbum SVD*, *CTC Bulletin*, *International Review of Mission*, *IDOC* papers and *Ministry Today*.

Contextual Theology in the Philippines 1800-2000 381

The subjects of such writings cover a very wide range, notably those of faith amid struggle; issues of Filipino Christology; Filipino spirituality; Filipino feminist theological method; biblical study; working for liberation; the religious life; openness to other faiths; patriarchy and violence; the Christian's role to know, suffer and contribute to humanization; and the stories, analysis and reflection of tribal and poor, urban and professional, lay and religious women. Writers here include - among many others - Myrna Francia Kumain, Carmela Abao, Teresita E. Nitorreda, Ma Cores P. Doyo, Margarita R. Cojuangco, Magdalena A. Villaba-Cue, Rita Mataragnan, Theresa Chong-Cariño, Mencie Karagdag-Peralto, Violeta Lopez-Gonzaga, Gladys d'Souza, Mary Regina Wallace sp, Pat Fox, Agnes Miclat-Cacayan, Marquita S. Mendoza, Ruth Panganiban, Carmelita M. Usog, Teresita M. Tchou, Susana R. Reyes, M. Aurora Augustine, Jurgette Honculada, Mariana Dimaranan, Edna Ortez, Lilith M. Usog, Norma Dollaga, Josephine Barrios, Ruth Panganiban-Billena, Jane Montenegro, Lidy Nacpil-Alejandro.

A selection of their writings appears below.

Selected References

Aguilar, Delia D. *The Feminist Challenge: Initial Working Principles Towards Reconceptualizing the Feminist Movement in the Philippines*. Malate, Manila: Asian Social Institute. In cooperation with the WACC, 1998.

Asedillo, Rebecca C. *Faith in struggle.* SPI series Faith and ideology C1-88. Manila: SPI, 1988.

Bragado, Erlinda H., ed. *Filipinas in dialogue: Muslim-Christian Women's Response to Contemporary Challenges*. Malate, Manila: De La Salle University, 1995.

Catli, Felicidad. "Retracing our Footsteps." In *Souvenir Program, 3rd joint NUCM-NCWA Quadrennial Convention*. Oroquieta City: n.p., 1990.

Constantino, Josefina D. *In faith and freedom*. Pasay City: Daughters of St Paul, n.d.

Corum, Mary Anicia. "The Call of Jesus Today in Journeying with the Spirit." In *A Commentary on PCP II*. Quezon City: Claretian, 1993.

Dural, Sr. Marie Therese. "Spirituality in the Roman Catholic Tradition." In *Response - Consultation*, edited by Ciriaco

Ma. Lagunzad, Jr. Quezon City: United Inter-Seminary Student Association, 1977.

Gaerlan, Kristina N. *Women Religious Now. Impact of the 2nd Vatican Council on Women Religious in the Philippines.* Manila: BPWC (1993).

Grenough, Mary. "The Non-Filipino Working for liberation." In *An Asian Theology of Liberation: the Philippines.* IDOC documentation participation project 5. New York: IDOC North America, 1973.

Honculada, Jurgette. "Notes on Women and Christianity in the Philippines." *In God's Image* (Oct. 1985).

Institute of Women's Studies, St. Scholastica's College. *Women Religious Now: Impact of the Second Vatican Council on Women Religious of the Philippines.* Manila: The Institute, c.1993.

José, Susana. *The Asian Religious Sensibility and Christian Spirituality.* 2 vols. Quezon City: Carmelite Monastery of St. Therese, 1983.

Kroeker, Wendy and Sharon R.J. Ruiz-Deremdes, eds. *Stories and Songs of Hope: Dance Amid Struggle.* Quezon City: AWIT, 1998.

Kumain, Francia Myrna. *Tayo! Let's Eat! Table-fellowship in Acts.* Theology in the Third World A-4. Manila: SPI, 1989.

Lascano, Lydia L. "Filipino Women and the Christ Event." *Kalinangan* 6.1 (1986).

Lucero, Rosario Cruz. *Herstory.* Manila: Institute of Women's Studies, 1990.

Madrigal, Ana Maria. "Batanes: The Melting Pot of Two Cultures". *Philippiniana Sacra* 18.53 (1983).

—. "The Theology and the History of the Commentaries of Paul's Letter to the Romans in the First Five Centuries." *Philippiniana Sacra* 17.49 (1982).

Mataragnan, Rita. "God of the Rich, God of the Poor." *Philippine Studies* 32 (1984).

Nacpil-Alejandro, Lidy. "Some Notes on Economic Alternatives from a Feminist View." *In God's Image* 14.1 (1995).

Nacpil-Manipon, Aida Jean. "Global Trends and Asian Women: of Saints and Icons in the Time of Globalisation." *In God's Image* 17.1 (1998).

Tengco-Labayen, Fe Corazâon. *In Every Woman: Asian Women's Journey to Feminist Awakening.* Manila: IWS, St. Scholastica's College, 1998.

Tauli-Corpuz, Victoria. "Reclaiming the earth-based Spirituality of Indigenous Women in the Cordilleras." *In God's Image* 12.3 (1993).

Tondo, Josefina. "Celebrating Filipino Woman Spirit: the Joys of Being a Woman." *Humig Ugnayan* 1.1 (1998/1999).

Women's Literature Committee. *Women's Power in the Pulpit.* Manila: United Methodist Women's Society for Christian Service, n.d.

2.5 Selected Theologians, Writers, Activists

2.5.1. Horacio de la Costa sj (1916-1977)

Horacio de la Costa studied at Novaliches (MA, 1939), Woodstock College and Harvard (PhD, 1951), and taught history, philosophy and theology principally at Ateneo de Manila. Initially a historian, he came to be an eminent theologian, civic leader, first Filipino provincial superior and adviser to the Jesuit Superior General, and editor of *Philippine Studies*. His major work upon the Jesuit history of the Philippines, has long been "the best overall history of 16th-18th century Philippines" (Schumacher 1978). De la Costa was dedicated to develop a Philippine historiography, to assemble the resources for this and to make them widely available (see *Readings in Philippine History,* 1965). But for over 40 years he also aimed to apply the social doctrines of the Church to the necessities of the Philippine islands: in writings and broadcast plays, and in social action which included spiritual assistance to laborers and labor leaders, mediation and conciliation, and in the promotion of healthy social organizations and institutions. His many writings include studies of Filipino nationalism and its leaders, the history of Filipino clergy and of church-state relationships, along with writings on faith, justice and human development, the "eastern Christ," inculturation and theologies of liberation, humanization and the local church.

Three main areas of his thought concerned the sources of Filipino identity; the unity of evangelism, human development, justice and liberation, and a liberating theology of the local church. He finds the central marks of Filipino identity in such deeply human values as *pakikisama* (willingness to share burdens and rewards), *pagkakaisa* (the building of community by people themselves) and *pagkabayani* (putting common good above private interest). Such commitments, found in India, China and throughout Asia, have always been the signs of God's presence in Filipino life, he affirms, and indeed "the eastern face of Christ." Regarding evangelism, justice and liberation, he makes a serious critique both of Spanish and US practices, as well as of Catholic social action which does not address the causes of massive economic injustice. Liberation from these is primary for him, but it is to be a self-liberation that utilizes the rich resources of Filipino civilization. A "theology of liberation" for de la Costa therefore, thinks "not so much in terms of timeless truths ... but of concrete happenings ... what men (sic) are doing or suffering, creating or destroying within the range of one's experience" (1976a). This is shaped by our particular landscape and community, by Philippine social realities and by the Spirit's life within our local church. This theological method is concluded, by the most diverse groups, by asking where in this history is the Holy Spirit working, and how may we join this work?

Selected References
Works by Horacio de la Costa
> *The Jesuits in the Philippines 1581-1768.* Cambridge, Mass.: Harvard University, 1961.
> *The Background of Nationalism and Other Essays.* Manila: Solidaridad Publishing House, 1965.
> *Readings in Philippine History: Selected Historical Texts.* Manila: Bookmark, 1965.
> *Asia and the Philippines.* Manila: Solidaridad Publishing House, 1967.
> *Liberation of all Men: Our Common Objective.* (Unedited texts). *Progressio Supplement* 2, 1973.
> *An Ignatian Witness.* (Unedited texts). *Progressio Supplements* 10 (1977), reprint, n.d.
> *Five Plays.* Quezon City: New Day Publishers, 1982.
> "Church-State Relationships: A Theological Perspective." *Philippine Priests' Forum* 2.4 (1970).
> "The Filipino National Tradition." In *Challenges for the Filipino,* by Horacio de la Costa, Edicio de la Torre and Pacifico A. Ortiz. Lenten lectures series, 1971. Manila: Ateneo Publication Office, 1971.

"Evangelization and Humanization." *Teaching all Nations* 3 (1973).

"Faith, Justice and Human Development." In *On Faith and Justice*, edited by P.S. de Achutegui. Loyola Papers 5. Manila: Loyola School of Theology, 1976a.

—, Antonio B. Lambino and C.G. Arevalo. *On Faith and Justice II: Faith, Ideologies and Christian Options*. Loyola Papers 7/8. Manila: Loyola School of Theology, 1976.

—, and John N. Schumacher. *Church and State: The Philippine Experience*. Loyola Papers 3. Manila: Loyola School of Theology, 1976b.

—, and John N. Schumacher. *The Filipino Clergy: Historical Studies and Future Perspectives*. Loyola Papers 12. Manila: Loyola School of Theology, 1980.

"In Memorium: Horacio de la Costa, S.J." *Philippine Studies*, Special issue vol. 26 (1978).

2.5.2. Catalino G. Arevalo sj (1925-)

Catalino Arevalo has been termed "the Dean of Filipino theologians" he has been a key theological consultant, writer and editor for both the Philippine Bishops' Conference and for the FABC since its inception in 1970 (see vol.1, chapter 3) and convenor of the Asian Bishops' Theological Advisory Commission. His studies were initially undertaken at Ateneo de Manila, Fordham University, New York, and the Gregorian University, Rome (ThD 1959). Along with many international assignments he has taught missiology, ecclesiology and Christology at San Jose Seminary, the East Asian Pastoral Institute and since 1965 at the Loyola (formerly Jesuit) House of Theology, Quezon City. Although his works have only sometimes appeared under his own name, Arevalo has written or drafted numerous articles and statements, for Bishops' Conferences, councils, ecumenical assemblies, and for Provincials. He edited the Loyola Papers series and also volumes such as *Toward a New Age in Mission* (1979) and *For all the peoples of Asia* (1994).

A central theological concern for Arevalo, deeply influenced by the Second Vatican Council, has been to "make the message and life of Christ truly incarnate in the minds and lives of our people ... building up a truly local church ... the realisation and enfleshment of the Body of Christ in a given people, a given place and time." This is to be through a threefold dialogue with people's culture, their religious traditions and with the destitute and poor, thus uniting the tasks of inculturation, inter-faith dialogue and a liberating human development, in "what-is-going-forward in our common journey as a people." It will mean responding to the concrete questions of Filipinos, and the constructing of local theologies, for every people in Asia has a vocation and contribution to hold the "dream of catholicity" and to realize themselves in their life and mission.

Arevalo has written major articles on liberation and development in Asia, on the "Signs of the Times" theology, on contextualizing theology, and on Filipino theology. Yet he insists that such a theology - "at the heart of 'history itself in the making'" - can itself only be one "gathered and scotch-taped together in hours of doing and suffering, in dialogue and confrontation, in reflections and prayer, in emptiness, in confusion and paralysis" (1998). In the collection of his articles, meditations, homilies and eulogies, *And They shall Name Him Emmanuel* (1999), a recurring note is that of the living presence of Christ in today's concrete situations: in actual suffering, in joys celebrated, in love directly shared, in service given where most needed, in the "depth" dimension of personal and community life. Here some of his own deepest reflections, often penned with affection and humor, are upon ordination, priesthood and apostolate, and upon Filipino theologians: that "we may learn to ... incarnate the word we must proclaim."

Selected References
Works by Catalino G. Arevalo

   And They shall Name Him Emmanuel. Manila: Claretian, 1999.
   "The Church on the Side of the Poor." *Philippine Studies* 19 (1971).
   "On the Theology of the Signs of the Times." *Philippine Priests' Forum* 4.4, 1972.
   "The Task of the Church: Liberation and Development." In *The Filipino in the Seventies. An Ecumenical Perspective*, edited by Vitaliano R. Gorospe sj and Richard L. Deats. Quezon City: New Day Publishers, 1973.
   "Prenotes to the Contextualization of Theology." *Philippiniana Sacra* 14.40 (1979).

"The Church in Asia and Mission in the 1990s." In *The Way of the Shepherd. Studies in Theology for His Eminence Jaime Cardinal Sin on the 25th Anniversary of his Episcopal Ordination*, edited by Socrates B Villegas. Manila: Salesiana Publishers, 1992.

"A Life in the Service of the Church in the Philippines and Asia." In *Yearbook of Contextual Theologies*, 1995: 7-52.

"Filipino Theology." In *Dictionary of Mission*, edited by Karl Muller et al. Maryknoll NY: Orbis Books, 1997.

"Some thoughts on Filipino Theology." *Landas* 12.2 (1998).

"God, The Compassionate Father." *Religious Life Asia* 1.2 (1999).

—, ed. *Evangelism in Asia Today*. Quezon City: Cardinal Bea Institute, 1974.

—, ed. *Toward a New Age in Mission*. 3 vols. Quezon City: Loyola School of Theology, 1979-1980.

—, with Aloysius B. Chang and Wendy Flannery. *Den Glauben neu Verstehen: Beiträge zu einer asiatischen Theologie* (Understand the faith again: an Asian theology). Freiburg: Herder, 1987 (1981).

—, and Gaudencio B. Rosales, eds. *For all the peoples of Asia: documents from 1970 to 1991, Federation of Asian Bishops' Conferences*. Maryknoll, NY: Orbis Books; Quezon City: Claretian, c1992.

Huang, Daniel Patrick. "On Catalino G.Arevalo S.J." *Landas* 12.2 (1998).

2.5.3. Vitaliano R. Gorospe sj

After study in the Philippines and the USA, Vitaliano R. Gorospe taught philosophy and from 1975 to the present has been full time theology professor of the School of Humanities, Ateneo de Manila University. Since 1971 he has also taught on theology of liberation, which aims to form "persons for others" in the promotion of social justice and a preferential option for the poor. His 1997 textbook entitled *Forming the Filipino Social Conscience* is a distillation of his 35 years' teaching. The Ateneo de Manila University Festschrift for Gorospe (1994), *Morality, Religion and the Filipino,* is a collection of essays on the four areas of Gorospe's lifelong concerns: namely, religious education, moral philosophy and theology, social justice and liberation theology, and Filipino popular religiosity. A full list of his publications are included.

Among Gorospe's more significant books *Filipino Values Revisited* (1988) is a collection of philosophical and theological essays on the moral and religious aspects of vital national issues. These have concerned especially the social ethics of violence and public policy, of social justice (poverty, environment, justice for women, human rights, the church, education, Christian-Muslim relations, peace, alternative model of a just society), of the challenge of a civil society, of advertising and commercial practice, of sexual morality, of scientific responsibility, and of revolution and the church of the poor. He has long been active also in fostering professional vocations, community development and student life.

Selected References
Works by Vitaliano Gorospe

Catechism of the Social Doctrine of the Catholic Church. Manila: Catholic Trade School, 1954.

The Morality of Demonstrations and Violence. Quezon City: Ateneo Publications, 1970.

The Filipino Search for Meaning; Moral Philosophy in a Philippine Setting. Manila: Jesuit Educational Association, 1974.

Filipino Values Revisited. Quezon City: National Book Store. 1988.

Banahaw: Conversations with a Pilgrim to the Power Mountain. Manila: Bookmark, 1992.

Forming the Filipino Social Conscience. Social Theology from a Filipino Christian Perspective. Makati, Manila: Bookmark, 2000 (1997).

"Christian Renewal of Filipino Values." *Philippine Studies* 14.2 (1966).

"Christian Koinonia and Some Philippine Cultural Forces." *SEAJT* 2 (1970).

"A Case for Violence Against Property." *Impact* 5 (1970).

"Toward a Filipino Spirituality for Justice." *Life Forum* 16/3 and 4 (1984).

"The Vatican Document and Liberation Theology in the Philippines." *Philippine Studies* 33 (1985).

"Mount Banahaw: The Power Mountain from Ritualism to Spirituality." *Philippine Studies* 40 (1992).

—, ed. *Theology of Development.* Quezon City: Ateneo Publications, 1970.

—, ed. *Faith and Justice and the Filipino Christian*. Alay Kapwa Lectures 1976. 4 vols. Quezon City: Cardinal Bea Institute, 1976.
—, ed. *Incarnation and Avatars in the World Religions*. New York: Harper and Row, 1985.
—, with Jaime Bulatao sj. *Split-Level Christianity: Christian Renewal of Filipino Values*. Quezon City: Ateneo de Manila University. 1967.
—, and Asandas D.Balchand. *Theology of Liberation for Today's Filipino Christian*. Manila: National Book-Store, 1990.

2.5.4. Julio Xavier Labayen ocd (1927-)

Julio Labayen gained his Lic.Theol. at Rome, and was made bishop in 1966. He has been national director of the CBCP National Secretariat of Social Action, Justice and Peace (NASSA); executive chair of the FABC Office for Human Development (1972-1986); and executive chair of the Socio-Pastoral Institute, Manila (see 2.6.7.8.). He also initiated the ACFOD for the Pontifical Justice and Peace Commission (1975), and has chaired the Philippines EBF. A long-time advocate for social justice and basic human rights, Bishop Labayen addresses these and the rights of the weak and vulnerable in the context of globalization. He is equally concerned for the theology and spirituality which sustains such ministries.

"Before a culturally imperialistic Christianity and of fundamentalist trends among religions," asks Labayen, "'To whom does God Belong?'" What is the true role of religions, of the Church amid diverse faiths, cultures and peoples? He finds answers in the incarnation in particular: supplying the common bond of humanity, beyond the conditioning of culture and situation, and revealing the "power of the human spirit and the human heart." Our humanity, he believes, is the place of creation and redemption, which "is the way of the Incarnation ... the way of the human ... the way of Inculturation." Different faiths may have different terms for "one and the same ultimate end," yet in assuming our common humanity Jesus Christ offers the supreme "meeting-place of God and humankind ... a joint life of God's Spirit and the human spirit *in the flesh* ..." (1990).

In his principal writings, Labayen seeks to clarify the implication of this for the church and the faithful, especially in its call to become "the Church of the Poor." In the "signs of the times" we see the 'absence' and presence of God, and the Church of the Poor affirms that saving presence and bears testimony to it among God's people "through their solidary hope in struggle." Paradigm shifts that he sees to be necessary for the church, include those from being objects to becoming subjects of the history of salvation; from the God of Christians to the one god of all peoples; from salvation of peoples to salvation of the whole cosmos; from patriarchal culture to a culture of care and nurture (eco-feminism); from a re-ordering of relationships after a revolution, to a re-ordering now through people's participation in Basic Christian Communities and community organization; from reason alone to reason that listens to the human spirit. He has also written on the role of priests, religious and laity in BCCs.

Selected References
Works by Julio Labayen

 Religion and Emerging Peoples' (Political) Struggles in Asia. Bombay: BUILD, 1983.

 To be the Church of the Poor. 2nd. ed. Manila: Communications Foundation of Asia, 1987.

 Wisdom and Compassion: the Message of Buddhism and Christianity for our Times. Theology in the Third World. Manila: SPI, 1989.

 Spirituality: Challenge to the Church of the Poor Today. Theology in the Third World. Manila: SPI, 1990.

 Solidarity from an Asian Perspective. Theology in the Third World. Manila: SPI, 1990.

 The Call of the Church of the Poor. Challenge to Christians Today. The Church and Social Transformation. Theology in the Third World. Manila: SPI, 1991.

 Revolution and the Church of the Poor. Manila: SPI and Claretian, 1995.

 "The Role of the Priest in Social Action." *Impact* 2 (1967).

 "A Christian Understanding of Economic Priorities." *Japan Christian Quarterly*, Winter (1977).

 "Filipino Christian Spirituality and Social Action Today." *Philippine Priests' Forum* 10 (1978).

2.5.5. Francisco F. Claver sj (1929-)

Francisco Claver was born in Bontoc, Mountain Province, and studied at Ateneo de Manila University and the University of Colorado (PhD 1973). He became Bishop of Malaybalay, Bukidnon (1969-1984), and later Bishop of North Quezon City (1991). He has taught at the East Asian Pastoral Institute, and is now bishop of the apostolic vicariate of Bontoc-Lagawe. Strongly influenced by the Second Vatican Council, he has often been a prophetic voice in the Philippines, despite government restrictions under martial law. (See for example, his weekly *Pastoral Letters* 1976-1978). Throughout his ministries he has given priority to the issues of social justice, human community, and to Basic Christian Communities as the key model for pastoral renewal and sustenance and for social change.

Claver applies theology directly to actual pastoral situations, in guidelines for forming Christian communities, for dialogue, for participation and co-responsibility for community-building, and even for land and income redistribution. He also presents methods for inculturation and pastoral action and committed active non-violence. Theology here, he affirms, requires reflection and discernment in a Jesus-like spirituality. To be contextual, it requires not only an "analysis of situations," cultural, socio-political - the people's whole social reality - it also requires an interpretation of faith values "in faith, with faith," using the sources of faith in order to strive for revolutionary change without violence, for forgiveness and reconciliation, and for holistic spirituality. So there is to be "a faith-justice pastoral" where people, becoming more just themselves, are the measure; and "a faith-justice method" by which activists, oppressors and victims become, in the process, more fully human. As found in the gospels, this is based on social discernment ("signs of times"). It lives out the paschal mystery through non-violence.

He therefore comes to a theology of the local church which is totally immersed in the life of the people, with the Catholic Church as a participatory communion of local churches which includes Basic Christian Communities and Pastoral Conferences. Both pastoral ministry and processes of inculturation and social transformation come, for him, from this participation - within the church, and of church within the life of people. In present history, the Church is thus to be with people in their struggles, suffering with them, vulnerable with them, and in the more difficult work of reconstruction. Yet restructuring society requires a corresponding reorientation of cultural values for lasting social change. The whole country, he declares, must become a "huge and voluntary re-education camp, taught by the people themselves ...," in the spirit of people power and people compassion. This is to be done by peaceful persuasion and free acceptance, *lakas-awa* (compassionate force), and to be carried into the social sphere for a "transmuting of the Filipino soul into a more and more authentic form of itself."

Selected References
Works by Francisco F. Claver

　　The Stones will Cry Out: Grassroots Pastorals. Maryknoll, NY: Orbis Books, 1978.
　　The Church and Revolution. Human Society 46. Manila: Human Development Research and Documentation, 1986.
　　Social Discernment and Theological Reflection. Human Society 53. Manila: Human Development Research and Documentation, 1988.
　　The Church in the Political Arena. Pulso Monographs 5. Manila: Pulso, 1991.
　　"Bukidnon Theory and Praxis: Beyond Ideology." In *The Philippines Today: Christian Faith, Ideologies ... Marxism.* Loyola Papers 10. Manila: Loyola School of Theology, 1978.
　　"Evolution of Theology in Asia." *IMCS Reprints*, Jan. 1980.
　　"Prophecy or Accommodation - The Dilemma of a Discerning Church." *Month* 13 (1980).
　　"Who's Afraid of Basic Christian Communities?" *Solidarity* 95 (1983).
　　"Cultural Analysis: Towards Social Change." *Pulso* 1 (1984).
　　"The Philippine Revolution a Year After." *Vidyajyoti* 51 (1987).
　　"People Power and Value Transformation: A Faith Perspective." In *Towards a Theology of People Power: Reflections on the Philippine February Phenomenon*, edited by D.J. Elwood. Quezon City: New Day Publishers, 1988, 49-61.
　　"Personal Thoughts on the Asian Synod." *EAPR* 35 (1998).

Fitzpatrick, Mary T. *The Theology of the Local Church in the Writings of Bishop Francisco F. Claver, S.J., 1972-90.* Manila: De La Salle University, 1993.

2.5.6. Peter G. Gowing (1930-1983)

Peter Gowing gained degrees in arts, theology (DTh Boston University) and in social science and Asian studies (PhD Syracuse University), and was an ordained minister of the UCCP. He taught at Silliman University, Dumaguete, for 11 years and was first director of Asian studies there. Following three years as regional professor for SEAGST, he was co-founder and first director of the Dansalan Research Center in Marawi City (1974-1983). His writings include studies of Philippine church history and of acculturation, with his chief works dealing with the history, beliefs and aspirations of Muslim Filipinos. Along with those listed below, he wrote articles on Christianity in the Philippines, Christian-Muslim understanding here, church and state in the early US period, and Moro responses to the US regime.

In early writings (1964), Gowing aimed to assist understanding of the challenge presented by Filipino Islam to Christian work and to expose false images so that new attitudes could be formed. He then undertook further studies and edited and wrote works in which he sought to analyze the causes of continuing conflict and consider the steps possible for "conciliation and national unity." In a major work, *Muslim-Filipinos: Heritage and Horizon* (1979), he presents a full study of Moro culture and religion, considers the options between "integration and secession," and outlines possible futures and objectives in Muslim-Christian relations. Along with tasks ahead he sees for Muslims chiefly to accept themselves as Filipinos, the tasks for Christians are those of much greater understanding and tolerance, employing the law and development programs to protect and enhance the livelihood, education and traditions of Muslims, and working towards some measure of genuine autonomy for Muslim provinces in the Philippines. Gowing's theology of Christian mission, throughout this and other volumes, remains one of servanthood, repentance and renewal, and of unconditional acceptance of others while being committed to the fullest human welfare of all in the communities of the south. See also Gomez 2.5.17.

Selected References
Works by Peter Gowing
  Mosque and Moro. A Study of Moslems in the Philippines. Manila: Federation of Christian Churches, 1964.
  Islands under the Cross; the Story of the Church in the Philippines. Manila: NCCP, 1967.
  Past and Present Postures in Christian-Muslim Relations in Insular Southeast Asia. Marawi City: Dansalan Research Center of Dansalan College, 1975.
  Muslim-Filipinos: Heritage and Horizon. Quezon City: New Day Publishers, 1979.
  "Resurgent Islam and the Moro problem in the Philippines." *SEAJT* 4.1 (1962).
  "Christians and Moros: the Confrontation of Christianity and Islam in the Philippines." *SEAJT* 10.2 & 3 (1969)
  "Muslim Filipinos between Integration and Secession." *SEAJT* 14.2 (1973).
  "Past and Present Postures in Christian-Muslim Relations in Insular Southeast Asia." *SEAJT* 18.1 (1977).
  —, ed. *Understanding Islam and Muslims in the Philippines.* Quezon City: New Day Publishers, 1988.
  —, and William Henry Scott, eds. *Acculturation in the Philippines; Essays on Changing Societies. A Selection of Papers Presented at the Baguio Religious Acculturation Conferences from 1958 to 1968.* Quezon City: New Day Publishers, 1971.

2.5.7. Virginia Fabella mm

Virginia Fabella has played a key role in the initiation and nurture of Asian theology, particularly through the programs and publications of EATWOT, its Women's Commission and the AWRCCT. She has taught in a women's college in Manila, has been a director of the Maryknoll Sisters' Mission Institute in New York and academic dean of the Institute of Formation and Religious Studies of the Philippines. She has been particularly concerned for a "progressive growth in the corporate theological consciousness of EATWOT women, from a limited male-defined liberation viewpoint to a more inclusive women's liberation perspective."

Much of Fabella's writing appears in the volumes she has written or jointly edited for EATWOT, for Orbis Books and for the AWRC. In these she presents liberation as a freedom from all bondage, especially androcentric practices in both society and church, along with "the imaginative construction of new relationships among human beings as well as ... with the earth." Contextual theologies which take this seriously, she affirms, involve serious analysis of people's actual situations, recognize both traditional culture and contemporary social struggles, draw on the transforming power of the Gospel, and seek the radical change of unjust structures and practices. This requires, however, strong critiques of the church's practices, recognition of the particular sufferings, and potentialities, of (especially) Asian women, a recovery of Mary as model of womanhood, and the following of new ministries, coalitions and forms of theology. In this theology there must be brought together an "experiential understanding" of "Asian-ness" and of "woman-ness", and studies of the ways in which "patriarchy has penetrated our cultural and religious structures and traditions ... the fabric of our daily life." There must also be a re-reading of the Bible as aware women. Without such theology, the central realities of Christian faith will be only half understood, Fabella believes.

Selected References
Works by Virginia Fabella
> *Beyond Bonding: a Third World Women's Theological Journey.* Manila: EATWOT and the Institute of Women's Studies, 1994.
> "Emerging Third World Theologies." *Kalinangan* 3 (1983).
> "Mission of Women in the Church in Asia: Role and Position." *In God's Image* Dec (1985)/Feb (1986).
> "Asian Women and Christology." *In God's Image* Sept. (1987).
> "Spirituality for Life: Women Struggle against Violence." *In God's Image* 12.3 (1993).
> —, ed. *Asia's Struggle for Full Humanity.* Maryknoll, NY: Orbis Books, 1980.
> —, and Sergio Torres, eds. *The Emergent Gospel: Theology from the Underside of History: papers from the Ecumenical*

Dialogue of Third World Theologians, Dar es Salaam, August 5-12, 1976. Maryknoll, NY: Orbis Books, 1978.

—, and Sergio Torres, eds. *Irruption of the Third World: Challenge to Theology*. Maryknoll, NY: Orbis Books, 1983.

—, and Mercy Amba Oduyoye, eds. *With Passion and Compassion: Third World Women Doing Theology: Reflections from the Women's Commission of the Ecumenical Association of Third World Theologians*. Maryknoll, NY: Orbis Books, 1988.

—, and Sun Ai Lee Park. *We Dare To Dream: Doing Theology As Asian Women*. Maryknoll, NY: Orbis Books, 1989.

—, Peter K.H.Lee and David Kwang-sun Suh, eds. *Asian Christian Spirituality: Reclaiming Traditions*. Maryknoll, NY: Orbis Books, 1992.

—, and R.S. Sugirtharajah, eds. *Dictionary of Third World Theologies*. Maryknoll, NY: Orbis Books, 2000.

2.5.8. Carlos Abesamis sj (1934-)

Abesamis has long been a creative Filipino scripture scholar, both in New Testament studies and in reconstructing the theologies of salvation, of Jesus Christ, of discipleship and of "heavenly" life. With strong commitment to working for personal and social transformation here and now - with special concern for poor and victimized people and in constant dialogue with them - he has developed a Filipino liberative theology and widely influenced the doing of contextual theology throughout the region and beyond. For Abesamis, the central message of the Gospel is that of a kingdom of justice and love to be built, not in another life, but in this life. Total salvation has a primarily historical reality, which can be recovered especially within the life of Asia's poor peoples. Contextual theology therefore commits itself to the proclamation of Jesus Christ, who is necessarily an Asian, at home in a world of pluralistic faiths, and offering a concrete alternative to "the unending demolition of poor people's shanties and the disenfranchisement of farmers from their lands in favor of golf courses." Such a theology engages in deconstructing old stories, weaving new narratives, and in challenging readers to go beyond their comfortable assumptions. It also recognizes the role of cosmic spirituality, of genuine religiosity in other living faiths, and in the struggles of the poor.

In his major work, *A Third Look at Jesus*, Abesamis presents the alternative Jesus as seen in continuity with Jesus' understanding of himself, and with the view of Jesus by and through the eyes of the poor people of the Third World: the "Third Look." The "Second Look at Jesus" is that of the Greeks, the Romans and the West since 50 CE, which is only a distant relative to Jesus' own self-understanding. Structured around a journey towards new understanding, the book discusses "concepts that need rethinking if one seeks to rediscover the story of Jesus and his mission." In other writings Abesamis has outlined the methods and tools by which the Bible can be re-read, and those by which a genuine Filipino theology can be constructed.

Selected References
Works by Carlos Abesamis
    Salvation - Historical and Total. Quezon City: JMC Press, 1978.
    Where are we going: Heaven or new world? Manila: Foundation Books, 1983.
    Exploring the Core of Biblical Faith. "A Catechetical Primer." Quezon City: Claretian, 1986.
    The Mission of Jesus and Good News to the Poor. Quezon City: Claretian, 1987.
    Ganoon Pala. A series of biblico-catechetical leaflets. Visayan translation: Ah Mao Diay. Quezon City: SPI, 1989.
    What is Inside the Wooden Bowl? (Ano Po ang Laman ng Mangkok?) Or: How Not To Move Towards a Contextual Theology. Manila: SPI, 1997; *CTC Bulletin* 15.1 (1998).
    A Third Look at Jesus: A Guidebook Along a Road Less Traveled. Quezon City: Claretian, 1999.
    What is in it for Mr and Mrs Pobre? The Jubilee Year and the Sabbatical Year of the Bible. SPI Series. Manila: SPI, 1999.
    "Doing Theology in a Philippine Context." In *The Emergent Gospel: Theology From the Underside of History: Papers From the Ecumenical Dialogue of Third World Theologians, Dar es Salaam, August 5-12, 1976*, edited by Virginia Fabella and Sergio Torres. Maryknoll, NY: Orbis Books, 1978.
    "Faith and Life Reflections from the Grassroots in the Philippines." In *Asia's Struggle for Full Humanity: Towards a Relevant Theology: papers from the Asian Theological Conference,*

January 7-20, 1979, Wennappuwa, Sri Lanka, edited by Virginia Fabella. Maryknoll, NY: Orbis Books, 1980, 123-129.

"Mark and the New World." In *Doing Theology with People's Movements in Asia. ATESEA Occasional Papers* 3, edited by Yeow Choo Lak and John C. England. Singapore: ATESEA/PTCA, 1986.

"Immersion in the Life and Struggle of the Poor (Some Theological Observations)." *Voices in the Third World* 10.3 (1987).

"Some Paradigms in Re-Reading the Bible in a Third-World Setting." *Mission Studies*, 17.1 (1990).

2.5.9. Leonardo N. Mercado svd (1935-)

Leonardo N. Mercado has pioneered in the study of Filipino philosophy, Filipino theology and of missiology, especially inter-religious dialogue, and has published books in all these areas. Following studies in Manila and Rome he taught at seminaries in Tagaytay City, Palo, Leyte, Vigan, Ilocos Sur, Manila, and in universities at Manila, and at Tacloban, where he was president. Mission exposure in Papua, New Guinea, prepared him for his assignment as coordinator of missiological education studies and research for the Divine Word Missionaries in the Philippines. He is chairman of the Asian Conference on Religion and Peace (Philippines), and currently the executive secretary of the Episcopal Commission for Inter-religious Dialogue, CBCP.

In many writings, Mercado has explored the elements, sources and methods of Filipino theology, and made particular contribution to the related studies of Filipino philosophy, psychology and traditional religion. In his major work on Filipino theology (1975), he moves from a study of basic Filipino ideas on religion to Filipino virtues in response to these, and then to the cultural symbolism and worship which expresses the fundamental spirit of harmony in every part of life. In a later work on inculturation (1992), he concludes with reflections on the historical, communal and cultic faces of the Filipino Christ, which he regards as central for Filipino theology. Regarding the central task of Filipino theology now, he believes that Filipino theologians who have been formed in western categories have to be re-rooted in their Filipino world view,

Contextual Theology in the Philippines 1800-2000

especially to be familiar with indigenous categories. Such categories must then be applied to pressing issues such as those which concern the four inter-related dialogues which are now necessary: with cultures, with non-Christian religions, with the poor and oppressed, and with the environment.

Selected References
Works by Leonardo N. Mercado
> *Elements of Filipino Theology.* Tacloban City: Divine Word University, 1975.
> *Elements of Filipino Ethics.* Tacloban City: Divine Word University, 1979.
> *Christ in the Philippines.* Tacloban City: Divine Word University, 1981.
> *Inculturation and Filipino Theology.* Manila: Divine Word University, 1992.
> *Spirituality on Creation According to Selected Philippine Indigenous Peoples.* Manila: Logos Publications, 1998.
> *From Pagans to Partners: The Change in Catholic Attitudes towards Traditional Religion.* Manila: Logos Publications, 2000.
> —, ed. *Filipino Religious Experience and Non-Biblical Revelation.* Manila: Divine Word Publications, 1992.
> —, ed. *Doing Filipino Theology.* Manila: Logos Publications, 1996.
> —, ed. *Experiencing the Spirit in the Faith-Culture of Kalinga. Proceedings of the Kalinga-Christian Dialogue 1998.* Philippine Inter-religious Dialogue 3. Manila: Logos Publications, 1999.
> —, ed. *Filipino Popular Devotions: The Interior Dialogue Between Traditional Religion and Christianity.* Manila: Logos Publications, 2000.
> —, and James Knight, eds. *Mission and Dialogue: Theory and Practice.* Manila: Divine Word University, 1988.
> —, and Michael T. Seigel, eds. *Towards an Asian Theology of Mission.* Manila: Divine Word University, 1995.

2.5.10. Lydia Nazario Niguidula

Lydia Niguidula has been a Christian educator, writer-enabler, ritual maker, feminist theologian and pastor of the UCCP. She has also taught in seminary and university (Silliman University), held local church pastorates, and exercised national and ecumenical leadership. In the 1970s and 1980s she was adviser to College Student Ministries (CSM) and in the 1990s, executive secretary in the Christian Education and Nurture Cluster of the UCCP. She has also edited *Liturgical Resources* for the UCCP.

Niguidula's experience as Christian educator, liturgist and theologian has enabled her to contribute over many years to pastoral theology and theological education which is experience-based, and renewal-oriented, and which stresses the role of field exposures and participatory educational process. She has also been concerned for setting this within church history, and for its celebration in renewed worship, along with the role and awareness of women in ministry and theology. Her writings therefore include studies of Reformed tradition, and of major Christian doctrines, feminist and educational studies, along with compilations of liturgies with brief historical background and biblical foundation. Her approach to worship and teaching is thus rooted in Christian tradition but also includes "openness to the world [and] openness to change." She has recently been cited for "blazing new trails in women's consciousness, liturgical renewal and transformation of faith communities."

Selected References
Works by Lydia Niguidula
- *The Shaping of Pastoral Theology in Philippine Theological Schools*. Boston: Boston University School of Theology, 1970.
- *Handbook for Christian Worship Celebration*. Quezon City: New Day Publishers, 1975.
- *The Heritage of the People of God*. Dumaguete City: Silliman University, 1977.
- "Field Education as a Process for Professional Theological Education." In *The Shape of Theological Education and Role of Field Experience in the 70s*, edited by Ciriaco Ma. Lagunzad Jr. Manila: Interseminary Program for Field Education, ?1971.
- "Women in Theology Revolutionising Liturgy." *CTC Bulletin* 4.3 (1982).
- "Problems and New Approaches in Mission and Evangelism." *Tugon* 3.2 (1982).

"Values Education from the Perspective of the NCCP." *Impact* 21.12 (1986).
"Four women." *Sunday Inquirer Magazine* 9.2 (1994).
"Women's Use of Power in Priesthood and Ministry." *In God's Image* 16.1 (1997).
"Reinterpreting the Creation Stories." *In God's Image* 16.3 (1997).
—, ed. *Mary, the Mother of Jesus.* Faith and Order Series 4. Quezon City: UCCP, 1993.
—, et al. *Being Reformed Christians in Asia Today*, edited by Yeow Choo Lak and Henry Wilson. Singapore: ATESEA, 1994.

2.5.11. Emerito P. Nacpil

Emerito P. Nacpil has been resident bishop in the Manila area for the United Methodist Church. He holds a PhD in systematic theology and the philosophy of religion from Drew University, Madison, New Jersey, and has also served as professor of theology at the Union Theological Seminary in Dasmariñas, Cavite. He earlier contributed to regional theological programs of the EACC and was director of ATESEA.

In earlier writings Nacpil has considered the challenge of secularization, politics and religion, and the relationship between processes of modernization and mission. He here concludes that the church must affirm the secular world, demystify its own language, structures and institutions in secular terms, and also exercise prophetic criticism upon secularism as an ideology. Regarding modernization, he places this within the inclusive perspective of God's mission which is larger than both the modernization process and the mission of the church, to which it is prior. The *missio dei* embraces creation, reconciliation and fulfillment for the church, humankind and the world. In writing of the Gospel for the new Filipino, Nacpil recognizes theological dimensions of Filipino aspirations, although in recent decades he has often opposed more contextual theologies.

In recent writings, such as *Jesus' Strategy for Social Transformation* (1999), he describes changes in Jewish society that Jesus sought to bring about, in the foundation of society, in people, in social structure, and in the formation of a new community. Based on Jesus' strategy for social transformation, the book offers a model of lay ministry for social reform in today's world, including a sharing in the vision of Jesus for society, in disciple-making and in the reform of social structure. For Nacpil, such ministry is not to be "an activity of the church through which it expresses its witness and service" to perpetuate itself. Rather, it is the means by which the church participates in the "mission which is prior in order and dignity to the church."

Selected References
Works by Emerito P. Nacpil
> *Mission and Change.* Manila: EACC, 1968.
> *Jesus' Strategy for Social Transformation.* Manila: United Methodist Church, 1998.
> "History and Theology Today." *SEAJT* 4.1 (1963).
> "Theological Education in a Changing Society - Some pointers and Indications." *SEAJT* 9.4 (1968).
> "Between Promise and Fulfillment." *SEAJT* 10.2&3 (1969).
> "In No Other Name" and "Whom does the Missionary Serve?" In *Sambayan '71: From Bondage to Liberation.* n.l. n.p., 1971.
> "Mission and Modernization." In *The Asian Meaning of Modernization,* edited by Saral K. Chatterji. Delhi: ISPCK, 1972.
> "Philippines: A Gospel for the New Filipino." In *Asian Voices in Christian Theology,* edited by G.H. Anderson. Maryknoll, NY: Orbis Books, 1976.
> "The Critical Asian Principle." and "Mission and Modernization." In *What Asian Christians are Thinking,* edited by Douglas J. Elwood. Quezon City: New Day Publishers, 1976.
> "Unity in Christ: A New Creation." *Tugon* 3 (1987).
> "Rethinking Ministry for a New Century." *Quarterly Review* 20.4 (2000).
> —, with Douglas Elwood, eds. *The Human and the Holy: Asian Perspectives in Christian Theology.* Quezon City, New Day Publishers, 1978.

2.5.12. Mariano C. Apilado (1936-)
Mariano Apilado gained his PhD from Vanderbuilt University Divinity School and is currently president of Union Theological Seminary, Dasmariñas, Cavite. He has been pastor to local churches

in North Central Luzon, to Cosmopolitan Church, Manila, and as chaplain of Silliman University. He has also served as Philippine area dean of the SEAGST; as president of Union Christian College in San Fernando City, La Union; and has held leading positions in councils of the UCCP. Amongst his earlier concerns was the compilation of bibliography for Asian theological writings.

The main sources for Apilado's work and thought are found in two principal books. In *Revolutionary Spirituality* (1999) he explores the inter-related questions of Protestant involvement in the abuses of colonialism in the Philippines, Protestant witness as prophets of a new order to guarantee liberation and self-assertion for development, and Protestant articulation of a new faith that included the goals of "national self-awareness and general betterment." What begins as a search by the author for his "identity and authenticity" as a Filipino and a Christian, becomes a comprehensive account of the Protestant role in the US's colonial rule in the Philippines, including analysis of the laborious efforts to bridge the diversities among early evangelical groups. In the sequel, *The Dream Need Not Die* (2000), he affirms that doing theology of struggle in the Philippines is doing theology in transit, a reflection upon "the struggle of the Filipino people towards the sublime ... and the humane of a people in community." He stresses the importance of remembering and storytelling as a unique way of doing theology of struggle within a community and discusses the tool, the task and the goal of a theology of struggle and revolutionary spirituality. Here he draws on biblical paradigms and presents three related schemes for methodology: "Faith: fulfilling the past"; "Hope: remembering the future"; and "Love: doing the present." These then lead on to "doing revolutionary spirituality persistently."

Selected References
Works by Mariano Apilado
> *Revolutionary Spirituality: A Study of the Protestant Role in the American Colonial Rule of the Philippines, 1898-1928.* Quezon City: New Day Publishers, 1999.
> *The Dream Need Not Die. Revolutionary Spirituality* 2. Quezon City: New Day Publishers, 2000.

"The Groaning of Life and Creation." *NCCP Magazine* 34.2 (1994).

"Why Theologians Tell Stories: Or Personal Notes Shared with a Special Friend." Report of a Consultation. *Asia Journal of Theology* 9.2 (1995).

"The United Church of Christ in the Philippines: Historical and Theological Essay." *Asia Journal of Theology* 10.1 (1996).

2.5.13. Mary John Mananzan osb (1937-)

Sr. Mary John Mananzan is a Missionary Benedictine Sister, currently the president of St. Scholastica's College, Manila. After obtaining advanced degrees in Rome and Münster, she has been actively involved in charting new paths in the academe, identifying with concerns of the masses, especially women, and in developing a distinct Third World theology. She has given birth to many women-centered programs, among which are the Institute of Women's Studies (IWS), the Women Ecology and Wholeness Farm, and the Women Crisis Center. She has been the national chairperson of GABRIELA, a broad alliance of women's organizations, for 15 years, has had leading roles in EATWOT, including convenorship of the Women's Commission (1983-1987) and has consistently pushed for a theology with a women's perspective. The commission has stimulated gender perspective in theologizing and initiated dialogues with both 'Third' and 'First' World theologians as well. The fruit of this dialogue is a book entitled *Women Resisting Violence: Spirituality for Life* (1996).

In her writings, Mananzan has included studies of Philippine church history in the Spanish period, of spirituality and the religious life, and of Christology and biblical sources. But her major work has focused upon the concerns and contribution of women - in Church, in theology and in social transformation. Here she provides in many writings not only theoretical framework and social analysis, but also reflective insight and theological construction, within both the Filipino and Asian contexts. Integral spirituality, social action and evangelization demands, she believes, "a life of prayer 'invaded' by the anguish of people ... an asceticism committed to justice," along with a "Church of the poor" and full participation in the necessary people's revolution.

Comprehensive renewal therefore also includes critical reinterpretation of scripture by women, and "fundamental questioning" of the church's hierarchical structures and discriminatory practices. Mananzan has published articles in many books and journals, including *Concilium, Review for Religious, NCCP Magazine, Lumen Vitae, Voices from the Third World,* and *International Review of Mission.* She has written three books for the Integral Evangelization Series: *Bible on Justice; Salvation: Historical and Total; There Shall be No Poor among You* (1978-1979), is a contributor to the *Dictionary of Third World Theologies* (Orbis Books, 2000) and is currently giving lectures and seminars in ecofeminist-creation-centered spirituality.

Selected References
Works by Mary John Mananzan
- *Woman Question in the Philippines.* Manila: IWS, St. Scholastica's College, 1997.
- *Challenges to the Inner Room.* Manila: IWS, St. Scholastica's College, 1999.
- "Who is Jesus Christ?" *Voices from the 3rd World.* (1988).
- "The Spanish Expansion and Christianity in Asia." In *Western Colonialism in Asia and Christianity,* edited by M.D. David. Bombay: Himalaya Publishing, 1988.
- "Redefining Religious Commitment in Philippine Context." In *We Dare to Dream,* edited by Virginia Fabella and Sun Ai Lee Park. Hongkong: AWRC, 1989.
- "Theological Perspectives of a Religious Woman Today." In *The Future of Liberation Theology: Essays in Honor of Gustavo Gutierrez,* edited by Marc H. Ellis and Otto Maduro. Maryknoll, NY: Orbis Books, 1989.
- "Feminist Theology in Asia. A Ten Year's Overview." *In God's Image* 14.3 (1995).
- "Towards an Asian Principle of Interpretation: A Filipino Woman's Experience." In *To be Fully Human; Women's Theologies.* Manila: EATWOT, 1998.
- —, et al., eds. *Women Resisting Violence: Spirituality for Life.* Manila: IWS, St. Scholastica's College; Maryknoll, NY: Orbis Books, 1996.
- —, ed. *Essays on Women.* Manila, IWS, St. Scholastica's College, 1987.

—, ed. *The Asian Women: Image and Status.* Singapore: CCA, 1988.
—, ed. *Women and Religion, A Collection of Essays, Personal Histories, and Contextualized Liturgies.* Manila, St. Scholastica's College, 1988. (3rd. Ed. 1999.)
—, ed. *"Sarilaya" Women in Arts and Media.* Manila: IWS, St. Scholastica's College, 1990.
—, ed. *Biblico Theological Reflections.* Manila: EATWOT, 2000.

2.5.14. Kathleen Coyle (1937-)

Kathleen Coyle is an Irish Columban Sister, a faculty member of the East Asian Pastoral Institute, Manila, and Editor of the EAPR. She also lectures at Maryhill School of Theology and the Institute of Formation and Religious Studies in Manila. She has published articles and books on mariology in contemporary perspective as well as on mission theology, ecology and on issues for women in church and theology.

Coyle's perspective in her writings is that of liberation and feminist theology, based on full study of the Bible and tradition. She is critical of excesses in Marian piety, finding the reasons for her divinization largely in patriarchal culture, and also of patristic contrasts between Eve and Mary. Mary emerges from these studies - and especially from the Lukan and Johannine material - as an independent and autonomous woman, and particularly in her "Song," the Magnificat, the model of a disciple of Jesus Christ serving the reign of God. Coyle also explores in some of her writings, new ways of doing and sharing theology which are more adequate to the concerns and capacities of women in church and society today.

Selected References
Works by Kathleen Coyle
> *Mary in the Christian Tradition: From a Contemporary Perspective.* Manila: Divine Word Publications, 1993 (Rev. ed. 1998).
> "Women in the Church." *EAPR* 23.3 (1986).
> "Marian Theology Today: Reinterpreting the Symbols." *EAPR* 26 (1989).
> "Tradition, Theology and Women in the Churches." *Asia Journal of Theology* 4.1 (1990).

"A theological reflection on Genesis 3." *EAPR* 27.1 (1990).
"Original Sin - Residue of Some Primal Crime?" *Doctrine & Life* 43 (1993).
"Reflection on a Theology of Mission: Insights for the Journey." *EAPR* 30 (1993).
"Renewing the Face of the Earth." *Asia Journal of Theology* 7.1 (1993).
"The Marian Tradition: a Rereading." *EAPR* 35.3/4 (1998).
"Mary Proto-disciple: A Lukan perspective." *EAPR* 35 (1998).
"Feminist Theology in Conversation." *EAPR* 36.3 (1999).

2.5.15. Pedro V. Salgado op (1937-)

Pedro Salgado obtained the PhD and LSth degrees and has taught at both the University of Santo Tomas, Manila, and at Philippine Dominican Center of Institutional Studies, Quezon City. He then worked with poor peasants in the municipalities of Soliven (1977-1982), Albano (1982-1985) and Santo Tomas (1995-). Teaching assignments in social philosophy and Marxism have continued, and his writings have included historical and sociological studies, along with writings on priesthood, biblical teachings and spirituality.

A major theological focus for Salgado has been the relationship of Christian faith to revolution. In *Christianity is Revolutionary* (1976), he expounds the revolutionary theology of the Bible and in the teachings of the Roman Catholic Church, demonstrating that God's concern is clearly also for people's material well-being and that faithful service to God is measured by this. He also argues for socio-economic justice, for which violence (in the last resort) may be necessary in order to stop inhuman abuse of the poor. For Christ is "a revolutionary figure," who struggled to uplift the downtrodden, and the church, worship and sacraments are therefore also to be revolutionary. In a later critique of the "new society" of Marcos under martial law, and in response to the CBCP's *Exhortation against Violence*, Salgado also gives detailed economic analysis as the basis for the necessary revolution, which in the last resort may require a mass uprising.

More recently he has published further studies of the spirituality which sustains the struggle for liberation. He contrasts the struggling spirituality of Jesus with the "spirituality of evasion" which ignores temporal conditions, and with patterns of Marian devotion which merely confirm the status quo. The essence of the religious life is for Salgado the service of God in God's poor within the temporal world which is being renewed by God. This will require purification, even the "dark night of the soul" and the intuitive vision and wisdom that comes from the unity of contemplation and action. He also presents the resources for this spirituality-in-struggle, in a re-interpretation of the classic religious vows, and in a full study of Christ-like prayer.

Selected References
Works by Pedro V. Salgado
    Christianity is Revolutionary. Quezon City: Garcia, 1976.
    Cory Aquino, Militarization and Other Essays. Quezon City. Garcia, c1986.
    Essays. Manila: Salgado, 1989.
    Essays on the Bases: Spirituality of Liberation. Quezon City: NCCP, 1989.
    Essays on Spirituality. Manila, Lucky Press, 1996.
    "Catholic Educational Association of the Philippines." *Philippiniana Sacra* 1.2 (1966).
    "The Truth on Teillard de Chardin." *Philippiniana Sacra* 3.7 (1968).
    "The Church and Social Involvement." *Philippine Priests' Forum,* June (1973).
    "To Worship is to Enter Politics." *Philippine Priests' Forum,* Sept (1975).
    "Revolution and the Church." In *With Raging Hope.* SPI Series 1. 2nd. ed. Manila: SPI, 1985.
    "Labor: A Historical Perspective." *Kalinangan,* June (1989).
    "Church and Violence: Philippine Experience." *CTC Bulletin* 10.1 (1991).

2.5.16. Lode Wostyn (1937-)

Lode Wostyn studied at the University of Louvain, at the study center of the CICM Missionaries in Louvain, and at the Facultés Catholiques de Lyon (STD 1968). He has taught systematic theology at San Carlos Seminary, Manila (1970-1972) and at Maryhill School of Theology, Manila (1972-1994) as well as at other theological schools in the USA and in the Philippines. He has collaborated closely in writing with Filipino colleagues such as José de Mesa, and some of his books are used as textbooks in theology courses in the Philippines. He later became director of the Institute of Philosophy and Religion, Saint Louis University.

Wostyn's theological emphases have included the development of alternative methods for the doing of theology in the life of Filipinos today, arising from the mutual interaction between transmitted Christian experience and the actual human situation. The hermeneutic necessarily proceeds from human experience; to "ideological suspicion" of our socio-cultural and historical structures, *and* of theology; then to new theological study which includes "exegetical suspicion"; which leads to re-interpretation of Bible, faith and Christian life. Such methods are fully elaborated, along with careful historical and biblical study, and are applied by Wostyn - often in cooperative works - to the reconstruction of Christology, ecclesiology and to catechesis in the Philippines.

Selected References
Works by Lode Wostyn
> *Doing Ecclesiology. Church and Mission Today*. Quezon City: Claretian, 1990.
> *Church: Pilgrim Community of Disciples*. Quezon City: Claretian, 1995.
> *A New Church for a New Age*. Quezon City: Claretian, 1997.
> "An Emerging Philippine Liberation Theology." *Japan Missionary Bulletin* 41.2 (1987).
> "Paradigm Change in Theology." *MST Review* 1.2 (1997).
> "The Filipino Conscience: Some Historical Indices." *DIWA* 23.1 (1998).
> "Jesus and the Culture of the Holy." *DIWA* 23.2 (1998).
> "The Catechism for Filipino Catholics: Some Considerations." *MST Review* 2.2 (1999).
> —, with José de Mesa. *Doing Theology. Basic Realities and Processes*. Quezon City: Maryhill School of Theology, 1982. Rev. ed. Quezon City: Claretian, 1990.
> —, with José de Mesa. *Doing Christology. The Re-Appropriation of a Tradition*. Quezon City: Claretian, 1989.

2.5.17. Hilario Gomez, Jr.

Hilario Gomez, Jr. obtained the degrees of MTh (SEAGST, 1969) and PhD in church and society, Princeton Theological Seminary (1977). He was formerly professor of the history of religion and Christian mission at Union Theological Seminary, Cavite (1977-1988), general secretary (1994-1998) of the UCCP, and chairperson of the NCCP. He also directed the Inter-Seminary Christian-Muslim Dialogue Program of the major seminaries of member-churches of the NCCP. He is currently co-convenor of the Bishops-Ulama Forum, an inter-faith organization composed of Roman Catholic and Protestant Bishops in Mindanao and the Muslim religious scholars of the Ulama League of the Philippines.

Gomez has long studied both the teachings and development of Islam and the particular history of Muslims in the Philippines. In a major study of the Moros of Mindanao (2000), Gomez provides a full history of their life and experience, along with the issues of "Christian-Muslim relations or, more exactly, Moro and non-Moro conflicts." The book answers the questions concerning the genesis and nature of the war still being waged by the Moro (Muslim) rebels against the Philippine government. In other writings Gomez has considered Christian approaches to the Filipino Muslim, Philippine socio-political conditions, issues of Muslim-Christian dialogue and Christian interpretation of Muslim beliefs. In portraying the Moro experience of Allah in their search for identity and social justice, he finds both a challenge to Christian theology and also meanings which "hopefully could deepen our faith in the God of Jesus." These include "the emphasis on *taqdir* as man's expression of the will of God," which has similarities to the message of Jesus in the Gospels; *amanah* as the trust of stewardship and responsibility for society; *zakat* and *puasa* as the tithe for the poor and readiness to suffer along with the hungry (see also Gowing 2.5.6.).

Selected References
Works by Hilario Gomez

> *The Moro Rebellion & the Search for Peace: A Study on Christian-Muslim Relations in the Philippines*. Zamboanga City: Silsilah Publications, 2000.

"A Christian Approach to the Filipino Muslim." *SEAJT* 13.1 (1972).

"Allah and the God of Jesus." In *Doing Theology with Religions of Asia,* edited by Yeow Choo Lak and John C. England. ATESEA Occasional Papers 4. Singapore: ATESEA/PTCA, 1986.

"Sources of Oppression in the Philippines." *Asia Journal of Theology* 1 (1987).

"Empowerment of People and Christian Mission." In *Towards a Theology of People Power: Reflections on the Philippine February Phenomenon,* edited by D.J. Elwood. Quezon City: New Day Publishers, 1988.

—, and Leomyr L. de Jesus, eds. *Commitment and Struggle: A Festschrift for Bishop Erme R. Camba.* Quezon City: UCCP, 1997.

2.5.18. Levi V. Oracion

Levi Oracion completed doctoral studies at the University of Chicago (DTh 1969) becoming dean of the School of Divinity, Silliman University, Dumaguete, and later president of Union Theological Seminary, Cavite. He has served the WCC (CCPD Office), been chairperson of the Institute of Religion and Culture, and now teaches again at Silliman University School of Divinity. He has long been concerned for the suffering of Filipino people under successive colonial and neo-colonial regimes along with the continuance of colonial mentalities in the churches. He is also concerned to develop the theologies of non-violence, struggle and liberation which will counter such mentalities.

For Oracion the basic theological theses are that "God is at work in our history"; "God identifies with the poor and takes up their cause"; and "that there is a perceptible dialectic of salvation that takes place in human history." Reflecting upon the history, experience and folk literature of the Filipino people he finds in these a continuing aspiration for just community life, often expressed in strongly nationalist movements for liberation. Such a history parallels key parts of the biblical story, which now requires of us that all action for socio-political change, all ideological involvement, be placed in an eschatological context, being judged and forgiven by God's liberating grace. To answer the question therefore as to how transformation is to come, "how is Jesus Christ to be made incarnate not only in our personal lives but also in the structures and forces that provide the dynamics and form of our societies?", Oracion presents a theology of struggle which moves from analysis of people's reality, to biblical reflection, to cooperative action, and to worship. This places the lives of Filipinos firmly in the setting of God's work and saving purpose. Yet he would also maintain that people's movements for justice are, though often unknowingly, "bearers of God's liberating grace,"and the struggle for justice itself can be genuinely transformative and purify the soul.

Selected References
Works by Levi Oracion

    Ideologies and People's Struggles for Justice, Freedom, and Peace: a Consultation Report. Geneva: WCC-CCPD 1989?

    Notes on Faith and Order. UCCP Study Series 1. Quezon City: UCCP, 1992.

    God with Us: Reflections on the Theology of Struggle in the Philippines. Dumaguete: Divinity School of Silliman University. Forthcoming.

    "A Theological perspective on Human Rights." *Wednesday Forum Journal* 1 (1979).

    "Living in Faith According to the Gospels. Four Bible Studies." In *Living in Faith. Report of the Asia Youth Resource Conference ... 1979*, edited by Soewarei Gadroen and Chris Tremewan. Singapore: CCA, 1980.

    "Religious Perspectives and the Social Imperatives of Education in the Philippines." *Tugon* 3.2 (1982).

    "How Emerging Theological Consciousness comes to Expression." *Kalinangan* 3.3 (1983).

    "People's Way out of the Nuclear Holocaust into Isaiah's Vision." *Kalinangan* 5.1 (1985).

    "Theological Reflections on Indarapatra and S. Sulayman." *East Asia Journal of Theology* 3.2 (1985).

    Ideologies and People's Struggles for Justice, Freedom, and Peace: a Consultation Report. Occasional Study pamphlet 2. Geneva: WCC, 1986.

    "Reflections on Ecclesiology in an Asian Context." *CTC Bulletin* 8.1&2 (1989).

    "Asian Theology in the Nineties: A Discussion Paper." *CTC Bulletin* 9.2 & 3 (1990).

2.5.19. Anscar Chupungco osb (1939-)

Anscar Chupungco gained his doctorate in liturgy at the Pontifical Institute of Liturgy (Rome 1970) and has been professor of liturgical inculturation at the Pontifical Institute of Liturgy and the Paul VI Institute of Liturgy (Philippines). He is currently president of San Beda College (Philippines). He has worked at different forms of liturgical inculturation for the Philippines, including the Eucharistic celebration and the rite of Christian marriage. Both are being used widely among Roman Catholics here.

Chupungco's work has for many years focused on Christian worship and the inculturation of liturgy. Formerly using such terms as indigenization, adaptation, contextualization, incarnation, and acculturation to express the relationship between culture and worship, under the influence of cultural anthropology he gradually came to use the term inculturation. This term expresses better, he writes, "the mutual integration that should take place when culture and worship interact." For him the inculturation of worship is basically a work of dynamic translation. "While pure creativity does not necessarily refer to existing liturgical text, symbol, or rite, inculturation requires them as the starting point for dynamic translation. Inculturation does not create a new liturgy but communicates its message through the local cultural medium of the worshiping assembly. In other words, inculturation preserves the liturgical tradition of the church at the same time that it hands it down in accord with the local congregation's cultural patterns, values, and institutions." He has constantly taken the mystery of the Incarnation as the basis of liturgical inculturation, believing it to be not merely a historical event (i.e. Christological), but also a continuing experience of the church (and therefore ecclesiological). "Thus, the church and its worship should be incarnated in a particular people in the same way that the Son of God was incarnated in the Jewish people."

Selected References
Works by Anscar Chupungco
> *Towards a Filipino Liturgy.* Manila: Bedan Research Foundation, 1976.

Cultural Adaptation of the Liturgy. New York: Paulist Press, 1982.
Liturgies of the Future. The Process and Methods of Inculturation. 2 vols. New York: Paulist Press, 1989.
Liturgical Inculturation. Sacramentals, Popular Religiosity, Catechesis. Collegeville: Liturgical Press, 1992.
Worship: Progress and Tradition. Washington: Paulist Press, 1995.
"Popular Religiosity and Liturgical Inculturation." *Ecclesia Orans* 8.1 (1991).
"Liturgical Inculturation in Multi-ethnic Churches." *Pastoral Music* (Feb.-Mar. 1993).
"Liturgical Inculturation and the Search for Unity." In *So We Believe, So We Pray. Toward Koinonia in Worship.* Geneva: LWF, 1995.
'Two Methods of Inculturation." In *Christian Worship: Unity in Cultural Diversity*, Lutheran World Federation Studies. Geneva: LWF, 1996.
"Ritual Language and Liturgy." In *Finding Voice to Give God Praise, Festschrift for G. Ostdiek*, 87-99. Collegeville: Liturgical Press, 1998.
"Liturgy and Inculturation." In *Handbook for Liturgical Studies*, vol. 2, 337-375. Collegeville: Liturgical Press, 1998.
"Baptism, Marriage, Healing, and Funerals: Principles and Criteria for Inculturation." In *Baptism, Rites of Passage, and Culture.* Lutheran Federation Studies. Geneva: LWF, 1999.

2.5.20. Louie G. Hechanova cssr (1940-)

Louie Hechanova took his first vows as a Redemptorist in 1957, and was ordained priest in 1962. Following studies in Manila, Bangalore and Rome (ThD), he taught theology in Ireland and the Philippines. But then "he allowed his heart to be seduced by the poor and immersed himself in the task of liberation." He will be best remembered by the sugar workers in Negros and the victims of human rights abuses because of his consistent advocacy and ministry with them. Hechanova, who was also a columnist in local and national papers, was elected to the General Council of the Redemptorists in Rome; was president of the AMRSP (1981-1985), and provincial superior of the Redemptorists of the Visayas and Mindanao in 1999.

For Hechanova, Christology, as with all Filipino theology, begins in confronting the actual - often destitute - life of the Filipino.

With colleagues and the faithful, he asked how can faith in a loving God and in the kingdom inaugurated in Jesus Christ "be reconciled with the harsh realities of life in rural barrios?" They then found that the "theology of the signs of the times" pointed to people's aspirations as a key source, and analysis of their situation released new truth from scripture and tradition and led to radical changes in both lifestyle and ministry, in which "responsible violence" motivated by love might even have a place. The beginnings of God's reign are revealed for Hechanova in two sacraments: "the world insofar as it is the material being transformed into the Kingdom"; and "the church insofar as it is the leaven for that total transformation." The human face of God, known in the Jesus of Nazareth sermon and in the Jerusalem cleansing, is to be the face of the church - therefore giving a *pro mundi vita* ecclesiology. But when this face is recovered again from the gospels in the life of his people, it also gives us a vulnerable but prophetic Christology. Here also, in scripture, tradition and present struggle, story-telling in faith is the integrating methodology, as it is also a key tool for mission.

Selected References
Works by Louie G. Hechanova
>*The Gospel and Struggle*. London: CIIR, 1986.
>*The Baclaran Story*. 2nd. ed. Quezon City: Claretian, 2000.
>"The Dynamic Role of the Priest Today." *Silliman Journal* 22 (1975).
>"Social Action: An Integral Part of the Pastoral Ministry." *Philippine Priests' Forum* 8 (1976).
>"Goal of Religious Formation within the Philippine Situation." *Philippine Priests' Forum* 9 (1977).
>"The Christ of Liberation Theology." *Diwa* 6.1 (1981); *Geist und Leben* 57.6 (1984).
>"Towards a Moral Theology of Violence." In *With Raging Hope. A Compilation of Talks on the Church involved in Social Transformation and its Emerging Theology*, by L. Hechanova et al. 2nd. ed. Manila: SPI, 1985.
>"Is there a God in the World? Notes from the Hacienda." In *Religion and society: Towards A Theology of Struggle*. Book I. Manila: FIDES, 1988.

2.5.21. Elizabeth Dominguez

Elizabeth Dominguez PhD, is a Filipina scholar of the Hebrew Scriptures, and has been professor of theology at Union Theological Seminary, Dasmariñas. In her teaching and writings a central concern is to reclaim the story and witness of women in the Old Testament as present resource for the struggles and concerns of Filipino women. She frequently points to biblical models for mutual empowerment and support, as well as for women's love for one another: in the resistance of Hebrew mid-wives (Ex. 15.1); in the story of unreserved sharing of love by Ruth and Naomi; or in the promise of the all-inclusive gift of the Spirit (Joel 2.28-29). But she is also critical of culturally determined or patriarchal aspects of the biblical record, including, for example, the condemnation of homosexuality as "violating the law of God" or the imposition of male-serving oppressive conditions upon women. More fully human criteria, drawn from the biblical record as a whole, must be applied so that moral judgments are made "only on the grounds that persons are degraded" or that women are not treated as fully human beings.

For Dominguez, key biblical teachings hold us responsible for each other, for society, and especially for the poor. Life cannot be fragmented to separate the issues of devotion, poverty, women's rights or US bases in the Philippines. Courage to take economic or political action is directly related to the faithfulness of God and the stewardship that God requires from us: to care for and empower all in the community.

Selected References
Works by Elizabeth Dominguez

"Sheep without a Shepherd." In *A Call to Vulnerable Discipleship*. CCA Seventh Assembly, 1981. Singapore: CCA, 1982.

"Some New Testament Reflections upon Political Power." *Kalinangan* 3.3 (1983).

"Signs and Counter-signs of the Kingdom of God in Asia Today." *Voices from the Third World* 7.2 (1984).

"Biblical Concept of Human Sexuality." *In God's Image* (March 1989).

"A Vision of Women." In *Realizing a Vision of Women in the Church. Proceedings of the NCCP Women's Seminar, Sept. 1989*. Quezon City: NCCP, 1990.

2.5.22. Teodoro C. Bacani (1940-)

Teodoro Bacani is auxiliary bishop of Manila and one of the most articulate and most quoted of Philippine bishops. His other roles include those of regular newspaper columnist and spiritual director for the Catholic Church of the charismatic movement El Shaddai. Along with statements and writings on personal faith, Bible study and evangelism, Bacani frequently highlights the vast disparity in wealth between the rich and the poor peoples who are "marginalised in Philippine society". He also speaks and writes on recent legislation regarding, for example, means to fight terrorism, which "are themselves the means to terrorize"; on the urgency of "bringing the Gospel to Asia"; and of the urgency for "a genuine encounter of the Gospel with our culture."

The encounter of Christian faith with Philippine culture is a central theme in his writing and addresses. He concludes from Philippine history and from contemporary social analysis that despite four centuries of evangelization and despite the fact that over 80% of Filipinos are Catholics, "our culture has not been sufficiently evangelized." As evidence he indicates the continuing injustice and inequities of Philippine society, the levels of corruption in government and commerce, and the abuse of Holy Week rituals, for example, as more "an entertaining movie" than a life-changing experience. Christianity in the Philippines, he affirms, has not touched hearts so much as heads, so the transformation of the whole person, in the whole life of the community has not been made. He has therefore been much concerned with Christian political witness, but although writing extensively of the church's role in politics, he also sees this as God's call to personal and communitarian holiness and has stressed this in his addresses. The role of Marian devotion, of Bible study and of a Filipino catechetics are also among the subjects of his teaching and writing.

Selected References
Works by Teodoro C. Bacani

Mary and the Filipino. Makati, Manila: St. Paul Publishing, c1985.
The Church and Politics. Quezon City: Claretian, 1991 (1987).
Katekesis Para sa Pilipino (Filipino Catechetics). Manila: n.p., 1990.

Towards the Third Millennium: The Vision of the Second Plenary Council of the Philippines. Manila: CBCP, 1991.
"The Renewed Integral Evangelization Envisioned by the Second Plenary Council of the Philippines." *Philippiniana Sacra* 28.83 (1993).
"The 'Humanae Vitae' in the Philippines: 25 years later." *Philippiniana Sacra* 28.84 (1993).
"A Re-evangelized and Re-evangelizing People." *Boletin Eclesiastico de Filipinas* 66.1 (1990).
"Genuine Marian devotion." *Philippine Graphic* 16 (Sept 1995).
"The Christian and Suffering." *Kergyma* 1 (2000).
—, and others. *Commentaries on Bible Diary and Daily Gospel.* Quezon City: Claretian, 2000.

2.5.23. Julita A. Quintos rc

Lily Quintos received her MA in theology from St. Xavier University in Chicago and became the first woman to defend her doctoral dissertation, granted magna cum laude, at the Faculty of Theology of the Catholic University of Leuven, Belgium. She has served as academic dean and professor of moral theology at the Franciscan School of Theology, Graduate Theological Union in Berkeley, California, director of the Cenacle Retreat House and Center of Spirituality, Quezon City, and is presently teaching at the Loyola School of Theology, Ateneo de Manila University. She continues to serve in international endeavors for renewal in religious life as well as in theological education.

Quintos's major studies have been of the moral system of Buddhism. Here she has investigated a specific Buddhist text, the *Milinda Panha*, regarded as representing the essence and mainstream of classical Buddha-dhamma. The particular aspect of ethics is emphasized with objectivity and "penetrating observations" (the Ven. Dr. H. Saddhatissa). Sensitive theological reflection is then given upon this classical Buddhist tradition as being a rich source for Christian understanding. Quintos has also written on other aspects of inter-faith dialogue, on the theology of social justice, as well as upon the struggles of women for their rightful place in church and in society.

Selected References
Works by Lily Quintos
The Moral System of Buddhism According to the Milinda Panha with a Christian Theological Reflection. Quezon City: Cardinal Bea Institute, 1977.
Buddhism in Dialogue. Quezon City: Cardinal Bea Institute, 1978.
"Buddhist Ethics in Christian Perspective." In *Ching Feng* (1974).
"Women and Culture: Women's Struggle for Equality in Church and Society." In *Doing Theology with Cultures of Asia*, edited by Yeow Choo Lak and John C. England. ATESEA Occasional Papers 6. Singapore: ATESEA/PTCA, 1988.
"Christian Responsibility for Pacific Civilization: Some Challenges From the Contemporary Philippine Context." In *Christian Responsibility for Pacific Civilization: Doing Theology in the Asian Region*, edited by Stephen S. Kim and John B. Cobb. Claremont CA: Asian Heritage Press, 1992.
—, with Tony van Santvoord. *Justice in the World: A Reflection on Four Major Documents of the Church.* Manila: Communication Foundation of Asia, 1974.

2.5.24. Feliciano Cariño

Feliciano Cariño was secretary and later national chairperson of the SCM in the Philippines, later gaining his PhD from Princeton University. He has served as general secretary of the WSCF (Geneva), taught at Philippine Christian University, Manila, and contributed leadership to many ecumenical and academic organizations in the Philippines. Following his appointment as general secretary of the NCCP - where he edited the journal *Tugon* - he was general secretary of the CCA. His particular contribution has been to hold theological, ideological and societal concerns and analysis in close union with formation, ministry and mission.

In articles and books of wide-ranging scope, Cariño has provided sociological and historical analysis of Philippine society and state, as the context in which the "self-identity of the Christian community and the shape of theological reflection and Christian existence" emerges. For him, such theological reflection is always to "clarify the meaning and shape of Christian responsibility in our present situation." In a collection of papers (1984), he finds "a paradigm of sacrifice" in recent historical incidents in the

Philippines; outlines theological bases for action amidst struggle and under authoritarian rule; and provides studies of praxis, ideology and theology. Theology here begins from the 'earth' (not 'heaven') where "human suffering and human hope meet." Theological method is intimately linked with the issue of method in human action, and although such 'practical theology' may be partial, it must first be efficacious for praxis, as it will be for the renewal of theology itself. Cariño has also written effectively on issues of ministry and formation, issues of ecclesial and ecumenical structure and goals, on the young Christ, on spirituality and on Christian response to particular political movements and events.

Selected References
Works by Feliciano V. Cariño
> *Sacrifice of the Innocent: Themes on Christian Participation in the Philippine Struggle.* Hong Kong: WSCF Asia/Pacific Region, 1984.
> *The Young Christ. A Social Biography.* Quezon City: NCCP, 1987.
> *Education for Ministry. Reflections from an Ecumenical Perspective.* Quezon City: UCCP, 1990.
> "The Willowbank Report: A Critical Response." *SEAJT* 19.2 (1978).
> "Praxis and Theology: Some Notes Toward a Practical Theology in the Asian Context." *SEAJT* 21-22 (1980-1981).
> "Some Recent Developments in Asian Theology." *Kalinangan* 3.3a (1983).
> "Political Context of the Church Mission." *Simbayan* 5.2 (1986).
> "Spirituality for Justice: Some Considerations from the Philippine Experience." In *Those Who Would Give Light Must Endure Burning. Consultation Report on Spirituality for Justice and Peace of the NCCP and WCC, November 1986,* edited by L. Bautista and S. Amirtham. Quezon City: NCCP, 1987.
> "The Encounter of Marxism and Christianity." *Kalinangan* 7.1 (1987).
> "Images and Self-Understanding of the NCCP." *Tugon* 7.2 (1987).
> "Towards A Culture of Freedom on Saying 'No' to the American Bases." *Kalinangan* 8.2 (1988).
> "Reflections on Culture and Religious Symbols." *Kalinangan* 8.3 (1988).

"The Theology of Struggle as Contextual Theology: Some Discordant Notes." *Tugon* 9.3 (1989). Also published by the Socio-Pastoral Institute (1990).

"Biblical and Theological Reflections on Current Economic Life." *Tugon* 10.2-3 (1990).

—, ed. *Like a Mustard Seed: Commentaries on the UCCP Statement of Faith.* Quezon City: UCCP Communications & Literature Desk, 1987.

2.5.25. Mary Rosario Battung rgs (1943-)

Mary Rosario Battung was born in Ibanag and studied in both the Philippines and New Zealand. She then shared in programs in the Philippines for renewal of religious life (1965-1971) and later in ministries in community organization on the Tondo foreshore. She was a founder of the Good Shepherd Community at Ilagan, has been a coordinator of FIDES (Forum for Interdisciplinary Endeavors and Studies), and since 1985, a recognized Zen teacher. She has worked in training programs, meditation and social action with BCCs, farmers' organizations, women's collectives, human rights movements, and also with the EBF (Ecumenical Bishops' Forum), EATWOT and THRUST. In all of these spheres her chief concern has been to develop an 'Asian spirituality' within the movements for social transformation. She has contributed to and/or edited many volumes on 'cosmic' spirituality, meditation, and integrated human development, along with feminist and indigenous resources for these.

From her many involvements with the urban poor, with religious, with social activists and indigenous women, Battung has gathered a range of diverse materials for her theology and spirituality of life, wholeness and transformation. Seeking to integrate "heart, mind, breath, one's people and the cosmos" for the people's struggles now, she finds central insights not only in creative traditions of Christian spirituality but also in the wisdoms of indigenous Filipino women, in Zen meditation and in imageries and experience of God the compassionate Mother. From tribal women, she finds a manifestly 'simple,' fully mutual and God-infused daily life; from Zen, the relation of breath to a life of contemplation and action in each moment. God the Mother here gives breath and wisdom, compassion and sustenance, gentle yet cosmic wholeness. There is a close link for Battung between the rich capacities of marginalized women and men for community life, spiritual insight and ecological wisdom, and the social vision and theological understanding which must guide all struggles for justice, human dignity, healing and survival. She also presents guidelines for patterns of life in community, for meditation and prayer, and for the reshaping of theology, regarding for example, a Filipino Mary, which such convergence provides.

Selected References
Works by Mary Rosario Battung

> *Pakikisang Hininga - Becoming One Breath with Humanity and the Cosmos - the Struggle for Wholeness of Life - "An Introduction to Asian and Indigenous Spirituality as a Way of Life and Transformation."* Manila: SPI, 1990.
> "Discovering Clear Water. A Spirituality of the Poor and Simple." In *Asia's Gift to a Total Christian Spirituality,* edited by M. Rosario Battung, Ruben Habito and Elaine MacInnes. Manila: Zen Center for Oriental Spirituality, 1988.
> "From Zen to God the Mother." In *God's Image* (March 1989).
> "Oneness of Breath." In *Women Religious Now. Impact of the 2nd National Council of Women Religious of the Philippines.* Manila: IWS, St. Scholastica's College, 1993.
> —, et al. *Toward an Asian Principle of Interpretation: a Filipino women's experience. Patriarchy in Asia and Asian Women's Hermeneutical Principle,* by EATWOT Women in the Philippines and Asia. Manila: IWS (St. Scholastica's College) and EATWOT , 1991.
> —, et al, eds. "On Being Fire: Seeing with Dumagat Eyes." In *Religion and Society: Towards A Theology of Struggle.* Book I. Manila: FIDES, 1988.
> —, et al., eds. *Witness and Hope amid Struggle. Towards A Theology of Spirituality and Struggle.* Book II. Manila: FIDES, 1991.
> Vivien Nobles et al. *The Womb of Mabuyan.* Davao: Women's Collective, 1998.

2.5.26. Teresa Dagdag mm (1944-)

Teresa Dagdag studied at Maryknoll College, Diliman, Quezon City, and at New York University (MA 1976), having joined the

Maryknoll Congregation in June 1966. She has taught at Diliman, Santiago, Isabela and Hong Kong, and was factory worker for a period. With other MM sisters she then organized Leadership Training Courses for young industrial workers and opened a tea house and Young Workers Center (1974) at Sau Mau Ping (Hong Kong). She was appointed CCA-URM coordinator for Women Workers Concerns in Asia (1979-1982), to document the plight of women workers throughout Asia. Dagdag was co-founder of the IGOROTA Foundation, Baguio, and edited *IGOROTA* (formerly *INGLAYAN*, see 2.6.8.6.), from 1985. Following work on the Central Governing Board of the Maryknoll Sisters (1990-1996), she is currently completing a PhD in Anthropology at the University of the Philippines.

Dagdag's theological thought has evolved from "simply being focused on justice-and-peace, to eco-feminism as an entry point into theology and spirituality." She sees this to be the area where the concerns for ecology and those of women converge and cross-fertilize. The new cosmology, she believes, calls us to go beyond any "anthropocentric visioning of our future" and to see the earth community with an eco-centric or cosmic vision, especially because women are able from their experiences to "perceive in a sharper and more sensitive way, the devastation and rape of the earth." Ecological anthropology here provides added resources both for ecological endeavors and for spirituality, sometimes called 'deep ecology.' Her study of multi-cultural diversity (in place of mono-cultural uniformity), of wise ecological management, and of feminist spirituality, have led her to "inner-depths" of life and ministry. She also finds here the resources by which inculturation may be a "rooting [of] the Gospel message in one's own culture," allied with both "gender awareness and sensitivity in the hope of challenging patriarchal structures," and "deep respect of the earth and of the universe to which our earth community belongs." Her writings have appeared in the Philippines, Hong Kong and in international periodicals, and addresses delivered internationally include those on "Women in Church and Society," "Solidarity Work with Women Workers in Asia" and the work of IGOROTA.

Selected References
Works by Teresa Dagdag

"To do Justice is to Know Yahweh. Righteousness in the Psalms." *Theology Annual* 3 (1979).

"The Glory of God is Man Fully Alive." *International Review of Mission* 68.272 (1979).

"Towards the Emergence of a People's Theology in the Philippines." *Ching Feng* 25:3 (1982).

"Emerging Christologies in the Philippines Today." *Kalinangan* III.3a (1983).

"IGOROTA Foundation: Some Pastoral Perspectives." *IGOROTA* Nov.-Dec. (1987).

"Why a Women's Unity Day? Why a Women's Movement?" *IGOROTA* Jan-Feb (1988).

See also: Cordillera Women's Education and Resource Center. *From the Eyes of the Cordillera Women.* Baguio City: Cordillera Women's Education and Resource Center, 1991.

and St Louis Univ. (USA) bibliographic entries on Cordillera women and development for IGOROTA Foundation.

2.5.27. Edicio de la Torre (1943-)

Edicio de la Torre taught systematic theology at SVD Seminary, Tagaytay; established a downtown "house-seminary" in Manila, and was one of the founders of Christians for National Liberation (CNL), which represented the far left in Philippine Christianity in the 1970s. A leader in social activism in the 60s and early 70s, he was also associated with radical movements for reform and was a leader in many programs of conscientization. De la Torre was National Chaplain to the Federation of Free Farmers, founding chairman of CNL and was imprisoned under martial law 1974-1980. He later worked as an animateur in urban mission and in movements for democratic education, and through the Education for Life Center he and colleagues worked for the development of leadership and empowerment for rice-roots and indigenous people. In the 90s, he was Director for Technical Education and Skills of the government's Development Authority (TESDA).

In these various fields de la Torre drew on a wide range of sources for thought and action, including contemporary Filipino theologians, both Catholic and Protestant, along with feminist pedagogy, basic Christian communities, popular theater and also liberation theology. His earliest writings were on the search for a Filipino theology and the pattern of priesthood required in current Philippine society. He also taught and wrote on a theology for social reform, biblical study, the role of Christians in struggles for national liberation, and the theology and strategies necessary for this, including "the passion, death and resurrection of the petty bourgeois Christian." Other writings spoke directly to the experience of exploited peasant farmers and to committed revolutionaries; those struggling, those missing, those in prison, all of whom need "the gift of final perseverance." In these writings he was concerned to reflect systematically, and both sociologically and theologically, on the living witness of the church in its diverse forms and to outline "a radically authentic Christianity." His considerable skill in both poetry and painting is seen in collections of work on the same themes, and in theological reflection on the relationship of politics, art, poetry and the search for justice. For de la Torre, the theology to be done within the struggle does not need to be only defensive (creating space for people); and purgative (liberating us from false concerns): it can also be "theology as companion," in solidarity with people and acknowledging that other movements (and ideologies) are "in the pilgrimage" to a new world.

Selected References
Works by Edicio de la Torre

> Documentation Committee. *Fr Ed. de la Torre: Excerpts from Speeches and Essays.* Manila: CNL, 1975.
> *Touching Ground, Taking Root. Theological and Political Reflections on the Philippine Struggle.* Manila: SPI; London: CIIR, 1986.
> *The Philippines: Christians and the Politics of Liberation.* CIIR Justice Papers 9. London: CIIR, 1986.
> "Living in Christ with the People." *Breakthrough* 4.3 (1981).
> "Renewing Spirituality, Strategies for Justice." In *23rd URM Meeting, Colombo, Feb. 1992.* Hong Kong: CCA-URM, 1992.
> "Theological and Political Reflections on Pluralism." *WSCF Journal,* July (1992).
> "Reflections on Matthew 9." In *24th URM Meeting, 1993.* Hong Kong: CCA-URM, 1993.

"Feeding the Hungry." In *Report of 26th URM Meeting*, Bangkok, 1995. Hong Kong: CCA-URM, 1995.

See also Avila, Charles. *Peasant Theology: Reflections by the Filipino Peasants on their Process of Social Revolution*. WSCF Asia book 1. Bangkok: WSCF Asia Region, 1976.

2.5.28. Melba Padilla Maggay

Melba Maggay is a Protestant who heads the ISACC (2.6.7.4), Diliman, Quezon City. She is well-known for her application of cultural studies to theological issues in the Philippines along with studies and writings on Filipino politics and mission and also Filipino psychology.

Maggay has been particularly concerned for the communication of the Gospel across cultural traditions and in the Filipino context in ways that take seriously both the features of Filipino consciousness and the urgency of social renewal. She has critiqued the "barren intellectualism in faith and worship" inherited from the USA and seeks a theological renewal and reorientation which will effectively communicate the Christian gospel. In her theological work, Maggay aims at more coherent articulation of theology, which is fully faithful to both text and context. For her, any contextual theologizing is begun by "perceiving the Biblical text," and by discerning the "signs of the times" in contemporary life. This is followed by communicating it in various contexts, recognizing the actual conditions of Filipino life and, in the light of such communication, facing and resolving any problems or conflicts resulting from process. God, she affirms, "works among us and through us in history" and the "coming of God's rule is always interwoven with what is human." There will therefore be both "reversal" in relationships and culture, and the "experience of deliverance" and empowerment. The rule of God always brings something new and unexpected: in "God-through-us-history" there is also something beyond our categories and understanding.

Selected References

Works by Melba P. Maggay

Communicating Cross-culturally: Towards a New Context for Missions in the Philippines. Quezon City: New Day Publishers, 1989.

> *The Gospel in Filipino Context.* 2nd. ed. Manila: OMF Literature, 1990.
> *A Faith for the Emptiness of Our Time.* Manila: OMF Literature, 1990.
> *US Military Presence in the Philippines and the Myth of Security.* ISACC Monograph Series 1. Diliman, Quezon City: ISACC, 1990.
> *Pagbabalik loob: Moral Recovery and Cultural Reaffirmation.* Diliman, Quezon City: Akademya ng Kultura at Sikolohiyang Pilipino; Quezon City: ISACC, c1993.
> *Transforming Society.* Oxford: Regnum, in association with Lynx Communications; Sutherland, NSW: Albatross Books, 1994.
> *Transforming Society.* Quezon City: ISACC, c1996.
> *Filipino Religious Consciousness: Some Implications to Missions.* Quezon City: ISACC, 1999.
> "Gringo and Habits of the Heart." *National Midweek* 3.7 (1987).
> "Signs of the Presence of the Kingdom of God in the February Revolution." In *Towards a Theology of People Power: Reflections on the Philippine February Phenomenon,* edited by D.J. Elwood. Quezon City: New Day Publishers, 1988.
> "Towards Sensitive Engagement with Filipino Indigenous Consciousness." *International Review of Mission* 87 (1998).
> —, ed. *Women, Culture and Revelation.* New Delhi: Regnum-Asia Books, 1994.

2.5.29. Evelyn Miranda-Feliciano

Evelyn Miranda-Feliciano is writer/trainer with the ISACC (2.6.7.4) and is also their resident writer and head of the Publications Department. She conducts seminars for writers, couples and women and is associate editor of the magazine *ISIP-ISAK*.

Miranda-Feliciano has been concerned, in teaching and writing, to uncover and foster the "quality living now that rests on the authenticity of who we are as Filipino Christians." This will come, she believes, from being rooted in the Word of God which is savored "in the recesses of our souls with Christ," as we respond to the impact of life in the world upon us. Once we find, in disciplined use of the Bible, in understanding of our world and in our Christian identity, the inner strength for life and action, we will be equipped and ready "for the future ... in whatever shape it will come." Regarding *Filipino Values* (1990), Miranda-Feliciano considers such concepts as *lakad* (social networking), *pakikisama* (equitable sharing) and *loob* (inner/whole person) and outlines their role in relation to Christian belief and life. In other works she discusses economic, political, socio-cultural issues and inequalities and shows alternative responses culled from biblical principles. She also critiques borrowed forms and styles of church worship in the Philippines, presenting indigenous concepts and elements as well. She has also published guides for Bible study, the spiritual life and the ministries of women.

Selected References
Works by Evelyn Miranda-Feliciano
> *All Things to All Men: An Introduction to Missions in Filipino Culture.* Quezon City: New Day Publishers, 1988.
> *Filipino Values and Our Christian Faith.* Manila: OMF Literature, 1990.
> "All on the Altar." *The Other Side* 33.2 (2000).
> "Public and Private Morality - Can a Line be Drawn?" *PATMOS Magazine* 15.1 (c.2000).
> Other volumes by Miranda-Feliciano which have been published by ISACC, Quezon City since 1990, include:
> *Unequal Words; Of Songs, Words and Gestures: Rethinking our Filipino Liturgy; Si Eba, Maria, Deborah and Maria Clara: A Bible Study Guide on Women; Courage to Live These Days.*

2.5.30. Oscar S. Suarez

Oscar Suarez gained his PhD from Princeton Theological Seminary and was formerly pastor of the Church of the Risen Lord at the University of the Philippines, Diliman, Quezon City. Later he was pastor of Cosmopolitan Church, Manila, and an adjunct faculty of Union Theological Seminary, Das Mariñas, Cavite. He is currently president of the Philippine Christian University. His first volume, a collection of sermons delivered at the Church of the Risen Lord (1981-1984), sought to communicate the dialectical unity of the personal and social dimensions of the faith, and for unlimited "prophetic judgement on the totality of human life." This he saw to be the Gospel of the "totally other" for the total person, and for this the pulpit is to be liberated. He has also written on the uses of power in society, on contemporary social policy, and on the "theology of struggle." For this last, he believes that the "hermeneutic privilege of the oppressed" exposes the conceptual inadequacy of much theology and indicates that new dimensions of spirituality can only come from those willing to "locate themselves in the struggle" for a liberated and creative people.

Suarez' principal work thus far is *Protestantism and Authoritarian Politics*, in which he analyzes the historical roots of Protestant evasion of politics in contemporary Philippine society and lays down a framework for reconstructing the Protestant vision by outlining important theological agendas for a new self-understanding of the church. He argues, through an analysis of NCCP statements and pronouncements, that Protestant churches and the ecumenical movement in the Philippines have become incoherent when the life and work of the Council is seen only as a "servant of the member churches in the search for and expression of their unity in Christ." This diminishes its accountability to society and thereby loses the claim of every church entity to be priest, pastor and prophet. "The church," says Suarez, "cannot be a voice of emancipation, nor can it be an effective instrument of healing and renewal by staying simply at the borders of struggle. It must earn its own way [and] ... embrace the discourse of politics as constitutive of its historical vocation." This will require more open and diverse theological methods, an ecumenical Christology, and the definition of mission and ministry "that champions the drive for human wholeness" and reunites the personal, the political, the historical and the sacred faces of life.

Selected References
Works by Oscar S. Suarez
> *Liberating the Pulpit: Selected Sermons.* Quezon City: New Day Publishers, 1984.
> *Protestantism and Authoritarian Politics: The Politics of Repression and the Future of the Ecumenical Witness in the Philippines.* Quezon City: New Day Publishers, 1999.
> "The Praxis of Freedom in the Philippine Society. A Restatement in Theological Perspective." *Tugon* 2.2 (1981).

"The Phenomenon of Power. Biblical and Theological Perspectives."
Tugon 5.1 (1985).
"Theology of Struggle. Reflections on Praxis and Location." *Tugon*
6.3 (1986).
"Re-reading Karl Barth for a Theological Reconstruction in Asia
and the Third World." *Tugon* 7.3 (1987*).*
"Church Agenda for a Post-Cold War Era." *Tugon* 11.3 (1991).
"Abundant Life for all: Quest for Justice and Peace." *NCCP
Magazine* 33.4 (1993).
"Theology of Struggle: Spirituality at the Borders of Life." *Asia
Journal of Theology* 10.2 (1996).
See also George R. Hunsberger, Shin Chiba and Lester Edwin J.
Ruiz, eds. *Christian Ethics in Ecumenical Context: Theology,
Culture, and Politics in Dialogue.* Grand Rapids: Eerdmans,
1995.

2.5.31. Benigno P. Beltran svd (1946-)

Following earlier studies in scientific subjects, Benigno Beltran gained his ThD at the Gregorian University, Rome (1985). He has taught at the Divine Word Seminary in Tagaytay City, the Catholic Theological Union in Chicago and the Johann Wolfgang Goethe University in Frankfurt. In the late 1970s he moved into the squatter settlement on the Tondo (Manila) rubbish dump - "Smoky Mountain" - in order to minister to scavenger communities there and "because it was good theology." Over the years, Beltran led in the formation of a vocational training center, and also of Basic Christian Communities committed to living out their faith communally by sharing their goods as well as joining in prayer, the Eucharist, protests and work for urban redevelopment.

Beltran's primary concern is the inculturation of Christianity in the Philippines in its intellectual dimension along with the changes for theologians that may be necessary if the Church is to effectively transmit her beliefs about Christ (in particular) to Filipino believers. Doing theology with a deep "faith seeking understanding" and with a committed love for the poor, Beltran aims in his major work - *Christology of the Inarticulate* (1987) - to find out first what people actually believe about Jesus, and then "to reflect critically and systematically on the findings to see whether they correlate with what the church wants to teach" (p. 24). He is also concerned that the "fruits of the reflection on the Christian faith" from the Basic Christian Communities "filter back to the professional theologians [just as] the works of professional theologians have to be communicated back to the people" in urgently needed dialogue.

"The Filipino," says Beltran, "conceives of humanity and personality as basically relation, dialogue and communion" (p. 226). So when God's presence is mediated to us through the humanity of Jesus it is already taken for granted that we realize our humanity through the mediation of other human beings. Filipino Christology must attempt to answer in its conceptual construction the questions as to who God is and what human beings can expect of God in the light of the belief that Jesus is the human being who is the embodiment of God's eternal, saving, gracious and loving presence. Christology from below, however, attempts to "come to terms with the new directions which the dynamic conception of reality has set. [It] puts the stress on the humanity of Jesus [which] is a more feasible approach towards articulating a rationale for the struggle for peace and justice in combating all forms of inhumanity" (p. 219).

Selected References
Works by Benigno P. Beltran

> *The Christology of the Inarticulate: An Inquiry into the Filipino Understanding of Jesus the Christ.* Manila: Divine Word Publications, 1987.
>
> *Philippinische Theologie in ihrem kulturellen und gesellschaftlichen Kontext.* Theologie interkulturell 3. Dusseldorf: Patmos Verlag, 1988.
>
> "Why Jesus Did Not Come Down From the Cross." *Simbahayan Website*: www.simbahayan.org/whyjesus.html <http://www.simbahayan.org/whyjesus.html>
>
> "The End is Nigh. Militant Millenarianism and Revolutionary Eschatology in the Philippines." *Diwa* 23.1 (1998).
>
> "The Alliance of Basic Christian Communities: People empowerment in a garbage dump"; "Toward a theology of holistic ministry"; and "Toward a theology of holistic ministry." In *Serving*

with the Urban Poor, edited by David Fanshel. Westport CT: Greenwood Publishing, 2000.

2.5.32. José M. de Mesa (1946-)

José M. de Mesa is a married lay theologian, whose interest in studies of religious matters was influenced strongly by the Brothers of the Christian Schools and CICM missionaries. He later studied in Quezon City, in Ottawa, Canada, and in Leuven in Belgium. His doctoral thesis was on inculturation, entitled "Providence in the Lowland Filipino Context." After teaching at Maryhill School of Theology, where he was also academic dean, and at the East Asian Pastoral Institute where he also edited the *East Asian Pastoral Review*, he now teaches systematic theology at De La Salle University, Manila, where he has introduced a lay-oriented program of applied theology. De Mesa is a member of the editorial board of the Leuven *Theological and Pastoral Monographs* and member of an advisory board for *Concilium.*

De Mesa's main theological interests revolve around the realities of Christianity and culture: inculturation and contextualization, the development of Filipino theology, and the inter-cultural dimensions of theologizing. Central concerns are "to give the Gospel a truly Filipino expression to the benefit of both the Church and the culture"; and uncovering in Filipino culture the "insight and wisdom which can serve as a worthy vehicle of the Gospel." For this he has made particular studies of religiosity, language and Christian teachings in the lowland Filipino context, and has developed theological models based on indigenous concepts such as *loob* (personhood in relation); *kagandahang-loob* (generous benevolence), *ginhawa* (total well-being in God), *pagbabangong dangal* (resurrection) and *utang na loob* (gratitude in common humanity). Jesus remains the source of *ginhawa*, which includes salvation and liberation: deliverance from both inner and outer suffering, along with both eucharistic and eschatological motifs. In this he presents a spirituality "which is not only indigenous but also responsive to situational imperatives" of Filipino life and struggle today. He has taught and tested his conclusions in many local settings.

Selected References
Works by José de Mesa

And God Said, "Bahala Na!": The Theme of Providence in the Lowland Filipino Context. Quezon City: Maryhill School of Theology, 1979.

In Solidarity with the Culture: Studies in Theological Re-rooting. Quezon City: Maryhill School of Theology, 1987. [German translation: Maginhawa: den Gott des Heils erfahren. Freiburg: Herder, 1992.]

Isang Maiksing Katesismo Para sa Mga Bata: A Study in Indigenous Catechesis. Quezon City: Wellspring Books, 1988.

Kapag Namayani Ang Kagandahang-Loob ng Diyos. Quezon City: Claretian, 1990.

Marriage is Discipleship. Quezon City: East Asian Pastoral Institute, 1995.

Following the Way of the Disciples: A Guidebook for Doing Christology in a Cultural Context. Quezon City: East Asian Pastoral Institute, 1996.

"Tasks in the Inculturation of Theology: The Filipino Catholic Situation." *Missiology* 26 (1998).

"Attending to the Cultural in Contemporary Filipino Theologizing." In *Liberation Theologies on Shifting Grounds,* edited by G. De Schrijver. Leuven: Leuven University Press, 1998.

"A Hermeneutics of Appreciation: Approach and Methodology." *MST Review* 4.2 (2000-2001).

—, with Lode Wostyn. *Doing Theology: Basic Realities and Processes.* Quezon City: Claretian, 1982. Reprint 1990.

—. *Doing Christology: The Re-Appropriation of a Tradition.* Quezon City: Claretian, 1989.

2.5.33. Karl Gaspar cssr (1947-)

Karl Gaspar is a lay Redemptorist Brother and activist and was a political prisoner during martial law. He has been executive secretary of the Mindanao-Sulu Pastoral Conference and worked for the CBCP's NASSA in-charge of development education. He has also written or edited theological, narrative and art works, as well as 13 religious plays produced by the Filipino theater foundation in the "theatre of conscientization (for the poor) and liberation (for theologians)."

Gaspar has written on the theology of struggle both from prison and within the movements for human rights, social justice and pastoral renewal. In *Prison Reflections* (1985) he presents the movement from cries of abandonment or rage to emerging hope and the birth of new awareness of God's presence. In later writing of a "theology of struggle" this emerges for him from the shared life and struggles of people for full human community, which, rather than doctrinal truths, are the raw material of theology. Through processes of social analysis, conscientization and reflection in "biblico-historical perspective," hope and intention are expressed in symbols from celebrations, rallies, liturgies and fiestas, as well as from imprisonment and suffering. Gaspar has therefore given special attention to the symbolisms and art-forms of such people movements, and also to the life and death stories and writings of many of their members. These songs, poems, posters, paintings and prayers have been a lived and celebrated theology. His book *A People's Option* (1991) is a "mission journal" which chronicles the experience of a local community in Davao del Norte, as they pursue a "theology of struggle" in Basic Christian Communities and in their striving for local justice, ecological care and human rights.

Selected References
Works by Karl Gaspar
> *How Long? Prison Reflections.* Quezon City: Claretian, 1985.
> *Pumipiglas: telohiya ng bayan: a Preliminary Sketch on the Theology of Struggle from a Cultural-liturgical Perspective.* Quezon City: SPI, 1986.
> *A People's Option - To Struggle for Creation.* Quezon City: Claretian, 1990.
> *Readings on Contemporary Mindanao Church Realities.* Quezon City: Claretian, 1994.
> *The Lumad's Struggle in the Face of Globalization.* Davao City: Alternate Forum for Research in Mindanao, 2000.
> "Struggle of Life in the Valley of Death." *Kalinangan* 6.1 (1986).
> "Doing Theology (in a Situation) of Struggle." In *Religion and Society: Towards A Theology of Struggle*. Book I, edited by M.R. Battung, et al. Manila: FIDES, 1988.
> Graham, Helen, and Breda Noonan, eds. *How Long? Prison Reflections of Karl Gaspar.* Quezon City: Claretian, 1985.

Gerlock, Ed, et al., eds. *You are not Forgotten: Symbols during Martial Law.*

2.5.34. Dionisio Marcello Miranda svd (1947-)

Dionisio Miranda is a religious missionary of the Society of the Divine Word. His studies included a survey of moral theology in the decade after Vatican II at the Accademia Alfonsiana in Rome (STD. 1984). He has taught at Maryhill School of Theology (Manila), Loyola School of Theology and East Asian Pastoral Institute (Quezon City), Fatuoaiga Pastoral Center (Samoa), Catholic Theological Union (Chicago), University of San Carlos (Cebu) and the Divine Word Seminary (Tagaytay). Within the Philippine SVD he has served as provincial councillor and seminary rector.

Miranda has written more than a dozen scholarly articles on Filipino psychology, culture and religious experience, and on Filipino values, conscience, moral theology and anthropology. He has also written on methods for inculturation, catechetical ministry, bioethics, social justice and the social encyclicals. In his major writings he has considered Filipino theological virtues and Filipino values; non-biblical revelation in Philippine culture; the development of a Filipino bioethic; and the sources for theology and ethics in Filipino psychology. In this he has focused upon Filipino understanding of the *loob*, as representing the whole person, or "the person within" as offering a basis for a moral theology. (See also de Mesa and Alejo on this, 2.5.32 and 2.6.3.) For methods of inculturation (for moral theology in particular) Miranda presents the resources for reconceptualization as being semantic or linguistic analysis, thematic exegesis (especially of the *loob*), social investigation and modular construction. Here he gives priority to "the indigenous rather than the contextual," with the first task being "to let the culture speak."

Selected References
Works by Dionisio Miranda
> Pagkamakatao *(Reflections on the theological virtues in the Philippine context).* Manila: Divine Word Publications, 1987.

Loob, The Filipino Within (A Preliminary investigation into a pre-theological moral anthropology). Manila: Divine Word Publications, 1989.
Buting Pinoy (Probe essays on value as Filipino). Manila: Logos Publications, 1992.
Pagkamakabuhay: On the Side of Life (Prolegomena for bioethics from a Filipino-Christian perspective). Manila: Logos Publications, 1994.
"On Judging the 1986 Philippine Presidential Elections." *DIWA* 11.1 (1986).
"The Meaning of Budhi." *DIWA* 12.2 (1987).
"The Papal Encyclicals on Labor." *DIWA* 16.1 (1991).
"A Daniw Theology of Revelation? Theological Comment." In *Filipino Religious Experience and Non-Biblical Revelation,* edited by Leonardo Mercado. Asia-Pacific Missiological Series 3. Manila: Divine Word Publications, 1992.
"Inculturation and Moral Theology." *The UST Journal of Theology* 11, June (1992); *Philippiniana Sacra* 28.83 (1993).
"Fragments of a Method for Inculturation." and "Outlines of a Method for Inculturation." *East Asian Pastoral Review* 30.2 (1993); *DIWA* 20.2 (1995).
"Social Justice, Health Care and the Poor." *DIWA* 19.1 (1994).
"Jesus and the Culture of the Holy." *DIWA* 23.2 (1998).

2.5.35. Melanio LaG. Aoanan

Melanio Aoanan obtained his PhD from Loyola School of Theology and is an ordained pastor of the UCCP, for which he has been a member of the Faith and Order Commission. Formerly dean of the College of Theology and Religious Studies of the Southern Christian College, Cotabato, he has taught at Union Theological Seminary, Cavite, and is now pastor of the Church among the Palms in the University of the Philippines at Los Baños, Laguna. He is also chairperson of the Philosophy and Religion Department at Silliman University.

In the volumes Aoanan has published, he has sought to integrate biblical interpretation, prophetic theology and spirituality, and concrete endeavors for just and compassionate society. In writing of God's liberating acts in the Hebrew scriptures (1988) he has aimed to relate the depth of the religious heritage received from the Bible to the emerging Filipino consciousness and identity. On spirituality (1988) he outlines a way of doing theology that integrates involvement in the continuing historic struggle of the Filipino people for liberation - and therefore a "theology of struggle" - with scriptural re-interpretation and spiritual development. In study material for inter-faith dialogue (1992) he is particularly concerned to outline pathways to Muslim-Christian solidarity for love, justice, freedom and economic sufficiency in the Southern Philippines. In his volume on the history of the UCCP (1998), his main aim is to describe the ecumenical and prophetic witness of the UCCP, to clarify the UCCP's self-understanding as church - with diverse heritages - and to develop an understanding of the concept of ministry that gives emphasis to this prophetic and ecumenical witness. He has also written in articles on these themes as well as on Filipino national:sm, a 'transforming Christology,' story-telling theology, and on Mary as 'mother of Jesus.'

Selected References
Works by Melanio LaG. Aoanan
> *God's Liberating Acts. Quezon City:* New Day Publishers, 1988.
> *Spirituality for the Struggle: Biblico- Theological Reflections from Mindanao.* Quezon City: E.C.T.E.E.P. 1988.
> *Strengthening Muslim-Christian Solidarity.* MIND Series 1. Davao City: SCC, 1992.
> *Pagkakaisa at Pagbabago: Ang Patotoo ng United Church of Christ in the Philippines. (Ecumenical and prophetic: the witness of the United Church of Christ in the Philippines).* Quezon City: New Day Publishers, 1996.
> *Ecumenical and Prophetic: The Witness of the United Church of Christ in the Philippines.* Quezon City: Claretian, 1998.
> "From Story-Telling to Social Transformation: Theologizing Through People's Movement." ATESEA Occasional Papers 3: *Doing Theology Through People's Movement in Asia,* edited by Yeow Choo Lak and John C. England. Singapore: ATESEA/PTCA, 1986.
> "Sharing in Struggle: The Philippine Experience." *CTC Bulletin* 3.3 (1989).

"Nurturing Nationalist Christians for the Nineties and Beyond." *Asia Journal of Theology* 4.2 (1990).

"Light Overcoming Darkness: A Biblico-Theological Reflection." *SCC Journal* 4-5 (1991).

"Salat and Sawm as Pathways to 'Chrislamic' Solidarity in Southern Philippines." *Tugon* 11.3 (1991).

"Transforming Christology in a Changing Church and Society." *CTC Bulletin* 13.3-14.1 (1995-1996).

2.5.36. Everett L. Mendoza

Everett Mendoza holds the MTh in pastoral care and counseling (1978) and DTh (1990) from the SEAGST. He is associate professor of theology and former dean of the Silliman University Divinity School, Dumaguete City. He is an ordained minister of the UCCP, which he concurrently serves as theological consultant (theologian in residence), was elected chairperson of the General Assembly of the UCCP (1998-2002) and is also national chairperson of *Kasimbayan*, an ecumenical nationalist organization of priests and pastors.

A prolific writer of short theological reflections and active as a speaker in progressive church circles, Mendoza has also written on the issues of Filipino freedom, Filipino theology and Christian ethics. He is currently working on a textbook of systematic theology. His major work, *Radical and Evangelical: Portrait of a Filipino Christian* (1999) provides foundations for systematic theological construction in the area of radical politics. In it Mendoza uses the 16th century principle of prophetic protest as a useful and critical tool in dialoguing with Roman Catholic theology. He affirms that Protestant Christianity, by and large, has been associated with political conservatism and therefore it has been used to bolster the political right. So how could Filipino Protestants become truly evangelical and politically radical at the same time? As one who is politically engaged in the struggle for Filipino national sovereignty and democracy, Mendoza's work emerges out of a "tortured conscience" because he recognizes that his political aspirations find no signification in the usual evangelical symbols of faith. Mendoza identifies the 'Protestant Principle' as a powerful dimension of evangelical theology, having a "critical function for a contemporary theological criticism and reconstruction" in dialogue with a Catholic theology of liberation. The book is described as "perhaps the first critique of Latin American liberation theology from a Protestant perspective in the Philippines."

Selected References
Works by Everett Mendoza
> *The Idea of Christian Freedom.* UCC Education and Nurture Series. Quezon City: UCCP, 1990.
> *Radical and Evangelical: Portrait of a Filipino Christian.* Quezon City: New Day Publishers, 1999.
> "Three Bible Studies on the Poor." In *Mission in the Context of Endemic Poverty,* edited by Lourdino Yuzon. Singapore: CCA, 1983.
> "The Struggle for Homeland. Liberty to the Captives." In *Mission of God in the Context of the Suffering and Struggling Peoples of Asia,* edited by Salvador Martinez. Osaka: CCA, 1988.
> "Peace, Justice and Power." *Tugon* 11.3 (1991).
> "Peace with Nature." *NCCP Magazine* 32.3 (1992).
> "Jubilee and the Filipino Quest for Freedom." *Tugon* (Jubilee Campaign Special Issue) 13.1 (1999).
> "Theology in the Philippines: the Future of Local Theologies in the Age of Globalization." *Tugon* (Jubilee Campaign Special Issue) 13.1 (1999).
> Refer also to George R. Hunsberger. *Christian Ethics in Ecumenical Context: Theology, Culture, and Politics in Dialogue,* edited with Shin Chiba and Lester Edwin J. Ruiz. Grand Rapids: Eerdmans, 1995.

2.5.37. Sharon Rose Joy Ruiz-Duremdes

Sharon Rose Joy Ruiz-Duremdes studied at Central Philippines University, the University of Hawaii and Berkeley Baptist Divinity School. She taught at the Central Philippines University College of Theology for 12 years and worked as regional coordinator of the Iloilo-based Western Visayas Ecumenical Council in 1985. She later became executive director of the Ecumenical Center for Development (1994-97), general secretary of the Kapatirang Simbahan para sa Bayan (1997-99), and general secretary of the NCCP in 1999. A political prisoner under the Marcos regime, Ruiz-Duremdes has been a consistent human rights advocate nationally and globally, being a convenor of the Ecumenical Jubilee 2000 Campaign Network and Church against Rising Tyranny.

Ruiz-Duremdes has written and lectured widely on ecumenical, theological and women's issues, as well as in Bible studies, political reflection and guides for spirituality. The starting-point of theology for her is "encountering Yahweh in the [objective reality of the] poor." Questions as to how to find God, or "what is God doing" in the middle of Filipino life then have a different locus, where social existence gives rise to theological consciousness and critical reflection. The reality is here the struggle between exploiter and exploited, oppressor and oppressed; and theology arising from the struggle is shaped by aspiration - "the *process* of attaining [liberation]." In this theology there is to be the full sharing of suffering, along with sociological analysis. People's hopes are then articulated and a theology of struggle is directed to discern Jesus Christ accompanying his people wherever justice, truth and love irrupt in the midst of their denials. To be with God is to be with people on their road to a new world. In applying this particularly to the life of women, Ruiz-Duremdes has worked for the support and solidarity of women in an integrated Christian life. She finds rich symbolism for spirituality of women in the elements of fire, blood and water, with which women are constantly in contact in their life-giving tasks. They also furnish rich sources for solidarity with nature, with the whole inhabited earth and with other women in particular. In the life-giving processes of women is also found the presence of the Mother God: constantly at work to preserve and continue life despite all abuses of land, wealth and community existence, and the injustices of patriarchy and class.

Selected References
Works by Sharon Rose Joy Ruiz-Deremdes

> *For The Life of the World - Bible Studies on Human Rights* (1986); *Land: A Grace from God, From its womb springs life* (1987); and *From Darkness to Light; Creative Studies for Women in the Churches* (1991). Booklet Series. Quezon City: NCCP.
> *A Christian Reflection on the National Situation.* Manila: PCPR, Kasimbayan, and EBF. n.d.

"A Search for a Relevant Asian Ecclesiology: Philippine Perspectives." *CTC Bulletin* 8.1 & 2 (1989); *Tugon* 9.3 (1989).
"The Role of Women in Theology and the Ecumenical Movement." *CTC Bulletin* 9.2 & 3 (1990).
"Sharing the Common Cup." *NCCP Magazine* 38.1 & 2 (1997).
"Women's Solidarity and Spirituality. A Theology of Life." *In God's Image* 16.3 (1997).
"Land: A Grace from God, from its Womb Springs Life." *People's Action for Cultural Ties* (PACT) ?1998.
"Peopling Theology." and "Three Men and a Woman." *In God's Image* 19.1 (2000).
—, and Wendy Kroeker, eds. *Stories and Songs of Hope: Dance Amid Struggle.* Quezon City: AWIT, 1998.

2.5.38. Muriel Orevillo-Montenegro (1954-)

Muriel Orevillo-Montenegro holds BThE (1979) and MDiv (1994) degrees from Silliman University in Dumaguete City and the STM (1999) and MPhil degrees from Union Theological Seminary, New York, where she is currently doing doctoral studies in theology. She has worked as pastor to churches in poor rural communities, and worked with urban poor communities in community organizing and community development programs for 13 years. She has also taught Christian education and religious studies at Silliman University's Religious Studies Department and the Divinity School (1989-1992 and 1994-1998).

Orevillo-Montenegro's main concern is to make a contribution to the nascent theological voices of women in Asia. Her involvement in the Philippine struggle for national democracy and frontier ministries in the church brought her to see "that the church and the movement have not fully addressed the roots of suffering of women, children and the weaker men." This led her to follow concerns such as re-reading the Bible, eco-feminism, rituals, indigenous spiritualities and their challenges to Christian theology, and women's theological methodologies. She has written in biblical studies and meditations on these themes as well as articles on Christian mission, human rights, violence against women, the land and women, community blessings, the history of the Protestant Filipina and on the challenge of indigenous spiritualities to Christian theology. Christology she believes, "has been used implicitly and explicitly by Christians in efforts to subjugate peoples whom they consider as the 'other' - the 'pagans,' the women, children, the gays/lesbians." It has been used to negate "other" religions, cultures; memories, and other forms of knowledge. Continual theological critique and reinterpretation are therefore necessary if Christology, which is the centerpiece of Christian theology, can become "truly relevant, liberating and meaningful in Asia."

Selected References
Works by Muriel Orevillo-Montenegro

"Deuteronomy's Rewards and Today's Dilemma." *Silliman Ministry Magazine* (August 1988).

"Seek Peace and Pursue It." In *Human Rights Ecumenical Observance,* edited by L. Bautista. Quezon City: NCCP, 1990.

"Come Holy Spirit!"; "The Christian Community: Rooted in God Who Gave Birth to Humanity"; and "Come Holy Spirit, Lead Us to Shalom!" In *Compilation of Bible Study for the 5th Quadrennial General Assembly of the United Church of Christ in the Philippines.* Quezon City: UCCP, 1994.

"A Great Challenge to Service: A Reversal of Roles." *Silliman Ministry Magazine* 60 (1997).

"Of Midwives and Mothers ... and the Call to Build a Community of Hope"; and "Sisterhood: A Model of Partnership in Keeping and Healing Creation." In *Dance amid Struggle,* edited by Wendy Kroeker and Sharon Rose Joy Ruiz-Duremdes. Quezon City: AWIT Publications, 1998.

"Doing Theology: Partnership of Women and Men in Keeping and Healing Creation." In *Proceedings of the Congress of Asian Theologians,* edited by F.V. Cariño. Hong Kong: CCA, Hanil Theological Seminary and Continuing Committee of CATS, 1998.

"My Love Story: Justice Work through the Path of Pain and Anger." In *Women's Concern Report, 44,* edited by Gwen Groff. Akron PA: Committee on Women's Concerns of Mennonite Central Committee, 1999.

"Why Are Some People Cast So Low? - Feminist Theology and the Problem of Evil." *Voices from the Third World* 23.1 (2000).

2.5.39. Elizabeth Padillo-Olesen

Elizabeth Padillo-Olesen was born in Hingotanan Island, Bohol, and has degrees in theological education and in the science of education from Silliman University, Dumaguete City. She has also studied at Selly Oak Colleges, Birmingham, England, and at the WCC Ecumenical Institute, Celigny, Switzerland. Her ministries have included those of teacher and pastor in the UCCP, teacher at Tribhuvan University, Nepal, as well as coordinator of Nepali women's literacy and conscientization program. She has also been administrative consultant to Central Visayas Ecumenical Fellowship Philippines, and social worker with multi-ethnic refugees and immigrants, contributing to the quarterly newspaper of the Intercultural Center, *Nyt på tværs*.

The main themes of Padillo-Olesen's work in art forms, poems, stories and music include human development and liberation, faith and creation, justice and peace. Particular subjects have been the sources of hope and courage in suffering, people's theology, compassion for Mother Earth, resurrection amid oppression and advocacy of "love and compassion in the midst of natural calamity, hatred and war." Her written works (in Cebuano, English and Danish) include plays of conscientization and faith for Filipino fisherfolk exploited by powerful multinational corporations, or exposing the situation of refugees and immigrants who are victims of discriminatory laws; and poetry which portrays the agonies of women and the suffering of children, realities of slavery and liberation, ethnic cleansing and the ways of compassion; along with the "altar of life" to replace war's altars of death. The core journey, she affirms, is the "journey to the heart ... lodged in the heart of our Maker" and where the wasteland is no more. In such poems - many of which have appeared in *In God's Image*, as well as in stories, art works, and anthologies, she presents expressions of "people's theology," forged amid their agonies and struggles. She is currently writing the biographical journey of a child's struggle for survival in the Philippine context of faith, despite sexual abuse, shame and poverty.

Selected References
Works by Elizabeth Padillo-Olesen

A Pulse for my Country People, Poems and Reflections on the Philippine Situation. Cebu City: CENDET, 1995.

Giya sa Nagmabdos nga Inahan. (A guide for pregnant mothers. Intended for mothers in the Philippine villages). Cebu City: CGS, 1997.

Burning of the Seaweeds Barn. (A play re-enacting the meaning of resurrection to the oppressed fishermen in the island of Hingotanan). *PRAXIS* (WSCF) c.1998.

25 Frames for exhibition in churches, each frame containing a poem that is illustrated by oil crayon, water colors, painting (acrylic), and collage. Intercultural Center of Denmark.

Intruders into Denmark's New Millennium. (A play). Copenhagen: the Danish Artist Association. Forthcoming.

"Doing Mission in Christ's Way." *In God's Image* (June 1990).

"Church Women's Response to Fire Victims." *In God's Image* 12.1 (1993).

—, et al. *Mugbong Sugilanon sa Matuod nga Hitabo sa Kangitngit og Kahayag* (True stories on light and darkness). Cebu City: CGS, 1995.

2.5.40. Sophie Lizares-Bodegon (1955-)

Sophie Lizares-Bodegon has an MSc in social development from Ateneo de Manila University and the MMin from Union Theological Seminary, Cavite. She lectures at Union Theological Seminary, is a consultant for Social Development Research and Communication, and is a member of the Faith and Order Commission, UCCP; the council of the Congress of Asian Theologians; and also of EATWOT. She is also vice-chair, Asia Regional Assembly, United Evangelical Mission, with concerns also in the Commission on Human Rights.

Most of Lizares-Bodegon's writing has been in practical theology, revolving around the vitalization of local congregations, particularly through strategic planning and liturgical renewal. For this, she draws together the disciplines of sociology, communication and pastoral ministry to challenge churches in rapidly urbanizing Asian countries in a globalizing world. Gender, family and children's issues are major themes here. She has written extensively on faith expressions and "transforming concepts of being Church" in particular churches, along with many study and planning resources for local congregations. These include liturgies for Lent and Easter, and on "Experiencing God"; for purposeful planning in a local church (weaving in ethical elements); and for "building community in a time of change." In sermons and meditations, which are often in the form of poetry, Lizares-Bodegon places biblical imagery directly within present Filipino experience. Here she portrays the one with "no beauty left" of Isaiah, in the "sampaguita girls ... barrio lads ... factory workers ...," and finds the call of Jeremiah coming in the work of student or teacher, the experience of laborer or mourning mother. Despite the realities of community or family tragedy in today's Philippines, she presents a "spirituality of enthusiasm"; the sense of the sacred in life; prayer "like a sunburst ..."

Selected References
Works by Sophie Lizares-Bodegon
> *Jubilee: Agenda for a Church in the City.* Policy Paper for the United Church of Christ in the Philippines - Ellinwood Malate Church. Manila: n.p. 2000.
> *Professing the Hope: A Living Way of Faith in Asia.* Paper delivered at the General Assembly of the United Evangelical Mission. Windhoek: n.p. 2000.
> *The Withered Fig Tree.* Meditation delivered at the Theological Consultation sponsored by the Uniting Church in Australia, Adelaide, July 2000. Mimeo'd, 2000.
> "Convent Girl Notes on Prayer." Mimeo'd, May 2000.
> —, ed. *The Isaiah Paradigm: Recapturing the Role of the Laity. Sermons by Joel L. Bodegon.* Quezon City: UCCP and Claretian, 1995.
> —, ed. *Quest for Church Renewal: One Baptism, One Faith, One Hope. Sermons by Joel L. Bodegon.* Quezon City: Crossroads Publications, 1998.
> —, et al, eds. *Religion and Society: Towards a Theology of Struggle.* Book I. Manila: FIDES, 1988.

2.5.41. Elizabeth Tapia (1955-)

From extensive studies in the Philippines and overseas, Elizabeth Tapia holds the MA, BRE, MDiv and PhD (Claremont 1989) degrees. She is an educator, ecumenist, preacher, Bible study leader and advocate for women's concerns as well as being an ordained elder of the United Methodist Church, Bulacan. She has taught theology at Union Theological Seminary, Philippine Christian University, Dasmariñas; as professor since 1991 and academic dean, since 1998. Her theological approach as a Filipina Christian woman is shaped by her upbringing in an economically disadvantaged rural family in a rural community of Bulacan, and from ministries in both the Philippines and in the West.

Tapia's main theological concerns focus upon the relationship between theology and ethics, Gospel and cultures, ecumenism and ecology, politics and economics. In these areas she presents feminist challenges for theologizing in method and approach. She also works for a "holistic, creative and dynamic mission" which includes the promotion of justice, peace and integrity of creation; the empowerment of women, youth and the indigenous peoples; as well as work towards an inclusive, participatory and democratic leadership in churches, workplaces and communities. She therefore describes herself as an eco-feminist liberation theologian. She is also concerned to promote the full personhood of Asian women along with their methods for doing theology, and their creative liturgies and rituals. For Tapia, theology must be dynamic and creative, feminist, simple and credible. It must also be contextual, community-centered and change-oriented. Doing theology, for her, arises in "the action-reflection of individuals and communities on their life situations, as prompted by their faith, contexts and commitment." Her writings include articles, poems, prayers and litanies, many of which have been published in *In God's Image*, and *Seeing Christ in Others*.

Selected References
Works by Elizabeth Tapia

"The Contribution of Philippine Christian Women to Asian Women's Theology." PhD Dissertation, Claremont Graduate University, Claremont, 1989.

"Asian Women Doing Theology: The Challenge of Feminism for Theologizing." A paper presented at the *CCA Colloquium* on *Methods of Doing Theology, April 14-19, 1996*. Mimeo'd, 1996.

"Asian Feminist Theology: Christian Women in Ministry and Women in the Ecumenical Movement." In *Behold I make all Things New. AWRC Study Workshop, October 1995*. Kuala Lumpur: AWRC, 1996.

"Reflections of a Filipina Christian." In *Ecclesiology and Ethics*, edited by Tom Best and Martin Robra. Geneva: WCC, 1997.

"My Life, My Passion." In *Women On Fire*, edited by Lorna Kalaw Tirol. Manila: Anvil Publishing, 1997.

"Globalization as Seen From the Eyes of Women." The Gumersindo Lecture, General Convention of the NCCP, Nov.22-26, 1999. Sta. Cruz, Laguna..

"A Filipino Woman's Vision for the Church of the Future." *Women's Magazine* (LWF) (March, 2000).

"Filipino Women's Liturgy: Pista Lakbayan." In *Dissident Daughters*, edited by Teresa Berger. Knox Westminster Press. Forthcoming.

2.5.42. Amelia Vasquez rscj (1959-)

Amelia Vasquez teaches church history at Maryhill School of Theology, Manila. Her work and writings evince a deep concern for the role of religious in today's world, for the form and content of formation and education now required by global "developments" and for the changes in spirituality and life necessary in order to fully respond to these. Writing on globalization, she recognizes massive forces of destruction in its commercial and political forms, but also finds in the multiplying networks of voluntary and non-government groupings, the "new internationality" which, in numerous Civil Society Organizations (CSOs), is "guiding us to new visions, building plausible alternatives, recombining mental and material factors that would create a responsibly shared future."

Regarding the spiritual life in such a context, Vasquez presents a spirituality of justice, interculturality, hospitality, radical education, and humanization. Justice is to be included as an intrinsic part of all programs of formation, as it is also integral to all evangelization, now to be put in the context of globalization. Interculturality is found both in appreciating one's own cultural identity and in readiness to critique one's culture according to the spirit of the gospel. Hospitality is expressed in making "the Stranger" of other people to be at home with change and diversity, and in helping the victimized and excluded to retrieve and interpret their cultural traditions. All such reciprocal giving and receiving transforms our own hearts and transforms the consciousness of both poor and well-to-do.

Globalization as a political-economic project is to be met, Vasquez believes, with equally hard-nosed political and economic action through support of local, community-based economies countering the direction of so-called "global development"; through international advocacy of a new vision that "sees the world with the eyes of God ... that knows that we are all interdependent and interconnected, and pressures international bodies for regulatory structures ..." These aspects of an integrated spirituality she anchors in a recovery of gospel imagery and power: in the foot-washing, in which "we serve in love and humility while doing away with [all] social or mental structures of superiority," and the open table, in which "there is no hoarding or clinging, where no one is excluded, and bread and life are shared to feed one another."

Selected References
Works by Amelia Vasquez

> *Women and the Church's Service to Life in Asia.* Sixth Plenary Assembly Workshop Discussion Guide (72h). Hong Kong: FABC Conference, 1995. Also in *Philippiniana Sacra* 30.89 (1995).
>
> "Women in the History of the Church: Invisible and Inaudible." *EAPR* 26.2 (1989).
>
> "Challenge for Religious Today." *MST Review*, Introductory Issue (1996).
>
> "Paradigm Shifts in Mission. Understanding and Praxis through the Centuries." *Religious Life in Asia* 2.1 (*Consecrated Life and the Church's Mission in Asia*) (2000).
>
> "The Society of the Sacred Heart in a Globalized World." *Religious Life in Asia* 2.4 (*Re-visioning Women in the Church*) (2000).

2.5.43. Agnes M. Brazal (1960-)

Agnes M. Brazal is a full-time faculty member at the Maryhill School of Theology and obtained her licenciate and doctorate at

Contextual Theology in the Philippines 1800-2000 449

the Katholieke Universiteit, Leuven. Her areas of research include feminist and liberation theologies and also the processes of inculturation. She has a particular concern for the role in Third World theologies of socio-economic and gender issues. In her writings she has also addressed the issues of epistemology in the Third World, of moral theology, and of feminist approaches to the inculturation of liturgy and to hermeneutic models. The issues of ideology and of women's labor, especially within the processes of globalization are also among her recent writings. She is currently a contributor on moral theology, as part of a team involved in preparing a *Filipino Theological Dictionary*.

Selected References
Works by Agnes M. Brazal

"John Paul II on Labor and Culture: An Assessment in the Light of Hegel and Marx." *Inter-Sectiones* 1 (1995).

"Inculturation: An Interpretative Model for Feminist Revisions of Liturgical Praxis?" *Questions Liturgiques* 1/2 (1996); *MST Review* 2 (1997). Also in *Liturgie en inculturatie. Verslagboek van het twaalfde liturgie colloquium van het Liturgisch Institut van de K.U.Leuven, Oktober 1995*, edited by J. Lamberts, 181-193. Leuven: Acco, 1996.

"Exploring Some Epistemological Implications of the Shift in Third World Theologies of Liberation." *Inter-Sectiones* 4 (1996). Also in *Liberation Theologies on Shifting Grounds: A Clash of Socio-Economic and Cultural Paradigms*, edited by Georges De Schrijver, 273-286. Leuven: Leuven University, 1998.

"A Response to Feminist Theology in Conversation." *Humig Ugnayan* 1.2 (1999).

"Feminist Ideology Criticisms, the Bible and the Community." *MST Review* 2.2 (1999).

"Patriarchal Relations: Reinforced or Undermined? Globalization and the Employment of Women's Labor." *MST Review* 4.1 (2000).

2.5.44. Hope S. Antone (1960-)

Hope Antone has degrees in mass communication (BMC) and divinity (MDiv) from Silliman University in Dumaguete City, in Theology (MTh) from the Presbyterian Theological College and

Seminary in Seoul, Korea, and the DEd from the Union Theological Seminary in Richmond, Virginia, USA. She has served local churches of the UCCP in the Visayas and Negros, and taught at Silliman University and at the Union Theological Seminary in Cavite. She now edits *In God's Image* and is publications secretary of the Asian Women's Resource Centre for Culture and Theology.

In her dissertation, "An Invitation to the Table Community: A Biblical and Cultural Image for Asian Christians' Theory of Religious Education that Takes Account of Religious Pluralism," Antone offers a contextual theory of education in religion, which might equip Asian Christians not only with the heritage of their own religious communities but also for the dialogue of life with Asians of other faith and religious commitments. As a means to recognize religious pluralism in religious education and to broaden all programs of Christian education in the churches, seminaries and colleges, she focuses on the imagery of sharing at the meal table. Taken both literally and figuratively, this image has biblical-theological and cultural bases and makes possible a "faith-shaping" in the context of dialogue and conversation with other faiths. Antone has also written a number of sermons and Bible studies on different themes and with feminist and pluralist perspectives for ecumenical and Asia-wide programs.

Selected References
Works by Hope Antone

"The Beatitudes of Jesus and Human Rights Teaching." In *Human Rights: Biblical and Theological Readings*. Manila: NCCP-HRD, 1988.

"A Christian Perspective of Women." In *Conceiving a New Creation, CCA-URM Grassroots Women's Leadership Formation* Report (Oct. 1990). Hong Kong: CCA-URM, 1991.

"Not Slaves but Co-Workers." In *Hope in God in a Changing Asia: Biblical and Theological Reflections*. Hong Kong: CCA, 1995.

"Finding Ties, Making Links: An Asian Woman's Gleanings from Womanist Theology." *In God's Image* 17.1 (1998).

"Christian Theologies from the Underside." *In God's Image* 17.1 (1998).

"Healed by Her Faith" and "Judith: A Woman's Steadfastness." In *Dance amid Struggle: Stories and Songs of Hope*, edited by Wendy Kroeker and Sharon Rose Joy Ruiz-Duremdes. Quezon City: AWIT, 1998.

"Ecumenical Decade: Churches in Solidarity with Women." *In God's Image* 17.4 1998.

"AWRC: Daring to Dream." *Ministerial Formation* 88 (2000).

—, with Yong Ting Jin and Esther Byu. "VLC (Vietnam, Laos, Cambodia) - a Sense of Hunger, a Note of Promise: Reflections on the Consultation of Indochinese Women." *In God's Image* 15.3 (1996).

2.5.45. Noriel D. Capulong

Noriel D. Capulong completed doctoral studies in the Hebrew Scriptures with the SEAGST (ThD) and is an ordained minister of the UCCP. He teaches at Silliman University and has served as dean of the Silliman University Divinity School. He is currently a member of the Faith and Order Commission of the UCCP. He is active as a popular Bible study facilitator and biblico-theological reflector and has written extensively on biblical study in the Philippines and its application to particular socio-political issues here.

A major focus of Capulong's theology is the interpretation of the Bible's prophetic tradition in the contemporary circumstances and struggles of the Filipino people. He has therefore brought his scriptural reflection to bear on a wide range of issues, including the basis of mission; spirituality for justice and peace; land ownership; national security and reconciliation; reading the Bible "through Filipino eyes"; the prophetic tradition of Protestantism; sanctuaries and community-building; the proclamation of Jubilee now; and the role of a prophetic theologian today. A "prophetic theology of history is one that is born out of crisis," he affirms, and the role of today's prophet is therefore to critically discern the socio-historical realities of extreme inequalities, injustice and victimization; responsibly appraise and apply her/his people's cultural traditions; and be advocate for all marginalized and oppressed.

In all this the central task is to be "faithful to the revealed word of God to one's own time," where history still holds the purposeful unfolding of God's rule. Capulong's biblically-based interpretation of history for Filipinos discerns in their movements against state repression, poverty, abuse of power, and for justice, freedom, equality and fulfillment, the movement of God's will for his people. Allied with this the prophetic church is to live out Yahweh's call, that all power is accountable, the voiceless are to be heard and succored, and the forces of continuing oppression are to be opposed. The mission of the church now, he declares, is "to reclaim and proclaim jubilee" for victims of indebtedness, land abuse and enslavement. The making of a "new Scripture tradition" synthesizing serious study and reflection will make possible the cultural and spiritual liberation of the Filipino people, he concludes.

Selected References
Works by Noriel Capulong
> *Where Lies Our Real Security? Two Bible Studies on the US Military Bases in the Philippines.* Quezon City: NCCP, 1988.
> *The Bible in the UCCP.* UCCP Study Series 13. Quezon City: UCCP, 1992.
> *Reading and Hearing the Old Testament through Philippine Perspective.* Quezon City: New Day Publishers. Forthcoming.
> "A Biblical-Theological Basis of Mission." *Tugon* 3.2 (1982).
> "Land, Power and People's Rights in the Old Testament: From a Filipino Theological Perspective." *East Asia Journal of Theology* 2.2 (1984).
> "Sanctuaries as Communities of Justice and Peace." *Tugon* 8.3 (1988).
> "Human Rights: A Theological and Historical Basis." In *Human Rights: Biblical and Theological Readings*, edited by Liberato Bautista. Quezon City: NCCP Human Rights Desk, 1988.
> "Towards a Prophetic Theology of History for Filipinos." *Tugon* 10.1 (1990).
> "From Swords to Ploughshares: A Foundation for Peace and Prosperity" and "Christ Our Peace: Building a Just Society." In *Bible Studies on the Theme of the Ninth Assembly of the CCA,* edited by Salvador T. Martinez. Hong Kong: CCA, 1990.
> "Reclaiming the Message and Spirit of Jubilee" and "The Year of Jubilee as an Occasion for Repentance." *Tugon* (Jubilee Campaign Special Issue) 13.1 (1999).

2.5.46. Luna Dingayan

Luna Dingayan wrote of a "Theology of Struggle" in post-graduate studies, and has been editor of *Kalinangan*, a progressive church magazine, published by the Institute of Religion and Culture (IRC). He has continued work in the area of the theology of struggle and contextual theology, with particular concerns also for the role of women in the church and for popular religiosity. He has served as dean of the College of Theology (and acting president) of Northern Christian College in Laoag City, and is currently the director of the UCCP Ecumenical Theological Seminary in Baguio City and member of the IRC Research Committee.

In reformulating Christology in the Philippine setting, Dingayan presents struggle and aspiration as the context, and struggling people as the doers, of Christology. He places this within the history and Christian experience of Filipinos, in "the struggle-context of Jesus and the early church, and in the context of contemporary Filipino imagery and writing." He concludes that such Christology will be radically different from traditional dogmas. It is only "the Christ who is truly human who can be truly divine"; Jesus' servanthood with people and his prophetic criticism of oppressive mentalities becomes central for understanding this. Here he empowered the "de-peopled to struggle," and in his death paid the price of struggle. His resurrection is the rising up of a suffering people. The continuing presence of God is found now where the actions of Jesus - to share, heal, feed, release - are continued through the struggle of his followers. This however requires conversion, not only personal, and in the structures of society, but also for the church - to become a people with people in the struggle. Any "second coming" of Jesus must be, affirms Dingayan, "the coming of a new heaven and new earth where people are re-born in Christ," when everyone comes to live Christ's life and teachings in a new community.

Selected References
Works by Luna Dingayan

"The Clenched Fist, the Barbed Wire and the Burning Candle." In *Doing Theology with People's Symbols & Images.* ATESEA

Occasional Papers 8, edited by Yeow Choo Lak and John C. England. Singapore: ATESEA/PTCA, 1989.

"Towards a Christology of Struggle: A Proposal for Understanding the Christ." *CTC Bulletin* 10.1 (1991).

"Popular Religion and Evangelization: A Philippine Experience." *International Review of Mission* 82 (1993).

"Women and Paul: An Inquiry into the Status of Women in the Early Church." *In God's Image* 16.3 (1997).

"The Road to Unity." *NCCP Magazine* 39.1 (1998).

2.6 Other Contributions to Contextual Filipino Theology

Comprehensive treatment of other contributions to contextual theology in the Philippines would require mention of many other theologians and groups, along with a range of Filipino poetry, fiction, art and music which expresses theological insight that arises from Filipino life. Only a little of that is possible here. However a selection of further theologians who have contributed to contextualizing Filipino theology must be given below, along with representative writings for some of their major concerns. This is done to make possible at least initial introduction to the very large body of contextual Filipino theology. Among the many women and men that should be noted here are theological teachers, pastors and religious, home-builders and parents, writers, activists, social workers, church leaders and missioners, scholars and researchers. (See also 2.3.) Writers are grouped according to their major concerns, although all are related to the formation of contextual theology in the Philippines and the work of individuals frequently overlaps several categories.

2.6.1. Contextual Theological Reflection and Spirituality

Rebecca C Asedillo is staff-member of the Institute of Religion and Cultures in the Philippines (IRC).

"A New Picture of Mary: A View From Below." *In God's Image* (April 1985).

Faith in struggle. SPI series. Faith and ideology. Manila: SPI, 1988.

Women of Faith: Bible Studies for Women's Group. Manila: IRC, 1996.

Charles Avila has written on philosophy, political economy, and on theological and sociological issues. He has also been an organizer of peasant and labor unions, cooperatives and community organizations.

—, comp. *Peasant Theology: Reflections by the Filipino Peasants on their Process of Social Revolution.* WSCF Asia series 1. Bangkok, WSCF Asia, 1976.

Ownership: Early Christian Teaching. Maryknoll, NY: Orbis Books; London: Sheed & Ward, 1983.

Nael Cortez (d. ca.1990) taught at Union Theological Seminary, before becoming general secretary of the WSCF (Asia-Pacific). With his wife Ruth he later founded the IRC (see 2.6.7.3.).

"Some Notes on the Theology of Struggle." *Kalinangan* 6.1 (1986).

—, et al. *The Struggle for Self-Reliance in Asia Today.* Bangkok: WSCF and IMCS Asia, 1976.

—, ed. *Faith and Social Justice.* WSCF Asia Book 4. Hong Kong: WSCF, 1978.

Benito M. Dominguez is a bishop of the UCCP, formerly coordinator of the Commission on Evangelism and Ecumenical Relations (CEER).

Tribal Filipinos: Fellow-Shapers of our Destiny as a Nation. Manila: People's Action for Cultural Ties, 1986.

A Theology of Struggle and the Jesus Tradition. Manila: SPI, ?1990.

"Theology of Struggle. Towards a Struggle with Human Face." *Kalinangan* 6.1 (1986).

"Heaven or New Earth." In *Witnessing Praxis in Mission. Proceedings of training Workshop for emerging URM Leadership, 1986.* Hong Kong: CCA-URM, 1986.

And No One Shall Go Hungry. Stewardship of all Creation. Quezon City: NCCP, 1988.

"God's Partners in the Kingdom." In *Turn Around. Called to Witness Together Amidst Asian Plurality CCA Asia Mission Conference, Seoul 1994.* Hong Kong: CCA, 1995.

Eleazar Fernandez is a UCCP pastor (Visayas) and has worked with the Socio-Pastoral Institute and with BCCs.

"Hermeneutics and the Bible in Liberation Theology: A Critique from Other Companions in the Struggle." *Tugon* 12.1 (1992).

Toward a Theology of Struggle. Maryknoll NY: Orbis Books, 1994.

"My Kingdom is Not of This World: Must We Abandon the Earth in Order to go to Heaven?" *Tugon* 9.3 (1991).

José Mario C. Francisco sj formerly taught at the Loyola School of Theology and is now director of the East Asian Pastoral Institute, Quezon City.

"Native Ground for Philippine and Theological Reflection." Mimeo'd. Quezon City: Loyola House of Studies, 1981.

Integrative or Decisive? Christian Symbols and Rituals in Philippine Society. Pulso Monograph 7. Manila: Institute on Church and Society Issues, 1991.

"Two Currents in Filipino Christianity." *Landas* 2.1; 2.2;(1988); 3.1 (1989).

"An Introductory Map of Narrative Theology." *Landas* 6.1 (1992).

"The Christ Story as the Subversive Memory of Tradition: Tagalog Texts and Politics around the Turn of the Century." In *Text and Politics in Island Southeast Asia*, edited by D.M. Roskies. Athens OH: University of Ohio, 1993.

"Interpreting Christian Symbols and Contemporary Events: The Hermeneutics of Traditional Tagalog Apocalyptic Groups." *Inter-Religio* 31 (1997).

"The Dynamics Between Catholicism and Philippine Society." *Inter-Religio* 37 (2000).

Judette Gallares rc a member of the Cenacle Congregation in the Philippines and a formator, spiritual director, writer and facilitator of workshops and retreats.

Images of Faith: Spirituality of Women in Old Testament. Maryknoll, NY: Orbis Books, 1992.

Images of Courage: Spirituality of Women in the Gospels from an Asian and Third World Perspective. Quezon City: Claretian, 1995.

Antonio Lambino sj formerly taught at the Loyola School of Theology, with particular concern for the relation of systematic theology to contemporary theological reflection and spirituality in Asia.

Towards "Doing Theology" in the Philippine Context. Quezon City: Loyola School of Theology, Ateneo de Manila University, 1977.

"Towards an Inculturated Theology in the Philippines." *SEAJT* 20.2 (1979).

"A Critique of Some Asian Efforts at Contextualization with reference to Theological Method." *SEAJT* 21.1 (1980).

"Inculturation in Asia: Going Beyond First Gear." *Landas* 1:72-80 (1987).

Arche Ligo is member of the faculty of the Institute of Formation and Religious Studies, Manila, and an active member of the AWIT and of the AWRCCT.

"Filipino Women's Quest for Healing and Integration." *In God's Image* 12.3 (1993).

"From Babaylan to Priests of Banahaw." *In God's Image* 11.4 (1992).

—, and Virginia Fabella, eds. *Dugo-Dugo ng Buhay* (Vital sap of life). Tagaytay City: Southeast Asia Conference of EATWOT, 1995.

—, and Rosario Battung. "Cosmic Spirituality for Wholeness of Life." *Lila - Asia Pacific Women's Studies Journal* 1/5/1995.

Ambrosio Manaligod, svd (d.1975) was for many years a leader in the movement to Filipinize the Catholic Church. He made particular studies of Aglipay and his work of Filipinization.

Gregorio Aglipay: Hero or Villain. Manila: Communication Foundation for Asia, 1977.

"Towards a Theology of the Local Church." *Philippine Priests' Forum* 2.1 (1970).

"Indigenization of the Church is Filipinization." *Philippine Priests' Forum* 3.3 (1971).

"Theological Basis of Filipinization." *Philippine Priests' Forum* 4.4 (1972).

"Progressive ecclesial Insights of the Paniqui Convention." *Philippine Priests' Forum* 4 (1972).

"Toward a Filipino Liberation Theology. Right, Center and Left." *Philippine Priests' Forum* 8 (1976) and 9 (1977).

Alfredo Salanga, is prize-winning poet, critic, essayist, novelist and playwright who has also explored in his works the Filipino search for God, and written on church history.

Chronicles & Dispatches. Quezon City: New Day Publishers, 1991.

Commentaries, Meditations, Messages, a Parable, Cycles and Confessions: poems 1969-1979. Quezon City: Aklat Peskador, 1985.

"Rebel Priests, Angry Bishops, Puzzled Laymen." In *Faith in Context* 1. Manila: SPI, 1983.

—, ed. *Corpus: An Anthology of Poets in Search of God.* Quezon City: New Day Publishers, 1989.

Rodrigo D. Tano (ca. 1933-) has taught at a number of colleges and been president of Ebenezer Bible College, Zamboanga. He has also pioneered studies of Filipino theology in a number of publications.

Theology in the Philippine Setting. A Case Study in the Contextualization of Theology. Quezon City: New Day Publishers, 1981.

"Theological Issues in the Philippine Context." *Evangelical Review of Theology* 19.4 (1995).

"Toward an Evangelical Asian Theology." In *Biblical Theology in Asia*, edited by Ken Gnanakan, 49-76. Bangalore: Asia Theological Association, 1995.

See also:

Delotavo, Allan J. "A Reflection on the Images of Christ in Filipino Culture." *Asia Journal of Theology* 3.2 (1989).

—. "Toward a Christ-Centered Way of Doing Theology in Asia." *Asia Journal of Theology* 3.1 (1989).

Harriman, Loretta. "Foundations for Theology: Establishing Perspectives for Understanding the Nature of Theology." *EAPR* 36.4 (1999).

—. "A Reflection on the Images of Christ in Filipino Culture." *Asia Journal of Theology* 3.2 (1989).

Nadeau, Kathleen M. *Liberation Theology in the Philippines: Faith in a Revolution.* Westport, Conn: Praeger. Forthcoming.

Sevilla, Pedro C. *People's Faith is People's Power. A Filipino Christological Catechism.* Quezon City: Loyola House of Studies, 1986.

—. "Christ at Edsa: the Filipino Faces of Christ and Christian Spirituality." *Landas* 2, 1988.

2.6.2. Regarding Philippine Church History

Apolonio M. Ranche is a historian of the Iglesia Filipina Independiente, concerned particularly for its nationalist and populist heritage.

"Inter-Caetera: A Reflection on Peace." *Tugon* 12.2 (1992).

"The Iglesia Filipina Independiente (IFI): A People's Movement for National Freedom, Independence and Prosperity." *Philippiniana Sacra* 35 (2000).

—, ed. *Doctrine and Constitutional Rules, Important Documents, Various Articles and Chronology of the Iglesia Filipina Independiente.* Quezon City: St. Andrew's Seminary, 1996.

John Schumacher has long been professor of church history at Loyola School of Theology and has completed major studies of nationalist Christian leaders and movements of the 19th century. He has also written on Catholic social doctrine.

The Propaganda Movement: 1880-1895. Manila: Solidaridad Publishing House, 1973.

Revolutionary Clergy: The Filipino Clergy and the Nationalist Movement, 1850-1903. Quezon City: Ateneo de Manila University, 1981.

Father Jose Burgos: a Documentary History with Spanish Documents and their Translation. Quezon City: Ateneo de Manila University, 1999.

"Syncretism in Philippine Catholicism: Its Historical Causes." *Philippiniana Sacra* 19.57 (1984).

"Social Teaching of the Church Revisited." *Landas* 4 (1990).

"Guidelines for the Study and Teaching of the Church's Social Doctrine in the Formation of Priests." *Landas* 41 (1990).

William Henry Scott (d. 1994) was a pioneering teacher of Filipino history and church history known for his critical acumen. He was also activist, linguist and essayist.

Cracks in the Parchment Curtain and other Essays in Philippine History. Quezon City: New Day Publishers, 1982.

The Discovery of the Igorots: Spanish Contacts with the Pagans of Northern Luzon. Quezon City: New Day Publishers, 1974.

Prehispanic Source Materials for the Study of Philippine History. Rev. ed. Quezon City: New Day Publishers, 1984.

Hollow Ships on a Wine-Dark Sea. Quezon City: New Day Publishers, 1976.

"The Philippine Independent Church in History." *East and West Review* 28.1 (1962); *Silliman Journal* 10.3 (1963).

"Worship in Igorot Life." *SEAJT* 4.1 (1963).

"History of the Inarticulate." *Diliman Review* July-Sept (1979).

T. Valentino Sitoy, Jr. is a prominent church historian with particular interests in both Catholic and Protestant history in the Philippines. He has been dean of the Silliman University Divinity School (1975-87).

The Initial Encounter: A History of Christianity in the Philippines. Quezon City: New Day Publishers, 1985.

Comity and Unity: Ardent Aspirations of Six Decades of Protestantism in the Philippines, 1901-1961. Quezon City: NCCP, 1989.

Several Springs, One Stream: The United Church of Christ in the Philippines. 2 Vols. Quezon City: UCCP, 1992, 1997.

"The Encounter between Christianity and Bukidnon Animism." *SEAJT* 10.2&3 (1969).

"The Catholic Teaching on Mariology, and Protestant Understanding of the Place of Mary in Christian Theology." In *Mary, the Mother of Jesus,* edited by Lydia Niguidula. Faith and Order Series 4. Quezon City: UCCP, 1993.

See also:

Pedro de Achutegui and Miguel A. Bernard. *Religious Revolution in the Philippines.* Manila: Ateneo de Manila University, 1960-1972: vol 4.

Deats, Richard L. *Nationalism and Christianity in the Philippines.* Dallas: Southern Methodist University, 1967.

2.6.3. Filipino History and Culture

Alexander Grant directed the Christian Institute for Ethnic Studies in Asia, Manila, from the 1960s to the 1980s, was active in ecumenical programs of cultural studies and acculturation, and edited *The Bulletin* of the Institute. See for example:

—, et al. *The Isneg of the Northern Philippines: A Study of Trends of Change and Development*, edited by Hubert Reynolds and Fern B. Grant. Dumaguete City: Anthropology Museum, Silliman University, c.1973.

—, ed. *Approaches to Mission in the Philippines*. (Theme Issue) *The Bulletin* 3.1-2 (1969).

—, ed. *Baguio Religious Acculturation Conference: Proceedings 1976-1979*. Manila: Christian Institute for Ethnic Studies in Asia, ?1980.

Albert E. Alejo is a theological teacher who believes that the exchange of faith is the basis of theologizing (not just theology), and that Filipino people are in some ways "living out a kind of theology that would be good to write down, but will not be dependent on it being written down."

Tao Po! Tuloy! Isang Landas Ng Pagunawa Sa Loob Ng Tao (Hello! Come in! A way of understanding the 'inside' of a person). Quezon City: Ateneo de Manila University, 1990.

—, ed. *Ang Mahalaga sa Buhay* (A handbook of Filipino values). Quezon City: New Day Publishers, 1992.

Jaime A. Belita cm is chiefly known for his work on the tasks and resources for a Filipino theology based in Filipino culture (1991).

From Logos to Diwa: A Synthesis of Theological Research in Catholic Graduate Schools in the Philippines, 1965-1985. Manila: De La Salle University, 1987.

The Way of Greater Self: Constructing a Theology around a Filipino Mythos. Manila: De La Salle University, c1991.

"The Santo Nino and the Nazareno: The Inculturation of Christ in Filipino Popular Religion." *EAPR* 30 (1993).

Kate C. Botengan is vice-president for academic affairs, Trinity College, Quezon City, and an editor of *Tugon: Ecumenical Journal of Discussion and Opinion*.

Bontoc Life-Ways. A Study in Education and Culture. Manila: Centro Escolar University, Research and Development Center, 1976.

"The Struggle of Ethnic Groups to be Free." In *Theology, Politics and Struggle*, edited by Feliciano Cariño. Quezon City: NCCP, 1986.

Bulatao, Jaime S. established the psychology department at Ateneo de Manila University, practiced as clinical psychologist and researched Filipino life extensively.

Phenomena and Their Interpretation. Quezon City: Ateneo de Manila University, 1992.

—, and Vitaliano R. Gorospe *Split-level Christianity and Christian Renewal of Filipino Values.* Quezon City: Ateneo de Manila University, 1966.

"Inculturating Christianity in East Asia" and "The Inculturation of the Faith." In *Inculturation, Faith and Christian Life.* Loyola Papers 6. Quezon City: Loyola School of Theology, 1978.

John J. Carroll sj has taught at the Ateneo de Manila University and has been director of research for the Institute of Social Order, Manila.

Looking Beyond EDSA. Parts I & II. Published as Human Society 42 & 43. Manila: Human Development Research and Documentation, 1986.

Philippine Values in Context. Human Society 22. Manila: Human Development Research and Documentation, 1989.

—, et al. *Philippine Institutions. The Challenges which Confront the Filipino.* Manila: Solidaridad Publishing, 1970.

"Faith Ideology and Social Action." In *Faith Ideologies and Christian Options.* Loyola Papers 7/8. Quezon City: Loyola School of Theology, 1978.

Henry Kiley (1936-) was formerly dean of St. Andrew's Seminary, Quezon City and the first Filipino to occupy that position.

"The Eucharistic Church." *Asia Journal of Theology* 4.2 (1990).

"Revelation Inside and Outside the Bible." In *Doing Theology with the Festivals and Customs of Asia.* ATESEA Occasional Papers 13, edited by Joseph Patmury, John C. England and Yeow Choo Lak. Singapore: ATESEA/PTCA, 1994.

—, ed. *Filipino Tribal Religious Experience II: Sickness, Death and after Death.* Biblical and Non-Biblical Revelation 2. Quezon City: Giraffe Books, 1994.

Lourdes R. Quisumbing (Mrs.) was formerly secretary of education, secretary general of the national UNESCO Commission, president of APNIEVE. (Asia Pacific Network for International Education and Values Education) and professor at Miriam College, Quezon City. She is also active in ecumenical networks.

"Religious Psychology of the Filipino Rural Adult." *DIWA* 2 (1977).

—, and Felice P. Sta. Maria, eds. *Values Education through History: Peace & Tolerance.* Pasay City, Manila: UNESCO National Commission of the Philippines, c1996.

An Instant is This Life: an Autobiography. Quezon City: Adarna Book Services, c1997.

Ramon C. Reyes has taught philosophy and ethics in various universities, with particular concerns for Filipino culture and human development.

"Rationalization and Culture." In *The Shape of Theological Education and Role of Field Experience in the 70s*, edited by Ciriaco Ma. Lagunzad Jr. Manila: Interseminary Program for Field Education, ?1971.

"Religious Experience in the Philippines: From Mythos through Logos to Kairos." *Philippine Studies* 33 (1985).

See also:

Bernard, Miguel. *Tradition and Discontinuity: Essays on Philippine History and Culture.* Manila: National Book Store, 1983.

Galdon, Joseph. "Education, Truth and Justice in Philippine Society." *Philippine Studies* 32 (1984).

2.6.4. Socio-political Theology and Concerns

Henry Aguilan has led many of the social and UIM ministries of NCCP since the late 1960s: in community organization, training and theological reflection.

"Nothing Less than Radical Change." *Ecumenical Review* 25 (1973).

See also: *Theology in Action*, edited by Oh Jae Shik and John C. England. Tokyo & Perth: EACC, 1972.

Liberato Bautista is co-ordinator of the Program Unit on Human Rights of the NCCP, with particular concerns also for social justice and peace-making.

"War, Peace, and the Ecumenical Movement in the Philippines." *Tugon* 9.3 (1991).

—, and S. Amirtham, eds. *Those Who Would Give Light Must Endure Burning. Consultation Report on Spirituality for Justice and Peace.* Quezon City: NCCP, 1987.

—, ed. *Human Rights: Biblical and Theological Readings.* Quezon City: NCCP Human Rights Desk, 1988.

José C. Blanco sj is director of AKKAPKA (Action for Peace and Justice), Manila, and Asia secretary of the Fellowship of Reconciliation.

"Aggiornamento and Works of Liberation." *Philippine Studies* 20.2 (1972).

"The Cultural Context of the Service of the Faith in the Promotion of Justice." In *Faith Ideologies and Christian Options.* Loyola Papers 7/8. Quezon City: Loyola School of Theology, 1978.

"The Gospel of Absolute Respect: A Spirituality of People Power." In *Towards a Theology of People Power: Reflections on the Philippine February Phenomenon,* edited by D.J. Elwood. Quezon City: New Day Publishers, 1988.

Mario V. Bolasco is a socio-political theologian who has taught at St. Scholastica's College, Manila.

Christianity and the Philippine Liberation Movement. Quezon City: SPI, 1986.

—, and Rolando Yu. *Church and State under Martial Law.* Manila, St. Scholastica's College, 1981.

—, and Edicio de la Torre, eds. *Points of Departure: Essays on Christianity, Power and Social Change.* Manila: St. Scholastica's College, c1994.

Erme Camba is a bishop of the UCCP and formerly its general secretary. He has been active in the EBF and in regional ecumenical programs. He has written on ecumenical and social issues including the struggle for justice and the quest for peace.

Faith Action and Politics. The Subir Biswas Memorial Lectures. Bangalore. NCC-UIRM, 1985.

"Emerging Ecumenical Co-operation - A New Ecclesiology?" *Japan Christian Quarterly* 52.1 (1986).

"End the Stranglehold of Debt on Impoverished People." *Tugon* (Jubilee Campaign Special Issue) 13.1 (1999).

Jose W. Diokno (d.1987) was formerly secretary of justice, peace negotiator for the President, and fearless campaigner for rights of the poor and the victims of abuse and injustice.

Justice under Siege. Five Talks. Manila: Nationalist Resource Centre, 1981.

"Rizal's Continuing Challenge." *Solidarity* 95 (1983).

See also: *Files on Notes and Clippings 1971-1987.* Quezon City: Jose W.Dioko Foundation, ?1988.

Fidel Galang (d. ca. 1980) was district superintendent for the United Methodist Church in troubled Pampanga district (1950s) and concerned for Christian action in disturbed areas.

"A Theory of Protestant Social Action." ThD Dissertation, School of Theology, Boston University, 1954.

"A Theory of Bible Translation in the Philippines." *SEAJT* 4.1 (1962).

Helen Graham mm is a Maryknoll sister who teaches at the Sister Formation Institute, Manila, and lectures throughout Asia.

"Empowerment of Women for Peace." In *Religion and Society: Towards A Theology of Struggle*. Book I, edited by Battung et al. Manila: FIDES, 1988.

"The Role of Faith in the Struggle." In *Currents in Philippine Theology*, edited by None S.Aviso et al. Kalinangan Book Series II. Quezon City: IRC, 1992.

"The Bible Tells it All." *NCCP Magazine* 34.3 (1994).

Jurgette Honculada has been active in student and ecumenical movements nationally and internationally and has been a president of the CCA.

"Notes on Women and Christianity in the Philippines." *In God's Image* Oct. (1985).

"Martha and Mary: The Burden and Blessing of Gender." In *Women of Courage in the Bible. Asian Women Reading the Bible*, edited by Lee Oo Chung et al. Seoul: AWRCCT, 1992.

"Winners and Losers: or the Triumphal Entry Revisited." *In God's Image* 15.1 (1996).

Romeo Intengan sj is a scholar critical of totalitarianism and concerned for human rights but believes the Gospel, not Marxism, provides the anthropology and the human rights necessary. Evangelism for him is an integral part of human development.

"Christians for Socialism and the Question of Christian-Marxist Relations: A Practical Philippine Perspective." *Teaching All Nations* 14.3 & 4 (1977).

"Christian Faith, Ideologies and Social Change." *Landas* 2.1 (1988).

"Human Dignity and Human Rights." *Landas* 7.2 (1993).

Luis Jalandoni was formerly a Cathedral priest in Negros, closely associated with ministries among sugar workers, and is a theological animateur.

"The Role of the Priest in Political Liberation." *Philippine Priests' Forum,* June (1972).

"Actual Conditions in the Rural Areas of the Philippines." In *An Asian Theology of Liberation: the Philippines*. IDOC documentation participation project 5. New York: IDOC North America, 1973.

"A Filipino Liberation Theology." *The Christian Century*, April 16 (1975).

Salvador T. Martinez was formerly dean of arts and sciences at Silliman University, and later staff member of CTC-CCA. He now teaches theology at Payap University, Thailand. He is also an artist and hymn writer, and edited *PTCA Bulletin* 1994-2000.

"On Doing Theology with the Economy and Cultures of the Philippines." *PTCA Bulletin* 11 (1998).

—, ed. *Mission of God in the Context of the Suffering & Struggling Peoples of Asia. Biblical Reflections: Asia Mission Conference 1989*. Chiangmai: CCA, 1988.

—, ed. *Peoples of Asia, People of God: A Report of the Asia Mission Conference 1989.* Osaka: CCA, 1990.

Jeremias U. Montemayor was formerly a leader in the work of the Federation of Free Farmers, and active in organizing, educating and writing.

Catholic Social Teaching. Manila: Rex Book Store, 1989.

"The Process of Development in Asian Society." *Solidarity* 5.10 (1970).

"Philippine Catholics and the Social Problem." In *The Encounter* by J.V. Braganza. Manila: Catholic Trade School, 1965.

—, ed. *Catholic Social Teaching and Philippine Social Problems.* Manila: Rex Book Store, 1987.

Valentino Montes (d. 1966) was a staff member of the National Council of Churches responsible for social ministries who pioneered approaches to urban and social mission in the Philippines.

"The Church and Social Questions." *Commentary on Industrial Evangelism* 12 (1960).

"Social Thinking of the Churches in the Philippines." *SEAJT* 4.1 (1962).

"The Christian and Politics" and "The Christian and Nationalism." In *Philippines Social Issues From a Christian Perspective*, edited by Richard Poethig. Quezon City: UCCP, 1963.

Jovito Salonga was formerly a prominent Philippine senator campaigning for effective and just democratic structures, and is a widely recognized lay theologian.

"The Christian Layman in the World of Politics." *Advance* (August 1960).

"Strategies in Christian Participation in Social Movements in Asia." *NCCP Social Education*, Mimeo'd, Sept. 1970.

"The Christian Gospel and Human Rights: An Ecumenical Perspective." In *Faith and Justice and the Filipino Christian*, edited by V.R. Gorospe. Manila: NASSA, LST & PACT, 1976.

See also:

Gerlock, Ed. *Signs of Hope: Stories of Hope in the Philippines.* Davao City: Philippine International Forum; Quezon City: Claretian, c1990.

Cecchini, Rose Marie. *Women's Actions for Peace and Justice: Christian, Buddhist, and Muslim Women Tell Their Story.* Maryknoll, NY: Orbis Books, 1990.

Fuliga, José B. "Law and Gospel: A Process of Preaching the whole Counsel of God." *SEAJT* 19.1 (1978).

"Church-State Relations and Civil Disobedience." *Asia Journal of Theology* 1.2 (1987).

Marasigan, Vicente. "Filipino Experience of Human Suffering." *EAPR* 21.4 (1984).

—, "Visions and Collaborative Practice." *Landas* 4.1 (1990).

Mendiola, Maria Ramona. "Participation of a Nation in Crisis in the Universal Mission of Christ." *Philippine Priests' Forum* 4 (1972).

—, "Human Rights: Context or Content of Mission?" *International Review of Mission* 66 (1977).

Tabing-Reyes, Corazon. "Towards a Theology of People's Solidarity." *East Asia Journal of Theology* 2.2 (1984).

2.6.5. Pastoral and Missiological Studies

Douglas J. Elwood has been professor of theology and ethics and coordinator of graduate studies at Silliman University Divinity School.

Faith Encounters Ideology: Christian Discernment and Social Change. Quezon City: New Day Publishers, 1985.

"Christian Theology in an Asian Setting." *SEAJT* 16.2 (1975).

—, ed. *Towards a Theology of People Power: Reflections on the Philippine February Phenomenon*. Quezon City: New Day Publishers, 1988.

—, and Patricia Ling Magdamo. *Christ in Philippine Context: a College Textbook in Theology and Religious Studies*. Quezon City: New Day Publishers, 1971.

Jesus V. Fernandes sj is a homiletics professor of long standing at the Loyola School of Theology, and one-time editor of the *Philippine Priests' Forum*, of *Life Forum* and of *Ministry Today*, all three publications considered to be then the voice of the local church of the Philippines. He has also been president of the Catholic Press Association of the Philippines.

"Theological Basis of Filipinization." *Philippine Priests' Forum* 4.4 (1972).

Fern Babcock Grant (d. ca. 1990), an expatriate missioner, was active from the 1950s to the 1980s in literature production and writing and an editor of both *Church and Community* and publications of New Day Publishers (formerly Christian Literature Society of the Philippines).

Ministries of Mercy. New York: Friendship Press, 1962.

—, and Hubert Reynolds, eds. *The Isneg of the Northern Philippines: a Study of Trends of Change and Development.* Dumaguete City: Silliman University, c1973.

—, et al., eds. *Muslim-Christian marriages in the Philippines: studies made in North Cotabato.* Quezon City: New Day Publishers, c1980.

James Kroeger mm is associate professor of systematic theology at Loyola School of Theology.

Human Promotion as an Integral Dimension of the Church's Mission of Evangelization: a Philippine Experience and Perspective since Vatican II, 1965-1984. Maryknoll NY: Orbis Books, 1985.

"Signs of the Times - A Thirty-year Panorama." *EAPR* 26 (1989).

"Catechesis in Popular Pageantry: Philippine Resurrection Rituals." *The Living Light* 26, Winter (1990).

"Living Mission in Asia." *EAPR* 29 (1992).

"Signposts of the Spirit for Mission." *Landas* 10.1 (1996).

—, ed. *Interreligious Dialogue: Catholic Perspectives.* Davao City: Mission Studies Institute, c1990.

Menelao D. Litonjua was for some years active in the activities of the Philippine Priests' Forum and earlier wrote regularly for them. He now teaches in the USA.

Liberation Theology: The Paradigm Shift. Lanham, MD: University Press of America, 1998.

"Double Fidelity in Evangelization." *The Philippine Priests' Forum* December (1977).

Series of "Theological Reflections." In *1976 Alay Kapwa Handbook.* National Lenten Action Program of the Catholic Church in the Philippines.

"Education for Justice: A Prophetic Task." *The Philippine Priests' Forum* June and September (1975).

"Dissent in the Church." *The Philippine Priests' Forum* September (1969).

Brendan Lovett is a St. Columban missioner and educator who has studied linguistic analysis and approaches in theology. His theological writings concentrate on the analysis of recent human development as cultural process.

Life before Death. Quezon City: Claretian, 1986.

On Earth as in Heaven: Corresponding to God in Philippine Context. Quezon City: Claretian, c1988.

It's Not Over Yet. Christological Reflections on Holy Week. Quezon City: Claretian, 1990.

"Religion and Popular Religiosity in the Philippines." *Asia Journal of Theology* 1.2 (1987).

Eli Mapanao was formerly president of Southern Christian College in Midsayap, Cotabato, and has initiated socially concerned programs of education and ministry.

"The Statement of Social Concern: Its Use and Relevance to the Local Church." *Commentary on Industrial Evangelism* 13 (1960).

"Ecumenical Education for Mission." In *Ecumenical Education for Renewal, Unity and the Mission of the Church in Changing Asian Societies*, edited by Pura P. Calo and Hope Antone. Singapore: CCA, 1988.

Change and Decay: The Either/Or of Christian Education. Quezon City: UCCP, 1989.

In the Valley of the Shadow of Death I Fear no Evil. Quezon City: UCCP, 1989.

Victoria Narciso-Apuan of Miriam College, Quezon City, is also a consultant of the PCP II Commission on the Laity.

"Spirit Speaks: the Good News according to PCP II. A Lay-woman's Perspective in Journeying with the Spirit." In *A Commentary on PCP II*. Quezon City: Claretian, 1993.

—, et al. eds. *Witness and Hope Amid Struggle. Towards a Theology and Spirituality of Struggle.* Book II. Manila: FIDES, 1991.

Jacob Quiambao (d. ca. 1985) was formerly president and professor of social ethics at Union Theological Seminary, Dasmariñas. He also conducted workshops in pastoral theology throughout the Asian region and taught later at Wesleyan College in Macon, Georgia.

"Toward Leadership in Family Planning." *Church and Community* 7.6 (1967).

"The Image of the Ministry we need in the '70's." In *The Image of the Ministry in the 70's*, edited by Ciriaco Ma. Lagunzad, Jr. Manila: Interseminary Program for Field Education, ?1970.

Cirillo A. Rigos (d. ca. 1998) was known firstly as a fine preacher, chiefly at Cosmopolitan Church, Manila, but also as an aware theologian contributing to writings and discussions on issues of church and state and of Filipino national identity.

Christians and Revolution: Sermons ... Manila: Cosmopolitan Church, 1972.

"To Be Filipino." In *Southeast Asians Speak Out*, edited by Barbara and Leon Howell. New York: Friendship Press, 1975.

Rebuilding on Broken Faith. Manila: Cosmopolitan Church, 1998. Includes the 3 vols.: *Rebuilding on Broken Faith* (1964), *Christians and Revolution* (1972) and *Love is Involvement* (1988).

Jaime L. Sin was consecrated bishop in 1967 and archbishop in 1974. He is known for his outspoken role in both religious and socio-political concerns.

Selected Writings on Church-State Relations and Human Development. Manila: Center for Human Development in Rural Areas, 1984.

"Human Rights and Poverty." *Philippiniana Sacra* 20.60 (1985).

"The Church in the Philippines 27 Years after Vatican II." *Landas* 2.1 (1988).

"Spanish Christianity: A Filipino Response." *Boletin Eclesiastico de Filipinas* 68 (1992).

"Women of Faith and the future of the nation." *Boletin Eclesiastico de Filipinas* 74 (1998).

"The Theologian as Gardener." *Landas* 13.1 (1999).

"'Carving out the Asian Face of Christ': Challenge to a New Ecclesiastical Faculty." *Landas* 13.2 (1999).

Lourdino Yuzon has been dean of the Divinity School, Silliman University, secretary for Mission and Evangelism for the CCA, and general secretary for the Council for Mission and Ecumenical Co-operation (COMEC), New Zealand.

"Building Communities of Justice and Peace in the Philippines." *Tugon* 10.2-3 (1991).

"Towards A Contextual Theology." *CTC Bulletin* 12.2, 13.1-2 (1994-1995).

"Communicating the Christian Message." *SEAJT* 23.1 (1982).

"God's Mission and Ours in Context." Mimeo'd. Auckland: COMEC, 1991.

"Communicating the Good News." *Asia Journal of Theology* 8.2 (1994).

—, ed. *Mission in the Context of Endemic Poverty and in Situations of Affluence. Papers of a Consultation.* Singapore: CCA, 1983.

See also:

Arichea, Daniel. *Despair and Hope - Bible Studies.* Quezon City: NCCP, 1973.

—. "Taking Theology Seriously in the Translator's Task." *Bible Translator* 33.3 (1982).

Clark, Francis X. "Making the Gospel at Home in Asian Cultures." *Teaching All Nations* 13 (1976).

—. *"Mission" and the Philippines: Past, Present, Future.* Manila: The Loyola School of Theology, 1981.

Gomez, Felipe. "Christology and Pastoral Practice From Below." *EAPR* 19.1 (1982).

2.6.6. Theological Education and Indigenization

Fausto B. Gomez op is dean of the faculty of sacred theology at the University Santo Tomas, Manila, and head of the Social Research Center, UST.

"Theological Formation in Context: Pastoral and Spiritual Dimensions." *Boletin Eclesiastico de Filipinas* 60 (1984).

"Paths of Liberation Towards Freedom." *Philippiniana Sacra* 21.62 (1986).

"The Holy Eucharist and Commitment to Justice and Solidarity." *Philippiniana Sacra* 22.66 (1987).

"Development through Solidarity: Reading and Commenting 'Sollicitudo Rei Socialis'." *Philippiniana Sacra* 25.71 (1989).

"Meaning of Justice, Peace and the Preferential Option for the Poor." *Philippiniana Sacra* 25.75 (1990).

Ciriaco Lagunzad, Jr. taught for many years at the St. Andrews Theological Seminary, Quezon City, and also directed the Office of Field Education there. He was later general secretary of the NCCP.

"A Critique of Theological Education." *Tugon* 4.2 (1984).

—, ed. "Situational Theology for Today." In *The Image of the Ministry in the 70's*. Manila: Interseminary Program for Field Education, ?1970.

—, ed. *The Shape of Theological Education and Role of Field Experience in the 70's*. Manila: Inter Seminary Program for Field Education, St. Andrew's Theological, Seminary, 1971?.

—, ed. *Experiential Theology*. Quezon City: St. Andrew's Theological Seminary, 1975.

Paul Lauby was associate professor in New Testament and Christian ethics, and chaplain, Silliman University; later he served as general secretary of the Associated Board for Christian Higher Education in Asia.

Sailing on Winds of Change: Two Decades in the Life of the United Board for Christian Higher Education in Asia, 1969-1990. New York: United Board for Christian Higher Education in Asia, 1996.

"The Protestant Ministry's Attitudes concerning the Economic Order in the Philippines." *SEAJT* 2.1 (1960).

"A Theological Core Curriculum with Reference to Asian Needs." *SEAJT* 3.4 (1962).

Richard Poethig was director of Inter-Seminary Urban Industrial Institute, Manila, and an animator in social ministries and theology.

Philippine Social Issues from a Christian Perspective. Manila: UCCP, Department of Christian Education, 1963.

Cities are for Living. New Day Booklet. Quezon City: New Day Publishers, 1972.

"The Protestant Ministry in a Period of High Social Mobility." *SEAJT* 6.2 (1964).

"Theological Education and the Urban Situation in Asia." *SEAJT* 13.2 (1972).

See also:

Esperito, Caesar. "The Intellectual and Spiritual Climate in the Asian University Today." *Student World* 55.3 (1962).

Ferriols, Roque J. *Pambungad sa metapisika*. Quezon City: Ateneo de Manila University, c1991.

—. *Magpakatao :ilang babasahing pilosopiko*. Quezon City: Ateneo de Manila University, 1999.

Gamboa, José, Jr. "Directing Christian Education Toward Urgent Social Action." *SEAJT* 12 (Autumn 1970).

—. "A Survey of Theological Education in Non-Traditional Styles." *East Asia Journal of Theology* 1.2 (1983).

2.6.7. The Contributions of Centers, Movements, Institutions
2.6.7.1. Catholic Bishops' Conference of the Philippines, Manila (CBCP 1945-)

The Catholic Bishops' Conference was first formed in 1945, although documents and pastoral letters of the Conference are so far available only since 1968. These, however, provide many of the "substantive Filipino theological texts of our generation" (Arevalo 1998). Pastoral Letters have been issued at least annually, on the apostolates for peace, evangelization, catechesis, pastoral ministry, social action and biblical study, as well as on civic, political and ecological responsibility, education for justice and non-violence and on current major events in the Philippines. As guides to pastoral and missionary activity they articulate, despite frequent sharp divisions within the conference, "an ecclesiology of transformative praxis in history" which has sought to make the Gospel effective in Philippine history. They have often done this by responding to socio-political realities using a "signs of the times" theological method which makes human promotion central to any integral evangelization. Documents from the Plenary Councils of the Philippines (1953 and 1991), in which approximately a quarter were bishops, have also shown, especially in the latter, "a search for an authentic and credible Christian living in contemporary

Philippine setting" (see for example, the special issue of *DIWA* 16.2, 1991.) Adviser-presenter theologians for the Conference have included Francisco Claver, Catalino Arevalo, Antonio Lambino, Teodoro Bacani and José Blanco.

A grouping of 17 more socially concerned bishops within the conference have initiated programs and issued documents since 1970 (see for example *Ut Omnes Unim Sint*, Davao, Nov. 4, 1976). A number of individual bishops, such as Francisco Claver, Teodoro Bacani and Julio Labayen, along with Archbishop Jaime Sin (for these see 2.5.5.; 2.5.22; 2.5.4.; 2.6.5.), have become known for their writings and incisive statements. A number of bishops have also cooperated with Protestant and Independiente colleagues in the EBF and in FIDES and EATWOT.

Selected References

Works from CBCP

> *Pastoral Letter of the Catholic Hierarchy of the Philippines on Evangelization and Development*, edited by Tiepisto V. Alberto et al. Baguio: CBCP, 1973.
>
> Catholic Episcopal Commission on Social Action, Justice and Peace. *A Decade of Social Action: A Commemorative of the 10th Anniversary of the Episcopal Commission and the National Secretariat of Social Action, Justice and Peace (NASSA), 1966-1976*. Manila: Apostolic Nunciature; NASSA, 1976.
>
> *The Philippines: Exhortation against Violence: A Joint Pastoral Letter of the Philippine Hierarchy*. Church in the World 6. London: CIIR, 1982?
>
> *Reflections on the Philippine Church*. (Bishops' Documents.) Human Society 19. Manila: Human Development Research and Documentation, 1983.
>
> "Philippine Bishops' Joint Pastoral Letter on the Biblical Apostolate." *Word Event* 15.59 (1985).
>
> "Church Power and the Revolution." *Ministry Today* 2.3 (1986).
>
> "Solidarity for Peace. Pastoral Letter of the Catholic Bishops' Conference." *Weltkirche* 2 (1988).
>
> *Letters and Statements, 1984-1990*. Quezon City: Cardinal Bea Institute, Loyola School of Theology, Ateneo de Manila University, 1990.

Pastoral Letter of the Philippine Catholic Hierarchy on 'Social Justice'. May 21, 1949. In *Ours to Share: An Approach to Philippine Social Problems*, by Jeremias Montemayor. Manila: Rex Bookstore, 1966.

"Exhortation on Philippine Politics. Pastoral Letter of the Catholic Bishops' Conference of the Philippines." *Catholic International* 9 (1998).

"Pastoral Exhortation on Philippine Culture." *Landas* 13.1 (1999).

Bacani, Teodoro. *Towards the Third Millennium: The Vision of the Second Plenary Council of the Philippines.* Manila: CBCP, 1991.

Bernier, P., and M.G. Gabriel, eds. *Journeying with the Spirit. A Commentary on PCP II.* Quezon City: Claretian, 1993.

Carroll, John J. and Francisco F. Claver. "The Pastoral Priorities of Philippine Bishops." *Ministry Today* 1.1 (1985).

Hardy, Richard P., ed. *The Philippine Bishops Speak (1968-1983).* Quezon City: Maryhill School of Theology. 1984.

—. *Ating mga kapatid* (To our brothers and sisters): *A Spirituality of the Catholic Bishops' Conference of the Philippines.* Quezon City: Maryhill School of Theology, 1984.

Josol, A. Ma C., ed. *Response to the Signs of the Times: Selected Documents of the Catholic Bishops' Conference of the Philippines.* Quezon City: Claretian; Cebu City: Redemptorist Press, 1991.

Kroeger, James. *Human promotion as an integral dimension of the church's mission of evangelization: a Philippine experience and perspective since Vatican II, 1965-1984.* Roma: Pontificia Universitas Gregoriana, Facultas Missiologiae, 1985.

Nemet, Ladislav. "Inculturation in the Philippines: A Theological Study of the Question of Inculturation in the Documents of CBCP and Selected Filipino Theologians in the Light of Vatican II and the Documents of FABC." Doctoral dissertation, Facultas Theologiae, Pontificia Universitas Gregoriana (Roma), 1994.

Santos, Ruperto C. "A Short History of the Catholic Bishops' Conference of the Philippines, 1945-1995." *Philippiniana Sacra* 32.96 (1997).

Three Bishops Speak. Human Society 22. Manila: Human Development Research and Documentation, 1989.

2.6.7.2. East Asian Pastoral Institute, Quezon City (EAPI 1961-)

Founded as an Institute of Missionary Apologetics by Johannes Hofinger sj to assist religious, laity and missioners in establishing "intelligent dialogue with the Asian community," it became in 1958 the Catechetical Center, and later the East Asian Pastoral Institute (1961). With collaborators such as Fr. Paul Brunner, José M\ua Calle, and Martin Ramsauer, besides Hofinger, it published the bimonthly review *Good Tidings* (1962-) and *Teaching All Nations* (1964-), plus other minor publications like *Amen* and the *Pamphlets For Training Catechists*. All these periodicals eventually merged into the *East Asian Pastoral Review* (1980-). Ateneo University, through the mediation of the Jesuit Provincials Francis Clark and Horacio de la Costa, offered facilities and from 1968, the Institute became more fully *pastoral* in wide-ranging courses based on the teachings of Vatican II which integrate faith and life within the cultural heritage of the Philippines and other Asian countries. Current editors of the *East Asia Pastoral Review* are Kathleen Coyle (2.5.14) ssc and Leticia A. Taberdo.

See also many similar institutes throughout the archipelago, including:

Cebuano Studies Center, University of San Carlos, Cebu City; Institute of Cotabato and Sulu Cultures (ICSC) and Peace Education Center (PEC), Notre Dame University, Cotabato City; San Carlos Pastoral Formation Complex, Makati City; Institute on Church and Social Issues, Ateneo de Manila University, Quezon City; St. Mary's Theologate, Center of Studies of Religion & Culture, Ozamiz City; De la Salle University Social Development Research Center, Manila; and the Institute on Church and Social Issues (ICSI), Quezon City.

Selected References

Clark, Francis X. "In Memoriam Johannes Hofinger S.J. (1905-1984). Life and Bibliography." *EAPR* 21.2 (1984).
King, Geoffrey J. "EAPI at Twenty-five: Evaluation, Mission Statement, Mission Plans." *EAPR* (1991).
O'Gorman, Thomas H. "At the Threshold of the Third Decade: The EAPI Looks Ahead." *EAPR* (1987).

2.6.7.3. Institute for Religion and Culture, Quezon City, Cebu City, Bukidnon (IRC 1980-)

The Institute for Religion and Culture was founded by Nael and Ruth Cortez (2.6.1, formerly of WSCF Asia-Pacific) and colleagues who were deeply committed to the transformation of church and society. Believing that "God is calling and empowering the Filipino people in their struggle to be truly a people," and that "faith can be a liberating force," they have initiated courses, seminars, consultations, work parties and publications which "motivate believers to participate in the transformation of church and society." Programs have included "Bible in Context"; "Leadership for Ministries"; "Study of Church and Society"; "Renewing the Earth"; along with Women's Orientation: "Women and Bible" seminars; "God-images, Language and Liturgy"; "Women and Men - co-disciples and co-ministers." The IRC has also cooperated in programs with Roman Catholic agencies such as the Catholic International Justice and Peace Commission.

Selected References
> The quarterly journal *Kalinangan* (since 1980) is directed to develop and enhance theology which is rooted in the concrete experiences and situations of Filipinos.
> Occasional volumes have also been published, notably:
> Aviso, Nonie S. et al. *Phillipine Society - Reflections on Contemporary Issues.* Kalinangan Book Series I. 1990.
> *Currents in Philippine Theology.* Kalinangan Book Series II. Quezon City: IRC, 1992.

2.6.7.4. Institute for Studies in Asian Church and Culture, Quezon City (ISACC)

This is a research and training organization working for community development, and in cross-cultural studies and missiology. Its purpose is to "creatively witness to the Lordship of Jesus in all of life by penetrating culture with the values of the Kingdom and engaging the powers towards social transformation." This is furthered by capacity-building programs; through research in social development issues; through research and training in Gospel and culture issues to enable the churches and mission organizations to more effectively witness in the context of Filipino and Asian cultures; and political advocacy through publications and various other media in, for example, popular education for good governance. Publications address, *inter alia*, the issues of Filipino culture and society; economic, political, socio-cultural inequalities, indigenous forms of worship and music; Filipino ways of communicating; biblical studies; and community development training. The Institute also publishes tri-annually the magazine, *PATMOS, A Vision for Our Times* on socio-political-cultural issues from a biblical perspective. See also 2.5.28, 2.5.29.

Selected References

Maggay, Melba Padilla. *Understanding Ambiguity in Filipino Communication Patterns.* Quezon City: ISACC.
—. *Pagbabalik-loob* (On Filipino culture) *Moral Recovery and Cultural Reaffirmation.* Diliman, Quezon City: Akademya ng Kultura at Sikolohiyang Pilipino; Quezon City: ISACC, c1993.
—. *Transforming Society.* Quezon City: ISACC, c1996.
—. *Filipino Religious Consciousness: Some Implications to Missions.* Quezon City: ISACC, 1999.
Miranda-Feliciano, Evelyn. *Unequal Words.* Quezon City: ISACC.
—. *Of Songs, Words and Gestures: Rethinking our Filipino Liturgy.* Quezon City: ISACC.
—. *Si Eba, Maria, Deborah and Maria Clara: A Bible Study Guide on Women.* Quezon City: ISACC.
—, et al. *Courage to Live These Days.* Quezon City: ISACC.

2.6.7.5. Institute of Women's Studies, St. Scholastica's College, Manila (1988-)

The Institute of Women's Studies was established as an affiliate unit of the college in 1988. The Institute's goals are: to awaken a consciousness to and provide an understanding of the woman question through a strategy of formal (institutional) and non-formal alternative education; engage in research and study on gender issues, and projects that uphold the cause of women; conduct outreach programs that serve women outside the formal educational institution. Programs include seminars and training programs, research and publication, resource and development and the Center for Women's Wholeness. The Resource and Development Program, or library, provides information to non-governmental and governmental organizations that need gender-oriented information. A main focus for the Institute is violence against women, along with the need to explore alternative and non-patriarchal sources of information both artifactual and archival. Publications include collections of articles on women's concerns, collections of poetry and story on the pains and difficulties a woman encounters as a result of her participation in a liberation movement, writings that explore the stage of feminist awakening as it redefines ancient epic and myths, and collections of liturgies, art forms and personal histories.

(Note also the Asian Christian Center for Women Studies at Asian Theological Seminary, Manila).

Selected References

Mananzan, Mary John. *Essays on Women*. Manila: IWS, St. Scholastica's College, 1987.
—. *The Asian Women: Image and Status*. Singapore: CCA, 1988.
—. *Challenges to the Inner Room*. Manila: IWS, St. Scholastica's College, 1999.
—. *Women and Religion, A Collection of Essays, Personal Histories, and Contextualized Liturgies*. Manila: St. Scholastica's College, 1988. (3rd. ed. 1999.)
Barrios, Josephine. *Ang Pagiging Babae ay Pamumuhay sa Panahon ng Digmaan*. Manila: IWS, St. Scholastica's College, 1990.
Bobis, M. *Ang Lipad ay Awit sa Apat na Hangin* (Flight is song). Manila: IWS, St. Scholastica's College, 1990.
Tengco-Labayen, Fe Corazâon. *In Every Woman: Asian Women's Journey to Feminist Awakening*. Manila: IWS, St. Scholastica's College, 1998.

2.6.7.6. National Council of Churches in the Philippines, Quezon City (NCCP 1963-)

Formed in 1963, on the earlier bases of the National Evangelical Union (1901) and the Philippine Federation of Christian Churches (see 1.7.2.). Since then the Council's work and membership has grown in many areas, under the leadership of José Yap, Ciriaco Lagunzad, Laverne Mercado, Feliciano Cariño, Roman Tiples and

Sharon Rose Joy Ruiz-Duremdes, and generations of committed staff-persons. Almost every aspect of the life and mission of churches in the Philippines has been nurtured, studied and resourced through the Council's many program departments and consultations. Regarding major social and political issues, the NCCP has also often maintained in its ecumenical obedience, a prophetic witness on behalf of the deprived and victimized in Philippine society.

The subjects of studies undertaken by the Council have included women's ministries, human rights, indigenous people's struggles, sustainable development, comity in mission, peace-making in the southern Philippines, 'theology of life,' Gospel and culture, mass media, and national and international debt. Statements or Policy Papers issued have included, among others, those on Martial Law, Warrantless Arrests, National Elections, Capital Punishment, Peace in the South, Extra-judicial Executions and Disappearances, Land Use, Taxation, and 'Abundant Life for All.' The NCCP has also regularly published *Tugon: Ecumenical Journal of Discussion and Opinion* and the *NCCP Magazine*.

Selected References

National Christian Rural Life Conference of the Philippines. *United Christian Witness for Rural Philippines: Report of the National Christian Rural Life Conference of the Philippines, December 17-20, 1954*, edited by Cornelio M. Ferrer. Manila: Dept. of Rural Life, Philippine Federation of Christian Churches, 1955.
Saunders, Albert. *Evangelical Ministry in the Philippines.* Quezon City: NCCP, for Union Theological Seminary, c1964.
Theology, Politics and Struggle, edited by Feliciano Cariño. Quezon City: NCCP, 1986.
Amirtham, Samuel and L. Bautista, eds. *Those who would Give Light. Consultation on Spirituality for Justice and Peace of the NCCP and WCC, November 1986.* Quezon City: NCCP, 1987.
Bautista, Liberato, ed. *Human Rights: Biblical and Theological Readings.* Quezon City: NCCP Human Rights Desk, 1988.
Realizing a Vision of Women in the Church. Quezon City: NCCP, 1989.
Yuzon, Lourdino, ed. *The Asia-Pacific Situation and the Ecumenical Response.* National Council of Churches in the Philippines

Readings on International Affairs 5. Manila: NCCP International Affairs Desk, 1989.

General Convention of the National Council of Churches in the Philippines. *Seek Peace and Pursue it: A Resource Book for the 14th General Convention of the National Council of Churches in the Philippines.* Quezon City: NCCP, c1989.

Formilleza, Prima S. *The Mission of God in the Context of the Suffering and Struggling People: a Report of the Philippine Mission Conference, January 15-19, 1990.* Quezon City: NCCP, 1990.

"Co-operatives: An Ecumenical Perspective." Policy Paper of NCCP General Council. *Tugon* 12.3 (1992).

Bautista, Liberato and Elizabeth Rifareal, eds. *And she said No!: Human Rights, Women's Identities and Struggles.* Quezon City: NCCP, 1990.

NCCP Booklets include: Cariño. *The Young Christ* (1987), Ruiz-Deremdes series: *For The Life of the World - Bible Studies on Human Rights* (1986); *Land: A Grace From God, From its Womb Springs Life* (1987); and *From Darkness to Light: Creative Studies for women in the Churches* (1991); with three further booklets in the series Creative Studies for Women in the Philippines: *From Darkness to Light; Mary of Magdala*; and *The Bible Speaks to Women* (Quezon City, 1993).

NCCP. "An Urgent Call to Resume Peace Negotiations" and "A Call for Restitution and Justice as Basis for National Reconciliation." *NCCP Magazine* 40.2 (1999).

2.6.7.7. Silsilah Foundation, Zamboanga

The Silsilah Foundation in Zamboanga City was established to foster relations between Christians and Muslims, to explore and nurture possibilities of peace in the southern Philippines, and to develop a pattern of inter-faith dialogue appropriate to the context. The Foundation has sponsored such dialogue in many forms, and hosts a regional exchange among Muslim and Christian academics and local leaders with the aim of reducing bias and promoting cooperation. The Interfaith Group, which is registered as a non-governmental organization, includes Roman Catholic, Islamic, and Protestant representatives who have joined together in an effort to support the Mindanao peace process through work with communities of former combatants. Silsilah, as well as scholars and leaders associated with it, have produced many important volumes, especially those of the Dialogue Forum Series.

Selected References

Carzedda, Salvatore. *The Quranic Jesus in the Light of the Gospel: Exploring a Way to Dialogue.* Zamboanga: Silsilah Publications, 1990.

The Vision of Dialogue of Bishop Bienvenido S. Tudtud.1931-1987. Zamboanga, Silsilah Publications, 1990.

Fitzgerald, M.L. and R. Caspar, eds. *Signs of Dialogue: Christian Encounter with Muslims.* Dialogue Forum 6. Zamboanga City: Silsilah Publications, 1992.

Silsilah Editorial Board, ed. *Inter-Religious Dialogue: A Paradox?* Dialogue Forum Series 4. Zamboanga: Silsilah Publications, 1991.

D'Ambra, Sebastiano. *Life in Dialogue*: (Pathways to Inter-religious Dialogue and the Vision and Experience of the Islamo-Christian Silsilah Dialogue Movement). Zamboanga: Silsilah Publications, 1991.

Nagasura T. Madale, and others, present the Islamic concept of Peace, and other essays in *Possibilities of Peace in Southern Philippines.* Zamboanga City: Silsilah, 1990.

Inter-Religious Dialogue: a Paradox. Zamboanga City: Silsilah Publications, 1991.

Gomez, Hilario Jr. *The Moro Rebellion and the Search for Peace: a Study on Christian-Muslim Relations in the Philippines.* Zamboanga City: Silsilah Publications, 2000.

Abubakar, Carmen. "Interreligious Dialogue and the Making of Civil Society: A Study of the Silsilah Movement." In *Civil Society Making Civil Society, Philippine Democracy Agenda, Vol 3.* Quezon City: Third World Studies Center, University of the Philippines, 1997.

2.6.7.8. Socio-Pastoral Institute, Manila (SPI 1980-)

The Socio-Pastoral Institute was established to help bishops, the clergy, religious and lay persons to develop a critical consciousness in favor of grassroots people and to creatively contribute to the integral transformation of church and society. As a formation and training institute, SPI helps develop socio-pastoral agents who assist in the promotion of justice, peace and integrity of creation. With

SPI's pastoral facilitation services, the institute accompanies local churches and congregations in becoming the Church of the Poor. Other SPI offerings include audio-video presentations, gender-sensitivity training, facilitation of immersions and retreats, and programs of publication.

Since its inception the SPI has regularly published booklets in four series: *Theology in the Third World*; *Church and Social Transformation*; *Faith and Ideology*; and *Special Issues*. Writers for these have included Julio Xavier Labayen, Myrna Francia, Michael Amaladoss, Carlos Abesamis, Mary Rosario Battung, Feliciano Cariño, Roland Simbulan, Christopher G. Tibong and many others. The Institute has also collaborated in joint publications of Filipino theological reflection, with the EBF, the FIDES, Claretian and the Asian Cultural Forum for Development.

Compare also the booklet series *Human Society* since circa 1978, published by Human Development Research and Documentation, La Ignacia Apostolic Center, Manila. Subjects here addressed have included: Spirituality and Social Justice, Looking Beyond EDSA, Social Discernment, Social Hermeneutic, Basic Christian Communities and the Apostolate of Theological Reflection.

Selected References

> Abesamis, Carlos et al. *A Philippine Search for a Liberation Spirituality*. Manila: SPI, 1990.
> Asedillo, Rebecca C. *Faith in Struggle*. Faith and ideology C1-88. Manila: SPI, 1988.
> Narciso-Apuan, Victoria et al., eds. *Witness and Hope Amid Struggle. Towards a Theology and Spirituality of Struggle*. Book II. Manila: FIDES, 1991.
> Mendoza, Maraquita S. and Zone C. Narito. *Spirituality, the Activist and the Social Movements*. Manila: Asian Cultural Forum on Development and SPI, 1992.
> Labayen, Bishop Julio X. *Revolution and the Church of the Poor*. Yapak Series I. Manila: SPI and Claretian, 1995.
> ———. *Linking the Church to the Struggle of the Poor*. Manila: SPI, ?1996.

Diaz, Josefina C. *Kababaiyan: Filipino Women in the Struggle for Freedom.* Manila: SPI, 1997.

Recently published materials of the SPI include booklets on *Faith in Struggle; The Theological Experience; Women Religious; Bases Free, Nuclear Free Philippines: the Moral Imperative of our Times; Globalization, Fundamentalism and Global Ecumenism as Humanity's Response; What is in it for Mr. and Ms. Pobre? The Jubilee Year ...; Being Church in a New Global Village - A Fresh Call for Renewal and Prophetic Witness; What is Inside the Wooden Bowl?; Into Workers' Clothes;* and *Linking the Church to the Struggle of the Poor.*

2.6.7.9. Supreme Council of Bishops, Philippine Independent Church (Iglesia Filipinas Independiente - IFI)

The Supreme Council of the IFI ,(1.6.5), under the leadership, for example, of Supreme Bishop Tito E. Pasco, and IFI leaders of lay movements such as the *Demokratikong Kilusan ng Magbubukid sa Pilipinas* (Democratic Peasant Movement in the Philippines), have continued the earlier Independiente traditions of social witness and reflection. The bishops have issued occasional statements and open letters on major social or political issues and also acted to support protest movements or to provide sanctuary for striking workers. Their statements have, for example, included Open Letters to the President of the Philippines and to other national leaders and movements calling for agrarian reform, for the end of foreign domination and for nationalist industrialization, for basic social services, human rights for all ethnic groups, and for peace and dialogue in southern Philippines.

Selected References

Works from IFI

"An Open Letter to President Aquino and the National Democratic Front." *Tugon* 11.1 (1991).

"Peasant Leader Reflects on Spirituality, Economy, Politics and Alternative Paradigm." *CCA News* 29.5&6 (1994).

"Pastoral Statement on the SPCPD and the Peace Process in Southern Philippines." *NCCP Magazine* 37.3 (1996).

"A Statement on the Visiting Forces Agreement. Steadfastly Guard our Heritage, Intensify our Response." *NCCP Magazine* 39.3 (1998).

Deats, Richard L. *Nationalism and Christianity in the Philippines.* Dallas: Southern Methodist University, 1967.
Manaligod, Ambrosio. *The Ecclesiality of the Philippine Independent Church.* Quezon City: National Priest Organization, 1988. This is the first in a 5 volume series of the IFI.
Ranche, Apolonio M. "The Iglesia Filipina Independiente (IFI): A People's Movement for National Freedom, Independence and Prosperity." *Philippiniana Sacra* 35 (2000).
Scott, William Henry. "The Philippine Independent Church in History." *East and West Review* 28.1 (1962); *Silliman Journal* 10.3 (1963).
Whittemore, L.B. *Struggle for Freedom: the History of the Philippine Independent Church.* New York: Seabury, 1961.

2.6.7.10. United Church of Christ in the Philippines (UCCP)

Since its foundation in 1948 - on the basis of the Evangelical Union (1901) and the United Evangelical Church (1929) (see 1.7.2 above) - the UCCP has issued a range of publications and statements on doctrinal, ecumenical and social concerns. These have included manuals and booklets on faith and order, Christian unity, evangelism and ecumenical relations, as well those on social and prophetic witness. Issues of faith and order were given their basic formulation in the *Basis of Union* (1948), along with its *Supplementary Statement* (1950) and the *Declaration of Union* (1948). Central to these was emphasis upon unity with autonomy, commitment to mission and ecumenical outreach, and to prophetic ministry.

UCCP Statements have therefore addressed specific issues of Christian witness in society, of human rights, democratic process, integrated human development, and of social and economic justice. There have also been broader statements on Church for the Life of the World, Peace with Justice, Healing ministry, and Stewardship of Creation. Many of the Philippines' most capable theologians have helped to shape these documents and together they provide a coherent and contextualized theology of mission, church and society. (For UCCP Statements of Faith, Social Concern and Statement on Transformation of Society, see Sitoy 1992 and Aoanan 1996.)

Selected References

Faith and Order; We Believe; Celebration Guides; Constitution and By-laws. (Four Series of Booklets). Quezon City: UCCP.

Aoanan, Melanio LaG. *Ecumenical and Prophetic: the Witness of the United Church of Christ in the Philippines* (Pagkakaisa at Pagbabago: Ang Patotoo ng United Church of Christ). Quezon City: New Day Publishers, 1996.

Cariño, Feliciano, ed. *Like a Mustard Seed: Commentaries on the UCCP Statement of Faith.* Quezon City: UCCP Communications & Literature Desk, 1987.

Dominguez, Ben. *We Believe in God.* Quezon City: UCCP, 1988.

—. *One Towards Life.* Quezon City: UCCP, 1988.

Quismundo, Jorge R., ed. *Manual for Mission and Evangelism.* Quezon City: UCCP, 1988.

Senturias, Alvaro Jr. *Human Rights Justice and Peace: A Manual for Reference.* Quezon City: UCCP, 1989.

Sitoy, T. Valentino, Jr. *Several Springs, One Stream: The United Church of Christ in the Philippines.* Vol. I. Heritage and Origins (1898-1948). Quezon City: UCCP, 1992, chapter 9.

United Church of Christ in the Philippines. *UCCP Statements and Resolutions (1948-1990).* Quezon City: UCCP, 1990.

2.6.8. The Contributions of Other Institutes and Associations

2.6.8.1. Association of Major Religious Superiors in the Philippines (AMRSP, 1974-)

The Association of Major Religious Superiors in the Philippines includes the associations for men and women formed in 1955, now representing approximately 240 congregations. The purpose of AMRSP is through "collaborative efforts [to] pursue the role of the prophetic witness of being religious in Philippine church and society." Justice and peace are therefore central concerns of its publications and it has held a particularly vital role during Martial Law and at times of national emergency since, providing key liaison and support roles for members of orders and congregations in frontier ministries. Along with its Mission Partners, the AMRSP has provided emergency assistance to workers, farmers, urban poor, women, human rights victims and political detainees.

Publications have included the periodicals *Signs of the Times*, and *ICHTHYS*, in which a flow of reports, statements and reflections have appeared. See also periodic statements and papers which include those on current political crises, conflict and reconciliation in the south, rehabilitation and development projects, military and legal abuses, cancellation of debt and proclamation of Jubilee.

See for example:
> *Filipino Women in Struggle*. Manila: Task Force Detainees, AMRSP. 1984.
>
> "Resignation for Impartial Investigation. Statement of the Association of Major Religious Superiors in the Philippines and its Mission Partners on the Recent Event in our Country, Oct 13, 2000." (regarding presidential abuses). Manila: AMRSP.

2.6.8.2. Association of Women in Theology (AWIT)

This is an association of women church workers, church educators, theologically trained women and women doing theology in the Philippines. Violeta A. Marasigan (d. 2000), who also co-founded GABRIELA (1984), was one of AWIT's founders. The main focus of AWIT's work has been the affirming of mutual support as they work to provide unconditional love and friendship to girl/women victims of violence and abuse. They undertake legal cases and advocacy, along with ecumenical networking, the study of feminist theology and collective theological reflection.

See for example:
> AWIT. "Of Secrets and Violence, Breaking the Silence." *In God's Image* 17.2 (1998).
>
> Kroeker, Wendy, and Sharon Rose Joy Ruiz-Duremdes, eds. *Dance Amid 'Struggle: Stories and Songs of Hope*. Quezon City: AWIT Publications, 1998.

2.6.8.3. Ecumenical Bishops' Forum (EBF)

A gathering of Roman Catholic, Protestant, Episcopal and Independiente bishops unified in their 'preferential option for the poor' and concerned with the struggles of the Filipino people for fullness of life. Bishop Julio Labayen (see 2.5.4.) has been for many years its chairperson. The Forum has studied, and issued statements on, significant issues for Filipino society. It has also cooperated with programs of the NCCP, FIDES, (THRUST) and (SPI).

See for example:
Abainza, Al. C., ed. *To Walk Humbly with God and Man. Statements of the Ecumenical Bishops' Forum*. Manila: EBF, 1996.

2.6.8.4. Forum for Interdisciplinary Endeavors and Studies (FIDES)

This group comprises men and women of different professions - economists, sociologists, anthropologists, educators, academics, political scientists and medical practitioners - who have been asked by the EBF to work with them in reflection on contemporary issues affecting the church and pastoral concerns.

See for example:
Battung, Mary Rosario et al. *Religion and Society: Towards A Theology of Struggle*. Book I. Manila: FIDES, 1988.
Narciso-Apuan, Victoria et al. *Witness and Hope Amid Struggle. Towards a Theology and Spirituality of Struggle*. Book II. Manila: FIDES, 1991.

2.6.8.5. Filipino Chapter of EATWOT

The Chapter has provided important leadership for EATWOT itself, in, for example, the Women's Commission, as well as in Asia-wide programs, and also undertaken projects related specifically to the Philippines.

See for example:
Abesamis, Carlos et al. *A Philippine Search for a Liberation Spirituality*. Manila: SPI, 1990.
Ligo, Arche and Virginia Fabella, eds. *Dugo-Duga ng Buhay* (Vital sap of life). Tagaytay City: Southeast Asia Conference of EATWOT, 1995.

2.6.8.6. Igorota Foundation (IF)

Founded in 1985 to work for the holistic development of women in the Cordillera, and to enable them to participate more effectively in the development of their own communities, IF activities include training services, community building, research, spirituality, marketing, publication and documentation. It has also promoted Asian networks for indigenous women. IF publishes the monthly

IGOROTA (formerly *INGLAYAN*) - the alternative women's magazine in the Cordilleras, and also annual booklet issues on particular themes (see also Teresa Dagdag 2.5.26.).

See for example:
> *IGOROTA Folktales and Myths*. Baguio: IF, 1988.
> *IGOROTA Weaving*. Baguio: IF, n.d.
> *Proceedings of the First Asian Indigenous Women's Conference 1993*. IF, 1993.
> *IGOROTA Annual* 10 (Tenth Anniversary), Baguio: IF, 1996.

2.6.8.7. Other institutes fostering theological formation and the writing of contextual Filipino theology include the following: Maryhill School of Theology (1972) stresses the missionary dimension, the Judeo-Christian tradition and creative Filipino theological scholarship, in its theological formation programs. The school is concerned also to bridge the gap between academic learning and Christian practice, and publishes the journal *MST Review*.

The Institute of Formation and Religious Studies (1963) promotes in its courses scriptural, theological and pastoral reflections rooted in human experience and contemporary issues. The aim is to bring the Gospel to bear as a historical force for the transformation of society, as well as for personal authenticity in a community milieu.

The Inter-Congregational Theological Center provides training for men and women religious through an incarnational and contextualized theology which is developed by identifying with the poor in their life struggles. Experiential, participatory and dialogical methods are used to develop theological understanding, and new cultural consciousness.

2.7 Supplementary Bibliography 2
2.7.1. Church History and Society

Aguilan, Henry. *Philippine UIM Projects*. Quezon City: NCCP-UIM, 1971-72.

Alonso, Isadoro et al. *The Catholic Church in the Philippines Today*. Manila: n.p., 1968.

Ante, Oscar A. *Contextual Evangelization in the Philippines: A Filipino Franciscan Experience.* Kampen: Kok, 1991.

Asedillo, R.C. and B.D. Williams, eds. *Rice in the Storm: Faith and Struggle in the Philippines.* New York: Friendship Press, 1989.

Association of Major Religious Superiors in the Philippines. *Political Detainees in the Philippines.* Manila: AMRSP, 1976.

Baye, Babaye. *A Primer About Women and for Women.* Manila: GABRIELA - Mindanao and Women Studies and Resource Center. 1986.

Because We Dare to Struggle: A Documentation Report on State Violence Against Women in the Philippines (1990- 1992). Manila: GABRIELA: Commission on Women's Political Rights. 1992.

Bennagen, Ponciano L. "Indigenous Responses toward Land and Natural Resources of Tribal Filipinos." *NCCP Magazine* 31.5 (1991).

Brand, Donald V. *The Philippine Independent Church: A Social Movement.* Microform. Thesis, Wheaton College, Illinois, 1980.

Chandlee, H. Ellsworth. *Isobelo de los Reyes Jr. Supreme Bishop in the Philippines.* New York: Episcopal Church, 1962.

Chant, Sylvia and McIlwaine, Cathy. *Women of Lesser Cost: Female Labour, Foreign Exchange and Philippine Development.* Manila: Ateneo de Manila University, 1995.

Covar, Prospero R. "General Characterization of Contemporary Religious Movements in the Philippines." *Tugon* 3.2 (1982).

David, Randolf S. "National Consciousness in a Dependent Society: A Brief Sociological Note on Philippine Culture." *Tugon* 3.2 (1982).

—. "Philippine Perspectives: From EDSA to Mendiola." *Simbayan* 6.2 (1987).

de Guzman, Emmanuel. *Filipino Base Communities: Description and Analysis of the Phenomenon in the Context of Local Church History.* Dissertation, Leuven, 1995.

Desquitado, Marivic. *Behind Shadows: Towards A Better Understanding of Prostituted Women.* Davao City: TALIKALA Inc., 1992.

Garbutt, John, ed. *The Unfinished Song - Voices of the Filipino People.* Hong Kong: DAGA; Manila: NCCP, 1986.

Garcia, Mila Astorga et. al. *Filipina II: An Anthology of Contemporary Women Writers in the Philippines: Essays.* Quezon City: New Day Publishers, 1985.

Gumban, Johnny. "The Christian Churches' Encounter with the *Iglesia ni Cristo* in the Philippines." *SEAJT* 10.1 (1968).

Hollensteiner, Mary, ed. *Society, Culture and the Filipino.* Quezon City: Institute of Philippine Culture, 1979.

Kerkvliet, B. "Additional Source Materials on Philippine Radical Movements." *Bulletin of Concerned Asian Scholars* (Fall 1971).

Kilusang Christiyano ng Kabataang Pilipino (Student Christian movement of the Philippines). Quezon City: KCKP, 1972.

Kinne Warren. *A People's Church?: the Mindanao-Sulu Church Debacle.* Studien zur interkulturellen Geschichte des Christentums Studies in the Intercultural History of Christianity 64. Frankfurt am Main; New York: P. Lang, 1990 (PhD thesis, University of Birmingham, 1989).

LalRousse, William. *Walking Together, Seeking Peace, The Local Church of Mindanao-Sulu Journeying in Dialogue with the Muslim Community. (1965-2000)* Quezon City: Ateneo Univ. Press, Forthcoming.

Lim, Hilario A. *Memorandum of my Appeal to his Eminence Valerio Cardinal Valeri on my Expulsion from the Society of Jesus.* La Ignaciana, Manila: n.p., 1958.

Lim, Paulino. *Requiem for a Rebel Priest.* Quezon City: New Day Publishers, 1996.

Lindis McGovern, Ligaya. *Filipino Peasant Women. Exploitation and Resistance.* Philadelphia: University of Pennsylvania, 1997.

Lua, Teresa Roco. "Developing a Holistic and Contextualized Discipleship Ministry among Urban Poor Adults in Metro Manila." *Journal of Asian Mission* 2.1 (2000).

Mulder, Niels. "Cultural Process in Lowland Christian Filipino Society. *Philippine Studies* 40 (1992).

—. "Localization and Philippine Catholicism." *Philippine Studies* 40 (1992).

Nacpil, Zenaida S. *A Critique of the Theology Program of the University of the Assumption*. San Fernando, Pampanga: University of the Assumption, 1983.

Philippine Human Rights Information Center, Manila. *In Defence of Human Rights*. 3.2 (1993).

Rosario, Simeon G. del. *Surfacing the Underground. The Church and State Today*. Quezon City: Monlapaz Publishing, 1976.

Ruiz, Lester Edwin J. "Towards Communities of Resistance and Solidarity: Some Political and Philosophical Notes." *Tugon* 7.3 (1987).

Tagle, Ramon A., Jr. *Towards Christian Democracy in the Philippines*. Manila: Christian Social Movement, 1984.

Tan, Samuel K. *Islam in the Philippines*. Mindanao Studies Reports 3. Marawi City: Mindanao State University, 1995.

Ty-Navarro, Virginia and Zafaralla, Paul C. *Carlos V. Francisco: The Man and Genius of Philippine Art*. Manila: Ayala Museum; Kyoto: Kansai Seminar House, 1985.

Villalba, Noel. "Philippine Ecumenism: Where to ?" *NCCP Magazine* 36.2 (1996).

2.7.2. Contextual Theology

A Pastoral Statement: Shaking the Foundations - Uprooting and Rebuilding. The College of Bishops, The United Methodist Church in the Philippines. (November 24, 1987).

Alampay, D. "Christian Mission amid Social Change." *Asia Focus* 5.2 (1970).

Andres, Tomas Quintin D. *New Dimensions in Philippine Christianity: 117 Themes for Reflection and Homilies*. S.l.: St. Paul Publications, ?1973.

Asian Seminar on Religion and Development. *Religion and Development in Asia: A Sociological Approach with Christian Reflections*. Baguio: Baguio FERES Seminar, 1976.

Aumann, Jordan et al. *Asian Religious Traditions and Christianity*, edited by Fausto Gomez. Thomasian 2. Manila: Faculty of Theology, University of Santo Tomas, 1983.

Cacayan, Alberto and Agnes Nelmida Miclat. *Let your Heart be Bold: A Reflection Paper on Church-Workers and National Security in the Philippines.* Hong Kong: Asian Centre for the Progress of Peoples, c1991.

Cariño, Feliciano, ed. *Theology, Politics & Struggle.* Quezon City: NCCP, 1986.

Contextualized Prayers. Quezon City: Clergy-Laity Formation of Northern Luzon (CLFP-NL), n.d.

Dais, Lolita T. "Woman: Symbol of Life." *Asia Journal of Theology* 3.2 (1989).

de Achutegui, Pedro S., ed. *The "Miracle" of the Philippine Revolution: Interdisciplinary Reflections: magkaisa ... magkakapatid lahat: a symposium organized by the Loyola School of Theology.* Manila: Loyola School of Theology, Ateneo de Manila University, 1986.

de Mesa, José M., ed. *Pastoral Agents and Doing Christology.* EAPR Special issue 29.2 (1992).

Demetrio, Francisco R. *Christianity in Context.* Quezon City: New Day Publishers, 1981.

Dominguez, Arsenio and Edith Dominguez. *Theological Themes for the Philippine Church.* Quezon City: New Day Publishers, 1989.

Edouarte, Salvador D. "Theologizing in a Crisis Situation: the Philippine Experience." *Asia Journal of Theology* 4.1 (1990).

"Filipino Patterns in Adult Catechesis." *DIWA* Special Issue 2.1 (1977).

Formilleza, Sammie P. *"Out of the Valley of Dry Bones": Faith-Life Reflections of Grassroot Christians.* Quezon City: People's Theology Publication, Ecumenical Center for Development, 1990.

Gener, Timoteo D. "Re-rooting the Gospel in the Philippines: Roman Catholic and Evangelical Approaches to Contextualization." MA thesis in Philosophical Foundations in Systematic Theology, Institute for Christian Studies (Toronto, Canada) 1998.

Gorospe, V.R., ed. *Faith and Justice and the Filipino Christian.* Manila: NASSA, LST & PACT, 1976.

Grant, Alexander, ed. *Baguio Religious Acculturation Conference: Proceedings 1976-1979.* Manila: Christian Institute for Ethnic Studies in Asia, ?1980.

Guzman, Edmundo Pacifico. "Creation as God's Kaloob: Towards an Ecological Theology of Creation in the Lowland Filipino Socio-Cultural Context." PhD in Religious Studies Dissertation, Faculty of Theology, Katholieke Universiteit Leuven (Louvain, Belgium), 1995.

Hollensteiner, Mary R. *Towards a People-Centered Endogenous Intellectual Creativity. Historical Testimony in the Philippines.* Tokyo: 1979.

Iniguez, Deogracias S. "Interreligious Dialogue in the Philippines." *Bulletin Pontificium Consilium pro Dialogo Inter Religiones* 24 (1989).

Lapiz, Ed. *Paano maging Pilipinong Kristiano* (Becoming a Filipino Christian) Makati City: Kaloob, c1997.

Maribao, Joel L. *Strategies for Empowerment: a Filipino-Christian Perspective.* Manila: Logos Publications, c1996.

Mateos, Juan. *Cristianos en fiesta* (Beyond conventional Christianity). Trans. from the Spanish original by Sr. Kathleen England osu. Manila: East Asian Pastoral Institute, c1974.

Maximiano, José M.B. *The Signs of the Times and the Social Doctrine of the Church: An Epistemological Basis.* Published by the author, 1991.

McDonagh, Sean. *To Care for the Earth: A Call to a New Theology.* Santa Fe: Bear and Company, 1986.

Natividad, Maria Lucia C. *Salvation History.* Quezon City: Ateneo de Manila, 1996.

Neo, Julma. *Towards a Liberating Formation of Christian Communities.* Quezon City: Claretian, c1988.

Ocampo, Renato A. et al. *Stories of Service: A Christian Spirituality for Agents of Social Transformation.* Pulso Monographs 9. Manila: Institute on Church and Social Issues, 1992.

Paguio, Wilfred. *Filipino Cultural Values for the Apostolate Utilization of Traditional Cultural Values of Filipinos.* Makati: St. Paul, 1991.

Pelingon, F.C., and A.M. Ramirez, eds. *Faith Experience in the Emerging Church of Mindanao-Sulu: The Testimony of a People in the Southern Fastnesses of the Philippines.* Manila: CFA Media Group, 1989.

Philippine Episcopal Church. "In Search for a Just, Prosperous and Peaceful Philippine Society." *Tugon* 9.2 (1989).

Pintig (Life-pulse in cold steel): Poems and Letters from Philippine Prisons. Hong Kong: Resource Center for Philippine Concerns, 1979.

Reese, Gunther. *Power shall be Given to the People. Thomas Muntzer and the Theology of Struggle*. Quezon City: UCCP, 1990.

Reyes, Taklin Soriano. "Theological Studies and Philippine Culture." In *A Search for a Liberating and Uniting Theological Education in the Philippines*. Quezon City: First Inter-Seminary Student Congress, 1975.

SCM of the Philippines. *Student Handbook*. Manila: SCM, 1960.

Sevilla, Victor J. *A Guide to Catholic Action in the Philippines*. Foreword by Vicente P. Reyes. Pasay City: n.p.,1953.

Solon, Bienvenido. *The Vision of Dialogue of Bishop Bienvenido S. Tudtud*. Zamboanga: Silsilah Publications, 1990.

Tan, Samuel K. *Selected Essays on the Filipino Muslims*. Marawi: Mindanao State University, 1982.

Tanseco, Ruben. *Disturbing Options in Quest of a Filipino Political Spirituality*. Quezon City: Ateneo University, 1992.

UCCP. *Mga Alawiton sa mga Hiniusang Iglesia ni Kristo sa Filipinas*. Dumaguete: Silliman University Press, 1963. (Hymns)

Vano, Manolo O. *Discovering the Original Jesus: A Biography of a Revolutionary Genius as He Was Actually Known to His Contemporaries*. Quezon City: New Day Publishers, 1998.

Villote, Ruben J. "Jesus Christ Today for the Filipino Christian." *Philippine Priests' Forum* June (1978).

Whelchel, James R. *The Path to Liberation: Theology of Struggle in the Philippines*. Quezon City: New Day Publishers, 1995.

Yatco, Nicomedes. *Jesus Christ for Today's Filipinos*. Quezon City: New Day Publishers, 1983.

2.7.3. Periodicals: A Selection Available for Research include:

The Asian Theologian, Asia Baptist Graduate Theological Seminary, Baguio (from 1995); *The Assembly Herald* (1899-1914); *Boletin Eclesiastico de Filipinas* (from ?1958-); *Church and Community,* UCC Division of Social Concerns (1960-); *Commentary on Industrial*

Evangelism, UCCP; *Diwa,* SVD Graduate Schools, Tagaytay and Quezon City (from 1975); *Human Society,* Human Development Research and Documentation, Manila; *Humig Ugnayan,* Intercongregational Theological Center and Institute of Formation and Religious Studies, Quezon City (from 1998); *ISIP-ISAK,* ISACC, Quezon City; *Journal of Asian Mission,* Asia Graduate School of Theology, Quezon City (from 1999); *Journal of the Philippines Annual Conference,* Methodist (from 1908); *Kalinangan,* IRC (from 1985); *Kinaadman,* Xavier University/Ateneo de Zamboanga, Cagayan de Oro (from 1978); *Landas* (The Way), Loyola School of Theology, Quezon City (from 1986); *MST Review,* Maryhill School of Theology (from 1997); *Ministry Today,* Loyola House of Studies (from 1985); *The Missionary Intelligencer* (1901-1918); *NCCP Newsletter,* formerly *Philippine Ecumenical Review* (from ca.1964); *Philippiniana Sacra,* University of Santo Tomas, Manila (from 1965); *Philippine Priests' Forum* (1969-1981); *Philippine Christian Advance,* Philippine Federation of Christian Churches, Manila (1949-1964); *The Philippine Presbyterian* (1910-1941); *Philippine Studies,* Ateneo de Manila University (from 1963); *Philippine YWCA Magazine*; *Pilipinas, Reflections for Philippine Christians*; and *Search* (Radical Christian, from 1970s); *Religious Life Asia,* Institute of Consecrated Life, Quezon City (from 1998); *Signs of the Times*; and *ICHTHYS* (AMRSP); *Silliman Journal* (from 1953); *Simbayan,* Ecumencial Development Center, Quezon City (from ca.1980); *Theology Series,* Ateneo de Manila, Quezon City (1971-); *Tribal Forum,* Episcopal Commission on Tribal Filipinos (from 1979); *Tugon: Ecumenical Journal of Discussion and Opinion,* NCCP (from 1980); *The Union Voice,* Dasmariñas, Cavite, Union Theological Seminary (1927-); *Wednesday Forum Journal* (ca.1975-1986).

— JCE, with JdeM, LAQ, MLaGA, RM

8 Contextual Theology in Thailand 1800-2000

(For Siam in the period 16th-18th centuries see chapter 2 of this volume.)

1 **Protestant History and Theology**
  1.1 Introduction
  1.2 A Selection of Writings containing Contextual elements (late 19th and early 20th centuries)
    1.2.1. Early Thai Ministers, Teachers, Translators and Writers; **1.2.2.** Expatriate Teachers, Ministers, Writers; **1.2.3.** Positive Assessments of Thai Culture and Religion; **1.2.4.** Women Educators, Writers
  1.3 Writings and Publications (1900-1950)
    1.3.1. Thai Ministers, Teachers, Writers; **1.3.2.** Ecumenical Co-operation;
  1.4 Women Doing Theology
  1.5 The Location of Protestant Theology in Thailand
  1.6 Key Themes in Protestant Theology in Thailand
    1.6.1. God as Patron and as Guardian Spirit; **1.6.2.** Jesus - Human and Divine; **1.6.3.** The Role of Works, Ceremony, Faith; **1.6.4.** Other Elements;
  1.7 Ecumenical and Social Witness and Reflection
  1.8 Selected Theologians
    1.8.1. Prakai Nontawasee; **1.8.2.** Koyama Kosuke; **1.8.3.** Maen Pongudom; **1.8.4.** Koson Srisang; **1.8.5.** Herbert R. Swanson; **1.8.6.** Other Theological Writers - Protestant.
  1.9 A Note on Regional and Tribal Theologies

2 **Roman Catholic thought and life**
  2.1 Introduction
  2.2 Theological Context
  2.3 Catholic Bishops' Conference of Thailand
  2.4 Participation in Social Development and Reflection

2.5 Christian Response to Buddhism
2.6 Spirituality, Ministry and Dialogue
2.7 Selected Scholars and Theologians
   2.7.1. Robert Ratna Bamrungtrakul; **2.7.2.** Augustin Moling sj; **2.7.3.** Mansap Bunluen; **2.7.4.** Kirti Bunchua; **2.7.5.** Seri Phongphit; **2.7.6.** Niphot Thienwiharn.
2.8 Other Catholic Contributions to Contextual Thai Theology

3 Supplementary Bibliography
   3.1 Monographs and Articles; **3.2** Periodical Sources for Research

1 Protestant History and Theology
1.1 Introduction

The first Protestant missionaries, the Rev'ds Carl Gutzlaff (Germany) and Jacob Tomlin (London), arrived in Siam, modern-day Thailand, in 1828. Over the next 30 years several American Protestant missionary agencies established themselves in Bangkok, for varying periods, until by the 1890s only the Presbyterian Church in the USA maintained active work in Siam. The first Presbyterian couple arrived in 1840, but the "Siam Mission" was not put on a permanent footing until 1847. Twenty years later, in 1867, the Presbyterians opened a separate mission in Siam's northern dependencies. It was known as the "Laos Mission," after the fashion of foreign residents who referred to those principalities as "Laos." The Presbyterians remained the dominant Protestant presence until the early 1960s. The American Baptists arrived in 1833 and established a small number of Chinese churches in Bangkok and the surrounding region and beginning in the 1880s, another small number of Karen tribal churches in the North.

In 1934, Thai Protestant churches gained nominal independence with the foundation of the "Church in Siam," later known as the Church of Christ in Thailand (CCT). Missionaries remained in many positions of authority and influence, however, until the 1970s and even into the 1980s. The CCT gained independence in 1957, but this only became full and meaningful some 25 years later. In the meantime, Thailand witnessed an explosion of evangelical and Pentecostal missions that led to the founding of a Southern Baptist convention as well as an umbrella organization for other evangelicals, the Evangelical Fellowship of Thailand (EFT). The EFT was established in 1969. Missionaries have maintained a strong voice in the councils of the EFT even down to the present.

Protestant theology in Thailand is therefore an outgrowth of two primary agencies, foreign Protestant missions and Thai culture. It can be fairly said that more formal expressions of Protestant theology in Thailand still draw largely upon foreign sources. The theology of the churches, however, is much more a product of the interaction of Protestant and Thai religious and cultural themes. Future research may well reveal that the Thai themes actually predominate. It remains a fact, however, that Thailand has produced relatively few formal theological works or theologians of any reputation. While any number of Thai Protestants have done advanced degree work in such fields as biblical studies, church history, and missiology, almost none have shown an interest in systematic theology. One of the few Protestant theologians of international stature to have contributed to theological reflection in Thailand is Kosuke Koyama. The work of Thai Protestants, such as Koson Srisang, or Prakai Nontawasee (for these and others see below), more well-known nationally, is much less well known outside of Thailand.

This is not to say, nonetheless, that there is no such thing as "Thai theology." This theology exists, partly in scattered writings; but more importantly in the worship, preaching, the personal faith and life of Thai churches and Christians. It is a theology that has received little attention, perhaps because it is not a "minjung" or a "dalit" theology, but is the theology of average people of varying economic and social conditions. Any structured study of Protestant theology in Thailand will have to look for that theology in two places. First, it will have to study the missionary and western sources. Second, it will have to examine how missionary religious thought interacted with Thai religious sensibilities in the context of the Protestant church in Thailand. What will become apparent is that "Thai theology," as lived and practised by Protestants in Thailand, has obtained a unique identity: like yet unlike western

Protestantism, while also like and unlike the religiosity of other Thais.

The predominant Presbyterian missions brought with them a theology as well as western technologies, practices and values. It was a uniquely American blend of Reformed Scholasticism (popularly known as "Calvinism"), Scottish Enlightenment philosophy, and evangelical revivalism that is generally known as the "Princeton Theology." In this body of thought, the intent was two-fold: first, to protect the church from impiety and unorthodox doctrines; and second, to expand Protestantism's influence and role in society, particularly among wealthy and middle class people (initially in America).

It should be emphasized in the context of Asian discussions on theological contextualization that the Princeton Theology was a thoroughly American brand of Reformed theological thought, combining biblical themes and European thought in a way that "made sense" to 19th century Americans. Ironically, the very fact of its success in the United States made it seem entirely "natural" and "right" in the minds of its missionary adherents. Yet that Princeton Theology proved itself more of a barrier to, than a facilitator of, contextualized theologies in Thailand.

Firstly, with only a few exceptions, the Presbyterian missionaries were entirely orthodox, Old School adherents to the Princeton Theology. It is what they preached, taught and inculcated into the churches they founded in Thailand. First, the Princeton Theology and western Protestant thinking in general introduced a profound concern with doctrines and right thinking. Where Thai Buddhism tends to be more focused on orthopraxis, the Princetonians put strong emphasis on orthodoxy. The churches learned that their salvation depends in part on adhering to a correct set of doctrinal propositions. As is usual for western religious consciousness, the Presbyterian missionaries articulated their orthodoxy in dualistic ideological terms such as "true" and "false," "right" and "wrong," or "saved" and "damned." Again, where Thai Buddhism values wisdom over belief, Protestantism in Thailand came to value living by faith over living by wisdom. Protestants speak constantly and at length about "belief" and "faith," and preachers affirm regularly that Christians are saved by faith alone. Wisdom is rarely mentioned.

Secondly, in keeping with the rigid western dualism of missionary theology, Protestants in Thailand from the beginning believed that Christianity alone is the "true" religion. All other religions are, by definition, "false." This simple and deeply held principle has had a profound impact on Protestant theology in Thailand. Protestantism has until recently actively avoided any religious forms or expressions that are in any way associated with Thai Buddhism and/or animism. The Thai Protestant community has lived in religious isolation from its neighbors of other faiths. Earlier generations of Protestants taught their children that it was "wrong" to even enter temple grounds, let alone attend religious ceremonies or even social activities there. In rural areas, Christians tended to live in separate areas of villages or even in predominantly Christian villages. From missionary times, Protestantism in Thailand has rejected the use of Thai religious vocabulary and concepts, preferring to use common words for such terms as "salvation." The Protestant church in Thailand, in sum, has limited itself at the conscious level to non-indigenous resources for theological reflection.

Thirdly, the Princeton Theology tended to emphasize head and reason over heart and also the "middle way" *(via media)* in all things. In this regard, it unwittingly proved itself compatible with indigenous Thai thinking which also tends to restrain the emotions, avoiding extremes of expression and behavior. Traditionally, then, Protestantism in Thailand has expressed itself in more subdued and restrained ways. Since the times of Presbyterian dominance, however, there have been missionaries and Thai Christians who have opted for the more outgoing, emotional expressions of revivalistic evangelicalism; and these expressions have gained growing prominence since the 1940s and especially since the rise of Pentecostalism in the 1980s. It is evident, then, that Protestants in Thailand have seldom nurtured inherent or potential similarities with the indigenous cultures of Thailand and that repeated infusions of western missionary influence have actually increased their social and theological isolation.

Fourthly, the Jesus of the Princeton Theology was a high and lifted-up figure of divinity and power. While this theological tradition is entirely orthodox in a formal sense, the paradox of the Incarnation has largely been lost to it. Jesus' humanity was affirmed only in a formal sense and always qualified with assertions of his sinlessness, his perfection, and his all-knowing nature. "Princeton's" Jesus was much more clearly the Son of God than a son of David. Interestingly enough, the Princeton view of Jesus has been a key point of contact between western theological thinking and the Thai religious and cultural context, as will be seen below.

Fifthly, Protestantism in Thailand has given women a substantially larger role in ecclesiastical affairs and theological reflection than is true of Thai Buddhism. Its churches ordain women to pastoral ministry and place them in teaching posts in Thai seminaries. In a similar fashion, it has made a greater place for those afflicted with leprosy, for those accused of demon possession, and for other social marginals. There seems, however, to have been only a small impact on overt theological expression and reflection as a result of earlier Protestant missionary concern for the liberation of the distressed and oppressed, and as a result of more recent ministries to poor farmers, workers or slum-dwellers.

Selected References

    Hughes, Philip J. *Thai Culture, Values, and Religion: An Annotated Bibliography of English Language Materials*. Chiang Mai: Manuscript Division, Payap College, 1981.

    Maen Pongudom. "Apologetic and Missionary Proclamation: Exemplified by American Presbyterian Missionaries to Thailand (1828-1978): Early Church Apologists: Justin Martyr, Clement of Alexandria, and Origen, and the Venerable Buddhadasa Bhikku, a Thai Buddhist Monk-Apologist." PhD dissertation, University of Otago, 1979.

    McFarland, George B. *Historical Sketch of Protestant Missions in Siam 1828-1928*. Bangkok: Bangkok Times Press, 1928. Reprinted Bangkok: White Lotus, 1999.

Saad Chaiwan. "A Study of the Impact of Christian Missions on Thai Culture from the Historical Perspective (1662-1985)." ThD dissertation, Presbyterian College and Theological Seminary, 1985.

Swanson, Herbert R. "This Heathen People: The Cognitive Sources of American Missionary Westernizing Activities in Northern Siam, 1867-1889." MA thesis, University of Maryland, 1987.

—. "A New Generation: Missionary Education and Changes in Women's Roles in Traditional Northern Thai Society." *Sojourn* 3.2 (1988).

—. *Towards a Clean Church: A Case Study in Nineteenth-Century Thai Church History.* Chiang Mai: Office of History, CCT, 1991.

—. "The Payap University Archives: A Resource for the Study of Thailand." *Sojourn* 6.1 (1991).

1.2 A Selection of Writings containing Contextual elements, late 19th and early 20th centuries [See chap. 2 above for Siam, 16th-18th centuries.]

1.2.1. Early Thai Ministers, Teachers, Translators and Writers

These formed indispensable partners for their expatriate colleagues but their preaching, teaching or letters have seldom been preserved. See references in the correspondence of e.g. Daniel McGilvary (1884), Robert S. Irwin (1904), A. J. Brown (1918). Those of whom more is known, include:

Boon Tuan Itt (1865-1903) from Bang-Pa Rajaburi, son of (Mrs) Acharn Mae Tuan. Educated at Williams College and Auburn Theological Seminary (USA), he joined the staff of the YMCA, and became a pastor, teacher and founder of churches. Some letters and fragments are extant for Boon as they are for Semo Wichai (fl.1890), pastor and theological teacher, and for Nai Poen (fl. 1895), assistant to Jonathan Wilson in translation and literary work, and compiler of a Lao Hymnal.

Nan Suwan (fl. 1870-). An ex-monk, medical worker, and evangelist, Nan was regarded as a founder of the Mae Dok Daeng Church and the "father" of Chieng Saen Church, although no writings of his have yet been identified.

1.2.2. Expatriate Teachers, Ministers, Writers

These were often competent linguists and scholars, laying a basis for much later Christian writing in Thai, Lao and Karen. But their own writings were almost wholly confined to western theological formulations. Prominent were:

Daniel McGilvary (1828-1911) teacher, pastor, diplomat. With Jonathan Wilson and colleagues he founded Chiangmai Presbytery in 1883 for the promotion of theological education. McGilvary Theological Seminary was later established in 1912. See his *A Half Century Among the Siamese and The Lao* (1911).

S.G. McFarland (d.1897) and Mrs McFarland were both effective educators. McFarland was also a printer and linguist, publishing his own *English-Siamese Dictionary*, a *Siamese Hymnal*, a number of textbooks and a Medical Dictionary.

J.B. Dunlap (in Siam 1888-1928), teacher and manager for the Presbyterian Mission Press 1891-1909, produced extensive Christian literature.

See also **Dan Deach Bradley (b.1804),** compiler of the *Thai Dictionary* and *Thai Old Testament* (1855) and editor of the *Bangkok Calendar* (1858) and the *Bangkok Recorder* (from 1865); **N.A. McDonald's** *A Missionary in Siam (1860-1870),* Bangkok, 1871, (reprinted Bangkok: White Lotus, 1999); and **Lyle J. Beebe** (fl.1920), linguist, who prepared a Thai Lu Bible, a hymnal, and other publications.

Samuel John Smith operated an independent printing press between 1869 and 1886, publishing periodicals, grammars, catechisms, along with Siamese prose and poetry.

1.2.3. Positive Assessments of Thai Culture and Religion

Howard Campbell (1866-1957) was a student of Siamese culture and religious literature, including Pali. He also co-sponsored the *Rural Economic Survey of Siam* (Harvard University, 1930-31). Mary Campbell, his wife, also held to a "mutual respect of religious beliefs" (Pongudom 1979: 74). With Dr Peoples, Campbell prepared the report *Monasteries and Buddhist Cults* (1907) which recognized their value in religious terms.

Evander B. McGilvary (fl.1900) was linguist, scholar and teacher of philosophy. He was also a sympathetic student of traditional religion, denied the verbal inerrancy of the Bible and was liberal in theological belief, recognizing salvific values in Buddhism. (Swanson 1984: 88f.)

C.C. Hansen, a contemporary of McGilvary, held a positive regard for northern Thai culture and religion and accepted that God "worked through Buddhism." (*Board of Foreign Mission Correspondence*, Swanson 1984: 88f.)

1.2.4. Women Educators, Writers

Few women, either national or expatriate, enjoyed the freedom to study or write extensively in the period until 1950, though some labored long at scholarly and educational tasks. Women's organizations such as the YWCA (from 1936) have also assisted the beginnings of theological reflection by women. Earlier women whose writings contained some contextualizing elements included the following:

Edna Jones whose *Memoirs* were published in Philadelphia in 1853;

Mrs D. McGilvary, effective evangelist and language tutor who collaborated to produce a translation of St Matthew's Gospel into Siamese ca.1875;

Edna S. Cole (c. 1855-1950), educator and school founder, who along with Kru Soowan edited *Daybreak* magazine (formerly edited by J.A. Eakin). In her letters (e.g. in 1883), and more in later years, she accepted Thai converts with diverse understandings of Christian belief, forbearing to impose rigid interpretations of doctrine.

Mary L. Cort (teacher 1874-1891), writer of *Siam the Heart of Further India* (New York: 1886).

Lillian Johnson Curtis's book *The Laos of North Siam Seen Through the Eyes of a Missionary* appeared in 1903, published in Philadelphia (reprinted Bangkok: White Lotus, 1998).

Memoirs of Jessie Mackinnon Hartzell for the years 1912-1928 are about to be published by the University of Hawaii Press.

Kru Tardt Pratipasena (fl.1905 -), edited *Daybreak* (in the early 1900s) and was later editor of *Khao Kristachak* (1932-1934).

1.3 Writings and Publications (1900-1950)
1.3.1. Thai Ministers, Teachers, Writers

In this period, nationals entered more fully upon the tasks of Church leadership, teaching, editing and writing (in Thai). The *Lao Press* had been published since 1891 and *Sirikitisap* (Lao Christian News), from 1903, and were edited now by nationals.

Boon Mark Kittisan (fl. 1935 -), minister, was one of the Thai delegates to the International Missionary Conference at Tambaram (1938), and later acted as Stated Clerk of the CCT General Assembly (1939-). His writings include: *Seven Proofs of the Cyclical Order of Birth and Death* (Bangkok: Boonreong Press, 1929); *The Living and the Dead* (Bangkok: Gene Hays Memorial School, 1939); *At the Pulpit* (Bangkok: Chareontham Press), Parts I and II, 1962); and *A Collection of the Teaching of the Holy Spirit* (Bangkok: Visult Press, 1973).

Simo Vichai wrote three volumes, entitled *Two Parties of Religion* (Chiangmai, Chareonmang Press), Part I, 1936; Parts II and III, 1937. A collection of his Letters is also extant.

For **Pluang Sudhikam (d.1942),** minister and teacher, who was later the first Moderator of the Church of Christ in Siam (1934), and **Kru Pannya** (fl.1900), a pastor at Chiangmai and also on the seminary staff as an instructor in theology, any extant writings have not yet been collected.

1.3.2. Ecumenical Co-operation, in steps towards indigenous Christian publication and Church witness included the following:

In 1929 the Committee on a *Living Indigenous Church* recommended the formation of a Siam Christian Council and the establishment of the Siam YMCA.

In 1932, the NCC commenced *Khao Kristachak* (Church News) with Kru Tardt Pradipasena as editor, to be later succeeded by Leck Taiyong. The National Protestant Church was formed in 1934, to be named The Church of Christ in Siam (now the Church of Christ in Thailand, CCT).

Thailand Discussion (Board of Foreign Missions, BFM, 1943) on post-war strategies for mission in Thailand, reflected some positive understandings of Thai religious traditions. Compare the later studies and writings in the 1960s, by for example, Theodore F. Rumig, Kosuke Koyama, W.J. Sinclair Thompson, Francis M. Seeley, Herbert Grether and Donald K. Swearer. (See Pongudom 1979: 69 ff., 76ff. and passim.)

Under the auspices of the CCT, the Thai Literature Committee was to consolidate its activities as the CCT Literature Dept. which was established in 1954, under the leadership of Acharn Charoen Wichai, the Rev'd Kenneth Wells and Ms Sarah Wylie. Early publications included studies and books on Christian faith and 3 periodicals, including *Khao Kristachak,* and *Guideposts*, edited by Koson Srisang. Since 1960 the CCT has provided a number of national ecumenical services, as well as facilities for regional ecumenical programs. Dialogues are currently being conducted between the Roman Catholic Church in Thailand and the CCT.

Selected References

Cressey, Earl H. *A Program of Advance for the Christian Movement in Thailand.* Bangkok: CCT, 1959.

Hughes, Philip. *Proclamation and Response: A Study of the History of the Christian Faith in Northern Thailand.* Chiang Mai: Manuscript Division, Payap College, 1982.

Maen Pongudom. "Apologetic and Missionary Proclamation."

Prasit Pongudom. *Nathaburi Si Nakh on Nan: prawattisat, sangkom, læ Khrit satsana* (History of Christianity in Nan Province, Northern Thailand). Chiangmai: CCT Office of History, 1996.

Saad Chaiwan. "A Study of the Impact of Christian Missions on Thai Culture from the Historical Perspective (1662-1985)."

Swanson, Herbert R. *Khrischak Muang Nua: A Study in Northern Thai Church History.* Bangkok: Chuan Press, 1984.

Wells, Kenneth E. *History of Protestant Work in Thailand.* Bangkok: CCT, 1958. Additional chapters, Mimeo'd, 1966.

1.4 Women Doing Theology

As in other country settings, Christian women in Thailand have served in almost all ministries and programs of the churches from their inception, yet recognition for their theological thought and spirituality, or access to publication for their writings, have seldom eventuated. In recent decades women theologians have been active in theological teaching both at Payap University, Chiangmai, and in the Bangkok Institute for Theology. Some have been active in commissions of the CCT, in the Student Christian Center and related movements, and in community organizations. Their role in Christian education in Thailand has been especially important, along with the preparation and publication of related materials. For the Protestant church, the work of Sarah Wylie in programs of the CCT from 1954 has been a notable example.

From the 1960s Prakai Nontawasee in particular has provided eminent leadership in the teaching of Christian education and related fields as well as in other areas of ecumenical and women's theology. (See 1.8.1.) Other theologians and scholars have included Kamol Arayaprateep - in biblical, historical and anthropological studies; Nantawan Boonprasat-Lewis - in mission, ethical and feminist studies; Chuleepan Srisoontorn-Persons - in indigenous pastoral theology and feminist reflection; and Esther Danpongpee - in the articulation of "tribal" theologies. Amongst others whose work includes contextual reflection are Samran Kwangwaena, Niramon Prudtatorn, Thanawadee Thajeen, Naiyana Supapung, Nantiya Petchgate, Lauran Bethell and Achara Yuphlee. (See for example the periodicals *In God's Image*, *Harvest Field*, *Reformed World*, *Asia Journal of Theology* and *HeRB Bulletin*.)

Women's centers and movements in which Christian women have been active include the New Life Center in Chiangmai (1987-), which provides education, vocational and craft training for tribal women, in association with the Thai government's Adult School program and the cooperation of a local seminary; the Church of Christ Social Development Department, and the Student Christian Center, Bangkok. Some professional Christian women have also been associated with the WE-TRAIN International House, Bangkok

(1990-) which includes emergency homes for women and children; the Women's Education and Training Center and the Women's Clinic, which supports the Association for the Promotion of the Status of Women. (For Catholic women see below 2.2 and 2.6)

Selected References

Batchelor, Martine. *Walking on Lotus Flowers. Buddhist Women Living, Loving and Meditating.* London: Thorson, 1994.

Boonprasat-Lewis, Nantawan. "A Study of Christian Mission in Thailand." *East Asia Journal of Theology* 2.1 (1984).

—. "Toward an Ethic of Feminist Liberation and Empowerment: a case study of prostitution in Thailand." In *Christian ethics in ecumenical context: theology, culture, and politics in dialogue*, edited by Shin Chiba, George R. Hunsberger and Lester Edwin J. Ruiz. Grand Rapids: Eerdmans, c1995.

Danpongpee, Esther. "Karen Stories of Creation." In *Doing Theology with Creation in Asian Cultures* Vol 1. Chiangmai: PTCA Regional Theological Seminar-Workshop, 2000.

Kamol Arayaprateep. "Covenant - Tool in Bible Study." *SEA Journal of Theology*, 18.1 (1977).

—. *Introduction to the Old Testament.* Bangkok: CCT, 1989.

Khin Thitsa. *Providence and Prostitution: Image and Reality for Women in Buddhist Thailand.* London: Change International, 1980.

Parichart Suwanbubha. "The position of women in Buddhism." *In God's Image* (June 1989).

Porntip Chaweephath. "Personal Spirituality in the Old Testament". 3 articles. Chiang Mai: Mimeo'd, 1999.

Prakai Nontawasee. "To Seek in Order to Give: Insiders, Not Outsiders." In *Faith in the Midst of Faiths*, edited by S.J. Samartha. Geneva: WCC, 1977.

—. "Liberation: The Thai Christian View." *Reformed World* 36.1 (1981).

Srisoontorn-Persons, Chuleepan. "A Contextual Approach to Pastoral Care and Counselling in Northern Thailand." ThD dissertation, Boston University, 1995.

—. "Thai Resources for Pastoral Counselling." *PTCA Bulletin*10.2 (1997).

1.5 The Location of Protestant Theology in Thailand

Because there has so often been little inclination to engage in formal theological reflection, the very term "Thai theology" carries little meaning for even theologically trained church leaders. The question then becomes one of ascertaining where Thai theologies are located and how they are expressed. It can be said that there are two key "places" where Protestant Christians in Thailand express their faith theologically, in liturgy and worship and in events and gatherings outside of worship. Wherever they meet to talk or to pray, in other words, Protestants in Thailand engage in the expression and creation of their theologies. One has to listen to their words and be sensitive to their actions in many places and on many occasions in order to discern the nature of those theologies.

One simple example will have to suffice here. A number of surveys of sermons have long pointed to the fact that Thai preachers largely limit themselves - and their theology - to the New Testament. The apostle Paul is widely honored, and theological students write repeated papers seeking to discover how he did ministry in the 1st century. If one examines those sermons again, one will find that almost none of them discuss the suffering or the death of Jesus. They focus on his greatness and glory and power. As we will see below, these homiletical and liturgical expressions of faith tell us much about the nature of Protestant theologies in Thailand.

We should pay particular attention here to liturgy and worship as a key resource for discovering the nature of Protestant theology in Thailand. Traditional Thai culture focused itself especially on the village temple and temporally and spiritually on the ceremonies and ritual of the temple (with an admixture of animistic ceremonies). Even today, one can frequently hear in the towns and villages of Thailand the modulated chanting of the monks as they officiate at house warmings, funerals, weddings, openings and other ceremonial occasions. Protestants in Thailand share this cultural inclination towards ceremony, worshipping frequently and on the same occasions as their Buddhist neighbors make merit.

At the same time, individual Protestants in Thailand not infrequently articulate a serious personal faith in God. They pray.

They turn to God in moments of need. They honor God. In the process, they express themselves theologically and point to their understanding of who God is and what God has done for them.

1.6 Key Themes in Protestant Theology in Thailand

In Protestant theologies in Thailand, we must understand that there is a fundamental division between tribal theologies and lowland, ethnic Thai theologies. This section deals only with ethnic Thai theologies, and even here the situation is more complex than it might appear to others. Apart from tribal and minority peoples, Thailand divides itself into four major geographic and cultural regions: the dominant Central region; the North; the North East, and the South. Each region has its own dialect, history and distinctive culture(s). The "Thai language" is actually a regional dialect turned into the state language by the Bangkok government through the exercise of superior power that has aggressively and intentionally sought to destroy the regional dialects as living languages. The theological issues dealt with here are those that arise out of the common and relatively recent historical experience of modern-day Thailand as embodied in the state language and culture of the nation. A number of these themes, however, would be common to the regional cultures as well.

1.6.1. God as Patron and as Guardian Spirit

Historically, Thai society has been a patron-client society, and the thought ways of a hierarchical and carefully structured social system remain potent in Thai thinking down to the present. In the past, the vast majority of people were commoners, peasants who each had a patron that they looked to for protection and to whom they gave honor and service. The lords, in their turn, always had lords above them until the apex of society was reached in the person of the King. It has been natural, thus, for Thai Christians to look to God as their King and Great Patron, although, of course, they do not voice this view overtly or consciously. Christians, nonetheless, understand themselves as those who are the servants and subjects of *phra phu ben chao*, that is, God. Great emphasis is laid on God's overarching care for those who "truly believe" in Him. (God in

Thai theological thinking is male. God's maleness reflects both cultural perceptions and an understanding inherited from the missionary past. See further below.) In the stories of everyday church members, then, one hears time and again of how God cared for them personally and individually. They were ill. God healed them. They had an accident. God saved them. They needed a job. God answered their prayers and provided one. Thai Protestants firmly believe that God is Benevolent, Righteous and Merciful. Many of them, however, would mix western exclusivistic notions into this understanding and thus affirm that God gives personal care only to Christians, because only Christians acknowledge God's sovereignty. Further, they add the spice of western personal piety to the mixture by emphasizing that "truly believing in God" is the means by which they demonstrate their loyalty to God the Patron.

God is not, however, simply their patron. God is the Great Patron, the Patron Above All Others, which effectively means that God is King. The image of the King has tremendous potency for Thais, particularly at present with the wide veneration of King Phumipol Adulyadet, known also as Rama IX. He has reigned as King since 1946 and is widely perceived as the greatest monarch in later Thai history, if not in all of Thai history. He has been given the title, "the Great" (Maharat) in addition to his other titles and honorifics.

Thai Protestants understand that God is God even over the King, which placed God at the very pinnacle of all reality and makes of God King of Kings and Lord of Lords in a potent, meaningful way that westerners can hardly appreciate. Mixed into this perception of God as King is an animistic appreciation of God as the Great Spirit. Thais still firmly believe in the spirit world, a world that is good as well as evil and to which people can turn in times of pressing need. God, thus, becomes a figure of great majesty and immense power, and is worthy of the highest of respect. At the same time, God's closeness is maintained through the patron-client motif by which God looks after individual Christians in a caring, personal manner.

1.6.2. Jesus - Human and Divine

In this context, the concept of God incarnate in one person, a lowly carpenter from west Asia, becomes a particularly difficult concept to maintain. Christians understand that Jesus was human in a formal sense only. If one asks Thai Christians whether Jesus was a man or God, most will answer quickly and firmly that Jesus was and is God. Some will maintain stoutly that he was never a human being. It should be noted that among a small number of theologically-trained Thai Protestants there has been a strong reaction against the generally held emphasis on Jesus' divinity, but that very reaction only serves to underscore the significance of the Divine Jesus for the vast majority of Protestants. Every evening Thais see television footage of the King and the royal family processing about the nation, graciously visiting and encouraging their subjects. That is the subliminal understanding they have of Jesus as well, most clearly expressed in the Thai term for processing, *kanrubsadet*. Advent is formally known as the Season of *Kanrubsadet*, that is the season of receiving the processing King. The image is precisely that of the Thai people themselves preparing for the gracious visit of their King, a matter of great honor and near frenzied preparation.

Thai Protestants, thus, place great emphasis on the divinity, majesty, power and sacredness of Jesus. These are his attributes, and included in them is the sense that this mighty and incredibly powerful person is the Patron of those who believe. The Thai language virtually forces those speaking the language to view Jesus, as well as God more generally, in the terms just described. The language has a special vocabulary devoted entirely to inhabitants of the realm of the sacred. It is used with the Buddha, with all divinities, and with the royal family. Christians speak of and to the Trinitarian God with this high vocabulary, thus lifting Jesus into the realm of the sacred and setting him apart from the realm of the mundane. Linguistically, Jesus simply cannot be associated with the mundane. Even the words used to describe his hands, eyes, or words are special words used only with sacred powers.

1.6.3. The Role of Works, Ceremony, Faith

Christian celebrations and their calendar of festivals reinforce this sense of the Sacred, Mighty Jesus. Christmas is the High Festival of Thai Protestantism, and it has only been in recent years that there has been a conscious attempt in some circles to give more emphasis to Easter. In the past, rural congregations would sometimes entirely forget Easter. Even where celebrated, Easter is seen as proof of the Great Power of Jesus as God. The cross, though hanging at the front of the sanctuary, is hardly mentioned. If Jesus' suffering is mentioned at all, again, the emphasis will be on how that suffering was intended for the good of those who believe in him.

Thai Protestants almost vehemently reject the concept of merit-making, one that is otherwise central to Thai religious consciousness. In a formal sense, they fully accept the common wisdom of international Protestantism by which merit-making is simply another way by which people try to win their own salvation. They accept and occasionally articulate the Protestant critique of Buddhism, namely that it is a system for winning salvation by human effort and is doomed to failure in the face of human sin. The habits of merit-making, however, have proven to be more difficult to dispense with. Thai Protestant piety expresses its loyalty to God in patterns that are strikingly similar to the ways in which their Buddhist neighbors make merit. Both Christians and Buddhists emphasize the central importance of building a variety of buildings for their church or temple. And on various occasions families will "donate" items to the church in a manner that precisely duplicates the patterns of making merit in Thai Buddhism.

As indicated above, Thai Protestants have also retained the centrality of ritual and ceremony that is a mark of Thai religious consciousness generally. Protestants state that there is a clear difference, however. "Other" Thais use their rituals as a form of merit-making, which is taken by Protestants to be self-serving. Thai Christians, in contrast, are showing their loyalty and their respect to God. By the same token, when they donate various articles to the church or support the church building fund, they are emphatically not making merit. As they see it, they are paying respect to God. It is at points like this that Thai Protestant theological reflection remains strongly Thai and yet unique also. Thai Protestants have taken an important Thai religious form, merit-making, and a central social concept, patronage, and combined them into a distinctive understanding of how one expresses one's loyalty to God.

It must be added that along with the above faith-practices, and while Thai Protestant churches generally show little interest in any form of outreach that is not evangelistic, there are many individuals and agencies that engage in impressive social, and educational outreach (see 1.7. below)

1.6.4. Other Elements

Thai Protestants have retained other elements of Thai religious consciousness as well, notably an emphasis on dhamma rather than grace. While there is a definite sense of the Compassionate Buddha in Thai Buddhism, the Buddha's compassion was located in his willingness to share his "way" and his teachings with others. However, the way and the teaching, the dhamma, are themselves fixed in the very nature of things. Each individual has to escape the cycles of life and death by her or his own efforts. Buddhism finds the idea that one can believe one's way into Heaven a naive and ultimately fruitless position. While Protestants in Thailand disagree and share traditional Christian understandings of salvation through faith and trust, individual Protestants sometimes believe that salvation is not really by grace. One has to live a proper life and have a deep, true faith in order to be acceptable to God. Effectively, one has to work out one's own salvation, but that salvation is not by merit but by showing a deep, consistent trust and faith in God. The expression of that trust, as already seen, often takes much the same form as do the merit-making activities of Thai Buddhists.

Much Thai Protestant theology must therefore be understood as functioning at two levels or in two modes simultaneously. In one mode or at one level, it is largely a western import. Its formal expressions of faith are taken from the West and when translated back into western languages sound entirely orthodox to other Protestants. In the second mode or at the second level, however, those same words when used in the Thai language and in the context of Thai culture and society take on meanings that are quite Thai. The theology of the people in the churches, then, is a highly contextualized theology for all its outward appearances. The situation that results is paradoxical. Much of the outward appearance of Thai Protestant practice seems quite alien to Thai eyes and ears. Thais not infrequently feel uncomfortable with the ways in which Christians worship because that worship is so different from what they are used to. Thai Protestantism, thus, appears alien. Yet, in fact, much of Thai Protestantism is in accordance with the religious values, attitudes and folk-ways of Thai culture, if reshaped and repackaged in somewhat unusual ways.

Selected References (See also1.8, Selected Theologians.)

Significant examples of Thai theological reflection which seeks to respond creatively to the Thai religious and social context include:

i) In Biblical Study:

Chaiwat Chawmuangman. "A Comparison of the Nature of Parables in the Synoptic Gospels and the Nature of Parables in the Thai Culture." ThD dissertation, Asia Baptist Graduate Theological Seminary, Philippine Branch, 1993.

Hamlin, John. *Joshua: the Conquest of the Promised Land*. Chiang Mai: Payap College, 1989.

—. *God: Builder of Society. the Importance of the Old Testament Prophets for the Southeast Asian Church*. Bangkok: Suriyabin, 1992.

Kamol Arayaprateep. "Covenant - Tool in Bible Study." *SEA Journal of Theology*, 18.1 (1977).

—. *Introduction to the Old Testament*. Bangkok: CCT, 1989.

Pisnu Akkapin. *Dictionary of the Bible*. (In Thai). Bangkok: Suriyabin, 1992.

Pradit Takerngrangsarit. "The Relevance of Western Biblical Scholarship to the Teaching of the Old Testament in the Thai Church: A Study of Selected Representative Texts and a Proposal for a Responsible Thai Scholarship." ThD dissertation, Melbourne College of Divinity, 1993.

Prasert Kusawadi. "Presenting the Gospel Using the Body, Mind, and Spirit Circles." *Lingo* 18 (1983).

Seree Lorgunpai. "World Lover, World Leaver: The Book of Ecclesiastes and Thai Buddhism." PhD dissertation, University of Edinburgh, 1995.

—. "The Book of Ecclesiastes and Thai Buddhism." *Asia Journal of Theology* 8.1 (1994).

ii) In Theological Studies:

Boonprasat-Lewis, Nantawan. "Asian Women Theology: A Historical and Theological Analysis." *East Asia Journal of Theology* 4.2 (1986).

Davis, John R. "Towards a Contextualised Theology for the Church in Thailand." Thesis, Birmingham, University of Birmingham, 1990. Published as *Poles Apart? Contextualizing the Gospel.* Bangkok: Kanok Bannasan, 1993.

Hovemyr, Anders P. "Towards a Theology of the Incarnation in the Thai Culture." *East Asia Journal of Theology* 1.2 (1983).

Seree Lorgunpai. "Thai Theology." In *Dictionary of Third World Theologies,* edited by Virginia Fabella and R.S. Sugirtharagah. Maryknoll, NY: Orbis Books, 2000.

Swanson, Herbert R. "Historical Perspectives on the Search for a Relevant Ecclesiology in the Church of Christ in Thailand." *Bulletin of the Commission on Theological Concerns, Christian Conference of Asia* 8.1 & 2 (1980).

—, ed. *To What Extent? Incarnation in the Thai Context.* Chiang Mai: Manuscript Division, Payap College, 1982.

Wanlapa Arurothayanon. "Justification by Faith Alone: A Comparison of Thai Buddhism's Concept of Righteousness with Luther's Idea of Justification." Thesis, Asian Center for Theological Studies and Mission, Seoul,1991.

iii) In Encounter with Thai Religion and Culture:

Baw Tananone. "A Call for Solidarity: A Thai Experience." *CTC Bulletin* 8.3 (1989).

Hughes, Philip J. "Christianity and Culture: A Case Study in Northern Thailand." ThD dissertation, South East Asia Graduate School of Theology, 1983.

—. "The Assimilation of Christianity in the Thai Culture." *Religion* 14 (1984).

—. "Christianity and Buddhism in Thailand." *Journal of the Siam Society* 73 (1985).

Pachara Chootoochana-Saengwichai. "Reflections on Communicating the Four Spiritual Laws in Thai Context." MTS thesis, Alliance Biblical Seminary, 1988.

Parichart Suwanbubbha. "Grace and Kamma: A Case Study of Religio-cultural Encounters in Protestant and Buddhist Communities in Bangkok and Its Relevant Environs, Thailand." ThD dissertation, Lutheran School of Theology at Chicago, 1994.

Saad Chaiwan. *The Christian Approach to Buddhists in Thailand*. Bangkok: Suriyaban, 1975.

Suk Prachayaporn. "The Encounter Between Buddhism and Christianity in Thailand: With Special Reference to the Question of the Uniqueness of Jesus Christ." Thesis, Norwegian Lutheran School of Theology, 1998.

iv) In Pastoral and Mission Studies:

Boonprasat-Lewis, Nantawan. "A Study of Christian Mission in Thailand."

Hughes, Philip J. *Proclamation and Response: A Study of the History of the Christian Faith in Northern Thailand*. Chiang Mai: Manuscript Division, Payap College, 1982.

Loh, I-To, ed. *Ak Phra Jao Rao Pen Thai* (The love of God sets us free). Quezon City: Asian Institute of Liturgy and Music, 1989.

Saad Chaiwan. "A Study of Christian Mission in Thailand." *East Asia Journal of Theology* 2.1 (1984).

Srisoontorn Persons, Chuleepan. "A Contextual Approach to Pastoral Care and Counselling in Northern Thailand." ThD dissertation, Boston University, 1995.

—. "Thai Resources for Pastoral Counselling." *PTCA Bulletin* 10.2 (1997).

1.7 Ecumenical and Social Witness and Reflection

The setting for this has been partly shaped by theologies which do not recognize the ecumenical thrusts of mission in either Christian and religious co-operation or in concerns for worldly and people-centered ministries. Individualistic and paternalistic practices in evangelism and welfare, along with institutions which often became elitist in practice, often fail to address many of the most pressing social needs and issues or to articulate the reflection arising from these.

However theological reflection by Thai Protestants upon the issues of society and development, particularly since the early 1960s, has arisen in many social, student and development ministries. These include the urban and rural mission programs of the Church of Christ in Thailand (Urban and Industrial League for Development) under such leaders as Samrit Wongsang; the Student Christian Movement and Student Christian Center, with leadership including Pisnu Akkapin, Koson Srisang, Pong Tananon and Tawin Sidhiphongse; education programs and publishing in social and political ethics by such theologians as Maen Pongudom and Koson Srisang; and the Co-ordinating Committee for Church and Society with such members as Witawan Kongkangdul and Kotom Aruya, both of Chulalongkorn University. The activities and publications of the East Asia Christian Conference when based in Bangkok under the leadership of Kyaw Than (1962-1973) made significant contributions to ecumenical and social ministries in Thailand.

The Thailand Theological Seminary (now McGilvary Seminary, Payap University) has prepared many for such ministries and reflection, and in association with the SCM, was instrumental in forming in 1968 a Religion and Society program for inter-religious co-operation on community issues. Among faculty members who have fostered theological reflection on such issues are (Ms) Prakai Nontawasee, (Ms) Samran Kwangwaena, Maen Pongudom, Kosuke Koyama, Kenihiro Mochizuki, Salvador Martinez and Seree Lorgunpai. Faculty members of the Bangkok Institute of Theology have also encouraged socio-theological reflection. (See also 1.8 and 2.4)

Selected References

Boonprasat-Lewis, Nantawan. "In Search of an Integral Liberation: a study on the Thai struggle for social justice from a Christian perspective: the contemporary Thai farmers' movement as a case study." Dissertation, Princeton Theological Seminary. Ann Arbor: UMI Reprint, 1982.

—. "Toward an Ethic of Feminist Liberation and Empowerment: a case study of prostitution in Thailand." In *Christian ethics in ecumenical context: theology, culture, and politics in dialogue*, edited by Shin Chiba, George R. Hunsberger, and Lester Edwin J. Ruiz. Grand Rapids, Mich.: Eerdmans, c1995.

Koson Srisang. "Dhammocracy in Thailand: A Study of Social Ethics as a Hermeneutic of Dhamma." PhD dissertation, University of Chicago, 1974.

Maen Pongudom with Pong Tanonon. *Christians and Politics. April 4th, 1976 - We.* Mimeo'd. Bangkok: 1976.

Pisnu Akkapin. "Present Status and Theological Foundations for Social Work in the Church of Christ in Thailand." STM thesis, Union Theological Seminary, 1961.

——. *Yut Trong Song Nati* (Stop and think two minutes - Meditations). Mimeo'd, ca. 1978.

Samrit Wongsang. "From Seminary to the Slum." *Church Labor Letter* 93 (1964).

——. *The Church's Industrial Work in Prapadaeng.* Bangkok: CCT Urban Industrial League for Development, 1971.

——. *Reports and Newsletters on CCT Urban Industrial Work in Thailand (UILD).* Bangkok: CCT, 1974- .

——. "Aim of our UILD Work in Thailand." Mimeo'd. Bangkok: 1975.

Tongkham Pantupongs. "The Social Influences of Buddhism and Christianity in the Life of the People of Siam." Typescript, Princeton University, 1951.

1.8 Selected Theologians

1.8.1. Prakai Nontawasee (1926-)

Prakai Nontawasee has been eminent in Thai theological education and Christian education, in women's work and theological reflection, and in both ecumenical and cultural studies since the late 1960s. She has taught at Thailand (now McGilvary) Theological Seminary, has been Dean of the Faculty of Humanities, at Payap University, Chiangmai, and has provided leadership in both the Southeast Asia Studies Program of the Institute for Southeast Asian Studies, and in Asia-wide networks of ecumenical scholars and church people.

In a wide range of leadership positions within the national and world church, she has contributed to the articulation of both theological and sociological understandings of the mission of Thai Christians within Thai culture and society. She has always placed biblical and sociological studies within the context of Thai experience and history where also, as in Israel, it is "God who initiates freedom for His people." The worldview of Thai Christians, their understandings of salvation and liberation, are to be reshaped by the recovery of Thai origins in Yunnan, she believes, as well as by the cultural history of northern Thailand and by reinterpretations of both the Bible and Christian tradition. The role of women in these tasks, for Prakai Nontawasee, is crucial and transformative, although always in mutual solidarity as oneness with others in the world church, to serve all people.

Selected References
Works by Prakai Nontawasee

"The Japanese Image in Thailand." *Japan Christian Quarterly* 41.2 (1975).

"To Seek in Order to Give: Insiders, Not Outsiders." In *Faith in the Midst of Faiths*, edited by S.J. Samartha. Geneva: WCC, 1977.

"Liberation: The Thai Christian View." *Reformed World* 36.1 (1981).

Bible Studies 1 and 2. In *Freed for Service in Vulnerable Situations in Asia: Bible Studies CCA 8th Assembly*. Singapore: CCA, 1985.

"Confrontation of Phii-ka and Christianity: A Case Study." *International Review of Missions* 76 (1987).

"Mission in Mutual Solidarity." *In God's Image* (Dec. 1989).

—, ed. *Change in Northern Thailand and the Shan States 1886-1940*. Singapore: Institute of SEA Studies, 1988.

—, with Chayan Hiranpun, eds. *A Study of the Role of Women in the Bible*. Chiangmai: Payap College, 1990.

1.8.2. Kosuke Koyama (see also under Japan, volume 3)

Kosuke Koyama is widely known in third-world theologies for his humane and provocative meditations on "neighbor-logical theology" (*Pilgrim or Tourist*, 1974), on "the crucified mind" (*No Handle on the Cross*, 1977), on the "direction of depth rather than distance" (*Three Mile an Hour God*, 1979) and on "a critique of idols" (*Mount Fuji and Mount Sinai*, 1984). His most influential work, however, remains the collection of papers, most of which were first published in mimeo'd form as a "Thai Theological

Notebook" (Singapore, 1970). This was to become the widely influential *Waterbuffalo Theology*, in which he presents the experience and reflections in Thailand which led to a (lifelong) reconstruction of theology in Asian contexts. He there affirms that "the theology that serves Jesus Christ in Northern Thailand ... begins and grows in Northern Thailand and nowhere else." He had decided that "the greatness of theological works is to be judged by the extent and quality of the service they can render to [Thai] farmers." Koyama would later expand some of his thought in *Waterbuffalo Theology* and in the book *No Handle on the Cross*. In the eyes of many Thai (and other) theologians Koyama's "open-ended" methodology - seeing the "pathos of God" in the lives of Thai people - has provided one of the most creative paths for Thai theology, and of course for many Asian theologies. His influence on Thai theology continues to be seminal.

Selected References
Works by Kosuke Koyama
> "'Wrath of God' vs. Thai Theologia Gloriae." *South East Asia Journal of Theology* 5.1 (1963).
> "Aristotelian Pepper and Buddhist Salt." *Practical Anthropology* 14.3 (1967).
> "The Mad Man Sits Down." In *Theology in Action 2*, edited by John C. England. Kuala Lumpur: EACC, 1973.
> *Theology in Contact*. Madras: Christian Literature Society, 1975.
> *Waterbuffalo Theology*. London: SCM Press, 1974. Most recently reprinted in revised and expanded edition as *Water Buffalo Theology*. Maryknoll NY: Orbis Books, 1999.
> "Thailand: Points of Theological Friction." In *Asian Voices in Christian Theology*, ed. by Gerald H. Anderson. Maryknoll, NY: Orbis Books, 1974, 65-86.
> Irwin, Dale T. and Akintunde E. Akinade, eds. *The Agitated Mind of God. The Theology of Kosuke Koyama*. Maryknoll NY: Orbis Books, 1996.

1.8.3. Maen Pongudom
Maen Pongudom studied theology in Thailand and Otago University, New Zealand (PhD, 1979). He is both church historian and theologian, has taught at McGilvary Theological Seminary and

Payap University, Chiangmai, and participated in scholarly and ecumenical programs throughout the region. He has long been concerned to reformulate more adequate Christian apologetic for Thailand, for in missionary proclamation he sees that the Thai religio-philosophical and cultural heritage has most often been ignored. Such an apologetic is necessary, Pongudom affirms, in order that Christian theology in Thailand may grow in continuity with Thai experience, and through a synthesis with Thai understanding.

Pongudom sees models for "the balance of freedom and faithfulness" required for this in both early Christian apologetics - in particular Justin Martyr, Clement of Alexandria and Origen - and in contemporary Buddhist interpretation (notably of Buddhadasa Bhikku). He concludes that in dialogue with Buddhist neighbors, Christians should (carefully) "adopt key Buddhist terms [and] explain them in a Christian Context." Resources for this will also come from creative elements in Thai history, Thai Buddhism, Thai folk stories and culture and from the social aspirations and struggles of the Thai people.

Selected References
Works by Maen Pongudom

"Progress and Problems of the Church of Christ in Thailand 1957-1971." *SEA Journal of Theology* 14.1 (1972).

"Apologetic and Missionary Proclamation: Exemplified by American Presbyterian Missionaries to Thailand (1828-1978). Early Church Apologists: Justin Martyr, Clement of Alexandria, and Origen, and the Venerable Buddhadasa Bhikku, a Thai Buddhist Monk-Apologist." PhD dissertation, University of Otago, 1979.

"Models of the Church in Church History." In *Tradition and Innovation: A Search for a Relevant Ecclesiology in Asia*, edited by CTC-CCA. Singapore: Commission of Theological Concerns, CCA, 1983.

"Creation of Man: Theological Reflections Based on Northern Thai Folktales." *East Asia Journal of Theology* 3.2 (1985).

—, with Pong Danonon. *Christians and Politics. April 4th, 1976 - We*. Mimeo'd. Bangkok: 1976.

1.8.4. Koson Srisang

From early participation in student movements, Koson Srisang became a founding leader in the Student Christian Center, Bangkok, where study and discussion of major issues facing Thai society were fostered in joint programs in which church, university and community groups collaborated. Following doctoral study, he has served as General Secretary of the Church of Christ in Thailand, staff member of the WCC-CCPD Geneva, General Secretary of The Ecumenical Coalition on Third World Tourism and a founder of the End Child Prostitution in Asian Tourism international campaign.

Among Koson Srisang's chief theological concerns has been the articulation of a contextual ethic which apply "freedom" and "compassion" - "the two most encompassing symbols in human life and history" - to human development and to concrete political and economic struggles. Also a key concern for him is the full participation of people, and of churches, in community-building, human development and politico-cultural renewal. He has therefore sought to bring together a Christian theology of society, with the "contributions of youth to the promotion of social goals and cultural values", and new "Asian paradigms" in social and political ethics. This has led to a re-interpretation both of Christian missiology and of Buddhist understanding of the Dhamma. In this he draws freely upon Asian and Third-World theologies, Thai scholars of culture and Buddhism, on Thai constitutional history, and the resources of ecumenical documentation.

Selected References
Works by Koson Srisang

> "Dhammocracy in Thailand: A Study of Social Ethics as a Hermeneutic of Dhamma." PhD dissertation, University of Chicago, 1974.
> "On Mission Identification with Thai Suffering and Hope." Manuscript Division, Payap College, 1976.
> "People are the Centre of Ministry." *Midstream* 18 (1979).
> "Recovering the Power of Life." *Ecumenical Review* 32.1 (1980).

"Cultural Heritage and Political Vision: Northern Thai Perspective on Political Ethics." *East Asia Journal of Theology* 3.1 (1985).

"On Reinterpreting the Dhamma: Towards an Adequate Thai Social Ethics." In *Radical Conservatism: Buddhism in the Contemporary World*, ed. by Sulak Sivaraksa. Bangkok: The Inter-Religious Commission for Development and International Network of Engaged Buddhists, 1990: 469-487.

"Free and Compassionate: A Perspective on Religious Foundations of Political Ethics." In *Doing Theology With Asian Resources: Theology and Politics*, edited by Yeow Choo Lak. Singapore: ATESEA, 1993: 69-102.

—, ed. *Perspectives on Political Ethics. An Ecumenical Enquiry.* Geneva: WCC; Georgetown: University Press, 1983.

—, ed. *Liberating Discovery: Asian Enquiry into Theological Reflection on Tourism.* Bangkok: Ecumenical Coalition on Third World Tourism, 1986.

1.8.5. Herbert R. Swanson

Herbert Swanson has worked for many decades in Thailand as historian, theologian and educator. His graduate studies were conducted at the University of Maryland (MA 1987) and for the PhD at the University of Melbourne. From early studies centered on the theologies brought to Thailand by western missionaries and their reception by Thai Christians, his research, writing and teaching have however developed to include all aspects of Thai theology and church history. In these areas he is now recognised internationally. From the beginning his work has been deeply rooted in careful study of Thai contexts and resources and to facilitate such studies he has pioneered the development of an archival center of regional importance for Thai materials - now the Payap University Archives. In full studies of Thai theology in its oral and written forms, he has written on the themes of Thai theology, on the contexts of Thai theology, on Thai ecclesiology and theological method.

Selected References
Works by Herbert R. Swanson
    Khrischak Muang Nua: A Study in Northern Thai Church History. Bangkok: Chuan Press, 1984.

Towards a Clean Church: A Case Study in Nineteenth-Century Thai Church History. Chiang Mai: Office of History, CCT, 1991.

HeRB Bulletin. Quarterly, Chiangmai (Herb Swanson e-mail: villager@loxinfo.co.th).

"Historical Perspectives on the Search for a Relevant Ecclesiology in the Church of Christ in Thailand." *CTC Bulletin,* CCA 8.1 & 2 (1980).

"This Heathen People: The Cognitive Sources of American Missionary Westernizing Activities in Northern Siam, 1867-1889." MA thesis, University of Maryland, 1987.

"A New Generation: Missionary Education and Changes in Women's Roles in Traditional Northern Thai Society." *Sojourn* 3.2 (1988).

"The Payap University Archives: A Resource for the Study of Thailand." *Sojourn* 6.1 (1991).

"Reflections on 'Christianity in the Thai Historical Context': A Conference of Catholic, Protestant and Buddhist Historians held in Chiang Mai, in March 1992." *Asia Journal of Theology* 7.1 (1993).

"What is It? Methods for Seeking Theology in Thai Contexts." (In Thai.) Chiang Mai: Workshop Documents Concerning Theology and Ministry in Thai Contexts, PTCA Workshop at the McGilvary Faculty of Theology, Payap University, 29 March-1 April 1999.

—, ed. *To What Extent? Incarnation in the Thai Context.* Chiang Mai: Manuscript Division, Payap College, 1982.

1.8.6. Other Theological Writers - Protestant

Amongst other theological writers to be noted - apart from theologians already mentioned - are Saad Chaiwan, John Hamlin, Pradit Takerngrangsarit, Philip Hughes, Seree Lorgunpai, Baw Tananone and Virat Setsoponkal. Saad Chaiwan teaches at Payap university, Chiangmai, and has long studied and written on the impact of Christianity on Thai Culture and on Christian-Buddhist relations in Thailand. John Hamlin was a scholar of the Hebrew scriptures and for many years principal of McGilvary Theological Seminary, Chiangmai. His writings place biblical exposition within the Thai and southeast Asian context. Pradit Takerngrangsarit has written on aspects of Thai culture and Thai church history. Philip

Hughes has written extensively on the encounter between Christianity and Thai culture and is now based in Australia. Seree Lorgunpai's Old Testament studies have been pursued in dialogue with Thai Buddhism, where he finds in Hebrew wisdom scripture a bridge between Buddhism and Thai Christianity.

Selected References

Hamlin, John. *Joshua: the Conquest of the Promised Land.* Chiang Mai: Payap College, 1989.

—. *God: Builder of Society. the Importance of the Old Testament Prophets for the Southeast Asian Church.* Bangkok: Suriyabin, 1992

Hughes, Philip J. "The Assimilation of Christianity in the Thai Culture." *Religion* 14 (1984).

—. "Christianity and Buddhism in Thailand." *Journal of the Siam Society* 73 (1985).

Pradit Takerngrangsarit. "The Relevance of Western Biblical Scholarship to the Teaching of the Old Testament in the Thai Church: A Study of Selected Representative Texts and a Proposal for a Responsible Thai Scholarship." ThD dissertation, Melbourne College of Divinity, 1993.

Saad Chaiwan. *The Christian Approach to Buddhists in Thailand.* Bangkok: Suriyaban, 1975.

—. "A Study of Christian Mission in Thailand." *East Asia Journal of Theology* 2.1 (1984).

Seree Lorgunpai. "The Book of Ecclesiastes and Thai Buddhism." *Asia Journal of Theology* 8.1 (1994).

—. "Thai Theology." In *Dictionary of Third World Theologies,* ed. by Virginia Fabella mm and R.S. Sugirtharagah. Maryknoll, NY: Orbis Books, 2000.

Baw Tananone. "A Call for Solidarity: A Thai Experience." *CTC Bulletin* 8.3 (1989).

1.9 A Note on Regional and Tribal Theologies

Northern Thais are heirs to a distinctive culture many centuries old which was once a high, impressive culture. Northern Thai Protestants have their own distinctive history as well, and in the "old days" worshipped and sang entirely in northern Thai. Some linguists claim that northern Thai was in its time a separate language from central Thai, with a greater difference between them than between Portuguese and Spanish, for example.

Contextual Theology in Thailand 1800-2000

It is a matter for speculation as to how a distinctive northern Thai theology might differ from that of central Thais. Northern Thai, for example, seems to have had no royal language. Northern Thai Christians referred to Jesus and God with terms of respect that could be applied to any respected person. Patterns of patronage were less formal although no less widespread. How would this affect northern Thai perceptions of God and Jesus? Historical research into northern Thai worship and hymnology shows that northern Thais sang almost exclusively western hymns; but they did so with a distinctive northern Thai accent that shifted notes in ways that musically-trained missionaries found impossible to accept - or to alter. We can only assume that northern Thais were equally adept at contextualizing missionary theology, but it is not clear how they did so. The problem with such "peoples' theologies," is that these theologies leave few formal records or traces that historians can easily rediscover, although it can be assumed that there are regional variations to the theological patterns described above, which may yield to research.

Much the same can be said for tribal theologies. Where American Presbyterianism has been a potent force for theological expression among the low-land Thai, the Presbyterians had little presence among the tribal peoples of Thailand. The first tribal Protestants were Karen Baptists in northern Thailand. As is the case generally, Baptist missionaries inculcated a deep disrespect for the religious heritage of the Karen so that in many ways Karen Protestants in Thailand today relate to their religious heritage in different ways from that of ethnic Thai Protestants. As with most other tribal churches, they are distinctively unlike other Protestants in many respects.

The religious and cultural context for Karen theologies, thus, is strikingly different from that of Thai Buddhism. The dialogue between Karen culture and Bible is in some ways much easier to conduct, the two partners being more obviously compatible than is the case with Buddhism. The theologian can bring many biblical passages straight into a Karen religious context with little need for adaptation, and it is quite easy to use the traditional poems, the *ta*, in tandem with biblical passages in preaching. At the same time, however, it soon becomes clear that Karen theism is quite different from Christian theism.

Future Karen Christian theologians will find a great number of issues to engage their attention. These include belief in Yua, the 'created' Creator (and sometimes absent) God, the relationship of Yua to Christian Trinitarian belief, the central place of the home with its elaborately detailed family ritual (*awe kwae*); the destructive impact upon Karen religious traditions of neo-colonial economic, cultural and political forces, along with the incursions of Buddhism and of Christianity which are insensitive to a people's selfhood.

Selected References

> Hayami Yoko. "Ritual and ReligiousTransformation among Sgaw Karen of Northern Thailand: Implications on Gender and Ethnic Identity." PhD dissertation, Brown University, 1992.
>
> Hovemyr, Anders. *In Search of the Karen King: A Study in Karen Identity with Special Reference to 19th Century Karen Evangelism in North Thailand*. Studia Missionalia Upsaliensia 49. Uppsala: Swedish Institute of Missionary Research, 1989.
>
> Htoo Hla E, ed. *The Golden Book*. (In Karen), 1955. Reprinted Chiang Mai: Thailand Karen Baptist Convention, n.d.
>
> Loo Shwe. "The Karen People of Thailand and Christianity." Mimeo'd. 1962.
>
> Marshall, Harry Ignatius. *The Karen People of Burma: A Study in Anthropology and Ethnology*. 1922. Reprinted Bangkok: White Lotus Press, 1997.
>
> Renard, Ronald. "Kariang: History of Karen-T'ai Relations from the Beginnings to1923." PhD dissertation, University of Hawaii, 1980.
>
> Swanson, Herbert. "What is It? Methods for Seeking Theology in Thai Contexts." (In Thai.) Chiang Mai: Workshop Documents Concerning Theology and Ministry in Thai Contexts, PTCA Workshop at the McGilvary Faculty of Theology, Payap University, 29 March-1 April 1999.
>
> Tanabe Shigeru, ed. *Religious Traditions Among Tai Ethnic Groups: A Selected Bibliography*. Ayutthaya: Ayutthaya Historical Study Centre, 1991.

Tapp, Nicholas. "The Impact of Christianity upon Marginalized Ethnic Minorities: the Case of the Hmong. *Journal of Southeast Asian Studies* 20.1 (1989).
The 2000 AD Culture Committee. *Cultural Handbook.* (In Karen). Karen Baptist Convention, 1996.

2 Roman Catholic thought and life

(For the period 16th-18th centuries see chapter 2 of this volume.)

2.1 Introduction

The Catholic Church had been slowly growing in Siam since the 17th century and the Missions Etrangères de Paris maintained a continuous presence there until the 20th century. In the late 18th century, the favor of the Kings for Catholic mission continued for Bishops Texier de Kerlay and de Lolière-Puycontat (1755), for Bishop Brigot, Father Corre (1769) and Mgr Lebon (1772-80). Fresh persecution from 1775 on however, greatly limited the Church's life under successive Bishops (Condé, Garnault and Florens). Further missionaries were only able to come in 1826 and 1830, among them Fathers Bouchot, Barbe, Bruguière, Vachal, Grandjean and Pallegoix. Fr Courvezy, who in 1834 was appointed Vicar Apostolic of Siam, was assisted by 11 European and 7 native priests. His successor, Bishop Pallegoix (1840-62), was a Siamese scholar and author of *Déscription du royaume Thai ou Siam* and *Dictionnaire siamois-latin- français- anglais.*

Under Kings Mongkut (1851-68) and Chulalongkorn (1868-1910), almost continuous peace was enjoyed by the Catholic Church in Siam under Pallegoix's successors, Bishops Dupont (1862-72) and Vey (1875-1909). The MEP had by now been joined by the Brothers of St Gabriel and the Sisters of St Paul de Chartres. Writings in this period were largely confined to "histories of mission," linguistic studies, or reports of Catholic communities and clergy, with only rare recognition of the Thai context other than the issues of religious liberty and Buddhist encounter.

In many aspects the Catholic Church in Thailand in the 20th century, remained a close reflection of the church in Europe, a character that was only underlined by the arrival since the 1920s of many other religious orders from the West. Italian Salesians arrived in 1926, and in the next few decades other orders and congregations also commenced work. These included the Ursuline, Carmelite, Capuchin and Salesian women's congregations, along with Redemptorists, Jesuits, Betharam Fathers, De La Salle Brothers, Oblates of Mary Immaculate and others. In the same period, nationalistic trends were shaping a new mentality in Thailand and the local Catholic communities and clergy shared in these movements. Japanese occupation gave added impetus to these trends, although the Catholic Church was still largely seen as being a "French Church". This foreign image was preserved in part through mission success among non-Thai minorities, along with the arrival of increased numbers of missionaries, especially expatriates from China after 1949.

Pastoral mission now included labor, refugee, social and student ministries, but despite extensive educational ministries, culminating in the formation of two Catholic Universities (Assumption, initially a college, in 1885; and St John's, formed a century later, 1989), the Church has made only small impact on the intellectual, cultural or political fields of national life. Until the 1970s, most local secular clergy had been formed in Penang (Malaysia) or in Rome, but in 1972 a Major Seminary was established and courses have been commenced in the Thai language. Only in 1975 were Thai Bishops consecrated and a significant number of Thai priests ordained. The fact that formation of clergy, religious and laity is done through Thai language has, however, a most important impact on the life of the church, especially as regards inculturation. (See below 2.2.)

Selected References

Bunchua Kirti. *The Catholic Parishes of the Portuguese and Annamite Descendants in Bangkok.* Bangkok, Chulalongkorn University, 1982.

—. "History of the Church in Thailand." In *Asia and Christianity,* edited by M.D. David. Bombay: Himalaya Publishing, 1985.

Launay, Adrien. *Histoire de la mission au Siam 1662-1811.* Bangkok: National Library, 1969 (2 vols.); Paris: Missions Etrangères de Paris, 2000 (3 vols.).

Love, R.S. "Monarchs, Merchants and Missionaries in Early Modern Asia: The Missions Etrangères in Siam." *International History Review*, 21.1 (1999).
Lux Mundi. *History of the Thai Catholic Church*. (In Thai) Bangkok: Samphran Major Seminary, 1990.
Mahoney, Irene. *A Far Country, Ursuline Mission in Thailand,1924-1945*. Bangkok: 1999.
Morrissy, Patrick. *The Redemptorists: 50 Years in Thailand*. <http://www.cssr.or.th/history/history.htm>.
Pallegoix, Mgr J.B. *Mémoire sur la Mission de Siam*. Beaune: Blodeau Dejussieu, 1853.
—. *Description du Royaume Thai ou Siam*. Paris: 1854: Bangkok: D.K. Book House, 1976.
Pezet, Edmund. "Mission Chrétienne en Thailande." *Spiritus* 28 (1987).
Pro Mundi Vita. *The Church in Thailand*. (PMV Bulletin); *A Church Survey in Thailand*. (PMV Dossier), 1976.
Seri Phongphit. *The Relation between the Catholic Church and Thai Society from 17c to today*. Jochi Daigaku Ajia Bunka Kenkujo 2.2. Tokyo: Sophia University, 1985.
Streit, R., and J. Dindinger, eds. *Bibliotheca Missionum*. Vol. 29 Missionsliteratur Suadostasiens 1910-1970. Rome: Herder, 1970.

2.2 Theological Context

Thai Catholics retain, with their compatriots, full respect for their culture which preserves many of their people's creative traditions, along with respect for those who teach these. The Thai language and culture also gives a priority to the order and harmony in society, and therefore gives much respect to rules and authority. Until recent decades, Thais have lived under a regime of royal absolutism, which along with the claims of hierarchical church leadership for Catholics, also exalts the role of authority and a corresponding passivity. Ideas of history as progress towards an eschatological future, or of human development as communitarian, have little meaning when compared to the personal improvement of the individual. And this is largely seen as an inward, not a historical, process. Jesus may take the place of Buddha for Christians, but the central concern remains that of individual conformity to an ideal of "spiritual" virtue.

Catholic tradition in Thailand has been shaped not only by the clericalism and orthodoxy of western missionaries but also by the rigor and piety of the Jansenist traditions which many of them brought. The maintenance of such a legalism, along with traditions of maintaining harmony and obedience has been strengthened by Roman centralism which has by its directives often obstructed the inculturation of theology. The history of the Church in Thailand in the 20th century has also been dominated by foreign priests, especially French, until Vatican II, and even after.

As theological teachers have all received their formation in Rome, the thought and categories for expressing the teaching of Jesus, and its theological interpretation, have remained highly westernized until recent decades. In the post-Vatican II period, increasing involvement in societal and inter-religious concerns, and in particular inter-faith programs of community development, have stimulated more contextualized theological reflection. In the 1980s, with the moves from foreign to Thai leadership, the Catholic Church has endeavored to become an integral part of Thai society. And in the last decade Thai Catholics have more widely accepted not only proposals for liturgical renewal, but also for fuller social involvement and inter-religious dialogue.

Only a few attempts at inculturation have, however, been seen in these years. Among these are a new awareness of the role of laity - as in the recent general assembly of the Church in Thailand preparing the "2000 Vision-mission Statement" - and in the recent initiation of reflection upon the meaning and use of symbols, now being undertaken by the National Liturgy Commission. Other attempts have arisen in the context of social development programs or in the closely-related programs of inter-religious collaboration and dialogue. (See below 2.4., 2.5., 2.6.)

Among many Catholic women who have been active in either lay movements or religious congregations some have also produced reflection and writing. Among these must be mentioned Mary Walter Santer osu, Irene Mahoney osu, Voranuch Parnommit, Rakawin Lee, Achara Somsangsruang, Porntip Chaweephath, Mary Hayden rgs and Carmencita Rojas. (See 2.6 below.)

Selected References

Bell, Sr. Francis Xavier. *A Socio-Religious Survey of the Catholic Church in Thailand*. (8 vols.) Bangkok: Catholic Research Centre of Thailand, mimeo'd, 1974. Summarized in *A Church Survey in Thailand*. PMV Dossier, 1976.

Cohen, Eric. "Christianity and Buddhism in Thailand: The 'Battle of the Axes' and the 'Contest of Power'." *Social Compass* 38.2 (1991).

Dusadee Angsumethangkur. "Catholicism and Thailand." *Inter-Religio* 11 (1987).

Hughes, Philip J. "The Assimilation of Christianity in the Thai Culture." *Religion* 14 (1984).

Mahoney, Irene. *A Far Country, Ursuline Mission in Thailand,1924-1945*. Bangkok: 1999.

Seri Phongphit. *The Catholics and Thai Society*. Bangkok: 1982.

— *The Relation between the Catholic Church and Thai Society from 17c to Today*. Jochi Daigaku Ajia Bunka Kenkujo 2.2. Tokyo: Sophia University, 1985.

— "Doing Theology with Asian Resources." *Seeds of Peace* 4 (1988).

Pro Mundi Vita. "La Thailande en période de transition: l'église dans un pays bouddiste." Brussels, PMV Bulletin 48. (Also in English) 1973.

Ratna Bamrungtrakal. "Inculturation and Mission." *Omnis Terra* 17.139 (1983).

Thabping, Joseph E.K. "The Conversion of Thai Buddhists: Are Christianity and Thai Culture Incompatible." Thesis, Ateneo University, Quezon City, 1974.

2.3 Catholic Bishops' Conference of Thailand

The Catholic Bishops' Conference of Thailand has been active since 1969 and currently operates through 26 Episcopal Commissions. Those for Pastoral Care of Christians include commissions for the Laity, the Apostolic Life, the Family, the Bible and for Pastoral Health Care. Those for Mission and Education include commissions for Evangelization of Peoples, Education, Missionary Works and for the Cultural Heritage of the Church. Those for Social Works include commissions for Human Development, Justice and Peace, Women, Ethnic Groups, Emergency Relief and Refugees, Migrants and Prisoners. The commissions for Religious and Cultural Relations are concerned for Christian Unity, Inter-religious and Cultural Dialogue and National Social Co-operation. There are also two commissions for Social Communications.

Periodical statements or pastoral letters are issued by each of these commissions to address current issues in society and church. These have included documents concerning inter-religious dialogue, human rights, education, social development and the practice of "jubilee." Most recently these place special stress on giving women and also youth equal share in the work of the church at every level. The documents also emphasize continuing study of the social doctrines of the church, including the materials of Vatican II, along with study of the religious and cultural values of Thai local traditions and indigenous wisdom. The CBCT also publishes *Udomsarn*, the Catholic Newsletter of Thailand, in both weekly and bi-annual formats.

Selected References

Publications of the Catholic Bishops' Conference of Thailand

> *Particular Norms for Thailand.* (Application and Modification of Canon Law). Bangkok: CBCT, 1991.
> *Inter-religious Dialogue in Thailand.* Bangkok: CBCT,1994.
> "For Christians in the Time of Economic Crisis." Pastoral Letters of the CBCT. Bangkok: CBCT, 1995 and 1999.
> "For the Great Jubilee." Pastoral Letter of the CBCT. Bangkok: CBCT, 2000.
> *Declaration of the Catholic Bishops' Conference of Thailand on the Pastoral Plan.* Bangkok: CBCT, 2000.
> *The Church and Human Rights* (In Thai). Human Rights Manual, Justice and Peace Commission, forthcoming.
> Mansap Bunluen. "The 8th National Economic and Social Development Plan and Human Development: the Christian Perspective." (In Thai). *Phu Thai 2.* (1996).
> Sirisuth, Joseph. *Inter-religious Dialogue in Thailand.* Bangkok: CBCT, 1994.
> Suwanna Satha-anan. "Catholic Schools and Human Rights Promotion." (In Thai: Seminar of the Catholic Education Council.) In *Justice & Peace Commission's Report, Feb. 1999.*

2.4 Participation in Social Development and Reflection

Missionaries had sometimes been accused of not "adapting their theology to meet the needs of the underprivileged," with church welfare programs remaining paternalistic and raising no challenge to social inequities. The image given of the church was often one of wealth and power, with priests seen as members of an elite. Christian schools, which were originally intended to educate children from all branches of society, have also become often elitist institutions. Concerns for these and wider social issues have gained the commitment of a number of Thai Catholic scholars and theologians over the past 30 years, and are leading to "reflection on the meaning of faith within the context and on the ground of the experience of village people in the framework of Social Development." Activities of the Young Christian Workers, led by lay people like Snan Vongsuthee, contributed to the revival of Thai labor movements in the 1960s, and along with Catholic students, to the growth of peasant and pro-democratic movements in the 1970s. Those involved in both social action and theological reflection at that time also included Paul Chamniern and Joachim Pranom Sion of the Social Action Center, Bangkok. Much action and reflection has been encouraged by the Commission of Thai Catholics for Development, Young Christian Workers (YCW), the International Movement of Catholic Students (IMCS), the Justice and Peace Commission of the Catholic Church (JPC), and the Thai Inter-religious Commission for Development (TICD).

Among those closely involved, from whom we have written theological reflections, are Bishop Michael Bunluen Mansap, Dr Seri Phongphit, Fr Niphot Thienwiharn, Dr Suwanna Satha-anan, Fr Vatcharin Samanjitre, Fr Vichai Phokthav and Dr Charoen Athitya. (See individual entries below.) At the Human Development Center and the Mercy Center in Bangkok, the staff comprises Fr Joseph Maier, Sr Joan Evans and Br Dang. A group of Catholic nuns are now also among those for whom direct participation in programs of rural development alongside farmers and their families has led to theological reflection upon such experience and the aspirations it embodies.

A number of eminent Buddhist leaders have also been committed to ecumenical work in human development and social reform, and have co-operated closely with Christian agencies since the 1960s. Among these are the late Buddhadasa Bhikku and Sulak Sivaraksa of the International Network of Engaged Buddhists, along with their colleagues and associated movements. (See, for example, Buddhadasa Bhikkhu. *Dhammic Socialism.* Bangkok: TICD, 1986; Sulak Sivaraksa. *A Socially Engaged Buddhism.* Bangkok: TICD, 1988; and the quarterly *Seeds of Peace,* of the International Network of Engaged Buddhists*).*

Selected References

Bobilin, Robert. "Thai Inter-religious Committee on Development and the Asian Cultural Forum on Development." In *Revolution from Below: Buddhist and Christian Movements for Justice in Asia. Four Case Studies from Thailand and Sri Lanka,* by Robert Bobilin. Lanham: University Press of America, 1988.

Chamniern, Paul. "Towards People's Organizations in Thailand." *Impact* (July 1972).

Charoen Athitya. *An Experience in Development According to Religion and Culture: Evaluation of the Work of the Committee for Human Development in Chiang Mai.* (In Thai). Chiang Mai: Catholic Diocesan Centre, 1997.

Seminar of Diocesan Social Action Centers' Directors. Pattaya: DISAC, April 1997.

Suwanna Satha-anan. "The Church and Human Rights in Philosophy Perspective." (In Thai). *Phu Thai* 42 (1997).

—. "Catholic Schools and Human Rights Promotion." (In Thai: Seminar of Catholic Education Council.) In *Justice & Peace Commission's Report, Feb. 1999.*

—. "Some Concerns of Thai Women on Peace Message 1995: Women the Peace Educator." (In Thai). *Phu Thai* 36 (1995).

Vatcharin Samanjitre. "Theology of Immersion." (In Thai). In *Report on the Occasion of Priests and Religious in Social Action VI's Seminar and Workshop.* CCTD, Nov. 2000.

Vichai Phokthavi sj. "The Church and the Poor." (In Thai). *Phu Thai* 3 (2000).

—. "The Church in the Social Crisis." (In Thai). *Phu Thai* 4 (2000).

2.5 Christian Response to Buddhism

It is still true that many Thai Buddhists see the Church as being powerful because of its foreign resources, ambitious for influence and skilful in disguising imperial claims by pretensions of being a spiritual presence. Mistrusting metaphysics and therefore all theology, they sometimes see Christianity as, at least partly, a form of animism. These understandings seemed in part to justify the attacks made on Catholic publications in 1957 and were also expressed in the criticisms by Buddhist monks and laity in the mid-1980s, of Catholic initiatives in dialogue and inculturation. (See *A Plot to Undermine Buddhism* by Phra Sobhon Ganabhorn. Bangkok: Siva Phorn, 1984.)

In return, many Catholics, certain of their own hold on 'the One Truth,' often shy away from self-confident Buddhist wisdom, and point to remnants of animism and superstition held by some Buddhists. Yet the tolerance shown to Christians, both officially and by countless Thai Buddhists, is notably genuine, based in the belief that all religion contributes to a more moral society. A minority of Christians show the same respect for Buddhist beliefs and practices, and many studies of Thai Buddhism have been undertaken by Thai Catholics. (See 2.7.)

Pioneers of inter-religious encounter and dialogue include Bishops Ek Thapine (d.1985) and Manat Chuabsamai, of Ratchburi diocese. In the 1980s a Buddhist-Christian group met regularly in Chiengmai and included Bishop Ratna Bamrungtrakal (see 2.7.1.), Acharns Saeng, Mukda, Baw and Seeley, and Sigmund Laschenski. A small number of Catholic priests and lay people have also recently undertaken to share the life and work of Buddhist monasteries in south and north Thailand as ventures in understanding and co-operation.

Although institutional Catholicism in Thailand does not always show enthusiasm for the encounter with Buddhism, there are important exceptions amongst scholars and those committed to integrated and indigenous social development. (See also above 2.4.).

Selected References

Anatriello, P. "Un bonze de Thailande dialogue avec les chrétiens." *Bulletin Secretariatus pro non Christianis* 5 (1970). Also in English.

Buddhadasa Bhikkhu. *Christianity and Buddhism*. Sinclair Thompson Memorial Lecture. Chiengmai: Thailand Theological College, 1967.

Cherdchai, Fr "Buddhist Pannya, A Study of Buddhist Theravada Ethics in dialogue with Christian Ethics." Doct. Thesis (published). Saentham College, Sampran, Nakornpathom, n.d.

Kirti Bunchua. *The Tripitaka for Thai Christians*. Bangkok: Chulalongkorn University, 1982.

—. *Indian Philosophy for Christian Philosophers*. Bangkok: Chulalongkorn University, 1982.

—. "Buddhist-Christian Interchange: An Attempt at a Definition." *Inter-Religio* 15 (1989).

Rivera, Jaime M. *A Differential Approach to the Christian Understanding of Buddhist Detachment*. Bangkok: Assumption University, 1997.

Seri Phongphit. "Liberative Elements in Theravada Buddhism in Thailand Today." *Inter-Religio* 18 (1990).

Thabping, Joseph E.K. "The Conversion of Thai Buddhists: Are Christianity and Thai Culture Incompatible." Thesis, Ateneo University, Quezon City, 1974.

Vivat, S. and J. Banchong Aribag. "Buddhism and Evangelization." In *The Far East: Culture, Religions, and Evangelization*. Rome: Dicastero per le Missioni, Salesiani, 1989.

2.6 Spirituality, Ministry and Dialogue

Always present within the life and thought of many Thai Catholics, is a deep concern for growth in the spiritual life, and for those resources in liturgy, Bible and prayer which sustain ministry and service. Although many of the sources that feed such concern come from (western) Roman Catholic traditions, there are now a small number of writers who find these within Thai traditions, or in association with Buddhists or with Christians of other communions. First articulation for such insights often occurs within the shared endeavors for social development or education, or within the encounters of inter-faith dialogue. (See also 2.3. and 2.4. above.) Resource leaders in these areas include Frs Silom Chaiyapheuk,

Vatcharin Samajitre, Manat Suphalak, Prayoon Phongphit, Vichai Phokthavi sj and Professors Suwanna Satha-anan and Yosa Santosombatr. (See also Augustin Moling 2.7.2.)

Women also are increasingly active in a wide range of ministries and in pastoral and theological programs. Few of their writings have yet gained publication, although the writing of women religious appears, sometimes anonymously, in the Bulletins or publications of their congregation. Among those whose writings are now available are Mary Walter Santer osu, Voranuch Parnommit, Rakawin Lee, Achara Somsangsruang, Porntip Chaweephath and Mary Hayden rgs. Carmencita Rojas has widened the scope of such participation by calling for "theological-pastoral reflection by both clergy and laity" and the recognition of lay theologians in various theological disciplines. (*UCAN Report*, Jan. 2000).

Selected References

Cecilio, Violeta. "A Buddhist-Christian dialogue in Thailand: Dialogue of Life." *Ugnay-Diwa* 15-16. 14 (1996),
Dhammachon (People of Dhamma). Quarterly Reflection on Life and Mission of the Church. Chiang Mai.
Moling, Augustin. "Die Heiligen Schriften der Buddhisten." *Ordensnachrichten* 103 (1977).
—. "OHM, Meditation uber den Dreifaltigen Gott." *Der Grosse Entschluss* 5 (1980).
Porntip Chaweephath. "Personal Spirituality in the Old Testament." 3 articles. Chiang Mai: Mimeo'd, 1999.
Ratna Bamrungtrakul. "Christian Asian Meditation; a Contribution to the Life of the Church." *Bulletin Secretariat pro non-Christianis* 17.2 (1982).
—. "Vous pouver changer vous-mêmes et changer le monde grace a la méditation chrétienne asiatique." *Eglise et Mission* 65 (1985).
—. "Dialogue at the Level of Experience in Thailand." *Bulletin Secretariat pro non-Christianis* 21 (1986).
Rojas, Carmencita. Workshop Report on "Lay Ministries in the Renewed Church in Asia." Seventh FABC Assembly, Jan. 2000. *UCAN Report*, Jan 12, 2000. (See also *FABC Paper* 92j, Jan. 2000).
See also *Saengtham Parithat,* Major Seminary publication, three times a year.

2.7 Selected Scholars and Theologians
2.7.1. Robert Ratna Bamrungtrakul (1916-2000)

Ratna Bamrungtrakul studied Buddhism in Thailand and Christian theology in Hong Kong and Leuven, and later was bishop in Chiengmai. He became widely known for his work and writings on catechesis, on faith and theology in Thailand, on meditation and on inter-faith dialogue. He also led in the formation of Buddhist-Christian dialogue groups, in the establishment of the Inter-religious Dialogue Center Chiengmai, and in preparations for a 'Buddhist Institute' in Bangkok designated as a Buddhist study center for Asia.

His writings appeared in many Catholic and ecumenical periodicals, and a collection of these has just been published (*Khom Sap Haeng Chirit* -The Treasure of Life). In these he affirmed that genuine spirituality reveals to us the universe's inner dimension, where Guiding Intelligence is operating within creation and animating all its various forms. This was the large context in which he saw the encounter of those of different faiths, their shared activity in Thai communities and their growing understanding of each other. For Christians this meant the inculturation of their theology and their prayer life, because for Ratna Bamrungtrakul both personal and social transformation can only come from a renewed and contextalized spirituality. His writings are much concerned with these issues.

Selected References
Works by Ratna Bamrungtrakul

 Ntaw Cog Qub Lus. Chiengmai: Ratna Bamrungtrakul, 1983.
 Khom Sap Haeng Chirit (The treasure of life), edited by Barnabas Chamniern Chitseriwong. 2 vols. Ratchburi: Diocesan Office, forthcoming.
 "Christian Asian Meditation; a Contribution to the Life of the Church." *Bulletin Secretariat pro non-Christianis* 17.2 (1982).
 "Inculturation and Mission." *Omnis Terra* 17.139 (1983).
 "Vous pouver changer vous-mêmes et changer le monde grace a la méditation chrétienne asiatique." *Eglise et Mission* 65 (1985).
 "Dialogue at the Level of Experience in Thailand." *Bulletin Secretariat pro non-Christianis* 21 (1986).

2.7.2. Augustin Moling sj (1924-1999)

Following some years' ministry in Taiwan and further theological study (1952-1959), Augustin Moling worked in Thailand until 1994. At the Major Seminary of Sampran, and in other institutes, he was spiritual director, theological teacher and inter-faith scholar. Strongly influenced by the documents of Vatican II, his particular studies were in liturgy, music, theology and Buddhism. He composed many hymns in Thai and wrote both 'Eastern Prayers' and a series of meditative articles on spirituality and inculturation.

In a lifelong ministry of spiritual direction, along with study and dialogue with Buddhist friends, Moling found a deep convergence of Christian and Buddhist thought and practice. For him, Love was present to a high degree in the "four sublime states of mind" of Buddhism, which also can assist Christians to recover the riches of their own mystical traditions. It is possible, he believed, to be Buddhist and to believe in God, *and* be Christian. This means a willingness to contemplate rather than know, to "let oneself go completely", receiving "salvation" wholly as gift. As the grace of Jesus Christ is present invisibly outside the church we can recognize the truth in other mystic experience, for it lies "deeply beyond our differences, in mystery." The key to dialogue as to inculturation, for Moling, was a living of the Gospel ever more fully and simply, amidst Buddhist friends. In Christian liturgy and practice he was passionately concerned to simplify, so that life lived close to ordinary people may be offered with Jesus for others. His writings, many as yet unpublished, present this life and the faith which sustained it in the form of occasional meditations.

Selected References

Works by Augustin Moling

"Die Heiligen Schriften der Buddhisten." *Ordensnachrichten* 103 (1977).

"OHM, Meditation uber den Dreifaltigen Gott." *Der Grosse Entschluss* 5 (1980).

"Christen und Buddhisten im Dialog. Erfahrungen und Uberlegungen aus Thailand." *Die Katholischen Missionen* 104 (1985).

"Inculturation in Thailand."; "'Old' and 'New' Spirituality, Is there a Choice?"; "The Simple Eye." Manuscripts in English, translated by Alfred and Mag. Pichler, Bozen, included in Frenes 2000, (below).

Frenes, Alfred. *Sudtirol: Thailand. Augustin Moling SJ.* Bozen: Verlagsantalt Athesia, 2000. (Includes many bilingual extracts of Moling's writings.)

Sturmer, Ernst. "Der Multi-Spezialist." *Alle Welt* (Jan.-Feb. 1996).

2.7.3. Mansap Bunluen

Mansap Bunluen, now Bishop of Ubon-Ratchathani Diocese, has been a leading figure in developing awareness of the issues of social and human development since the early 1970s. Along with his many pastoral and episcopal ministries he has engaged in numerous national and international programs directed to education and animation for human development, in both Catholic and ecumenical regional networks, including especially the FABC and the CCA.

His theological concerns have largely focused upon the nature of integral, human development, the theological basis for social action, and the role of the church in national development, democratic process and the fostering of peace and justice. In these he advocates a "down-to-earth theology," the "hiding" of the institutional church, and openness to respond to the "signs of the times" in the desires of peoples. This has sometimes required criticism of western economic and military initiatives, and proposals for new forms of collaboration in sharing resources and information. For Mansap Bunluen, alliance with the people in their struggles requires also struggle within the church, in order to incarnate the Gospel within Asian culture and Asian people. And this in turn may help to rejuvenate the world church. (See also "Interview," *Development News Digest* 14, 1975).

Selected References
Works by Mansap Bunluen

"Development from Within." In *Report of an Asian Ecumenical Consultation on Development: Priorities and Guidelines.* Singapore: CCA, 1974.

"My Impressions of the BISAs (Bishops' Institutes for Social Action)." In *The Bishops' Institutes for Social Action,* by Bishop Julio X. Labayen, et al., FABC Paper 6, 1978.

Contextual Theology in Thailand 1800-2000 545

"Pastorale D' Ensemble." (In Thai.) In *Social Action Theology Study Group.* Bangkok: CCHD, Sept. 1988.
"The Progress of Development in the Catholic Church in Thailand." (In Thai.) In issues of *Phu Thai* 1990s.
"The Significant Elements and Agreement of FABC VI." (In Thai.) The 27th General Assembly, Report of Catholic Commission for Human Development. Bangkok: CCHD, 1994.
"To Build up the Real Democracy." (In Thai.) *Phu Thai* 1 (2000).
"Religious values bring Peace." (In Thai.) *Phu Thai* 4 (2000).
"The Church and Human Rights." (In Thai.) The Seminar of Catholic Education Council, Feb. 2000; and "The Catholic Mission in the Third Millennium." (In Thai: Seminar on the year 2000 Peace Message.) In *Justice & Peace Commission's Report.* Bangkok, CJPC, Feb.-March 2000.

2.7.4. Kirti Bunchua

Kirti Bunchua is professor and Dean of the Graduate School of Philosophy and Religious Studies, Assumption University, Bangkok. He is also Fellow of the Royal Institute in Thailand, President of the Asian Conference of Religion and Peace, president of the International and Inter-religious Federation for World Peace (IIRFWP), Thailand, and an editor of the *Journal of Contextual Philosophy and Religions.* He is, in addition, the founder and director of the Spirituality Ashram, Bangkok, and is recognized as a leading philosopher for Thailand.

Kirti Bunchua's scholarly work and writings embrace many fields: history, philosophy, both eastern and western, Thai church history, the indigenization of Christianity in Thailand, Buddhist studies and Buddhist-Christian dialogue. He has been particularly concerned to make available to Christians the resources of Asian religious and philosophical traditions, and to foster inter-religious study and collaboration for peace and social action, both in Thailand and internationally. His philosophical studies have led him to recognize Thai terms and imageries as sources for Thai people in their reflection, along with a "new level of self-understanding and new possibilities for directing their life." For Kirti Bunchua, Thai church history is to be "a history of the Christian community in its spiritual as well as mundane aspects," in ways that make possible the understanding both of Christianity's impact upon Thai society, and of the Buddhist way of life in Thailand. In this, as in all his philosophical and religious work, he declares that the basis for all study and relationships must be the full mutual understanding that makes possible co-operative work in the community.

Selected References
Works by Kirti Bunchua
> *The Tripitaka for Thai Christians.* Bangkok: Chulalongkorn University, 1982.
> *Indian Philosophy for Christian Philosophers.* Bangkok: Chulalongkorn University, 1982.
> *The Catholic Parishes of the Portuguese and Annamite Descendants in Bangkok.* Bangkok: Chulalongkorn University, 1982.
> "Social Change and Cooperation among Various Faiths in Thailand." In *Development Issues in Thailand (Papers Presented at the First International Conference on Thai Studies, 1981, New Delhi),* ed. by B.J. Terwiel. Gaya: Center for South-East Asian Studies, 1984: 227-36.
> "History of the Church in Thailand." In *Asia and Christianity,* ed. by M.D. David. Bombay: Himalaya Publishing, 1985.
> "Buddhist-Christian Interchange: An Attempt at a Definition." *Inter-Religio* 15 (1989).
> "Dialogue Situation in Thailand." *Bulletin Pontificium Consilium pro Dialogo Inter Religiones* 24 (1989).
> "Is There a Thai Philosophy?" *Journal of Contextual Philosophy and Religions* 1 (1998).
> "Creation of New Philosophy in the Age of Global Village." *Dialogue and Universalism* 7-8 (1999).
> —, et al. *The Bases of Values in a Time of Change: Chinese and Western.* Cultural Heritage and Contemporary Change, series 3, Asia; V.016. Washington, DC: Council for Research in Values and Philosophy, c1999.

2.7.5. Seri Phongphit

Seri Phongphit is a historian, a scholar of religion and, as an 'engaged academic,' an animateur in community development. He is active in national and international movements for inter-faith dialogue and has contributed to the work of both the Thai Inter-religious Commission for Development and the International Network of Socially Engaged Buddhists.

Seri Phongphit has particular concern for the role of Catholics within society and in relation to other living faiths and works closely with non-government and Buddhist agencies in this. Apart from research in Thai Church and religious history, he has undertaken a number of pioneering studies on the basis of extensive fieldwork, both of the problems and needs of particular localities and of the models in theory and praxis for authentically religious response to these. Apart from those works mentioned below he has contributed to a number of collaborative volumes on related concerns, published only in the Thai language.

Selected References
Works by Seri Phongphit

> *The Catholics and Thai Society.* Bangkok: 1982.
> *The Relation between the Catholic Church and Thai Society from 17c to today.* Jochi Daigaku Ajia Bunka Kenkujo 2.2. Tokyo: Sophia University, 1985.
> *Religion in a Changing Society: Buddhism, Reform and the Role of Monks in Community Development in Thailand.* Hong Kong: Arena, 1988.
> "The Problem of Religious Language: A Study of Buddhadasa Bhikku and Ian Ramsey as Models for a Mutual Understanding of Buddhism and Christianity." Thesis, Munchen University, Saengtum Catholic Seminary, 1978.
> "The Impact of Interreligious Encounter in Thailand." *Inter-Religio* 5 (1984).
> "Church in Asia: Past, Present and Future." *Seeds of Peace* 1.1 (1985).
> "Dialogue and Development: A Buddhist-Christian Search for Alternative models for Development." *East Asia Pastoral Review* 22.4 (1985); *Seeds of Peace* 2.1 (1986).
> "Liberative Elements in Theravada Buddhism in Thailand Today." *Inter-Religio* 18 (1990).
> "Doing Theology with Asian Resources." *Seeds of Peace* 4 (1988).
> —, ed. *Back to the Roots: Village and Self-reliance in a Thai Context.* Bangkok: Rural Development Documentation Center, Village Institution Promotion, 1986.
> —, et al. *Setthakit chumchon: thanglu'ak phu'a thanglot sangkhom Thai.* Krung Thep: Mahawitthayalai Thurakitchabandit, 1999.

2.7.6. Niphot Thienwiharn

Niphot Thienwiharn has been engaged for almost 25 years as parish priest, teacher of theology and pastoral animateur in Chiengmai Diocese. He has also been a leading figure in the work of Catholic Human Development. Along with such colleagues as Dr Charoen Athitya, Niphot Thienwiharn has organized special programs of educational formation and reflection on the issues and basis of community development which is grounded in the life and values of Thai people. Many of these programs are jointly arranged with Protestant, Muslim and Buddhist groupings including both clergy and laity.

Niphot Thienwiharn has particular concern for the recognition and study of Thai cultural traditions as a major resource in all programs for human and community development and has written on not only the pastoral and communitarian aspects of these but also on the studies necessary to sustain them. His writings therefore present theological bases for such work and also report the insights and experience resulting from concrete programs when the realities of Thai culture are both the context and the resource for work in total human development.

Selected References
Works by Niphot Thienwiharn

"Culture and Development: Why do we Study Culture in Development Work?" (In Thai.) *Sangkhom Pattana* 4 (1983).

"Community-Based Development in the Buddhist Context, Religion and Culture Values of People." In *Colloquium on the Social Doctrine of the Church in the Context of Asia, Jan. 21, 1993*. Manila: FABC Office for Human Development, 1993.

"Rice: the Mystery Transmitter from Life to life." (In Thai.) *The 25th Anniversary of Rev. Cyril Niphot Thienwiharn's Consecration, 1975-2000*. Chiengmai: Chang Phuek Publishing House, 2000.

"Pastoral Work in the Context of Thai Society which has Diversity in Culture." In *The 25th Anniversary of Rev. Cyril Niphot Thienwiharn's Consecration, 1975-2000*. Chiengmai: Chang Phuek Publishing House, 2000.

2.8. Other Catholic Contributions to Contextual Thai Theology

2.8.1. Joseph Chusak Sirisuth was formerly Secretary to the Episcopal Commission for Inter-religious Dialogue of the Catholic Bishops' Conference of Thailand. In this capacity he wrote a series of volumes on the understanding and practice of inter-faith dialogue "according to Thai Catholics." All written in Thai, these included reports of seminars and conferences, guidebooks to principles and approaches, and works of theology. He has also contributed to documents of the FABC, and a collection of his articles is about to be published.

Selected Works:

Inter-religious Dialogue in Thailand. Bangkok: CBCT, 1994.
The Approach of the Catholic Church to Other Religions. Bangkok: CBCT, 1995.
Basic Thought Concerning Inter-religious Dialogue. Bangkok: CBCT, 1996.

2.8.2. Sigmund Laschenski sj has taught theology at Chiengmai and at the Major Seminary, Samphran, Bangkok. He has also been active in Christian-Buddhist and in ecumenical dialogue in both northern and southern Thailand.

Selected Works:

"Doing Theology on the Mountain-Tops." *SEAJOT* 21.1 (1980).
"The Meaning of the Incarnation for the Church in Thailand." *East Asia Journal of Theology* 2.1 (1984).
"Towards Christian Unity." (Doctrinal dialogue with the Church of Christ in Thailand) *Saengthan Review* 1 (forthcoming).

2.8.3. Siripong Charatsri now teaches at the Major Seminary, Samphran, Bangkok, and in his writings is mainly concerned for dialogue, both ecumenical and inter-religious.

Selected Works:

"The Spirit at Work in Inter-religious Dialogue in the Asian Context." Study Paper, Pontifical University of St Thomas, Rome. (May 1999).
"Ecumenical Dialogue." (Vatican II, WCC, Ut Omnes Unum Sint, Dialogue and Proclamation). Study Paper, Pontifical University of St Thomas, Rome (2000).

2.8.4. Other Theologians and Writers include Bishop Louis Chamniern Santisukniran, along with the scholars and writers Surichai Chumsriphan, Dusadee Angsumethangkur, Joseph E.K. Thabping, Suwanna Satha-anan, Vatcharin Samanjitre, Vichai Phokthavi sj, Bruno Arens and Somsri Saphapramai. Along with these are Francis Cais, Jean Dantolin and others of the Samphran Seminary. The seminary has issued *Saengtham Parithat* (The Light of Teaching Review) tri-annually since 1975. This has included articles by both nationals and expatriates on biblical subjects, Thai church history, on moral and ethical theology, spirituality and evangelization.

Selected References

Dantonel, Jean. "La Naissance d'une Société Missionnaire en Thailande." *Echos de la Rue du Bac* (1990).

Dusadee Angsumethangkur. "Catholicism and Thailand." *Inter-Religio* 11 (1987).

Suwanna Satha-anan. "The Church and Human Rights in Philosophy Perspective." (In Thai.) *Phu Thai* 42 (1997).

—. "Catholic Schools and Human Rights Promotion." (In Thai: Seminar of the Catholic Education Council.) In *Justice & Peace Commission's Report, Feb. 1999*.

—. "Some Concerns of Thai Women on Peace Message 1995: Women the Peace Educator." (In Thai.) *Phu Thai* 36 (1995).

Thabping, Joseph E.K. "The Conversion of Thai Buddhists: Are Christianity and Thai Culture Incompatible." 1974.

Vatcharin Samanjitre. "Theology of Immersion." (In Thai.) *Report on the occasion of Priests and Religious' in Social Action VI's Seminar and Workshop*, CCTD, Nov. 2000.

Vichai Phokthavi. "The Church and the Poor." (In Thai.) *Phu Thai* 3 (2000).

—. "The Church in the Social Crisis." (In Thai.) *Phu Thai* 4 (2000).

3 Supplementary Bibliography
3.1 Monographs and Articles

Bayet, Claudius. *"Une Lumière s'est levée. Historique de l'evangelisation au Nord-est de la Thailande et au Laos.* Bangkok: Chamras Karnphim, 1985.

Bunarunraksa, Simona Somsri. "Monseigneur Jean Baptiste Pallegoix (1805-1862) Imprimeur et Ecrivain." Thesis at the Sorbonne, Ecole Pratique des Hautes Etudes, 2000.

Callahan, William A. *Imagining Democracy: Reading "The Events of May" in Thailand*. Singapore: Institute of Southeast Asian Studies, 1998.

Chanson, Philippe. "Father Yves, an Essential Figure in the History of Hmong Christianity." *Exchange* 22 (1993).

Chappoulie, H. *Aux origines d'une église: Rome et les missions d'Indochine au XVIIe siecle*. Tome I. Paris, Bloud et Gay, 1943.

Cohen, Eric. "Christianization and Indigenization: Contrasting Process of Religious Adaptation in Thailand." In *Indigenous Responses to Western Christianity*, edited by S. Kaplan: 29-55. New York: New York University, 1995.

de Bèze, P. *Memoir*. Translated and edited as *1688 Revolution in Siam*, by E.W. Hutchinson. Hong Kong: Hong Kong University, 1968.

Fonner, Michael G. "Transforming Religious Language: Experiment in Pattaya." *Areopagus* 2 (1988).

Franklin, Stephen T. "A New Christian Community and its Surrounding Culture in Northeast Thailand." *Missiology* 11 (1983).

Fuller, Paul H. "The Christian Approach to Hinayana Buddhism in Siam." BTh thesis, San Francisco Theological Seminary, 1929.

Fux, Pierre-Yves, ed. *Rencentre avec un Sage Bouddhiste*. Paris: Ad Solem et Cerf, 1998.

Grether, Herbert. "The Cross and the Bodhi Tree." *Theology Today* 16.4 (1960).

Hoare, Timothy Douglas. "On the Aesthetic and the Religious Dimensions of the Classical Theatre of Thailand: Performance as a Theological Agenda for Christian Ritual Praxis." PhD dissertation, Graduate Theological Union, 1992.

Hohnecker, Susanne. "The Contextualization of the Biblical Story of Creation in Thai Culture: A Model for Contextualization." MA thesis, Columbia International University, 1995.

Holden, Peter, et al. *Tourism: An Ecumenical Concern*. Bangkok: ECTWT, 1988.

Horn, E. "Traditional and Biblical 'Phii' Concepts Within the 'Church of Christ' in Northern Thailand." DMin dissertation, Columbia International University, 1996.

Hutchinson, E.W., tr. & ed. see de Bèze, P. *Memoir*.

Kammerer, Cornelia Ann. "Customs and Christian Conversion among Akha Highlanders of Burma and Thailand," *American Ethnologist*, 17.2:(1990.)

—. "Transformations in Kinship Among Akha (Hani) Christians of Highland Northern Thailand." In *Proceedings of the 4th International Conference on Thai Studies*, Vol. 1: 330-338. Kunming, China: Institute of Southeast Asian Studies, 1990.

Karunan, Victor P. *If the Land Could Speak it Would Speak for us. Volume 1: A History of Peasant Movements in Thailand and the Philippines*. Hong Kong: Plough Publications, 1984.

Keyes, Charles F. *The Golden Peninsula: Culture and Adaptation in Mainland Southeast Asia*. New York: Macmillan, 1977.

Klausner, W.J. *Thai Culture in Transition: Selected Writings*. Bangkok: Siam Society, 1997.

Kongsamuth Dulayapinun. "A Comparative Study of the Roles of a Buddhist Monastery and an Organization of the Roman Catholic Church in promoting Social Justice for People of Low Income: a Case Study in Nakornratchasima." Thesis, Mahidol University, 1987.

Larqué, Victor. *History of the Catholic Church in Thailand*. (In Thai). Bangkok: 1967.

Launay, Adrien. *Siam et les Missionnaires Francais*. Tours: Alfred Mame, 1896.

Makela, Jaakko. *Krischak Issara: The Independent Churches in Thailand, their Historical Background, Contextual Setting and Theological Thinking*. Abo, Finland: Abo Akademi University, 2000.

National Christian Council Guide to Missions in Siam. *The Siam Outlook. Guide Book* (1931). Bangkok: Siam Press, 1931.

Parichart Suwanbubbha. "A Comparative Study of the Status and Roles of Theravada Buddhist and Roman Catholic Nuns: case study in the community of Bangkok." Thesis, Mahidol University, 1983

Popp, Richard L. "American Missionaries and the Introduction of Western Science and Medicine in Thailand, 1830-1900." (bibliography). *Missiology* 13 (1985).

Purnell, Herbert C., Jr. "Thai Response to the Gospel." *Practical Anthropology* 4 (1985).

Seely, Francis M. "Thai Buddhism and the Christian Faith." *SEAJOT* 10.2-3 (1968-1969).

Smith, Alex G. *The Gospel Facing Buddhist Cultures*. Asian Perspective Series. Taichung, Taiwan: Asia Theological Association, 1980.

—. *Siamese Gold: A History of Church Growth in Thailand*. Bangkok: Kanok Bannasan, 1982.

Somsri Saphapramai. "A comparative study of the Theravada Buddhist and Roman Catholic Concepts of Love: Case Study at Baan Mai and Thakham subdistricts, Samphran district, Nakorn Pathom Province." Thesis, Mahidol University, 1984.

Sulak Sivaraksa. "Christianity in the Reflection of Buddhism." *Seeds of Peace* 2.2 (1986).

Surichai Chumsriphan. "The Great Role of Jean-Lois Vey, Apostolic Vicar of Siam (1875-1909) in the Church History of Thailand ..." Dissertation, Pontifical Gregorian University, Rome, 1990.

Swanson, Herbert. "Reflections on 'Christianity in the Thai Historical Context': A Conference of Catholic, Protestant and Buddhist Historians held in Chiang Mai, in March 1992." *Asia Journal of Theology* 7.1 (1993).

Taylor, Stephen. "A Study of The Relationship Between Christian Education and the Belief System Of Thai Christians." DMin dissertation, International Theological Seminary, Los Angeles, 1999.

"The 'Sollicitudo Rei Socialis' in Thailand." *East Asia Pastoral Review* 26 (1989).

Thongchai Winichakul. *Siam Mapped: A History of the Geo-body of a Nation*. Honolulu: University of Hawaii, 1994.

Wan Petchsongkram. *Talk in the Shade of the Bo Tree*. Translated and edited by Francis E. Hudgins. Bangkok: Thai Gospel Press, 1975.

Wells, Kenneth E. *Theravada Buddhism and Protestant Christianity*. Sinclair Thompson Memorial Lectures 14-15, November 1963. Bangkok: Chareon Tham Printing Press, 1963.

—. *Thailand and The Christian Faith*. Bangkok: CCT, Department of Christian Education, 1968.

Wichian Wattageejaroen. *The Prophets*. (In Thai). Bangkok: Bannasan, 1990.

Win, May Kyi and Harold E. Smith, eds. *Historical Dictionary of Thailand*. Lanham MD: Scarecrow Press, 1995.

Wipa Tanhassaitong. "Women's Ministry in the Baptist Church in Thailand." Thesis, Lutheran Theological Seminary, Hong Kong, 1994.

—. *Thailand and the Christian Faith*. Bangkok: CCT, 1968.

Wisely, Thomas N. "Dynamic Biblical Christianity in the Buddhist/Marxist Context: Northeast Thailand." PhD dissertation, Microform, Princeton, 1984.

Zehner, Edwin. "Church Growth and Culturally Appropriate Leadership: Three Examples From the Thai Church." Unpublished paper, School of World Mission, 1987.

—. "Merit, Man and Ministry: Traditional Thai Hierarchies in a Contemporary Church." *Social Compass* 38.2 (1991).

—. "Thai Protestants and Local Supernaturalism: Changing Configurations." *Journal of Southeast Asian Studies* 27.2 (1996).

3.2 Periodical Sources for Research

Bangkok Recorder (1844-1867); *Bangkok Calendar* (1859-1872); *Siam Repository* (1869-1884); *Sayam Siam* (1882-1886); *Daybreak Magazine* (from ca. 1870); *Sirikitisap (Lao Christian News,* from 1903); *Lao News* (1904-, later *North Siam News* 1917, and *The Siam Outlook* 1921)

Khao Kristachak (Church News, from 1932. Until the 1950s, included poetry in traditional form by Christian writers.)

Co-ordinating Committee on Religion and Society. Occasional journal.

Dhammachon (People of Dhamma). Quarterly Reflection on Life and Mission of the Church, Chiang Mai.

HeRB Bulletin. Chiangmai (Herb Swanson <villager@loxinfo.co.th>)

Journal of Contextual Philosophy and Religions. Assumption University, Bangkok.)

Justice & Peace Newsletter. Catholic Church of Thailand.

Phu Thai (Liberator) (Justice & Peace Commission Magazine)

Prajna Vihara, the Journal of Philosophy and Religion. Assumption University, Bangkok.

Saengtham Parithat (The Light of Teaching Review), Samphran Seminary.

Sangkhom Pattana. Bangkok: Committee of Thai Catholics for Development.

Seeds of Peace. International Network of Engaged Buddhists (INEB), Bangkok.

Udomsarn. Catholic Newsletter of Thailand.

Vice Provincial News. Newsletter of the Bangkok Redemptorist Vice-Province.

— JCE & HRS with AS, BA, JD,

9 Contextual Theology in Vietnam 1800-2000
(For Christian Reflection in Vietnam prior to 1800 see chap 2 above.)

1 **The Period 1800-1908**
   1.1 Introduction: Christianity and Context
   1.2 Theological Reflection
   1.3 Giáo Lý Tam Phu (Doctrine of the 'Three fathers' [*Ba Cha*])
   1.4 Nationalist Scholars and Reformers (19th century)
      1.4.1. Phêrô Nguyên Vãn Tu (1790-1838); Micae Nguyên Huy My (1804-1838); Phêrô Ðinh Công Quý (1826-1859);
      1.4.2. Ðãng Ðúc Tuân (1806-1874); **1.4.3.** Nguyên Truòng To (1827-1871); **1.4.4** Truòng Vinh Ký, Petrus (1837-1898); **1.4.5.** Huỳnh Tinh Cua, Paulus (1834-1907); **1.4.6.** Pierre Huu Triêm (Trân Luc, Father 'Six') 1825-1899);
      1.4.7. Expatriate Writings and Biographies

2 **The Period 1908-1940**
   2.1 Nationalist or Revolutionary Christian Writers
      2.1.1. Mai Lão Bang ['Gia Châu'] (?-1945); **2.1.2.** Hàn Mac Tu (Nguyên Trong Trí, 1912-1940); **2.1.3.** Other nationalist Christian poets of the late 19th/early 20th centuries
   2.2 Journals and Periodicals
   2.3 Theological Writings
   2.4 Writings in History and Culture

3 **Mid-20th Century**
   3.1 Historical and Religious Context
      3.1.1. Vietnamese Traditions, Catholicism and Colonialism
      3.1.2. Theological Locus and Response of Vietnamese Catholics 1940s to 1975

Contextual Theology in Vietnam 1800-2000

3.1.3. NOTE: Christian publishing and distribution in Vietnam
3.1.4. Theological Reflection in Journals and Periodicals 1

3.2 The Writers and Doers of Theology
   3.2.1. Catholic Intellectuals and Activist Theologians
   3.2.1.1. Pham Hân Quỳnh (fl. 1950); **3.2.1.2.** Nguyên Văn Trung (fl. 1955); **3.2.1.3.** Nguyên Khac Chính (b.1922); **3.2.1.4.** The *Hành Trình* (Journey) group of Catholic Intellectuals; **3.2.1.5.** Parallel groups in France; **3.2.1.6.** Buddhist-Catholic Co-operation
   3.2.2. Peace-makers and Patriots
   3.2.2.1 Vu Xuân Ky (b.1886); **3.2.2.2.** Hô Thành Biên, John-Baptiste, 1890 -1976; **3.2.2.3.** Hoàng Quỳnh
   3.2.3. Parish Priests, and Lay People
   3.2.4. Cultural, Historical and Church Historical Studies 1

4 Theological Understanding and Movements to 2000

4.1 Overview

4.2 Theological Reflection in Journals and Periodicals 2
   4.2.1. *Chính Nghia* (Right Cause); **4.2.2.** *Đôi Diên* (Face to Face); **4.2.3.** *Công giáo và Dân tôc* (Catholic and Nation); **4.2.4.** *Tuyên Tâp Thân Hoc* (Theological Selection)

4.3 Theological Scholars, Leaders and Animateurs
   4.3.1. Peter Nguyên Xuân Tín (1918-); **4.3 2.** Nguyên Văn Bình, Archbishop (1910-1995); **4.3.3.** ₫) Văn Thiên. (1929-); **4.3.4.** Francis Xavier Nguyên Văn Thuân, Archbishop (1927-); **4.3.5.** Stephen Nguyên Khac Duong (?1928); **4.3.6.** Hoàng Si Quý sj (1926-); **4.3.7.** Bao Tinh Vuong Đình Bích (1928-); **4.3.8.** Mai Thành (1928-); **4.3.9.** Truờng Bá Cân (1928-); **4.3.10.** Nguyên Ngoc Lan (?1930-) and Chân Tín (1921-); **4.3.11.** Thomas Trân Thiên Câm op (1933-); **4.3.12.** Amelie Nguyên Thi Sang; **4.3.13.** Nguyên Hông Giáo ofm (1937-); **4.3.14.** Joseph Đinh Đúc Dao; **4.3.15.** Phan Khac Tù (1940-); **4.3.16.** Nguyên Chính Kêt (1952-); **4.3.17.** Hoàng Gia Khánh (1955-)

4.4 Other Theologians and Groups
4.4.1. Other Women Scholars and Writers; **4.4.2.** Episcopal Conference of Vietnam; **4.4.3.** Catholic Poets; **4.4.4.** Other Theologians, Scholars, Writers
4.4.4.1. Theology, Spirituality and Mission; **4.4.4.2.** History, Culture and Religion 2

5 Protestant Presence and Writing
5.1 Historical Background.
5.2 Contextual Protestant Theology

6 Supplementary Bibliography

1 The Period 1800-1908
(For the 16th to 18th centuries see *Indochina, Burma, Siam*, chapter 1 above.)

1.1 Introduction: Christianity and Context
The present population of Vietnam numbers almost 80 million, 85% of whom are Vietnamese with significant minorities of tribal peoples and of Chinese. The vast majority of Vietnamese follow a form of Confucian tenets and practices, with approximately 80% being Buddhist, 5.3 million Christian (4.8 million Roman Catholic) and 3 million Caodaoists. Historically, early dynasties in Vietnam were followed by periods of Chinese domination until 968 CE, during which, however, the Lý and Ngô dynasties established temporary rule. They were succeeded by a series of National Dynasties (968-1945), of which the longest-reigning were the Lý (1009-1225), the Lê, ending with rule by the Trinh (in the North) and Nguyên (South) families (1428 -1787), and the Nguyên (1802-1945). Dutch, Portuguese and French traders were present from the 17th century on, but from 1802, however, French influence steadily increased, with their conquest of all Vietnam completed between 1858 and 1883. Despite the attempts of some Governors to extend education, and to ameliorate abuses, French rule became increasingly exploitative and brutal throughout the century, and in turn provoked increasing resistance and the growth of nationalist movements and consciousness.

Contextual Theology in Vietnam 1800-2000

Christianity had been known in Vietnam, in the 'modern' period since the first decades of the 16th century, and early Roman Catholic missionaries included Dominicans (1580), Franciscans (1583) and Jesuits (1615). Of the latter, the most prominent was Alexandre de Rhodes (1591-1660) who established a network of lay catechists, contributed to the romanizing of the Vietnamese script (*quôc ngu*) and worked for the establishment of a Catholic hierarchy in Vietnam. (See *Indochina, Burma, Siam,* chapter 1 above, 1.2). The following two centuries saw Catholic communities grow in identity and numbers, but only under severe difficulties caused by dynastic, clan and North-South conflicts. Disputes between missionaries of the Portuguese *padroado royale* and those appointed by the Propaganda Fide Congregation, along with the impact upon Vietnam of the controversy concerning Chinese Rites (in Vietnam until 1964), also caused continuing dispute and confusion in jurisdiction, pastoral care and catechetics. The severe persecutions of previous centuries was also continued in the 19th century, with over 100,000 being killed between 1820 and 1885. Yet throughout this period Christian communities survived and individual Christians played significant roles in church and community. The Catholic Church in Vietnam remained until 1954 an integral part of France ecclesiastically, with the first bishop only being appointed in Vietnam in 1933.

French colonial domination, although often cruelly oppressive, was also in many ways culturally fructifying. For Catholic communities it brought increasing numbers of expatriate clergy and religious and a measure of freedom in religious practice unknown before. Christian scholars, both national and expatriate, studied and recorded much of Vietnamese religious and cultural traditions, and would in the next half century greatly expand the publishing of monographs and journals, including specifically Christian materials. Education for Vietnamese Catholics in France, and careers in languages and literature, for example, would follow for some, and the best of French culture and of Catholic liberalism would provide stimulus for 'modernizing' scholars and movements.

Yet in the 70-year period until 1954, many Christians shared the resentment, and participated in the resistance, which French rule provoked. Along with others, many Catholics would teach and write on nationalist subjects, and for anti-imperial causes, which colonial authorities could not tolerate; while others participated in local uprisings against the French and suffered imprisonment or worse for their struggle. By 1930, divisions within Vietnamese society were greatly increased by the growing numbers of large landowners and landless peasants; by the French refusal to develop Vietnamese industries; and by the fragmentation of nationalist movements as Communist support grew. Japanese aggression in East Asia and the French defeat in Europe then completed the conditions for the dominance in Vietnam of a strongly nationalist form of Communism. In the years immediately after 1945, many Catholics, along with others, had become fearful of possible Communist oppression, so that on the division of the country in 1954, approximately 3/4 of the priests (800) and 2/5 of the faithful (600,000) left North Vietnam for the south.

(See further 3.1 below.)

Selected References

Buttinger, Joseph. *Vietnam. A Political History.* New York: Praeger, 1968.
Durand, M.M. and Nguyên Trân Huân. *An Introduction to Vietnamese Literature.* New York: Columbia University, 1985.
Launay, Adrien. *Histoire de la Mission de Cochinchine 1658-1823: Documents Historiques.* 3 vols. Paris: Tequi, 1923-1925.
—. *Histoire de la Mission du Tonkin: Documents Historiques.* Vol. 1, 1658-1717. Paris: Libraire Orientale, 1927.
Le Contexte Historique du Viêt-Nam. HCMV, Comité National des Sciences Sociales du Viêt-Nam, 1988.
Marr, David. *Vietnamese Anticolonialism 1885-1925.* Berkeley: University of California Press, 1971.
Nguyên Huu Trong. *Les origines du clergé vietnamien: Le clergé national dans la fondation de l'Eglise au Vietnam.* Saigon: Section historique, Groupe litteraire Tinh Viêt, 1959.
Phan Phát Huôn. *Viêt-Nam giáo-su* (History of Catholic Church in Vietnam 1533 -1960). 2 vols. Saigon: Cuu The Tùng-Thý, 1965. English version, vol. 1 forthcoming. Refer bibliography.
Truòng Bá Cân, Lê Văn Khuê and Nguyên Nghi. *Bibliography of Books, Documents and Articles on Catholic Christianity in Vietnam, Held in Vietnam.* HCMV: mimeo'd, 1989.

Whitfield, Danny J., ed. *Historical and Cultural Dictionary of Vietnam*. Metuchen, NJ: Scarecrow Press, 1976.

1.2 Theological Reflection

From the earliest period, features of Vietnam's living faiths had been studied and valued by exceptional Christian scholars and missionaries and this was to contribute to much later theology. The experience of occupation by the French and the challenges of reconciling a devout Christian allegiance and acceptance of aspects of western knowledge with a growing resistance to colonial greed and oppression, were also to become central concerns for many Christians. These contextual issues, in a theology reflecting the realities which have shaped the life of Vietnamese, would find expression in the writings of the most diverse range of believers, both national and expatriate. The best of French culture would be absorbed by many, and traditions of Catholicism would be treasured and developed, while increasingly the reflection and practice of the most creative Christians became more critical, and for many, revolutionary.

Although Vietnamese Christians seem to have given more priority to the practice and living out of their faith than to reflection and writing on it, yet from the beginning, they have published countless religious writings. These include catechisms and treatises, extensive collections of letters and poetry, of devotions and of testimonies (frequently of those later martyred), along with newsletters, magazines and journals. The great majority of these are directed to instruction in the faith to assist religious practice and to encourage the religious devotion of believers. However, Vietnamese Catholics have also reflected on their Christian belief amidst the realities of their life and culture in works of theological significance. These reflect on, and present, the Christian faith through the familiar images, symbols, expressions and thoughts of Vietnamese people, or depict the concern of Christians for the social, economic, political and cultural issues facing Vietnamese people in particular contexts and periods.

Among such writers as these we will find clergy and lay people, both national and expatriate, who wrote and reflected as nationalist scholars and reformers, as parish priests, mandarins or poets, journalists, theological teachers or revolutionaries. Specifically contextual theology arises for them both in the continuing encounter with Vietnam's living faiths and philosophies, and in response to the exigencies of colonial oppression, and the struggle for livelihood and community survival. Throughout this period such writings remain subject to sporadic censorship and prohibition by colonial authorities, so that many are found only in often short-lived periodicals or in privately printed and circulated booklets and documents.(See 3.1.3.)

Much work remains to be done in order to unearth and interpret a full range of theological reflection in these sources, but sufficient is now known for us to study major movements and traditions. These include the recurring tradition of "the three fathers"; contribution to the movements for social reconstruction; the translation and teaching of traditional Catholic doctrine; study and advocacy for Vietnamese cultural tradition; ardent nationalist writings and radical critique of imperialism.

Selected References

Bibliography on Christianity in Vietnam. Saigon: Directorate of National Archives and Libraries, 1966.

Hoàng Gia Khánh. "Three Hundred Years of Catholic Writing in Vietnam." In *Tuyên Tâp Thân Hoc* (Selected theological writings). April, 1993.

Modras, Ronald. "The Inculturation of Christianity in Asia: from Francis Xavier to Matteo Ricci"; and Peter C. Phan. "Alexandre de Rhodes' mission in Vietnam: evangelization and inculturation." In *Theology and Lived Christianity,* ed. by David M. Hammond. Annual Publication of the College Theology Society 45. Mystic, CT: Twenty-Third Publications / Bayard, c2000.

Nguyên Huu Trong. *Les origines du clergé vietnamien: Le clergé national dans la fondation de l'Eglise au Vietnam.* Saigon: Section historique, Groupe litteraire Tinh Viêt, 1959.

Nguyên Vãn Trung et al. *Ve Sách Báo cua Tác Gia Công Giáo: The Ky XVII-XIX* (Books and newspapers by Catholic authors, 17th-19th centuries.) HCMV: University of HCMV, 1993.

Phan Huy Lê et al. *La Canonisation des Martyrs dans le Contexte Historique du Vietnam.* (In French.) HCMV, Comité Nationale des Sciences Sociales du Vietnam, 1988.

Sõ thao muc luc thu tich ve Thiên Chúa Giáo o Viêt Nam (A bibliography on Christianity in Vietnam). Saigon: Bo Vān hóa , 1967.

Trân Anh Dung. *Sõ thao thý muc Công giáo Viêt Nam* (The Catholic Church in Vietnam: brief bibliography of sources in Vietnamese). Paris: Trân Anh Dung, c1992.

Truòng Bá Cân , Lê Vān Khuê and Nguyên Nghi. *Bibliography of books, Documents and Articles on Catholic Christianity in Vietnam.*

Võ Long Tê. *Lich-sy Vān-hoc Công-giáo Viêt Nam* (History of the Vietnamese Catholic Literature). 3 Vols. Saigon: Tý-Duy, 1965.

1.3 *Giáo Lý Tam Phu* (Doctrine of the 'Three fathers' *[Ba Cha]*)

This is the earliest tradition in Vietnamese theology and one which would continue to be important throughout this century and after. Its sources lie in the rich traditions of Sino-Vietnamese religion and morality and in the writings of Alexandre de Rhodes and his colleagues, especially to be seen in the *Phép Giang Tám Ngày* (Eight days' catechism) of de Rhodes. The thought there had been in part mediated to Vietnam through the work in inculturation of Matteo Ricci and others in China. Within the encounter of a missionary church with Vietnamese culture, filial piety was central and came to recognize not only the 'lower' father of a family, and the 'middle' father of King, but also the supreme Father, the lord and creator of all. Here it recognized the three major religious and ethical traditions already present in Vietnam - Taoism, Buddhism and Confucianism - along with their sources in India and China. To these it added the vision of the one Creator and Lord, who had set the true Dao already in the hearts of Vietnamese. de Rhodes also referred to the *Tam Phu* as Three Superiors, Three Rewarders and Punishers, and spoke of three tasks (or duties). This supreme Father, the "Three-in-One," was to be worshipped with *latria* and also in bodily and community life.

The doctrine of *Ba Cha* would therefore long appeal to the reason as well as the faith of Vietnamese. It was further developed in the 18th century (see *Hoi Dong Ty Giáo* from the Meeting of Four Religions, ca.1790 - vol. 1, chap.2, 5.8). In the 19th century it appears in the writings of Christian poets like Phêrô Nguyên Vãn Tu, Micae Nguyên Huy My, Phêrô Dinh Công Quý, (for these see 1.4.1.) and Dang Dúc Tuân (See 1.4.2.), as well as in the treatises of Nguyên Truòng To (1.4.3.). It would also reappear in the work of 20th century writers such as Nguyên Chính Kêt and Hoàng Gia Khánh. Such a theology made it possible to express full gratitude to one's ancestors, yet within a Christian faith which was deeply personal and socially responsible. Placing the Creator of all even above the King, however, would prove highly controversial to many and as a usurpation to the royal court. It would also stimulate fuller expressions of the *Giáo Lý Tam Phu* and a wide range of insights concerning the relationships between religion, family and the state.

Selected References

De Rhodes, Alexandre. *Phép Giang Tám Ngày* (Catechism explained in eight days). Ho Chí Minh: Tu Sách Dai Kêt, 1993 (1651).

Hoàng Gia Khánh. "Three Hundred Years of Catholic Writing in Vietnam."

—. "Filial Piety Against the Background of the Doctrine of Tam Phu - Triple Fatherhood." In *Filial Piety and Christian Faith in Vietnam, Papers from the Seminar held under the Auspices of Archbishop Stephen Nguyên Nhý Thê at Huê, 1999*, ed. by Hoàng Gia Khánh. HCMV: Institute for the Study of Religion, 2000.

Nguyên Huu Lai, Joseph. *La tradition religieuse, spirituelle et sociale au Vietnam: Sa confrontation avec le christianisme*. Paris: Beauchesne, 1981.

Phan, Peter C. *Mission and Catechesis: Alexandre de Rhodes & Inculturation in Seventeenth-Century Vietnam*. Faith and Culture series. Maryknoll, NY: Orbis Books, 1998.

Truòng Bá Cân, ed. *Nguyên Truòng To 1830-1871*. 3 vols. Ho Chí Minh: Trung Tâm Nghiên Cuu Hán Nôm (Institute of Research on Chinese and Vietnamese Culture) 1991.

Vu Dình Trác, Petrus. *Công giáo Viêt Nam trong Truyên Thong Vãn hóa Dân toc* Vietnamese Catholicism in the Tradition of Its People's Culture). Thoi Diêm Công giáo: Orange County, California, 1996.

1.4 Nationalist Scholars and Reformers (19th century)

1.4.1. Phêrô Nguyên Vãn Tu (1790-1838), Micae Nguyên Huy My (1804-1838), Phêrô Ðinh Công Quý (1826-1859)

These Christian poets among others, expressed aspects of *Giáo Lý Tam Phu* in writings that portrayed both intense personal experience and a whole-hearted Christian devotion in which both traditional loyalties and transformed relationships were reconciled.

Micae Nguyên Huy My was both a poet and the writer of a well-organized catechism, who also later became a lay Christian martyr. He was known to enter deeply into every aspect of life with verve and sensitivity even during times of persecution, and remained "passionate for the Tao" even while in prison. This he considered the proper place for prayer and for rejoicing. In poems written there he expresses clearly both his deep Christian devotion and his reverence for both 'middle' and "supreme" fathers:

> "Even the cold warms me, three rings at my neck fatten me,
> The law of the King I obey with Tao. Grateful to the Lord and the King
> I readily accept all that will come and confide all to the Lord of Heaven."

Phêrô Dinh Công Quý expresses a similar devotion and theology in his prison poetry, when addressing his Mother and Father in a positive resignation.

> "Even though in manacles, I accept,
> For my loyalty to the King, and piety to you, father,
> I try hard to be grateful to the Lord, and to you my parents.
> Mother do not be saddened, but accept,
> So that the Father may be Glorified."

Phêrô Nguyên Vãn Tu more explicitly refers to all three Fathers in his poetry, the *Thýong Phu* (Superior Father), *Trung Phu* (Middle Father) and *Ha Phu* (Lower Father), declaring in one poem:

> "...One cannot for parents kill the King,
> Nor for the king reject the Supreme Father."

Other Roman Catholic intellectuals and activists of the mid-19th century cooperated in the loose movement *Giai Tác, giai hành* (Act Together, go together): described as "a credo in crisis time."

Among these, the poet and priest Tran Luc (fl. 1860 - see 1.4.6 below) whose poems were recited by peasant farmers, mediated in conflicts between the King and local Catholic communities. Dinh Văn Diên (fl. 1865), Catholic scholar and writer submitted petitions similar to those of Đang Đúc Tuân (see 1.4.2.) on methods by which France could be repulsed in both trade and warfare.

Selected References

Công giáo. *Tinh Hoa Công giáo Ái quoc Viêt Nam* (The genius of Catholic patriotism in Vietnam). Saigon, 1970 (Reprint).

Hoàng Gia Khánh. "Three Hundred Years of Catholic Writing in Vietnam."

—. "Filial Piety Against the Background of the Doctrine of Tam Phu - Triple Fatherhood."

Nguyên Huu Lai, Joseph. *La tradition religieuse, spirituelle et sociale au Vietnam: Sa confrontation avec le christianisme.*

Phan Huy Lê et al. *La Canonisation des Martyrs dans le Contexte Historique du Viêt-Nam.* HCMV: Comité National des Sciences Sociales du Viêt Nam, 1988.

Võ Long Tê. "Contribution a l'étude d'un des premiers poèmes narratifs d'inspiration catholique en langue Vientnamienne Romanisée: Ine Tu Dao Văn ou le Martyre d'Agnes. *BSEI* 42.4, Saigon.

1.4.2. Đãng Đúc Tuân (1806-1874)

From the province of Nghia Bình, Dang Dúc Tuân was accepted for study at the Seminary in Penang (Malaysia), and later ordained. After six years, however, he was arrested and imprisoned during the prohibition of Catholicism (1862). Already a celebrated poet, he now addressed a series of petitions to the Emperor Tu Duc, denouncing French oppression and advocating the mobilization of all cultural and military resources in order to end this. He continued writing after his release, both poetry and extensive petitions, which foreshadowed many later nationalist writings.

His *Confession to the King* clearly links worship of the lord, with loyalty to the King and piety to one's Father, and calls these the "Three Fathers." In other works such as *Hoan Mê Khúc* (Answer to criticism) he again presents this doctrine, along with that of the "three periods": of natural religion, of scriptural religion and of present obedience to the law of heaven. This faith he declares, is not of the West, but the religion of the Lord and Creator of the Universe. "If [one is] to do good and return to [one's] natural being, [there are] ten commandments and three worships..." (of the three Fathers).

In "Strategy for Repulsing the French and Western Repression ... by a poor scholar living in a thatched hut," Dang Dúc Tuân declares that "we Catholics will be the first to fight the French" (!) and calls the wealthy and privileged to greater discipline and simpler styles of life. Mandarins especially are to cease their fine feasts and welcome poor writers, sleeping "on bare boards and eating the bread of hardship."

In other documents he condemns the French abuse of religion in justifying aggression and insists that to betray people is to sin against God. "The French may be our co-religionists but culturally they are strangers to us," he wrote.

Selected References

Công Giáo. *Tinh Hoa Công giáo Ái quoc Viêt Nam* (The genius of Catholic patriotism in Vietnam).

Chuong Thau. "Quelques Figures des Catholiques Vietnamiens du Temps Contemporain ...." in Phan Huy Lê, et al. *La Canonisation des Martyrs dans Martyrs dans le Contexte Historique du Vietnam. Selection des Contributions au Symposium National, Ho Chi Minh Ville, June 1988.*

Hoàng Gia Khánh. "Filial Piety Against the Background of the Doctrine of Tam Phu - Triple Fatherhood."

Lâm Giang and Võ Ngoc Nha. *Dang Dúc Tuân, Tinh Hoa Công giáo Ái quoc Viêt Nam.* Saigon: published by the Authors, 1970.

Võ Duc Hanh, E. *La Place du catholicisme dans les relations entre la France et le Vietnam de 1851 à 1870.* 2 vols. Amsterdam: Brill, 1969. Part 2, Les Documents.

1.4.3. Nguyên Truòng To (1827-1871)

Nguyên Truòng To was a Chinese classical scholar, a teacher, architect, reformer and prolific Catholic writer. He travelled in Europe, read widely, also in Korean and Chinese writings, and as a "practicalist Confucian" gave much time to preparing the strategies for social reform. Returning to Saigon in 1861, he submitted a stream of memorandums to Emperor Tu Duc, advocating extensive reforms in the administration of justice, taxation, the army and international affairs, to make possible equitable incomes, indigenous production and elimination of corruption. Natural forces and the elements, he declared, must be studied first, for they were created by God for the betterment of humanity. So scientific study and economic production come before literature, laws and customs. He also, therefore, proposed mass education, the reform of festivals in honor of popular divinities and the inclusion of western studies in school and college. 'Urgent measures' in which he personally also worked included the formation of co-operatives, of creches and hospices and the development of irrigation and land settlement schemes.

Such proposals by a passionate Roman Catholic patriot constituted an assault on almost every vested interest in Vietnamese society and proposed "more ambitious reforms than any ... between the 1880s and 1945." They followed directly from Nguyên Trýòng Tô's "practicalist" (*silhak*) view of filial piety and its relation to Vietnamese culture, and were based on carefully enunciated theological principles concerning God as Creator, the nature of humanity and religious freedom, the importance of the 'middle father' (see 1.3.) and the relationship of 'earthly' well-being to 'spiritual' blessing. His thought would have continuing influence upon Vietnamese thinkers, reformers and theologians.

Selected References

    Hoàng Gia Khánh. "Filial Piety Against the Background of the Doctrine of Tam Phu - Triple Fatherhood."

    Hoang Thanh Dam. *Nguyên Trýòng Tô, Thòi Thê và Tý duy Cai cách* (Nguyên Trýòng Tô, His Time and Reformist Thinking). HCMV: Vãn Ngh?, 2000.

    McLeod, Mark W. "Nguyên Truong To: A Catholic Reformer at Emperor Tu-Duc's Court." *Journal of Southeast Asian Studies* 25.2 (1994).

    Phan Phát Huôn. *Viêt-Nam giáo-su* (History of Catholic Church in Vietnam 1533 -1960). 2 vols.

Social Sciences Institute and the Culture Information Department of Ho Chi Minh Ville. *Nguyên Truòng To and the Country's Reforms: Proceedings of the Symposium on Nguyên Trÿòng Tô, a Great Reformer of the Nation.* HCMV: Centre for Chinese and Nom Languages, 1992.

Truòng Bá Cân , ed. *Nguyên Trÿòng Tô 1830-1871. Con Ngýoi và Di Thao* (Nguyên Trÿòng Tô 1830-1871. The man and his writings). 3 vols. HCMV: Trung Tâm Nghiên Cuu Hán Nôm (Institute of Research on Chinese and Vietnamese Culture) 1988-1991.

Truòng Buu Lâm. *Patterns of Vietnamese Response to Foreign Intervention 1858-1900.* New Haven: Yale University, Southeast Asian Studies, 1907. (Includes translations of 20 key documents of Nguyên Trÿòng Tô).

1.4.4. Truòng Vinh Ký, Petrus (1837-1898)

Truòng Vinh Ký attended the College General at Pinhalu and Penang (until 1858) but his linguistic skill (proficient then in twelve languages) led to his appointment as interpreter for the Cochin-China government in negotiations with France. After teaching and diplomatic appointments, he devoted his time to writing and teaching. In these he advocated measures for peace (with France) while also criticizing much of French thought, the reform of traditional (Confucian) education and government, the development of agriculture and the dissemination of publications in *quôc ngu*.

His writings were to include dictionaries and grammars, collections of folklore and of classical Vietnamese literature, biography, history, geography, science and language education, along with collections of poems (71 volumes in all). In works like *Annamite Customs and Proprieties* (1883), Truòng Vinh Ký presented Annamite civilization in its historical and international context. Traditional values and also social reform are found in writings such as *Fisherman and Woodcutter* and *Rich and Poor* (1885). His plays on biblical themes, such as *Joseph* (1888), were in the classical form of Vietnamese drama. Both Confucian and Roman Catholic teachings inform his works on education and morality. More meditative reflection is found in *L'invariable Milieu* (1875) and *Le Precieux Miroir de Coeur* (1893), and also in his Latin manuscript *Vita Jesus*.

Selected References
Works by Truòng Vinh Ký

L'invariable Milieu. Saigon: Collège des Stagiaires,1875.
Voyage to Tonkin in the Year At-Hoi (1876). Trans. and ed. by P.J. Honey. London: School of Oriental and African Studies, 1982.
Fais ce que Dois Advienne que Pourra (Do that which is duty come what may). Saigon: Guilland et Martinon, 1882.
Les Convenances et les Civilités Annamites (Annamite customs and proprieties). Saigon: Guilland et Martinon, 1883.
Pêcheur et Bucheron (Fisher and Woodcutter). Saigon: Imprimerie de la Mission, 1885.
Le Précieux Miroir de coeur. (Precious mirror of the heart). 2 vols. Saigon: Rey, Curiol et Cie,1893.

Bouchot, J. *Petrus Truòng Vinh Ký: Erudit Cochinchinois.* Saigon: Bibliographies Cochinchinoises, 1925. Includes full bibliography of Ky's writings.
Durand, M.M. and Nguyên Trân Huân. *An Introduction to Vietnamese Literature.* New York: Columbia University, 1985.
Không Xuân Thu. *Truòng Vinh Ký (1837-1898).* Saigon: Tân Viêt, 1958.
Lê Thanh. *Truòng Vinh Ký biên khao.* Hanoi: Tân Dân, 1943.
Nguyên Văn Trung et al. *Ve Sách Báo cua Tác Gia Công Giáo: The Ky XVII-XIX* (Books and newspapers by Catholic authors, 17th-19th centuries.) HCMV: University of HCMV, 1993. Chapters 11, 12, 14 & 15.

1.4.5. Huỳnh Tinh Cua, Paulus (1834-1907)

Sometimes grouped with Nguyên Truòng To and Truòng Vinh Ký as Roman Catholic intellectuals, and as one of the three most eminent scholars and reformers of 19th century Vietnam, he is also known as Vietnam's pioneer journalist. He also collected Vietnamese stories, publishing them in *quôc ngu* under the title *Truyên giai buon* (Stories to dispel sadness). Huỳnh Tinh Cua collaborated with Truòng Vinh Ký in publishing the first daily newspaper in *quôc ngu,* the *Gia Dinh Nhât Báo* (Gia Dinh Daily). He compiled the first national dictionary for contemporary Vietnamese and proposed to the Emperor that newspapers be established. He also founded the journal *Gia Dinh Báo,* and later received the rank of provincial governor.

Like Truòng Vinh Ký, Cua was accomplished in Chinese, Vietnamese and French, fostered the spread of *quôc ngu* as the national language, and advocated reforms in education and communication. For these purposes he employed a flowing colloquial style in much of his writing. Although most of his writings were on Vietnamese culture and language, his understanding of Christian faith is expressed in deep concerns for the education and culture of his people and for the reform of Vietnamese society.

Selected References
Works by Huynh Tinh Caa
>Huynh Tinh Cua, Paulus. *Dai Nam quoc âm tu vi* (Dictionnaire Annamite). Saigon: Khai Trí, 1974.
>*Truyên giai buon* (Stories to dispel sadness). 2 Vols. Saigon: 1880, 1885.
>*Truyên giai buon.* Dong Nai: Nhà xuat ban Đong Nai, 1992.
>*Đai Nam quôc âm tu vi.* TP. Ho Chí Minh: Nhà xuat ban Tre, 1998.
>Durand, M.M. and Nguyên Trân Huân. *An Introduction to Vietnamese Literature.* New York: Columbia University, 1985.

1.4.6. Pierre Huu Triêm (Trân Luc, Father 'Six,' 1825-1899)

Huu Triêm was ordained deacon in 1858, during a period when Christians suffered persecution. Although imprisoned and exiled by Tu Duc he later enlisted widespread support for the King in the face of rebellion. Parish priest of Phát Diem, he drained marshes to build a cathedral there, using local patterns and craftsmanship, local wood and stone. Though never more than assistant Dean, he was consulted by the Royal Court, and received in 1899 the highest mandarin dignity. He was revered by local people as holding both spiritual and political power, and his work, though sometimes ambiguous in motivation, attempted to preserve national values.

His writings included a passion play in indigenous form, prayers in Annamese language and rhythmic chants, letters and memorials. He also wrote long didactic poems in *quôc ngu* on filial piety and behavior to be read by the less educated, and for them also wrote in *nôm* guidance for their dealings with Mandarins.

Selected References

Olichon, A. *Father Six*. Paris: Bloud et Gay, 1941; London: 1954.

—. *Le Baron de Phat Thiên (Histoire d'un Prêtre Tonkinois)*. Paris: Bloud et Gay, ?1950.

Jarrett-Kerr, M. *Patterns of Christian Acceptance*. London: Oxford University Press, 1972. Chapter 14.

Nguyên Gia De et al. *Tran Luc*. (USA) 1996. (Includes Tran Luc's three didactic poems).

1.4.7. Expatriate Writings and Biographies

The many writings by expatriate missionaries in this period - in letters, tracts and treatises - reflected mainly orthodox Roman Catholic doctrine and often also French cultural and imperial aspirations. They include accounts of travel and mission work, testimonies under persecution, catechetical materials, theological treatises, brief bibliographies and historical studies. Contextual elements occur in some of these.

Among the letter collections extant are those of Theophane Venard (1829-1861) - from Tonkin 1845-1861 (See J.A. Walsh, ed. *A Modern Martyr: Theophane Venard*. New York: Catholic Mission Society, 1913); of Dominique Lefebre – 1862-1865 (first Bishop of Saigon *BSEI*, 23, 1943), and the *Lettres Circulaires* (1873-1902) *de la Societé des Missions Etrangère de Paris* (M.E.P.), 1902.

Doctrinal writings in *quôc ngu* came from such missionary priests as Jean -Louis Taberd and Jean-Claude Miche (1871), Pierre Lallement (1887), Guillaume Masson (1899), Charles Lhomand (1897), Marcel Ravier and Mgr Lefebre (1899). In particular, Taberd's work in the *Documenta Rectae Rationis* includes a treatment of the "Three Fathers" teaching and concepts (See 1.3.).

Many biographical studies of prominent missionaries are extant, for example those of Theophane Venard (1861), Benique Vachet (1868), Jean Louis Bonnard (1891), Mgr Puginier (1894), and P.J.G. Pigneau de Behaine (1900), to mention only a few of those more significant.

The lives of other notable Vietnamese Christians are also available to us. Among many others they include those of Phan Thanh Gian (1796-1867, in *BSEI* 22, 1941), Princess Marie Minh

Dúc Vuong Thai Phi (16th century, in *TBAVHM* 1939 and 1941), Maria Nguyên Duy Ton (d.1944), Geronimo Liêm (1861-1951), and H. Chappoulie (1961). A collection of Vietnamese lives is given in *Ngýoi Công giáo trýoc thoi dai (Churchmen of former times)* by Nguyên Viêt Cý (Saigon: Dao và Doi, 1961). See also Nguyên Huu Trong, *Les Origines du Clergé Vietnamien. Le clergé national dans la fondation de l'Église au Vietnam*. Saigon: Groupe Littéraire Tinh-Viêt, 1959.

Historical writings from this period are extensive, and notably include F.M. de Montezou, *Mission de la Cochinchine et du Tonkin*. Paris: Charles Douniel, 1858; Paul Antonin, *L'Annam, Le Tonkin et L'intervention de la France en Extreme-Orient*. Paris: Bloud et Barrel, n.d.; L.E. Louvet. *Les Missions Catholiques au XIXè siècle*. Lilles: Desclec, 1908, Pierre Dourisboure, *Les Sauvages Bahnar*. Paris: 1870.

Selected References

Dourisboure, P., and C. Simonnet. *Vietnam: Mission on the Grand Plateaus*. Maryknoll, NY: Orbis Books, 1967.
Launay, A. *Histoire de la Mission de Cochin-Chine 1658-1823*. 3 vols. (Documents Historiques included.) Paris: P. Tequi, 1923-1925.
—. *Histoire de la Mission du Tonkin*. Paris: Libraire Orientale, 1927.
Lettres Edifiantes et Curieuses. Nouvelle Edition. Tome 16. Paris: 1781.
Louvet, L.E. *Cochinchine Religieuse*. 2 vols. Paris: Challamel Ainé, 1885.
Pallu, Francois. *Histoire de l'établissement du Christianisme dans les Indes Orientales par les évêques français aux autres missionnaires apostoliques*. Paris: 1803.
Taberd, Jean-Louis. *Documenta Rectae Rationis seu Forma Instructionis*. 3rd Ed. Hong Kong: Typis Societas Missionum, 1914.
Trân Anh Dung. *Sõ thao thý muc Công giáo Viêt Nam* (The Catholic Church in Vietnam - a brief bibliography of sources). Paris: n.p., 1992.
Truòng Bá Cân, Lê Văn Khuê and Nguyên Nghi. *Bibliography of Books, Documents and Articles on Catholic Christianity in Vietnam, Held in Vietnam.*

2 The Period 1908-1940
2.1 Nationalist or Revolutionary Christian Writers
Here too there would appear a wide variety of priests and poets, bishops and reformers, nationalists, scholars, activists and educators. Some would remain in the work of parish priests, like Dâu Quang Linh (see 2.1.3.); some would be members of the Société du Modernisme; Hàn Mac Tu (2.1.2.) would become a poet of national stature, and others end their lives in prison. Mgr Nguyên Bá Tòng, Bishop of Phát Diem, composed a long eulogy to Dang Dúc Tuân (1.4.2.) along with many nationalist articles and homilies, while the politically active Mgr Lê Huu Tý became counsellor to Ho Chí Minh, and in his diocesan letters advocated nationalist policies. Even more directly involved in revolutionary activities was Mai Lão Bang (below).

2.1.1. Mai Lão Bang ['Gia Châu'] (?-1945)
Born in the province of Nghe Tinh to a Catholic family, Mai Lão Bang studied in the major seminary of Xa Doai. Leaving with six others to join La Societé du Modernisme, he became a close associate of Phan Bôi Châu, the most eminent of early revolutionary leaders, and in 1908 led a delegation of Roman Catholic students to Japan. His writings at this time included the poems *Conseils de Lão Bang* and *Exhortation à l'unanimité*, addressed to fellow Catholics in Vietnam and advocating unity despite and beyond personal interest, in the cause of revolution. Here he cited the example of Lê Loi and his men 400 years earlier, enduring privation in the pursuit of destroying the Ming colonial system. Poems such as these of his were widely recited amongst nationalist groups.

From 1913-1917 he was imprisoned along with Phan Bôi Châu and three other Catholic priests, and afterwards exiled until 1933. He continued to write poetry which was widely used by nationalist and revolutionary groups. 'Khuyên Dông Tâm' for example, calls for an end to all animosities, and for unity in struggle, again citing as model Lê Loi and his followers. He is included in recent studies of nationalist Catholic writers and respected as a Christian patriot.

Selected References
Works by Mai Lão Bang
"Khuyên Dông Tâm". In *Văn Thõ Cách Mang Viêt Nam Dau Thê Ky XX*, by Dang Thái Mai, Hanoi: 1964.

Dang Thái Mai. *Văn Thõ Cách Mang Viêt Nam Dau Thê Ky XX* (Vietnam's Revolutionary Prose and Poetry in the early 20th Century), Hanoi, Nxb Văn Hoc, 1964.

Marr, David. *Vietnamese Anticolonialism 1885-1925*. Berkeley: University of California Press, 1971.

Phan Huy Lê et al. *La Canonisation des Martyrs dans le Contexte Historique du Vietnam. Selection des Contributions au Symposium National, Hochiminvolle, June 1988*. HCMV: Comité National des Sciences Sociales du Vietnam et al, 1988.

Phan Phát Huôn. *Viêt-Nam giáo-su* (History of Catholic Church in Vietnam 1533 -1960). 2 vols.

Vu Dình Liên et al., eds. *Hop Tuyên Tho Văn Viêt Nam 1858-1930* (A Collection of Vietnamese Poetry and Prose 1858-1930). Hanoi, Nxb Văn Hoc, 1963.

2.1.2. Hàn Mac Tu (Nguyên Trong Trí, 1912-1940)

Regarded as the most eminent Catholic poet in the first half of the century, Hàn Mac Tu came from a Catholic family of Quang Bình province, but died of leprosy while still young. His other pen-names were Minh Duê and Lê Thanh. One of a group of 'young intellectuals of the town,' he became a leader in the movement of "New Poetry" and was later acknowledged as a significant literary pioneer. His writing formed a breakthrough in poetic style and language, in lucidity, emotion and mysticism. Moving love poems, along with others deeply shaped by his own suffering, are included in his oeuvres, many of which also possess spiritual symbolism. See for example:

> Dream of the traveller on the long road ... the long road
> Her garments are too white ... how shall she be known to him?
> Here mists and smoke smother human forms.
> Oh Heart of love, who may ever sound its secret depths?
> (Nguyên Khac Viên and Huu Ngoc, c.1976.)

His 'theo-poetry' is thus highly symbolic and mystical and much of it 'hymned the Christian faith' with fervor and was called by him *tho dao hanh* (religious-pious poetry) or *tho cau Nguyên* (praying poetry). Among his religious poems, some are in praise of Mary, while he also used Buddhist imagery in his poetry. His published works include *Thõ Diên* (Mad poem), *Dau Thýõng* (Feel deep grief), and *Chõi Gua Mùa Trãng* (Playing in the middle of the moon season), although his volume *Gái Quê* (Peasant girl, 1936), is the only work which has been published in its entirety. His poems have been partially collected in *Thõ Hàn Mac Tu* (Poems of Hàn Mac Tu).

Selected References
> Durand, M.M. and Nguyên Trân Huân. *An Introduction to Vietnamese Literature.* New York: Columbia University, 1985.
> Hàn Mac Tu. *Thõ Hàn Mac Tu* (poems by Hàn Mac Tu). Hanoi: n.p.1949.
> Hoàng Diêp. *Hàn Mac Tu.* Saigon: Khai-Trí, 1968.
> Nguyên Khac Viên and Huu Ngoc. *Vietnamese Literature - Historical Background and Texts.* Hanoi: Foreign Languages Press, c.1976.
> Pham Xuân Tuyên. *Di Tìm Chân Dung Hàn Mac Tu* (In Search of Hàn Mac Tu's Portrait). Hanoi: Nxb Vãn Hoc, 1997.
> Thái Vãn Liêm and V.L. "A Great Vietnamien Poet." *Asia* 4.16 (1955).
> Võ Long Tê. "L'expérience poétique et l'itinéraire spirituel de Hàn Mac Tu." *BSEI* 47.4, 1972.

2.1.3. Other nationalist Christian poets of the late 19th/early 20th centuries

Nguyên Tuong (1853-1911), Nguyên Huu Bài (1863-1935) and Dâu Quang Linh (1867-1919).

Under colonial rule and its often severe censorship, poetry assumed a vital role both for resistance and religious movements. Although voicing immediate concerns for the fate of Vietnam or the suffering of its people, the writing of nationalist Christian poets also reflects deep convictions of the dignity of human life, the requirements of justice, and the redemptive power of shared struggle and agony.

Nguyên Tuong was another priest member of La Société du Modernisme; also a poet and also imprisoned, along with Dâu

Quang Linh and Nguyên Thanh Dông. While there, and in late exile, he continued his writing in poems which expressed deep concern for his people's suffering and strong love for his country.

By the 1930s, the Catholic mandarin **Nguyên Huu Bài** was writing extensively both in poems and in treatises which contributed to an emerging Vietnamese theology. In the following years he compiled with others a wide-ranging theological and philosophical dictionary. He and his colleagues resisted colonialist attempts to remove the King, coining the widely used proverb "Giêt Vua Không Khá" (To kill the King, No!). He also established the *Ngu Tàu Du Hoc* association to provide overseas study for Vietnamese students.

Dâu Quang Linh was a scholar in Chinese and Latin from the province of Nghê Tinh. While a parish priest he also read and translated reformist books by non-Vietnamese and also became a member of La Société du Modernisme. During imprisonment he wrote many poems expressing resolve to free his people and to restore true religion. In response to the question of his captors as to how as a priest he could give himself to such 'piracy,' he wrote:

> For the cause of the Whites
> In the pulpit, at the site of the executions
> Life is sometimes sweet, sometimes bitter
> Throughout the trials and tribulations
> As citizens, we are determined to assume the responsibility.
> From the same yellow race, the many well-read
> And other personalities
> Some incarcerated, others in exile
> All have been condemned
> Letting their bitter blood drip
> We amount to only one with them.......

Selected References

Dang Thái Mai. *Vān Thõ Cách Mang Viêt Nam Dâu Thê Ky XX.* Hanoi: 1964.

Durand, M.M. and Nguyên Trân Huân. *An Introduction to Vietnamese Literature.*

Nguyên Huu Bài. *Tho Nôm Phuóc Môn.* Edition Tái ban. United States: s.l., 1997 (ca 1932). Poems translated from the Nôm script.

Nguyên Khac Viên and Huu Ngoc. *Vietnamese Literature - Historical Background and Texts*. Hanoi: Foreign Languages Press, c.1976.

Phan Huy Lê et al. *La Canonisation des Martyrs dans le Contexte Historique du Vietnam. Selection des Contributions au Symposium National, Ho Chi Minh Ville, June 1988*.

2.2 Journals and Periodicals

The early 20th century saw the development by political moderates, of weekly and monthly journals which regularly included theological articles and discussion. In 1906, reformist Confucian scholars initiated the *Dong-Kinh Nghia-Thuc* (literally 'Hanoi unpaid teaching' movement) in order to bring free education to the mass of ordinary Vietnamese. It included women and girls, surprisingly, and used the vehicle of Vietnamese in *quôc ngu* script. Key leaders were Luong Vãn Can and Phan Bôi Châu along with Catholics like Nguyên Vãn Vinh. The movement proved so popular, with four or five hundred at evening lectures, that it was suppressed by the French after nine months. But nevertheless seeds of social and cultural awareness had been widely sown, later to yield a nationalist harvest.

Priests and lay people also participated in other patriotic movements before 1945 such as *Cân Vuong* (For the King), *Quang Phuc Hôi* (Association for the Reconquest of Independence). These included Fr Mai Rinh (Thanh Liêm Dist.), Fr Võ Thành Trinh (Hanoi), and Thái Vãn Lung (Thi Nghè).

In 1907 the first of many periodicals began, *Dang-co tuân báo*, which like the later *Dông Duong tap chí* (from 1913) was edited by Nguyên Vãn Vinh. These, along with the larger *Nam Phong* (from 1917) were notable for the inclusion, along with mandatory articles on French culture, of a wide range of writings on literary, philosophical and theological subjects, and all in *quôc ngu*. Under the editorship of Pham Quynh, *Nam Phong* extended this range, retaining the inclusion of theological writings.

Scholarly journals had been initiated by Roman Catholic missionaries by the 1880s and these came to include a wide range of literary, historical, biographical and theological studies by both expatriates and Vietnamese.

The *Bulletin de la Société des Études Indochinoises* (BSEI) began c.1885 and included among local authors Huỳnh Tinh Cua in a lengthy study of Annamite traditions and on filial piety(1888-1908); Michael Tinh concerning the life of Lê Văn Gâm (1903-); Lê Văn Phúc on Annamite documentation (with Pierre Daudin, 1938-); and N. Truòng Vinh Tông on Truòng Vinh Ký's writings (1929-1932).

Local contributors to the *Bulletin des Amis du Vieux Huê* (BAVH) included in the years 1914-1944, biographical studies by Bao Thái Thanh, Nguyên Dình Hòe and Ngô Dình Diem (1915-1919); historical studies by Bùi Văn Cung (with H. Peysonnaux, 1920), Nguyên Dình Hòe and Trân Xuân Toan (1921), Lê Thanh Canh (1928-1932) and Pham Quynh (also editor of *Nam Phong*, 1936).

The *Bulletin de L'École Française d'Extrême-Orient* (BEFEO) begun in 1903, includes few Vietnamese writers in this period.

Selected References

Doàn Thi Dô. "Le journalisme au Viêt-Nam et les Periodiques Vietnamese de 1856-1944." *Bulletin d'Informations de A.B.F.* 25.3 (1958).

Durand, M.M. and Nguyên Trân Huân. *An Introduction to Vietnamese Literature*. New York: Columbia University, 1985: Chaps. 10, 11.

Hill, R.D. *Index Indochinensis*. An English and French Index to *Revue Indochinoise, Extrême-Asie, Extrême-Asie-Revue Indochinoise,* and *La Revue Indochinoise Juridique et Economique*. Hong Kong: University of Hong Kong Asian Studies, 1983.

Marr, David. *Vietnamese Anticolonialism 1885-1925*. Berkeley: University of California Press, 1971: Chaps. 6-9.

Truòng Bá Cân, Lê Văn Khuê and Nguyên Nghi. *Bibliography of books, Documents and Articles on Catholic Christianity in Vietnam, Held in Vietnam*.

2.3 Theological Writings

The majority of works in Vietnamese on Christian belief from the first decades of the century remain anonymous, issued under L'Impr.

de la Mission, in Saigon, Qui Nhon, Hà Nôi or Hong Kong. In the period 1910-1940, Roman Catholic publications were a significant, but declining proportion of the 20% of all *quôc ngu* publications of religious materials. They included articles, tracts, prayer-books, treatises, catechisms.

Almost all explicitly theological or moral writings reflected the gradual assimilation of Confucian precepts - regarding, for example, 'the five relationships' - yet they also maintained traditional Catholic doctrines on, for example, 'original sin,' martyrdom, confession and marriage. And in contrast to many other Christian writings, formal theological works regularly condemned any rejection of 'constituted authority' whether Roman or French, along with 'free thought,' 'utilitarianism' or even 'egalitarianism.' The Catholic Weekly from Huê, *Vì Chúa* (For the Lord), includes many such critical articles in the 1930s.

However, from the many Vietnamese writers of theology in this period came volumes showing a wide spectrum of theological, moral and political belief. A small selection would include the following:

Pierre Dô Dình (fl. 1935) published the long poem *Le Grand Tranquille* (The Great Calm) in 1937, presenting the 'interior debate' of a Vietnamese convert to Catholicism.

Nguyên Văn Thích (fl.1935) was a priest in Huê who wrote volumes in largely traditional moral theology as well as editing *Tuân Báo Vì Chúa* (Vì Chúa Review) ca. 1936.

Joseph Thích lamented widespread moral decline - in materialism, disobedience in the five relationships, labor strikes, revolution and Communism (*Today's Ethical Questions,* 1930.) For Thich, all talk of rectifying inequalities was dangerous since the "lower orders" would only disobey, pillage and fight among themselves.

Between such reactionary thought, which often included more extreme defenses of French colonization on the one hand, and the revolutionary commitment of Mai Lão Bang or Dâu Quang Linh on the other (above), many diverse positions were held.

Simon Chính devoted volumes to Confucian themes, such as "First study ritual, then study literature," which preserved traditional hierarchic distinctions. He also wrote and translated many works of doctrine and moral theology between 1907 and 1932.

Vu Dãng Khoa insisted on the unity of religious faith and moral behavior and on the belief in God and in the after life as essential to moral instruction. However he also offered teaching as to how Christians and non-Christians 'might be able to live together peacefully.' (*New Code of Ethics,* 1930.)

Members of the Missions Étrangère de Paris writing in *quôc ngu* on doctrinal and moral theology in the period 1907-1921 include: Philemon Jeanningross, Jean-Pierre Martin, Auguste Feillon, Charles La Motte, Jean A.P. Macou, and Victor Pierre Martin. The Dominicans Santiago Hemandez and Victor Coloma also contributed works in moral theology.

Selected References

Chinh, Simon. *Con Nít Hoc Nói* (Children Learning how to Speak). Qui Nhõn: Công giáo, 1924.

Chuong Thi. *Vãn Duc Bà* (Hymns to our Lady). Ha-Noi: Nhac Doàn Tiêng Chuông Nam, 1952.

Dô Dình, Pierre. *Le Grand Tranquille* (The great calm). N.p. 1937.

Nguyên Hýng. *Sõ thao thý muc Công giáo Viêt Nam* (Bibliography of Vietnamese Catholic books written in Nom and Demotic Script). N.p.

Thich, Joseph. *Vân dê Luân Lý Ngày Nay* (Today's ethical questions). Qui Nhõn: Công giáo, 1930.

Trân Anh Dung. *Sõ thao thý muc Công giáo Viêt Nam.* (The Catholic Church in Vietnam: a brief bibliography of sources in Vietnamese). Paris: Bibliothèque Asiatique M.E. et al., 1992.

Truòng Bá Cân , Lê Vãn Khuê and Nguyên Nghi. *Bibliography of books, Documents and Articles on Catholic Christianity in Vietnam, Held in Vietnam.*

Vu Dãng Khoa. *Luân Lý Tân Ca* (New code of ethics). Hanoi: 1930.

2.4 Writings in History and Culture

Expatriate writing on Vietnamese literary, historical and cultural subjects in the period 1928-1941 included Jean Bouchet (1928),

G. Taboulet (1936-1943), Henri Verdeille (1935-1936) - all in the *BSEI*; Leopold Cadière (1906-), Paul Pelliot (1922) - in *BEFEO;* and in *BAVH*, such scholars as H. Cosserat (1917-1927), A. Salles (1919-1923) and most notably L. Cadière (1915-1941).

Cadière's prolific work in both *quôc ngu* and French includes many diverse linguistic historical and biographical studies, both in 'secular' and in church history. His major volume is an exhaustive study of Annamite religious tradition: *Croyances et Pratiques Religieuses des Annamites* (Hanoi and Paris).

Jean Bouchot published also three studies of Petrus Truòng Vinh Ký (1927-1928) and George Taboulet later completed archival collections (1955) and historical works.

Early history of Christianity in Tonkin in the period 1884-1959 came from, amongst others, Romanet du Caillaud, A. Bonifacy, André Migot, Henri Chappoulie, Adrien Launay. André Migot also studies the relation of Christianity to Buddhism and other religious traditions, as do Maurice Price, and Cadière (above). Works in history and church history (in *quôc ngu* and French) also included, among many others, those of Eugene Louvet, Leon Joly, Charles Maybon, Philippe Grandjean and Marcel Caratini, Francis Trochu, Bernard de Vaulx and Charles Gayou.

Notable works by Vietnamese historians include:

> Lê, Nicole Dominique. *Les Missions Étrangères et la Pénétration Française au Viêt-Nam*. Publications de l'Institut d'études et de recherches interethniques et interculturelles 5. Paris: Mouton, 1975.
>
> Lê Thành Khôi. *Le Vietnam, Histoire et Civilisation. Le Milieu et l'Histoire*. Paris: Les editions de minuit, 1955.
>
> Nguyên Hiên Lê. *Dông Kinh Nghia Thuc* (Eastern capital public school). Saigon: N.H.L., 1956.
>
> Nguyên Huu Trong. *Le Clergé National dans la Fondation de L'Église au Vietnam. Les Origines du Clergé Vietnamien*. Saigon: Tinh Viêt, 1959.
>
> Nguyên Khac Viên. *The Long Resistance, 1858-1975*. Hanoi: Foreign Language Publishing House, 1975.
>
> Phan Huy Lê, et al. *La Canonisation des Martyrs dans le Contexte Historique du Vietnam. Selection des Contributions au Symposium National, Ho Chi Minh Ville, June 1988*.

Phan Phát Huôn. *Viêt Nam Giáo Su* (History of the Church in Vietnam). vol. I (1533-1933). Saigon: Dong Chúa Cúu Thê, 1958.

Trân Thi Liên. *Les Catholiques Vietnamiens pendant la Guerre d'Independence (1945-54): Entre la Reconquête Coloniale et la Resistance Communiste*. Paris: Institut d'études politiques de Paris, 1996.

Võ Duc Hanh, Etienne. *La place du Catholicisme dans les Relations entre la France et le Vietnam de 1851 à 1870*. Leiden: Brill, 1969.

Additional References

Cadière, L. *Croyances et Pratiques Religieuses des Vietnamiens*. vol. I, Hanoi: Imprimerie d'Extrême Orient, 1944; Vols. II and III, Paris: Ecole Francais d'Extrême Orient, 1955 and 1956.

Grandjean, Philippe, and Marcel Caratini. *Le Clergé Indigene du Tonkin et ses Prêtres Martyrs*. Paris: Missions Étrangères, 1925.

Launay, A. *Histoire de la Mission du Tonkin*. Paris: Libraire Orientale, 1927.

Migot, A. *Mission et Cultures non-chrétiennes*. Paris: Desclée and Brouwer, 1959.

Streit, Robert, and Johannes Dindinger. *Bibliotheca Missionum*. Munster i. W., Aachen: 1964 (1916): vols.6, 8. Missionsliterature Indiens / Indochinas.

Trân Anh Dung. *Sõ thao thý muc Công giáo Viêt Nam* (The Catholic Church in Vietnam - a brief bibliography of sources).

Truòng Bá Cân, Lê Vãn Khuê and Nguyên Nghi. *Thý Muc Sách Và Các Bài Báo Vê Lich Su Công giáo Viêt Nam Có Tai Viêt Nam* (Bibliography of books, documents and articles on Catholic Christianity in Vietnam, held in Vietnam).

3 Mid-20th Century
3.1 Historical and Religious Context
3.1.1. Vietnamese Traditions, Catholicism and Colonialism

By the 1940s religious traditions had been greatly weakened and fragmented under colonial rule. Confucianism then has been described as "little more than a set of moral platitudes," while Buddhism found itself in tension with a "social Darwinism which linked objective analysis of class struggle with an ethical vision of new society." Roman Catholicism remained closely linked with France in ecclesial organization, conceptualization and allegiance as "the French Church abroad"; Catholic school texts described the French as "liberators" after 1946; and social privileges were still accorded to the Roman Catholic faithful. Termed "the way of heaven," not "the way of man," Catholicism was seen by many to be part of the colonial system and sharing its wealth and power. It also accepted many features of a class system socially and politically, while nonetheless advocating a harmony of classes. The Catholic hierarchy remained closely associated with the French government and military, and forbad Catholics from joining the Communist party or allied organizations.

By 1954, the previous decade of French occupation and of the first Indo-China war had greatly increased rural destitution. The jungle war had brought heavy casualties on both sides, along with atrocities against civilians and "the indiscriminate destruction and contamination of much of the landscape." The French administration was now largely corrupt; education was in collapse; and despite attempts by the Department of Mass Education from 1946, widespread illiteracy exacerbated the severe inequalities and conflicts. By 1950 it was therefore to be expected that Vietnamese Catholicism included movements both of collaboration with France and of nationalist support for the Viêt Minh.

The exodus of many - Catholics, Buddhists and others - from North Vietnam in 1954 was followed by the passing there of the Law on Religious Freedom (1955). Under this and other measures, activities of the Church in the North suffered increasing restrictions during the next 20 years of conflict, despite the attempts of some Catholics - in for example the Liaison Committee of Patriotic Catholics (1955) - to bridge the ideological gulfs, or to explore ways of rapprochement and "Vietnamization." (Examples appear below). The Liaison Committee was early supported by Bishop Hoang Văn Doàn, and later by some other bishops and formed the basis for the later Committee for the Union of Catholics (1983). By 1965 there were committees in all provinces, with the aims of "encouraging resistance to aggression" and to "restore national dignity." It also had the aim of bringing a theological re-orientation towards Vietnamization and also towards relationships with "liberation and socialist movements."

In the South, both Catholics and Buddhists faced many dilemmas in allegiance in the face of escalating conflict in these decades: whether to support the positions of government, of hierarchy or of the National Front; whether to espouse nationalism despite its growing association with communism, or to acquiesce in the policies of an often corrupt government, its policies of "strategic hamlets" and other repressions, along with its subservience to American policies. Despite continuing movements to establish a basis for peace, to oppose corruption and to establish a "third way" between communism and capitalism, "neutralism" was officially outlawed, and divisions sharpened not only throughout society but within the major religious traditions. This would be further embittered by the "absolutist" Catholicism of President Diêm. After 1963, in addition to those Catholics who were directly involved in organizations of the National Liberation Front, other priests and lay people came to oppose the Thiêu and later administrations and their policies. Under the influence also of Vatican II, and often in close association with Buddhists and other activists, many Catholics were active in movements for peace and democracy and in work for a different role for the Church within society and nation. (See 3.2.1.6.).

Following unification of the country in 1975, all institutions of the churches in the South were confiscated, as they had been in the North in 1954. Catholic organizations were disbanded, and the numbers of priests ordained was greatly limited. The imprisonments of a number of priests and intellectuals followed - as it had under both the Diêm and Thiêu regimes; the publication of Christian writings was officially prohibited and seminary libraries except those of Dalat and Saigon, were largely destroyed. By 1988 restrictions on Catholic seminaries were partially lifted and six were allowed to re-open, followed by two more in 1993. Confrontations with government - sometimes over church property - and occasional imprisonments, still occur and the bishops continue to request the end of all restrictions on organizations, pastoral work, ordinations and publication.

Selected References

Beyond Aid and Development. Future of the Missionary Enterprise 18. Rome: IDOC, 1976.

Bibliography on Christianity in Vietnam. Saigon: Directorate of National Archives and Libraries, 1966.

"Catholics and the National Movement". *Vietnamese Studies* 53, Special Issue (1977).

Công-Huyên Tôn-Nu Nha-Trang. "Women Writers of South Viêt Nam 1954-1975." *Vietnam Forum* 9 (1987).

Duiker, William J. *Vietnam: Revolution in Transition.* 2nd ed. Boulder: Westview Press, 1995.

Eisen, Arlene. *Women and Revolution in Vietnam.* London: Zed books, 1984.

Gheddo, Piero. *Vietnam Christiani e communisti.* Torino: Editrice international, 1976.

Hunger, Wilhelm, sj. "Kirchenkampf in Vietnam. Die Rolle des 'Unionskomitees Patrioscher Katholiken." *Die Katholischen Missionen* 104 (1985).

Jamieson, Neil L. *Understanding Vietnam.* Berkeley and London: University of California Press, 1993.

Kotte, Heinz & Nguyên Mai Tam. *Christen und Sozialisten in Viêt Nam.* W. Germany: IDOC 12063, 1976.

Le Contexte Historique du Vietnam. HCMV: Comité Nationale des Sciences Sociales du Vietnam, 1988.

Marr, David. *Vietnamese Tradition on Trial 1920-1942.* Berkeley: University of California Press, 1981.

Phan Phát Huôn. *Viêt Nam Giáo Su* (History of the Church in Vietnam). vol. I (1533-1933). Saigon: Dong Chúa Cúu Thê, 1958; English trans. Long Beach: Cúu Thê Tùng Thu, 2000.

Thích Nhât Hanh. *Vietnam - Lotus in a Sea of Fire.* London: SCM Press, 1967.

Trân Thi Liên. *Les Catholiques Vietnamiens pendant la Guerre d'Indépendence (1945-54): Entre la Reconquête Coloniale et la Résistance Communiste.* Paris: Institut d'Études Politiques de Paris, 1996.

3.1.2. Theological Locus and Response of Vietnamese Catholics 1940s to 1975.

Before the 1960s theology for much of the Catholic Church of South Vietnam was traditionally orthodox, triumphalist, strongly anti-communist, and in its relation to the state, comprador.

Contextual Theology in Vietnam 1800-2000 587

Clericalism was strong, "a spirit of martyrdom" was fostered, and in rural Vietnam, life in the village for Catholics was "a community life based on the Christian group." Public village demonstrations for the faith were frequent, as was the undertaking of pilgrimages, and the cult of the Virgin had central place for many. In following years, the condemnation by the majority of progressive Catholic thought would be fostered by the Diêm regime, along with anti-reformist preaching, the development of a "personalist" state philosophy and government subsidies given to dioceses in return for collaboration. The Church became admired in its public "face" for its organization, and feared for its power and apparent wealth, both largely the inheritance of the colonial era. Widely used chants, poems and hymns of the 1950s and 1960s spoke of the church as a "castle" or fortified citadel, as if God was a monarch remote from ordinary people and requiring defense. Scholars such as Trân Thiên Câm spoke of "les deux visages de l'Église [which is] a mystery to non-Christians" and asked "after three centuries ... is it a religion or a state?"

In North Vietnam in this period, similar traditionalism, clericalism and anti-communism are prominent features, and for many these were strengthened by an attitude of "self-imposed withdrawal ... in order to preserve the faith." Isolation from the wider church, and particularly from the *aggiornamento* under way elsewhere, hardened the adherence to traditional forms and the 'letter' of Catholic belief for many. There were, however, numbers of priests and laity for whom the socio-political context of North Vietnam called forth thought and action that was both nationalist and people-centered (see 3.2.3. and following).

In the context of increasing nationalism and the tentative recoveries of Vietnamese traditions, and despite the continuance of widespread teaching and writing on European Catholic tradition, the development of specifically Vietnamese theology in coming decades would therefore be inseparable from growing reformist, anti-colonial and "patriotic" sentiment. Creative theological reflection in both the North and the South in these years thus came more and more to focus upon Vietnamese historical experience, upon sources within Vietnamese culture, and upon faith insights arising from within the struggles and hopes of Vietnamese people.

The larger intellectual context also favored the growth of a localized theology. "New Poets" in the North who had begun writing in the early 1940s, incorporated popular Vietnamese imagery and themes, recognizing their patriotic character. There was also a rewriting of Vietnamese history "from the inside," by, for example, Hoang Thuc Tram (1944). Journals such as *Tri Tan* (To Know the New) also used *quôc ngu* rather than French, in articles on Vietnamese history, culture, religion and language. For Vietnamese literati, the earlier debates in such areas as ethics, language, women's rights and Vietnamese history, and the long tradition of their involvement in political affairs, now led to a questioning of the relation of knowledge to action as understood in much western or classical Chinese thought. Instead, Phan Văn Hum presented a full exposition of Wang Yang Ming's "unity of knowledge and action," while Phan Bôi Châu and others advocated "a dynamic creative integration of knowledge and action." For revolutionaries and theologians alike this was to provide important groundwork for contextualizing insights.

There had been beginnings for contextual theology in the work of 19th century nationalist priests (see 1 above and following), but historical and theological reflection was now sharpened amid heightening armed conflict and social disturbance. By 1954 groups of priests and lay people were studying and disseminating writings on Vietnamese heritage, national identity and patriotism. Some from the South were working with groups in the North to continue "their struggle for a Catholicism which would not break with the nation and socialism." Among these were the priests Hô Thành Biên, Trân Quang Nghiêm, Vu Thanh Binh, Luong Minh Ky and Nguyên Hiêu Lê (for these see 3.2). Some bishops and clergy, influenced in part by the Vatican Council, chose to adopt a simple and modest lifestyle as well. Many Catholics in the South were also influenced by national struggles, and by the reforming initiatives of Vatican II, believing that earthly life within nation and society is integral to the kingdom of God. The council also contributed to the emerging movement of *Dông Hành* ("the Church with nation and people"), stimulated by critiques, such as those by Nguyên Ngoc Lan and Chân Tín (see 4.3.10.) of the *Lâu dài - Pháo dài* ("block-house and castle") images used by the church. *Dông Hành* also advocated the return to national culture in liturgy, architecture and in the struggle to transform society.

Contextual theology was also emerging from Catholic movements such as the Young Catholic Workers (founded by Fr Vacquier mep, in 1937), which conducted courses in Christian formation and on social issues; from intellectual groups such as Pax Romana; and from the Social Secretariat (founded by Fr Parrel mep, 1953) which undertook training in the Church's social teaching and documentation on major social problems, publishing the journal *Economie Humaine*. By the early 1960s many other movements in the South were contributing to Vietnamese theology. These included: groups of Catholic nationalists who studied the socio-cultural milieu of Vietnam in order to give the faith "a Vietnamese character and color." And Catholic Study weeks were held in Saigon and Dalat for these purposes. Writings arising from these movements were both stimulated by, and published in, such journals as *Sông Dao, Chon* and *Tin Mùng Hôm Nay* (see 3.1.4.).

By the late 1960s, there were more calls for Catholics to "go back to our national roots" and to "accept that we are Catholic Vietnamese" (see 3.2.1.f). Such thought was accentuated by the escalating international conflict and the fragmentation of religious constituencies. Along with the burgeoning publication of "approved" Christian and related historical works, in this decade, the works of concerned scholars, priests and activists appeared in a wide variety of formats (see 3.1.3.). By the early 1970s more groups and networks of clergy and lay people were articulating a more open theology of Christian presence in Vietnamese society.

Selected References

Cadière, L. "Organisation et Fonctionnement d'une Chrétienté Vietnamienne." *Bulletin MEP* (1955).
"Catholics and the National Movement." *Vietnamese Studies* 53 (1977).

Công Nguyên Bão and Harry Haas. *Vietnam: the other conflict.* London: Sheed and Ward, 1971.

Denney, Stephen. "Religion and Communism in Vietnam 1975-1992." In *Render unto Caesar - The Religious Sphere in World Politics*, edited by S.P. Ramet and D.W. Treadgold. Washington, DC: American University Press, 1995.

Gheddo, Piero. *The Cross and the Bo-Tree: Catholics and Buddhists in Vietnam.* Trans. by Charles Underhill Quinn. New York: Sheed and Ward, 1970.

—. "La Chiesa del Vietnam dieci anni dopo il Vaticano II." *Humanitas* 30 (1976).

Haas, Harry. "Catholics in North Vietnam." *Commonweal* 87 (1968).

Houtart, Francois. "Les Catholiques au Sud-Vietnam." *Foi et Dévelopement* 51 (1977).

Lange, Claude. "L'Église Catholique au Sud-Vietnam de la 'Libération' à la 'Réunification'." *Echos de la Rue du Bac*, Series of 3 articles, 1976. English version in *Teaching All Nations* 14 (1977)

Lê Tiên Giang. *Công giáo Kháng chiên Nam bô 1945-1954* (Catholic Church resisting in South Vietnam 1945-1954). Saigon: Chon, 1972; Paris: Công giáo Dân toc , 1980.

National Catholic Action Committee. "Declaration." *L'Osservatore Romano,* Sept 26 (1963).

—. "Communism and We Christians." Saigon: Mimeo'd, 1965.

Thích Nhât Hanh. *Vietnam - Lotus in a Sea of Fire.* London: SCM Press, 1967.

Trân Anh Dung. *Sõ thao thý muc Công giáo Viêt Nam* (The Catholic Church in Vietnam - A Brief Bibliography of Sources). Paris: Trân Anh Dung, 1992.

Trân Tam Tinh. *Catholics in the History of Vietnam.* Rome: Editrice Coines, 1976. (Also in Italian and French editions).

Truòng Bá Cân, Lê Vãn Khuê and Nguyên Nghi. *Bibliography of books, Documents and Articles on Catholic Christianity in Vietnam, Held in Vietnam.*

3.1.3. NOTE: Christian publishing and distribution in Vietnam

Throughout the 20th century, under colonial rule and during later prolonged conflict, the publishing of Christian writing has been an uncertain and often hazardous work. This was especially so in North Vietnam from 1954, and in the South after 1975, and in the case of any writings that aspired to relate Christian faith to contemporary

Contextual Theology in Vietnam 1800-2000

history and social conditions, or to Vietnamese culture and aspirations. Until the late 1960s of this period, a diversity of historical, biographical, doctrinal and bibliographical volumes were published in the South (see references in Supplementary Bibliography below), but as in the North, it was to become increasingly difficult, especially after 1975, to publish specifically Christian material other than for 'private circulation.' Many theologians, scholars and commentators - their ranks swelled by many who had been fully trained for priesthood but prevented from exercising this - have continued to issue their writings in booklet or document form. These usually have no designated publisher or printer and are often also pseudonymous. But they often attain wide distribution and for this half century number many hundreds. References below will therefore include a larger than usual proportion of "privately circulated" or "mimeo'd" materials.

The other chief outlets for contextual writing have been provided by a wide range of periodicals, only a few of which have achieved official sanction - from either Church or government regime - for at least a part of their period of publication. Many of these have also suffered change of location, name or format in order to survive censure, and many articles again appear only under pseudonyms. The sections below on journals in which Christian theological reflection has appeared are therefore, although highly selective, also of more than usual importance if we are to obtain any adequate view of Vietnamese theological endeavors.

3.1.4. Theological Reflection in Journals and Periodicals 1
(See also Journals and Periodicals 2, below).

During the 1940s more than 20 Catholic magazines were being published, but only in the late 1950s do we see periodicals that provide a wider range of writing that includes both theological and contextual elements. Theology in these periodicals was now stimulated and shaped by the social, political and economic realities of Vietnam and especially by the conflicts after 1954. Within such a context, it is very often the socio-theological reflection of those seeking to act according to their faith in the issues and turmoils of their society rather than of those studying established doctrines or wishing to construct any 'systematic' theology. Their commitment of life and actions must therefore be studied along with their writings. Many journals which included Catholic reflection became in this period vehicles for a growing awareness of Vietnamese Christian identity, for criticism of the Church's role within a colonial and puppet state, as well as for the development of a Vietnamese theology.

Dating from the French colonial period, one of the earliest was the periodical **Mission,** edited by Pham Hân Quynh from 1952. (See 3.2.1.1.) This advocated the development of an indigenous Catholicism which would be Vietnamese in leadership, in language and liturgy, imagery and writing, as well as in its music, its theology and philosophy. Such a church would be able to live in and for Vietnamese society, instead of aping the European churches, Quynh and his colleagues affirmed in numbers of diverse articles. But this, they thought, would require changes to the hierarchy, to the Mass, and most of all to the attitudes of clergy and faithful, so that Vietnamese Catholics might fully live in Vietnamese society.

The weekly magazine **Sông Dao** (Living the faith), Saigon, 1962-1966, was initiated by Nguyên Dình Dâu and Nguyên Duc Phong with the collaboration of a number of Catholic intellectuals such as Lý Chánh Trung, Nguyên Vãn Trung, Trân Vãn Toan, and Nguyên Thi Oanh. A number of priests, including Nguyên Ngoc Lan, Truòng Bá Cân and Trân Viêt Tho, also collaborated. In the light of the Gospel and the requirements of Christian faith, especially in the light of the second Vatican Council, *Sông Dao* consistently raised issues concerning the role of the Catholic Church in the social and political situation of South Vietnam in the midst of war. Although subject to suspicion from both church and government, its writers addressed the growing inequalities between poor and rich in South Vietnamese society. They therefore called upon the Church and Catholic believers to take up the concerns of the poorest. Because of the escalating deaths of Vietnamese and the destruction of Vietnamese moral values in the war, they also advocated the firm choice and action of Catholic believers to work along with those of other faiths for a peace which both ends war and creates a new order of justice.

Dât Nuóc (Country), Saigon 1967 - 1970, was initiated by a Catholic writer, Thê Nguyên, with a group of writers and teachers including a number of Catholics. *Dât Nuóc* was not a specifically religious magazine, nor was it produced primarily for Christian readers. However, many Catholic writers contributed articles on subjects such as "Religion pursued by politics" (Nguyên Vān Trung, February 1969), "Catholic Questions Raised to the Nation", "The National Question Raised for Catholics" (Nguyên Tý Lôc), and "Two Images of the Church in Vietnam" (Lý Chánh Trung). Such articles continued to profoundly question the role of Catholics and the Church in face of the problems of the nation, critically placing the Church's life and theology in historical context. "Maybe during these three centuries," wrote Lý Chánh Trung, "we took the wrong way. We helped the poor while eating together with the rich. We loved our nation while standing by the enemies of our country. We gave but never sacrificed ..."

Chon (Choice), Saigon, 1970-1975, was directed by Fr Truòng Bá Cân and Fr Vu Xuân Hiêu, and was a thematic collection of documents published irregularly. The focus for *Chon* was more upon the internal problems of the Catholic Church, but set in the context of the realities of the country and the world. Among the themes for particular issues were: "The Material Problems of Young Laborers ..." (Nos 1, 2, 3); "Peace for the Fatherland" (No 5); "South American Catholic Church on the Liberation Way" (No 6); "Church and Communism" (No 7); "Church and Labor" (No 8); "The Church and New Problems" (Nos 11, 12); "Justice in the world" (No 18); "Propagating Faith Yesterday and Today" (No 20); and "Catholicism and Socialism' (No 21). The discussion of these Church-world issues presented a new and progressive orientation for Christians in Vietnam and called for a change in Vietnamese Catholic theology and orientation.

Tin Mùng Hôm Nay (Gospel today), Saigon 1974-1975, was published (in Roneotype) by Catholic labor and student Chaplains, including Huênh Công Minh, Phan Khac Tù, Nguyên Nghi, Nguyên Vān Bình, Bui Thoang Giao, Truòng Bá Cân and Trân Thê Luân. Its purpose was to offer "documents and news to help Christians reflecting, acting and participating in the changes of the nation, according to the demand of love." For this it drew on the Gospel - with regular Biblical studies - and on the teachings of Vatican II, in the light of the revolutionary realities in the world and in Vietnam. Articles therefore interpreted the Christian faith in response to concrete social, political and environmental problems, and to human rights issues such as the exploitation and repression of labourers in a textile factory or the arrest and torture of dissidents by the Thiêu Government. In each case the problem is raised here for reflection very concretely.

Amongst other periodicals including theological reflection were **Nhip Câu** (Bridge), **Dùng dây** (Uprising) and **Chính Nghia** (Right Cause) - (See also below, Theological Reflection in Journals and Periodicals 2).

Typical of their approach are the words of Hô Výong in *Nhip Câu* (Bridge, 1969): "Jesus was not involved in directly political activity and had no temporal ambition. He built the Church with poor workers. But he mourned for the fate of his people and it was first of all to them that he gave the grace of salvation. ... The mature churches of the west have a well-marked national character and link their destiny to that of their country ... [and] the western missionaries came to convert us without forgetting their national interests. Why should I, a Vietnamese Catholic, have to sacrifice my country and live on its margin if I want to defend my faith? ... Our compatriots must try to return to the heart of the nation and join our Lord from there."

Similar reflections appeared in the statement by Nguyên Tu Lôc in *Dât Nuóc* (Homeland, 1968), that Vietnamese Catholicism had traditionally relied upon "the colonial power for its existence and development, and aped western religion ... not only were Vietnamese Catholics used for inadmissable ends by colonialism but they were deviated by Christianity itself, which, mistaken in its religious essence, is unable to blossom in spirit."

Nhip Câu also carried articles critical of Church dignitaries living in "islets of abundance amidst an ocean of hungry and wretched people" and called on them to leave aside "the power and prosperity of a self-interested Church" for "the gospel of a church returning to the heart of the nation and the working people."

This is a "profound change for the church and not a purely formal transformation" it declares. Otherwise the "Good News would risk being only a false news, offering neither redemption nor salvation. ..." (*Nhip Câu*, No. 3, Aug., 1969.)

Articles in *Dúng dây* (Uprising) sometimes reflected further on the nature of the church and its work if it was to be thus changed. The "true Catholic," wrote one author, must be the "tiny seed sprouting in the national soil to become the eternally flourishing tree of love, the grain of salt giving poignancy to the love binding people of the same country." (*Dúng dây*, No. 71, 4 July, 1975) Rather than a 'fortress" or 'castle' therefore, the church is to be an open 'way' of love in the community. (See Nguyên Ngoc Lan 4.3.10.)

The theological and pastoral review *Sacerdos*, was also edited by a group of priests in Saigon during the 1960s and early 1970s, concentrating upon more traditional concerns for Catholic clergy and people. Few references were included to the current sociopolitical context, or to critical rethinking of the faith.

Selected References

Earlier Christian Student periodicals include *Articles du Journal L'Avenue du Tonkin* (1923-), *L'Évangile en Indochine Française* (1923-), *Viêt Nam Thanh Niên Tap Chí* (1922-1924), *Annamites, Au Travail!* (1926-).

Articles (1952-1975) in *Mission, Nhip Câu* (Bridge), *Dât Nuóc* (Homeland), *Dùng dây* (Uprising), *Chính Nghia* (Right Cause), *Tin Mùng Hôm Nay* (Gospel Today), *Sông Dao* (Living the Faith), *Dói Dien* (Face to Face), *Chon* (Choice).

"Catholics and the National Movement." *Vietnamese Studies* 53, Special Issue (1977).

Cau, F. et al. "Công Bình Trên Thê Gian" (Justice in the world). Trans. and Notes on the Document of the Synod of Bishops, Rome, 1971. Privately Printed ca. 1972.

Nguyên Tý Lôc. "The National Problem as it Appears to Catholics," *Dât Nuóc*, Dec. 8 (1968).

Vu Xuân Ky. "Why Join the Revolution?" *Chính Nghia*, 2 Sept. (1976).

Výong. "Going back to National Roots". *Nhip Câu* 2 (1969).

3.2 The Writers and Doers of Theology
In the years 1954-1975, a wide spectrum of Catholic lay people, scholars and clergy came to write and act on behalf of movements which they saw to be faithful to the church, patriotic to the nation or laying foundations for peace. Others were most concerned to re-interpret scripture or tradition in ways which recognized new theological insights, such as those of Vatican II, along with creative sources in Vietnamese tradition and the social realities of their people amid protracted conflicts. Theological and ideological positions were similarly most diverse and ranged from those of 'traditional French Catholicism' through many gradations to ardent and socialist nationalism. The periodicals published in both the North and the South before 1975 show this diversity and it is to be expected that most contextual theological thought is found in writers who share some form of nationalist vision for both church and country. That many of them also understood this to require a more just and egalitarian society was inevitable in a post-colonial society which was made the battle-zone between capitalism and communism. It is important however to recognize that those doing theology now included not only theological teachers or bishops, but also Catholic intellectuals, social activists, both men and women religious and parish priests, journalists and teachers, student or worker leaders, and workers for peace and inter-faith co-operation.

Among the many writers in theology as an academic discipline in the twenty years before 1975, few ventured beyond the presentation of traditional theological teachings or ventured to relate these to the history and experience of Vietnamese. Those who did so, at least in part, included: Diên Phong, a layman influenced by John Wu and a writer of Christian reflection on Buddhism; and the philosopher and prolific writer Thiên Phong Buu Duong op, who contributed to the development of "personalist" philosophy in Vietnam. Much contextual thought and life are however found in the movements of Catholic intellectuals, students, lay people and priests.

3.2.1. Catholic Intellectuals and Activist Theologians
In the 1950s and 1960s, many Catholic intellectuals and writers, both in the North and in the South, were being influenced not only

Contextual Theology in Vietnam 1800-2000

by major political conflicts and movements and the impact of continuing armed conflict, but also by nationalist writings and movements in which Catholics were playing leading roles. Diverse and often conflicting currents of thought within movements for peace and for justice also contributed to the theological reflection and action of well-educated Catholics. Many documents are extant from the period 1954-1975 in which groups of Catholic intellectuals advocated specific policies for peace with justice and for genuine democracy. Other influences included such cultural reforms as the use by Pham Dình in *Văn Dàn* (Literary tribune) of contemporary Vietnamese language and style; the innovations of Fr Ngo Duy Linh in music and dramatic art; the activities of such "literary" associations as *Tinh-Viêt Văn-Doàn*. Catholic journals such as *Nhip Câu, Dât Nuóc, Chính Nghia, Dùng Dây, Sông Dao* and *Mission* were often both the stimulus and vehicle for Catholic theologians and intellectuals committed to peace-making and egalitarianism. (See 3.1.4. and 4.2.)

Spokespersons for groups of Catholic students and younger intellectuals who shared these concerns in the 1960s included: Chân Tín, Nguyên Ngoc Lan, Huênh Công Minh, Nguyên Duy Trinh and Trân Kim Giám.

A small selection of individual figures would include the following:

3.2.1.1. Pham Hân Quynh (fl. 1950)

Pham Hân Quynh was a diocesan priest in Hai Phong and returned to North Vietnam from France (1954). He became a strong critic, through for example the journal *Mission*, of the Vietnamese church as being merely the French - Spanish, or Canadian - church abroad. This was because of the very small number of Vietnamese bishops and the fact that "all key posts and functions are in the hands of foreign missionaries." But it is also true because "the style of speech and writings of the church, its music, its theology and philosophy are those of a foreign country. The fact is" he concludes, "that the Vietnamese Catholics are not living amid the Vietnamese society"(1952).

3.2.1.2. Nguyên Văn Trung (fl. 1955)

Nguyên Văn Trung was a professor in Saigon University's Faculty of Letters who was also concerned at the gap between the life of Vietnamese Catholics and that of the surrounding population from which they appeared alienated. This, he says, was largely caused by the ghetto-like forms of church activity as well as by unthinking submission to, and imitation of, French traditions of Christianity. "Our form of worship, our art, our religious practices" he wrote, "have turned us into strangers ... when a Vietnamese becomes a convert he has to ... abandon his native cultural heritage, with which he may assert his Vietnamese identity. ... In the end, the Catholics have had to live as foreigners amid their countrymen [sic]"(1958).

3.2.1.3. Nguyên Khac Chính (b.1922)

Nguyên Khac Chính graduated from Sorbonne Law School in Paris, practised as an attorney-at-law at the Saigon Superior Court, and was a former member of the National Party. He was imprisoned in a re-education camp from 1975 until 1992, and has since acted as Minister of Information of the GFVN (Government of Free Vietnam). Despite frequent illness, he has continued to be a prolific Catholic writer and a member of PEN and of the International Writers Association (IWA) which assisted in his release. He is the author of 19 novels as well as of plays and poetry, which are imbued with Christian nationalism, and also of political articles which strongly advocate a free and democratic Vietnam.

3.2.1.4. The **Hành Trình** (Journey) group of Catholic Intellectuals, was particularly concerned at the deepening conflict in the early 1960s, and addressed intellectuals overseas on the need for a non-communist and democratic movement, "not aligned with any power bloc, [and] in which ... Communists and non-communists can co-operate to build a progressive society according to the ideals of justice and freedom." Their aims and activities were closely parallel to other movements which insisted that "a third way" between orthodox Communism and Capitalism - and their military/political policies - was possible, while also recognizing that non-Communists frequently neglect social justice.

Groups of Catholic priests also shared deeply these concerns, writing on the sufferings of their people, calling for more sustained efforts for peace, and condemning the continued escalation of conflict and arms production. See especially the *Manifesto* of eleven Vietnamese priests of January 1966 (Mimeo'd).

3.2.1.5. Parallel groups in Europe included *Fraternité Vietnam* - originally *Communauté Vietnamienne*, formed in Paris 1963. Activities included publications, conferences and advocacy programs (both in France and Vietnam) for peace and independence, for humanitarian aid and organizational support. Among its leaders was Fr Nguyên Dình Thi, who was committed to the collaboration of Christians and revolutionaries, and to the realization of "all that Jesus preached ... in a concrete political context." By 1970 the Fraternité's publications included translations - in English and French - of theological letters such as those by Bao Tinh Vuong Dình Bích (see 4.3.7.), the newspaper *Mien Nam Di Toi* (The South Moves Forward), and with co-publisher, *Gong Giao va Dan Toc* (Catholics and the Nation - see 4.2.3. below), along with the bi-monthly bulletin *Vietnam Info*. In the 1960s and early 1970s the *Vietnam Solidarieta*, based in Bologna and led by Onesta Capene and her colleagues, worked closely with the *Fraternité Vietnam* and also groups in Vietnam, to disseminate letters and theological reflections.

3.2.1.6. Buddhist-Catholic Co-operation. By 1964 Buddhist and Catholic intellectuals and activists were co-operating, despite the tensions of the Diêm years, on the common basis of "their desire for peace and national independence," and their shared vision of a fully democratic and equitable society in Vietnam. This grew rapidly in the early 1960s through collaboration in education programs and demonstrations: for the promotion of peace, and in campaigns against corruption and for more democratic processes in government. Vietnamese Catholic Action from 1963 fostered communication and co-operation between younger Buddhist and Catholic leaders: Catholic "presence" being close, in understanding, to Buddhist "engagement," and two years later acknowledged Communist criticisms of a church heedless of injustice. An array of peace and reform movements such as that of Catholiques pour

Paix and the Committee for the Union of Vietnamese Catholics (see 3.1.1, 4.2.3) were active in these causes, and such dialogue also often included Marxists and anti-Marxists. Inter-faith cooperation also brought insight into each other's faith traditions and this is found both in many Christian writings in the journals mentioned above (3.1.4.), and in longer studies (see 4.3.6.), as well as in the writings of eminent Buddhists such as Thích Nhât Hanh and Thích Minh Châu, among many others.

Selected References

Beyond Aid and Development. Future of the Missionary Enterprise 18. Rome: IDOC, 1976.

Boudarel, Georges. "Intellectual Dissidence in the 1950s: the Nhân Văn Giai Phâm Affair." *Vietnam Forum* 13 (1991).

"Catholics and the National Movement." *Vietnamese Studies* 53, Special Issue (1977).

Gheddo, Piero. *Vietnam Christiani e communisti*. Torino: Editrice internat. 1976.

IDOC Newsletter (Rome from 1965).

Informations Catholiques Internationales 188 (1952).

Lê Tiên Giang. *Công giáo Kháng chiên Nam bô 1945-54* (The Catholic Resistants in South Vietnam 1945-1954). Paris: Công giáo Dân Tôc, 1980.

Monteunis, Gustave. *Mouvement des Catholiques pour la Paix au Sud-Vietnam, Étudiants et Lycéens en Prison*. Saigon: n.p., 1972.

Nguyên Ngoc Ngai, Anselme, et al. *Bouddhisme et Christianisme. Temoignages* (Paris) 20 (1949).

Nhân Dinh I. Nam-Son, Saigon (1958).

North-Vietnam's Undisciplined Intellectuals. S.l.: s.n, COLLA, 1959.

Vietnam, Vietnam. No.1, edited by Lê Văn Hao (July 1965.)

Thích Minh Châu. *Nhung loi dây cua Duc Phât vê Hoa Binh hoa hop va giá tri con nguòi* (Some teachings of Lord Buddha on peace and harmony and human dignity). Bilingual. HCMV: Dharma Executive Council, 1984.

Thích Nhât Hanh. *Vietnam - Lotus in a Sea of Fire*. London: SCM Press, 1967.

—. *Living Buddha, Living Christ*. New York: Riverhead Books, 1995.

3.2.2. Peace-makers and Patriots
3.2.2.1 Vu Xuân Ky (b.1886)

Ordained in 1921, Vu Xuân Ky ministered at An Lôc in the northern Nam Dinh province, and developed a strong nationalist and revolutionary commitment. For him there was a unique role for Catholics in working for social change, although this also required the co-operation of government holding similar aims. He came to work closely with the Catholic Liaison Committee of which he was later president.

Vu Xuân Ky had established many communities of Catholic families prior to 1945, based on the faith "that the light of the Gospel would diminish social injustice, crime and suffering." Yet after some years he came to feel that such activities by the faithful only, were far too limited in effect on the wider community and that "social life around me had not changed at all." Reflecting on this later he wrote of hopes and struggles for a just society in the years following, including articles on the subject "why join the revolution?" To this his answer was: "I began to realise that the humanity, the aspirations and the truth of religion could only be achieved with the support of a progressive political regime." He thus posited a close alliance between church and state not only in order to achieve social justice but also to establish the human reality of religious truth.

3.2.2.2. Hô Thành Biên, John-Baptiste, 1890 -1976.

Hô Thành Biên was ordained in 1921, at Sa Keo, in Soc Trang province, served as priest both in the South and the North (1954-1975), as well as in Pnom Penh. He also participated in the Sa Keo anti-colonial revolt for which he was arrested by the French. He later organized groups of patriotic/nationalist Catholics and later again represented them in the National Assembly (*Liên Viêt Tinh*). He became Vice-President of the Assembly, President of the National Catholic Liaison Committee and was prominent in international socialist meetings. With Vu Xuân Ky he founded the paper *For God and Country,* writing on such theological themes as "The Gospel and National Independence and Liberation," "God and the Motherland," "Socialism and Freedom of Religion" and "Religious Practice and Production".

In his last statements (Hanoi, 30th August 1973) Hô Thành Biên affirmed that "I have tried to lead our Catholic community along the path charted by the Gospel and our Lord Jesus Christ: to align ourselves with the nation and to ensure a decent material standard of living for everybody, especially the workers."

3.2.2.3. Hoàng Quỳnh

Following ministries in North Vietnam, Hoàng Quynh became, in the late 1950s, spokesman for many refugees from the North, yet combined a strongly anti-communist approach with "the revolutionary impetus for social justice in favour of the most miserable classes." He was a Christian socialist committed to work for radical agrarian reform, the abolition of caste and class privileges, for the establishment of trade unions and co-operatives and for the nationalization of the sources of production. For these ends he would, however accept no dialogue with Communist or 'pro-Communist' groups. In 1964 Hoàng Quỳnh founded the Catholic Committee for the Struggle - to counter anti-Catholic discrimination - which in 1965 became the politically active *Dai Doàn Kêt (*Movement for greater solidarity). In this the aims were to achieve greater social justice, while still opposing Communism. In co-operation with Buddhist colleagues and those of other faiths, he then founded the Front for Citizens of all Faiths to oppose the regime's coercive policies and to work for a non-military government. After 1968 he returned to parish ministry amongst the poor in the slums of Saigon, while still co-operating with Buddhist bonzes who were politically active.

He also called for the full commitment of Catholics, working with others, to obtain true peace "since brotherhood is the raison d'être of Christianity"; and for the co-operation of nationalists and those of different faiths in establishing "a juridically-based government supported by the people ... [and] to contribute to the creation and safeguard of the peace."

(For Refs. see below.)

3.2.3. Parish Priests and Lay People

Others active in nationalist and 'patriotic' movements, or in association with the Liaison Committee in the 1960s and 1970s, include many priests engaged in parish ministries. Among these were the Frs Dinh Thi Thuc, Nguyên Duy Trinh, Nguyên Thái Bá, Doàn Thuc Su, Võ Thành Trinh and Trân Kim Giám. Only occasional or fragmentary writings appear to be extant from many such priests, or from laymen such as Lý Thiên Kim, or the journalist Trân Huu Thanh (cssr), who wrote and worked to oppose corruption and injustice under the Thiêu regime. These were published in such journals as *Nhip Câu, Chính Nghia, Chon, Mission, and Chính Nghia,* mentioned above (3.1.4.), in newspapers or in mimeographed form.

Typical of the thought and commitment of many such Catholics is that of Doàn Thuc Su, who had continued work in the North and later reported on the development of the churches there. This he described as being "a new style with the best way of living and the most reasonable faith nearest the truth," for he sees the red vestments of clergy symbolizing "the blood of patriotic martyrs fallen" in the struggle for the end of warfare and injustice. For him it symbolizes also the life "of many patriotic Catholics who know how to reconcile love of their country with their faith." Nguyên Duy Trinh also declared before his death that to "worship the Lord, love my country and peace" is "to realise one of the Lord's commandments." He and others staunchly supported the work of the Catholic Liaison Committee as "an originator of new life" (Trân Kim Giám) and "a source of light, a grain of salt, a yeast ... bringing out all the best in each Vietnamese Catholic" (Lý Thiên Kim). (See also 3.2.2.) Others deplored the fact that there has been "little study in depth of Vietnamese culture because [we] have never acknowledged the value of the culture." To become a Christian has meant "to stop being Vietnamese." Other writers on Church and society issues in the 1950s and 1960s, included Gérard Gagnon cssr (Dalat), Vu Công (Saigon), Pham Dình Khiêm (Saigon), Pham Châu Diên (Saigon), Tâm Ngoc cssr (Dalat) and Thanh Lao Công (Saigon).

However these positions were expressed, or later modified, they still represent a theological wrestling with the concrete life-situation of their people and with the present implications of the life and deeds of Jesus Christ. There was also often a passionate conviction that the church and its theology must now break decisively free from colonial forms of thought, practice and social control.

Selected References (3.2.2, 3.2.3)

Chính Nghĩa (Justice) 12.2. (1976), 10.3. (1977), 17.3. (1977), et seq.

Công giáo và Dân tôc (Catholicism and nation) 20.3. (1976).

Hô Thành Biên "Ultima Verba." *Chính Nghĩa,* 9 Sept. (1976).

Hoàng Quynh. "An Appeal to Vietnamese Christians." *Kipa-Konzil,* Communiqué of May 5th, 1967.

Gheddo, Piero. *The Cross and the Bo-Tree: Catholics and Buddhists in Vietnam.* Trans. by Charles Underhill Quinn. New York: Sheed and Ward, 1970.

Lê Minh Dúc. *Les Catholiques en République Démocratique du Vietnam.* Hanoi: Éditions en langues étrangères, 1963.

Monteunis, Gustave. *Mouvement des Catholiques pour la Paix au Sud-Vietnam, Étudiants et Lycéens en Prison.* Saigon: 1972.

Nguyên Khac Viên. *The Catholics and the National Movement.* Hanoi: Xunhasaba, 1978. See also "Catholics and the National Movement." *Vietnamese Studies* 53, Special Issue (1977).

Nguyên Văn Bình. "Homage to the Reverend Father Hô Thành Biên." *La Vie Catholique,* 22.8 (1976).

Vu Xuân Ky . "Why Join the Revolution?" *Chính Nghĩa,* 2 Sept. (1976).

3.2.4. Cultural, Historical and Church Historical Studies 1

Many articles appeared in such journals as the *Bulletin de l'École Francaise d'Extrême-Orient (BEFEO)* , and the *Bulletin de la Société des Études Indochinoises (BSEI),* taking further the researches of scholars like Truòng Vinh Ký, Lê Thành Khôi, Phan Phát Huôn, L. Cadière and André Migot. Authors included: Maurice Durand on Alexandre de Rhodes (*BSEI* 32, 1957), Võ Long Tê on the Catholic contribution to early Vietnamese narrative poetry (*BSEI* 42, 1967) and on Hàn Mac Tu (see 2.1.2 above), Jean Pilliozat reviewing Võ Duc Hanh's work on Catholicism and the French (*BEFEO* 58,1971), and Nguyên Huu Dang on Christianity and Colonialism (*BEFEO* 59, 1972).

Sr Tô Thi Ánh produced her monograph study of Confucianism, Taoism and Buddhism under the headings of The Cult of Harmony, The Cult of the Person, and Conflict or Harmony (1975). This study would later be extended by the work of such scholars as Joseph Huu Lai (4.4.4.2.), Hoàng Si Quý (4.3.6.), Pierre Nguyên Vãn Tôt (Ref. under 4.4.4.2.), Kim Dinh (4.4.4.2.) and Trân Thiên Câm (4.3.11.).

Writings in the church history of Vietnam by Vietnamese in this period include among many others, those of Hông Lam (1944); the editor, activist, poet and historian Pham Dình Khiêm (fl. 1955); Trân Minh Triêt, writing on the history of persecution in Vietnam (1955); Nguyên Huu Trong who wrote extensively upon the history of Vietnamese clergy (1959); and Dô Quang Chính, concerning de Rhodes and early Jesuits in Vietnam.

Two historical writers should be further noticed for the theological dimensions of their narratives. Fr Trân Minh Triêt has written both in monographs and articles on the church history of Vietnam, and in particular on the period since 1945. He is careful in this to study a range of letters and documents which record the varying roles of the bishops, the Vatican and clergy during the following 30 years of warfare. Actions of government and church since 1954 are outlined, along with the new roles required now of the church in Vietnam. These are to become 'vietnamized' he believes, to return to the Gospel of Jesus Christ which is indeed good news to the poor. Catholics in particular are now offered the vocation to participate with brother and sister Vietnamese in the formation of new men and women in a new society.

Jean Maïs mep was Bishop in Huê and analyzes the ways in which the history of Christianity in Vietnam since the 1930s has been rewritten by the revolutionary government since 1975, using "the three languages of authority" (toleration, legislation, pragmatism). He outlines both the repressions which this has brought and also the diverse movements of response by the church in following years. Acknowledging the gaps between the position of the hierarchy, the clergy and the faithful, and within each of these groups, he presents the dilemmas being faced by all Christians regarding the acceptance or rejection of socialism as a desired goal, or as it is interpreted by government. Only free dialogue between all groupings, he believes, will offer the way forward for Vietnam.

Selected References

Maïs, Jean. *Church-State Relations in Vietnam*. Brussels, PMV Dossier 4, 1985.

—. "Les Droits de L'homme sont la Loi de Dieu." *Echos de la Rue du Bac (1986).*

—. "Des voix Prophétiques au Vietnam." *Spiritus* 33 (1992).

Nguyên Huu Trong. *Le Clergé National dans la Fondation de l'Église au Vietnam. Les Origines du Clergé Vietnamien.* Saigon: Tinh Viêt, 1959.

"Note sur les chrétiens montagnards du Nord-Vietnam." *Eglises d'Asie. Dossiers et documents 2* (1993).

Pham Dình Khiêm. "La Bibliothèque de la Conference Episcopale du Vietnam." *Études Interdisciplinaires sur le Vietnam* 1.2 (1974).

Tô Thi Ánh. *Eastern and Western Cultural Values, Conflict or Harmony?* Manila: East Asia Pastoral Institute, 1975.

Trân Anh Dung. *Sõ thao thý muc Công giáo Viêt Nam* ("L'Église catholique au Vietnam: bibliographie sommaire en langue vietnamienne"[The Catholic Church in Vietnam: brief bibliography of sources in Vietnamese]). Paris: Trân Anh Dung, c1992.

Trân Minh Triêt. *Histoire des Persecutions au Vietnam*. Paris: Thiêu Dung, 1955.

Trân Minh Triêt. *Catholics in the History of Vietnam*. Rome: Editrice Coines, 1976. (Also in Italian and French editions).

Truòng Bá Cân, Lê Văn Khuê and Nguyên Nghi. *Bibliography of Books, Documents and Articles on Catholic Christianity in Vietnam, Held in Vietnam.*

4 Theological Understanding and Movements to 2000
4.1 Overview

In the period since 1975, the "low-key and informal" work of many movements formed in the previous decades, continued in both North and South, in spite of continuing restrictions upon theological teaching, writing and publishing. Principal concerns have ranged from scholarly study of theology of the "Three Fathers" to critical reflections amid warfare or imprisonment; from nationalist theologies of society and culture to a mysticism which through the "prism of the heart" comes to know the Way. Despite also continuing tensions within the Church, and between "patriotic" Catholics and the Vatican, many Catholic movements of renewal, dialogue and Christian "publication" flourished, albeit informally and unpublicized, though only two Catholic periodicals have been permitted to publish (see 4.2.). In addition, from experiences in prison and labor camp have come a series of meditations (see 4.3.10. and 4.4.1.); from the Catholic hierarchy a series of pastoral statements in response to current circumstances (see 4.4.2.); and from priests, bishops and lay people have come homilies, statements, articles and reflections upon the present forms of Christian faith and life. Scholars have published full studies of Vietnamese religious tradition, or of Vietnam's church history and theology. (See for example 4.4.4.2.) Not least in importance here is the almost unchartable expanse of semi-underground writing and publishing which has come largely from those fully trained for priesthood but prevented from formally exercising such ministry. (See for example 4.3.3, 4.3.17, and also 3.2.1.)

Vietnamese theology in this period has been increasingly stimulated by fuller study of the documents of the Second Vatican Council - now fully translated by the Faculty of Theology of the St Pius X Pontifical College, Dalat - and more recently the Asian Synod of Bishops (1998). But equally important for a number of Vietnamese has been the work of theologians and activists in other countries of the Asian region. This is seen not only in the writings of individual Vietnamese bishops, and also theologians like Trân Thiên Câm (4.3.11.), Mai Thành (4.3.8.), or Hoàng Gia Khánh (4.3.17), but also in journal translations of Asian theological writings and in the seminar and publishing programs of the Committee for the Union of Vietnamese Catholics. And although very few Christian writings can as yet be formally published in Vietnam, restrictions have been relaxed in the last five years to allow more private printings and seminary libraries are able to accession a number of volumes from overseas. Considerable numbers of both journals and monographs of Vietnamese Christian writing are being published outside Vietnam, especially in the USA, and a number of web-sites, notably that of Vietnamese theologians teaching in Taiwan, provide useful examples. (See 4.4.4.1.)

Selected References

An Phong. "Catholicism in Vietnam and Catholic Reintegration into the National Community." *Vietnam Courier* 66 (1977).

"Chrétiens au Vietnam" et seq. *Missi* 528 (1991).

Digan, Parig. *Churches in Contestation. Asian Christian Social Protest*. Maryknoll, NY: Orbis Books, 1984.

Hông N'Guyên, Jiao. "La formation à la vie religieuse au Vietnam aujourd'hui." *Eglises d'Asie* 153 (1993).

Huênh Quang Sanh, Stéphane. "Benedictine Monasticism in Vietnam and Inculturation." *A.I.M. Bulletin* 70 (2000).

Lange, Claude. "La Situation de l'église au Vietnam." *Echos de la Rue du Bac*, Series of 3 articles, 180-182, (1987).

Nguyên, An. "The role of the laity in the development and expansion of the church in Vietnam under the Communist regime from 1975 to 1989." STL Thesis, Jesuit School of Theology at Berkeley, 1998.

Nguyên Van Tuyên, Antoine. *La nouvelle évangélisation de l'Eglise du Vietnam: Face au problème du développement dans la perspective du Synode des Eveques pour l'Asie*. Romae: Pontificia Universitas Sanctae Crucis, 2000.

Trân Anh Dung. *Sõ thao thý muc Công giáo Viêt Nam* (The Catholic Church in Vietnam - a brief bibliography of sources).

Trân Thiên Câm. "Vietnam Church since April 30th 1975." *L'Hebdomadaire Catholique et Nation* 19.6. (1997)

Truòng Bá Cân, Lê Văn Khuê & Nguyên Nghi. *Bibliography of books, Documents and Articles on Catholic Christianity in Vietnam, Held in Vietnam*.

4.2 Theological Reflection in Journals and Periodicals 2

(See also Theological Reflection in Journals and Periodicals 1, above.)

4.2.1. For writers in **Chính Nghia** (Right Cause) in the early and later 1970s, the "open 'way' of love in the community" for the

Church meant that "as we want reconciliation with the workers, we must 'lower' ourselves to live their lives, to reconcile ourselves with the revolutionaries [and] revolutionize our own lives ... only those who dare truly to live the Christian faith can effectively reconcile themselves with the national revolution ..." In the years immediately following 1975 others, including both priests and lay people in the North, would write on the changes in attitude and involvement of Catholics in the Christian witness and reflection of previous decades: Fr Dinh Thi Thuc questioned whether the recommendations of church authorities have been useful for the country and the people ... or should one "show one's independence of thought ... and choose the path charted by the patriots?"; Fr Nguyên Thái Bá had been "happy to remain in the North ... on this soil of the Gospel, so as to contribute to building a Catholic congregation attached to the nation and freed from the vestiges of colonialism ..."

Chính Nghia also reported the "three theological lessons" from the previous 17 years, as seen by an enlarged conference of more than 100 delegates in April 1971: "By its temporal activities, the Church is in close touch with people and society ... [as] Christ stood by the side of the exploited and oppressed ... ; socialism ... creates the conditions enabling Catholics to assert the fundamental spirit of Christ; all Vietnamese Catholics who are anxious to fulfil their duty toward Christ and the Fatherland must unite with the entire people" to fight aggression and bring independence and prosperity." The theological conference of the Catholic Liaison Committee in 1976 called for, amongst other things, a "return to the national roots," just as "Jesus mourned for the fate of his people"; and a "return to the spirit of the Gospel" which affirms that the kingdom of God includes as well as the future life, life here below in nation and society. (*Chính Nghia* , Jan.10, 1977.)

Other writers outlined the new sources for theological reflection and action which had come from recent experience, or in their articles they sometimes encapsulated a wholistic faith and vision. Fr Võ Thành Trình summarized the experience and learnings of many Catholics in the North, who have now "a storehouse of precious theoretical knowledge concerning the relationship between theology and the reality of a new society ... [and] a whole system of organization and experience of social and political activities based on the worship of the Lord and on patriotism [with] ... completely new conventions on religious practices ..." The primitive Gospel, social transformation and the perfecting of people, are held together by Fr Vuong Dình Ái: "... there exists in Vietnam" he wrote (*Chính Nghia*, 7 April, 1977) a Catholicism which returns to the spirit of the Gospel, fights against social injustices, stresses the role of the workers and puts itself at their service ... to transform society and to liberate it from the exploitation of man by man in order to pave the way for the emergence of a society in which mutual assistance and encouragement make it possible to advance to perfection."

4.2.2. Đôi Diên (Face to Face), Saigon 1969-1978. Directed by the priests Chan Tín, Nguyên Ngoc Lan and Nguyên Nghi, this was forbidden and confiscated by the Saigon government, but continued to appear under different names, namely *Đôi Diên, Dông Duong, Dông Dao* and *Dùng Dây*. Inspired by the Vatican II Council, *Dôi Diên* had both 'secular' and Christian readership, advocating ecumenical co-operation with those of other faiths, and participation in people's response to the human, political, economic and social realities of Vietnam. Many articles reflected on the role of the Church in relation to nation, peace and social justice, in the light of the Gospel and in the Christian faith.

4.2.3. The magazine **Công giáo và Dân tôc** (Catholic and nation), has continued weekly publication in HCMV from July 1975 until now, and in a monthly edition also from 1994. *Công giáo và Dân tôc* is the organ of the City Catholic Union Committee, an organization that belongs to the United Front, and is one of the two Catholic magazines permitted by government. The other magazine, *Ngyòi Viêt Nam Công giáo* (The Catholic Vietnamese) is also an organ of the Catholic Union Committee on the national level, published in HCMV and edited now by Fr Truòng Bá Cân (formerly by Frs Huênh Công Minh and Vuong Dình Bích).

Công giáo và Dân tôc continues to share thought as to living the Christian faith in the realities of Vietnam. Its orientation is towards fostering a Christian understanding of socialism and of the policies of the Vietnamese government as the concrete way to realize the demands of the Gospel for society and people. Drawing on biblical teaching the magazine calls on Vietnamese Catholics to work for the building of God's kingdom in this world in which all are loved and respected, working with all those of good will whatever their faith or ideology.

4.2.4. Tuyên Tâp Thân Hoc (Theological Selection) began in the late 1980s as a collection of theological documents. From 1994 it was edited by Nguyên Nghi, Không Thành Ngoc, Hoàng Minh Thúc, Gia Trân and Trân Công Thach. The journal has been temporarily in recess since 1998.

In the Christmas issue of 1995, the introduction of Nguyên Nhý Quang presents the main goals of the journal: *"Theological Selections would wish to be a place of meeting for Christian faith which faces the realities of human life day - not however separated from the past of this land, but held in relation to world realities far and near: a place of searching effort to realize and respond. The Word has become male and female 'in the image and after the likeness of God' (Gen.1:26), and became flesh 'and dwelt among humankind' (John1:14). In becoming flesh the Word brings 'theology' directly into human life."* *Tuyên Tâp Thân Hoc* therefore searches for truth in human life, and for liberation in all efforts to satisfy human necessities, material and spiritual, "in the eating, the drinking, the clothing" and housing of all. The 12 issues of 1993 for example, contain papers which seek to newly portray the image of God in the human, not only through church teachings, but also through the resources of Vietnamese literature and mythology.

Selected References

   Articles (1975 - 2000) in the journals *Chính Nghia, Dôi Diên, Công giáo và Dân tôc, Ngýôi Viêt Nam Công giáo,* and *Tuyên Tâp Thân Hoc.*

   A Bibliography of Overseas Vietnamese Periodicals and Newspapers, 1975-1995 (Muc Luc Báo Chí Viêt Nam Hai Ngoai, 1975-1995). Compiled by Nguyên Hùng Cuòng and Nguyên Anh Tuân. Washington, DC: Southeast Asia Resource Action Center, 1997.

   Other periodicals and related publications to be recognized for research in this period include :

Nhà Chúa (Domus Dei - God's house) periodical series pre- 1975.

Hop Tuyên Thân Hoc (Anthology of theology) published by the Vietnamese Theological Association (Paris, San Diego, Vienna).

Nghiên Cùu Tôn Giáo (Research in religions) published by the Institute of Religious Studies, HCMV.

4.3 Theological Scholars, Leaders and Animateurs

4.3.1. Peter Nguyên Xuân Tín (ca.1918-)

Nguyên Xuân Tín has long been a brilliant theologian, a student of other faiths and a courageous innovator in contextual thought. In many writings he has, despite episcopal censure (later removed), explored new directions for Christian theology and catechetics, drawing on both the teachings of Vatican II and those of eastern faiths and philosophies. He has strongly criticized aspects of traditional Catholic theology which he considers often incomprehensible and advocated an alternative theology based on eastern wisdoms. This he has presented in new interpretations of Christology - studying the Apostles' Creed, the Ten Commandments and the Lord's Prayer; in a new pattern of catechetics; and in reflections upon contemporary (and personal) experience of ecclesial policies and authority along with "theological solutions" for such problems. He has also written a "theological memoir," and works on catechetics and metaphysics. His writings have had wide recognition, especially by other theologian priests in Vietnam, with many younger theologians acknowledging him as mentor.

Selected References (1980-1990)

Works by Nguyên Xuân Tín

Thân Hoc trong sa mù (Theology in a fog). Privately printed, n.d.

Kitô hoc siêu hình [hoc cái gì tôn tai] (Metaphysical/existential christology). 2 vols. Privately circulated, nd.

Ngýòi Kitô Huu là ai? (Who is a Christian?). Privately circulated, n.d.

Tôi biêt Dýoc nhung gì (What I know). Privately circulated, n.d..

4.3.2 Nguyên Vãn Bình, Archbishop (1910-1995)

Nguyên Vãn Bình studied in Saigon and Rome, becoming bishop of Can Tho on the Mekong plain. Appointed Archbishop of Saigon/HCMV in 1960, he was to become one of the most widely respected church leaders of recent decades. Since the early 1960s he exercised a prophetic and also conciliatory ministry in the midst of unceasing turmoils and conflict - both in nation and church. Prior to 1975 he took a clear position against state interference and oppression of any religious groups, and sought to moderate both government policies and Catholic or Buddhist politicization. He also sought to maintain separation of church and state and also the religious peace which had long reigned between Christians and Buddhists, and had a passionate concern for the health and well-being of all Vietnamese. At the time of great tensions between the pro-Catholic Diêm government and the larger Buddhist community, he declared in a pastoral letter that just as the Church at times had its limitations, so also should the State accept limitations. "We freely practise our religion in South Vietnam" he wrote. "Let us rejoice in this freedom. But let us not try to add to it exaggerated rights and priviliges. Let us not confuse the spread of the faith with the development of political influence or social prestige" (Sept. 1963).

After 1975 Nguyên Văn Bình continued to defend the Church's autonomy in "the field of divine things" and was deeply committed to supporting priests, and lay-people in numberless local tensions and confrontations. He affirmed the differences between Marxism and Christianity, but also maintained a position of dialogue and openness in many attempts to reach a modus vivendi with the Communist government. At the same time he initiated agricultural programs of re-orientation for priests and lay leaders to assist in the understanding and living of the faith in a Marxist milieu. In speeches, pastoral letters and other writings (in e.g. *Công Giáo và Dân Tôc*), he depicted faith and its witness in everyday life as the practice of "justice, love to one's neighbour and one's country," through the teaching and sacraments of a church that is "open to collaborate in a ... modest and very loving fashion with all those who are in the service of human beings" (*Being Christian Today*, 1978). He helped shape the open letter of the Vietnamese bishops in 1980 (see 4.4.2.) which laid the basis for co-operation between church and state in helping to rebuild a new Vietnamese society. His goal remained the development of a "devout people [who could] harmoniously contribute to national construction along with other people." In a later interview (1995) he assessed how far that had been possible and lamented the persistence of many restrictions on church activity which had not disappeared, not least upon the number of priests educated and ordained.

Selected References
Works by Nguyên Văn Bình

    Articles and pastoral letters (1960s and 1970s) in *Fides* (Rome), *La Vie Catholique* (Paris), *Échos de la Rue du Bac* (Paris), *La Documentation Catholique* (Paris). Post 1975, his articles also appeared in such periodicals as *Tripod* (Hong Kong), *Weltkirche* (Munich) and, by far the majority, in *Công giáo và Dân tôc* (HCMV) in Vietnamese. For a small selection, see below.

  "Two Years after Liberation." *Công giáo và Dân tôc* 96-97, (8.5.1977).
  "Catholic and Nation are One." *CGvDT* 158-159 (16.9.1978).
  "The Concrete Meaning of Retreat (work-camp)." *CGvDT* 165-166, (3.10.1978).
  "We Must Love our Country." *CGvDT* 508-509, (31.3.1985).
  "Twelve Years under the Socialist Regime." *CGvDT* 608, (19.04.1987).
  "Living in the society." *CGvDT* 681, (2.10.1988).
  "Serving in Favor of the Poor." *CGvDT* 706, (30.04.1989).
  "Make the Society Healthier." *CGvDT* 898, (14.03.1993).
  "Letter of Thanks and New Year's Sharing." *CGvDT* 995, (12.02.95).

Gheddo, Piero. *The Cross and the Bo-Tree: Catholics and Buddhists in Vietnam.*
Lange, Claude. "La Situation de l'Église au Vietnam." *Échos de la Rue du Bac.* Series of 3 articles, 180-182, (1987).
Trân Tam Tinh et al. *Being Christian Today in Vietnam.* (In French and English, includes 3 papers by Nguyên Văn Bình). Zurich: Second International Assembly for healing the Wounds of War, 1978.
Truòng Bá Cân. *Duc Tong Giam muc Phao lo Nguyên Van Binh.* HCMV, 1995.

4.3.3. Vũ Văn Thiên (1929-)

Following studies for the priesthood and ordination, Vu Văn Thiên worked in the 1960s with the Jorai people of the Vietnamese highlands. From this ministry grew his particular interest in Jorai culture and its story-tellers and religious story-singers. He was later laicised and until illness restricted his work in the mid-1990s, was Curator of the 'House of Tradition': the historical museum of the Catholic Church of Vietnam, HCMV. His writings include works in moral theology and collections of stories and poetry of the Jorai. In moral theology Vu Vãn Thiên interprets central concepts such as love and law on the basis of a thorough analysis of biblical texts. Drawing on his experience with tribal Montagnards and with a concern for the development of indigenous theology, he presents love - for God and man (sic) - as the one supreme law, liberating us from all other law. For Vu Vãn Thiên, the life and teaching of Jesus frees us to love more and more, although this always remains a "mystery of love." Here also we are freed to form a conscience for love and also to form a community of love.

Selected References
Works by Vu Vãn Thiên

Tiêng Jorai - Huênh Olê (Collection of brotherly sons and poems). Mimeo'd, 1969.

Lê Lụât Lýõng Tâm Tình Yêu (Law, conscience and love). HCMV: Uy Ban Doàn Kêt Công Giáo (Catholic Committee for Religion and Society), 1992.

4.3.4. Francis Xavier Nguyên Vãn Thuân, Archbishop (1927-)

Francis Xavier Nguyên Vãn Thuân was Bishop of Nha Trang in 1967, and appointed by Rome coadjutor of bishop of Saigon (1975). He was then arrested and imprisoned by the Vietnamese government until 1988, held in house arrest until 1991, and then expelled from Vietnam. He went to Rome to become Vice President of the Pontifical Council for Justice and Peace, and since 1998, has been its President. Although politically and theologically conservative, and not involved directly in the development of contextual Vietnamese theology, Vãn Thuân's writings contain many contextual elements, especially in the stories he recounts of relationships and events while confined in prison.

His books and articles are largely based on his prison experience which he confesses "enlarged" his heart and brought him to new experiences both of spiritual truth and of life with others, specifically the friendship of prison guards and fellow prisoners. While there he was able to smuggle out his writings to be published, the first of which was *The Road of Hope*. In this and following books the "road of hope" remains a central symbol: a road which is followed amid suffering, sustained by the Eucharist and dedicated to serving others. Vãn Thuân pictures such a road in his "ten rules of life," which include: living the present moment to the fullest; discerning between God and God's works; holding firmly to one secret: prayer; seeing in the Holy Eucharist the only power; carrying out a revolution by renewal in the Holy Spirit; speaking one language and wearing one uniform: charity. More recently he has become concerned for the future of humankind in Asia and the Pacific: the area surrounding the ocean which he names the Mare Nostrum of the Third Millennium. In this context he calls all faithful to discern the signs of the times and to commit themselves to serve the cause of Justice and Peace.

Selected References
Works by Francis Xavier Nguyên Vãn Thuân
>The first five books written in prison and 'privately' published (1977 -1988):
>>*The Road of Hope.* (Vietnamese, English, French, Italian, German and Spanish).
>>*The Pilgrims on the Road of Hope.*
>>*The Road of Hope in the Light of God's Word and the Vatican Council.*
>>*Five Loaves and Two Fish.*
>>*About to Zizania.* (Index of religious vocabulary in Latin, French, English, Italian, Spanish and Chinese with Vietnamese definitions).
>>*Testimony of Hope.* Boston: Paulines Press, 2000.
>Pruzinsky Mumola, Lynnea. "We are with Jesus: In captivity and in freedom, Vietnamese archbishop has found strength in Eucharist". *The Catholic Standard*, Nov. 9, 2000.

4.3.5. Stephen Nguyên Khac Duong (?1928)

Coming from a Mandarin family, Nguyên Khac Duong became a Catholic convert, studied in France and returned to teach philosophy in Saigon and Dalat. Both as a teacher and also as a poet he has had wide influence on younger generations in particular. Long associated with the United Catholic Committee (see 3.1.1, 3.2.1.6, 4.2.3) he has written for its journal (*Theological Selections* - see 4.2.4) and been active in teaching, writing and non-formal education programs for the promotion of genuinely Vietnamese approaches to the contemporary tasks of both philosophy and theology. Some years before 1975, he was the Dean of the Department of Literature at the University of Dalat and also Professor of Philosophy. In the years immediately following 1975, he was placed in a Re-education Camp with numbers of other intellectuals.

For Nguyên Khac Duong, theology is not primarily about doctrine but rather concerns the poetry of life and belief. The keyword for theology in Asian contexts is "worship" - in life and thought and community. And this is both an ongoing wrestle and authentic search. In western terms such a quest and worship may be "non- theology," and in fact for the transformation of people and society in Vietnam, theology as it has been known must die, to become again truly good news of and for human life. For this many creative traditions of Vietnamese culture fuse with central biblical insights (such as the covenant with Noah) to fructify and enlighten Christian understanding of such doctrines as evangelization, salvation and the Communion of Saints. Vietnamese wisdom and experience, past and present, is integral to this theology: "however exalted one is" says Nguyên Khac Duong, "the greatest pain would be to not know who one's mother was."

Selected References
Works by Stephen Nguyên Khac Duong
> *Autobiographical Memoir*. (In Vietnamese). Saigon: Privately Printed, ca. 1978.
> Articles in *Tuyên Tâp Thân Hoc* (Theological selections) (1988 - 1998).

4.3.6. Hoàng Si Quý sj (1926-)

Hoàng Si Quý gained his doctorate in philosophy from the Université de Sorbonne, Paris, for his studies in Indian philosophy. He later taught at the University of Saigon and at the Pontifical College of Dalat. He was founder of the Movement for the Revival of the Religious Spirit and Eastern Culture, editor of the periodical *The East*, and regional convenor for Theological Reflection of the Jesuit Commission of Inculturation and Dialogue of the Religious for Vietnam. In extensive research on Asian cultures Hoàng Si Quý came to focus on East Asian theology and "the depth of its mystery." His writings therefore include studies of *yin-yang* dialectics as a basis for theology, applications of the Tao for ascetic practice and the transcendant self of the Vedanta. Other writings consider spiritual theology, the problems of inter-religious dialogue, the psychology of inculturation in Vietnam, the way of knowledge (*jnaâna*) and the way of love or devotion (*bhakti* or *amida*).

For Hoàng Si Quý the inculturation of Christian theology and spirituality must be rooted in Indian culture and Chinese civilization, Vietnamese history and also contemporary scientific thought, all of which shape life in Vietnam. He therefore lays particular stress upon the principles of complementarity and reciprocity found in other faith traditions, which allow us to go beyond dualism and opposition to a "softer position" in belief and practice. A *yin-yang* dialectic in theology allows us to accept apparent opposites as "part of the psyche, the community and of theology itself." Christian spirituality rooted in graeco-roman traditions can be reshaped by Confucian morality, Zen meditation and practice of the Taoist "way of water." Similarly reflection upon the recent insights of science can greatly extend our understanding of the creative process and purpose. As well as his academic work, which issues in full-scale volumes or articles in learned journals such as the *Annals of Musée Guimet* (Paris), Hoàng Si Quý has regularly initiated (or edited) both publications and movements through which such insights can be disseminated more widely. These include the newsletter *Interculturation and Religious Dialogue*, the journal *The East*, and many booklets and off-prints. Prior to 1975, he and his colleagues have also applied principles of inculturation in the liturgy by organizing "Eastern" masses in Huê and Saigon, and after 1975, they worked through groups of clergy and lay people to adapt Christianity to the new conditions of life. Hoàng Si Quý continued to celebrate his "Mass incarnée" weekly at Saigon (1973-1980).

Recent writings have included *Invitation to Philosophy* (1993), *Compendium of Dogmatic Theology* (1997) and *Invitation to the Philosophy of Languages* (2000), published privately in HCMV.

Selected References
Works by Hoàng Si Quý

> *Le moi qui me dépasse selon le Vedanta: étude du concept d'atman chez Sankara et dans les Upanisad sous son aspecte de densité et d'intériorté.* Series: Bibliothèque de philosophie H.G.V.D. Saigon: Éditions Hýng Giáo Văn Đông, 1971.
> *Vân dê Dôi Thoai Tôn Giáo* (The problem of inter-religious dialogue). Saigon: 1972.
> *Théologie Spirituelle*. 2 vols. Saigon: 1995; (4th ed.) Berkeley: University of California Press, 1997.
> "A principle of Ascesis: The Way of Water." *Recueils théologique* 11, edited by P. Nguyên Văn Minh and Filipe Gomez. (Also published in *Hop Tuyên Thân Hoc*).
> "Inculturation and Bases of the Vietnamese Psyche", in *Recueils théologique 16*. (Also published in *Hop Tuyên Thân Hoc*).
> "Avec les Nouvelles Sciences, Il Faut Revoir Plusieurs Conceptions Philo-Théologiques." *Recueils théologique 23*. (Also published in *Hop Tuyên Thân Hoc*).

4.3.7. Bao Tinh Vuong Đình Bích (1928-)

The home of Fr Bao Tinh Vuong Dình Bích was situated in the zone of the Xô Viêt Nghê Tinh insurrection, but his family "practiced conservative traditional piety." He studied in both Vietnam and France (1954-1961), joined the Benedictine order and returned to Vietnam in 1970. Studies in social philosophy had shown him social injustice and problems of class, and this he saw as a reality that existed even in religious congregations and throughout the Church also. In Vietnam he was appointed to teach young religious, while the war continued its devastation about them. Having contact with some revolutionary groups before 1975, and "conscious of the national dimension of the faith and of the religious life," he participated in the movement "Against War And For Peace" in Saigon. Along with colleagues, in 1975 he also founded a Catholic magazine (*Ngyòi Viêt Nam Công giáo* - see 4.2.3.), to foster the patriotism of Vietnamese Catholics. Bao Tinh Vuong Dình Bích is now senior priest of the Fraternity of the Virgin of the Poor. He is nationally known, and has played important and often controversial roles in the leadership of indigenous movements within the Catholic Church.

His prolific writings include letters, articles and sermons, which have continued to appear in mimeographed papers or privately printed books and booklets, since 1970. His primary aim throughout has been to unify 'worldly' and 'religious' concerns and to foster "national reconciliation between Catholics and non-Catholics, through an interpretation of God's Word in the Asian dialectics of a Vietnamese Christian." He has done this while living in a small Fraternity which "practices contemplation within society itself, side by side with the poor and the unfortunate, and according to the guideline 'For Jesus and His Religion of Good News.'" His scores of articles provide theological reflection upon major Christian doctrines and concerns within the daily context of Vietnamese life, in neighborhood, society and Church. Issues of national life, of Church policy and of personal discipleship are alike subjected to incisive Gospel critique, and illumined by celebration of the Christian year. Bao here draws on Vietnam's Christian history and the insights from Vatican II to discern the life of Christ within the contemporary experience of Christians in Vietnam. He thus presents a critical theology which transcends western dualisms, is open to other faiths, is nationalist as well as universalist, and which is grounded in just and compassionate community life.

Selected References
Works by Bao Tinh Vuong Dình Bích

All booklets and articles (in Vietnamese or French) have been privately printed and circulated (1970-2000). They include:
1. On Return and Vietnamese Identity:
"Return to meet the Nation"; "Why the Virgin of the Poor?"; "Life in our Community"; "An Unprecedented Retreat"; "Family,

Nation and World Community"; "Community determines Happiness"; "Relying on the Holy Spirit."
2. On Doing Theology in Vietnam:
"May Jesus Christ be Praised for Ever!"; "Becoming Human Beings"; "Theology and the Cause of the Nation"; "Viêt Theology"; "Viet-Christianity"; "Service of Society"; "Faith the Motive Power."
3. On The Religious Life:
"He came from Heaven to Earth"; "Two Beats of a Single Heart: Heart and Mind - Yin and Yang"; "Evangelical Pedagogy of the Celibate Vocation"; "Poor One of Yahweh"; "Religious life : Grace Given."
4. On The New Resurrected Life:
"Easter: Celebrating the Mystery of Universal Salvation"; "Passion Related to Resurrection"; "Holy Week - Nativity of the Christian Faith"; "Easter: Divinization of Humanity".
5. On A Life of Faith and Worship:
"On the True Eucharist"; "Live the Loving Presence"; "People of the New Covenant"; "Praying in Accordance with Christ's Gospel"; "The Christianity of Prayers"; "Passing Beyond."

4.3.8. Mai Thành cnd (1928-)

Sr Mai Thành was educated at Huê and Paris, and entered the Congregation de Notre Dame (CND) ca. 1950. In France she obtained her Theology Licence from L'Institut Catholique and her doctorate in Philosophy from the Sorbonne. She also studied media production at Cambridge and on return to Vietnam directed educational television at the Centre Alexandre de Rhodes (1970-1975) and for HCMV (1975-1984). Mai Thành also worked with Jeunesse Étudiante Catholique (JEC), was a member of the Conseil Genéral of CND, and has become internationally known for her writings and work in education.

Thành was early concerned to develop methods of dialogue with other faiths and with Marxism, and for the doing of Asian theology. This, she declares can only be a theology of the heart, speaking the language of the heart which is that of love, known in the supreme lover, Jesus Christ. In his fullest humanity is seen the love by which women and men can also become fully human, and being refined by this love makes possible friendship with all, regardless of creed or ideology. We find the Holy Spirit ahead of us in all people and places, all religious traditions, all partners in active human concern. Thành writes also of the humanism found in both Buddhism and Christianity, and sees the coming of Buddhism, Confucianism and Taoism to Vietnam as preparations for the Christian Gospel. But she returns again and again to speak of that full love which is life itself, so that the more we love, the more we come to fullest humanity. And in this we find the divinity of that full humanity. In other writings, Thành presents detailed studies of Vietnamese culture and religion, of inter-religious dialogue, and of reflections on such apostolic documents as *Ecclesia in Asia*.

Selected References
Works by Mai Thành

> Thõ Hýõng Nguyên (Incense of Prayer, Poems 1953-1999). HCMV: Privately printed, 1999.
>
> —, ed. *Consécration et Service* (Consecrated Life in Vietnam 1975-1990). HCMV: Liksin, 1989.
>
> "Vietnamese Culture and Civilization." Conference Paper. Mimeo'd, 30.7.73.
>
> "Justice et Dialogue Interreligieux en Asie." *Revue Congrégation Notre Dame* (1992).
>
> "Vie Religieuse et Dialogue Interreligieux en Asie." *Revue de Unim Internationale des Supérieures* (1993).
>
> "Aspects du Christianisme au Vietnam." *Concilium* 246 (1993).
>
> "Filial Piety in the Confucianist Ethic and in the Gospel." In *Filial Piety and Christian Faith,* edited by Hoàng Gia Khánh. Papers delivered at the Seminar in Huê, November, 1999. Forthcoming.

4.3.9. Truòng Bá Cân (1928-)

A scholar in theology, literature and history, Truòng Bá Cân was active in the Third Force for peace and against corruption, and YCW Chaplain from the early seventies. He has long been active as writer, editor and bibliographer, and now edits the journal of the Catholic Union Committee *Công giáo và Dân tôc* (Catholic and Nation - weekly since 1975, monthly since 1994 (See 4.2.3.). Truòng Bá Cân has maintained deep concern in writing, education and activism, for not only Catholic Christian identity and tradition in Vietnam, but also for its expression in movements for peace, for an appropriate form of socialism and for active Christian citizenship. His theological vision is of a fully liberated Vietnamese people within which the church draws on the best of creative Catholic, socialist and national tradition to make possible full human life in community for all. His work as animateur, publicist and scholar has often led to censure by church and sometimes imprisonment by government, but his prolific writings continue to be widely read.

Prior to 1975 Truòng Bá Cân wrote regularly for such journals as *Tâp San Chon* (What You Choose) and *Dât Nuóc* (The Nation), and among his articles in *Tâp San Chon* which had wide influence were "My Church in the Situation of the Nation's Conflict," "Memoir in the Prison of the Regime," and "Christmas of the Poor." A key paper in *Vietnam Information* focusses particularly on the departure of foreign missionaries in 1975, in the context of evangelical, liberating and missionary tasks in a liberated Vietnam. His books in the same period include a study of the Second Vatican Council, and writings on peace and social justice. Since 1975, and apart from regular journal articles, he has collected and edited the writings of Nguyên Truòng To (see above 1.4.3.), written volumes on particular periods in the church history of Vietnam, and with others compiled a bibliography of Christian writings in Vietnam. His writings in *Công giáo và Dân tôc* since 1975 have included articles on the Vietnamese Christian, national unification, socialism, Catholic citizenship, Christian history in Vietnam, ways of implementing the Bishop's Pastoral Letter of 1975, as well as on contemporary socio-political issues.

Selected References
Works by Truòng Bá Cân

> *Sac lênh: Tông Dô Giáo Dân / Công Dông Vatican II*. Saigon: Nhà Sách Dùc Me 1970).
>
> *Hòa Bình cho Quê Hÿõng* (Work for peace). Saigon: Chon xuat ban, 1971.
>
> *Tin Mùng Hôm Nay* (Good news for today). Saigon: Mimeo'd, 1972-75.

Nguyên Truòng To - Con Nguòi và Di Thao (Nguyên Truòng To - The man and his writings). Hochiminh Ville: Nga Xuat Ban Thanh Pho,1988.

Công giáo Dàng Trong Thói G.M. Pigneau (Catholic church in the South in the time of G.M. Pigneau, 1771-1799). HCMV:1992.

Catholicism after 50 years of Activities (1945-1995). HCMV: Công Giáo dân tôc, 1996.

"Being Christian and Vietnamese." *Công giáo và Dân tôc* 20 (29.11.75).

"What is Socialism?" *CGvDT* 34 (28.02.76).

"One can be Catholic and Citizen." *CGvDT* 603 (15.03.87).

"Conflict between Atheism and Catholicism." *CGvDT* 607 (12.04.87).

"From October Revolution to August Revolution." *CGvDT* 932 (7.11.93).

"In Order to say Farewell to the Past." *CGvDT* 1142-1143 (25.1.1998).

— with Me Gia. "Témoignage d'une religieuse" *Vietnam Information* (Sept 1975).

— with others. *Tâp San Chon* (What You Choose). Saigon: Chon, 1972.

— with Lê Vān Khuê and Nguyên Nghi. *Thý Muc Sách Và Các Bài Báo Vê Lich Sy Công giáo Viêt Nam Có Tai Viêt Nam* (Bibliography of books, documents and articles on Catholic Christianity in Vietnam, held in Vietnam). HCMV: Mimeo'd, 1989.

4.3.10. Nguyên Ngoc Lan (?1930-) and Chân Tín (1921-)

Nguyên Ngoc Lan was for many years the chief editor of the Redemptorist journal *Dôi Diên*, founded in 1969 (*Dôi Diên* - Face to Face: see 3.1.4. Sel. Ref., and 4.2.2.). A skilful writer, he has been able in his main writings to pioneer a 'breakthrough' for contemporary writing in the noblest Vietnamese style. This is seen also in his theological reflections, which have evinced a strong commitment to the renewal of the church and the development of its broader mission to Vietnamese society. He is widely known for his penetrating satirical writings on the Catholic Church in Vietnam in the late 1960s, in which he contrasted its fortress mentality and practice with the "way pursued by the wandering Rabbi Jesus." In more recent writings he has provided a critical commentary on many of the specific observances of the institutional church, in the light of this way of Jesus. Along with large numbers of journal articles and meditations, Nguyên Ngoc Lan has also published volumes which present more fully the contrasts he sees between Jesus' way and the church's defense of its "blockhouse."

A close colleague of Nguyên Ngoc Lan in such prophetic writing and publishing, along also with Nguyên Nghi, has been Fr Chân Tín cssr. Chân Tín was the first theologian to introduce the insights of liberation theology to Vietnamese audiences in the 1960s, and soon became a leading dissident against political imprisonment and other human rights violations in South Vietnam pre-1975, which led to his arrest by the Thiêu regime in 1972. He later protested against Communist re-education camps, and decrees which limited religious freedom (1981) and publicly dissented from a government-organized campaign to oppose Vatican plans to canonize 117 Vietnamese martyrs (1988). Despite censure he continued preaching and writing, in samizdat editions, on behalf of human rights, and called upon the government to "repent" of their failure to protect these. Further statements and homilies led to his arrest, along with Nguyên Ngoc Lan (1990-1993), and following release he continued his writing and advocacy, addressed to both the government and the Vietnamese Bishop's Council. In September 1999, Father Chân Tín joined leaders of the Buddhist, Hòa Hao, and Cao Dài faiths in letters requesting the government to respect religious freedom. He is reportedly now under house arrest in HCMV.

Selected References

Nguyên Ngoc Lan. *Way or Blockhouse* (In Vietnamese). Saigon: Privately circulated, ca. 1968.
—. *Rosy Sunday. Meditations on the Inner Life* (In Vietnamese). HCMV: Privately circulated, 1998.
Chân Tín. *Repent to the Nation*. Privately printed. 1990.
—. "Fr. Chân Tín's Critique of Dô Myói Speech". *Vietnam Insight*, Vol. V.10, (October 1994).
—. "Voice of the Masses. Letter from Father Chân Tín." *Vung Tau*, July 10 (1998).
Tôn That Manh Týong. "Chân Tín: A Non-violent Struggle for Human Rights in Viêt Nam." *Viêt Nam Generation* 5.1-4 (1994).

4.3.11. Thomas Trân Thiên Câm op (1933-)

Thiên Câm grew up in a rural district of Nam Dinh Province, and studied in both Vietnam and France, gaining his doctorate from the Sorbonne. He has been parish priest, teacher of oriental philosophy at Dalat and of medieval philosophy at the University of Saigon. He also teaches Asian Theology in HCMV and is currently national Director of Studies for the Dominican order. He is active in Catholic movements concerned for the social witness of Christians and for the development of Vietnamese theology. Strong influences upon him have included the documents of Vatican II, contemporary Asian theology and also specialist studies in Asian literature, in particular the poetry of Rabindranath Tagore. For Thiên Câm, theology begins in human and community experience, and theology is 'done' in the wrestle with human problems "on the spot" while committed to people's well-being. It is also fed by the life and wisdom of one's own people for, he quotes C.S. Song, "unless a worm eats mulberry leaves it will not produce silk."

Thiên Câm's writings include scores of articles and booklets, along with three books, published in Vietnamese. They include studies of eastern religions, of the Incarnation and the Trinity, major essays on Christology, papers on salvation as justice and as liberation, on Ho Chí Minh and on government policies, on good news for the poor, a church of jubilee, women's role in the church, the use of power, and on elements of a 'basic church,' among many others. A central image for Christian life and faith for Thiên Câm is that of mountain-climbing, on "the Way." This is a risky adventure, requiring courage, skill, endurance and wisdom, but "speaking in terms of Zen," he writes, "this is to live one's life in such a natural way as the flow of a steady stream, the blossoming of a tree, the singing of a bird." We do not already possess all truth of the Way, nor can religious doctrines - of any faith - do more than point to the way. Yet the challenge to Vietnamese Christians is to not only point to it, but in the midst of daily struggle and aspirations, to also build the Way with others, and then strive further to become the way. For this we must rediscover the concrete life of Jesus as the bridge span, the human-divine ladder between God and humankind.

Contextual Theology in Vietnam 1800-2000

Selected References
Works by Thomas Trân Thiên Câm

Kitô giáo voi các tôn giáo khác (Christianity and Other Religions). Saigon: Da Minh, 1970.

Quan niêm Giai thoát trong Phât giáo cu (The Idea of deliverance in early Buddhism). Saigon: Da Minh, 1970.

Hoa Trong Ke Dá (Flowers out of crevices - Hoa trong ke da). San Francisco: Dong Huong, 1993.

Co Moc Ven Duóng (Plants at the edge of the road). 2 vols. HCMV: Privately printed, 1989. 2nd ed., 1997.

Nhâp Hôi Hoa Dãng (Mingling at the carnival of the lamps). HCMV: Privately printed, 1997.

Tiêng hát môi dòng sông (The song of each river). HCMV: Privately printed, 1999.

Giáo Hôi trýóc th?m nãm 2002 (The Church at the threshold of the year 2000). HCMV: Privately printed, 1999.

"Coming Home." *Understanding* (Saigon Catholic Students' monthly). Ca. 1962.

Articles in *Công giáo và Dân tôc* (in Vietnamese) include:
"Revolution, Change of Life?" *CGvDT* 1, 10.7.1975.
"Good News for the Liberated Country." *CGvDT* 3, 30.7.1975.
"Time for Reconciliation." *CGvDT* 604, 22.03.1987.
"Reflections on the Capacity of Reconstruction." (2 articles.) *CGvDT* 695, 22.1.1989.
"Once again about Inculturation." *CGvDT* 1035, 26.11.1995.
"Equality of women." *CGvDT* 9/1995, 3.14 1995.
"To be Vietnamese." *CGvDT* 21/1996, 6-1 1996.
"Doing theology." *CGvDT* 29/1997, 26.10.9 1997.
"Independence of the Church." *CGvDT* 33/1997, 6.19.1997.
"The Revolution and Renewal." *CGvDT* 35/1997. 6.2.1997.
"The Reality of Asian Churches." *CGvDT* 51/1998, 9.3.1998.
"Live the Gospel through signs." *CGvDT* 57/2000, 5.5.2000.

4.3.12. Amelie Nguyên Thi Sang cnd

Amelie Nguyên studied theology, languages and biblical studies in Saigon, Paris and Jerusalem, entering the CND in France. She worked as a missioner in Hong Kong (1969-1974) and returned to Vietnam to undertake extensive work in Bible translation, along with theological reflection on the Chinese classics. Central in her thought and work has been the search to give human expression

- in Chinese and Vietnamese - to biblical texts and her discovery of the close "similarity of expression between Hebrew and Chinese/Vietnamese." In this she has been concerned to bring together Chinese wisdom and Christian scripture as parallels of our spiritual journey today, and also to provide models for new forms of biblical translation into Vietnamese which embody Vietnamese culture and idiom. For in these there is already a "pre-sympathy for every personality." With the "Liturgy of the Hours Group" which included scholars from many religious congregations (formed 1971), Amelie Nguyên worked to develop Vietnamese masses using similar principles in translation and writing, for popular festivals in Vietnam such as New Year and the eighth month Full Moon.

In her theological writing Amelie Nguyên finds the signs of compassion and of joy in self-sacrifice, and of communitarian concern, in the best traditions of Vietnamese and Chinese cultures, as she does in the commitment of 'ordinary' Vietnamese people to neighborhood, to voluntary work for social justice and peacemaking. The Gospels clearly declare that the actions of Jesus, which sign-posted the coming of God's reign are expected from every human being, she writes. And here in these ways even "those who do not know Him" act out such signs! - evidencing that "everybody is under illumination." The "mystery of the coming of God's kingdom" may be that though "[the] Christian's action is limited; the non-Christian's, [is] unlimited; God's kingdom must have its way to come, in spite of all obstacles, through all events."

Selected References
Works by Amelie Nguyên Thi Sang
"Untitled Paper" (Chinese is important). *Union of Catholic Asian News* (UCAN). (29.3.1999)
"Doing Asian Theology. Some experiences and reflections about an informal coming of God's Kingdom in Vietnam." Conference Paper, Mimeo'd, Nov. 1999.
Thánh Lê theo Truyên Thông Dân tôc (Eucharistic celebrations on traditional Vietnamese festivals). Saigon: Liturgy of the Hours Group, 2000.
"The unfolding of God's Kingdom in Vietnam." *UCA News* 3.5.2000.
Thành, Mai, ed. *Consécration et Service* (Consecrated life in Vietnam 1975-1990). HCMV: Liksin, 1989.

4.3.13. Nguyên Hông Giáo ofm (1937-)

Nguyên Hông Giáo has devoted much of his ministry to fostering the social ministries of Catholics in the community and to assisting in their education and equipment for these. He has been closely associated with a number of movements for church renewal and for socio-political participation in the Church of Vietnam, including the United Catholic Committee. In his writings for Vietnamese periodicals, in particular for *Công Giáo và Dân Tôc*, he has provided a wide range of theological comment concerning faith and life within the present social conditions in Vietnam. Here he has provided re-interpretations of Resurrection, Incarnation, the Eucharist, spirituality, repentance, reconciliation and jubilee; all within the vocation of living totally for God and His kingdom, in the world: "living the present for the future." He has also reflected on ecological issues, on patriotism, on honoring ancestors, the relationship between faith and science, and upon history and historical movements. In addition he has collaborated in the publication of writings by women religious of 43 congregations in South Vietnam.

Selected References
Works by Nguyên Hông Giáo

"Les Religieux à HCMV." In *Consécration et Service* (Consecrated life in Vietnam 1975-1990), edited by Mai Thành. HCMV: Liksin, 1989.
Articles in *Công giáo và Dân tôc* (in Vietnamese) include:
"The Eucharist in a State Farm." *CGvDT* 102 (12.06.77).
"Easter for the Whole Life." *CGvDT* 143-144 (2.1.1978).
"Religious Life in the World." *CGvDT* 388-390 (26.1.1982).
"We want to Live Totally." *CGvDT* 570 (27.07.1986).
"A Vietnamese Church." *CGvDT* 831 (3.11.1991).
"Reflexion on the Street." *CGvDT* 935 (28.11.1993).
"National Culture in the Open Gate Era." *CGvDT* 939 (2.1.1994).
"Living his Faith in his Social Milieu." *CGvDT* 1039 (7.1.1996).
"Catholics and the Nation." *CGvDT* 1217 (23.7.1999).
"All the Beautiful Aspects of the World." *CGvDT* 1270 (4.8.2000).
"The Jubilee and Repentence." *CGvDT* 1241 (14.1.2000).

4.3.14. Joseph Đinh Đúc Dao

Joseph Dinh Dúc Dao, who is now based in Rome, has been Vice Director, International Center of Missionary Animation (CIAM) and also director of the pastoral office for Vietnamese in the diaspora. Along with continuing study of the life of the Vietnamese church, and also of missionary animation, he has been particularly concerned for issues of inculturation especially as these can be met, and furthered, in the spiritual life. He has written many articles published internationally, on inculturation, meditation - both Christian and Buddhist - and on the practice of mission in contemporary Vietnam and Asia. Đinh Đúc Dao advocates a "dialogical reflection" with Asian cultures in order both to understand the present forms and goals of Christian mission and also to overcome such critical problems in western theology as that of epistemology. He holds closely with this the contribution to both inculturated theology and inculturated mission, of renewal in Christian prayer and contemplation. But this is to be prayer and contemplation which receives fully the insights of Asian sensibilities, and which is enriched by other faiths. He has also written on missionary spirituality, on catechetics, and on aspects of Asian church history and is a regular reviewer for *Bibliographia Missionaria* (Pontifical Urban University).

Selected References
Works by Joseph Dinh Dúc Dao

> *Preghiera rinnovata per una nuova era missionaria in Asia Roma, Centro "Culture e religioni"* (Prayer renewed for a new missionary era in Asia). Inculturation Series 15. Rome: Center for "Cultures and religions," Pontificia Università Gregoriana, 1994. Bibliographical references.
>
> "Inculturation of the Prayer Life of the Church in Asia: the Case of Zen Meditation. In *Inculturation: Working Papers on Living Faiths and Cultures 7*, edited by A.R. Crollius. Rome: Pontifical Gregorian University, 1986.
>
> "La Chiesa Vietnam. Segnali d'esperanza." *Omnis Terra* 24 (1990).
>
> "Spiritualita Missionaria." In Cristo, Chiesa, Missione. Rome: Urbaniana University Press, 1992.
>
> "Dialogo Interreligioso di Fronte alla Mentalité e Sensibilita Asiatica" (Inter-religious conversation with Asian mentality

and sensibility). *Omnis Terra* 16 (In English, *Omnis Terra* 32) (1998).

4.3.15. Phan Khac Tù (1940-)

Phan Khac Tù was born in Haiphong and was later strongly influenced both by the Second Vatican Council and by progressive priests gathering in Výon Xoai Church who pioneered the newspaper *Sông Dao* and also the Vietnamese Young Catholic Workers. In the 1960s he became a student leader and worked in the YCW, and from 1970 contributed to the People's Gaining Peace Front and related Third Force and students' movements for peace and justice and against corruption. Convinced that churches could not remain "rich islands in an ocean of hunger and misery" but rather should be churches of the poor, Phan Khac Tù labored as a worker priest with litter collectors from 1972 and was for a period imprisoned. He later co-operated with the Marxist-led Committee of Protecting Labor Rights and with the Buddhist-led People's Saving Hunger Front (from 1974) working closely with Buddhist colleagues in many cities throughout Vietnam. Since 1980 Phan Khac Tù has been parish priest of Výon Xoai (Garden of Mangoes) Church, a Delegate to Parliament, and Vice President and Secretary of Vietnam's United Catholic Committee (see 3.1.1.). He has also led the work of the Dai Kêt center, HCMV, in its promotion of specifically Vietnamese theology through national seminars, publishing and ecumenical networking.

Early writings of Phan Khac Tù expressing the above concerns appeared in the journal *Chon* (Choice - see 3.1.4. above) which was independently published by a group of clergy and lay people - Roman Catholic, Protestant, Buddhist and Cao Dài - who wrote and organized for peace, lay participation, and in opposition to policies of the South Vietnamese government and the U.S. He also wrote for the journal *Dôi Diên* (Face to Face), and in the volume *Tâp San Chon* (What You Choose) published by the Chon group.

Selected References
Works by Phan Khac Tù
    Ngô Hai Phông. (Gate of Hai Phong). HCMV: Privately Circulated, 2000.

"Interview with Phan Khac Tù, Kiêu Mông Thu, Ngô Bá Thành and Francoise Demeure - as leaders of Third Force regarding their role in revolutionary activities." HCMV: IDOC Document 06252, August, 1975.

"A Process of Serving People." Mimeo'd, 2000.

— with Truòng Bá Cân and Trân Thê Luân. *Tù Cua Chê Đô* (Prisoner of the regime). Chon, 1972. Also in *Tâp San Chon* (What You Choose) ed. by Truòng Bá Cân et al. Saigon: Chon, 1974.

— with Truòng Bá Cân, Vu Xuân Hiêu and Huênh Công Minh. *Cong Binh Tren Thê Giói*. (Justice in the World). Saigon: n.p., 1971.

Nguyên Thành Vinh. "Trente Années de poursuite de l'Évangile (1945-1975)". HCMV: 1975.

4.3.16. Nguyên Chính Kêt (1952-)

Nguyên Chính Kêt of HCMV, is a younger scholar in Vietnamese religion and culture and also of eastern philosophy, as well as a prolific author on the inculturation of Christianity in Vietnam. Among his writings are studies in ontology and epistemology in which he contrasts western logic and conceptualization with more flexible and non-dualistic approaches in Vietnam. Regarding inculturation, Chính Kêt stresses the need for contemporary patterns of localized theology which draw on the principles evolved by Matteo Ricci and similar pioneers. Such a theology will require contemporary prophets and will grow from reflection upon the realities of human life in Vietnam: the practice of filial piety and ancestor 'worship'; encounter and dialogue with those of other living faiths; the festivals of the New Year, of ancestors and of La Vãng; the lives and struggles of those now suffering privation and injustice. It will also be shaped by the more dynamic and flexible insights of Asian wisdom that allow many aspects of the 'one' - the *yin* and the *yang* - to be held at the same time.

Chính Kêt gives his deepest concern in his writings to presenting the bases and the processes of genuine inter-religious dialogue. Beginning with the principal attributes of an Ultimate Reality, as these are recognized in all major religions, he then distinguishes subordinate attributes which differ: the personal creator God of Christianity, and the impersonal 'suchness' of

Buddhism which is one with the cosmos. Here there are different conceptualizations, sometimes apparently contradictory, which however describe the same reality, he believes. If personal experience of that 'ultimate reality,' rather than theoretical knowledge, is shared, the true dialogue occurs. For the purpose of inter-religious dialogue, Chính Kêt affirms, is not the construction of final and agreed philosophical statements, but rather the quality of meeting and acceptance which makes possible shared work and love for the welfare of all. "The Christian way of seeing the unique and unchanging God and other religions has continuously changed in the past" he affirms, so that we should hesitate to claim finality for inherited or present categories. The central priority remains the discovery and fostering of those religious values which make possible personal and social transformation.

Selected References
Works by Nguyên Chính Kêt
> *Dôi Thoai Tôn Giáo* (Inter-religious dialogue). HCMV: Privately printed, 1992.
> *Linh Hanh Phât giáo dôi chiêu vói linh hanh Kitô giáo* (Buddhist spirituality in comparision with Christian spirituality). HCMV: Privately printed, 1997.
> *Thích Úng và Hôi Nhâp Vān Hóa trong Truyên giáo* (Adaptation and inculturation in mission). HCMV: Privately printed, 1998.
> *Thuc Tai Tôi Hâu Trong Các Tôn Giáo* (The Ultimate Reality in religions). HCMV: Privately printed, 1999.
> *Ngôn Sú Thòi Dai Mói* (The contemporary prophets). HCMV: Privately printed, 2000.
> "Inculturation of the Christian Message in Asia." Mimeo'd, 1997.

4.3.17. Hoàng Gia Khánh (1955-)

Hoàng Gia Khánh studied philosophy and theology in Dalat, and now bases his work in teaching, translation and writing in HCMV. He is an accomplished linguist and a recognized scholar in the history and theology of Christianity in Vietnam. His particular areas of research and writing have been the history of Vietnamese theology and of inculturation in Vietnam. Of special interest for him is the theological tradition of "the Three Fathers" (*Giáo Lý Tam Phu*, see above 1.3.), which blends Christian faith with

Vietnamese practices of filial piety and national loyalty. This is found in the work of Alexandre de Rhodes and colleagues (see chapter 1.1. - 1.3.) and applies the thought of Matteo Ricci in China; to add honor to the 'supreme Father,' the Lord of Heaven, to 'loyalty to the king' and honor to parents - the 'middle' and 'lower' fathers. Hoàng Gia Khánh has written and lectured widely on the implications of such a theology for the development of contextual theology in Vietnam.

In other writings, Hoàng Gia Khánh proposes that theology in Asia requires and demonstrates new models, for in many ways it has been "a pagan science practised by Christians." One such model is found in careful study of folk literature - such as the Buddhist folksong "Mother accepts the wet place to lie on" - by which one reflects on the sacrificial love of parents as an image of divine love, and moves from folktale to God-talk. The larger framework for such a theology, he believes, is the inter-cultural convergence which is found in deeply held parallel traditions of Confucianism, Buddhism, Islam and Christianity. This is already partly seen in the works of Ricci and de Rhodes but in the situation of Vietnam, the convergence is also to be recognized in Taoism and Marxism, even though Marxism is now unable to provide an ethic for the whole society. The parallelism is found not only in regard to love and wisdom but in the realities of "pistis," "prajna" and "praxis", which are to be felt "as one passion, wrestling within the one flame of theology."

In his poetry Hoàng Gia Khánh seeks to portray a cosmic experience wherein "the lord is so gentle, courteous, and beautiful, coming in the moments of subtle intimations and awareness - unbearable; and in deep awareness of suffering ..." And regarding the role of the church and Catholic intellectuals in Vietnam, he proposes the image of Ruth who was 'foreign' yet wholly identified with the land. "If the church is similarly a 'daughter-in-law,' her husband is undoubtedly the people!"

Selected References
Works by Hoàng Gia Khánh

"Three Hundred Years of Catholic Writing in Vietnam." In *Tuyên Tâp Thân Hoc* (Selected theological writings) April, 1993.

"Hiêu Thao Trong Bôi Canh Giáo Lý Tam Phu" (Filial piety against the background of the doctrine of triple fatherhood). In *Filial Piety and Christian Faith in Vietnam, Papers from the Seminar held under the Auspices of Archbishop Stephen Nguyên Nhý Thê at Huê, 1999*, edited by Hoàng Gia Khánh. HCMV: Institute for the Study of Religion. Forthcoming.

"The Sage from the West." Paper for the 350th Anniversary of Alexandre de Rhodes' Catechism. Forthcoming.

Trần Uyên Thi et al. *Mùa Hoa Sýu Tâp Tho* (Flower Season - anthology of poetry). Dalat: Privately printed, ca. 1991.

4.4 Other Theologians and Groups

4.4.1. Other Women Scholars and Writers

Women have been everywhere present and active in the churches of Vietnam, as religious, parish staff, teachers, social workers, health professionals, interpreters, evangelists, catechists and parishioners. Most are directly concerned in the lives and struggles of their Vietnamese sisters in particular, with whom they live out a theology of compassion, empowerment and hope, not only in daily commitment to family and neighborhood but many also in social action and organization. Their published writings are unfortunately few, although the poems and reflections of a number have been circulated in various formats. Apart from Mai Thành (4.3.8.) and Amelie Nguyên Thi Sang (4.3.12.), many religious women, of which there are over 40 congregations in Vietnam, have for example, written articles in periodicals, booklets or reports. Along with those mentioned below, they include Antoine de Thái-Hà-Âp, Marie Bùi Thi Nga, Tô Thi Ánh (3.2.4.), and Elizabeth Trôn Thi Quỳnh Giao.

No collection or survey of such writing has yet been made, although the unusual volume *Consécration et Service* (1989) provides both overviews of women's congregations and the reflections and reports of individual sisters. It includes the writing of Hô Thi Chính, Pham Thi Khân and Lê Thi Nhiêu (Amantes de la Croix); Nguyên Thi My (St Vincent de Paul); Nguyên Thi Chung (Notre Dame des Missions); Nguyên Thi Thu Huâng and Nguyên Thi Kiêu Diêm (Carmelite); Phan Thi Nghi and Trân Thi Quỳnh Giao (Franciscan); and Nguyên Thi Thê (Daughter of Charity).

The full introduction by Mai Thành, "Aspects Essentiels de La Vie Religieuse" (see 4.3.8.) stresses that religious vocation today is different only in function, not quality, from the ministry of all believers and places the ministries and spirituality firmly in the context of contemporary Vietnam.

Selected References

> Barry, Kathleen. *Vietnam's Women in Transition.* International Political Economy Series. Basingstoke and New York: Macmillam/St. Martin's Press, 1996.
> Bergman, A.E. *Women of Vietnam.* London: London School of Economics, 1975.
> Bùi Thi Nhu Kha, Marie. "Religious Life in Vietnam. Opportunity and Challenge." *Tripod* 49 (1989).
> De Maleissye, Marie-Thérèse. "Les religieuses au Vietnam d'aujourd'hui." *Église et Mission* 60.217 (1980).
> Mai Thành, ed. *Consécration et Service* (Consecrated life in Vietnam 1975-1990). HCMV: Liksin, 1989.
> Tô Thi Ánh. *Eastern and Western Cultural Values, Conflict or Harmony?* Manila: East Asia Pastoral Institute, 1975.
> Trân Cuu Chân. *Les grandes poétesses du Viêt-Nam: études littéraires: Đoàn-Thi-Điêm, Bà Huyên Thanh-Quan, Hô-Xuân-Hýõng, Sýõng Nguyêt-Ánh.* Saigon: Imprimerie de l'Union Nguyên-Vãn-Cua, 1950.
> Trân Thi Quỳnh Giao, Elizabeth. "Religieuse au Vietnam." In *Femmes en Mission,* edited by Marie-Thérèse de Maleissye. Lyon: Editions Lyonnaises, 1991.
> —. "Religieuse dans l'Église du Vietnam." *Spiritus* 31 (1990).
> Trân Uyên Thi et al. *Mùa Hoa Sýu tâp Thõ* (Flower season - anthology of poetry). Dalat: Privately printed, ca. 1991.
> "Vietnam." *In God's Image* 11.1 (1992).

4.4.2. Episcopal Conference of Vietnam

The bishops of Vietnam, first constituted as a hierarchy in 1960, have frequently issued statements corporately and individually, both for the guidance of the faithful and to make public the church's position and concerns for major issues facing the nation. An early statement in this period appeared in the joint letter of the episcopate (1954) declaring that the Church "is not subjected to any political party and is not opposed to any regime that recognises the inalienable rights of the Church ... Catholics are free to join any political group or movement of their choice ... [according to] ... the imperatives of the duly enlightened Catholic conscience ..." In the south, the majority of bishops in fact supported both the Diêm administration and those which followed (until 1975). The Pastoral Letter of three bishops who had prematurely returned from Rome following the Saigon coup of 1963, also declared their solidarity with Vietnamese people in the wake of Catholic reversals and interfaith tensions. It was to be "acceptance of humiliations ... [and] obedience to government," along with "collaboration with all for the welfare of the country ..."

The collective Lenten Pastoral Letter of 1964 was a much fuller exhortation to the faithful, charting a new theological and political path for the church. All Catholics are called to "make a special effort toward unity" for the national community; to accept the discipline in action that love requires; to undertake a "revision of life" - regarding "reciprocal love, the spirit of service and the forgiving of wrongs" in the spirit of Vatican II; and to carry this out in tolerance and understanding in their civic behaviour for "the collective whole." Pastoral letters for major church festivals and national occasions were issued in the following years and among their major themes were the unity and reconciliation of Catholics as well as of the nation; new patterns of mission and evangelization; removal of restrictions on religious freedom; worship and communion; and commitment to the purposes of peace and reconstruction.

The Pastoral letter of 1980 was of particular importance for its appeal to all Catholics to "live the Gospel amidst the Vietnamese People." This stressed solidarity with all Vietnamese people - "because this people is the community which God has entrusted to us" - along with concrete acts of love and service. These were summarized as being "to contribute to the defense and edification of the nation [and] to construct a lifestyle and a way of expressing our faith which will conform to the traditions of our people ..." The letter encouraged many levels of participation in community service and reconstruction, and became the theme for many later programmes and writings.

Yet the Vietnamese bishops have also continued to express criticism of the government's religious policy stating (in the early 1990s) that although some changes in this have promised reform, restrictions have in fact increased. "Of all human rights, the right to religious freedom is the most important. Therefore, it must be respected as a right, and not as a privilege." The Pastoral Letter of 1991 requested more tolerance of religious practice and dissent by the government, and also criticized increased corruption and inequalities. Letters in 1993, and annually since 1996, which have received belated replies from government officials, continued to stress these issues, and particularly the continuance of surveillance and lack of full religious freedoms. In almost all their documents the bishops are careful to outline the theological, and sometimes humanitarian, bases upon which their statements and appeals are founded. In their response to the *Lineamenta* (Preparatory document from the Vatican for the Asian Synod of 1998), these included a critical statement which emphasised the particular situation and theological insights of Vietnamese and Asian churches.

Work of the Bishops' Conference for the inculturation of the liturgy is directed by Bishop Peter Trân Đình Tú and aims to incorporate elements of Vietnamese culture in liturgy and festivals. The basis for this is in a theology which "allows us to see those of other faiths as the children of God", for the values of other religions are also from God, declares Trân Đình Tú.

The Pastoral Letter issued by the bishops at their annual general assembly in Hanoi, October 2000, highlighted the study and implementation of *Ecclesia in Asia* (post-Asian synod document); the impulse to evangelization; the ongoing formation for clergy and religious; special care for laity and families; and social outreach to the needy, the exploited, the excluded. The Conference also affirmed that the Vietnamese Church has matured and is now taking responsibility to proclaim the Gospel "in a Vietnamese way," and called upon laity to infuse the "'mind of Christ' into the mentality, customs, laws and structures of the secular world in which they live." And "since Jesus identified himself with the hungry, the poor, the handicapped, the marginalized," living the faith requires also commitment to serving and transforming society. (Bishop

Barthelemy Nguyên Son Lâm of Thanh-Hóa, is now secretary of the Bishops' Conference).

Selected References

"Lettre Pastorale de la Conférence épiscopale." *Missi* 6 (1954).
"Lenten Pastoral Letter." *Fides* 19.2. (1964).
"Communiqué de la Conférence épiscopale du Vietnam." *La Documentation Catholique* 50e Année. 65 (1968).
"L'Evangélisation au Vietnam. Lettre Pastorale de la Conférence épiscopale." (Epiphanie 1975). *La Documentation Catholique* 57.9 (1975).
"L'Église est mystère de communion. Lettre Pastorale de la Conférence épiscopale." *Weltkirche* (1990).
"La Conférence épiscopale Chrétiens a dix ans. Fidélité à l'Église et Fidélité au Vietnam. In *Chrétiens au Vietnam: Missi* 528 (1991).
"Pastoral Letter of the Vietnamese Conference of Bishops. To all the Vietnamese Priests, Religious and Laity". HCMV: May1980. Also in Pham Đình Thái, "Christians in Vietnam; Dialogue and Social Commitment in the New Social Context." Dissertation, University of Edinburgh, 1992.
"La Liberté de l'Église au Vietnam: nouvelle demandes de l'Episcopat. *La Documentation Catholique* 75 (1993).
"Lettre Pastorale de la Conférence épiscopale à M.Võ Văn Kiêt, chef du gouvernement de la République Socialiste du Vietnam." *Mission Étrangères de Paris* (1996).
"L'Evangile revit dans le peuple de Dieu. Lettre Pastorale de la Conférence épiscopale." *Weltkirche* (1998).
"Lettre Pastorale de la Conférence épiscopale adressée aux prêtres, religieux, religieuses, séminaristes et è l'ensemble des fidéles." *Églises d'Asie* 274 (1998).
"Les Inquiétudes et les difficultés des catholiques." Lettre de évêques du Vietnam au gouvernement. *La Documentation Catholique* 80 (1998).
"Living, witnessing and proclaiming the Good News in the Life of Christians." Pastoral Letter of the Conference of Bishops Vietnam. *Fides* 11.10 (2000).

4.4.3. Catholic Poets

Vietnam is especially rich in the number of Catholic poets in this period, as in the 19th and early 20th centuries (see 1.4.ff and 2.1.3.).

Much of this verse is deeply imbued with theological insight and must be recognized as integral to the body of contextual theological reflection in Vietnam. It is only possible here to make brief mention of a selection of those who have published poetry to their credit, although this has almost always been printed and circulated only privately. Among priests, bishops, lay people and religious, who are recognized as Christian poets, some of whom are very widely known, are:

Xuân Ly Bãng, Lê Dình Bang, Vinh An Nguyên Văn Sõn, Trân Uyên Thi, Linh Hoàng, Liêu Giang, Nguyên Ca Nguyên, Thanh Sâm, Nguyên Thi Xuân, Hýõng Kinh, Dông Thi Vân Khanh, Pham Phù Sa, Dô Văn Trân, Lê Khánh, Trâm Tý, Võ tá Khánh (Trăng Thâp Tu), Mai Thành and Hoàng Gia Khánh (For latter two see 4.3.8. and 4.3.17.).

Others include: Khat Vong, Cho Mong, Chut Duyen Tho, Noi Niem Khuc Hat An Tinh, Noi Niem, Chum Tho Dai, Dap Lai Tinh Yeu, Deo Van Tran, Que Huong Va Tinh Dao, U Tim.

The work of many of these poets is available only in mimeographed or even manuscript form, but a number had their work privately printed in the pioneer volume *Flower Season* (1991). This was a large anthology of contemporary Catholic poetry, in a wide range of traditional and 'free' form, but anonymous regarding either editors or publishers. Here again much work remains to be done if an adequate range of Catholic poetry, along with its theological significance, is to be assembled and studied in Vietnam.

Selected References

> All the volumes below have been privately circulated, and most of them were printed or roneo'd, in Saigon/HCMV.
> Mai Thành. *Tho Huong Nguyên* (Incense of Prayer, Poems 1953-1999). 1999.
> Lê Dình Bang. *Hành Huong* (Pilgrimage). 1994.
> —. *Quy truóc Dên vàng* (Kneeling in front of Golden Temple). 1998.
> —. *Lòi Tu Tình cua Biên Trân Gian* (Sensing the ocean of the world). 1999.
> Trân Uyên Thi et al. *Mùa Hoa Suu tâp Tho* (Flower season - anthology of poetry). Dalat: Privately printed, ca. 1991.

Contextual Theology in Vietnam 1800-2000

Vinh An Nguyên Văn Sõn. *Lòi Dâng* (Words of offering). 2000.
Xuân Ly Bãng. *Thõ Kinh* (Prayers in verse). 1956.
—. *Hýõng Kinh* (Perfume of prayers). 1958.
—. *Trâm Tu* (In Reflexion). 1959.
—. *Nôi niêm* (Innermost feelings). 1961.

4.4.4. Other Theologians, Scholars, Writers

An extensive listing of published Christian writings in Vietnamese is provided in the bibliography by Lm. Trân Anh Dung, *Sõ thao thý muc Công giáo Viêt Nam* (The Catholic Church in Vietnam - a brief bibliography of sources), 1992. This covers most traditional subjects of Catholic writing, including dogmatics, church history, moral theology, biblical studies, liturgy and sacramental theology, catechetics, hagiography and Marian studies. Only a few examples of contextual reflection are included, however, either in this or other bibliographies thus far produced. For some decades, the Nguyên Bá Tòng printing house of Saigon/HCMV has printed many books and pamphlets for the purposes of catechetics and priestly formation, with increasing concern in recent years for inculturation in an Asian setting. There are also a large number of theologians, scholars and writers in this period - other than those mentioned above - whose thought also contributes to a contextual Vietnamese theology. A short selection of these must be at least briefly mentioned.

4.4.4.1. Theology, Spirituality and Mission

Joseph Miettes sj was former Jesuit Superior in Vietnam from whom we have a collection of homilies, *Bánh Vun* (Crumbs of bread), and a volume of biblical meditations reflecting on his experience of years in a labor camp. Recalling Jesus' words on responding to persecutors, he readily entered fully into the demanding labor and refused to escape: praying "for the disabled, the wanderers, the suffering, the hungry, let me be good fortune ... Do with me as you will ..."

Mgr Nguyên Kim Diên has given many lectures and homilies, and although few have been published, contributions he has made to the Conference of Bishops and to FABC discussions are recorded. With a theology that recasts the traditional roles of dogma and of sacrifice, he has advocated a much fuller Catholic commitment to the life and hopes of Vietnamese people. "Many priests and religious have been ready to die for the faith," he declared to fellow bishops, "but few have been willing to die for the people."

Trân Duy Nhiên, is a dramatist and lay theologian whose plays on Christian themes have been privately printed by the Redemptorist Pastoral Center and whose articles appear mainly in *Công giáo và Dân tôc* (HCMV) and in *Dinh Huóng* (Alsace). Concerning a Vietnamese theology, he questions the necessity to begin with logical explication of Christian dogma about God, and gives priority to thought and writing which discerns the ways in which "God is manifest, in his Christ, to the peoples of Asia." Such a theology will portray in "the most faithful way possible, the living God who saves and who liberates in concrete reality" men and women in Asian lands.

Vincent Trân Vãn Doàn, now of the National Taiwan University, has circulated a number of papers on the internet on "Towards a Viêt Theology." The method for this theology, he writes, is not 'systematic' but is sensual more than rational, relational and dialectic rather than Cartesian and analytic, praxis-oriented rather than abstract. Viêt Theology is a tool for realizing mutual and reciprocal relationships with God - and with each other - rather than an 'objective' study. God is to be humanized rather than absolutized: the human being seen as a co-creator in theology, and the "relational point between God and earth" rather than passive recipient.

Peter C. Phan gained his STD from Salesian University and his PhD and DD from London University, UK, and has been Professor of Religion and Culture at the Catholic University of America and President of the Catholic Theological Association of America. His teaching is in the areas of systematic theology, missiology and interfaith dialogue. He is the author or editor of some 20 books and 250 essays, amongst them important writings on Alexandre de Rhodes, the "Asian face of Jesus", and upon the recent Asian Synod of Bishops (1998). His writings also include volumes on social thought, and on grace and the human condition, and on wider diversities within the beliefs and theology of the Church. He has also edited volumes on a wider ecumenism, on ethnicity, nationality and religious experience, as well as on Asian-American theology, ecclesiology and eschatology.

Pham Dình Thái (1952-) studied theology, philosophy and languages in Saigon and later studied Christian Social Ethics at Edinburgh. A layman, he writes regularly for both Vietnamese and international Catholic journals and assists in programs of theological seminars and publication in Vietnam. In a full study of the background, theological basis and contemporary situation of Christian social commitment in Vietnam, he focuses upon the present and future participation of Christians in human development in Vietnam. He concludes that renewed Bible study, social analysis, inter-faith dialogue and pastoral praxis will make possible a living Vietnamese theology and bring about a church with an Asian face, identified with the Vietnamese people. This, however, will require, he believes, a radical change in Catholic world views, in "the spirit of renewal and reconciliation promoted by the Second Vatican Council."

Among many others who have contributed to a localized Vietnamese theology with articles in Christian magazines in recent years, are Không Thành Ngoc - a journalist writing regular reflections upon the everyday life and situation of Christians in Vietnam, for the weekly *Công giáo và Dân tôc*; Norbert Nguyên Văn Khánh sf - teacher at the Major Seminary in Nha Trang, who also writes on issues in the inculturation of the faith; Msgr Bùi Tuân - known for his letters and addresses on the Vietnamese church and methods of mission in Vietnam; Nguyên Thái Hop op - who has written on liberation theology in the Vietnam context, following ministries in South America; Dê Văn Nguyên - who has written a critical interpretation on the Gospels from the perspective of the 'underside'; Hoàng Minh Tuân - in volumes of biblical reflections and hermeneutics; and Guy-Marie Nguyên Hông Giáo - teacher of philosophy in HCMV, who has written on discerning "God's actions in historical events."

Others to be named here are Thiên Phong Buu Duong op, Nguyên Khac Chính, Hô Thành Biên, Nguyên Ngoc Lan, Nguyên

Tâm Thuòng, Msgr Paul Bùi Vãn Doc, Nguyên Hông Giáo, Trân Thanh Cao, Nguyên Vãn Nôi and Lý Chánh Trung.

Selected References

Bùi Tuân. "Nhung Con Duòng Truyên Giáo" (Ways of missionary work). Mimeo'd, October 1991.

Dê Vãn Nguyên. *Matthäus auf der Reise nach Vietnam: Notizen zum Evang elium.* Stuttgart: Radius-Verlag, 1979.

Miettes, Joseph. *Ecrits au Camp Travail 1985-1990.* HCMV: Privately Printed, ca.1991.

Nguyên Thi Oanh et al. *Vietnamese Catholics Amidst of the Nation.* HCMV: Committee for the Union of Patriotic Catholics, 1989.

Pham Dình Thái. "Christians in Vietnam; Dialogue and Social Commitment in the New Social Context." Dissertation, University of Edinburgh, 1992.

Phan, Peter C. *Mission and Catechesis: Alexandre de Rhodes & Inculturation in Seventeenth-Century Vietnam.* Faith and Culture series. Maryknoll, NY, Orbis Books, 1998.

— "Jesus Christ with an Asian Face." *Theological Studies* 57.3 (1996).

— "How Much Uniformity Can We Stand? How Much Unity Do We Want? Church and Worship in the Next Millennium." *Worship* 72 (May 1998).

Trân Anh Dung. *Sõ thao thu muc Công giáo Viêt Nam* (The Catholic Church in Vietnam - a brief bibliography of sources). Paris: Trân Anh Dung, 1992.

Trân duy Nhiên. "Thân Hoc Á Châu, Môt Thách Thúc?" (An Asian theology: a challenge?) *Công giáo và Dân tôc* .... (Jan 2000)

See also:

www.catholic.org.tw/vntaiwan/theology/vietnam.htm <http://www.catholic.org.tw/vntaiwan/theology/vietnam.htm> - June 1999 - for writings of Vietnamese theologians currently working in Taiwan.

4.4.4.2. History, Culture and Religion 2

Joseph Nguyên Huu Lai is known as the writer of the fullest study of Vietnam's religious and cultural traditions, and the history of Christian encounter with them. In his work *La Tradition Religieuse, Spirituelle, Sociale au Vietnam* (1981), he first presents chapters on the major religious traditions and then narrates the history of

Jesuit response and the more recent experience especially since 1954. The documents of Vatican II are also studied along with the creative values of other faiths in Vietnam. He concludes that these are still of relevance and are in fact fulfilled in Jesus who is "the way, the truth and the light" of all.

An Sõn Vi is a scholar of oriental traditions and has written much on inculturation and the integration of Christian life and faith within Vietnamese culture and religion. His writings include studies of the processes necessary for this, the models given in the Pastoral Letter by the bishops in 1980, and also of applications of particular Hindu or Buddhist insights, such as Zen meditation and yoga asanas, in the life of Christians.

Nguyên Viêt Cu (d.?1980) was Director of the Catholic Center in Saigon in the 1960s and later Secretary to the Bishops' Conference. His many writings in journals and newspapers during the1960s and 1970s were in the main reflections and exhortations for the peace of the nation and the reconciliation of Church and people during conditions of war.

Kim Dinh has written many volumes in the field of oriental philosophies, and especially upon Vietnamese religious, cultural and philosophical traditions. These have included such traditions as those of kingship, of sacred reality and of communal village life (*Triêt lý cái dình*), as well as the humanist traditions of Vietnam (*Nhân ban*). Since 1975 he has continued writing in the USA.

Vu Kim Chính sj, of the Fujen Catholic University, Taiwan, has circulated papers on the internet containing extensive reflections upon the emerging relationships between the Catholic Church and the state in Vietnam, and upon the "Mission of the People of God in the World." Regarding church-state relations, he outlines their recent history, interprets the role of Marxism and of Communist policies and proposes that through greater measures of co-operation could come a "mutual liberation." Other Vietnamese theologians whose writings upon Vietnamese theology have been issued in Taiwan include Ban Biên Tâp, Vu Dình Trác, Trân Vãn Doàn, and Trân Cao Tuòng.

Among other scholars and church leaders who must be mentioned are Fr Cao Vãn Luân - founder and Rector of the University of Huê and courageous in his concern for a just peace, for inter-religious amity, and for freedom from the aggression of both North Vietnam and the USA, Dang Thanh Minh - parish priest and teacher at Huê Seminary, writing on Buddhism and Inculturation; Nguyên Thê Thoai - parish priest and adjunct Professor at Nha Trang Seminary, teaching Social Documents and Theology of Religions; the church historian Dô Huu Nghiêm; and Nguyên Hung who has produced a bibliography of Vietnamese Catholic books written in Nom and Demotic Script.

Selected References

An Sõn Vi. *Kitô giáo di vào Vãn hóa Viêt Nam* (Christianity integrating into Vietnamese culture). Hochiminh City: Uy Ban doàn kêt Công giáo yêu nuóc, 1990.

—. *Lô di yên tinh* (Quiet path). Hochiminh City: Uy Ban doàn kêt Công giáo yêu nuóc, n.d.

—. *Thiên Kitô Giáo* (Christian Zen). HCMV: Committee for Religion and Society, 1992.

Cao Vãn Luân. "Theses of the Progressive Catholics." In Piero Gheddo *The Cross and the Bo-Tree: Catholics and Buddhists in Vietnam.* Trans. by Charles Underhill Quinn. New York: Sheed and Ward, 1970.

Nguyên Huu Lai, Joseph. *La Tradition Religieuse, Spirituelle, Sociale au Vietnam.* Paris: Beauchesne, 1981.

Nguyên Vãn Tôt, Pierre. "Le Boudha et le Christ. Paralleles et Resemblances dans la Littérature Canonique et Apocrypha Chrétienne." Dissertation, Collectio Urbaniana 3284. Rome: Pontifical Urban University, 1987.

Trân Anh Dung. *Sõ thao thu muc công giáo Viêt Nam* ("L'Église catholique au Vietnam: bibliographie sommaire en langue vietnamienne; The Catholic Church in Vietnam: brief bibliography of sources in Vietnamese") Paris: Trân Anh Dung, c1992.

Truong Bá Cân, Lê Vãn Khuê and Nguyên Nghi. *Bibliography of Books, Documents and Articles on Catholic Christianity in Vietnam, Held in Vietnam.* HCMV: mimeo'd, 1989.

See also:
  www.catholic.org.tw/vntaiwan/theology/vietnam.htm <http://www.catholic.org.tw/vntaiwan/theology/vietnam.htm> - June 1999 - for writings of Vietnamese theologians currently working in Taiwan.

5 Protestant Presence and Writing
5.1 Historical Background

Participation by Protestants in cultural, political or ecumenical life had been limited since the 'late' arrival in Vietnam in 1911, of the Christian and Missionary Alliance (CMA) from Canada (to Laos 1902 and to Cambodia 1922). Edwin F. Irwin was a pioneer missionary for the CMA (1914-1960), who with his colleagues, was committed to establishing an "indigenous and autonomous church." The *Hôi Thánh Tin Lành Viêt Nam* (Evangelical Church of Vietnam - "Tin Lành" ["Good News"] churches) was formed in 1927 as a national although loosely linked association. By 1945 most churches were able to support themselves, although many congregations were led by expatriates. By 1965, 104 nationals had been ordained, including such leaders as Lê Vãn Thái, Ông Vãn Huyên and Doàn Vãn Miêng. Many other Protestant missions became active in South Vietnam after 1955, often establishing a range of social ministries. Although traditionally holding a theology which limited church activities to "spiritual" goals, the *Tin Lành* now also came to accept that ministry to social, medical and educational needs was necessary if Christian witness was to be authentic.

In the period of greater American involvement the CMA intensified activities particularly amongst the highland ethnic minorities of South Vietnam. There were approximately 200,000 Protestant Christians in Vietnam by 1975, of whom one-third were Montagnard. Numbers in North Vietnam however may not have exceeded 2,000, largely due to severe restrictions upon their activities. Some pastors associated with the Vietnam Protestants' Association, formed in 1955 under government auspices, have participated politically but the majority have refused co-operation. Protestant seminaries in Hanoi and Nha Trang, along with other church institutions, and over 100 churches, were closed in 1975. Ninety pastors were sent to re-education camps and few conferences either district or national were allowed. Most churches in the highlands remained closed between 1975 and 1986, and scores of pastors were imprisoned until 1988 (some again in 1991). But church leaders, such as Bui Hoanh Thu of the Protestant Alliance in Hanoi, have affirmed that it is "no more contradictory to live [as Christians] in a socialist state than any other." Tribal Christians suffer not only continuing state-condoned persecution but also continuing expropriation of lands by ethnic Vietnamese. Yet it is now estimated that in addition to over 300 recognized churches there are many hundreds of "underground" churches meeting (especially in the highlands), with a total of nearly 800,000 members. Not until 2000 was it possible for the *Tin Lành* to obtain government recognition for some 250 congregations in the southern half of the country. This is expected to bring permission to open new churches and for activities other than public worship. Whether it will be possible to open more seminaries and Bible schools appears more doubtful.

Provisions of the new Decree on Religious Freedom being prepared may also bring a measure of liberty for Protestant mission, teaching and publishing.

Selected References

Archives: Reformed Churches Documentation. Compiled by Lukas Vischer and Jean-Jacques Bauswein 1991-1999. Geneva: WCC Library. These contain folders: Christian Church in Vietnam, Protestant Church of Vietnam, Theological Schools of Vietnam.

Dowdy, Homer. *The Bamboo Cross. Christian Witness in the Jungles of Vietnam.* New York: Harper and Row, 1964.

Huynh Thiên Buu. *Niên Giám Hôi Thánh Tin Lành Viêt Nam* (Yearbook of the Evangelical Church of Vietnam). HCMV: Privately Printed, 1999.

James, Violet B. "American Protestant Missions and the Vietnamese War." PhD dissertation, University of Aberdeen, 1989.

Lê Hoàng Phu. *Lich Sy Truyên Giáo* (History of missions). 1995.

Manikam, Rajah B. and Winburn T. Thomas, eds. *The Church in Southeast Asia.* New York: Friendship Press, 1956.
Pham, Xuân Tín. *Ngu Vung Thân Hoc. Hôi Thánh Tin Lành Viêt Nam,* 1973 (A brief account of the Evangelical Church of Vietnam). Elkhart, Ind: n.p., 1973.
Reimer, Reginald E. "The Protestant Movement in Vietnam." M.A. thesis, Fuller, 1972.
Roeck, R. De. "Vietnam, Cambodia and Laos: The Church at the Crossroads of Chaos". In *Christ and Crisis in Southeast Asia,* edited by Gerald Anderson. New York: Friendship Press, 1968.
Smith, Mrs Gordon H. *Victory in Vietnam* (Missions behind the headlines). Grand Rapids: Zondervan, 1965.

5.2 Contextual Protestant Theology

Little theological writing or publication has been undertaken by members of the *Tin Lành* during the last 70 years - especially that which might draw on, or respond to specifically Vietnamese issues or experience. This is largely because of theological and ideological positions which are strongly conservative. The church's mission and purpose has been interpreted as being solely "spiritual" so that any involvement or ministry regarded as "social" or "secular" has been avoided as much as possible. Only a small number of letters, testimonies and reports have appeared from Protestant pastors or lay people over recent decades, some smuggled abroad, but little if any contextual reflection is included in them. A few pastors only have in recent years sought to participate in ecumenical theological programs such as those of the United Committee's center in HCMV.

From 1954, however, many international ecumenical agencies had established relief and development programs in Vietnam, including those of the Mennonites, the Lutherans and Christian World Service, which were united as Vietnam Christian Service by 1965. The Asian Christian Service of the East Asia Christian Conference (EACC, later CCA) co-ordinated a wide range of emergency and community programs in which many nationals were employed and/or trained. From this Christian presence, most Protestant reflection - both theological and contextual - has come. Among a wealth of reports and stories arising from the often tragic experiences of both nationals and expatriate co-workers, a number of significant theological reflections can be found.

By 1968, published collections of stories and reflections included the following:

A New Song, edited by Kenneth de Lanerolle (1968), provides people-stories, along with images of 'being found,' of rescue, restoration and healing, of worship in ruined churches, and of "a little love" amidst brutal warfare .

Fragments of War, by Jill Perkins (1970) presents prose and poetry which portray courage under bombardment, the demanding work of feeding, healing and teaching, the reunion of families, teamwork in emergency, "joyful surgery," the vitality of life in a refugee camp, light found in tragedy, the confidence and resilience of refugees, along with glimpses of remaining beauty in the land.

Signs of Christian Presence ed. by Ruth Cadwallader (1971 and 1972) recount the story of Asian Christian Service work with those on both sides of the conflict in Vietnam. In particular, vol. 1 includes 'Why we serve' by Samuel Isaac: "We follow Him - the healer, social reformer, bringer of a new social order based on love ..." along with what became a widely used 'Manifesto for Christians in the midst of Conflict' - the anonymous writing of a group of ACS staff. (See below.)

The theology emerging in such collections as these is one of Christian presence in situations of conflict, destitution, massacre and conflagration. Finding inspiration in pursuing hope-in-action and in dedicated teamwork, this understanding is nourished by the life, and death, of Jesus in the gospels, and discerns his presence with all life-giving, peace-making partners; in rescue and restoration, re-uniting, and reconciliation, friendship and reconstruction. It is articulated first in letters, in stories gathered, in occasional meditations, and in brief affirmations which sometimes arise from co-operative reflection. See particularly the "Manifesto for the Christians in the Midst of Conflict" (1972) in which Beatitude is announced for example, on those "who are humble enough - to receive the judgement ... who are sensitive enough - to bear the sorrows of others as their own ... open to seek a new way - other than aggressive assertion ... who hunger after integrity and justice ... who are single-minded to eschew the injustices done by sophisticated corridors of the powers ... Blessed are those who are ready to endure the persecution which attends the single-minded pursuit of justice and peace in the face of intransigent power ..."

Booklets were later regularly issued by the ACS, the CCA and the WCC, some of which contain narrative and theological reflection: see for example *Nurturing an Asian Christian Presence in Indochina* (1983), and *Indochina Today: A Consultation on Emerging Trends* (1994).

A small number of doctoral and masters theses have been completed overseas by Protestant Vietnamese since the late 1960s and a selection of these appear below and in the Supplementary Bibliography. Concerns for Christian education, and for theology, which is rooted in Vietnam are prominent among these.

Selected References

Between Two Tigers: Testimonies of Vietnamese Christians. Bartlesville, Okla.: Living Sacrifice Book Co., c.1996.

Cadwallader, Ruth, ed. *Signs of Christian Presence* (vol. 1, 1971, vol. 2, 1972). Bangkok: East Asia Christian Conference.

de Lanerolle, Kenneth, ed. *A New Song*. Saigon: Asian Christian Service, 1968.

Herendeen, D.S. "Conversion and Indigeneity in the Evangelical Church of Vietnam." D.Miss. Dissertation, Fuller, 1975.

Lê Dông Thiên. "The Bamboo Cross: Toward a Vietnamese Theology and Christian Educational Ministry in Vietnam." S.T. Thesis, Claremont, 1994.

"Manifesto for the Christians in the Midst of Conflict." In *Vietnam Beyond Aid and Development*. FME/IDOC 18, 1976.

Mathews George Chunakara, ed. *Indochina Today: A Consultation on Emerging Trends*. Hong Kong: CCA-WCC Indochina Programme, 1994.

—, ed. *Ecumenical Response to Indo-China*. Hong Kong: CCA, 1995.

Perkins, Harvey. *Sounds of the Song: Report of a team visit to Vietnam August-September 1978*. Singapore: CCA, 1978.

Perkins, Jill. *Fragments of War*. Hong Kong: Chinese Christian Literature Council for the Asian Church Women's Conference, 1970.

Yap Kim Hao et al. *Nurturing an Asian Christian Presence in Indochina*. Singapore: CCA, 1983.

Documents of ACS and related agencies are listed in Dorothy M. Harvey's *... there is no end: Check list of EACC-CCA Publications ... 1948-1981*. Singapore: CCA, 1981.

Reports and reflections of Vietnamese Protestants appear on occasion in such sources as *CCA News*, *Praxis* (WSCF Asia Pacific), and *Christianity Today*.

6 Supplementary Bibliography

Bensberger Kreis. *Die Christen und der Krieg in Vietnam: ein Memorandum deutscher Katholiken*. Mainz: Grünewald, 1969.

Bùi Dúc Sinh op. *The Catholic Church in Vietnam*. (In Vietnamese). 3 vols. 2nd ed. Calgary: n.p. 1998.

Chunakara, Mathews George, ed. *Indochina: From Socialism to Market Economy*. Hong Kong: CCA, 1996.

Chuong Thâu, Phan Bôi Châu. *Thiên Hô! Dê Hô! (Tròi ôi! Chúa ôi!)* (O Heaven! O Lord!). Hà Nôi: Khoa hoc xã hôi, 1978.

Cuenot, Claude. "Le Reverend Pere Emile Licent, S.J." *Bulletin de la Societe des Études Indochinoises*, 41.1 (1966).

"Cùng Nhau Tiên Dên Thiên Niên Ky Thú Ba" (Come forward together; some notes on the edge of conflict). Ho Chí Minh: Uy Ban Doàn Kêt Công Giáo Yêu Nuóc, 1990.

Dao, Joseph, op. *L'Église du Vietnam dans l'épreuve* (The church in Vietnam under trial). Montréal: Presse Dominicaine, 1955. Also *Revue dominicaine* 61.2 (1955).

Descours-Gatin, Chantal et al. *Guide de recherches sur le Vietnam: bibliographies, archives et bibliothèques de France*. Paris: L'Harmattan, c1983.

Doàn Doc Thu and Xuân Huy. *Giám muc Lê Huu Tù & Phát-Diêm, 1945-1954*. (Bishop Lê Huu Tù and Phát Diêm [his diocese], 1945-1954). S.l.: s.n., 1973.

Duiker, William J. *Historical Dictionary of Vietnam*. 2nd. ed. Lanham, Md.: Scarecrow Press, 1997.

―. *The Rise of Nationalism in Vietnam, 1900-1941*. Ithaca: Cornell University Press, 1976.

Éditions "Vie ouvrière." *L'Église et les mouvements révolutionnaires. Vietnam, Amérique latine, colonies portugaises Bruxelles*. Paris: Editeur Les Éditions ouvrières 1972.

Elbert, Joan. "How the Church is Faring in Vietnam." *Christian Century* 98 (May 20, 1981).

Giáo Hôi Trong Con Lôc Lich Sy: Tuyên Tâp Thân Hoc (The Church in the whirlwind of the new times: selection of writings by Vietnamese and foreign authors). HCMV: Committee for Union of Vietnamese Catholics, 1990.

Halley, Cyril. "The Catholic Church in South Vietnam." *ABA Newsletter* 27 (1976).

Haas, Harry. "South Vietnam's Catholics and the War." *Christian Century* 85 (March 20, 1968).

Hoàng Quý. *Cam nghiêm sông lòi Chúa: phân thuc hành* (Experiencing how to live out the word of God: practical aspects). S.l.: Thanh tien, 1991.

Huu Ngo, et al. *Tu Diên Vãn Hóa Cô Truyên Viêt Nam: Muc Tù xêp theo Dê Tài, và A B C, Có Minh Hoa* (Dictionary of Vietnamese traditional culture). Hà Nôi: Thê Giói, 1995.

Karnow, Stanley. *Vietnam: A History*. New York: Viking Press, 1984.

Ky yêu dia phân Bùi Chu: ky yêu ghi nhó 50 nãm dia phân Bùi Chu duoc trao hoàn toàn cho hàng giáo si VN (1936-1986) (Bui Chu Diocese summary: summary in remembrance of the 50 year time during which the Bui Chu diocese was being entirely entrusted to the Vietnamese clergy (1936-1986)). Santa Ana, Calif.: Hôi ái Huu Gia Dình Bùi Chu tai Hoa Ky, 1987?

Lê Huu Dân. *Tài liêu soi sáng su thât* (Evidence of truth). Fremont, CA: Lê Huu Dân, 1995.

"Lettre ouverte à l'Union des Supérieurs généraux religieux de HCMV." *Église et Mission* 60.217 (1980).

Lý Chánh Trung. *Tôn giáo và Dân toc* (Religion and the nation). Saigon: Lua Thieng, 1973.

Merrell, Betty J. and Priscilla Tunnell, eds. *Stories that Won't Go Away. Women in Vietnam 1959-1975*. Birmingham AL: New Hope, 1995.

Nguyên Minh Quang. *Religious Problems in Vietnam: Questions and Answers*. Hanoi: Thê Giói Publishers, 2000.

Nguyên Thê Anh. *Bibliographie Critique sur les Relations Entre le Vietnam et l'Occident* (Ouvrages et Articles en Langues Occidentales). Paris: Maisonneuve and Larose, 1967.

Nguyên, An Tôn. *Công giáo miên Nam Viêt Nam sau ngày 30-4-1975* (Catholicism in South Vietnam after April 30th 1975). Gretna: Dân Chúa Xuât Ban, 1988.

Osborne, Milton E. *The French Presence in Cochinchina and Cambodia: Rule and Response (1859-1905)*. Ithaca: Cornell University Press, 1969.

Pham Kim Vinh. *The Vietnamese Culture: an Introduction*. [Calif.?]: The Pham Kim Vinh Research Institute, 1990?

Shortland, John R. *The Persecutions of Annam: A History of Christianity in Cochin China and Tonking*. London: Burns and Oates, 1875.

Singleton, Carl. *Vietnam Studies: an Annotated Bibliography*. Lanham, Md.: Scarecrow Press; Pasadena, Calif.: Salem Press, 1997.

So Tak Tsang. "Christian Education of Adults in Vietnam." Thesis, Evangelical Lutheran Seminary, Hong Kong, 1970.

"Socialisme et Religion au Vietnam Nord." *IDOC International* 35 (1970).

Studies on Vietnamese Language and Literature: a Preliminary Bibliography. Nguyên Dình Tham. Ithaca, NY: Cornell University, Southeast Asia Program, 1992.

Suy Niêm Tin Mùng Nãm B: Mùa Vong, Mùa Giáng Sinh, Tâp 1 (Meditations on Bible Readings Year B: Advent and Christmas Seasons 1). HCMV: Committee for Union of Vietnamese Catholics, 1990.

The Vietnamese Theological Dictionary. (In Vietnamese). Taipei: Quangchi Press, 1996.

Thích, Joseph. *Vân dê Công San* (The question of Communism). Qui Nhõn: Công giáo, 1927.

Tuck, P.J.N. *French Catholic Missionaries and the Politics of Imperialism in Vietnam 1857 - 1914. A Documentary Survey*. Liverpool: Liverpool University Press, 1987.

"Vatican-Vietnam Talks." (Vietnamese Catholic bishops visit Rome) *Christian Century* 108 (January 2-9 1991).

Verwey, W.D. *Hel en Hemel, De rol van de Katholieken in Vietnam.* Baarn: Bosch and Keuning, 1971.

Vu Duy Tú. *Der Beginn der christlich-europäischen Einflussnahme in Vietnam.* Mitteilungen der Deutschen Gesellschaft. Hamburg: Gesellschaft fur Natur- und volkerkunde Ostasiens, 1976.

Young, Stephen B. and Nguyên Ngoc Huy. *The Tradition of Human Rights in China and Vietnam.* Lac Viet Series 10. New Haven CT: Yale Center for International and Area Studies, 1990.

- JCE with HGK, NVN, NCK.

Key Bibliographical Sources

Asia Journal of Theology
Includes regular section on Asian bibliographical resources.
P.O. Box 4635, 57 Miller's Road, Bangalore 560 046, India.

Bibliographia Missionaria
Annual classified listing of new publications on non-western Christianity, by country worldwide.
Pontifical Missionary Library, Pontifical Urban University, 00120 Vatican City.

Exchange
Journal of Missiological and Ecumenical Research, issued three times a year. Occasional special issues or bibliographical articles on Asian resources.
c/o Exchange IIMO, Interuniversity Institute for Mission and Ecumenical Research, Heidelberglaan 2, 3584 CS Utrecht, The Netherlands.

International Review of Mission
Quarterly. Includes a regular classified bibliography of mission and church studies from a selection of Asian journals and books.
World Council of Churches,150 route de Ferney, 1211 Geneva 2, Switzerland.

PTCA Bulletin - now Journal of Theologies and Cultures in Asia
Bi-annual publication of the Programme for Theology & Cultures in Asia.
c/o Theology Division, Chung Chi College, Chinese University of Hong Kong, Shatin N.T., Hong Kong SAR.

Theological Book Review
Issued three times a year - classified listing of theological publications primarily from Europe and North America.
Feed the Minds, Albany House, Sydenham Road, Guildford, Surrey GU1 3RY, England.

Theology in Context
Published three times a year. Annotated Bibliography, including summaries and surveys of "Third World" periodicals, books, articles. Lists and abstracts from approximately 50 Asian journals, along with selected books. The print version of Theology in Context will be discontinued at the end of 2002, but MWI-Missio's Yearbook is to be expanded and published annually in German and in four other languages (English, Spanish, French and Portuguese). In addition, the MWI data base will be freely available on the Internet. Up-to-date details from: Institute of Missiology (MWI), Missio, P.O. Box 11 10, 52012 Aachen, Germany.

Contributors to Volume 2

AMSP - Dr Anna May Say Pa, Lecturer in Biblical Studies and Principal of Myanmar Institute of Theology, Insein, Myanmar/Burma.

AP - Mr Alan Po, Librarian, Myanmar Institute of Theology, Insein, Myanmar/Burma.

AS - Achara Somsaengsruang, of the Ubon-Ratchathani Diocesan Office, Thailand.

BA - Fr Bruno Arens, Bishop's Office, Nakhonsawan Diocese, Thailand.

DK - Ms Delia Kwong, Seminari Teologi Malaysia, Seremban, Malaysia.

ED - Ms Esther Danpongpee, Payap University, Chiangmai, Thailand.

FJJ - Fr Fung Jojo sj, formerly Research Fellow at the Catholic Research Centre, Kuala Lumpur; now of the Arrupe Jesuit Community in Taman Rinting, Johor, Malaysia.

GS - Ms Gwynneth Squires, University of Phnom Penh, Cambodia.

HGK - Hoàng Gia Khánh - Historian of Theology and poet, Ho Chi Minh Ville, Vietnam.

HRB - Dr Herbert R Swanson, Office of History, Church of Christ in Thailand.

HS - Dr Hermen Shastri, General Secretary of the Council of Churches of Malaysia.

JCE - The Rev'd John C. England, formerly Assoc. Dean, Programme for Theology and Cultures in Asia; Co-ordinating Editor.

Contributors to Volume 2

JD - Fr Jean Dantonel, Professor at the Major Roman Catholic Seminary, Samphran, Bangkok.

JdM - Dr Jose de Mesa, De La Salle University, Manila; and East Asia Pastoral Institute, Quezon City, Philippines.

JMP - Dr John M. Prior svd, Secretary of Puslit Candraditya, Maumere, Flores, Indonesia, and Consultor to FABC Commissions and Vatican Congregations.

LAQ - Dr Lily A. Quintos rc, formerly Dean of Franciscan School of Theology, Berkeley, USA; Director, The Cenacle, Quezon City, Philippines.

MLaGA - Dr Melanio LaG. Aoanan, Union Theological Seminary, Philippine Christian University, Das Marinas, Cavite, Philippines.

NCK - M. Nguyên Chính Kêt - Theological scholar and writer, Ho Chi Minh Ville, Vietnam.

NvN - M. Nguyeãn Nghò (Nguyen van Nghi), Institut des Sciences Sociales, Ho Chi Minh Ville, Vietnam.

PJ - The Rev'd Peter Joseph, Executive Secretary of the Association for Theological Education Myanmar/Burma.

RM - The Rev'd Reuel Marigza, Divinity School, Silliman University, Dumaguete City, Philippines.

TD - Dr Pradit Takerngransarit, Vice-President, Payap University, Chiangmai, Thailand.

TDN - Tran Duy Nhien, Professor in the University of Law, and humanitarian worker, Ho Chi Minh Ville.

Editors

Janice Wickeri was a mission co-worker with the PCUSA in Taiwan and Hong Kong, was formerly managing editor of the Research Centre for Translation of the Chinese University of Hong Kong and has been the editor of the *Chinese Theological Review* since 1985. She is the translator of many literary and theological works from Chinese to English. Recent publications include: *Love Never Ends: Papers of K.H. Ting* (ed. & tr., 2000), named one of Fifteen Outstanding Books in Mission Studies 2000 ; *Plurality, Power and Mission* (ed., with Philip Wickeri and Damayanthi Niles, 2000); and *The Oxford Guide to Literature in English Translation* (member of Advisory Board and editor of China section, 2000).

David Kwang-sun Suh, holds a PhD in Religion from Vanderbilt University, and taught theology and philosophy in Ewha Woman's University in Seoul, Korea. A founding member of the Korean Minjung Theology movement, he has written numerous articles for national and international ecumenical theological journals along with books in Korean and English. His representative work is *Korean Minjung in Christ.* (1991). He was recently Henry Luce Visiting Professor of World Christianity at Union Theological Seminary in New York and Visiting Professor of Asian Theology at Drew University. He is currently working for the Asian Christian Higher Education Institute of the United Board for Christian Higher Education in Asia.

Dr Lily A. Quintos rc , is a religious of the Cenacle and is Director of the Cenacle Retreat House and Center of Spirituality, Quezon City, Philippines. She was the first woman to defend her doctoral dissertation at the Faculty of Theology of the Catholic University of Louvain, Belgium, magna cum laude, and has served in international programmes for renewal in religious life as well as in *theological education*. Her writings and teachings in many countries have included also Buddhist and feminist studies. She has served as Academic Dean and Professor of Moral Theology at the Franciscan School of Theology, Graduate Theological Union in Berkeley, California, and now also teaches at the Loyola School of Theology, Ateneo de Manila University.

John Mansford Prior svd (PhD Birmingham) has worked in eastern Indonesia in cross-cultural mission since 1973. He is Executive Secretary of Candraditya Research Centre for the Study of Religion and Culture, Maumere, Flores, and has lectured in Asian *theology* in many countries. Since 1987 he has published scores of articles in Indonesian and other journals,; 16 original book chapters in collections, and edited or co edited more than 20 books. He has been lecturer at St. Paul's Major Seminary, Maumere, Flores, Executive Secretary of the SVD Asian Pacific Missiological Education and Research Programme(1994-99) and founding member and first Secretary of SVD Asian Pacific Association of Mission Researchers (ASPAMIR). Since 1992 he has also worked closely with the FABC Office for Evangelization.

Jose Kuttianimattathil sdb, is Professor of Systematic Theology at Kristu Jyoti College, Bangalore, India and holds a Doctorate in Systematic Theology from the Pontifical Gregorian University, Rome. He has taught philosophy at the Salesian College, Yercaud, Tamil Nadu (1978-1981), systematic theology at Kristu Jyoti College, Bangalore (1987-1990, and 1994-), and is currently Rector for theology students at Kristu Jyoti College. He is the editor of *Kristu Jyoti*, a youth pastoral, theological and catechetical journal. His previous publications include *Jesus Christ: Unique and Universal* (1990), *Practice and Theology of Interreligious Dialogue* (1995) and a number of articles in scholarly journals.

John C. England has been a staff member of the EACC/CCA, Programme Co-ordinator for Tao Fong Shan Ecumenical Centre, Hong Kong, and Associate Dean for the Programme for Theology and Cultures in Asia (PTCA). Since 1970 he has worked with centres, movements and seminaries throughout the region, co-ordinated programmes of post-graduate theological education for the Asian region and lectured in Asian theologies in many countries. Along with many articles in international journals, he edited the PTCA Bulletin from 1987-1994, and has written or edited five volumes for EACC/CCA, along with *Living Theology in Asia* (1981, 1982, the annual series of Occasional Papers of *Doing Theology with Asian Resources* (Singapore), and the *Hidden History of Christianity in Asia* (1998).

INDEX OF PERSONS

A

Abdu'llah bin 'Abdu'l-Kadir 251, 253f.
Abednego, Benjamin Agustinus 220
Abellera, Juan A. 359
Abesamis, Carlos H. 315, 396f.
Abineno, Johannes L. Ch. 169f.
Abraham, Dulcie 273, 276, 290
Adisucipto 156
Admund, D. 92
Aglipay, Gregorio 348, 350f., 354f.
Aguilan, Henry 463
Aguinaldo, Emilio 350
Ah Mya, Francis 40, 47, 53, 54, 64f.
Ahmed bin Hussein Shah 270
al Ghazali 260
Alejo, Albert E. 461
Aliah Umbukun, Jessica 277, 278
Allen, Clabon 270
Alopen 2
Amaladoss, Michael 315
Amba-Oduyoye, Mercy 219
Amstutz, Hobart 261, 267, 268
An Sôn Vi 645
Andrus, J. Russell 37
Ano, Stephen 100
Antone, Hope S. 449f.
Antonin, Paul 573
Aoanan, Melanio LaG. 436f.
Apilado, Mariano C. 402f.
Appleton, George 37, 63f.
Aquino, Melchora 340
Arevalo, Catalino G. 385f., 475
Arey, Leslie B. 34
Aritonang, Jan S. 221
Arur Sok Nhep 114
Asa Kiman 144f., 145, 147

Asedillo, Rebecca C. 454
Atlas, Laureano 19
Atmadja-Hadinoto, Nieke 129
Augurlion 95
Aung Hla Tun, Wilfred 95
Aung Hla, John 47
Aung Khin, Joseph 95
Aung San Suu Kyi 46
Aung Soe Myint, William 98
Avila, Charles 454f.
Aye Kyaw, John 99
Aye Maung, Grace 59
Aye Myat Kyaw 92
Aye, Peter 95

B

Ba Mau, Peter 47
Ba Maung Chain, Mrs 40, 59, 66
Ba Than Chain 40
Ba Thann Win 78f.
Ba, Vivian 42, 97
Bacani, Teodoro C. 417, 475
Bagongbanta, Fernando 21
Baines, H.W. 261
Balavendrum, Royopen 262
Balchin, Frank 322f.
Balhetchet, Robert 320
Ban Biên Tâp 645
Ban, James K. 95
Banawiratma, Johanes Baptista 125, 127, 136, 174, 205, 206ff.
Bao Thái Thanh 579
Bao Tinh Vuong Đình Bích 599, 619f.
Bargent, Dianne 278
Basilio Ai Theik 101
Battung, Mary Rosario 421f.

Batumalai, Satayandy 273, 302f.
Bautista, Liberato 463
Baw Tananone 527
Bayet, Claudius 120
Be Bin Htu, Simon 95
Beebe, Lyle J. 505
Belita, Jaime A. 461
Beltran, Benigno P. 430f.
Bento Thien 11
Beurel, Jean Marie 263
Biem Lap 268
Bigandet, Ambrois 42
Blackmore, Sophia 256, 275
Blanco, Jose C. 464, 475
Blasdell, Robert A. 253, 260
Bolasco, Mario V. 464
Bones-Fernandez, Angeline 273, 282, 294f.
Bong, Sharon A. 278
Bonifacy, A. 582
Bonnadr, Jean Louis 572
Boon Mark Kittisan 507
Boon Tuan Itt 504
Borie, Pierre 255
Borri, Christoforo 13
Borrong, Robert Patannang 221
Botengan, Kate C. 461
Bouchet, Jean 581f.
Bounthanong Somsaiphon 119
Bowers, Russell 114
Bradley, Dan Deach 505
Brazal, Agnes M. 448f.
Brewster, Grace 271
Brooke, Rajah 248
Browning, P. 263
Brunner, Paul 477
Buddhadasa Bikku 538
Bui Hoanh Thu 648
Bùi Thi Nga, Marie 635
Bui Thoang Giao 593
Bùi Tuân 643
Bùi Văn Cung 579
Bukaneg, Pedro 21
Bulatao, Jaime S. 462
Burgos, José Apolonio 346
Burke, DeAnn 113, 114
Burke, Todd 113, 114
Bwa, Rosalind 59
Byu, Esther 53, 59, 94

C

Caballero, Caroline Lopez 282
Cadière, Leopold 582, 604
Cahill, Sharon 282
Calderon, Cicero 367
Calle, José Mª 477
Camba, Erme 464
Campbell, Howard 505
Camphuys, Johannes 15
Cao Văn Luân 646
Capene, Onesta 599
Capulong, Noriel D. 451f.
Caratini, Marcel 582
Cardon, R. 263
Cardoza, Jacinta 278
Cariño, Feliciano 419f., 480
Carpenter, C.H. 32
Carroll, John J. 462
Casper, Linda Ty 341.
Castagneda, Hyacinth 9
Castro, Jose Luna 367
Catherine (Man Tai) 11
Chamniern, Paul 537
Chan Soon Seong, James 284
Chân Tín 589, 597, 610, 624f.
Chan, Edwin 271
Chan, Francis 284
Chan, Simon 319
Chandra Muzaffar 273
Chang, William 222
Chappoulie, Henri 573, 582
Charbonnier, Jean 281
Charles, G.P. 37
Chelliah, D.D. 261, 267, 287
Chen, Paul 54, 94
Cheng, Elizabeth 276
Cheng, Vincent 272
Chew Beng Lan 271, 276
Chew, Maureen K.C. 276f.
Chew, Peter 267

Index of Persons

Chhmar Salas, Joseph 109
Chia, Edmund 273, 313f.
Chia, Grace 278
Chia, Roland 273, 316f,
Chính, Simon 581
Cho Cho Win 59
Chong Yak Jong 3
Choo Kee Goh, Jeffery 322
Chooi Mun Sou 323
Choong Chee Pang 273, 321
Chou Su Teng, Ivy 322, 276
Chuleepan Srisoontorn-Persons 509
Chum Awi 94
Chunakara, Mathews George 113
Chung Chi-an 268
Chung Hoan Ting, Peter 284
Chung Hyun Kyung 219
Chung Song Mee 277
Chupungco, Anscar 413
Chusak Sirisuth, Joseph 549
Clasper, Paul 40, 70
Claver, Francisco F. 315, 391f., 475
Colbeck, J.A. 32
Cole, Edna S. 506
Colin, Francisco 22
Colivier, Fr. 251
Coloma, Victor 581
Combes, Francisco 22
Compain, Alice 113
Contesse, Gabriel 117
Cook, J.A.B. 262
Cooke, Sophia 256, 262f., 275
Coolen, C.L. 142f., 149
Cooley, Frank 133
Cope, J Herbert 37
Cormack, Don 113, 114
Correa, Juan 19
Cort, Mary L. 506
Cortez, Nael 455, 478
Cortez, Ruth 478
Cosserat, H. 582
Coueron, Raymond 113
Courvezy, J.P. Hillary M. 251, 255
Coyle, Kathleen 406, 477
Cruz, Hermenegildo 354

Cuarteron, Don Carlos 254f.
Cung Lian Hup 90f.
Curtis, Lillian Johnson 506

D

d'Amato, Joseph 12
D'Oliviero, Anne 278
Dagdag, Teresa 422f.
Đang Đức Tuân 564, 566f.
Dang Thanh Minh 646
Dang, Peter 9
Danil, Francis 272
Dankaets, S. 15
Danuwinata, Francis Xavier 222
Darmaputera, Eka 128, 195ff. 204
Dâu Quang Linh 574, 577, 580
David, V. 272
Daw Aye Tin 34
Daw Cecilia Sar Yee 34
Daw Hla Shein 34, 59
Daw Htu Raw 34
Daw Htwa Yee 34
Daw Kai 34
Daw May Si 34
Daw Mi Mi 34
Daw Myat Yan 47
Daw Nellie Mya Yee 34
Daw Nyein Tha 59
Daw Ohn Mya 34
Daw Saw Tint 34
Daw Tee Tee Luce 34
Daw Than 34
Daw Thaung Tin 34, 59
Daw Win Mya 34, 40, 59
de Behaine, P.J.G. Pigneau 572
de Belen, Aquino 3, 22
de Bobadilla, Diego 22
de Castro, Jeronimo Correa 19
de Cevallos, Ordonnez 9
de Choisy, Francoise 12
de Espinosa, Gomez 20
de Federich, Gil 9
de Jesus, Felipe 22
de la Asuncion, Jeronima 21, 340
de la Costa, Horacio 364, 365, 383f.

de la Cruz, Apolinario 337, 343
de la Cruz Bagay, Nicholas 19
de la Motte, Lambert 13
de la Torre, Edicio 424f.
de Lanerolle, Kenneth 650
de los Reyes y Florentino, Isabelo, Sr 350, 352, 355
de Marini, Jean Phillipe 13
de Mesa, José M. 432
de Montezou, F.M. 573
de Rhodes, Alexandre 10, 13, 563, 634, 642
De Roeck, René 120
de Rosario Binh, Philipe 11
de S. Justa Y Rufina, Basilio Sancho 20
de Salazar, Domingo 20
de Santa Justa, Sancho 345
de Tavera, Joachim Pardo 346
de Thái-Hà-Âp, Antoine 635
Dê Vǎn Nguyên 643
de Vaulx, Bernard 582
de Vera, Juan 19
Decorvet, Jeanne 120
del Carmen, Cirilo 367
del Espirito Santo, Ignacio 21, 340
del Pilar, Marcel 348
Delaney, John Patrick 337, 365
Destombes, Emile 109
Diên Phong 596
Dim Khaw Cing 31
Din, Greeta 59
Dingayan, Luna 453
Dingrin La Seng 95
Đinh Đúc Dao, Joseph 630
Dinh Thi Thuc 603, 609
Dinh Vǎn Diên 566
Diokno, Jose W. 465
Dô Dình, Pierre 580
Dô Huu Nghiêm 646
Dô Quang Chính 605
Do Sian Thang.94
Doàn Thuc Su 603
Doàn Vǎn Miêng 647
Doh Say 95
Dok Ket 119
Dominguez, Benito M. 455

Dominguez, Elizabeth 416
Doraisamy, M.R. 259
Doung Champa 119
Dourisboure, Pierre 573
Driyarkara, Nicolaus 126, 160, 173f.
du Caillaud, Romanet 582
Dun, Mary 53, 59, 81
Dunlap, J.B. 505
Durand, Maurice 604
Duroiselle, Charles 42
Dutton, Denis 268, 269, 322f

E

Ee Chooi, Theresa 273, 276, 292f.
Eh Wah 77f.
Eh Wah Hpaw 95
Eichner, David 270
Eiichi Kamiya 263
Ek Thapine 539
Ellison, David 109
Ellison, J. Paul 113
Ellison, Mrs David 109
Elwood, Douglas J. 468
Encina, Francisco 22
Erari, Karel Phil 132, 133, 212f.
Eschels-kroon 17
Esther Danpongpee 509
Evans, Grant 120

F

Fabella, Virginia 394f.
Falière, Albert 42
Feillon, Auguste 581
Ferguson-Davie, C.E. 263
Fernandes, Angela 276
Fernandes, Jesus V. 468
Fernandez, Eleazar 455
Fernandez, Irene 271, 276
Fernando 278
Fleming, John R. 261, 268, 286
Florimond, Fr. 271
Francisco, José Mario C. 456
Fransz, Tine 129
Fuentes, Francisca 21, 340

Index of Persons

Fujiyoshi, Ron 270
Fukansai Fabian 3
Fung Jojo 273, 315f.

G

Gagnon, Gérard 603
Gainza, Francisco 345
Galang, Fidel P. 367, 465
Galia, Donato 367
Gallares, Judette 456
Galvao, Antonio 15
Garnault, Bp 255
Gaspar, Karl 433f.
Gayou, Charles 582
Ge Gui Shing, Eugene 98
Gernault, P. 17
Gia Châu, see Mai Lão Bang
Gia Trân 611
Gian Maria Zau 12
Gibson, L.C. 267
Gibson, T. Campbell 261
Gilhodes, Charles 42
Glar Taw 95
Gobius, Jan Frederick 17
Goh Hood Keng 263
Goh Keat Peng 273, 320
Gomes, William Henry 258
Gomez, Fausto B. 472
Gomez, Hilario 410
Gomez, Mariano 345, 346
Gorospe, Vitaliano R. 387f.
Gowing, Peter G. 393f.
Graham, Helen 465
Grandjean, Philippe 582
Grant, Alexander 460
Grant, Fern Babcock 468
Grawng, Paul Z. 50, 99
Guansing, Benjamin 359
Guevarra, José 345
Gutzlaff, Carl 499

H

Hadiwijono, Harun 134, 167f.
Hamlin, John 527

Hammond, Arthur 109
Hammond, Mrs Arthur 109
Hàn Mac Tu 574, 575
Hanna, A.C. 37
Hansen, C.C. 506
Hardawiryana, Robert 136, 175, 178f.
Hartoko, Dick 215, 223
Hartono, Christophorus Thoekoel 223
Hartzell, Jessie Mackinnon 506
Hechanova, Louie G. 414f.
Hemandez, Santiago 581
Henkel, Merv 271
Hka Nau, Lilian 59
Hkan Naw, L. 95
Hkawn Aung, L, 95
Hkum Paw Lu, N. 95
Hla Thwin 92
Hla, Grace 53
Hlaing Bwa 95
Ho Fuk Tong 254
Ho Seng Ong 259
Hô Thành Biên, John-Baptiste 588, 601f.
Hô Thi Chính 635
Ho, Samuel 271
Hoàng Gia Khánh 564, 607, 633f.
Hoàng Minh Thúc 611
Hoàng Minh Tuân 643
Hoàng Quynh 602
Hoàng Si Quý 605, 618f.
Hoang Thuc Tram 588
Hoang Văn Doàn 584
Hofinger, Johannes 477
Hogan, Walter 364, 365
Hoi Kyin, Daniel 47
Honculada, Jurgette 465
Hông Lam 605
Honor Nyo 95
Hosokawa, Gracia 3
Howard Malcom, Howard 32
Howe, Bp. 50
Hre Kio, Stephen 47
Hsane Hgi, John 99
Hsar Min Htaw 95
Hsi Ya Da 95
Hsu (Xu), Candida 3

Htin Ya, David 47, 95
Hting Nan, K. 95
Htu Ra, C. 59
Huai Man Cing 59
Huang Hsing Peng 268, 296
Huênh Công Minh 593, 597, 610
Hughes, Philip 527
Hutabarat-Lebang, Henriette Tabita 216f.
Huu Lai, Joseph 605
Huu Triêm, Pierre 566, 571
Huỳnh Tinh Cua, Paulus 570f., 579
Hwa Yung 273, 303f.

I

Ihromi 134, 179f.
Ihromi-Simatupang, Tapi Omas 179f.
Ing Hua 270
Ing, Cecilia 276, 278
Intengan, Romeo 465f.
Irwin, Edwin F. 113, 647
Isaac, Samuel 113, 650

J

Jacobs, Tom 136, 175, 183f.
Jalandoni, Luis 466
Jambunathan, K. 267, 269, 287f.
Jara-Martinez, Josefa 341, 360f.
Jayasooria, Denison 273, 298f.
Jeanes, Sylvia M. 277
Jeanningross, Philemon 581
Jesudason, Samuel 267
John of Yedana 12
John, Sebil 270, 272
Johnson, Elisabeth 219
Jojo Fung, see Fung Jojo
Joly, Leon 582
Jones, Edna 506
Joseph, Peter 95
Judson, Ann 34

K

Kamol Arayaprateep 509
Katoppo, Henriette Marianne 127, 133, 200f.

Keasberry, Benjamin 251, 253f.
Kei Serey Vuthi 110
Kelleher, Jeremiah 42, 50
Khaing Oo, Esther 59
Khaing Thiri 59
Kham Ciang 31
Khamsé Vithavong, Jean 120
Khen Cham 95
Khin Khin, Katherine 34, 58, 59
Không Thành Ngoc 611, 643
Khoo, Aileen 277
Ki, Thomas Lucy 9
Kien, Paul 9
Kieser, Bernard 224
Kiley, Henry 462
Kim Dinh 605, 645
Kirti Bunchua 545f.
Kler Taw 92
Knight, Arthur 32, 37
Ko Ko Naing 94, 95
Ko Lay, Arthur 53, 76f.
Ko Pai San 32
Ko Thah-Byu 31
Koh Peck Chiang, Roland 268, 269, 285
Koson·Srisang 500, 525
Koyama Kosuke 500, 522f.
Kroeger, James 469
Kru Pannya 507
Kru Tardt Pratipasena 507
Kung En Hmung, Joseph 101
Kyaw Htun Lin 95
Kyaw Mya, George 47
Kyer Baw Nai 92
Kyin Nang 59

L

La Motte, Charles 581
Labayen, Julio Xavier 389f., 475, 488
Lagunzad, Ciriaco, Jr. 473, 480
Lahu, A-Teh-Pu-Cu 32
Laisum, David 53, 88
Laivet Mami 59
Lakawa, Septemmy Eucharistia 128, 218f.
Lal Rawng Bawla 95

Index of Persons

Lallement, Pierre 572
Lambino, Antonio 456, 475
Lamont, Archibald 261, 263
Laneau, Mgr 13
LaPel, Christopher 114
Laschenski, Sigmund 549
Latuihamallo, Peter D. 171f.
Lau King Lang, Sabrina 277
Lau, Rinnie 278
Laubach, Frank C. 341, 359, 366f.
Lauby, Paul 473
Launay, Adrien 582
Lay, William 53, 92
Lazuk dau Hkawng 95
Le Blanc, Marcel 13
Lê Huu Tý 574
Lê Loi 574
le Paz Liem, Vincent 12
Le Tessier 255
Lê Thanh Canh 579
Lê Thành Khôi 604
Lê Thanh, see Hàn Mac Tu
Lê Thi Nhiêu 635
Le Turdu, Bp 255
Lê Văn Thái 647
Leck Taiyong 507
Ledi Sayadaw 61
Lee Bee-teik 277
Lee Tzu Pheng 276, 306f.
Lee, James 270
Lefebre, Dominique 572
Legge, James 254
Leimena, Johannes 127, 163f., 180
Letondal, Fr. 251
Levasseur 113
Levy-Bruhl, L. 162
Lhomand, Charles 572
Li Esther Aye Aye Thein 95
Lian Sakhong 95
Lian, Philip 98
Liciniana, Mathieu 9
Liem Khiem Yang 225
Liêm, Geronimo 573
Liem, Vincent 9
Liew, Samuel 319

Ligo, Arche 457
Lim Chin Chin, Theresa 272
Lim Mah Hui 321
Lim, Fr. 271
Lim, Marilyn 278
Lim, O.C. 323
Lin Lin Shwee 59
Ling, Ricky 270
Liong Yuk Chong 272
Litonjua, Menelao D. 469
Lizares-Bodegon, Sophie 444f.
Lockerbie, Jeannette 113, 114
Loh Soon Choy 321
Lopez, A. 337
Lopez, Juliana 340
Lopez-Jaena, G. 348
Lourdes, Patricia 272
Louvet, L. Eugene 573, 582
Lovett, Brendan 469
Lozano-Santander, Sra, of Cebu 340
Lu Y Doan 3, 10
Luering, H.L. Emil 255
Lumentut, Agustina 128, 133, 194f.
Lung No 95
Luong Minh Ky 588
Luong Văn Can 578
Lwin, Esther 59
Lwin, M.K. 59
Lý Chánh Trung 592, 593
Lý Thiên Kim 603
Lyons, Adrian 113

M

Ma Lay Lone 59, 92
Ma Rita, Patricia Mary 58, 59
Mabini 350
MacCarthy, initial?? 337
Maclead Wylie, Mrs 34
Macou, Jean A.P. 581
Maen Pongudom 523f.
Maggay, Melba Padilla 426
Magnis-Suseno, Franz 126, 136, 190f.
Maha Sila Viravong 119
Mahathir Mohammed 264
Maher, Debbi 114

Mai Hoa 9
Mai Lão Bang 574, 580
Mai Rinh 578
Mai Thành 607, 621f., 636
Maïs, Jean 605f.
Manaligod, Ambrosio 457
Mananzan, Mary John 404f.
Manat Chuabsamai 539
Manghisi, Pietro 97
Mangunwijaya, Yusuf Bilyarta 125, 127, 128, 151, 174, 181f. 205, 215f.
Manna, Paolo 97
Mansap Bunluen 544
Mantegazza, Gaetano 12
Manuel, chief of Hatiwi 15
Mapanao, Eli 470
Mar Gay Gyi 86
Maran Yaw 95
Marasigan, Violeta A. 488
Marco, Prof. 101
Mardiatmadja, Bernhard 225
Marquez , Natividad (Ana Maria Clavez) 341
Marsden, William 17
Martin, Jean-Pierre 581
Martin, Victor Pierre 581
Martinez, Patricia 273, 276, 312f.
Martinez, Salvador T. 466
Masson, Guillaume 572
Mastra, Wayan 186ff.
Mastrili, Francisco 20
Maung Bo, Charles 51, 99
Maung Coompany 32
Maung Doe, Mark 95
Maung Lat, Johnny 53
Maung Maung Yin 94, 95
Maung Pe, John 95
Maung Win, Joseph 99, 103
Mawia, Bp. 95
Maybon, Charles 582
McDonald, N.A. 505
McDougall, Harriette 262
McFarland, S.G. 505
McGilvary, Daniel 117
McGilvary, Daniel 505

McGilvary, Evander B. 506
McGilvary, Mrs D. 506
Meachem, Stewart 271
Means, Nathalie 277
Meh Kha Khway, see Khin Khin, Katherine
Mendoza, Agustin 345
Mendoza, Everett L. 438f.
Menger, J. Matt 120
Mercado, Laverne 480
Mercado, Leonardo N. 398f.
Merentek-Abram, Sientje 211
Micae Nguyên Huy My 564, 565
Miche, Jean-Claude 572
Miettes, Joseph 641
Migot, André 582, 604
Miles, Glenn 114
Miller, Charles 17
Milne, William 251, 252f., 254
Min Thide, Justine 99
Minh Dúc Vuong Thai Phi, Marie 573
Minh Duê, see Hàn Mac Tu
Miranda, Dionisio Marcello 435
Miranda-Feliciano, Evelyn 427f.
Moelia, T.S.G. 127, 133, 155, 161f.
Moling, Augustin 543
Montemayor, Jeremias U. 466
Montes, Valentino 467
Moo Paw 59
Moor, John Henry 254
Morais, Elaine 278
Morrison, Robert 252
Morrow, Honore 34
Mott, John 155
Mu Mu Kyu 59
Mulry, Joseph A. 365
Muthiah, Lionel 271
Muthuswami, R.S. 263
Mya Han, Andrew 47, 95
Myint Maung 95

N

Nababan, S.A.E. 133, 175
Nacpil, Emerito P. 401f.
Nair, Girija 278

Index of Persons

Nakhon Sawan 120
Nan Suwan 504
Nang Ngaih Pau 95
Nantawan Boonprasat-Lewis 509
Narciso-Apuan, Victoria 470
Nat-shin-naung 12
Navarro, Cipriano 357, 359
Naw Eh Tar Gay 95
Naw Grace 59
Naw Hosanna 95
Naw Kyin Nang 95
Naw Ming, L. 95
Naw San Dee, K.D. 95
Nawl Uk 95
Nena 340
Ng Kam Weng 273, 310
Ng, Cecilia 272
Ngabei Judasarta 17
Ngai Gam 95
N-Gan Tang Gun 95
Ngô Dình Diem 579
Ngo Duy Linh 597
Ngun Ling, Samuel 89f.
Nguyên Bá Tòng 574
Nguyên Chính Kêt 564, 632f.
Nguyên Dình Dâu 592
Nguyên Dình Hòe 579
Nguyên Dình Thi 599
Nguyên Duc Phong 592
Nguyên Duy Ton, Maria 573
Nguyên Duy Trinh 597, 603
Nguyên Hiêu Lê 588
Nguyên Hông Giáo 629
Nguyên Hông Giáo, Guy-Marie 643
Nguyên Hung 646
Nguyên Huu Bài 577
Nguyên Huu Dang 605
Nguyên Huu Lai, Joseph 644f.
Nguyên Huu Trong 605
Nguyên Khac Chính 598
Nguyên Khac Duong, Stephen 617
Nguyên Kim Diên 641f.
Nguyên Nghi 593, 610, 611
Nguyên Ngoc Lan 589, 592, 595, 597, 610, 624f.
Nguyên Nhý Quang 611
Nguyên Son Lâm, Barthelemy 639
Nguyên Thái Bá 603, 609
Nguyên Thái Hop 643
Nguyên Thê Thoai 646
Nguyên Thi Chung 635
Nguyên Thi Kiêu Diêm 635
Nguyên Thi My 635
Nguyên Thi Oanh 592
Nguyên Thi Sang, Amelie 627f.
Nguyên Thi Thê 635
Nguyên Thi Thu Huong 635
Nguyên Trong Trí, see Hàn Mac Tu
Nguyên Truòng To 564, 567f., 623
Nguyên Tu Lôc 594
Nguyên Tuong 576f.
Nguyên Tý Lôc 593
Nguyên Văn Bình 593, 612f.
Nguyên Văn Khánh, Norbert 643
Nguyên Văn Thích 580
Nguyên Văn Thuân, Francis Xavier 615f.
Nguyên Văn Tôt, Pierre 605
Nguyên Văn Trung 592, 593, 598
Nguyên Văn Vinh 578
Nguyên Viêt Cu 645
Nguyên Xuân Tín, Peter 612
Nhkum Lying Nang 95
Nhkum Pau Tu 95
Nicholson, William 364
Niguidula, Lydia Nazario 399f.
Nilar Win 95
Niphot Thienwiharn 548
Nunes, Nicolo 15
Nunuk Prasetyo Murniati, Agustina 130, 198f.
Nyce, Ray 271, 288f.
Nyi Win Hman 95
Nyun, Marie 50
Nyunt Nyunt Thein 59
Nyunt Wai, Maurice 100

O

Olcomendy, Bp 251
Ông Văn Huyên 647
Oorjitham, Victor 270, 273

Oracion, Levi V. 411f.
Orevillo-Montenegro, Muriel 441f.
Ortiz, Pacifio 364
Osias, Camilo O. 359
Ossorio, Pedro 21
Othman, Jamaluddin 272
Outhine Bounyavong 119

P

P'do Ba Tun Tin 91
Pa Nai 119
Padillo-Olesen, Elizabeth 443
Pakianathan, S.S. 259
Pang Ken Phin 277, 278
Pang Yan Whatt 257
Panganiban, J 348
Parrel, Fr 589
Pasco, Tito E. 485
Pau Khan En, Simon 53, 85
Pau Suan 31
Pelaez, Pedro 344f., 346
Pellako, Thomas 32
Pelliot, Paul 582
Penafort, Robert 282
Penfold, Helen 113
Peoh, K.C. 267
Percoto, J.M. 12
Pereira, Patricia 278
Perez, Asuncion Arriola 341, 360f.
Perez, Mateo 22
Perkins, Jill 113, 120, 650
Peysonnaux, H. 579
Pham Châu Diên 603
Pham Dình 597
Pham Dình Khiêm 603, 605
Pham Dình Thái 643
Pham Hân Quynh 592, 597
Pham Quynh 578, 579
Pham Thi Khân 635
Phan Bôi Châu 574, 578, 588
Phan Khac Tù 593, 631
Phan Phát Huôn 604
Phan Thanh Gian 572
Phan Thi Nghi 635
Phan Văn Hum 588

Phan, Peter C. 642f.
Phêrô Dinh Công Quý 564, 565
Phêrô Nguyên Văn Tu 564, 565
Pieris, Aloysius 205, 315
Pihan, Jean 113
Pilliozat, Jean 604
Pinpin, Tomas 19
Piong, Cornelius 284
Pluang Sudhikam 507
Po Ba, George 47
Po, Claribel Irene, see Ba Maung Chain, Mrs
Poblete, Pasqual H. 357
Poerwowidagdo, Judowibowo 192f.
Poerwowidagdo, Timur I. 193
Poethig, Richard 473
Polbete, Sra, of Manila 340
Politi, Giancarlo 113
Ponce, M. 348
Ponchaud, Francois 113, 114
Poniah, Gnanamani 259
Pradit Takerngrangsarit 527
Prakai Nontawasee 500, 509, 521f.
Pranom Sion Joachim 537
Prasetyo Murniati 128
Price, Maurice 582
Prior, John Mansford 136, 209f.
Puginier, Mgr 572
Pum Suan Pau 95
Putranta, C.B. 225

Q

Quiambao, Jacob 470f.
Quintos, Julita A. 418
Quisumbing, Lourdes R. 462f.

R

Radermacher, J.C.M. 17
Rajah, Solomon 324
Rajendra, Cecil 273, 300
Ramousse, Yves 113
Ramsauer, Martin 477
Ranche, Apolonio M. 459
Ratna Bamrungtrakul, Robert 542

Index of Persons

Ratnam, Martha 270, 278
Ratnam, Perala 120
Ravi Jayakaran 114
Ravier, Marcel 572
Rebello, Gabriel 15
Reyes, Ramon C. 463
Ricci, Matteo 632, 634
Rigos, Cirillo A. 471
Rillstone, Thomas 42
Rizal, Jose 349f.
Rochat, Georges 120
Rodgers, J.B. 341
Rodriguez, Proculo 359, 367
Rofe, G. Edward 117
Rogers, Anthony 272, 273, 305, 313
Roman Tiples 480
Rondineaux, P. 113, 114
Roxas, Manuel 347
Roxborogh, John 319f.
Ruiz-Duremdes, Sharon Rose Joy 439f., 481
Ruyl, Cornelius 139

S

Saad Chaiwan 527
Saccano, Metello 13
Sadrach Surapranata 127, 147f., 154
Salai Hla Aung 95
Salanga, Alfredo 457
Salgado, Pedro V. 407f.
Salles, A. 582
Salonga, Jovito 467
Salvador, Felipe 343
San Crombie Po 38, 40
San Hoo 47
San Min Tun 95
San Si Tay 54, 95
San Tay, Eleanor 34
Sang Awr 95
Sanlone, Victor 53, 72f.
Santhau, Christiane 278
Savarimuthu, John 271, 287, 323
Saw Laban 95
Saw Lader 47
Saw Lar Ba 95

Saw Michael 98
Saw Quala 31
Saw San Po Tin 40
Saw Taw 92
Saw U, Alan 53, 87
Saw Yaw Han, John 100
Say Pa, Anna May 53, 59, 82f.
Saya Shia Kyaw 31
Saya Thun Aung 32
Saya U Tha Din 39
Schuessler-Fiorenza, Elisabeth 219
Schumacher, John 459
Scott, William Henry 459
Seng Bu 95
Seng Kyaw 95
Seree Lorgunpai 527f.
Seri Phongphit 546f.
Sevilla, Mariano 347
Sevilla, Philipe 19
Shaou Tih 254
Sharp, A.F. 263
Shastri, Hermen 273, 320
Shea, Alice M. 278
Shearburn, Victor G. 92
Shellabear, William 251, 253, 257, 260
Shum, Swinnie 278
Shwee, Rebecca 34, 58
Si Maria 340
Sidjabat, W.B. 226
Silang, Gabriela 340
Simanjuntak, Lieke 129
Simatupang, Tahi Bonar 127, 133, 156, 165f.
Simo Vichai 507
Sin, Jaime L. 471, 475
Sindhunata, Gabriel Possenti 126, 174, 215f.
Sing Khaw Khai 95
Singgih, Emanuel Gerrit 213f.
Siripong Charatsri 549
Sitompul, Adelbert Agustin 226
Sitoy, T. Valentino, Jr 460
Sjarifoeddin, Amir 156, 157f.
Smith Dun 40
Smith Ngulh Za Thawng 95

Smith, Samuel F. 36
Smith, Samuel John 505
Snan Vongsuthee 537
Sng, Bobby E.K. 320
Sobary, Mohamad 182
Sobrepeña, Enrique C. 359, 361f.
Soegijapranata, Archbp. 181
Soejatno, Ardi 227
Soekoto, Leo 152
Song Ong Siang 263
Soosai, Fr. 99
Sotero Phamo, Bp. 100
Sotto, Sra. Vicente, of Cebu 340
Spurgeon, Augustus 95
Squires, Gwynneth 113
Sramu Alice 34
Sramu Luella San Gyaw 34
Steendam, Jacob 16
Street, Margaret 114
Su Mo Mo Win 59
Suarez, Luis 19
Suarez, Oscar 428f.
Sue, Patricia 98
Sugijapranata 152
Sulaiman bin Muhammad Nur 257, 258
Sulak Sivaraksa 538
Sumartana, Th. 133, 202ff.
Sutton, James 268
Swanson, Herbert R. 526

T

Taberd, Jean-Louis 572
Taberdo, Leticia A. 477
Taboulet, G. 582
Tailum Jan 32, 34
Talaivasingham, A. 263
Tâm Ngoc 603
Tan Chee Ing, Paul 273, 297f.
Tan Chee Khoon 320
Tan Jin Huat 323
Tan Kim Huat 273, 321f.
Tan Teck Soon 263
Tan Yak Hwee 278
Tan, Jonathan 317f.
Tan, Stephen 271, 273, 323f.

Tanja, Victor Immanuel 188f., 203
Tano, Rodrigo D. 458
Tapia, Elizabeth 445f.
Tarrosa-Subido, Trinidad L. 341
Taylor, Brian 263
Teh, Bernadette 278
Teo Bong Kwang 322
Tep Im Sotha, Paul 109, 113
Thái Văn Lung 578
Than Tun 95
Thanbyah, Theodore 32
Thanh Lao Công 603
Thar Do Thon Kyaing, see Saw Michael
Thaung Shwee, Joseph 100
Thaw Tu 92
Thê Nguyên 593
Thein, Marcheta 59
Thetgyi, John 47
Thevathasan, S.M. 261
Thích Minh Châu 600
Thích Nhât Hanh 600
Thích, Joseph 580
Thiên Phong Buu Duong 596
Thio Chan Bee 320
Thomas, P.D. 267
Thomson, Alan 227
Thra Asa Htoo Tha 92
Thra Ba Tay 39
Thra Chit Maung 39
Thra Mooler The 40, 47
Thra Tha Hto 40
Thra Tu Saw 92
Thramu E Byu 34
Thramu Laura 34
Thramu Naw Paw 34
Thramu Pyu May 34
Thu En Yu 273, 300f.
Thu, Luke 9
Thuam Hang 31
Tin Hla Kyi 59
Tin Maung Shwe 95
Tin May 58, 59
Tin Tin Hla, Dorothy 47
Tin Tin Win, Rosie 58, 59
Tin Win, Mark 99

Index of Persons

Tinh, Michael 579
Tint Lwin 94, 95
Titaley, John 227f.
Tô Thi Ánh 605, 635
Tolentino, Aurelio 353f.
Tomlin, Jacob 262, 499
Torrevillas, Rowena Tiempo 341
Tosari, Paulus 143f., 145, 147, 148, 154
Trân Cao Tuòng 645
Trân Công Thach 611
Trân Dình Tú, Peter 638
Trân Duy Nhiên 642
Trân Huu Thanh 603
Trân Kim Giám 597, 603
Tran Luc, see Huu Triêm, Pierre
Trân Minh Triêt 605
Trân Quang Nghiêm 588
Trân Thê Luân 593
Trân Thiên Câm, Thomas 587, 605, 607, 626
Trân Văn Doàn, Vincent 642, 645
Trân Văn Toan 592
Trân Viêt Tho 592
Trân Xuân Toan 579
Trang, Joseph 12
Trinity, Mary 98
Trochu, Francis 582
Trôn Thi Quynh Giao, Elizabeth 635
Truòng Bá Cân 592, 593, 610, 622f.
Truòng Vinh Ký, Petrus 569, 570f., 604
Truòng Vinh Tông 579
Tschu, John 262
Tun Hlaing, Esther 59
Tun Meh 95
Tun Myat Aye 95
Tunggul Wulung, Ibrahim 145f., 147
Turner, Marie 278

U

U Aung Khin 47, 95
U Ba Aye 47, 95
U Ba Hmyin 40, 53, 67
U Ba Ohn 95
U Ba Yin, Stephen 99
U Chit Maung 47, 94
U Chit Pe 40, 92
U Di Aung Yi 93f.
U Dun 47
U Hla Bu 40, 53, 62f., 87
U Khin Maung Din 53, 73f.
U Kyaw Than 40, 53, 68f.
U Maung Kaung 97
U Maw Naw 28
U Mya Than Tint 95
U Mynt Hla 47, 92
U On Kin 40, 91
U Pan Yi 39
U Pe Maung Tin 40, 54, 60f., 87
U Pe Thwin 40, 53, 71
U Tun Aung Chain 75
U Win, Joseph 49
Ukur, Fridolin 133, 156, 185f.
Uon Seila 114
Usher, Patrick 42

V

Vachet, Benique 572
Vacquier, Fr 589
van Bogendorp, Dirk 16
van der Haghen, Admiral 15
van Hoorn, Pieter 16
Van Kung 95
Van Lal Vena 95
van Lith, Francis 125, 148, 151f., 160, 173, 174
van Minh, Philippe Phan 11
van Outshoorn, Vlaming 15
van Papendrecht, P.C. Hoynck 17
Vasquez, Amelia 447f.
Venard, Theophane 572
Vendargon, Dominic 283f., 297
Verdeille, Henri 582
Vergara, Mario 97
Vey, Jean-Louis 116, 120
Victorine 278
Vierow, Duain 271, 319
Villacampa, Sra. Carmen, of Negros 340
Virat Setsoponkal 527
Viset Savengseuksa 119

Vismara, Clement 97
Võ Long Tê 604
Võ Thành Trinh 578, 603, 609
Voon Choon Khing 277
Vu Công 603
Vu Dăng Khoa 581
Vu Dình Trác 645
Vu Kim Chính 645
Vu Thanh Binh 588
Vu Văn Thiên 614f.
Vu Xuân Hiêu 593
Vu Xuân Ky 601
Vung Za Thang, J.Z. 95
Vuong Dình Ái 610
Vuong Dình Bích 610

W

Walker, E.A. 263
Walters, Albert 272, 307f.
Wang Yang Ming 588
Watson, Rosemary A. 120
Way, Bernard 97
Weiss, Arthur 364
West, George 37
Whitehorn, R.D. 261
Widyatmadja, Josef P. 228
Wilson, J. 120
Wilson, J.C. 263
Wilson, J.L. 267
Wilson, Leonard 261
Win Mya 59
Win, Kanbawza, see Ba Thann Win
Winn, Mrs William 59
Winn, William 40, 92
Wismoady, Wahono S. 229f.
Wittenbach, H.A. 261
Wong Hoon-hee 268
Wong Meng Chow 272
Wong, David 319
Wong, James 271
Wong, Michael 271
Woodward, Frank J. 366

Wostyn, Lode 408f.
Wu, John 596
Wylie, Sarah 509

X

Xavier, Irene 278
Xu, Candida, see Hsu, Candida

Y

y Novicio, A.L. 348
Yaha Laylayla 95
Yan, Maria 278
Yang Ting Yun 3
Yang, Joshua 95
Yap Kim Hao 291f.
Yap, Jose 480
Yasudian, J.S. 258f.
Yeo, Patrick C.S. 319
Yeoh Seng Guan 273, 311f.
Yeow Choo Lak 293f.
Yeow-Teo Giok Lian 277
Yewangoe, Andreas Ananggguru 133, 204f.
Yin Yin Maw 59
Yoho-ken, Paul 3
Yong Ting Jin 273, 276, 308f.
Yos Em Sithan 110
Youngquist, Neal 114
Yuzon, Lourdino 471

Z

Za Bik, Edmund 53, 79f.
Za Theh Lo 95
Zago, Marcel 120
Zamora, Jacinto 346
Zamorra, Nicolas 357
Zau Lat, Lahpai 53, 83f.
Zau Yaw, Sara 59
Zaw Min Tun 95
Ziello, Pasquale 97
Zung Ceu, Mike 95

INDEX OF SUBJECTS

A

Alopen documents 2
Anonymity 11f., 56
Apologetics 3, 10f., 297
Association of Major Religious Superiors in the Philippines 380, 487f.
Association of Women in Theology, Philippines 373, 380, 488

B

Batavian Society of Arts and Sciences 17
Biblical study and Hermeneutics passim
    Southeast Asia 10, 16, 17
    Burma/Myanmar 32, 40, 53, 61, 72, 74, 77, 80, 81, 82, 84, 85, 94, 99, 102,
    Cambodia, Laos 114
    Indonesia 136, 143, 146, 159f., 170, 172, 187, 194, 199, 202, 211, 213f.
    Malaysia, Singapore 252, 254, 257, 277, 299, 309, 316, 321f., 324
    Philippines 363, 367, 375, 379, 381, 396f., 404, 407f., 409, 411f., 416, 425, 426f., 434, 436f., 441, 445, 450-452, 462, 474, 479
    Thailand 500, 509, 517f., 522, 527, 529, 550, 551ff.
    Vietnam 569, 594, 610, 615, 617, 627, 641, 643
Biographies passim, 31, 58, 65, 66, 93, 97, 135, 141, 184, 254, 258, 262f., 321, 340, 347, 443, 569, 572, 578, 582, 591
Biographies, pre 1800 9, 13f., 18, 19, 23
Buddhism, Christian response to
    Southeast Asia, pre 1800 2, 10, 11, 12
    Burma/Myanmar 36, 37f., 39, 42, 50, 52, 54, 57, 61f., 63f., 65, 69, 70f., 73f., 76, 79, 81, 82, 85f., 89f., 92, 98, 100
    Cambodia, Laos 114, 119
    Indonesia 124, 203
    Malaysia, Singapore 252, 265, 274, 302, 310, 318
    Philippines 418, 421f.
    Thailand 501ff., 505f., 511, 514, 515f., 518f., 524, 525, 527f., 529f., 531, 533, 538, 539, 542-547, 549
    Vietnam 563, 576, 582ff., 585, 596, 599f., 602, 605, 613, 622, 625, 630-634, 645

C

Catechesis 10f., 12, 17, 33, 49, 53, 97, 99, 113, 143, 151, 186f., 225, 250, 258f., 336f., 340, 397f., 409, 417, 435, 474, 477
Catholic Bishops' Conferences. See also Catholic regional associations
    Burma/Myanmar 47, 102f.
    Cambodia, Laos 120
    Indonesia 130, 135-137, 176, 178, 206, 209
    Malaysia, Singapore 280f., 283f., 326
    Philippines 373, 385, 474f.
    Thailand 535f., 549
    Vietnam 636-639

Catholic regional associations 6f., 52, 100, 273, 292f., 305, 314, 318
Catholic social teaching and Apostolate 20, 21, 53, 99, 102f., 271f., 281
Catholic students. See Student Movements, Christian
Chinese manuscripts, pre-1500 2
Christian art 3, 16, 19
Christian Conference of Asia / East Asia Christian Conference 6f., 61, 68f., 72, 94, 115, 118, 286f., 291f., 309, 319, 323
Christian Institute for Ethnic Studies in Asia 373f
Christian music. See Hymns and Lyrics
Christian Muslim dialogue. See Interfaith encounter / Dialogue
Christian poetry 3f., 11, 12, 16, 20, 21f., 30, 93, 114, 157f., 290, 296f., 300, 306f., 316. See also Hymns and Lyrics
Christian student movements. See Student Movements, Christian
Christian writings, pre-1500 1f.
Christian Writings 1500-1800 9-24
Christians for National Liberation, Philippines 373
Christology. See Jesus Christ, Christology
Church and Mission, Missiology passim, 2, 6, 13, 15. See also Ecclesiology; Evangelism
  Burma/Myanmar 50f., 53f., 58f., 63, 68f., 72f., 78f., 80f., 84, 86, 87, 89, 90f., 92, 94f., 97f., 99
  Cambodia, Laos 108ff., 114, 116f.
  Indonesia 124, 132, 141, 142f., 149f., 151f., 154f., 156, 161f., 169, 174, 176, 185, 187f., 203f., 209, 218, 228,
  Malaysia, Singapore 249, 254f., 260, 261, 265f., 167ff., 271ff., 280f., 286, 291, 296, 301, 304, 310, 318, 320, 323f.,
  Philippines 338, 356f., 358f., 366f., 374, 386, 393, 397f., 401, 406, 415, 419f., 424, 426, 429, 441, 446, 451f., 468ff., 481f., 486
  Thailand 499, 509, 519f., 521f., 526, 531, 532, 534, 535f.,
  Vietnam 572, 587, 592, 601, 603, 613, 624, 630, 637, 641ff., 645, 649
Church and Society, Social concern. See Catholic social teaching and Apostolate.
  Burma/Myanmar 39f., 50, 51, 52, 63, 65f., 73, 75, 76, 78f., 81, 84, 87, 94, 95
  Cambodia, Laos 110
  Indonesia 127f., 129, 130, 142, 146, 151, 153f., 158, 163f., 165f., 172, 173f., 175f., 179f., 181f., 189, 190f., 196f., 198f., 201, 203, 205, 208, 209, 213f., 222, 228
  Malaysia, Singapore 249, 258f., 260, 261, 265f., 267ff., 271ff., 276, 287f., 288f., 291, 293f., 296, 297f., 299f., 302f., 305, 307f., 310, 315f., 318, 321f., 324
  Philippines 340, 342f., 346, 347f., 349-355, 360f., 362, 363f., 365-367, 371f., 373-375, 377f., 380f., 383f., 387f., 389, 391f., 395, 396, 401f., 403, 404, 407f., 411f., 414f., 416, 417, 419, 425, 528-431, 433f., 439f., 451f., 453, 463ff., 474f., 478, 481, 483ff.
  Thailand 503, 509, 517, 519f., 521f., 524, 525, 532, 533f., 536, 538, 544, 545-548
  Vietnam 565-568, 574-577, 587ff., 591-595, 597-604, 608-611, 613f., 623, 624f., 629, 631, 637ff., 643
Cofradia 337
Committee for Union of Viet Catholics (Liaison Committee / United

Index of Subjects

Catholic Committee / Union Committee) 584ff., 600, 601, 603, 607, 609f., 917, 622, 629, 631, 649

Confucianism 10, 11, 16, 222, 249, 318, 563f., 568f., 580f., 605, 618, 622, 633f.

Congress of Catholic Action, Philippines 363f.

Contextual theology passim, 4f., 6. See also Indigenisation / Inculturation

    Burma/Myanmar 35ff., 52ff., 73f., 76f., 79, 80f., 82f., 84, 85, 87, 88f., 92f., 100

    Cambodia, Laos 114

    Indonesia 16f., 125f., 127f., 132, 134, 136f., 139, 142-148, 154f., 160, 164-168, 171-174, 175ff., 181f., 187f., 196, 203, 205, 206ff., 213ff., 315f., 218f., 220-228

    Malaysia, Singapore 249, 251f., 259, 268, 272f., 276f., 281f., 287-294, 297-308, 310ff., 315f., 319-324

    Philippines 22, 359, 365f., 366f., 373-375, 380, 383f., 387f., 395, 396f., 404, 407f., 421f., 424f., 426, 429, 435, 437-440, 445, 446, 451f., 453, 454ff., 486, 490

    Thailand 511f. 516f., 520, 521-524, 525, 529f., 534, 539f., 542f., 544, 548, 549ff.

    Vietnam 10, 561f., 563f., 588f., 591ff., 596, 607f., 608ff., 612, 617, 620, 621f., 626, 630, 632-634, 637f., 640, 641ff., 649f.

Cordillera Women's Education and Resource Center 380, 489f.

CPDSK 47, 78

Cultural studies passim, 12f., 17, 22, 29f., 36f., 39, 88f., 94f., 100, 113, 120, 253, 255, 257, 260, 272f., 280, 287-290, 301ff., 311ff., 314, 315f.

D

Dawkalu association (Burma) 32

E

East Asia Christian Conference. See Christian Conference of Asia

East Asia Pastoral Institute 373, 477

EATWOT 130, 176, 199, 201, 206, 374, 380, 395, 404, 421, 444, 475, 489

Ecclesiology. See also Church and Mission

    Burma/Myanmar 521

    Indonesia 134, 160, 178, 185, 220, 225

    Malaysia, Singapore 281f., 284, 291, 301, 315, 322

    Philippines 385, 409, 412, 413, 415, 420, 457, 474

    Thailand 518, 526, 534

    Vietnam 584, 587, 592f., 612, 626, 636ff.

Ecology 300, 404, 406, 422, 423, 434, 444, 474

Ecumenical associations and theology passim

    Burma/Myanmar 27f., 37, 39, 47, 52ff., 58, 60, 62, 66, 67, 68, 72, 73, 77, 82, 87, 91f.

    Cambodia, Laos 110

    Indonesia 129, 130, 132-137, 150, 154, 156, 159, 162, 166, 175, 180, 185, 194f., 201, 209, 211, 212, 217

    Malaysia, Singapore 260f., 265, 267-269, 270ff., 275f., 285ff., 288f., 290, 291, 296, 298f., 305f., 308f., 314, 322f.

    Philippines 340, 359, 361f., 366, 371f., 373ff., 380, 385f., 394f., 399f., 411f., 419f., 421f., 428f., 437, 439f., 443, 446, 450, 460, 463, 464f.

    Thailand 499, 507f., 519f., 521f., 525, 538, 542, 544, 546f., 549

    Vietnam 610, 631, 642, 643, 649

Ecumenical Bishops' Forum, Philippines 488
Episcopal Synod for Asia (1998) 195, 209, 638
Eucharist 268, 413f., 430, 432, 473, 616, 618, 628, 629,
Evangelical Fellowship of Thailand 500
Evangelism. See also Church and Mission
 Burma/Myanmar 32, 40, 52f., 58, 72, 74, 86, 90, 100
 Indonesia 142, 144-148, 150, 151, 167, 210
 Malaysia, Singapore 248f., 256, 304, 258, 261
 Philippines 357, 378, 384, 400, 404, 417, 447, 466f.
 Thailand 504, 516, 519, 535, 550
 Vietnam 617, 635, 637f.

F

Federation of Asian Bishops' Conferences 6f., 52, 100, 305, 514, 318
Federation of Free Farmers 365, 373
Federation of Free Workers 365, 373
Forum for Interdisciplinary Endeavours and Studies 374, 489

G

GABRIELA 380, 488
Graduates' Christian Fellowship / Graduate Students Fellowship. See Student Movements, Christian

H

Hinduism 265, 274, 288, 295, 302, 312, 324, 618, 645
Holy Spirit 69, 81, 82, 90, 384, 442, 507, 616, 621, 622
Hukbahalap movement 367, 371
Hymns and Lyrics. 30, 31, 37, 113, 144, 258, 337, 466, 504f., 529, 543, 575, 581, 587. See also Christian poetry

I

Igorota Foundation 380, 489f.
Indigenisation / Inculturation passim, 5, 9, 12f., 14
 Burma/Myanmar 38, 41f., 47, 51, 53, 55, 89
 Cambodia, Laos 114
 Indonesia 16, 125, 144, 148, 152, 194, 199
 Malaysia, Singapore 259, 264, 272, 277, 287f., 303f., 308, 315f., 322f.
 Philippines 336ff., 343, 351, 352, 374, 383f., 385f., 391, 398, 413, 423, 430f., 432, 435, 449, 457, 461, 478f.
 Thailand 502, 507, 509, 536, 539, 545
 Vietnam 571, 792, 615, 620, 647
Indigenous religion 301, 315, 320
Institute for Religion and Culture, Philippines 374, 478
Institute for Studies in Asian Church and Culture 374, 478f.
Institute of Social Order, Philippines 364, 365, 373
Institute of Women's Studies, St. Scholastica's College 380, 479f.
Inter-faith encounter / Dialogue
 Burma/Myanmar 39, 50, 52ff., 60f., 62ff., 65, 69, 70, 73f., 76, 79, 80f., 85, 87, 89f.
 Cambodia, Laos 109
 Indonesia 134, 137, 182, 184, 187f., 189, 191, 197, 203, 208
 Malaysia, Singapore 265, 302, 312f., 315, 318
 Philippines 379, 387f., 393f., 398f., 410, 418, 421, 437, 450, 482f., 485
 Thailand 524, 528, 534, 536, 539f., 542, 543, 545, 546f., 548, 549f.
 Vietnam 563f., 599f., 618f., 621, 630, 631, 632f., 633f., 642, 643

Index of Subjects

International Movement of Catholic Students. See Student Movements, Christian

International Network of Engaged Buddhists 526, 538, 546

Inter-Seminary Urban-Industrial Institute, Philippines 374

Islam, Islamic, Muslim 17, 124, 125, 144, 145, 146, 147f., 149f., 164, 166, 168, 171, 182, 184, 189, 197, 208, 302f., 308f., 310, 313, 393, 410, 482, 634. See also Inter-faith encounter / Dialogue

J

Jesus Christ, Christology passim
   Burma/Myanmar 32, 52f., 64, 67f., 70, 74, 80, 81, 85f., 89f., 96
   Indonesia 134, 143f., 148f., 184, 187, 199, 207, 228,
   Malaysia, Singapore 256, 260, 261, 267ff., 270ff., 297f., 286, 290, 291, 296, 302f., 310, 319, 320, 324,
   Philippines 21f., 337, 342f., 348f., 356, 381, 385, 389, 395f., 401, 404, 408, 409, 410, 411f., 413, 414f., 429, 430, 432, 437, 440, 442, 453, 478
   Thailand 511, 514ff., 523, 528f., 533, 543, 499ff.
   Vietnam 11, 594, 599, 604f., 609, 611, 612, 615, 620, 621, 624, 626, 628, 638, 641f., 645, 650

K

Karen theology 27f., 31f., 38-40, 58f., chapter 3 passim, 528-530

Kachin 28, 42, 50, 99

Katipunan 334, 337, 349

Khao Kristachak 507

Kingdom / Reign of God 132, 258, 396, 415, 527, 478, 588, 609, 610, 628, 629

L

Laos Press 507

Liberation theology 79, 90, 94, 158, 272, 319, 375, 387, 425, 439, 446, 449, 625, 643

Liturgy, Worship, Prayer
   Burma/Myanmar 61, 64, 70, 76
   Indonesia 16, 169f., 181, 143, 146, 148
   Malaysia, Singapore 258, 276, 282, 296, 305, 318
   Philippines 19, 337, 338, 343, 352, 374, 386, 400, 404, 408, 413, 422, 430, 434, 478, 480, 444, 445, 446, 449
   Thailand 511ff., 529, 540f., 542, 543
   Vietnam 565, 571, 580, 613, 616, 621, 622, 630

M

Malayang Kilusan nh Bagong Kababaihan 373, 380

Marxism, Marxian 190, 392, 407, 449, 465f., 600, 613, 321, 631, 634, 645

Mary, Marian 218, 395, 401, 406, 408, 417, 422, 437, 454, 576

Mission and Evangelism. See Church and Mission; Evangelism

Muslims. See Islam

Mysticism, mystery 67, 141, 146, 149, 152, 160, 168, 171, 257, 296, 306, 391, 413, 543, 575, 607, 615, 618, 628

N

National Christian Councils. See Ecumenical associations

Nationalism and theology passim, 4f.
   Burma/Myanmar 28, 38, 65, 67, 75, 88
   Indonesia 139, 148, 151f., 153f., 156f., 157f., 161f., 165f., 172, 181, 196
   Malaysia, Singapore 258f., 260, 285, 302, 305,

Philippines 337ff., 341, 342f., 344-355, 357, 358ff., 373ff., 383, 411, 424f., 437 438, 441, 459, 467, 471, 481, 485
Vietnam 359, 561f., 565-571, 574-577, 584, 587ff., 596ff., 601f., 603, 607f., 619f., 631 636f.
Nestorian theology 1f.

P

Pancasila 125, 160, 166, 170, 177, 189, 196f.
Pastoral theology passim, 10f., 20, 21. See also Church and Mission
  Burma/Myanmar 51, 54, 58, 65, 73f., 76ff., 87, 92, 94, 99f.
  Indonesia 134f., 137, 142ff., 169f., 176f., 180, 194, 199, 222
  Malaysia, Singapore 255, 275f., 281, 285, 287f., 295, 297f., 299, 315, 319f.
  Philippines 362, 365, 367, 373f., 391, 400, 414, 430f., 444f., 468ff., 472, 474f., 477, 481, 483f., 485f.
  Thailand 509, 519f., 535f., 540f., 548
  Vietnam 580f., 589, 592ff., 608ff., 613, 619f., 623, 636ff., 645, 650
Pasyon tradition 3, 4, 21f., 338, 342f., 348, 363
People's theology passim
  Burma/Myanmar 33, 38, 53, 58f., 75, 79, 82, 84, 87f.
  Indonesia 142-148, 151, 176, 181f., 191, 196f., 199, 209, 215f., 219, 228f.
  Malaysia, Singapore 259, 271ff., 275f., 290, 295, 294, 299, 319, 321, 323
  Philippines 354f., 373, 396, 411, 415, 421, 423, 424, 430f., 434, 440, 453, 455

Thailand 509, 511ff., 520, 525, 528f., 537, 544
Vietnam 561, 570f., 578f., 591ff., 596f., 603, 608ff., 623, 631, 635, 642, 650
Periodicals
  Burma/Myanmar 35f., 55f., 97f.
  Cambodia, Laos 114, 120
  Indonesia 137f.
  Malaysia, Singapore 325f.
  Philippines 380f., 496f.
  Thailand 507, 554f.
  Vietnam 578f., 591-595, 608-611
PERSETIA 127, 131, 134f., 138, 180
PERWATI 127, 131, 138, 219
Prayer. See Liturgy, Worship, Prayer

R

Rotinese prayers 16

S

"Signs of the Times"..80, 164, 224, 375, 379, 386, 390, 391, 415, 426, 474, 544, 616
Silsilah Foundation 482f.
Social concern and reform. See Church and Society
Socio-Pastoral Institute, Philippines 373, 483f.
Spirituality passim
  Burma/Myanmar 51, 53, 70, 76, 77, 87, 92, 94, 98, 102
  Indonesia 137, 153, 190, 199, 217, 219
  Malaysia, Singapore 255, 277f., 293, 294, 295, 296, 308, 310
  Philippines 340, 362, 375, 378, 379, 381f., 388, 389, 391, 396, 403, 404f., 407, 420, 421f., 423, 429, 432, 436, 440, 441f., 445, 447, 451, 454-458, 484
  Thailand 543, 540f., 542, 545, 550
  Vietnam 565, 580, 613, 616, 618, 628, 629, 630, 636, 641-643

Index of Subjects

Student Movements, Christian 27, 37, 59, 62, 68, 110, 152, 162, 174, 176, 180, 190, 195, 247, 249, 267f. 271f., 273, 276, 287, 296, 309f., 320, 321, 324, 359f., 361f., 365, 400, 419, 465, 509, 520, 525, 537, 574, 596, 597, 627, 631

Student Christian Movement. See Ecumenical associations; Student Movements, Christian

Supreme Council of Bishops Philippine Independent Church 485

T

Tambaram Conference (1938) 39, 162, 163, 507

Taoism 247, 563, 605, 622, 634

Theological libraries / librarians (in text only) 35, 55f., 184, 188, 198, 224, 253, 277, 281, 302, 480, 526, 585, 608

Theological method. See also Contextual theology

    Burma/Myanmar 74, 79, 80, 81, 82f., 85, 89

    Indonesia 132, 160, 172, 173, 175, 182, 184, 187, 196f., 199, 205, 207, 213f., 219

    Malaysia, Singapore 276, 286, 287f., 290, 291f., 294, 296, 299, 302, 308, 311f., 315f., 318, 319, 322

    Philippines 366f., 373f., 379, 381, 383f., 386 391f., 395, 397, 403, 404, 409, 412, 414, 415, 420, 421f., 425, 426, 429, 430f., 432f., 435, 440, 441f., 446, 474, 490

    Thailand 512, 523, 524, 525, 526, 537, 540f., 543, 544, 548

    Vietnam 580, 592f., 603f., 609f., 611, 613, 616, 617, 621, 630, 633, 634, 637f., 642, 643

Theology in Action 127, 270, 463

Theology of Reality / Realism 80, 94

Theology of religions 52, 85, 89, 171, 187, 204, 209, 288, 324, 389, 393, 410, 418, 545f., 618, 632f., 638, 645

Three Fathers Theology, Vietnam 10, 562, 563-565, 566,f., 572, 607, 633f.

Tribal Theologies 209, 212, 375, 378, 381, 398f., 421, 462, 509, 512, 528ff., 615. See also Indigenisation / Inculturation

U

Underground writings 56, 591, 607, 625, 648

V

Vatican II 52f., 98f., 132, 157, 175, 178, 183, 207, 297, 305, 373ff., 385f., 391, 435, 477, 534, 536, 543, 585, 588, 592, 596, 607, 610, 612, 620, 623, 626, 631, 637, 643, 645

W

Waterbuffalo Theology 523

Wednesday Forum, Philippines 374

Women doing theology passim

Southeast Asia 7

    Burma/Myanmar 25, 27, 32, 33f., 36, 47, 50, 57ff., 66, 77f., 81ff., 92, 94, 95f., 98

    Cambodia, Laos 110, 113f., 115

    Indonesia 129, 130f., 160, 194f., 198f., 200f., 211, 218

    Malaysia, Singapore 244, 256f., 271f., 275f., 277ff., 290f., 292f., 294f., 306f., 308f., 312f., 322

    Philippines 340f., 373, 380, 379f., 380, 394f., 404f., 406, 416, 418, 421f., 422f., 426-428, 439-450, 462f., 465, 468f., 470, 479f., 481, 488, 489f.

Thailand 499ff., 506f., 509f., 517ff., 521f., 534, 537, 541
Vietnam 596f., 605, 621f., 627f., 629, 635f., 640, 650
Women writing, pre-1800 3, 21, 23f.
World Student Christian Federation, Asia-Pacific. See Student Movements, Christian
Worship. See Liturgy, Worship, Prayer

Y

Young Christian Workers (YCW) 271, 276, 423, 589, 622, 631
Young Men's Christian Association (YMCA) 27, 37, 49, 62, 92, 249, 265, 268, 307, 361, 370, 504, 507
Young Women's Christian Association (YWCA) 27, 58, 66, 249, 256, 265, 268, 361, 506

WITHDRAWN

BT 30 .A8 A774 2002 v.2 c.2

Asian Christian theologies